Mental Retardation

Foundations of Educational, Programming

Linda Hickson
Teachers College, Columbia University

Leonard S. Blackman
Teachers College, Columbia University

Elizabeth M. Reis
Bernard M. Baruch College, The City University of New York

Allyn and Bacon
Boston London Toronto Sydney Tokyo Singapore

To Dana and Jeremy
Frances, Julie, Gary, and Mark
Ding, Jason, and Madeleine

Series Editor: Ray Short
Series Editorial Assistant: Christine Shaw
Production Administrator: Ann Greenberger
Editorial-Production Service: Barbara J. Barg
Composition Buyer: Linda Cox
Cover Administrator: Suzanne Harbison
Marketing Manager: Ellen Mann

Copyright © 1995 by Allyn & Bacon
A Simon & Schuster Company
160 Gould Street
Needham Heights, MA 02194

Library of Congress Catalog-in-Publication Data
Hickson, Linda (Prior to 1993, publications by Linda Hickson appeared under the name Linda Hickson Bilsky)
    Mental retardation: foundations of educational programming/
Linda Hickson, Leonard S. Blackman, Elizabeth M. Reis.
        p.   cm
    Includes bibliographical references and index.
    1. Mentally handicapped children—Education—United States—Case studies.   2. Special education—United States—Case Studies.   3. Curriculum planning—United States—Case studies.
    I. Blackman, Leonard S.   II. Reis, Elizabeth M.   III. Title.
LC4631.H53   1995
371.92—dc20   94–6849
                                                                                                          CIP

ISBN: 0–205–14016–5

Printed in the United States of America

10   9   8   7   6   5   4   3   2   1   99   98   97   96   95   94

See page 422 for text and photo credits

Contents

CHAPTER 10
Basic Life Skills: The Motor and Self-Help Domains   251

CHAPTER 11   Cognitive Infrastructure of the Academic Program   281

CHAPTER 12   Reading   313

Preface

This text is designed to introduce students to the nature and needs of individuals with mental retardation from an educational perspective. The book is based on a critical analysis of existing special education approaches representing both cognitive and behavioral orientations to determine the degree to which their effectiveness has been demonstrated with various segments of the population with mental retardation. The first half of the proposed text presents foundational issues in mental retardation including history, etiology, characteristics and functioning levels, assessment, curriculum analysis, design of Individualized Education Programs (IEPs), instructional principles from both cognitive and behavioral perspectives, and inclusion and placement in the Least Restrictive Environment (LRE). In the second half of the text, these foundational issues are discussed in terms of their relevance to specific educational programming applications, including early intervention, motor and self-help development, the cognitive infrastructure of the academic program, academic instruction in reading and arithmetic, and transition to employment and life in the community. The scope of the book will encompass all levels of mental retardation and the range of age levels covered by PL94–142—early childhood through age twenty-one.

The case studies are an important feature of this book. They are included to provide practitioners new to special education with a true-to-life context in which to anchor their understanding of principles and practices in the field. Toward this end, we have included descriptions of a number of students with mental retardation who represent a wide range of ages, abilities, and instructional placements. Some basic characteristics of the eight students whose case studies appear throughout this text are presented in Table P–1.

The book is divided into two parts. Part I provides an introduction to foundational issues in the education of students with mental retardation. The eight chapters in Part I are intended to provide a framework for the more specific educational applications in the remainder of the book. Chapter one provides a historical and social context for the material which follows while chapter two establishes the scope of the book in terms of labels, definitions, and functioning levels. Chapters three and four focus upon the foundations of assessment and the practical applications of assessment in the educational process, respectively. These chapters examine the wide range of ways in which assessment from intelligence testing to curriculum-

Table P–1   **Basic Characteristics of the Eight Case Studies**

Name	Age (Years)	IQ	Level of Mental Retardation	Discussed in Chapters
Tony	16–0	65	Mild	3, 5, 6, 7, 13
Sonia	7–7	<15	Profound	3, 5, 6, 7
Alicia	3–6	20	Profound	3, 5, 6, 7, 9
Scott	18–0	33	Severe	3, 5, 6, 7, 13, 14
Karen	15–1	47	Moderate	3, 5, 6, 7
Juan	9–0	55	Mild	3, 5, 6, 7, 13
Tanisha	7–3	58	Mild	3, 4, 5, 6, 7, 11, 12
Norman	5–5	64	Mild	3, 5, 6, 7, 10

based assessment can be used to guide the education of students with mental retardation. Chapter three uses salient issues in measurement to introduce assessment summaries for each of the eight case studies that will be further developed in subsequent chapters. In chapter four, an assessment model is presented to aid teachers in linking assessment to curriculum and instruction. Chapter five focuses upon the selection and development of curricula for persons with mental retardation. In that chapter, curriculum trends and characteristics are examined and principles of curriculum design and evaluation are presented. Chapter six consists of an in-depth treatment of how the IEP requirement of PL 94–142 is used in the development of educational programs for students with mental retardation. In chapter seven, some key instructional strategies required for effective teaching are presented. In chapter eight, the placement alternatives available to students with mental retardation are discussed along with their implications for effective program delivery. In essence, Part I of this text is designed to provide both the foundations and some of the key components of the specific educational programs discussed in the remainder of the book.

Part II of the book consists of six chapters concerned with specific aspects of educational programming for students with mental retardation. In chapter nine, the emphasis is upon early intervention approaches and their efficacy. Chapter ten is devoted to techniques for fostering the development of motor and self-help skills. Chapter eleven examines the cognitive infrastructure of the academic program. Instructional considerations relating to reading are the focus of chapter twelve. In chapter thirteen, frameworks and approaches for instruction in number skills and arithmetic are presented. Chapter fourteen targets transition to employment and community living.

Acknowledgements

We would like to express our sincere appreciation to Terrence Calnen and Ishita Khemka for their important contributions to the preparation of this text, including developing case study examples, conducting library research, requesting copyright permissions, and assisting with a variety of editorial tasks. Betty Engel provided an invaluable service through her conscientious word processing of major parts of the manuscript and her helpful comments.

The students who participated in a field test of the manuscript while enrolled in the Nature and Needs of Persons with Mental Retardation course at Teachers College, Columbia University provided generous feedback. Helpful library research was provided by the three cohorts of students who were supported by the Secondary Level Focus Training Grant in Mental Retardation. We also wish to thank Tiina Urv for her assistance with proofreading and the many other students who contributed enthusiastically to this project.

We are also grateful to our friends and colleagues who provided encouragement and helpful comments, especially Frances P. Connor, Ding Gerzog, Ignacy Goldberg, and Ellen Karsh. We are grateful to Penny Colman for her valued suggestions and photography. For arranging photography sessions and/or providing us with photographs, we wish to thank Louise Fougner, Pat Lavin, Hedy Leutner, and Frances D. Meyer, as well as Bancroft Inc., a private non-profit agency based in Haddonfield, NJ, which provides educational, vocational and residential programs to children and adults with developmental disabilities and traumatic brain injuries, and the Cooke Foundation for Special Education, a not-for-profit corporation in New York City, which provides school and education for children with mental retardation and developmental delays.

We wish to thank those professionals in the field who reviewed the manuscript for Allyn and Bacon: Mary Lynne Calhoun, The University of North Carolina at Charlotte; David W. Test, The University of North Carolina at Charlotte; Charlotte Erickson, University of Wisconsin–LaCrosse; Thomas P. Lombardi, West Virginia University; and Barbara Gartin, University of Arkansas.

Chapter 1

Historical Perspectives:

Educational and Social Issues

Mental retardation has existed since the dawn of civilization. The definition, manifestations, and treatment of mental retardation, however, have clearly varied with the characteristics of each society. Although individual differences in ability have existed in every society, the values and expectations of each society have determined who was classified as deviant and the social consequences of that deviance. For example, individuals assigned the label of mild mental retardation today might not have been singled out in many earlier societies as long as they were able to perform the hunting, fishing, and/or farming activities required by their society. Although the treatment of individuals with low ability has changed dramatically over time, a few critical issues have emerged as recurrent themes in the history of mental retardation. The current newsclippings presented throughout the chapter as Issue Updates highlight the fact that most of these issues continue to be controversial.

In this chapter, the emergence of educational programming for individuals with mental retardation is traced back to some of its historical roots. Because the treatment of people with mental retardation is heavily influenced by the social climate at any given point in time, a brief synopsis of the social context precedes a discussion of the status of education for persons with mental retardation for each historical period.

The Earliest Civilizations

Social Climate

During prehistoric times, it is likely that few infants with severe disabilities survived infancy since infanticide was widely practiced. Even then, however, some tribes sustained and protected these infants. Most early civilizations varied in their treatment of infants with disabilities. Within ancient Greece, for example, practices differed dramatically from Sparta to Athens. In Sparta, with its premium on physical strength and endurance, each newborn infant was examined by a state council of inspectors. Any child suspected of being defective was hurled from a cliff to die on the rocks below. During Athens' Golden Age, although infanticide did occur, many unwanted infants were placed in earthen jars near a temple in case anyone wished to adopt them. In ancient Rome, the extent to which infanticide was practiced fluctuated with economic and social conditions. During the first century A.D., the state provided wet nurses to feed unwanted infants left for possible adoption at the Columna Lactaria. Unfortunately, many of these infants were taken and mutilated to increase their value as beggars or sold into slavery. In the second century A.D., individuals with disabilities were sometimes purchased to serve as a source of household amusement. By the end of the Roman era, the influence of Christianity had become apparent and Roman emperors issued edicts prohibiting infanticide and the selling of children into slavery (Scheerenberger, 1983).

From prehistoric times through the ancient civilizations of Mesopotamia, Greece, and Rome, the treatment of people with disabilities was characterized by its variability. Mental retardation was not usually differentiated from other handicapping conditions. The responses of societies to individuals with disabilities ranged from kindness to extreme cruelty. As reflected in the widespread practice of infanticide, a key issue during this period was whether infants with disabilities should be allowed to survive. Although overt infanticide is no longer sanctioned, Issue Update 1-1 illustrates that today's society continues to agonize over the extent to which the survival of infants with severe disabilities should be supported by modern medical intervention. The "right to survival" of these infants remains an unresolved issue.

Education

Education was not a consideration for individuals with mental retardation during this early period. Amelioration of disabling conditions was rarely attempted. At best, physical care and maintenance were provided.

The Middle Ages through the Enlightenment

Although societies throughout the world have responded to the phenomenon of mental retardation, the roots of the treatment of individuals with mental retardation in the United States can be traced most directly to the events in Europe which are the focus of the present chapter.

Social Climate

The Middle Ages
The Middle Ages are generally viewed as encompassing the nearly one thousand year period from the conquest of Rome by invading tribes in A.D. 476 to the beginning of the Renaissance in Italy during the 1300s. During this period, characterized by the central role of the Church in society, the fates of individuals with mental retardation varied. On the positive side, people with mental retardation were sometimes viewed as "innocents of God" and provided with humane care either at home or in monasteries. In the largely agrarian economy of medieval Europe, children were highly valued and infanticide was rarely practiced. Many individuals with mental retardation supported themselves by working in the fields or were maintained by their neighbors (Scheerenberger, 1983). On the negative side, however, mental handicaps were sometimes viewed as visitations of the devil and victims were subjected to exorcism and torture (Hewett & Forness, 1977). Beginning in the latter years of the Middle Ages and continuing through the eighteenth century, many individuals were persecuted and executed for practicing witchcraft. There is little question that individuals with mental retardation were among them (Scheerenberger, 1983). Living conditions were harsh for all throughout the Middle Ages, but were undoubtedly more so for individuals with mental retardation. Some scholars showed an awareness of mental retardation (e.g., Avicenna, 980–1037; Maimonides, 1135–1204), but manifested little understanding of the condition.

The Renaissance
Although conditions for individuals with mental retardation probably did not improve substantially during the Renaissance (approximately 1350–1550), major changes in society occurred which set the stage for future developments. The dominance of the

Parents of 'Baby Jane Doe' Win Ruling Against Surgery

by David Margolick
Published in *The New York Times*, October 29, 1983
Copyright © 1981/83/85 by The New York Times
Company. Reprinted by permission

New York's highest court, using unusually strong language, yesterday upheld a Long Island couple's right to withhold corrective surgery for their 17-day-old daughter, born with debilitating defects.

The State Court of Appeals, in a unanimous opinion, backed the right of the parents to determine the treatment for the child and described the lawsuit that challenged that right as "offensive."

"Confronted with the anguish of the birth of a child with severe physical disorders, these parents, in consequence of judicial procedures for which there is no precedent or authority, have been subjected to litigation through all three levels of our state's court system," the unsigned five-page opinion said. "We find no justification for resort to or entertainment of these proceedings."

U.S. Agency Held Inquiry

Last night, an Assistant United States Attorney General said the Justice Department's Civil Rights Division was considering a lawsuit to require the hospital where the baby is being treated to provide the Government with medical records of her case. The official, William Bradford Reynolds, said the department's involvement came after an inquiry into the case by the Federal Department of Health and Human Services. The hospital has declined to turn over its records up to now.

The infant, identified as Baby Jane Doe, was born on Oct. 11 in Port Jefferson, L.I. She suffers from spina bifida—a failure of the spinal cord to close properly—along with hydrocephalus, or excess fluid in the brain. Without surgery, doctors say, she is likely to die within two years; with it, she could survive into her 20's but would be severely retarded and bedridden.

The parents, identified as "Mr. and Mrs. A," decided to forgo surgery after consulting with neurosurgeons, social workers and clergymen.

A private lawyer, Lawrence Washburn of Albany, then challenged the parents' decision in court.

Paul Gianelli, the lawyer for the parents, commended the court's ruling. "What the opinion says is that the state is not going to second-guess parents," Mr. Gianelli said from his Smithtown, L.I., office. "It presumes that parents make these decisions with love and thoughtfulness, and that strangers, however whimsical or well-intentioned, cannot subject them to this outrageous kind of proceeding."

Mr. Washburn, who lives in Vermont, did not return calls to his office.

William E. Weber, the baby's court-appointed guardian, said the decision ran counter to state public health laws, which guarantee handicapped children the same medical services as healthy children.

The court's opinion treated the issue as a matter of procedure, holding that the proper course in cases of this kind was not through the courts, but through child-neglect proceedings initiated by a child protective agency.

While it did not mention Mr. Washburn by name, it reserved its harshest criticism for him. The court said that he "had no disclosed relationship with the child, her parents, her family or those treating her illnesses" and had failed to communicate his concerns to the State Department of Social Services—the agency with jurisdiction over child-neglect cases.

"It would serve no useful purpose at this stage," the opinion states, "to recite the unusual, and sometimes offensive, activities of those who have sought, in the interests of Baby Jane Doe, to displace parental responsibility for and management of her medical care."

The court further discounted the control over the baby asserted by Mr. Weber, who had been appointed guardian by Justice Melvyn Tanenbaum of State Supreme Court.

Mr. Weber had argued that the parents' constitutional right to privacy "was not so broad that it gives them the freedom to bring about their children's death by deliberate medical neglect."

Baby in Stable Condition

To permit him to exercise control over the baby, the court said, "would be to recognize the right of any person to institute judicial proceedings which would catapult him into the very heart of a family circle, there to challenge the most private and most precious responsi-

ISSUE UPDATE 1-1   Right to Survival *(Continued)*

bility vested in the parents for the care and nurture of their children."

The baby was reported in stable condition yesterday, at the hospital, in Stony Brook, L.I., which was named as the defendant in this case.

David M. Fishlow, a spokesman for the State Attorney General, Robert Abrams, whose office represented the hospital, said: "The Attorney General was pleased that the court upheld the right of a family to make a decision of such profound consequence in consultation with the medical authorities and without the interference of an outsider." ■

Who'll Pay the Bills for Baby Doe?

Published in *The New York Times*, July 9, 1984
Copyright © 1981/83/85 by The New York Times Company. Reprinted by permission

Just how much and what kind of care a severely handicapped infant should get is a question that's been agitating the nation ever since the death of one called Doe in 1982. Baby Doe, born with Down's syndrome, died of starvation after his parents, supported by the Indiana courts, chose not to feed him. The Federal response to the public outcry was an ill-advised attempt to create a spy system in hospital nurseries.

Last year, the parents of another Baby Doe decided against surgery for their multiply handicapped daughter because, while it might prolong her life, it could not correct her severe retardation. Though that decision had the support of physicians, clergy and social workers, the parents were hauled through court after court by the Reagan Administration. The courts upheld the Does, and their daughter is doing reasonably well.

The deeper question of how to proceed in such situations, however, remains unanswered. The Department of Health and Human Services contributed some useful guidelines last January to encourage the creation of hospital review boards. Made up of medical experts and community representatives, they would look over any decision by parents and doctors to forgo treatment.

Then the House voted, rather sweepingly, to deny funds for child-abuse prevention to any state that fails to set up procedures to investigate and report the withholding of "medically indicated treatment" from handicapped infants. Just what such treatment might be wasn't defined—leaving the burden of interpretation to the states.

Last week, after months of work with groups on all sides, six Senators who span the political spectrum came up with definitions. "Medically indicated treatment" would mean those steps that physicians believe most likely to correct or ameliorate a handicapped infant's life-threatening conditions. But doctors and hospitals would not be asked to make heroic efforts to save the irretrievably comatose, or provide treatment that would only prolong dying.

The next step should be obvious. A society that, understandably, wants doubtful cases resolved on the side of life also has an obligation to those for whom such life may be extremely painful: the infants and their immediate families. Pending amendments in Congress ask for study of the best ways to provide Federal financial support for the treatment of disabled infants. But who will pay for an adequate level of *continuing* care? ■

Whatever happened to Baby Jane Doe?

By Nat Hentoff
Published in the *Washington Post*, December 11, 1990
Reprinted by permission of the author

Seven years ago, the national press was much taken with a battle between the United States and the parents of a New York infant invariably described by the press as severely deformed (as if she were the Elephant Man). She was a child with spina bifida.

Spina bifida is a lesion in the spinal column. If it is not repaired through immediate surgery, there is danger of infection that can lead to permanent brain damage. Usually accompanying spina bifida is an accumulation of spinal fluid in the brain. If a shunt is

Continued

not inserted to drain the fluid, the pressure on the brain often leads to mental retardation.

The parents, however, chose to give the child—known in the headlines as Baby Jane Doe—only "conservative treatment." No surgery, and for a long time, no shunt. After all, as nearly all the reporters and nearly all the editorial writers assured their readers and viewers, it really did not matter what was done for Baby Jane Doe.

Either way, she wouldn't live all that long and as long as she did live, she would be profoundly retarded and in constant pain, would always be bedridden, would never be able to learn anything, and would never be able to recognize anyone, even her parents. In grim sum, her quality of life would be so low—the press implied—that her departure would be a blessing to her parents and, of course, to herself.

The only problem with this prognosis was that a number of leading pediatric neurologists—based on what they knew of Baby Jane Doe's condition—told me it wasn't true. I talked with, among others, **Dr. David McLone**, chief of neurosurgery at Children's Memorial Hospital in Chicago. He said that his extensive experience with spina bifida children gave him confidence that if she were treated at his hospital, she would grow up to have normal intelligence and would be walking, probably with some bracing.

Also much interested in the case was **Dr. C. Everett Koop**, then the Surgeon General—and for many years before, one of the more renowned pediatric surgeons in the country. He wanted to see the hospital records, which had been sealed because of so much national attention to the case.

The federal government brought suit—under Section 504 of the *1973 Rehabilitation Act*—to find out from the records whether Baby Jane Doe was being discriminated against because of her handicap. Section 504 says that where federal funds are involved, there can be no such discrimination. Therefore, said the government, handicapped infants—like all other infants in the nursery—must get appropriate medical treatment.

The legal team for the parents included the attorney general of New York as well as the New York Civil Liberties Union. They maintained that the privacy rights of the parents and of the infant must be protected at all costs against "Big Brother."

Supporting the government—though there was little notice of these allies in the press—were the American Coalition of Citizens with Disabilities, the Association for Persons with Severe Handicaps, the Disability Rights Education and Defense Fund and the Disability Rights Union.

Unlike many able-bodied Americans, the people with disabilities know that treatment based on "quality of life" can strip you forever of all your civil liberties, and your life.

The government lost in the courts all the way. The privacy rights of the parents and the infant getting "conservative treatment" prevailed. The "intruders" were routed.

In the years since, it has been learned that the child's real first name (we've never known the last) is **Keri-Lynn**. And in a recent *Newsday* story by **Kathleen Kerr**, it turns out that Keri-Lynn is not in pain, that she laughs and plays with her parents and other children, and recognizes her parents with no trouble at all.

But she cannot walk. She attends special classes; her intelligence is considered between low-normal and educable.

What would have happened if the government and Dr. Koop had won in 1983 and Keri-Lynn had received what is called "aggressive treatment?" Kathleen Kerr of *Newsday* asked Dr. Koop. He said to her, as he has said to me, that if Keri-Lynn had been able to get full treatment through the anti-discrimination provisions of the federal Rehabilitation Act, "she would be in a considerably different condition today."

It never occurred to the American Civil Liberties Union, which was protecting the right of the parents to be the sole decision-makers in the case, that Keri-Lynn was not a fetus and had her own due process and equal protection rights under the Constitution. By their own principles, the civil libertarians, were on the wrong side. Keri-Lynn was being discriminated against because she was handicapped. But the ACLU saw her, and still does, as being an extension of *Roe v. Wade*. ■

Church began to erode, accompanied by a decrease in society's preoccupation with religious beliefs. This preoccupation was replaced by a spirit of free inquiry and curiosity about human beings and nature. Although widespread understanding of mental retardation would not be seen until much later, at least one Renaissance individual, Paracelsus (1493–1541), proposed a definition of mental retardation which clearly differentiated it from mental illness.

The Seventeenth and Eighteenth Centuries

During the seventeenth and eighteenth centuries, which encompassed the Age of Reason and the Enlightenment in Europe and the colonial period in America, understanding of brain function and certain types of mental retardation (e.g., cretinism and hydrocephalus) increased. However, the treatment of individuals with mental retardation seemed to reach an all-time low.

In Europe, begging was so widespread that it began to be viewed as a public nuisance. For example, it is estimated that during the Thirty Years' War, there were more than 100,000 beggars in Paris alone. It became more and more common for individuals with mental retardation to be confined to institutions (e.g., foundling homes, hospitals, prisons). The death rate of children placed in these facilities was appallingly high, often exceeding 75 to 80 percent. Conditions for adult residents of institutions were similarly inhumane. People with mental retardation were incarcerated with criminals and individuals with mental illness. Food, clothing, and sanitation were blatantly inadequate. Extreme overcrowding, disease, and brutality were rampant. In fact, it was believed by many that individuals with mental retardation and mental illness were actually insensitive to cold, heat, hunger, and pain. A few humanitarian individuals did attempt to improve conditions. Philipe Pinel (1745–1826), for example, is well known for his efforts to unchain the inmates and initiate humane care in the institutions of Salpetrière and Bicêtre near Paris. He advocated the "moral management" of individuals with mental retardation and mental illness, an approach involving humane care, gentle treatment, and freedom from physical abuse and chains (Scheerenberger, 1983).

During this same period in colonial America, generally dismal conditions prevailed for people with mental retardation. It has been reported that individuals with mental retardation were among those accused of witchcraft and executed in Salem. More typically, however, they were required to work long hours as indentured servants or apprentices, or, if unable to work, put in jail or "placed out" in the care of a local family with support from the town. Increasingly, individuals with mental retardation and mental illness were confined together in prisons and hospitals under generally inhumane conditions.

Eventually, advocates of humane care for these individuals, began to come forward. Benjamin Rush (1745–1813) was one early reformer in the United States who called attention to the widespread abuse of people with mental retardation and mental illness in institutions (Scheerenberger, 1983).

The question of precisely what constitutes humane treatment for people with mental retardation continues to be the focus of widespread debate, as illustrated in Issue Update 1-2. Although the legitimacy of the Behavior Research Institute program referred to in the Issue Update has been upheld in the courts, the media coverage surrounding the case reflects the existence of widely diverging views on the nature of humane treatment.

ISSUE UPDATE 1-2   Right to Humane Treatment

Death During Treatment

Published in the *Boston Herald*, July 26, 1985
Reprinted by permission of the *Boston Herald*

PROVIDENCE, R.I. (AP)—The death of an autistic twenty-two year old man who passed out after being shackled and forced to listen to "white noise" has renewed the controversy over a type of aversion treatment for behavior disorders.

Vincent Milletich, who lived in a group home in Attleboro, Mass., may be the first person ever to die from the controversial therapy, said the American Society for Children and Adults with Autism.

Authorities say Milletich's death Tuesday has not positively been linked to the "white-noise visual screen" treatment. He became unconscious while being treated at a Seekonk, Mass., group home operated by the private Behavior Research Institute.

A preliminary investigation found that "at this time, there is no indication of any inappropriate action by the staff," according to Michael Coughlin of the Massachusetts Office for Children, which licenses BRI's homes.

However, the Massachusetts Department of Education on Thursday ordered the BRI to discontinue the therapy on residents of that state until the investigation is completed, a spokeswoman said.

Autism is a form of childhood schizophrenia char-

acterized by acting out and withdrawal from reality. Symptoms can include bizarre, self-destructive and animalistic behavior in otherwise normal-appearing children—victims have been known to spend hours in repetitive activities such as flushing a toilet.

---

may be first person ever to die from . . . "white noise."

During the aversion procedure, a patient is helmeted, shackled hand-and-foot, and forced to listen to static through earphones, Coughlin said Thursday.

He said aversive therapy is "treatment that uses a system of rewards and consequences to modify behavior. The consequences involve physical punishment to control aggressive and other inappropriate behavior on the part of severely disturbed children."

Coughlin defined "white noise" as "sounds quite similar to the static of a television or radio not tuned in to a station. If turned up to a high enough level, it can drown out all other transmissions into one's ears."

The therapy is "controversial and frequently misunderstood," said Donna Cone, assistant director for program standards at the state Department of Mental Health. "But I think they've got a very fine program." ∎

Letters: Behavior Modification Defended

Robert and Mary Flanagan
Port Washington, L.I. Printed in *The New York Times*, Thursday, October 31, 1985

To the Editor:
As parents of an autistic person at the Behavioral Research Institute in Providence, R.I., we disagree with the use of the word "punishment" in your Oct. 13 report on efforts to close the institute's seven homes by the Massachusetts Office for Children. Indeed, whether or not the behavior-modification methods of the institute are "punishment" is the crux of the dispute.

To illustrate, consider a self-abusive person (a frequent condition among the autistic) who will hit his head on the floor until he is bruised and bleeding. At

B.R.I., they will first attempt to stop this behavior through rewards. But if those do not work, he will be subjected to some form of aversive therapy each time he tries to bang his head. For example, he could be doused with cold water. As a result of this treatment, the head banging will ultimately be eliminated. We have seen this happen.

Now compare the treatment for head banging at most state institutions. It will be heavy drugging. There will be no improvement in behavior. We believe it dangerously loads the terms of the debate to use the word "punishment" about the cold water at B.R.I. and not about the medication at the institution.

B.R.I.'s approach is designed to avert and eliminate dangerous behavior. It replaces such behavior with

ISSUE UPDATE 1-2   Right to Humane Treatment *(Continued)*

more appropriate behavior, like classroom and vocational work, swimming and competing in the special olympics. Our son arrived at the Behavior Research Institute after a variety of other programs had failed to handle him despite the use of straitjackets and life-threatening drugs. Not to mention the casual, hidden abuse that occurs behind institution walls and is very rarely admitted by the sort of state bureaucracy that is now attacking B.R.I.

Today, our son lives in a group home on a normal suburban street. B.R.I. has taught him to dress himself, fold laundry, to make his bed and sandwiches for his lunch. And to put it in purely economic terms, he does not need the services of an expensive state institution.

Of course it takes a tough mental effort to accept the use of aversives. It is easy to say that parents are letting their children be tortured, that we either hate our children or are indifferent to them. It is also convenient for society to think that. Rotting in a stupor does not offend the sensibilities of politicians as aversives do.

We do not consider the program at the Behavior Research Institute to be simply the lesser evil—although the alternatives are in most cases dreadful. We consider it instead to be remarkably successful in treating certain very difficult cases that have been rejected by every other program. This program has given autistic people a chance to learn how to live a happier and more normal life. ■

Court Imposed Restrictions on State Agency Regulation of Behavior Modification Programs

By Roderick MacLeish, Jr.
Published in *Psychology in Mental Retardation*,
Division 33 Newsletter, Vol. 11(3), Spring 1986
Reprinted by permission of the American
Psychological Association

While the Supreme Court has yet to announce whether there exists a broad, constitutionally based, "right to treatment," it is now beyond dispute that handicapped citizens possess minimal rights to appropriate treatment and training. In *Youngberg v. Romeo*, decided in 1982, the Court decided that those minimal rights encompassed the right "not to regress" while confined to state institutions, as well as the right "to habilitation." The latter term can include educational options, medical intervention, and behavior modification programs.

The law in this area is in a decidedly evolutionary state. There is great uncertainty as to how far the federal and state courts will go in interpreting habilitation rights. Most claims will inevitably arise in lawsuits against understaffed and overpopulated state institutions, many of which have failed to provide even safe conditions of confinement, let alone any program which could be appropriately characterized as "treatment."

The right to minimally adequate treatment may well have applications in other areas. In late January of this year, a Massachusetts Probate Court judge issued a decision authorizing a private residential school to resume a form of behavior modification which the school had been banned from using by order of a state agency. The decision raises the right to habilitation in a slightly different context—are there constitutional limits on the state's regulatory authority to proscribe certain treatment options?

In the Massachusetts case, the proposed form of treatment had been the subject of significant controversy. The school in question, the Behavior Research Institute (BRI), provides an educational and treatment program to some of the most seriously handicapped clients in the United States; adolescents and adults with extreme levels of self-abuse and violence who have frequently arrived at the School from state schools and hospitals. In certain cases, BRI's treatment includes the use of *physical aversives*, including finger pinches and spanks. The students in the program are cleared for this treatment by a physician and are monitored daily by a nursing staff. The program enjoys virtually uniform support from parents and guardians.

Continued

ISSUE UPDATE 1-2   Right to Humane Treatment *(Continued)*

Last September, a state agency in Massachusetts banned physical aversives at BRI, citing health and safety concerns. In January, the parents of six BRI students brought suit in the Probate Court, requesting a resumption of treatment. The legal vehicle chosen by the parents was a "substituted judgment" action, in which the court decides what treatment an incompetent individual would elect if that individual were competent.

After hearing extensive testimony and conducting a "view" of BRI, Probate Court Judge Ernest Rotenberg issued orders authorizing the school to resume treatment for the five clients, including treatment which was banned by the Office for Children's order. The Judge found that BRI indeed was a *last resort* for the students and that the failure to return those students to the treatment program would be *life-threatening*. The state has appealed the Probate Court's order but its motion for a stay was rejected by the Massachusetts Appeals Court.

This case raises again the time-honored question, Who should decide? Clearly, parental views should carry great weight, but are not absolute. However, should state agencies possess an even greater authority than parents by being able to arbitrarily prohibit certain forms of treatment?

It is submitted that state regulatory agencies should not be granted this authority. Parents, guardians and professionals should be free to petition for court authorization for treatment otherwise prohibited by regulatory agencies. This conclusion is justified for several reasons.

First, state agencies and their employees are ill-equipped to make important treatment and habilitation decisions for handicapped citizens. As a recent article in the Yale Law Journal notes, even "the most well-intentioned [state] social workers do not have to live with their decisions in the way parents do." Parental choices require a sensitivity which the state, as an impersonal institution, cannot have.

Second, the record of the state in providing treatment for clients committed to its care raises serious questions of the state's competence in this area. For example, while one Massachusetts agency purports to have the expertise to preclude certain treatment, other human service agencies of the state find themselves almost continually in court faced with allegations of unconstitutional conditions and gross insensitivity to the needs of the handicapped. Four state schools for the retarded are under federal court consent decree, the U.S. Justice Department has brought suit against the state over conditions in one hospital and Massachusetts was recently ranked 41st in quality of services for the mentally ill. Yet the state continues to presume that it knows best.

Finally, permitting the courts to order treatment prohibited by regulatory agencies will prevent clients from being denied needed treatment, while at the same time allowing such agencies to show, on an *individual* basis, the reasons for their decisions.

In a recent case, the California Supreme Court struck down a state statute prohibiting sterilization of incompetents on the grounds that the statute could interfere with an individual ward's right to habilitation. The Court found that if the state withholds from a handicapped individual the only safe and reliable method of contraception, it necessarily limits her opportunity for habilitation and her freedom to pursue a fulfilling life. As the Court stated: "True protection of procreative choice can be accomplished only if the state permits the court-supervised *substituted judgment* of the [guardian] to be exercised on behalf of a [ward] who is personally unable to exercise this right" (emphasis supplied). The California decision, like the decision in the BRI case, shows the danger of broad-based statutes and regulations purportedly drafted to "protect" the handicapped. For most handicapped citizens, sterilization or restrictive behavior modification techniques are undoubtedly inappropriate. Yet, in individual cases, such procedures may not only be appropriate, but sometimes necessary to vindicate the right to habilitation or even to save lives. Unless the courts retain the ultimate authority to order treatment otherwise prohibited by state law, regulation, or administrative order, some of our most handicapped citizens will become victims of their self-appointed state protectors. ∎

Education

From the Middle Ages through the eighteenth century, virtually no progress was made in education for people with mental retardation. However, the Renaissance did mark the beginning of a more scientific, or rational, approach to mental retardation which paved the way for future progress. During the seventeenth and eighteenth centuries in Europe and America, people with mental retardation were not provided with schooling (Scheerenberger, 1983). The majority of intellectually average people, however, probably did not fare much better. In colonial America, for example, it is estimated that less than half of the population received formal schooling. For all but the most privileged members of society, education often took place in the home or through apprenticeships (Cremin, 1977). Serious educational gains for persons with mental retardation did not take place until well into the 1800s.

Nineteenth Century Beginnings: 1800–1850

Social Climate

The history of the systematic treatment of individuals with mental retardation begins in the nineteenth century. The dramatic progress during this period was probably stimulated by at least three factors. First, by the beginning of the nineteenth century, mental retardation was becoming a much more conspicuous social problem than it had been in earlier times. Major changes were occurring in society that undoubtedly served to increase the visibility of individuals with mental retardation. As the industrialization of society increased, opportunities for a simple agrarian existence decreased. With technological advances, the requirements for employment became more complex. The simplest jobs disappeared, and a more intelligent, adaptable workforce was required. Urbanization, an accompaniment of industrialization, imposed additional demands. Clearly, survival in the city was considerably more complex than survival in the country. During this same period mass education was becoming more common, placing further complex demands upon the less intelligent members of society. It became apparent that formal education was not equally effective with all children. Ultimately, it was the inability of some children to handle the school curriculum that led to the identification of mild mental retardation. Maloney and Ward noted that "man had not only discovered mild mental retardation, he may in fact have created it" (1978, p. 25). Mild mental retardation emerged as a meaningful concept only in the face of the school-imposed demands for widespread literacy and high-level mathematical thinking.

Second, from the beginning of the nineteenth century, scientific developments began to support a more clearly defined conception of mental retardation. Considerable progress was made during this period in both medicine and psychology. Specifically, the distinction between mental retardation and mental illness was clearly established. Many of the clinical types of mental retardation were identified, and classification systems were proposed. For example, Esquirol (1782–1840) designated mental retardation as *amentia* and mental illness as *dementia*. He proposed a two-level classification system for mental retardation. *Idiots* were the lowest functioning and *imbeciles* were closer to average. It was also during this period that J. Langdon Down (1828–1896) proposed his ethnic classification, which included a detailed description of what is now called Down Syndrome.

Third, society was developing a social conscience. Reform movements began to appear in both Europe and the United States. In Switzerland, Guggenbühl (1816–1863) established a model residential facility for "cretins." In the United States, Samuel Gridley Howe (1801–1876), Charles Sumner (1811–1874), Horace Mann (1796–1859), and Dorothea Dix (1802–1887) called attention to the intolerable conditions endured by most individuals with mental retardation and mental illness. One fruit of their efforts was the opening of an experimental wing of the Perkins Institute for the Blind in 1848 to serve ten "idiot" children. The major aim of these reformers was to urge the states to provide humane treatment in the form of well-designed, specialized, residential facilities for individuals with mental retardation and mental illness.

Education

Before the nineteenth century, well-intentioned humanitarians such as Pinel and Rush believed that individuals with mental retardation were not educable. Apparently, even the nineteenth-century reformers did not aspire to cure mental retardation. Scheerenberger (1983) pointed out that there is no historical evidence to support the frequent assertion that Howe and other early leaders aimed to cure mental retardation. In fact, Howe spoke of "improvement," but not cure.

It was Jean-Marc-Gaspard Itard's publication in 1801 of *De l'Education d'un Homme Sauvage* that marked the beginning of the professional literature on the education and training of individuals with mental retardation (Davies & Ecob, 1964). In that book, Itard described his efforts to educate a boy who had been found living naked and wild in the forest near Aveyron, France. Although Pinel, who had been Itard's teacher, diagnosed the boy as an "idiot," Itard believed that the boy was simply untaught and took on the challenge of his education. Naming the boy Victor, Itard took him into his home and worked with him for approximately six years. Itard exposed Victor to a carefully developed sequence of activities aimed at training his senses, intellectual functions, and emotions. However, Itard was disappointed by Victor's slow progress. Finally, when at puberty Victor became increasingly unmanageable, Itard terminated his lessons and concluded that the experiment had been a failure. Although it was apparent that Pinel's initial diagnosis of Victor had been correct, Itard had demonstrated that progress could be made even with individuals with mental retardation. Furthermore, he left a legacy of methods and materials suitable for use with individuals of low intelligence (Scheerenberger, 1983).

Unfortunately, the general care and treatment of individuals with mental retardation in the early nineteenth century was not significantly better than it had been during the previous century. However, the economic, scientific, and social developments of this period were setting forces in motion which would eventually culminate in sweeping change. Mental retardation was finally acknowledged as an important social problem, distinct from mental illness. Considerable scientific interest centered upon this new specialty. Most importantly, professionals began to consider the possible benefits of educating individuals with mental retardation. Although all children with mental retardation in the United States are now entitled to a "free appropriate education," the extent to which resources should be allocated to the education of people with mental disabilities continues to be controversial, as illustrated in Issue Update 1-3.

ISSUE UPDATE 1-3   Right to Education

Justices Restrict a 'Bill of Rights' for the Retarded

By Linda Greenhouse
Excerpted from *The New York Times*, April 21, 1981
Copyright © 1981/83/85 by The New York Times
Company. Reprinted by permission

High Court calls U.S. law
only advisory for States

WASHINGTON, April 20—The Supreme Court ruled today that a Federal "bill of rights" for the mentally retarded, enacted six years ago, did not oblige the states to provide any particular level of care or training for retarded people in state institutions.

The 6-to-3 decision reversed key portions of a highly publicized Federal court ruling in Pennsylvania under which the Pennhurst State School was effectively placed under management of the United States Court of Appeals for the Third Circuit.

Release of Retarded People

In the case involving the retarded, the appeals court had ruled that the 1,200 residents of Pennhurst, a state institution, were being deprived of their right to treatment under the least restrictive setting possible. The court interpreted that right to include a presumption in favor of release from the institution and treatment in small community facilities.

While today's decision left some aspects of the appeals court ruling unresolved, the Supreme Court substantially blunted the 1975 law as a judicial tool for restructuring state care for the retarded.

The decision is likely to affect pending litigation around the country, including separate lawsuits by advocates for the retarded against New York, New Jersey and Connecticut. All three states had joined Pennsylvania in urging the Supreme Court to reverse the Third Circuit decision. The states argued that the Third Circuit's analysis would require them to spend tens of millions of dollars for "deinstitutionalization."

'Findings' in 'Bill of Rights'

The Federal law at issue was the Developmentally Disabled Assistance and Bill of Rights Act of 1975, which last year channeled $65 million to the states for care of the retarded.

The law contains a "bill of rights" section, setting forth as Congressional "findings" the right of a retarded person to "appropriate treatment" in an environment "that is least restrictive of the person's liberty."

The Pennhurst case was brought as a class-action lawsuit by family members of residents of the institution. They did not originally invoke the 1975 law, and they won their case in the United States District Court on other grounds. The appeals court, however, based its affirmation of the trial court's ruling on the "bill of rights" section, concluding that at least as a condition of the receipt of Federal funds states were required to provide the specified rights. ■

Two Aides Quit Education Dept.
in Dispute Over Views on Disabled

By Stephen Engleberg
Excerpted from *The New York Times*, April 19, 1985
Copyright © 1981/83/85 by The New York Times
Company. Reprinted by permission

WASHINGTON, April 18—Two Education Department officials resigned today after their criticism of Federal programs for the handicapped evoked angry protests from members of Congress and groups representing the disabled.

A spokesman for the department said that the two, Dr. Eileen M. Gardner and Lawrence A. Uzzell, had submitted their resignations to Education Secretary William J. Bennett. Earlier, Mr. Bennett said in a letter that some of Dr. Gardner's comments on the handicapped were "insensitive and repugnant." He had previously disavowed Mr. Uzzell's advocacy of abolishing major Federal education programs, including those affecting the handicapped.

The spokesman said that Mr. Bennett had not

Continued

demanded that the two officials step down. But he said, "The Secretary felt that their ability to be effective here in the Department had been compromised because of what happened."

A coalition of 16 groups representing the handicapped as well as several members of Congress had called for Dr. Gardner to resign. The coalition, in a letter to President Reagan, called her comments "an outrage and an insult to the fundamental principles of American democracy." Representative Tony Coehlo, a California Democrat, said that anyone holding such "prejudiced" opinions was unfit to serve "this or any other administration."

The controversy arose Tuesday when Senator Lowell P. Weicker Jr., the Connecticut Republican, confronted Mr. Bennett with a 1983 draft of a paper Dr. Gardner wrote for the Heritage Foundation, a research group where she was working as an analyst. The paper said that Federal programs for the handicapped were "selfish" and "misguided." They "drained resources from the normal school population," she said. ∎

Education for Persons with Disabilities Well Worth Extra Cost

By Robert Bernstein, a lawyer with the tax division of the U.S. Department of Justice. The original version of this article first appeared in the *Atlanta Journal and Constitution* on May 5, 1985

Eileen Marie Gardner apparently never met Ed Roberts. If she had, it might have saved her from losing her high policy post with the Reagan administration.

Eileen served briefly as a special consultant to Secretary of Education William J. Bennett. She resigned after an attack by Senator Lowell P. Weicker (R-Connecticut) for what Weicker called the "callousness" of her views on people with handicaps.

She had written that persons with handicaps have "selfishly drained resources from the normal school population" and that many people with disabilities simply "seek to have others bear their burdens."

The critical failing in these opinions, however, is not that they are callous. It is that they are fiscally irrational.

A prime justification for enactment of the Education of All Handicapped Children Act in 1975 was that the extra costs would represent sound economic investment. The added expense of educating a child with handicaps, by every thoughtful analysis, is minuscule compared to that of the alternative: maintaining the person for life as a helpless government ward, on welfare or in an institution.

The fate of Edward V. Roberts of Berkeley, California, could have been instructive to Eileen. Ed had polio as a teenager and still sleeps in an iron lung. During the day, he breathes with the aid of a respirator attached to the motorized wheelchair on which he reclines in a semi-horizontal position.

The family doctor told Ed's parents their son would always be "a vegetable." The California Department of Rehabilitation, a la Eileen, denied him educational funds on the ground he was medically "non-rehabilitable."

Later, for a period of eight years, Ed was the director of the same state agency. Today, he heads the World Institute on Disability, and was recently awarded a coveted "no-strings" MacArthur Foundation grant.

To be sure, not every person with severe disabilities can muster the drive and creativity of an Ed. But the vast majority can be productive to some degree, if they don't buy misguided medical and bureaucratic pronouncements of uselessness. The need, therefore, is to alter social expectations of persons with handicaps, rather than to deny them the opportunity to become self-supporting.

Eileen's crucial, but commonplace, error is her apparent belief that the function of the disability rights movement is simply to obtain handouts for its constituency. It is an interesting irony that handicapped activists are in fact more closely attuned to fiscal conservatism—and to prevailing administrative thinking—than is political appointee Eileen.

Thus, the ultimate aim of many disability leaders is one close to the conservative heart: to move as many of their constituents as possible off welfare rolls and into productive work. Far from asking others to "bear their

ISSUE UPDATE 1-3   Right to Education *(Continued)*

burdens," people with handicaps yearn most of all to become taxpayers instead of tax users. But they face enormous obstacles of encrusted prejudice, architectural, and transportation barriers.

The activists have found sympathetic listeners in the Reagan administration, at levels well above that of the departed Eileen. Vice President George Bush, for example, has demonstrated his support for the cause of people with handicaps on numerous occasions.

Most recently, Vice President Bush invited sixty-four disability leaders of the National Council of Independent Living Programs—directors of community efforts to maximize the self-reliance of their citizens with handicaps—to an April White House meeting.

Vice President Bush there expressed his personal admiration for the independent living movement (which, incidentally, was conceived and initiated by Ed).

Michael Uhlmann is a former White House aide who probably reflects the thinking of many Reaganites. He feels strongly that an important asset in avoiding a potential national labor shortage, and a serious Social Security crunch, is the latent productivity of people who are handicapped and/or elderly.

Undeniably, as Eileen suggests, it costs more to educate a person with a handicap than an able-bodied one. But, as Ed could have told her, it costs even more not to do it. ■

Systematic Treatment: 1850–1900

Social Climate

During the middle of the nineteenth century, progress in the United States was disrupted by a bitter civil war and the difficult period of reconstruction that followed. By the latter part of the century, the country was straining its resources to accommodate and assimilate peak numbers of immigrants. Although this was an extremely stressful period for the nation, dramatic gains in the understanding and treatment of people with mental retardation began to be apparent.

Understanding of mental retardation increased considerably, although some misconceptions remained. Definitions of mental deficiency, then commonly called *idiocy*, clearly differentiated the condition from mental illness and other disabilities. Many distinct etiological categories were identified and described (e.g., Down Syndrome, cretinism, hydrocephaly, microcephaly), although the causes of many of these conditions were poorly understood (Scheerenberger, 1983).

Throughout the latter half of the nineteenth century, the treatment of individuals with mental retardation continued to vary considerably. In rural areas, most people with mental retardation worked alongside their parents in the fields. In the cities, where most of the newly arrived immigrants were concentrated, many people with mental retardation worked in menial jobs or roamed the streets. Jails and almshouses continued to house those who got into trouble or who could not be supported and cared for by their families. However, the response of reformers to the deplorable conditions in these facilities finally culminated in the establishment of the first institutions designed as educational facilities for people with mental retardation.

Education

Remarkable gains were made during this period in the education of people with mental retardation. Eduoard Seguin (1812–1880), building upon the work of his teachers, Esquirol and Itard, was the first to translate a strong belief that "idiocy" was treatable into the explication and application of a detailed teaching approach specifically aimed at the amelioration of mental retardation. Born in France, Seguin was an adherent of Saint Simonism, a philosophy supporting the elevation of the poor and lowly through mass education (Seguin, 1866; Talbot, 1967). In addition, Seguin's early work with a boy with mental retardation was supervised and influenced by Itard. In 1837, Seguin founded in Paris the first successful school specifically for the education of children with mental retardation. In 1848, Seguin, fleeing the political upheaval surrounding the French Revolution and responding to the urging of Samuel Gridley Howe and others, emigrated from France to the United States. Here, he played a major role in the establishment of the first residential facilities for individuals with mental retardation, where his physiological method was widely applied as the dominant treatment approach.

The two most basic components of the physiological method were muscle training and sense training. Mastery of these motor and sensory skills then formed the basis for the acquisition of the more cognitive skills of drawing, reading, and writing, and culminated in extensive moral training. Seguin's method was a precursor of practices currently in use in that it utilized common, functional activities and relied upon techniques such as imitation and positive reinforcement. Punishment was rejected as inappropriate for use with individuals with mental retardation. Although not promising to cure *idiocy*, Seguin was generally quite optimistic in stating the anticipated outcomes of his approach:

> True, idiots have been improved, educated, and even cured; not one in a thousand has been entirely refractory to treatment; not one in a hundred who has not been made more happy and healthy; more than thirty per cent have been taught to conform to social and moral law, and rendered capable of order, of good feeling, and of working like the third of a man; more than forty per cent have become capable of the ordinary transactions of life under friendly control, of understanding moral and social abstractions, of working like two-thirds of a man; and twenty-five to thirty per cent come nearer and nearer to the standard of manhood, till some of them will defy the scrutiny of good judges when compared with ordinary young women and men (Seguin, 1866, pp. 74–75).

Seguin expected that teaching methods developed for children with mental retardation would ultimately be applicable to all children. His prediction was realized in the work of Maria Montessori (1870–1952), who was inspired by Seguin. Her approach, first delineated in a series of lectures to teachers of children with mental retardation, has been widely applied to children without disabilities throughout the world. The essence of Montessori's educational philosophy was that learning is spontaneous. Her method emphasized the use of a structured environment and didactic materials to maximize opportunities for spontaneous learning (Lane, 1979).

During the last half of the nineteenth century, the idea that individuals with mental retardation could benefit from education and training finally came into its own. Shortly after the establishment of Howe's wing for "idiots" in the Perkins Institute, several states in the Northeastern United States established state-supported institutions for the education and training of individuals with mental retardation. By 1876, the Association of Medical Officers of American Institutions for Idiotic and Feeble-Minded Persons, now known as the American Association on Mental Retardation, was formed, with Seguin as its first president. The early institutions were designed to educate children with mental retardation so they could return to society at the end of their school years to live as independent adults. The establishment of these early residential facilities was guided by the following principles (Crissey, 1975):

1. The institutions were to be small, with no more than 150–200 children.
2. They were to be located in rural areas with fresh air, milk, and good food.
3. The educational programs were designed to proceed sequentially from basic to more complex skills and from play to vocational activities.
4. The children were to be observed and studied to discover the causes of their defects.
5. There was to be close contact with the communities to which the residents would return at the end of their school years.

Unfortunately, by the turn of the century, these small educational facilities had been replaced by large, overcrowded, and primarily custodial institutions. Of the many factors contributing to this shift, perhaps two were most central. First, the attitudes of society towards people with mental retardation worsened as the condition was increasingly attributed to hereditary factors. Public opinion began to support the segregation of people with mental retardation as far as possible from the mainstream of society, particularly women of child-bearing age. Second, it was apparent that many of the trainees would not be able to live fully independent lives if released. In the absence of community programs for adults with mental retardation, the parents of these adults begged that they be allowed to remain in the institutions (Scheerenberger, 1983).

In spite of the trend toward institutionalization, many people with mental retardation continued to live at home with their families. The first public day-school classes for children with mental retardation in the United States are generally thought to have started in Providence, Rhode Island in 1894 (Legarde, 1903). Although some special educators believed that special classes should prepare individuals with mental retardation to enter institutions, Rhoda Esten, in Providence, aspired to train the students to become self-supporting citizens. Her program included four components: (1) sense training; (2) modified academic subjects; (3) industrial training; and (4) nature study (Scheerenberger, 1983). After seven years of operation, the Providence special classes were judged to be highly successful by Ellen Legarde, the director of physical training for those classes. The following paragraph conveys the essence of her assessment:

> It is safe to say eighty per cent of the children are cured. By cured one does not mean made into Edisons, Marconis or Roosevelts, but lifted up to better things. Oscar, who greets me in the big department shop where he is a cash-boy, is able to be an intelligent cash-boy, slow of speech to be sure, but patient and painstaking. Angelina May, who at fourteen used to follow me noisily on the streets and insist I note her new gown or shoes, is now at twenty in a jewelry shop packing cheap jewelry and putting what

was once a restless, talkative, never concentrated self into quiet, well directed, energetic labor. Jacob and Annie will never be any better, but they can read and write, know right from wrong and have been taught that cleanliness is a necessary part of life, as well as good manners. John and Susie and Maude are back in the grades, not brilliant but doing as well as their limited abilities will allow. Not disgraced because they were "born short" but aided and encouraged to make the best possible of what is in them. Such are the types. Few are lost, many saved, all improved (Legarde, 1903, p. 38).

As we have seen, the period from 1800 to 1850 was characterized by dramatic progress in the treatment of individuals with mental retardation. For the first time, the cause of mental retardation had attracted the talents of numerous able and influential champions and promising methods of education had been developed. Disappointingly, this initiative did not long survive the turn of the century. By the early 1900s, considerable momentum had been lost and negative attitudes and pessimism had begun to replace the early optimism. Issue Update 1-4 illustrates the continued ambivalence of society about whether people with mental retardation should be segregated from or accepted into the community.

ISSUE UPDATE 1-4   Right to Participate in Society

Court to Rule on Texas Zoning Ban for Retarded

Published in *The New York Times*, November 27, 1984
Copyright © 1984 by Associated Press. Reprinted by permission

CLEBURNE, Tex., Nov. 26 (AP)—It is a nice small-town neighborhood with solid, working-class people. And it is a nice old house, with fresh beige paint and a broad, inviting porch.

But no one lives there. And no one will until the United States Supreme Court makes a decision.

The owners of the house at 201 Featherston wanted to provide a home for mildly retarded people and have challenged a city zoning ordinance that excludes "hospitals for the feeble-minded" from the neighborhood.

The Court is to decide whether excluding such homes through zoning laws violates the civil rights of the retarded. The Court's decision, expected by July, could have a vast effect on the rights of the mentally retarded.

One of Many Neighborhoods

Experts say hundreds of neighborhoods across the country have faced similar disputes since mental health institutions and state schools have come under pressure from the courts to return mildly or moderately retarded people to the community.

"It would not have been worth it to fight this battle if we were the only ones who would benefit," said Jan Hannah, 42 years old, who owns the house. "I didn't intend to be a crusader, but I've kind of taken on that characteristic."

Mrs. Hannah, who has worked with the retarded for 18 years, bought the house in 1980 and asked the City Council for a permit to use the home to house 13 mentally retarded men and women, who would receive 24-hour supervision.

Neighbors objected, fearing violence from the home's residents, a drop in property values or trouble between the residents and students at a junior high school across the street.

ISSUE UPDATE 1-4   Right to Participate in Society *(Continued)*

Attitude of Some Neighbors

Joe Marchbanks, 65 years old, who lives three doors away, said: "If these people get by with this, all cities might as well do away with their laws. We've lived here all our lives and I don't know why we should be subjected to this."

Residents would be mildly to moderately retarded, Mrs. Hannah said, and would not have tendencies toward violence. There would be no curfew or security system at the residence.

Frank Hyde, principal of the junior high school, said he accepted Mrs. Hannah's assurances. However, he worried about the reactions of some students. "Seventh- and eighth-grade kids might not always be the kindest people," he said.

Cleburne, a city of about 19,000 people 25 miles south of Fort Worth, classified the house as a "hospital for the feeble-minded" because of the 24-hour care.

Mrs. Hannah and her company, Cleburne Living Centers, which owns and operates three smaller homes for the mentally retarded in neighboring towns, sued the city in Federal District Court after it rejected her application.

The court threw out the suit, saying the city's ordinance was "rational."

Parallel With Sexism Seen

However, the United States Court of Appeals for the Fifth Circuit, in New Orleans, ruled for Mrs. Hannah, saying laws that placed the mentally retarded in a different category must be judged as are those treating the sexes differently.

The case was accepted by the Supreme Court after Cleburne officials appealed the higher court's ruling.

Mayor George Marti of Cleburne said city officials would not comment on the case while it is before the Supreme Court.

Jim McKenna, director of administration for the Arlington-based Association of Retarded Citizens, said the case was crucial to efforts to move patients out of institutions and into communities.

Mrs. Hannah said she had a waiting list of 30 mentally retarded people now living with their families or in institutions who were capable of handling life in the home and holding down jobs at a nearby workshop. ■

Retarded Denied a Special Status

Excerpted from *The New York Times*, July 2, 1985
Copyright © 1981/83/85 by The New York Times
Company. Reprinted by permission

But High Court Holds a City in Texas Unlawfully Rejected Bid for a Group Home

WASHINGTON, July 1—While ruling that the Constitution does not give the mentally retarded special protection against official discrimination, the Supreme Court nonetheless concluded today that a Texas city's denial of a zoning permit for a home for the retarded was so irrational as to be unconstitutional.

All nine Justices agreed that the zoning permit was unconstitutionally denied. The Court divided 6 to 3 on the underlying question of what constitutional standard to apply in analyzing the problem.

Advocates for the mentally retarded around the country had looked to this case, which concerned a proposed home for 13 people in Cleburne, Tex., as a key

constitutional test of the rights of the retarded under the equal protection guarantee of the 14th Amendment. The message the Court delivered, in an opinion by Associate Justice Byron R. White, was a mixed one.

On the one hand, the Court said, "mere negative attitudes," "vague fear" and "irrational prejudice" may not form the basis for official action that places the retarded at a disadvantage. The Court found that those factors were at the heart of Cleburne's decision not to permit the home in an area already zoned for apartments, fraternity houses and convalescent homes.

'Heightened Scrutiny' Denied

On the other hand, Justice White said for the 6-to-3 majority that the retarded as a group do not have the characteristics that had led the Court to accord "heightened judicial scrutiny" to official actions that affect such groups as racial minorities, aliens, illegitimate children and women. It is difficult for a law to survive a constitutional challenge once the heightened standard is applied.

Continued

Under "heightened scrutiny," a law that singles out members of these groups for particular treatment will be declared unconstitutional unless it serves an "important" or, in the case of race or national origin, "compelling" governmental interest. ■

Group Homes Up; Need Still Unmet

By Susan Landers
Published in *APA Monitor*, May 1988

Thanks to the support of state legislatures and federal and state courts, community group homes for people who are mentally ill or mentally retarded increased tenfold between 1972 and 1982.

But Arlene Kanter, staff attorney for the Mental Health Law Project, a Washington-based advocacy group, warned those at a February meeting of the President's Committee on Mental Retardation not to relax their vigilance because local opposition to group homes is still strong.

Kanter said there were 611 group homes for 16 or fewer residents in 1972. By 1982, there were 6,500. But despite that increase, she said, "group homes are not keeping pace with the need."

Thirty-five states, she said, have now passed statutes to allow for residential facilities for up to 16 individuals who are mentally ill or have developmental disabilities. Those laws, which take precedence over local zoning ordinances, however, exclude homes for former drug or alcohol abusers in many cases.

Federal and state courts have also been ruling in favor of group homes. In 1985, the U.S. Supreme Court struck down a zoning ordinance in Cleburne, Texas that had required special permits for group homes for people with mental retardation.

In a decision handed down last December, the U.S. District Court in Ashland, Ky. repealed two local zoning ordinances that kept mentally ill people from living in Ashland's residential neighborhoods.

When Pathways, Inc., a nonprofit organization serving mentally ill people in eastern Kentucky, was denied permits to build housing for mentally ill people, four prospective residents of the proposed apartment building filed an $8.5 million lawsuit against the city. The Dec. 17 decision in its favor has allowed Pathways to proceed with its plans to open an apartment building this year that will house 15 individuals.

However, even as the courts slash away at local zoning regulations and states pass the necessary laws to circumvent them, would-be neighbors of group homes continue to find new tactics to oppose them.

In 1984, several homeowners in Greenwich, Conn. asked for and received a reduction in their tax assessments when they claimed that the location in their neighborhood of a half-way house for people with mental illnesses would lower property values.

The state attorney general filed suit against the tax board, claiming that by lowering the rate, it had discriminated against the half-way house residents.

The case was settled out of court last May, with the town of Greenwich agreeing to readjust the assessments without admitting to any wrongdoing. The Superior Court in Stamford, however, did find that "It is impermissible under the United States and Connecticut Constitutions and the Connecticut General Statutes to rely upon the mental disabilities of the residents of the Davis Avenue Group Home as a factor in assessing the effects of a group residence upon property values or to use as a basis for lower assessments any such factor."

Other well-to-do property owners have seized upon the tactic of buying properties that they learn are being considered for group use. In Alexandria, Va., several families bought a home for more than its asking price while the city council was still debating whether to allow it to be used as a group home for people with mental illnesses. No court action resulted, and a different property was successfully purchased for the group home.

However, when a group in New York tried that same ploy earlier, New York courts disallowed the neighbors' purchase and ruled that the would-be buyers had to pay all court costs.

These actions, noted Kanter, are usually motivated by unfounded fears that could be overcome through education.

For instance, community residents' most common concern is that a group home in the neighborhood will devalue property, but several studies have found that property values are not affected. The District of Columbia Association for Retarded Citizens found no change in the pattern of housing sales or the sale prices of homes in neighborhoods with group homes for people who are mentally retarded. The neighborhoods were sound and stable and the appearances of the group homes matched or exceeded the quality of private homes nearby, their study showed.

Another study by the Governor's Planning Council on Developmental Disabilities in Chicago looked at 2,000 residential properties and determined that group homes for people with developmental disabilities affect neither the value of residential property in the surrounding neighborhoods nor the stability of the neighborhood.

Other erroneous beliefs, said Kanter, are that the presence of a group home will destroy the tranquility of their neighborhoods, or that people with mental retardation are dangerous, but studies show the opposite is true. The Chicago study followed the activities of 2,200 people with disabilities and found the crime rate for those living in group homes was substantially lower than that of the general population. ■

For additional information, contact the Mental Health Law Project, 2021 L St. N.W., Suite 800, Washington, DC 20036.

Source: Susan Landers, APA Monitor, May 1988, pp. 32–33. Copyright 1988 by the American Psychological Association. Reprinted by permission.

The First Half of the Twentieth Century

Social Climate

The Peak of Pessimism: 1900–1929

From 1900 through the 1920s, optimism concerning the prospects of ameliorating mental retardation was replaced by profound pessimism:

> The first decades of the twentieth century represented the nadir of professional sensitivity toward mentally retarded persons, at least as a class or subpopulation (Scheerenberger, 1983, p. 138).

Education and training efforts in institutions were largely replaced by custodial care. The belief that mental retardation was caused by environmental factors was replaced by a belief that mental retardation was caused by hereditary factors. The view expressed by Edgar Doll was perhaps typical:

> In approximately two-thirds of the cases investigated, feeble-mindedness has been traced to biological inheritance of defective germ-plasm (Doll, 1917, p. 34).

Positive attitudes toward individuals with mental retardation were replaced by negative attitudes. Numerous scientific and social developments, both within and beyond the field of mental retardation, were responsible for these changes. However, two particular developments were, perhaps, of central importance: the eugenics movement and the development of mental testing.

Sir Francis Galton heralded the beginning of the eugenics movement with his 1901 paper entitled, "Possible Improvement of the Human Breed." Building upon the theories of Darwin, Galton introduced the concept that individual differences in intelligence are determined by heredity. With the widespread acceptance of this position, mental retardation was no longer considered remediable. Even more devastating was the related idea that the human race could be improved through eugenics (Maloney & Ward, 1978). In the United States, data interpreted as supporting these theories were taken from several family history studies, the most famous of which traced several generations of two families, the Jukes and the Kallikaks. Although Dugdale's study of the Jukes was originally published in 1877, it was reprinted and reinterpreted in 1910. Dugdale studied the offspring of five sisters, and reported a high incidence of criminality and indigence. Although Dugdale specifically identified only one case of mental retardation, later interpretation of his work by Arthur Estabrook of the Eugenics Records Office asserted that one-half of the Jukes were feeble-minded. Furthermore, Estabrook concluded as follows:

> All of the Juke criminals were feeble-minded, and the eradication of crime in defective stocks depends on the elimination of mental deficiency (Estabrook, 1916, p. 85).

Goddard's study of the Kallikaks was published in 1912. In it he traced the ancestors of Deborah Kallikak, a resident of an institution for individuals with mental retardation, back to Martin Kallikak, a Revolutionary War soldier. Martin apparently sired two lines of descendants. Goddard traced one line of offspring, the majority of whom were judged to be of subnormal intelligence, back to Martin's union with a woman whom he had met in a tavern and who apparently had mental retardation. The other line of offspring, all judged to be normal and generally successful, were traced to Martin's marriage to a woman of average intelligence. Goddard was led by his data to the following conclusions:

> We find on the good side of the family prominent people in all walks of life and nearly all of the 496 descendants owners of land or proprietors. On the bad side we find paupers, criminals, prostitutes, drunkards, and examples of all forms of social pest with which modern society is burdened.
>
> From this we conclude that feeble-mindedness is largely responsible for these social sores.
>
> Feeble-mindedness is hereditary and transmitted as surely as any other character. We cannot successfully cope with these conditions until we recognize feeble-mindedness and its hereditary nature, recognize it early, and take care of it (Goddard, 1912, pp. 116–117).

Although these findings were widely accepted in their time as concrete evidence of the hereditary nature of intelligence, more recent critics (e.g., Smith, 1985) have noted the unreliability of these retrospective estimates of mental retardation as well as the plausibility of environment-based interpretations of the findings.

The eugenics movement received further support from the widespread belief that individuals with mental retardation were more fertile and reproduced at a much higher rate than individuals of average intelligence. The anticipated increase in the proportion of individuals with mental retardation was perceived as a threat to society. It was reasoned that previous generations had escaped this danger through "natural selection" and the "survival of the fittest." The present society's efforts to protect persons with mental retardation were viewed as violations of the natural order likely to foster undesirable increases in the population with mental retardation (Davies & Ecob, 1964).

In 1911, the Research Committee of the Eugenics Section of the American Breeder's Association considered various possible solutions ranging from laissez-faire to euthanasia. Although they rejected euthanasia, they recommended that two remedies be generally applied to reduce the menace of mental deficiency. The committee's primary recommendation was that mentally defective people should be segregated from society for life, or at least during their reproductive years. Second, sterilization was recommended as an adjunct to segregation. Both remedies were applied widely during the first half of the twentieth century, although never universally. Institutions grew rapidly in size, but they were never adequate to serve the entire population with mental retardation. Sterilization laws proliferated in many states, and were supported by the Supreme Court in 1927 as constitutional. At that time, Justice Oliver Wendell Holmes stated:

> It is better for all the world, if instead of waiting to execute degenerate offspring for crime, or to let them starve for their imbecility, society can prevent those who are manifestly unfit from continuing their kind. The principle that sustains compulsory vaccination is broad enough to cover the cutting of the Fallopian tubes. . . . Three generations of imbeciles are enough (Sloan & Stevens, 1976, p. 135).

More than half of the states eventually enacted sterilization laws, some of which remain in effect today. As shown in Issue Update 1-5, controversy continues to surround the issue of mandatory sterilization of people with mental retardation.

In Germany, the eugenics movement was carried to its ultimate extreme with respect to disabilities as well as ethnicity. In 1939 Hitler authorized physicians to grant release to incurably ill patients through euthanasia. Institutionalized people with mental retardation and mental illness were initially starved to death. Later they were gassed, until eventually 70,000 of these individuals died in gas chambers. This active euthanasia program was officially terminated in 1941 in response to public protests, but continued more discreetly as a prelude to the holocaust (Scheerenberger, 1983).

The influences of the development and widespread application of mental tests were intertwined with those of the eugenics movement. The intelligence test developed in France in 1905 by Binet and Simon was intended to select slow-learning children for special educational treatment and was developed in the belief that intelligence was modifiable (Scheerenberger, 1983). The test was brought to the United States and translated by Goddard, who was impressed by its usefulness for differentiating among the ability levels of the residents with mental retardation at the Vineland Training School in New Jersey. The Binet-Simon test was soon employed as a means to seek out and identify individuals with mental retardation so that society could be protected from them, not as a means to enhance their

ISSUE UPDATE 1-5   Right to Reproductive Freedom

Sterilization Now a Power of Courts

By Harvey Fisher
Published in *The Bergen Record*, February 19, 1981
Reprinted by permission of The Record of Hackensack, N.J.

Courts now can order the incompetent sterilized

TRENTON—Courts have the power to decide whether mentally incompetent people should be sterilized for their own benefit, the New Jersey Supreme Court has ruled.

In a landmark decision yesterday the high court, however, said judges may consider sterilizations only when individuals, because of their mental impairments, are incapable of deciding for themselves if they should have children.

Individuals' interest cited

The ruling was immediately hailed by Deputy Public Advocate Herbert Hinkle, who originally opposed such sterilizations unless rigid standards and safeguards were applied. "This decision protects the rights of the retarded from abuse in this area but at the same time gives them the right to choose, through a surrogate, whether to have a family," he said.

The seven Supreme Court justices emphasized court-authorized sterilizations like tubal ligations on women and vasectomies on men will be allowed only when such procedures are in the best interests of the individuals. That sterilizations of mentally incompetent persons might be of benefit to the parents, the state, or society as a whole should in no way enter into the decision, they said.

Factors to be considered

What should be considered, they noted, are such factors as the possibility the incompetent person could become pregnant and psychological damage might result, the person's present and future capacity to understand reproduction or contraception, and the person's ability to care for children.

Thus judges, for example, not only will be considering whether persons with mental disorders are capable in the future of raising children, but also whether they will be able to do so with the aid of a spouse.

The justices established a nine-point test for judges in the Chancery Division of Superior Court to determine if sterilization is in the incompetent person's best interests.

"By applying the standards we have developed, courts will be able to protect the human rights of people least able to protect themselves," Justice Morris Pashman said in a 54-page opinion that was based heavily on an individual's right to privacy. He said the ruling is a natural outgrowth of the court's decision five years ago in the celebrated Karen Ann Quinlan case in which the court allowed the parents of the comatose woman to disconnect artificial life-support systems.

The latest decision came in a case involving 19-year-old Lee Ann Grady, a mentally retarded Sparta woman whose parents and court-appointed guardian have been trying to have her sterilized for her own good. She is said to function at the level of a 4-year-old, and experts see no likelihood there will be any medical breakthrough in the near future in treating her disorder, known as Down's Syndrome or mongolism.

Superior Court Judge Bertram Polow previously had authorized the sterilization. Although agreeing with much of Polow's decision, the Supreme Court ordered a reversal solely on grounds that it wants him to reconsider the case in light of the newly established standards.

Miss Grady's court-appointed attorney-guardian for the case, Richard Kahn, declined comment.

Pashman, who over the years has been one of the most liberal members of the court, repeatedly said the decision should not be interpreted in any way as approving compulsory sterilization.

"Lee Ann should have the opportunity to lead a life as rewarding as her condition will permit," he wrote. "Courts should cautiously but resolutely help her achieve the fullness of that opportunity. If she can have a richer and more active life only if the risk of pregnancy is permanently eliminated, then sterilization may be in her best interests. Upon a clear and convincing demonstration, it should not be denied to her."

Although there is nothing to indicate the woman has had any sexual encounters, her parents, Edward and Luann Grady, have been giving her birth control pills for the past four years. They say they are planning soon to send her to a coed home for the retarded and it is conceiv-

ISSUE UPDATE 1-5   Right to Reproductive Freedom *(Continued)*

able she might have sexual experiences there. She takes the pills only under her mother's supervision. The case developed after Morristown Memorial Hospital refused to perform the sterilization without court authorization.

Referring to the Quinlan case, Pashman said an individual's personal right to control her own body and life is a right of privacy that overrides the state's general interest in preserving life. "If one can decide to forgo artificial life-preservation and thereby sacrifice life, then one certainly can decide to forgo reproductive capacity and thereby relinquish the ability to procreate," he reasoned.

Continuing, he said: "The right to choose among procreation, sterilization, and other methods of contraception is an important privacy right of all individuals. Our courts must preserve that right. Where an incompetent person lacks the mental capacity to make that choice, a court should ensure the exercise of that right on behalf of the incompetent in a manner that reflects his or her best interests."

In so ruling, the New Jersey Supreme Court

departed from decisions in many other states in recent years, where courts have declined to order sterilization of incompetent individuals because there was no state law granting such authority.

In the Quinlan case the court was told the comatose 22-year-old woman would die once the artificial life-support apparatus was turned off. To the amazement of medical experts, however, she is still alive in a coma. Once a judge has decided that sterilization is in the best interest of an incompetent person, he must appoint a lawyer, who, along with the judge, must pursue all avenues to make sure the right decision is being made. Unless the Supreme Court modifies its decision in the future, only the parents can initiate the sterilization request, and they will have the burden of proving by "clear and convincing evidence" that their child lacks the capacity to consent or withhold consent. The clear and convincing standard of proof is much stricter than normally required in civil cases.

Associate Justice Alan Handler issued a separate but concurring opinion. ■

Court Authorizes Forcing Sterility

Excerpted from *The New York Times*, February 18, 1988. Copyright © 1988 by Associated Press. Reprinted with permission

---

Iowa Ruling Permits Action for the Mentally Retarded

DES MOINES, Feb. 17 (AP)—The Iowa Supreme Court said today that lower courts could authorize the sterilization of mentally retarded people but refused to say when the procedure was appropriate.

In a narrowly drawn opinion, seven of the eight justices agreed that courts could act on a request that mentally retarded people be sterilized even though a state law providing for such action was repealed in 1977.

"We conclude that our district courts possess subject matter jurisdiction over, and accordingly may hear and determine, applications seeking authorization for sterilization of a mentally incapacitated ward," the

high court said in an opinion written by Justice Bruce Snell.

In his dissent, Justice K. David Harris said the court was wandering into a subject "shot through with searching social and ethical questions."

Limits Seen on Court Fitness

"In taking this first wide leap, the majority commits itself to the eventual resolution of a twisted conglomeration of attendant social and ethical issues," Justice Harris said. "Future litigants, faced with unanswered questions of great social and ethical dimensions, or with missing ingredients of a vague application process, will continue to press us for determinations we are singularly unfit to reach."

But the majority rejected that reasoning.

"We do not believe our courts lack jurisdiction over a case merely because the case is important or unavoidably includes a constitutional dimension," the court said.

The decision came in the case of Jan and Tekla

Continued

Matejski, who are the legal guardians of their 33-year-old mentally retarded daughter, court records said. When the couple filed an application in Polk County Court seeking authorization to have their daughter sterilized, a lawyer appointed by the court to guard the daughter's rights objected, saying there was no provision in Iowa law allowing sterilization.

Ground Rules Were Asked

The county judge, Glenn E. Pille, agreed and dismissed the application.

Both sides appealed, arguing over whether courts have the power to order sterilization and asking the high court to set ground rules.

Lawyers for the retarded woman noted that in 1977

the Legislature repealed a law providing for sterilization of people "who are mentally ill or retarded, syphilitic, habitual criminals, moral degenerates, or sexual perverts and who are a menace to society."

But while agreeing that lower courts can decide such requests, the high court refused to specify guidelines.

"We are not persuaded that such action is appropriate given the posture of the present case," the court said, adding what was being asked was "in the nature of an advisory opinion."

Justice Harris said the decision would haunt the justices. "At what level of mental retardation can sterilization be compelled?" he said. "What board or body, if any, will suggest statewide standards?" ■

education. The concept of IQ constancy inherent in the testing movement provided further justification for the abandonment of education and training efforts (see Chapter 3). Because the new test facilitated the identification of mild mental retardation, the ranks of people labeled mentally retarded swelled dramatically. Although the advent of mental tests undoubtedly increased the precision of our knowledge of mental retardation, it also served to increase the perceived menace to society (Maloney & Ward, 1978).

Moderation: 1930–1950
The period between 1930 and 1950 has been described as "The Great Lull" (Maloney & Ward, 1978), during which little progress was made in the field of mental retardation. This characterization overlooks important progress in at least two areas: attitudes and treatment.

In the wake of the Great Depression, the political and social concerns of most Americans shifted to issues relating to economic recovery. This shift is undoubtedly responsible, at least in part, for drawing attention away from the menace of mental retardation. However, numerous other developments during this period also contributed to the tempering of attitudes toward individuals with mental retardation. The examination of data from a variety of sources cast doubt upon previous conceptions of the nature and origins of mental retardation. The notion of IQ constancy was challenged. Terman, in 1919, had observed sizable shifts in IQ scores with repeated testing. Now, research data consistent with Terman's observations began to appear. Bayley's (1949) longitudinal studies demonstrated that intelligence continues to develop with increasing age. Skeels and Dye (1939) reported that orphaned infants classified as mentally retarded and placed under the attentive care of female residents of an institution for individuals with mental retardation gained dramatically in IQ. Infants originally classified as average and dull normal who remained in the relatively unstimulating orphanage environment declined in IQ. In spite of serious methodological shortcomings (Longstreth, 1981), the widely publicized findings of this study clearly stimulated further efforts to challenge the notion of IQ constancy.

The above research also contributed to a declining belief that heredity alone was responsible for the majority of cases of mental retardation. In addition, studies of the offspring of individuals with mental retardation failed to confirm expectations of a high incidence of the condition. In fact, they tended to find that the intellectual level of the children was generally superior to that of their parents. Considerable progress was also made during this period in identifying various causes of mental retardation, including phenylketonuria, toxoplasmosis, and glandular, enzyme, vitamin, and protein deficiencies. Many of these causes were associated with primarily environmental, as opposed to hereditary, factors. According to Scheerenberger (1983), by the early 1930s, the proportion of mental retardation attributed to hereditary causes had declined to about 30 percent from nearly 100 percent at the turn of the century.

Finally, it became apparent that rates of crime and delinquency among individuals with mental retardation were not as high as had been feared. Studies typically yielded estimates of between 10 and 24 percent. Although these rates were higher than delinquency rates for the general population, it was acknowledged that less intelligent individuals were more vulnerable to arrest (Doll, 1962). In addition, as institutions expanded their services into the community, professionals became aware of a segment of this population that was well-adjusted to home and community. Numerous instances of successful parole and community placement programs were reported (Doll, 1962; Scheerenberger, 1983). Even Fernald (1919), in a follow-up study of former residents of Waverly, concluded that "a few defectives do not need or deserve life-long segregation" (p. 31). His conclusion was based upon the results of his survey, which indicated that many individuals did quite well upon return to the community and that rates of criminality and sex offense were lower than expected.

Together, the events of this period led to a weakening of the belief in IQ constancy, the heritability of intelligence, and the association of crime and delinquency with mental retardation. By 1930, leading professionals such as Goddard and Fernald had made dramatic turnabouts in their initially pessimistic views of mental retardation. By 1950, a widespread improvement in public attitudes toward mental retardation had become apparent. Mental retardation was no longer viewed as a menace to society. It was clear that individuals with mental retardation did not inevitably become criminals and they did not necessarily produce offspring with mental retardation. Even more important, the realization that IQ was not fixed reopened the possibility of effective education and training.

Education

Progress during the first half of the twentieth century in education for people with mental retardation, although perhaps less dramatic than in the previous century, was no less important. Residential and community programs were established that determined the direction of future developments in the field. Although some educational progress continued to be made in residential settings, this progress was mitigated by an emphasis on custodial care, the domination of a medical treatment model, and overcrowding and understaffing. Even when educational programs in institutions were maintained, student-teacher ratios were often as high as 70 to 1 (Scheerenberger, 1983). In spite of decreasing scientific and ideological justification for the confinement of persons with mental retardation, institutional populations grew at a phenomenal rate during this period, increasing from 40,000 in 1925 to 128,000 in 1950. Many factors appear to have contributed to this increase. First, medical science was becoming more successful at increasing the survival rate of infants with birth defects. Second, a pattern of institutional care had become well-established. Third, society's perception of mental retardation as a threat was slow to yield to disconfirming scientific evidence. Finally, and most important, the economic strains of the Great Depression and the two world wars created hardships leading families to seek the existing relief offered by state facilities (The President's Committee on Mental Retardation, 1977). During the first half of the twentieth century, the focal point of progress in the education and training of individuals with mental retardation gradually shifted from the institution to the public school special class. Although only a few special classes had existed at the turn of the century, by 1930, sixteen states had either permissive or mandatory legislation regarding the establishment of special classes. (Scheerenberger, 1983).

One early leader in the special class movement was Elizabeth Farrell (1870–1932). With Lightner Witmer, she conducted a model special class at the University of Pennsylvania (Doll, 1962). She also taught at New York University and Teachers College, Columbia University, and served as Inspector of Ungraded Classes for New York City. During the summer of 1922, while teaching at Teachers College, she was instrumental in founding the Council for Exceptional Children. She served as its first president for four years. Farrell advocated classes for children with IQs below 50 as well as trade schools for older students with mental retardation.

Scheerenberger (1983) has identified at least three divergent educational philosophies that were represented in the education of children with mental retardation during these years. The most conservative approach emphasized the limitations of individuals with mental retardation and advocated only limited education. The guiding principle of this approach, as stated by E. R. Johnstone was: " 'Happiness' first, all else follows" (Johnstone, 1924, p. 54).

A second philosophy, characterized as "progressive," emphasized social and emotional growth. The curriculum was oriented toward individual needs and interests with an emphasis on those skills needed for independent living.

Finally, the most flexible and optimistic approach was advocated by J. E. Wallace Wallin (1924). Wallin recommended separate classes for three categories of children: trainable children, children with mild mental retardation unsuitable for return to a regular class, and children with mild mental retardation who might be returned to a regular class.

The emerging field was also influenced by several widely used textbooks (Descoeudres, 1928; Ingram, 1935; Inskeep, 1926; Wallin, 1949). Toward the end of this period, Strauss and Lehtinen (1947) published their influential book on teaching methods which were designed for children with mental retardation due to brain injury. Their approach emphasized controlling the environment to minimize distractions and focus attention on the material to be learned. Techniques included covering classroom windows, isolating children in distraction-free cubicles, using short assignments, and enhancing foreground stimuli.

It should be noted that, in spite of the rapid growth of special classes, many children with mental retardation, especially those with IQs below 50, were excluded from the public schools. Home instruction was sometimes offered as an alternative. Although school board decisions were challenged by some parents, courts were generally supportive of the school boards. During the period between 1930 and 1950, firm foundations for the field of special education were laid. At the same time, seeds of discontent were sown that ultimately blossomed into the powerful parent movement of the 1950s.

Recent Developments: 1950 to the Present

As illustrated in the Issue Updates throughout this chapter, most of the key social issues relating to the treatment of people with mental retardation that have challenged past societies continue to be relevant today. In spite of the continuing controversy surrounding many of these issues, the period since 1950 has seen the emergence of a strong national commitment to the education of people with mental retardation. The remainder of this chapter is devoted to tracing this emergence.

The 1950s

During the 1950s, children with moderate mental retardation emerged as a focus of concern, largely through the efforts of increasingly well-organized parent advocacy groups. The majority of these children were excluded from public school programs. In the spring of 1950, a group of parents attending the annual meeting of the American Association on Mental Deficiency planned an organizing convention that was held in Minnesota in September of that year. The meeting was attended by representatives from state and local organizations already in existence in about fourteen states. This group founded a national organization called the National Association of Parents and Friends of Mentally Retarded Children. Subsequently, the organization has undergone several name changes, becoming the National Association for Retarded Children in 1952, the National Association for Retarded Citizens in 1974, the Association for Retarded Citizens of the United States in 1980, and most recently, in 1991, "The Arc." Although the formation of a national parent association was an event of far-reaching consequence, not all parent activity was coordinated through that organization. Many state and local groups were emerging simultaneously during this period (Katz, 1961).

The eventual admission of children with "trainable" mental retardation, as children with severe to moderate mental retardation were then labeled, to public school programs is generally credited to the effective parent initiatives of that period. However, Ignacy Goldberg pointed out in an interview with Rubenfeld (1983) that this shift to public education was not always accomplished smoothly. In 1958, Goldberg had been commissioned by the National Association for Retarded Children to survey special education for trainable children across the United States. This survey, itself a reflection of the parents' seriousness, seemed to serve as a stimulus to further program growth (The President's Committee on Mental Retardation, 1977). Goldberg observed that many parent groups had, by then, established their own programs. However, the dedicated although sometimes untrained teachers and the parent-developed curricula of these programs were not always welcome in the public schools. Furthermore, the professionals themselves were divided as to the merits of including trainable children in public school programs.

Many educators believed that it was inadvisable to provide a public school education for trainable retarded children (Williams & Wallin, 1959). Institutional care and treatment were frequently recommended. For example, in Goodenough's (1956) textbook, she asserted that "the ordinary modern home is not a suitable place in which to rear a feeble-minded child" (p. 233). She recommended training in "attitudes, habits, and some form of useful work" (p. 266) and felt that this training could be best provided in the institution. The philosophical underpinnings of this position were clearly articulated by Cruickshank (1958) in his debate with Goldberg. Cruickshank pointed out that, first, public education had been established to educate those with the ability to learn. Second, public education was based on the assumption that those educated would return something to society. Third, placement of these retarded children in public schools could mislead parents into expecting that their children would become normal. Cruickshank concluded that because none of these goals were attainable by trainable retarded children, there could be no benefit to the individual or to society in admitting them to the public schools. He recommended improved residential services for this population. Goldberg (1958) defended the opposing view that both the trainable retarded individual and society could benefit from admitting these children to public school programs. He argued that trainable children had the right to develop to their fullest potential and that public schools were best equipped to provide that opportunity. The latter position eventually won out, with increasing numbers of public school systems accepting responsibility throughout the 1950s for educating trainable mentally retarded children.

The public education of trainable children eventually led to concern over their post-school placement options. Although the results of several evaluation studies, reported by Connor (1958), indicated that children with IQs above 20 did tend to profit from the programs, it was clear that most would not be able to function as completely independent adults. Connor pointed out that it was essential to make plans to provide the support services they would need throughout life. The urgency of this need was also reflected in the priorities of the parent organizations. These organizations advocated the creation of a variety of community programs for adolescents and adults with mental retardation, such as vocational training, sheltered employment, and social clubs (Weingold, 1952).

Also during the 1950s, the federal government began to make explicit provisions for advancing scientific knowledge in the area of mental retardation, as well as improving the quality of educational services for individuals with mental retardation. Federal grant programs were initiated to support research and research training. For example, in 1954 the Cooperative Research Program was established by the passage of PL83–531. When funds were finally appropriated to implement this program during the 1957 fiscal year, two-thirds of those funds were designated to foster cooperative research between the government and institutions of higher education on the education of individuals with mental retardation (Conrad, 1958). In 1958, the first federal law specific to mental retardation, PL85–926, was enacted. It provided for the training of teachers and other professionals to work with individuals with mental retardation (LaVor, 1976). This decade is, perhaps, best characterized by the reemergence of mental retardation as an area of national concern.

The 1960s

The 1960s were dominated by a concern for the rights of minority individuals, including individuals with mental retardation. As president, John F. Kennedy turned the national spotlight upon mental retardation. He was acutely sensitive to this issue as the brother of a woman with mental retardation, and immediately urged the country to launch a full-scale attack on the problem. In 1961, President Kennedy appointed the President's Panel on Mental Retardation. In 1962, the Panel issued a report that exerted a major impact on the field. The Panel's recommendations emphasized the need for research and urged a shift toward comprehensive community-based services for individuals with mental retardation. The development of a continuum of educational programs to serve children with even the most severe mental retardation was recommended, as was the expansion of adult services (The President's Panel on Mental Retardation, 1962). The report represented the first statement of a national policy on mental retardation. This policy provided important direction for the rapid expansion of mental retardation programs and facilities that occurred during the ensuing years (Maloney & Ward, 1978). In the wake of Kennedy's assassination, an effort was made by his successor, Lyndon B. Johnson, to honor the national commitment to progress in the area of mental retardation. An ongoing mechanism for revising national policy and monitoring progress in the field of mental retardation was provided by the establishment of the President's Committee on Mental Retardation (PCMR) by President Johnson in 1966. This committee issued annual reports to the president. Throughout the 1960s federal laws were enacted, federal agencies were created, and federal grant programs were established to implement the national policies on mental retardation. Some of the legislation that has benefitted people with mental retardation is summarized in Table 1-1 on page 32.

The federal policies and initiatives of the 1960s were supported by several developments within the fields of education and psychology. As resources were allocated to the education of people with severe and profound mental retardation, effective training techniques were devised. These methods were successful at providing previously custodial individuals with a repertoire of self-care skills permitting greater independence in dressing, feeding, and toileting. The emergence of improved training methods went hand in hand with a renewed national commitment to the humane treatment of people with mental retardation. In an influential 1969 publication by the President's Committee on Mental Retardation, edited by Kugel and Wolfensberger, several essays on the problems of United States institutions and proposed solutions were compiled. In this volume, Bengt Nirje from the Swedish Association for Retarded Children summarized his reactions to a tour of United States institutions for individuals with mental retardation in the following way:

> I have reacted with disbelief and bewilderment to what I saw. I found it difficult to understand how a society which is built on such noble principles, and which has the resources to make these principles a reality, can and will tolerate the dehumanization of a large number of its citizens in a fashion somewhat remindful of Nazi concentration camps (Nirje, 1969b, p. 53).

Nirje's reactions were based on visits to large public institutions in several states where he observed overcrowding, a total absence of programming, the excessive use of restraint,

TABLE 1-1   **Major Federal Laws Directly Relevant to Mental Retardation**

Public Law No.	Enactment Date	Title/Purpose
83–531	7/26/54	To authorize cooperative research in education; two-thirds of the funds were earmarked for mental retardation
85–926	9/6/58	To encourage the training of teachers of children with mental retardation; established the Institute of Child Health and Human Development, with mental retardation as an explicit priority area
88–156	10/24/63	Social Security Act Amendments of 1963, the first bill to implement the Kennedy mental retardation program
88–164	10/31/63	Mental Retardation Facilities & Community Mental Health Centers Construction Act of 1963
89–10	4/11/65	Elementary & Secondary Education Act of 1965, as amended
89–97	7/30/65	Social Security Amendments of 1965; authorized funds to implement state plans to combat mental retardation
89–105	8/4/65	Mental Retardation Facilities & Community Mental Health Centers Construction Act of 1965
89–313	11/1/65	Federal Assistance to State Operated & Supported Schools for the Handicapped
90–170	12/4/67	Mental Retardation Amendments of 1967
91–695	1/13/71	To assist lead-based paint elimination programs
93–112	9/26/73	Rehabilitation Amendments of 1973
93–151	11/9/73	Lead-Based Paint Poisoning Prevention Amendments
93–380	8/21/74	Education of the Handicapped Amendments of 1974
94–142	11/28/75	Education for All Handicapped Children Act; entitled all children with handicaps to a free, appropriate education
98–199	12/2/83	Amendments to the Education of the Handicapped Act
99–457	10/8/86	Amendments to the Education of the Handicapped Act; extended provisions of PL94–142 to preschool children; established incentives for infant & toddler programs, transition programs, and technology for persons with disabilities
101–336	7/26/90	Americans with Disabilities Act (ADA); asserted civil rights of persons with disabilities in employment, public services, public accommodations, transportation, and telecommunications
101–476	10/30/90	Individuals with Disabilities Education Act (IDEA); renamed and amended the Education of the Handicapped Act; emphasized minorities with disabilities

Adapted from *Public policy and the education of exceptional children* by LaVor, M. L., 1976, pp. 103–111. Copyright 1976 by The Council for Exceptional Children. Reprinted with permission.

and other inhumane treatment. In another essay in the same volume, Nirje (1969a) provided a detailed discussion of the normalization principle which had already been applied extensively in Scandinavia. In Nirje's words, "the normalization principle means making available to the mentally retarded patterns and conditions of everyday life which are as close as possible to the norms and patterns of the mainstream of society" (p. 181). This principle was clearly compatible with many of the recommendations of the President's Panel, especially the movement toward comprehensive community services. The ideal of normalization became the guiding theme for many of the changes in services for people with mental retardation that took place in the United States during the 1970s.

The 1970s

Optimism about mental retardation continued into the 1970s. President Nixon outlined the following goals for the 1972 PCMR (The President's Committee on Mental Retardation, 1973):

- To reduce by half the occurrence of mental retardation in the United States before the end of this century.
- To enable one-third of the more than 200,000 retarded persons in public institutions to return to useful lives in the community. (Krause, 1986, p. 14)

Richard Nixon

The rights of individuals with mental retardation remained a central concern during the 1970s. The principles established in the civil rights struggle of black Americans in the 1950s and 1960s were invoked in litigation to gain the rights of individuals with mental retardation. In particular, the landmark case of *Brown v. Board of Education* (1954) set an important precedent which influenced the outcomes of several cases during the 1970s concerning the rights of persons with disabilities. In the Brown decision, which mandated desegregation of the Topeka schools, the principle of equal opportunity for education was established. Subsequent cases applied this principal to the rights of individuals with mental retardation. In the *Mills v. Board of Education* (1972) case in Washington, D.C., it was ruled that no child could be denied a free public education because of mental, behavioral, emotional, or physical handicaps. The *Pennsylvania Association for Retarded Children (PARC) v. Commonwealth of Pennsylvania* (1971) class action suit resulted in a consent agreement stipulating that all children with mental retardation had a right to a "free program of education and training" regardless of degree of deficit. This agreement was followed by further class action suits on behalf of the residents of Pennhurst, a Pennsylvania state institution. In 1977, Federal Judge Raymond J. Broderick rendered a 72-page decision ruling that Pennhurst failed to provide minimally adequate habilitation for its residents. In 1978, Judge Broderick (*Halderman v. Pennhurst*) ruled that all institutions violated the right to habilitation of persons with mental retardation and must be expeditiously replaced by community programs (Howse, 1981). This decision was followed by a series of appeals which eventually reached the United States Supreme Court. In 1981, the U.S. Supreme Court, in a 6 to 3 decision, failed to uphold the 1978 decision on the basis of insufficient legal arguments (Greenhouse, 1981). Although considerable momentum had already been gained in the deinstitutionalization movement, the Supreme Court decision was a serious blow to that effort. Finally, in 1984, a settlement was reached in which the state of Pennsylvania agreed to close Pennhurst by July 1, 1986.

Litigation in other states centered upon similar issues. In the *Wyatt v. Stickney* (1972) decision in Alabama, the court issued a statement of 49 minimal constitutional standards of care, treatment, and habilitation, in which the rights of individuals with mental retardation to habilitation and treatment were affirmed. As in Pennsylvania, this decision was followed by a series of appeals. In 1978, a motion to modify some of the original standards was filed. Expert testimony on both sides of the argument was provided by professionals from the field of mental retardation. Two of the most controversial issues concerned whether an institution could constitute the least restrictive environment for some individuals and whether an "enriched environment" would be more appropriate than continued intensive training for residents who had made only minimal progress over an extended period of time. In 1979, Judge Frank M. Johnson ruled to retain some of the 1972 standards but to modify others. The judge clarified that community placement decisions rested with professionals. However, the "enrichment" modification was denied on the grounds that it might endanger the rights of some individuals (Cavalier & McCarver, 1981).

Similarly, in New York State, class action suits by parents and advocates, citing widespread abuse and neglect of residents at Willowbrook State School, culminated in the 1975 Willowbrook Consent Decree. In that ruling, Federal Judge Orrin Judd ordered the reduction of the Willowbrook population from 5,400 to 250 and an emphasis on training individuals for life in the community.

The principles established in these court cases were reflected in two far-reaching federal laws expanding the rights of individuals with disabilities. In 1973, amendments to the Vocational Rehabilitation Act (PL93–112, Section 504) prohibited discrimination solely by reason of handicap in any program or activity receiving federal financial assistance. In 1975, the Education for All Handicapped Children Act (PL94–142) was passed. In addition to granting *all* children with handicaps the right to a free, appropriate education, the law established several additional rights:

1. The right to due process
2. Protection against discriminatory testing
3. Education in the least restrictive environment
4. Individualized Education Programs (IEPs)

This law was structured to support an active role for parents in every phase of the educational process.

The 1980s and the 1990s

In the 1980s, the education and training of children and youth with mental retardation was transformed by the implementation of PL94–142. For the first time in history, all children, regardless of the severity of their mental retardation or other disabilities, were entitled to a free, appropriate education. Parents were guaranteed a central role in all educational decision-making regarding their children, with clear appeal procedures in the event of dissatisfaction. Educational programs were designed by collaborative teams, including parents, to meet the needs of each child. The mandate to provide education in the least restrictive environment resulted in the placement of children with mental retardation in an expanding array of educational settings. The 1983 (PL98–199) and 1986 (PL99–457) amendments to the Education of the Handicapped Act extended the provisions of PL94–142 to preschool children, established voluntary grant programs for infants and toddlers, supported the improvement of secondary and transition programs, and increased the availability of technology to individuals with disabilities.

In 1990, PL101–476, the Individuals with Disabilities Education Act (IDEA), was passed, renaming the Education of the Handicapped Act and amending and reauthorizing its provisions. This law adds autism and traumatic brain injury to the disabilities served by special education. In addition, it mandates that a transition component be added to each student's IEP by age 16, emphasizes meeting the needs of minorities with disabilities, and extends the availability of assistive technology. Another major piece of federal legislation, the Americans with Disabilities Act, or the ADA (PL101–336), was also adopted in 1990. This law, which focuses upon adults with disabilities, asserts their civil rights in employment, public services, public accommodations, transportation, and telecommunications.

In the wake of these sweeping legislative mandates, more recent progress may appear less dramatic. However, the increasing complexity of the challenges facing the field in the 1990s and beyond will require an intensified effort to provide educational programming that meets the needs of students with mental retardation. It has been projected that the number of children living in poverty will continue to rise dramatically (Cohen, 1992). Because many of the concomitants of poverty are contributing factors to mental retardation, prevention and treatment programs must be put in place to minimize the impact. It is also projected that the proportion of children from minority language and ethnic groups will continue to increase until it constitutes nearly half of the school population by the turn of the century (e.g., Ramirez, 1988). The increasing cultural and linguistic diversity of children both with and without mental retardation will pose many challenges to educators. Ultimately, the success of educational programs for individuals with mental retardation will depend upon the adequacy of educators' responses to these challenges, as well as the ability of society to resolve the key issues that have dominated the history of mental retardation.

References

Bayley, N. (1949). Consistency and variability in the growth of intelligence from birth to eighteen years. *Journal of Genetic Psychology, 75,* 165–196.

Brown v. Board of Education. (1954). 347 U.S. Supreme Court 485.

Cavalier, A. R. & McCarver, R. B. (1981). Wyatt v. Stickney and mentally retarded individuals. *Mental Retardation, 19,* 209–214.

Cohen, D. L. (August 5, 1992). Despite widespread income growth, study finds increase in child poverty. *Education Week,* 24.

Connor, F. P. (1958, September). Education in the field of mental retardation. In *Proceedings of the Conference on Research and Training in the Field of Mental Retardation* (pp. 129–141). Colony, VA: Lynchburg Training School and Hospital.

Conrad, H. S. (1958). Introduction. In *Cooperative Research Projects, Fiscal 1957.* Bulletin 1958, No. 5, Washington, DC: U.S. Department of Health, Education, and Welfare, Office of Education.

Cremin, L. A. (1977). *Traditions of American education.* New York: Basic Books.

Crissey, M. S. (1975). Mental retardation: Past, present, and future. *American Psychologist, 30,* 800–808.

Cruickshank, W. M. (1958). [Debate with Ignacy Goldberg.] The trainable but noneducable: Whose responsibility? *Journal of the National Education Association, 47,* 622–623.

Davies, S. P. & Ecob, K. G. (1964). *The mentally retarded in society*. New York: Columbia University Press.

Descoeudres, A. (1928). *The education of mentally defective children*. [Translated from the second French edition by Ernest F. Row.] Boston: D. C. Heath & Co.

Doll, E. A. (1917). *Clinical studies in feeble-mindedness*. Boston: Richard G. Badger.

Doll, E. E. (1962). A historical survey of research and management of mental retardation in the United States. In E. Trapp & P. Himelstein (Eds.), *Readings on the exceptional child* (pp. 47–97). New York: Appleton-Century-Crofts.

Dugdale, R. (1877). *The Jukes: A study in crime, pauperism, disease, and heredity*. New York: G. P. Putnam [Reprinted by Arnos Press, 1970].

Dugdale, R. (1910). *The Jukes: A study of crime, pauperism, disease, and heredity*. New York: G. P. Putnam.

Estabrook, A. (1916). *The Jukes in 1915*. Washington, DC: Carnegie Institute of Washington.

Fernald, W. E. (1919). After-care study of the patients discharged from Waverly for a period of twenty-five years. *Ungraded, 5*, 25–31.

Goddard, H. H. (1912). *The Kallikak family: A study in the heredity of feeble-mindedness*. New York: Macmillan.

Goldberg, I. I. (1958). [Debate with William Cruickshank.] The trainable but noneducable: Whose responsibility? *Journal of the National Education Association, 47*, 622–623.

Goldberg, I. I. (1983, October). [Interview with Phyllis Rubenfeld.] In P. Rubenfeld, *Education in public schools for cerebral palsy and mentally retarded children: The parent movement in New York City, 1946–1975*. Unpublished doctoral dissertation. Teachers College, Columbia University, New York.

Goodenough, F. L. (1956). *Exceptional children*. New York: Appleton-Century-Crofts.

Greenhouse, L. (1981, April 21). Justices restrict a 'Bill of Rights' for the Retarded. *The New York Times*.

Halderman v. Pennhurst State School and Hospital. (1978). 466 F. Supp. 1295, U.S. Third Circuit Court of Appeals.

Hewett, F. & Forness, S. (1977). *Education of exceptional learners* (2nd ed.). Boston: Allyn & Bacon.

Howse, J. (1981, May). Chronology of the Pennhurst case. Paper presented at the Annual Convention for the American Association on Mental Deficiency, Detroit.

Ingram, C. (1960). *Education of the slow learning child*. New York: The Ronald Press.

Inskeep, A. D. (1926). *Teaching dull and retarded children*. New York: Macmillan.

Johnstone, E. R. (1924). Social objectives for subnormals. *Training School Bulletin, 21*, 49–57.

Katz, A. H. (1961). *Parents of the handicapped*. Springfield, IL: Charles C. Thomas.

Krause, F. (Ed.). (1986). *Historical review of the President's Committee on Mental Retardation*. Washington, DC: Government Printing Office.

Kugel, R. B. & Wolfensberger, W. (Eds.). (1969). *Changing patterns in residential services for the mentally retarded*. Washington, DC: President's Committee on Mental Retardation.

Lane, H. (1979). *The Wild boy of Aveyron*. Cambridge, MA: Harvard University Press.

La Vor, M. L. (1976). Federal legislation for exceptional persons: A history. In F. J. Weintraub, A. Abeson, J. Ballard, & M. L. La Vor (Eds.), *Public policy and the education of exceptional children* (pp. 96–111). Reston, VA: The Council for Exceptional Children.

Legarde, E. (1903). Should the scope of the public school system be broadened to take in all children capable of education? *Journal of Psycho-Asthenics, 8*, 35–38.

Longstreth, L. E. (1981). Revisiting Skeels' final study: A critique. *Developmental Psychology, 17*, 620–625.

Maloney, M. P. & Ward, M. P. (1978). *Mental retardation and modern society*. New York: Oxford University Press.

Mills v. The Board of Education. (1972). Civil Action No. 1939–71, U.S. District Court of the District of Columbia.

Nirje, B. (1969a). The normalization principle and its human management implications. In R. B. Kugel & W. Wolfensberger (Eds.), *Changing patterns in residential services for the mentally retarded* (pp. 179–195). Washington, DC: President's Committee on Mental Retardation.

Nirje, B. (1969b). A Scandinavian visitor looks at U.S. institutions. In R. B. Kugel & W. Wolfensberger (Eds.), *Changing patterns in residential services for the mentally retarded* (pp. 51–57). Washington, DC: President's Committee on Mental Retardation.

Pennsylvania Association for Retarded Children v. Commonwealth of Pennsylvania (1971). Civil Action No. 71–42, 3-Judge Court, E. D. Pennsylvania.

President's Committee on Mental Retardation. (1973). *MR72: Islands of excellence.* Washington, DC: U.S. Government Printing Office.

President's Committee on Mental Retardation. (1977). *MR76, Mental retardation: Past and present.* Washington, DC: U.S. Government Printing Office.

President's Panel on Mental Retardation. (1962). *A proposed program for national action to combat mental retardation.* Washington, DC: U.S. Government Printing Office.

Ramirez, B. (1988). Culturally and linguistically diverse children. *Teaching Exceptional Children, 20*(4), 45–51.

Rubenfeld, P. (1983). (Text of interview with Ignacy I. Goldberg). *Education in public schools for cerebral palsy and mentally retarded children: The parent movement in New York City, 1946–1975.* Unpublished doctoral dissertation. Teachers College, Columbia University.

Scheerenberger, R. C. (1983). *A history of mental retardation.* Baltimore: Brookes.

Seguin, E. (1866). *Idiocy and its treatment.* New York: William Wood & Company.

Skeels, H. & Dye, H. (1939). A study of the effects of differential stimulation on mentally retarded children. *Journal of Psycho-Asthenics, 44,* 114–136 [Reprinted in M. Rosen, G. R. Clark, & M. S. Kivitz (Eds.). (1976). *The history of mental retardation: Collected papers. Vol. 2.* Baltimore: University Park Press.]

Sloan, W. & Stevens, H. A. (1976). *A century of concern: A history of the American Association on Mental Deficiency, 1876–1976.* Washington, DC: American Association on Mental Deficiency.

Smith, J. D. (1985). *Minds made feeble: The myth and legacy of the Kallikaks.* Rockville, MD: Aspen.

Strauss, A. A. & Lehtinen, L. E. (1947). *Psychopathology and education of the brain-injured child, Vol. 1.* New York: Grune and Stratton.

Talbot, M. (1967). Edouard Seguin. In E. E. Doll (Ed.), Historical review of mental retardation: 1800–1965, A symposium. *American Journal of Mental Deficiency, 72,* 184–189;

Terman, L. M. (1919). *The intelligence of school children.* Boston: Houghton-Mifflin.

Wallin, J. E. W. (1949). *Children with mental and physical handicaps.* New York: Prentice-Hall.

Wallin, J. E. W. (1924). Classification of mentally deficient and retarded children for instruction. *Journal of Psycho-Asthenics, 29,* 166–182.

Weingold, J. T. (1952). Parents' groups and the problem of mental retardation. *American Journal of Mental Deficiency, 56,* 484–492.

Williams, H. M. & Wallin, J. E. W. (1959). *Education of the severely retarded child: A bibliographical review.* Washington: U.S. Government Printing Office.

Wyatt v. Stickney. (1972). Civil Action No. 3195–N, U.S. District Court, Middle District of Alabama, North Division.

Chapter 2

Labels, Definitions, and Functioning Levels

The purpose of this chapter[1] is to describe the characteristics of individuals with mental retardation at different levels of severity and at those developmental stages that are germane to our efforts to deliver quality educational programs and services to them. There are any number of texts that have defined mental retardation and described those characteristics—psychometric, behavioral, and psychosocial—that are typically found at different classification levels. The intent of this book is to discuss curriculum and instructional strategy issues concerning preschool to young adult individuals with mild to profound levels of mental retardation. Given this wide-ranging intent, the following sections will emphasize, wherever possible, the educational and later life adjustment implications of mental retardation in its many manifestations. The first section reviews the labels assigned to mental retardation and their impact on adjustment and classroom performance. The second section discusses definitions of mental retardation and their role in facilitating or inhibiting educational planning. The third section describes the functional characteristics of children at different classification levels. It also outlines the potential interface of classificatory and pedagogical criteria. The fourth section offers some recommendations for achieving successful educational outcomes for students with different levels of mental retardation.

Labels

The labels assigned to different groups of individuals with mental retardation have varied as a function of the perspectives of those doing the labeling. Over the years, the generic labels most often applied to individuals with significant intellectual deficits have been as follows: mentally defective, mentally deficient, mentally handicapped, and mentally retarded (Blackman, 1985a). Traditionally the labels *mentally defective* and *mentally deficient* have been used to describe those individuals who were more seriously involved. The label *mentally defective* suggested that the source of the deficit was some damage to those central nervous system mechanisms responsible for mediating intellectual functions. The label *mentally deficient* implied the absence of critical structural components of the brain responsible for the expression of intelligence.

The terms *mentally handicapped* and *mentally retarded*, while not completely synonymous, have often been used interchangeably. The terms usually refer to the milder levels of mental retardation and imply that an individual's potential for normal intellectual development has been curtailed, either by cultural or socioeconomic disadvantage or both, or by a mild and difficult-to-diagnose form of neurophysiological dysfunction. Since the practice of labeling children with mental retardation has come under recent criticism, there seems to be little point in making generic label distinctions. For the purposes of this book, therefore, the label of *mental retardation* will be used exclusively to refer to any manifestation of the condition at any level of severity and as a result of any etiological factor or

---

[1]Sections of this chapter have been taken from two entries entitled "Mental Retardation" (pp. 3308–3313) and "Mild Mental Retardation" (pp. 3363–3365) authored by Leonard S. Blackman in the *International Encylopaedia of Education*. This material has been reprinted with kind permission from Husen/Postlethwaite, *International Encyclopaedia of Education*, Copyright 1985, Pergamon Press, Headington Hill Hall, Headington, Oxford, OX3OBW.

factors. In line with current practice, this book except when reflecting historical usage will not use the noun *mental retardate* or the adjective *mentally retarded*. The construction to be used whenever possible is person with *mental retardation*. This construction, while sometimes awkward, does underscore the fact that mental retardation is only one of an individual's many characteristics.

In selecting one label for the purposes of this book, it should be noted that over the long history of professional concern for individuals with mental retardation, many different labels have been applied (Gelof, 1963). These labels have reflected a variety of biases and purposes. Some, mirroring the distorted public view of mental retardation in the latter part of the nineteenth century, used highly pejorative labels. The American Association for the Study of the Feebleminded used the terms *moron, imbecile*, and *idiot*. These labels, long ago discarded into the garbage heap of offensive terms, were used to describe individuals with mild, moderate, and severe mental retardation, respectively.

Reflecting an optimistic educational perspective, educators introduced the terms *educable* and *trainable* to describe children with mild and moderate mental retardation and to reflect their good prognoses for improvement in effective school settings. The National Association for Retarded Citizens, a parent organization, announced its concerns and hopes for the social development of children with mental retardation when it introduced the terms *marginally independent* (mild mental retardation), *semi-independent* (moderate mental retardation), and *dependent* (severe and profound mental retardation). Society's apparent need to mark deviance by the use of labels—both understood and misunderstood—(Guskin, 1978) is born out of prejudice and fear on the one hand, but also out of compassion and a sense of rehabilitative purpose on the other.

There has been a long-standing controversy over whether labeling children as having mental retardation results in negative expectations and stigmatization that might have a deleterious effect on school achievement and life adjustment in general (MacMillan, 1982). The psychological aspects of this issue have been complicated by administrative, legislative, and funding concerns. In most states, administrative mechanisms and funding sources for special services for children cannot be set in motion until the children have been classified and labeled. However, with the advent of PL94–142, the mandate that special needs children be educated in the least restrictive environment, a ripple effect has begun to wash over the practice of labeling. There is a growing trend to label special needs children in a less restrictive way. Instead of using the stereotypic labels associated with categories of exceptionality and severity levels, many school systems are changing to designations that emphasize the degree of modification required in the child's instructional program. For example, in New York State, special classes carry such designations as MIS (Modified Instructional System) 1 and MIS 2 to reflect the extent of educational adaptations that the children in these classes require. This change in classificatory orientation is, in fact, a harbinger of very recent changes in definition and classification proposed by the American Association on Mental Retardation (AAMR) (1992).

An excellent review and analysis of the labeling literature appears in MacMillan (1982). The current trend toward delabeling children with mental retardation is a natural outgrowth of the view that labels are uniformly stigmatizing (Reynolds & Balow, 1972) and consistently result in lower self-concepts (Jones, 1972), rejection by peers, and reduced teacher expectations (Meyers, MacMillan, & Yoshida, 1974). On the other hand, there is an equally impressive array of evidence that finds labeling "not guilty" of many of these negative social and school outcomes.

Some studies found no decrease in self-concept as a result of labeling (Bacher, 1965; Goldberg, Passow, & Justman, 1966). This may have been due to the fact that labeling occurred concurrently with placement in a special class where the children enjoyed a more favorable competitive position and a more patient teacher. Other studies (Guskin, 1963; Siperstein, Budoff, & Bak, 1980), found that labels seemed to protect children with mental retardation from the low opinion of peers without mental retardation. Unexplained poor behavior and inadequate academic performance in unlabeled children was not well tolerated by normal peers because of their inability to account for this performance in any reasonable way. Since the label of mental retardation provided an "explanation" for unacceptable behavior or slow academic progress, peers without mental retardation were prepared to be more understanding. In general, there is little conclusive evidence that the use of labels is consistently damaging to individuals with mental retardation. Indeed, there is some evidence that labels, under certain circumstances, may function as aids to understanding by individuals without mental retardation. Past experience, however, would suggest that research evidence is not always the surest road to practical application. It is likely that social and political considerations, as well as empathy with parent feelings, will maintain and perhaps accelerate the delabeling trend.

Definitions

There have been many definitions of mental retardation over the period of professional concern for this population. The definition presented by the AAMR in 1983, reflecting the state of our understanding of this condition at that time, was as follows:

> Mental retardation refers to significantly subaverage general intellectual functioning existing concurrently with deficits in adaptive behavior, and manifested during the developmental period (Grossman, 1983, p. 1).

"General intellectual functioning" was estimated from an IQ score obtained from an individual intelligence test. "Significantly subaverage general intellectual functioning" meant that a child had been found to have an IQ score that was at least two standard deviations below the mean for the test used. On the Stanford-Binet, this meant an IQ below 68; on the Wechsler, below 70. "Adaptive behavior" was defined as the degree to which an individual met the standards of personal independence and social responsibility expected of his or her age and cultural group. Deficits in adaptive behavior varied in terms of the individual's developmental level. For example, deficits in adaptive behavior at the preschool level were generally manifested in the late acquisition of maturational benchmarks such as sitting, walking, talking, and toilet training. During the school period, adaptive behavior problems were typically defined in terms of the child's inability to respond adequately to the demands of the academic environment. After the school years, deficits in adaptive behavior were more often reflected in unsuccessful social and vocational adjustment.

The developmental period within which mental retardation had to manifest itself was between birth and eighteen years of age. If an individual past the age of eighteen suffered significant regression in intellectual functions and adaptive behavior as a result of emotional disturbance or a severe brain injury caused by trauma to the head or a stroke, the diagnosis of mental retardation would no longer be applicable. It should be carefully noted that the diagnosis of mental retardation could only be made in the presence of all of its defining characteristics: a significantly subaverage IQ score, a deficit in adaptive behavior, and onset during the previously defined developmental period.

A significant modification in the 1983 definition of mental retardation from Doll's definition in 1941 was its "here and now" orientation. Whereas the earlier definition alluded to essential incurability as a defining characteristic of mental retardation, the 1983 AAMR definition was pointedly silent on the issue of prognosis. If a child was diagnosed as having mental retardation by the most reliable instrumentation available, then he or she had mental retardation. Whether this child would always have mental retardation was a separate issue related to the etiology of the condition and the availability of effective educational, psychological, and/or medical interventions.

Given the current state of medical intervention, for example, it is likely that an individual born with only one-half of a badly damaged cortex will always have profound mental retardation. If in the future, however, science fiction becomes scientific reality and brain transplants become possible, even that dire prognosis could be reversed.

On the other hand, an individual who was considered to have mental retardation because of a serious emotional disturbance or because of socio-economic disadvantage might, after the remission of emotional symptoms or under more favorable conditions of intellectual stimulation, progress to the point where he or she was no longer considered to have mental retardation. In short, the 1983 AAMR definition, although not explicit in this regard, had opened the door for both professionals and parents to consider the potential for improvement of individuals at all levels of mental retardation under maximally effective training conditions (Blackman, 1985b). While the definition provided the prognostic leeway so important to the field, it should be noted that the results of efforts made to date to improve the intellectual functioning of children with mental retardation can be described as ranging from unsuccessful to only marginally successful (Spitz, 1986). The quest, however, continues (Blackman, 1988).

The "here and now" position of the 1983 definition offered educators and other professionals in the field an important incentive. Special educators could now aspire toward improving the functioning of individuals with mental retardation without challenging unnecessary definitional assumptions (Blackman, 1972). Similarly, other professional disciplines have begun to discuss the possibilities of and difficulties inherent in actually "curing" some forms of mental retardation (Blackman & Lin, 1984; Menolascino, Neman, & Stark, 1983; Spitz, 1986).

The 1992 AAMR Definition

In 1992, the AAMR promulgated its most recent position on describing this population. It is presented in a manual and workbook entitled *Mental Retardation: Definition, Classification, and Systems of Supports*. The new definition is as follows:

Mental retardation refers to substantial limitations in present functioning. It is characterized by significantly subaverage intellectual function (IQ of 70–75 or below), existing concurrently with related limitations in two or more of the following applicable adaptive skills areas: communication, self-care, home living, social skills, community use, self-direction, health and safety, functional academics, leisure and work. Mental retardation manifests before age 18 (AAMR, 1992, p. iii).

Four assumptions are described as essential to the application of the definition. These assumptions are as follows: (1) valid assessment considers cultural and language diversity, as well as communicative and behavioral factors; (2) limitations in adaptive skills occur within a context of community environments; therefore, each person requires a statement of that person's individualized needs for supports; (3) specific adaptive limitations typically coexist with strengths in other adaptive skills or personal capabilities; and (4) with appropriate supports over a sustained period, the life functioning of a person with mental retardation will generally improve.

This definition continues the steady progression of optimism that has occurred over the years in the prospects for individuals with mental retardation. Doll's earliest definition of mental retardation in 1941 proclaimed "essential incurability." Grossman's 1983 definition had a "here and now" orientation that dealt with the issue of prognosis only by inference. It suggested that diagnosis, etiology, and intervention were separate issues, and that the potential of intervention to ameliorate mental retardation should be taken more seriously. The 1992 AAMR definition expresses open optimism that, given the application of appropriate support systems specified by the diagnostic process, the individual with mental retardation is likely to improve.

The 1992 definition is also described as a multidimensional approach to diagnosis, classification, and systems of supports. Dimension I establishes the existence of mental retardation by evaluating intellectual functioning and adaptive skills. Dimension II considers the individual's psychological and emotional characteristics. Dimension III involves the individual's health and physical well being. Dimension IV analyzes the individual's current environment and identifies those aspects of the environment, with its systems of supports, that will facilitate the individual's adjustment to and integration into the community.

Finally, the 1992 AAMR Manual describes the implementation of a three-step process of diagnosis, classification, and recommendations for systems of supports. In the first step, the diagnosis of mental retardation is made if the person meets these three criteria: age of onset (under eighteen years of age); significantly subaverage intellectual abilities (IQ below 70 to 75); and limitations in two or more of the adaptive skill areas. The second step describes the individual's strengths and weaknesses with reference to the four dimensions described earlier. The third step develops a profile of the support needs appropriate to each of the four dimensions. Each support recommended in the third step is assigned a level of intensity. These levels of intensity are called *intermittent*, *limited*, *extensive*, and *pervasive*. Intermittent supports are typically temporary and provided on an as-needed basis. Limited supports are usually provided on a regular basis for a short period of time. Extensive supports reflect an ongoing and regular involvement. Finally, pervasive supports are characterized by their constancy and high intensity in terms of time and involvement of personnel. In short, the new definition does not stop at telling us what mental retardation is. It goes on to tell us how to ameliorate its negative effects.

Alternative Approaches to Definition and Diagnosis

Efforts have been made to revise and qualify the understanding of intelligence in ways that ascribe less importance to IQ and adaptive behavior scores. For example, Mercer (1973) viewed mental retardation from a social systems perspective, taking the position that individuals can be considered to have mental retardation only if they are so defined by the social system to which they belong. In most instances of mild mental retardation, it is the social system of the school that assigns a child to the role of a person with mental retardation. This role is defined mainly in terms of the acquisition of academic competencies. At the same time that this assignment of status is going on in the school, there may be no such assignment in the child's home or neighborhood. This must inevitably lead to some degree of role confusion for the child and frustration for the school, as well as disjunctive expectations on the part of the family.

Others, from the perspective of behavior analysis (Bijou, 1966, 1992; Throne, 1972), have rejected psychometric indices of mental retardation as too closely tied to genetic and biological conceptions of the cause of the condition, and irrelevant to what should be the primary concern: rehabilitative intervention. They contend that mental retardation is the result of "the reduction, withholding, or noncontingency of reinforcement; and [of] the restriction of opportunities for learning" (Robinson & Robinson, 1976, p. 29). While this view seems more credible when applied to individuals with mild as opposed to severe or profound retardation, it does avoid blaming the victim. Rather, it places the onus for this condition on society in general, and on the child's non-responsive and non-reinforcing immediate environment in particular. Of course, well-trained special education teachers will be critically important participants in educational interventions designed to reverse these early environmental failures.

Finally, an ahistorical view of intelligence that continues to be widely used, which stresses a child's potential for learning on particular, contemporary learning tasks, has been presented by Feuerstein (1979) and Budoff, Meskin, and Harrison (1971). For example, on Feuerstein's Learning Potential Assessment Device (LPAD), a child is asked to perform on a cognitive task such as the Organization of Dots. This task consists of groups of apparently scattered dots that can be organized into a square and two triangles by linking the dots that form the outlines of the model figures. After the child has completed the task, he or she is coached so as to correct any errors. The child is then readministered the task. The degree of learning potential or modifiability of the child is estimated from his or her ability to profit from coaching. Where poor learning ability is detected, Feuerstein (1980) implicates the absence of an effective mediated learning environment in the child's early developmental history. He then offers his "Instrumental Enrichment" (IE) program as the appropriate intervention for remediating underlying cognitive deficits that stand in the way of satisfactory school performance. As with other attempts to repair the cognitive infra-structure, relative success in accomplishing the "repairs" has not yet been consistently reflected in classroom progress (Blackman & Lin, 1984; Mann, 1979).

Levels of Mental Retardation and Educational Expectations

Although the 1992 definition of mental retardation dismisses the 1983 classification categories of mild, moderate, severe, and profound in favor of categories of levels of support needed to improve adaptive skills in environmental contexts, that definition is too new to know what its fate will be in terms of field implementation and acceptance. Consequently, to facilitate this transition, this section reviews functional and educational expectations for individuals with mental retardation based on the 1983 categories. We will illustrate the new procedures and forms associated with the 1992 AAMR definition when we analyze the case studies presented in Chapter 3 and beyond.

Those individuals who have been diagnosed as having mental retardation based on IQ scores at least two standard deviations below the mean and poor performance on adaptive behavior scales have been further classified in terms of the severity of their mental retardation. Table 2-1 presents the IQ score ranges associated with different classification levels.

In the same sense that society in general and professionals in particular have deemed it important to differentiate people with and without mental retardation, wide-ranging differences among individuals with mental retardation themselves led professionals to break this group down even further into classification categories labeled mild, moderate, severe, and profound. Educators have assigned prognostic meaning to these labels by referring to persons with mild mental retardation as "educable" and persons with moderate mental retardation as "trainable." People with severe mental retardation, while eventually capable of developing low-level skills that might allow them to function in a sheltered or supported work environment, are considered uneducable for the purpose of developing academic competencies. Individuals with profound mental retardation will require care and supervision all of their lives. Their major problems concern the maintenance of critical life functions and the development of self-care skills wherever possible. Physicians, nurses, and physical therapists may play a role equal to educators in the care and the training of these individuals.

Assigning children to different classification levels serves these two purposes: first, making curriculum choices informed by the level of conceptual and behavioral functioning expected at each level, and second, facilitating administrative decisions regarding proper placement, assignment of resources, and application of support services for children at different classification levels. The following subsections will speak to the defining char-

TABLE 2-1   Mental Retardation Classification Levels

	Obtained IQ	
Classification Level	**Stanford-Binet (SD=16)**	**Wechsler (SD=15)**
Mild	52–67	55–69
Moderate	36–51	40–54
Severe	20–35	25–39*
Profound	below 19	below 24*

*Extrapolated

acteristics, primarily from an educational perspective, of students representing different classification levels.

Mild Mental Retardation (Educable)

The mild, or educable, level of mental retardation falls between two and three standard deviations below the mean: an IQ from 52 to 67 if the Stanford-Binet is used, or from 55 to 69 if one of the Wechsler scales is used. However, state departments of education or local school districts frequently deviate from these IQ ranges for reasons of tradition or administrative convenience. Perhaps the most common range for defining mild mental retardation has been 50 to 75. Even with this range, some controversy exists. Some professionals feel that 50 may be too low to consider a child educable, and others feel that children with IQs as high as 80 should be included in this category. The deficits in adaptive behavior required to confirm the diagnosis of mild mental retardation are often justified in terms of insufficient progress in school. The full constellation of deficits in adaptive behavior typically includes inattentiveness and disruptive behavior in the classroom as well.

With respect to classroom behaviors, the child with mild, or educable, mental retardation has been seen as one

who, because of slow mental development, is unable to profit in any degree from the program in the regular classroom, but has the following potentialities for development:

(a) minimum educability in reading, writing, spelling, arithmetic, and so forth;
(b) capacity for social adjustment to a point where he or she can get along independently in the community;
(c) minimum occupational adequacy such that he or she can later become self-supporting partially or totally at a marginal level (Kolstoe, 1976, p. 10).

Special Class and Mainstream Efficacy Studies

Few practitioners in the 1950s and 1960s questioned the need for special classes or even special schools to educate children with mild mental retardation. At about the same time, however, research reports (Blackman & Heintz, 1966) began to appear which found that children with mild mental retardation educated in special classes performed no better in terms of academic skill development than those who remained in regular classes.

This was a disappointing finding for professional special educators who believed that the specially trained teachers, the special curriculum and methods, and the small classes would certainly produce outcomes in these children that would be superior to those that a regular class could provide. While there were sometimes serious methodological problems in these special class efficacy studies, it became clear by the late 1960s that the system of using special classes for teaching individuals with mild mental retardation was not fulfilling the promise made when these programs were first initiated. An even better-designed and more comprehensive study of the effects of special classes conducted by Goldstein, Moss, and Jordan (1965) did little to improve the credibility of special classes.

Attacks on the value, both academic and social, of special classes for children with mild mental retardation also came from another direction. The civil rights movement in the United States, energized by the 1954 Supreme Court decision supporting desegregation, turned its attention to what seemed to them to be yet another flagrant violation of the now legally validated principle of desegregation. Most special classes for children with mild mental retardation, particularly those in large urban centers, were comprised heavily and disproportionately of minority group children (Reis, 1986); perhaps as high as 80 percent in some cities. The pedagogical and administrative aspects of that issue aside, these classes were often perceived by civil rights groups as yet another way that the educational power structure had contrived to segregate minority children. This message presented a challenge to the regular education system to accept children with mild mental retardation back into regular classes in the hope that these children would earn both acceptance and competence in this more democratic, albeit less protected and more competitive educational environment.

Even after the passage of PL94–142, which insisted on the education of children with mild mental retardation in the least restrictive environment possible, progress in placing these children into regular classes, typically referred to as mainstreaming, or more recently as inclusion, has been uneven. In many school districts where mainstreaming was introduced, there had been little preparation of regular teachers, children without mental retardation, or their parents. Regular teachers and administrators felt stressed at having to assume the educational burden of children with mental retardation. Early research studies (Gottlieb, Agard, Kauffman, & Samuel, 1976) designed to evaluate the effectiveness of mainstreaming in accelerating the social and academic skills of these children were inconclusive in some important respects.

There seems to be insufficient evidence currently available to conclude that achievement is a function of whether individuals with mild mental retardation are educated in segregated or mainstreamed settings. The current emphasis is on evaluating the effects of the resourcefulness of their teachers and the quality of the educational system (Corman & Gottlieb, 1978).

Reading Performance

At least partial evidence for a general lack of high quality educational programming comes from the observation that many educable youngsters, whether in special or regular classes, do not seem to perform up to their intellectual potential in academic areas. For example, by the time most adolescents with mild mental retardation reach the age of sixteen, their mental ages (MAs), determined by the number of items passed successfully on an intelligence test, should be in the range of nine to twelve years. Translating these MA scores into achievement expectations, these youngsters should be able to read at the fourth- to sixth-grade levels, respectively. While some earlier studies of reading in students with mild mental retardation found that they were capable of reading at their MA expectancy levels (Kirk, 1940; 1964), later work has suggested that they tend to fall far short of those levels. Semmel, Gottlieb, and Robinson (1979) reported that the highest reading grade level found for children with mild mental retardation has been 3.8. Even more disappointingly, Blackman and Capobianco (1965) found that most of these youngsters do not get beyond the second- to third-grade levels. Similarly, if IQ were to be considered as a rate of growth measure, although this would be somewhat oversimplistic, youngsters with mild mental retardation would be expected to progress at the rate of one-half to three-quarters of an academic year for each full academic year that they spend in school. Experience and research (Blackman,

Burger, Tan, & Weiner, 1982) reveal that these children, in academic subjects, are more likely to grow at the rate of only two- to three-tenths of a year for each full academic year.

Arithmetic Performance

The performance of children with mental retardation in arithmetic has not received as much programmatic or research attention as has their performance in reading. It has been noted, however, that adolescents with mild mental retardation perform well below their MA expectancy in verbal arithmetic problem solving (Bilsky & Judd, 1986; Cruickshank, 1948). Studies have generally found that students with mild mental retardation perform up to MA expectations in computation but not in arithmetic reasoning or comprehension (Bilsky & Judd, 1986; Dunn & Capobianco, 1954). Their deficits in arithmetic reasoning are clearly related to their inability to comprehend and remember what has been read (Bilsky & Judd, 1986; Goodstein, Cawley, Gordon, & Helfgott, 1971).

Social Adjustment

In addition to the acquisition of reading and arithmetic skills, the development of social adjustment skills has traditionally been the third component of the special education curriculum for students with mild mental retardation, particularly those in segregated settings. Among several approaches designed to improve the social skills of children with mild mental retardation, Goldstein's (1969) Social Learning Curriculum emphasizes what they need to know in order to become well-adjusted adults. While the methodological aspects of this approach stress an inductive teaching method designed to stimulate critical thinking skills, the major thrust is in developing those competencies required for good social and occupational adjustment in adult life.

In mainstreamed settings, opportunities to provide social adjustment training as a formal part of the curriculum may be limited or non-existent. In those settings, social adjustment often becomes a pre-condition for an inclusionary placement. Social adjustment in the regular classroom would be reflected in the extent to which intellectually average children accept and support those students with mental retardation. Disappointingly, the record of mainstreamed education in this regard is poor. Students with mild mental retardation are rejected more frequently than students without mental retardation (Goodman, Gottlieb, & Harrison, 1972; Iano, Ayres, Heller, McGettigan, & Walker, 1974). This rejection occurs more often in integrated than in segregated settings (Gottlieb & Budoff, 1973). While there have been a few studies that have found some cause for optimism with respect to the adjustment of children with mild mental retardation in integrated classes (Bruininks, Rynders, & Gross, 1974), these students seem to sink a bit more than they swim in terms of at least one index of their social adjustment—the degree to which they are accepted by their normal classmates.

Cognitive Strategy Use

One of the more important theoretical and research issues for children and adolescents with mild mental retardation is whether it is possible to improve through training their use of cognitive strategies such as rehearsal, imaging, verbal mediation, and others. It is now clear that many of these strategies, useful in problem solving, remembering, and classification tasks, can be not only successfully produced through training, but also maintained by these youngsters over relatively long periods of time (Blackman & Lin, 1984).

A key question is whether youngsters with mild mental retardation can be taught to generalize the cognitive strategies that they acquire in one setting to others. After several years of frustration with this line of research (Campione & Brown, 1977), a few researchers have published findings indicating that some forms of generalization can be produced by training (Brown, Campione, & Barclay, 1979; Burger, Blackman, Clark, & Reis, 1982).

Moderate Mental Retardation (Trainable)

The moderate or trainable level of mental retardation falls between three and four standard deviations below the mean: an IQ from 36 to 51 if the Stanford-Binet is administered or from 39 to 54 if one of the Wechsler scales is used. Whereas the causes of mild mental retardation are typically attributed to environmental disadvantage, a variety of biological factors, or some interaction between the two, moderate mental retardation is almost always due to some form of biological insult or specific and isolatable genetic anomalies. For example, maternal infections such as rubella during the first trimester of pregnancy, or post-natal infections such as encephalitis in the infant, can cause moderate levels of mental retardation. Down Syndrome, associated with the chromosomal defects of nondisjunction, translocation, and mosaicism, is the most frequent cause of moderate mental retardation (Pollard & Haisley, 1985).

Children who have moderate mental retardation are typically more visible physically, behaviorally, and educationally than children with mild mental retardation. Physical stigmata and significant behavioral deviations appear to be the consistent accomplices of biologically and genetically mediated deficits in the central nervous system. Individuals with moderate mental retardation have more limited educational and postschool social and vocational adjustment expectations than individuals with mild mental retardation.

Early efforts to evaluate the efficacy of special classes for children with moderate mental retardation in terms of IQ growth and adaptive behavior did not produce encouraging results (Cain & Levine, 1963; Goldstein, 1956). While programming seems to have improved in quality over the years, efficacy studies have gone out of style. One encouraging development, however, seems to be a result of the growing trend to maintain children with Down Syndrome in their own homes and communities. Most of these children are enrolled in very early infant stimulation programs, and later, early childhood programs. Both professionals and parents are observing more rapid rates of development in these children than would have ordinarily been anticipated. There is an increasing number of reports of many children with Down Syndrome entering school with readiness skills sufficient for placement in classes for students with mild rather than moderate mental retardation.

Children with moderate mental retardation typically experience early delays in a number of developmental areas, including sitting, walking, communication, toileting, social adjustment, and self-help. Eventually, all or most of these developmental bench marks are achieved, but considerably later than in children who do not have mental retardation. The majority of children with moderate mental retardation do not develop functional academic skills, often achieving second-grade levels in reading and arithmetic (Gearhart & Litton, 1979). Early reading instruction typically emphasizes helping the children acquire a "survival" reading vocabulary. Essential for functioning in the community, this vocabulary might include: Men's Room, Women's Room, Exit, Bus Stop, Beware of Dog, and Danger, among many others. The professional consensus, informed by parents' experiences, is that individuals with moderate mental retardation, as adults, will lead semi-independent lives in the community.

Severe and Profound Mental Retardation

Although children classified as having severe and profound mental retardation may differ somewhat in motor and language skill development, and the extent to which other disabilities are present, they overlap sufficiently in characteristics to be discussed together. Their IQs are more than four standard deviations below the mean of 100. People with severe mental retardation have IQs in the 20 to 35 range, and people with profound mental retardation have IQs below 20. Individuals with severe mental retardation may ultimately achieve MAs as high as four or five, while individuals with profound mental retardation will generally not develop beyond an MA of three. People with profound mental retardation are also more likely to have multiple disabilities. More useful assessment information, in terms of program planning, is generally obtained from adaptive behavior measures and early developmental screening tests (Baken, 1985).

Severe and profound mental retardation are typically caused by chromosomal abnormalities, as well as prenatal and perinatal trauma. The severity of injury to the brain, and the systemic pathology that occurs in these children, is often associated with multiple physical and sensory disabilities.

Finally, while the early assessments of children with severe and profound mental retardation may not often stimulate optimism, the epilogues of some of their educational journeys have been more gratifying than their prologues would have suggested. As a result of improved medical techniques for maintaining life, increasingly effective classroom interventions, better long-range planning, and growing public awareness, some individuals with severe and profound mental retardation are living satisfying lives in the community with support.

Recommendations

The psychometric and functional characteristics of individuals with mental retardation at all classification levels have been presented as a way of highlighting the scope of this book. Curricula and methods will be described and discussed for individuals with mental retardation across age and severity levels. The success of the educational process for meeting the individual needs of people with mental retardation will depend on the implementation of the following five recommendations:

1. Focus on the new procedures for diagnosing and classifying individuals with mental retardation in terms of support systems required to improve performance.
2. Apply good scientific theory and reliable data to the continuing modification of curricula and methods for students with mental retardation.
3. Carefully select and train teachers and administrators.
4. Urge the government to commit to the equitable distribution of resources to individuals with mental retardation.
5. Promote public awareness of the needs of people with mental retardation.

References

American Association on Mental Retardation, Ad Hoc Committee on Terminology and Classification. (1992). *Mental retardation: Definition, classification, and systems of support* (9th ed.). Washington, DC: American Association on Mental Retardation.

Bacher, J. H. (1965). The effect of special class placement on the self-concept of the adolescent mentally retarded in relation to certain groups of adolescents. *Dissertation Abstracts, 25*, 2846–2847.

Baken, J. W. (1985). Severe and profound mental retardation. In T. Husen and T. N. Postlethwaite (Eds.), *The International Encyclopedia of Education, 8(S)*, 4530–4532.

Bijou, S. W. (1966). A functional analysis of retarded development. In N. R. Ellis (Ed.), *International Review of Research in Mental Retardation, 1*. New York: Academic Press.

Bijou, S. W. (1992). Concepts of mental retardation. *The Psychological Record, 42*, 305–322.

Bilsky, L. H. & Judd, T. (1986). Sources of difficulty in the solution of verbal arithmetic problems by mentally retarded and nonretarded individuals. *American Journal of Mental Deficiency, 90*, 395–402.

Blackman, L. S. (1988). Review of Spitz, H. H. *The raising of intelligence: A selected history of attempts to raise retarded intelligence. Teachers College Record, 89*, 446–450.

Blackman, L. S. (1985a). Mental retardation. In T. Husen & T. N. Postlethwaite (Eds.), *The International Encyclopedia of Education, 6 (M–O)*, 3308–3313.

Blackman, L. S. (1985b). Mild mental retardation. In T. Husen & T. N. Postlethwaite (Eds.), *The International Encyclopedia of Education, 6 (M–O)*, 3363–3365.

Blackman, L. S. (1972). An active-passive dimension in the definition of mental retardation. *The Journal of Special Education, 6*, 67–70.

Blackman, L. S., Burger, A. L., Tan, N., & Weiner, S. (1982). Strategy training and the acquisition of decoding skills in EMR children. *Education and Training of the Mentally Retarded, 17*, 83–87.

Blackman, L. S. & Capobianco, R. J. (1965). An evaluation of programmed instruction with the mentally retarded utilizing teaching machines. *American Journal of Mental Deficiency, 70*, 262–269.

Blackman, L. S. & Heintz, P. (1966). The mentally retarded. *Review of Educational Research, 36*, 5–36.

Blackman, L. S. & Lin, A. (1984). Generalization training in the educable mentally retarded: Intelligence and its educability revisited. In P. H. Brooks, R. Sperber, & C. McCauley (Eds.), *Learning and cognition in the mentally retarded*. Hillsdale, NJ: Lawrence Erlbaum Associates.

Brown, A. L., Campione, J. C., & Barclay, C. R. (1979). Training self-checking routines for estimating test readiness: Generalization from text training to prose recall. *Child Development, 50*, 501–512.

Bruininks, R. H., Rynders, J. E., & Gross, J. C. (1974). Social acceptance of mildly retarded pupils in resource rooms and regular classes. *American Journal of Mental Deficiency, 78*, 377–383.

Budoff, M., Meskin, J., & Harrison, R. H. (1971). Educational test of the learning-potential hypothesis. *American Journal of Mental Deficiency, 76*, 159–169.

Burger, A. L., Blackman, L. S., Clark, H. T., & Reis, E. (1982). The effects of hypothesis testing and variable format training on the generalization of a verbal abstraction strategy in EMR learners. *American Journal of Mental Deficiency, 86*, 405–413.

Cain, L. F. & Levine, S. (1963). *Effects of community and institutional school programs on trainable mentally retarded children*. Washington, DC: Council for Exceptional Children.

Campione, J., & Brown, A. L. (1977). Memory and metamemory development in educable retarded children. In R. Kail & J. Hagen (Eds.), *Perspectives on the development of memory and cognition*. Hillsdale, NJ: Lawrence Erlbaum Associates.

Corman, L., & Gottlieb, J. (1978). Mainstreaming mentally retarded children: A review of research. In N. R. Ellis (Ed.), *International Review of Research in Mental Retardation (vol. 9)*. New York: Academic Press.

Cruickshank, W. M. (1948). Arithmetic ability of mentally retarded children: I. Ability to differentiate extraneous materials from needed arithmetic facts. *Journal of Educational Research, 42*, 161–170.

Doll, E. A. (1941). The essentials of an inclusive concept of mental deficiency. *American Journal of Mental Deficiency, 46,* 214–219.

Dunn, L. M. & Capobianco, R. J. (1954). A comparison of the reading processes of mentally retarded and normal boys of the same mental age. *Monographs of the Society for Research on Child Development, 19,* 7–99.

Feuerstein, R. (1980). *Instrumental enrichment: An intervention program for cognitive modifiability.* Baltimore, MD: University Park Press.

Feuerstein, R. (1979). *The dynamic assessment of retarded performers: The Learning Assessment Potential Device.* Baltimore, MD: University Park Press.

Gearhart, B. R. & Litton, F. W. (1979). *The trainable retarded: A foundations approach.* St. Louis, MO: Mosby.

Gelof, M. (1963). Comparison of systems of classification relating degree of retardation to measured intelligence. *American Journal of Mental Deficiency, 68,* 299–301.

Goldberg, M. L., Passow, A. H., & Justman, J. (1966). *The effects of ability grouping.* New York: Teachers College Press.

Goldstein, H. (1969). Construction of a social learning curriculum. *Focus on Exceptional Children, 1,* 1–10.

Goldstein, H. (1956). Lower limits of eligibility for classes for trainable children. *Exceptional Children, 22,* 226–228.

Goldstein, H., Moss, J. W., & Jordan, L. J. (1965). *The efficacy of special class training on the development of mentally retarded children.* Urbana, IL: University of Illinois Press.

Goodman, H., Gottlieb, J., & Harrison, R. H. (1972). Social acceptance of EMRs integrated into a nongraded elementary school. *American Journal of Mental Deficiency, 76,* 412–417.

Goodstein, H. A., Cawley, J. F., Gordon, S., & Helfgott, J. (1971). Verbal problem solving among educable mentally retarded children. *American Journal of Mental Deficiency, 76,* 238–241.

Gottlieb, J., Agard, J., Kauffman, H., & Semmel, M. (1976). Retarded children mainstreamed: Practices as they affect minority group children. In R. L. Jones (Ed.), *Mainstreaming and the minority child.* Reston, VA: Council for Exceptional Children.

Gottlieb, J. & Budoff, M. (1973). Social acceptability of retarded children in nongraded schools differing in architecture. *American Journal of Mental Deficiency, 78,* 15–19.

Grossman, H. (1983). *Classification in mental retardation.* Washington, DC: American Association on Mental Deficiency.

Guskin, S. L. (1978). Theoretical and empirical strategies for the study of the labeling of mentally retarded persons. In N. R. Ellis (Ed.), *International Review of Research in Mental Retardation,* (*vol. 9*), 127–158. New York: Academic Press.

Guskin, S. L. (1963). Measuring the strength of the stereotype of the mental defective. *American Journal of Mental Deficiency, 67,* 569–575.

Iano, R. P., Ayres, D., Heller, H. B., McGettigan, J. F., & Walker, V. S. (1974). Sociometric status of retarded children in an integrative program. *Exceptional Children, 40,* 267–271.

Jones, R. L. (1972). Labels and stigma in special education. *Exceptional Children, 38,* 553–564.

Kirk, S. A. (1964). Education. In N. Stevens & R. Heber (Eds.), *Mental Retardation.* Chicago: University of Chicago Press.

Kirk, S. A. (1940). *Teaching reading to slow-learning children.* Boston: Houghton Mifflin.

Kolstoe, O. P. (1976). *Teaching educable mentally retarded children (2nd ed.).* New York: Holt, Rinehart, & Winston.

MacMillan, D. L. (1982). *Mental retardation in school and society.* Boston: Little, Brown, and Company.

Mann, L. (1979). *On the trail of process.* New York: Grune & Stratton, Inc.

Menolascino, F. J., Neman, R., & Stark, J. A. (1983). *Curative aspects of mental retardation: Biomedical and behavioral advances.* Baltimore, MD: Paul H. Brooks Publishing Co.

Mercer, J. R. (1973). *Labeling the mentally retarded: Clinical and social system perspectives on mental retardation.* Berkeley, CA: University of California Press.

Meyers, C. E., MacMillan, D. L., & Yoshida, R. K. (1974). *Preliminary findings on the decertification of inner city EMRs.* Paper presented at the Annual Joint Convention, American Academy of Mental Retardation and the American Association of Mental Deficiency, Toronto.

Pollard, N. E. & Haisley, G. E. (1985). Moderate mental retardation. In T. Husen & T. N. Postlethwaite

(Eds.), *The International Encyclopedia of Education, 6 (M–O)*, 3389–3394.

Reis, E. M. (1986). Minority disproportionality in special placements as an assessment and programming issue. *Journal of Instructional Psychology, 13*, 135–140.

Reynolds, M. C. & Balow, B. (1972). Categories and variables in special education. *Exceptional Children, 38*, 357–366.

Robinson, N. M. & Robinson, H. B. (1976). *The mentally retarded child: A psychological approach* (*2nd ed.*). New York: McGraw-Hill.

Semmel, M. I., Gottlieb, J., & Robinson, N. M. (1979). Mainstreaming: Perspectives on educating handicapped children in the public schools. In D. Berliner (Ed.), *Review of research in education* (*vol. 7*). Washington, DC: American Educational Research Association.

Siperstein, G. N., Budoff, M., & Bak, J. J. (1980). Effects of the labels "mentally retarded" and "retard" on the social acceptability of mentally retarded children. *American Journal of Mental Deficiency, 84*, 596–601.

Spitz, H. H. (1986). *The raising of intelligence*. Hillsdale, NJ: Lawrence Erlbaum Associates.

Throne, J. (1972). The assessment of intelligence. *Mental Retardation, 10*, 9–11.

Foundations of Assessment

The intent of Chapter 3 is to trace the evolution of assessment practices used with individuals with mental retardation. Early on, the concentration was on measuring intelligence for the purpose of excluding difficult-to-teach children from school. More recently, the emphasis has been on curriculum-based assessment specifically designed to find effective ways of maintaining children in the educational process. This chapter is organized into the following eight parts: (1) the definition of assessment; (2) the history of the movement from an exclusionary to an inclusionary orientation in assessment philosophy and procedures; (3) the construct of intelligence; (4) the contribution of tests to the diagnosis of mental retardation and the measurement of achievement and adaptive behavior; (5) bias in formal testing; (6) introduction to case studies: sample assessments; and (7) recommendations.

The Definition of Assessment

Traditionally, the assessment of children with mental retardation had been rather narrowly defined by the use of psychometrically sophisticated and typically well-standardized instruments. These instruments were used to measure the child's intellectual status, adaptive behavior, educational achievement level, communication skills, and other aspects of development deemed important for understanding his or her current deficits and potential for training. More recently, the concept of assessment has been expanded to include the acquisition of information from a wide variety of more informal and typically curriculum-based evaluation procedures. According to Simeonsson, the reason for extending the meaning of assessment is that:

> (a) the psychometric base for psychological testing of many special children is inadequate, and (b) the idiosyncratic and complex problems of special children may require appraisal that needs to be flexible and comprehensive (Simeonsson, 1986, pp. 4–5).

To concretize the point, assessment is here defined as the generic concept that subsumes several sources of data likely to contribute to an understanding of the strengths and weaknesses of the child with mental retardation, as well as his or her potential for habilitation. These sources of data include formal or norm-referenced testing, informal or criterion-referenced appraisals, observations, interviews, and analysis of case records. This expanded definition of assessment is for the purpose of asking questions and collecting information so that more informed educational decisions can be made.

The Journey from Exclusionary to Inclusionary Assessment

The history of formal assessment procedures for special needs children probably dates back to the development of the first intelligence test (Binet & Simon, 1908). This test was developed for use with children with mental retardation, or at least for use with those children whose poor school performance led to concerns about their ability to profit from traditional instruction. The nature of this development supports the observation that no scientific activity takes place in a sociopolitical vacuum. The sociopolitical necessity that stimulated the invention of the intelligence test was the conviction held by Paris educators that slow-learning children had no place in the regular classrooms of the public schools (Binet & Simon, 1905). An objective instrument for measuring intelligence was needed to scientifically substantiate acts of educational exclusion from schools designed to serve so-called normal children. This instrument needed to yield results that would be free of teacher bias or halo effects, and convincing in the face of parent pressures.

The use of assessment devices to undergird exclusionary educational and social processes was not restricted to French schools. Pearson and Moul (1925) used a simplified test of sensory-motor functions, then widely considered to be a reasonable approximation of overall intellectual functioning, as a way of scientifically establishing the intellectual inferiority of Jewish immigrants attempting to enter England after the European pogroms of the early 1900s. The Army Alpha and Beta tests, developed in 1917, identified those recruits during World War I who were to be excluded from military service because of intellectual limitations that might endanger themselves or their comrades. The much respected, feared, and widely used Scholastic Aptitude Tests may also result in excluding from college those students whose scores do not reach levels that are ostensibly predictive of success. Thus, until quite recently, assessment has had a negative connotation in the sense that its impact was widely perceived as exclusionary rather than inclusionary.

With the passage of the Education for All Handicapped Children Act (PL94–142) in 1975, assessment procedures used with children with special needs are now applied in the service of the "zero reject" principle. Under the provisions of the act, the emphasis of assessment has shifted. Earlier, the emphasis was on classifying children as having handicaps, and therefore ineligible for regular education classes. Since the passage of this act, the emphasis has been on assessment as a logical and necessary precursor to individualized programming for *every* child with mental retardation. The emphasis has shifted from *whether* to include a child in a particular educational program to *how* to include the child in that program. More recent assessment concerns, therefore, have been oriented less toward the exclusionary activities implied by labeling and classifying, although some of that still persists, and more toward inclusionary activities such as designing educational interventions likely to fit a particular child's level and style of intellectual functioning.

This characterization of assessment procedures as either exclusionary or inclusionary in impact has been described in other ways. Halpern, Lehman, Irvin, and Heiry (1982) made a similar distinction, but labeled the ends of the bipolar dimension of assessment as traditional versus contemporary. According to Halpern et al.:

> contemporary assessment refers to those practices that clearly link the purposes and outcomes of assessment with the goals and techniques of instruction and other forms of service intervention. Traditional assessment, on the other hand, is viewed as a practice the primary intent of which, at least in the field of mental retardation, has been to label and classify people (Halpern et al., 1982, p. 1).

Similarly, Payne and Patton (1981) have discussed assessment procedures that are oriented toward establishing interindividual differences and other assessment procedures that are more concerned with issues of intraindividual differences. A focus on interindividual differences reflects a concern for classifying, labeling, and ultimately grouping children in special classes or ability level groups. On the other hand, a focus on intraindividual differences reflects an interest in organizing instructional programs designed to cater to a particular child's learning strengths and weaknesses in the context of a particular educational objective.

Despite the emphasis on instructionally useful assessment procedures, in many cases children must still be classified as having mental retardation before placement decisions can be made and appropriate funding released. This classification is generally made on the basis of a standardized intelligence test. Tests are no longer used to keep children out of school, but they continue to be used often to determine eligibility for services and access to funding.

In one sense, it can be argued that assessment practices created the milder forms of school-based mental retardation. There were no quantitative benchmarks that defined the upper end of the mental retardation continuum until Binet and Simon (1908) initially, then Terman and Merrill (1937) and Wechsler (1944) developed tests that allowed psychologists to use IQ numbers for that line of demarcation. The lower end of the continuum never needed test scores to spotlight the phenomenon of mental retardation. At that level, mental retardation is cruelly unmistakable. Indeed, the impact of severe and profound levels of mental retardation has been to render most of the more frequently used intellectual assessment devices conceptually inappropriate and psychometrically unstable.

Almost inevitably, the history of assessment in the area of mental retardation has been closely intertwined with issues of the definition of intelligence and the diagnosis of intellectual insufficiency. Mental retardation, since its diagnostic independence from mental illness was established (see Chapter 1), has been consistently viewed as a behaviorally demonstrable failure in intellectual functioning.

The Intelligence Construct

There are many different perspectives from which the construct of intelligence can be viewed. An awareness of individual differences in intelligence certainly predated the advent of quantitatively oriented testing instruments. "Common sense," or the ability to share in common social understandings and to participate in social, religious, and vocational functions that contributed to the common welfare and were publicly appreciated, was probably an early view of intellectual capacity. At a non-professional and non-technical level, that conception of intelligence still has its adherents today. Intelligence as a "common sense" construct, then, is the ability, at some level, to acquire generally known information, share common understandings, and accept widely valued perspectives. The marked failure of an individual to share these cognitive responsibilities led the Greeks to apply the word *idiot* to those individuals who, for whatever reason, stood outside the boundaries of "common sense."

Before the development of intelligence tests, there was little refined understanding of the continuum of intellectual capacity that ranged from giftedness through normalcy to mental retardation. The usual "rough and ready" indices of intellectual capacity were the following: fluency in communication skills, the capacity to learn in a reasonable amount of time and to retain what had been learned, and the ability to reason and use good judgment in academic, social, and vocational domains.

In the wake of the burgeoning scientific and industrial revolution during the latter part of the nineteenth century and the early part of the twentieth, quantification of psychological phenomena, particularly intellectual ability, assumed great scientific value. Psychometrics—a systematic approach to quantifying intellectual behavior by the administration of so-called intelligence tests—made its entrance into a professional world starving for numbers that would objectively validate "more than" and "less than" judgments about children's mental capacities. It was not long before the enthusiasm for quantifiable data swept psychologists into rampant operationalism, a point of view that suggests that constructs can be defined in terms of the instruments that are used to measure them. Intelligence, then, became defined as what an intelligence test measures.

If one questioned that simple statement of faith by carefully examining what the most commonly used intelligence tests of that day did, in fact, measure, one discovered that the "potpourri" phenomenon made it impossible to define intelligence. For example, the second revision of the Stanford-Binet (Terman & Merrill, 1937) contained 129 different tests. These tests ranged across items that measured comprehension, perception of absurdities, object identification, form board skills, the ability to establish differences and similarities, and memory for digits, among a host of others. Similarly, the original Wechsler Bellevue Intelligence Tests (Wechsler, 1944), as well as later versions, produced verbal, performance, and combined IQs derived from measures of general information, general comprehension, arithmetical reasoning, picture arrangement, vocabulary size, and memory for digits, among others.

It became obvious that no single comprehensible definition of intelligence could be extracted from the maze of subtests comprising the Binet or the Wechsler. This, however, did not stop the major psychometricians of the day from trying. Terman and Merrill (1937) leaned heavily on abstract thinking as the central core of intelligence. Wechsler (1944) bravely offered a definition of intelligence as "the aggregate or global capacity of the individual to act purposefully, think rationally, and to deal effectively with his environment" (p. 3).

There have been other instances when definitions of intelligence and the tests used to measure it have been "like ships that pass in the night." Clearly, no one expected psychometricians to develop point-to-point relationships between what is required to pass a test and how intelligence is defined. Perhaps it was simply never possible to reflect the majesty of the construct called intelligence in the pedestrian tasks that might be accessible to the skills of children.

The psychometric era provided IQ scores and a numerical continuum for estimating differences in children's intellectual capacity. It offered demarcation points (Binet IQ under 68; Wechsler IQ under 70) for enabling decisions about the educational, social, and vocational futures of children classified as having mental retardation because their IQs fell below those demarcation points. Some professionals had reservations about these IQ scores and fretted over their internal reliability (Anastasi, 1976), stability over time (Honzik, Macfarlane, & Allen, 1948), and the fairness with which they measured the intelligence of children who were not adequately represented in the population on which the tests were initially standardized (Baca & Cervantes, 1984). Nevertheless, on the side of validity, most professionals were comforted by the fact that these IQ scores were moderately predictive of school performance (Mussen, Dean, & Rosenberg, 1952). As long as intelligence, if not altogether synonymous with school achievement, was regarded as its inseparable companion, the sanctity of IQ scores went unchallenged. As a result of both scientific and sociopolitical pressures, however, the insularity of IQ scores from criticism would not last forever. That discussion will come later.

Factor Analytic Movement

If the psychometric era and the IQ score put the power to classify and segregate into the hands of psychologists and educators, they also left us the legacy of a widening conceptual gap between what intelligence really is and the operations used to measure it. An effort to close that gap was characterized as the *factor analytic movement*. Essentially, investigators used a statistical procedure called factor analysis (Cattell, 1971) in an effort to extract the core meaning of intelligence. This involved identifying the relationships among a wide variety of intelligence test items as the basis for identifying a smaller number of dimensions that define intelligence.

Although it is not clear that the essence of pure intelligence has ever been extracted, Thurstone (1938) did break away from IQ, which was based on adding up a composite of widely varying abilities, as a generic index of intelligence. In its place, he suggested that intelligence could be defined in terms of a finite number of independent primary mental abilities. These abilities, at least statistically, seemed to constitute the cognitive infrastructure that supported performance on the more polyglot items that comprised intelligence tests. They included visual-spatial skills, memory, reasoning, comprehension, and word fluency. Intelligence was no longer to be construed as a unidimensional (the Stanford-Binet IQ score) or even a bidimensional construct (the Verbal and Performance IQs of the Wechsler scales). It was, according to Thurstone, an eight-pointed profile of independent abilities. The problem of multiple intellectual reference points was further compounded by Guilford (1959, 1967), who defined the "three faces of intellect" as a cubed matrix that interlaced five intellectual operations (memory, cognition, divergent thinking, convergent thinking, and evaluation) acting on four content types (figural, semantic, symbolic, and behavioral) to produce six cognitive products (units, classes, relations, systems, transformations, and implications). This 4×5×6 matrix predicted that each intellectual act could be classified as one or more of a possible 120 different combinations of operation, content, and product.

The intellectual soup had thickened considerably. If the original purpose of factor analysis had been to systematize and simplify, that was no longer apparent to the typical test administrator and interpreter. He or she was now required to measure and understand the intelligence of children along eight ostensibly independent dimensions (Thurstone, 1938; Thurstone & Thurstone, 1965) or, even more mind boggling, along 120 dimensions (Guilford, 1967). As a result of this proliferation of intelligences, the factor analytic contribution to understanding intelligence lost much of its glitter. Even though it was muddy in its meaning, suspect in its impartiality, and unpromising in its ultimate validity as a measure of intelligence, the less scientific but more comprehensive IQ score never lost its salience in psychometrics as either an operational definition or a diagnostic marker. The single, generic IQ score seemed to better fit the common conception that the law of nature with respect to intelligence was correlational rather than compensatory in its impact. The correlational argument is that smart people tend to be smart about most things. Similarly, people with mental retardation tend to be slow in most things. The IQ score, although conceptually and psychometrically fragile from its inception, reflected that belief system better than the compensatory argument for a set of multiple, independent intelligences that allowed ability to be expressed in terms of a profile of high and low points in unrelated dimensions.

Up to this point, the construct of intelligence had evolved from a monistic conception reflected originally in Spearman's (1927) "g factor" theory to the pluralistic conceptions put forward by Thomson (1939), Thurstone (1938), and Guilford (1967). Whether one defined intelligence as unitary in meaning and comprehensive in influence or put forward the notion of a profile of multiple and independent intelligences, the basic data from which these positions were distilled consisted of intellectual products. That is, the focus was consistently on the responses of individuals to varieties of test items reflective of culturally defined important information and commonly accepted wisdom.

Another conception of multiple intelligence (MI) that attempts to span the theoretical gap between product and information processing perspectives was proposed by Gardner (1983). MI theory rejects the notion of a generic intelligence and argues for "the existence of a number of relatively autonomous human intelligences" (Gardner & Hatch, 1989, p. 5). These intelligences are Logical-Mathematical, Linguistic, Musical, Spatial, Bodily-Kinesthetic, Interpersonal, and Intrapersonal. The assessment implications of this approach are that separate instruments will be required to evaluate the capacity of children in each of these intelligences. This follows from the supposition that information about every form of intelligence has equal legitimacy in helping to make sound educational decisions. The curriculum implications of MI theory are that schools should design instruction around those intelligences for which students are "at promise" while avoiding, when possible, those for which they are "at risk." It is not yet clear whether most students with mental retardation, particularly those at the mild and moderate levels, are likely to have low, flat profiles on these intelligences or manifest some of the "peaks and valleys" often found in normal children as well as in so-called idiot savants, children with autism, and children with learning disabilities.

Information Processing Theories

We suggested earlier in this chapter that science tends to parallel major socio-political and economic movements. It can be argued that the transition over the last few decades from a manufacturing, product-oriented society to one concerned with the most effective ways of transmitting information has had an impact on shaping the renaissance of a new scientific inquiry into the nature of intelligence. The new emphasis has shifted from finding out *how smart people are* to finding out *how people are smart*.

Prior concern with differentiating people intellectually so that they might be rank ordered for educational and, some might argue, for social and political purposes as well, has changed gradually to a concern with how individuals process information (Sternberg, 1979). The "new wave" assessment issue is less the ability of children to produce intellectually acceptable products in response to culturally appropriate problems and more one of determining how children formulate those products. A focus on the ratio of the number of right answers earned on IQ tests to the number of years of life experience has given way to an analysis of how information is decoded, encoded, stored, and retrieved. This analysis is done in response to a narrow range of problems with varying cognitive demands. These problems are specifically selected and systematically altered to facilitate making inferences about the quality of those information processing components.

Finding out how the intellectual machinery works through a process assessment (Meyers, Pfeffer, & Erlbaum, 1985) has far more potential benefit for our efforts to design effective instructional environments for children with mild and moderate mental retardation than simply knowing an IQ score. Understanding the cognitive infrastructure that supports classroom learning for each individual with mental retardation is often the key to making special education really special.

Sternberg (1984) has been influential in recasting the discussion of generic intelligence, as measured by IQ scores, into more analytical terms. He has shifted the perspective of researchers and practitioners in the area of intelligence away from a concern with general intelligence and its expression in academic performance and the development of real world skills, to an effort to identify and understand the operation of those so-called "microcomponents" responsible for managing and manipulating the information processing system.

These microcomponents include metacomponents responsible for identifying the problem to be solved and managing the selection, organization, application, and monitoring of those cognitive strategies most likely to achieve problem solution. They also include performance components used in the execution of a particular task strategy, as well as acquisition, retention, and transfer components. The latter three components have to do with the storage of new information, retrieval of old information, and the transfer of old information to new situations, respectively.

The major contribution being made by investigators in the area of process assessment is that they have shifted the focus from counting the number of correct products of thinking to understanding the quality of the thinking process itself. While one would ordinarily expect a high correlation between the quality of the information processing mechanism and the size of its inventory of stored and retrievable products, there are circumstances in which that relationship could be suppressed. Foremost among them is an intellectual environment that is so sparse that it provides insufficient "fuel" for even an inherently adequate information processing system to operate effectively. The product consequences of intellectual deprivation for any particular child are predictable, but they contribute less to good educational planning than does knowledge of the intactness of that child's information processing system and its capacity for responding to remedial intervention.

It should be pointed out that an approach to assessment through an analysis of how children with mental retardation think or process information is probably less readily applied to individuals with severe and profound mental retardation. In children with extremely low functioning levels, the repertoire of potential responses is often so limited that it is difficult to present the type and level of problem that will permit meaningful "think-watching." With respect to children with severe and profound mental retardation, therefore, the degree of intelligence is typically assessed by taking an inventory of behaviors produced in response to simple stimuli in uncomplicated settings. Efforts to study the covert cognitive routes to those expressed behaviors are often frustrated by the inability of these children to be introspective about their own problem-solving activities, as well as by our inability to design problems from which cognitive inferences can be drawn.

Piagetian Theory

Yet another approach to understanding how intelligence develops and works in children with mental retardation was suggested by Piaget and Inhelder (1947). As a former biologist, Piaget was comfortable in describing the dynamics of intellectual development in terms of the emergence of a series of staged intellectual patterns, probably genetic in their source. Powering the transition from one stage to the next is exposure to environmental data that initially support the intellectual schema characteristic of that stage and later raise questions about their validity. Piaget referred to these intellectual adaptations as assimilation and accommodation, respectively. Assimilation occurs when the child's understanding of the world is reinforced by environmental events. Accommodation occurs when current intellectual structures are no longer capable of interpreting and integrating environmental events.

When conceptual thesis confronts antithesis, the individual is ultimately forced to find a new equilibrium by moving on to the next intellectual stage, which can encompass and make sense out of what had been competing perspectives. In this way, the child moves through the following stages: sensorimotor (Birth to two years); preoperational (two to seven years); concrete-operational (seven to eleven years); and formal-operational (over twelve years). For a concise but clear description of these stages, see Siegler and Richards (1982).

One of the helpful contributions of this theory is that the characteristics of mental retardation, at its different levels, need not be pinioned to a range of IQ scores derived from performance on a number of intelligence test items that seem to have little cohesive meaning. Rather, a particular level of mental retardation can be associated with one of Piaget's stages, thereby allowing a qualitatively richer description of the intellectual features of that level. For example, severe and profound levels of mental retardation are associated with the sensorimotor and preoperational stages of intellectual development. At the other end of the continuum, adults with mild mental retardation are not likely to go beyond concrete operations. For that matter, some so-called normal adults never progress to formal operations either.

The essential feature of Piaget's stage analysis of intellectual development as it pertains to individuals with mental retardation is that these individuals progress more slowly through the stages, and never progress beyond concrete operations. In one sense, mental retardation can be viewed as perseverative assimilation in that there is both a greater reluctance to discard outmoded and obsolete schema, thereby delaying the transition to succeeding stages, and an inability to master the abstract thinking and hypothetico-deductive reasoning essential for formal operations.

There are still a number of unresolved issues around Piaget's theory of intellectual stage development that have implications for understanding mental retardation. First, while the invariance of stage development has been consistently supported by research (Flavell, 1977; Weisz & Kigler, 1979), there is some question as to whether individuals operate at the same stage for every problem type. A phenomenon referred to as "decalage" (Piaget, 1972) occurs in those instances in which an individual may function at the concrete-operational stage in response to one problem type and at the preoperational stage in response to another. A second major issue generated by the intriguing possibility of remediating intelligence in individuals with mental retardation is whether specifically designed intervention programs can force access to hitherto unattained stages of intellectual development (Blackman & Lin, 1984; Detterman & Sternberg, 1982; Feuerstein, 1980). To date, the results of such efforts have ranged between discouraging and indeterminate (Spitz, 1986). As Blackman has suggested, however, the work is likely to continue, because:

> optimism has been the constant hand-maiden of research into the educability of intelligence in the mentally retarded. That fascination and that optimism will not long be restrained by Spitz's well-substantiated account of the impotence of the effort to date. From the point of view of the mentally retarded and their families, the human need is too pressing. From the point of view of program designers and service providers, the stakes are too high (Blackman, 1988, p. 450).

Instrumental Enrichment Theory

A major research and development effort currently under way to improve the intellectual and educational functioning of young people with mild mental retardation is being directed by Feuerstein (1980). His theoretical premise is that mental retardation, as a diagnostic category, or ineffective thinking, as a more generic issue, can be traced to poor quality mediated learning experiences. Feuerstein makes a critical distinction between learning through direct exposure and learning at the hands of a well-intentioned mediator. In direct exposure learning, the child learns as a result of direct contact with the environment. Mediated learning, however, more crucial to normal intellectual development, is defined as:

> the interactional processes between the developing human organism and an experienced, intentioned adult who, by interposing himself between the child and external sources of stimulation, 'mediates' the world to the child by framing, selecting, focusing, and feeding back environmental experiences in such a way as to produce in him appropriate learning sets and habits (Feuerstein, 1979, p. 71).

Consistent failures in mediated learning, whether due to an unqualified mediator or some pathological condition in the child that resists even the best mediational efforts, can lead to a wide variety of cognitive deficits that Feuerstein (1980) argues are reversible under appropriate training conditions. Before these deficits can be "repaired," however, a dynamic assessment is required to pinpoint their location (Feuerstein, 1979). The argument is put forward that conventional psychometric instruments, such as standardized intelligence or achievement tests, are essentially designed to confirm a child's depressed intellectual and educational status. Little information is provided on how the child got that way and the specific areas of cognitive malfunction that are inhibiting learning in the classroom.

According to Feuerstein (1979), what is needed is an instrument and a set of procedures that can provide a contemporary assessment of the child's potential for learning in optimally appropriate instructional settings. This is a concept that evolved from Budoff's (1968) earlier "test-teach-test" approach to assessment in which children were tested, trained on the test items, and then retested to evaluate the extent of their improvement. Stated too simply, children who made significant gains as a result of the teaching could be considered to have good potential for educability, irrespective, within limits, of such status measures as IQ or grade level achievement scores.

The instrument developed and now being widely used by Feuerstein and his associates is the Learning Potential Assessment Device (LPAD). This instrument is purported not only to estimate the extent of the child's modifiability under appropriate training conditions but, more analytically, to identify debilitating cognitive deficits, preferred perceptual modalities and cognitive strategies, and, perhaps most critically, the generalizability of strategies stimulated by the modification efforts to new tasks.

In addition to being more sensitive to the workings of the cognitive mechanisms that support the more complex forms of classroom learning, the LPAD has other special features. It is less concerned with the child's history of intellectual and academic failure and more oriented toward how the child is functioning right now and the specific instructional circumstances under which improvement might be possible. Put another way, it eschews the use of standardized instruments that have been accused by some of being culturally biased (Baca & Cervantes, 1984). It aims to minimize the consequences of cultural deprivation, and emphasizes the possibilities of accelerating children's intellectual development and educational progress. According to Instrumental Enrichment (IE) theory (Feuerstein, 1980), this acceleration can be expected when the functioning of underlying cognitive mechanisms is understood, and instructional interventions, tailored to those mechanisms, are effectively applied. It goes without saying that this approach to assessment will be confirmed only when the interventions based on the information that it provides result in the significant gains anticipated. While numerous field trials have been done, and some are currently in progress that are designed to evaluate the effectiveness of the LPAD/IE connection, it is probably fair to say that "the jury is still out."

The Diagnostic Role of Intelligence, Achievement, and Adaptive Behavior Tests

Up to this point, the emphasis in this chapter has been on reviewing competing definitions of the construct of intelligence and the implications of these definitions for assessment. It is now important to discuss the effectiveness of intelligence tests and their diagnostic partners, adaptive behavior scales, in assessing intellectual adequacy. Chapter 4 will be devoted to curriculum-based assessment for the purpose of designing more efficient instruction for learners with mental retardation at all levels. Therefore, it is first necessary to develop an anchoring orientation to this field; that is, how adequately and with what degree of impartiality are children identified as having mental retardation in the first place? This orientation builds on the premise that among our important educational values are those committed to differentiating children from one another with respect to their capacity to learn and their ability to be instructed by ordinary means.

Intelligence Tests

The Wechsler Scales

Among the most frequently used intelligence tests are the Wechsler Scales (1974). In 1949, the Wechsler Intelligence Scales for Children were developed for children 6 to 16 years of age. These were later revised into the WISC-R (Wechsler, 1974). The 1991 revision (Wechsler, 1991), named WISC III, maintains the essential content and structure of WISC-R. It retains the 125 subtests from the WISC-R and adds a new one, Symbol Search. This revision has changed the number of items for many of the subtests; it has also updated the subtests and evaluated them for cultural bias. In 1955, the Wechsler Adult Intelligence Scale was constructed for individuals sixteen years of age and older. Finally, in 1967, the Wechsler Preschool and Primary Scale of Intelligence (WPPSI) for children from four to six and a half years of age joined the inventory of Wechsler tests (Wechsler, 1967). This instrument was revised again in 1989 (Wechsler, 1989). The tests have proven to be adequately reliable and significantly correlated with the Stanford-Binet Scale of Intelligence (Terman & Merrill, 1973).

One of the major appeals of the Wechsler tests is that many school psychologists feel that the three IQ scores (Verbal, Performance, and Full Scale) provide the test interpreter with more school-relevant diagnostic material than the one IQ score derived from the Stanford-Binet. The Verbal IQ score is a composite of scale scores obtained from subtest measures of Information, Similarities, Arithmetic, Vocabulary, and Comprehension. Digit Span can be used as a supplementary subtest in estimating Verbal IQ. The Performance IQ is contributed to by subtests measuring Picture Completion, Picture Arrangement, Block Design, Object Assembly, and Coding. A Mazes subtest can be used as a supplement in this category. Although the reliability and validity of the WISC-R and WISC III are considered adequate, their floors, or the conceptual levels of their easiest items, are not low enough to make them useful instruments for very young children or for children at the severe and profound levels of mental retardation. The AAMR definition of mental retardation rates performance of less than IQ=70 as significantly below average on both the WISC-R and WISC III.

The Stanford-Binet Intelligence Scale

The other widely used test of intelligence is the Stanford-Binet Intelligence Scale (Terman & Merrill, 1973a, 1973b). While it is no longer used as extensively as the WISC-R, the Stanford-Binet, with its fuller complement of easier items, is useful with young children as well as individuals with more severe levels of mental retardation. There is a wide variety of subtests ranging from form boards and picture and object identification at the younger ages to memory, vocabulary, verbal absurdities, similarities, and reasoning at the upper age levels. The Stanford-Binet Form L–M, revised for the third time in 1960 and renormed in 1972, starts at age two and ranges through the Superior Adult level. It provides both a mental age and an IQ score. The AAMR definition of mental retardation rates performance of less than IQ=68 on the Stanford-Binet as significantly below average.

The fourth revision of the Stanford-Binet Intelligence Scale, brought out by Thorndike, Hagen, and Sattler (1986), represents by far the most significant conceptual and psychometric departure from the original instrument. Influenced by recent theoretical developments in cognitive psychology, the new Stanford-Binet offers "a diverse set of cognitive tasks that call for relational thinking in a diversity of contexts" (p. 6). In an effort to evaluate those cognitive abilities most predictive of school success, the instrument measures verbal reasoning, quantitative reasoning, abstract/visual reasoning, and short-term memory. Appropriate for individuals from age two to adult, the scales provide scores for each of the cognitive abilities mentioned above, as well as a composite score intended to reflect general reasoning ability.

Among other objectives, the test constructors designed the instrument to: (1) distinguish between students with mild mental retardation and students with learning disabilities; and (2) help clarify the underlying cognitive reasons for school difficulties. Since the test is not yet being widely used, there are insufficient data and experience to determine whether those important goals are indeed being achieved.

Other Ability Measures
Although they are not specifically referred to as intelligence tests, there are a number of other individually administered scales that are applicable to individuals with mental retardation. These focus on more specific aspects of cognitive, perceptual, and motor abilities, often at particular developmental levels. Illustrative of some of the more frequently used instruments are: the Bayley Scales of Infant Development (0 to 30 months) (Bayley, 1969); the Boehm Test of Basic Concepts (5 to 7 years) (Boehm, 1986); the McCarthy Scales of Children's Abilities (2.5 to 8.5 years) (McCarthy, 1972); the Coloured Progressive Matrices (5 to 11 years) (Raven, Court, & Raven, 1977); the Peabody Picture Vocabulary Test—Revised (2.5 to 40 years) (Dunn, 1981); and the Columbia Mental Maturity Scale (3.5 to 10 years) (Burgemeister, Blum, & Lorge, 1972).

Group Intelligence Tests
It has long been recognized that, under most circumstances, group tests, except as very preliminary screening devices, are inappropriate for use with individuals with mental retardation (Salvia & Ysseldyke, 1988). This is due primarily to the heavy demand that group tests typically place on the skills required to read and understand both the directions and the test items themselves. Reading is not a strong point even for students with mild mental retardation. As we descend the IQ ladder into the moderate, severe, and profound levels of mental retardation, group tests become increasingly inappropriate. If they are used at all, it should only be under very special conditions that include the close monitoring of small groups of children by well-trained proctors.

Assessment of School Performance

Successful academic performance remains an important goal for students with mild mental retardation. Efforts to mainstream these youngsters into regular classes and programs whenever possible began with the advent of PL94–142 in 1975. One of the assumptions underlying the passage and implementation of that landmark piece of legislation was that many youngsters with mild mental retardation, too many of them from minority groups (Reis, 1986), had been misdiagnosed by biased intelligence and achievement tests that were insensitive to cultural diversity (De Avila & Havassy, 1974). As a result of that misdiagnosis, many of these youngsters had been short-changed instructionally.

The rush to atone for years of segregated special education by placing as many of these youngsters as possible in regular classes was soon slowed by an opposing trend called *the educational reform movement* (McKinney & Hacutt, 1988; Passow, 1984). One of the principles of that movement, concerned with a return to high academic standards, insisted that everyone, nonretarded and newly mainstreamed students with mental retardation as well, had to acquire minimum academic competencies before they could graduate from high school and receive a regular diploma. From the outset, it was clear that many of the mainstreamed students with mental retardation would not achieve the minimum academic competencies required for graduation. The reasons for the failure of many mainstreamed students to demonstrate that they were educable by ordinary means in regular classes are not clear.

One argument is that their prior years of educational disadvantage and discouragement in a segregated special education system had taken them beyond the critical period when one might reasonably expect a reversal of poor school performance. Another argument is that earlier diagnoses of mild mental retardation did indeed reflect the existence of school learning problems that were not entirely associated with socioeconomic disadvantage, minority group status, test and instructional bias, and segregated education. Furthermore, it was suggested that these problems were not likely to yield easily to instructional techniques currently in use.

In either case, most high schools responded to failed expectations with respect to their mainstreamed students with one of the following: (1) to exempt these students from competency test requirements; (2) to redefine academic requirements by excluding some of the more demanding subject matter areas and replacing them with subjects such as Personal Affairs Management, Functional Reading and Arithmetic, and a Part-time Job Practicum; or (3) award an alternative diploma or certificate of attendance that makes it clear to potential employers and the public-at-large that they must attach a different significance to the alternative diploma or certificate than they do to the diploma generally awarded.

It should be pointed out that the discussion of whether or under what circumstances mainstreaming works for students with mild mental retardation is really not applicable to students with moderate, severe, or profound mental retardation. There is a growing movement in this country and elsewhere to include children with more severe mental retardation in regular classes. However, the intention of some of the professionals who designed these programs has been less to accelerate academic development and more to improve the opportunities for the social integration of these children, as well as to improve the attitudes of their nondisabled peers toward them. The assessment of adaptive behavior, to be described in a later section, may be more germane to monitoring the progress of some of those students.

Individual Achievement Tests
As alluded to above, achievement tests are designed to give some approximation of the level of academic achievement that a child has reached, as well as some indication of the child's strengths and deficits in the use of strategies applicable to school learning (McLoughlin & Lewis, 1986). The Peabody Individual Achievement Test–Revised (PIAT-R) (Dunn & Markwardt, 1970; Markwardt, 1989) and the Wide Range Achievement Test–Revised (WRAT-R) (Jastak & Wilkinson, 1984) are among the most frequently used achievement tests for students with mental retardation.

The PIAT-R was normed on students from kindergarten to twelfth grade. It measures performance on five subtests: Mathematics, Reading Recognition, Reading Comprehension, Spelling, and General Information. With the exception of Reading Recognition and General Information, the PIAT-R uses a multiple choice format. The examinee responds to a problem situation by selecting one of four possible responses. The PIAT-R provides three age scores: age equivalents, percentile ranks related to the age of the student, and normalized scale scores with a mean of 100 and a standard deviation of 15. Similarly, three grade scores are provided: grade equivalents, percentile rank for the grade in which the student is currently housed, and normalized standard scores with the same mean and standard deviation parameters as the age scores.

The Wide Range Achievement Test (WRAT-R) is used by both educational practitioners and researchers who need an easily administered instrument to provide a rough estimate of grade equivalence in spelling, arithmetic, and reading. It is divided into Levels I (CA 5–0 to 11–11) and II (CA 12–0 to adulthood). Raw scores obtained from each of the subtests can be quickly converted to grade equivalent scores which, in turn, can be transformed into standard scores and percentile ranks according to age.

Group Achievement Tests

As with group tests of intelligence, group achievement tests are generally considered inappropriate for use even with youngsters with mild mental retardation. It goes without saying that they are grossly inappropriate for use at lower levels of mental retardation. Every assessment experience with children with mental retardation requires close, individualized supervision. Test proctors must know when any particular child is not following directions, is responding randomly, or has simply "fatigued out" of the test. It is very difficult to offer that kind of supervision with a group test. The achievement levels of individuals with mental retardation have tended to be underestimated significantly in those instances when group achievement tests have been used.

Students with mental retardation typically confront group achievement tests when they are used as a general school screener. Those students who do poorly on these tests should be and generally are referred for more intensive individual assessment. Among the most frequently used group achievement tests are the Metropolitan Achievement Tests (MAT) (Prescott, Balow, Hogan, & Farr, 1985, 1986, 1987) and the Stanford Achievement Test (SAT) (Gardner, Rudman, Karlsen, & Merwin, 1982). Other group achievement tests used frequently in the schools include the California Achievement Tests (CTB, 1985, 1986, 1987) and the Iowa Tests of Basic Skills (Hieronymous, Hoover, & Lindquist, 1986).

While many standardized instruments are available, an effective assessment program requires a careful matching of what information is needed with what a particular test is capable of delivering. There is also the question of whether tests should be modified in ways that would maximize the performance of children with disabilities. Finally, there is the issue of discriminating between "good" and "poor" tests from the perspectives of reliability, validity, fairness, adequacy of standardization, and ease of administration. The Tenth Mental Measurement Yearbook (Conoley & Kramer, 1989) is a useful resource for practitioners required to make these decisions.

Adaptive Behavior Measures

The motivation for adding the adaptive behavior criterion to the definition of intelligence was to take intellectual assessment, at least in part, out of the rarefied atmosphere of the traditional IQ test and to add a dimension of real-life "smarts" associated with real-life activities. From the beginning, one of the major difficulties associated with obtaining valid measures of adaptive behavior or personal and social adjustment has been the "rubber ruler" quality of that assessment. Simply put, the quality of an individual's adaptive behavior is inevitably related to the demand of the physical and social context in which it occurs. For example, good adjustment or an adequate level of adaptive behavior in an isolated rural setting or in a highly structured institutional environment can be quite different, along some absolute scale, from what is required to achieve acceptable adaptive behavior as an integrated member of a complex urban community. For a young man with mental retardation, moving about in a farm community where everyone knows him and his family is quite a different activity than taking public transportation to school or work in the often impersonal and potentially confusing environment of a large city.

The precautions required for interpreting the meaning of adaptive behavior scores are associated with questions such as "adaptive behavior where?" or "adaptive behavior accompanied by what level of family or school or work setting support?" Despite these concerns, the call for more ecological validity in the assessment of competence has resulted in a proliferation of adaptive behavior instruments. Among the more widely used tests of adaptive behavior or social competence are the AAMR *Adaptive Behavior Scales-School* (Lambert, Nihira, & Leland, 1992) and the Vineland Adaptive Behavior Scales (Sparrow, Balla, & Cicchetti, 1984). Both of these tests rely on the reports of parents or teachers or both if the youngsters are at home, or on staff members responsible for the immediate supervision of individuals in residential facilities. The Vineland Adaptive Behavior Scales measure behavior across four domains: communication, daily living skills, socialization, and motor skills.

Other frequently used instruments are the Cain-Levine Social Competency Scale (Cain, Levine, & Elzey, 1977), the Balthazar Adaptive Behavior Scales (Balthazar, 1976), and the Adaptive Behavior Inventory for Children, which is part of a series of instruments called the System of Multicultural Pluralistic Assessment (SOMPA) designed with the intention of reducing bias in testing (Mercer, 1979; Mercer & Lewis, 1977).

The Diversity and Bias Issue

The 1954 Supreme Court decision, which found that segregated education for black children was inherently inferior education, has had ripple effects for special as well as regular education. After segregated education for blacks had been declared unconstitutional, it did not take long for civil rights groups and other observers of the educational scene to note that minority group children made up a heavy majority of children placed in classes for students with mild mental retardation. This was particularly true in large urban centers. African American and Latino children in the large cities of the Northeast, and Mexican American children in southern California and other states of the Southwest found their way in large numbers into these classes. Finally, the children of Native American families have been assigned in disproportionate numbers to special classes in some states and districts.

The controversial issue is whether educators and psychologists have used assessment procedures, too often designed and standardized with a middle-class orientation to unfairly classify and label children from culturally and linguistically diverse backgrounds as individuals with mental retardation who require special education services. It has been suggested that there are strong elements of bias against minority children in the referral, diagnosis, and placement system (Baca & Cervantes, 1984). These arguments largely contend that the poor performance of minority children in classrooms that often leads to their referral by teachers for assessment in the first place is due less to intellectual limitations and more to inadequate educational opportunities. This problem is often compounded by limitations in English proficiency, and lack of confidence in schools and formal learning experiences. Some of the same reasons are given for their marginal performance on intelligence and achievement tests during the diagnostic process. In addition, these tests have been criticized as too often contentually irrelevant to the experience and concerns of inner-city minority children (Dew & Perlman, 1980), linguistically inappropriate (Cervantes, 1974), and interpersonally more threatening to these children in their administration than they are for middle-class children (Dew & Perlman, 1980; Laosa, 1977).

There is some controversy over whether most cases of mild mental retardation and placements in programs requiring special educational services can be accounted for in terms of an assessment bias against intellectually intact minority and disadvantaged children. Some professionals suggest that at least some of these children may have intellectual limitations that require special programming. This controversy can not be fully resolved by data currently available. Educators and psychologists remain divided with respect to the degree of their optimism about the intellectual and scholastic remediability of children who manifest early problems in school.

Perhaps the most elaborate, if as yet incompletely validated, set of procedures for attempting to minimize assessment bias was developed by Mercer (1979) and her colleagues (Mercer & Lewis, 1977). Known as the System of Multicultural Pluralistic Assessment (SOMPA), the procedure involves collecting a wide variety of data from different sources. These data reflect on one of the key conceptual contributions of the system; namely, comparing the child's performance not to national norms that too often do not include the population segment that the child represents, but to his or her own sociocultural peers. For example, if a child earns an IQ of 100 and comes from a sociocultural cohort with an average IQ of 80, this ostensibly normal IQ may in fact reflect the potential for higher intellectual and academic performance than an IQ of 100 might ordinarily suggest. To illustrate, if a particular environment typically produces an average IQ of only 80, the child who overachieves intellectually in that environment by 20 points might be a child with special abilities. On the other hand, a child who earns an IQ of 60 in an 80 IQ environment might be evidencing less impairment than his or her IQ of 60 would indicate.

In an effort to achieve a balanced and complete view of the child's assets and liabilities, both intellectual and physical, the SOMPA requires the collection of current medical information as well as a health history. Despite the widespread wariness toward the meaning of IQ scores, WISC-R IQ scores are obtained as well as a measure of adaptive behavior. The IQ score as related to national norms leads to an estimate of School Functioning Level. This same IQ score, as viewed from the perspective of comparable sociocultural norms, leads to an Estimated Learning Potential. In theory, combining reliable and valid assessment information on both current school functioning and potential for learning should lead to more sensitive and more effective educational decisions for children. Since evaluation of learning potential is more tenuous in its measurement and validity than evaluation of current achievement levels, efforts to combine these two sources of assessment information for purposes of educational planning typically suffer from appropriate weighting and unequal reliability and validity problems. Although it represents the boldest effort to date, insufficient evidence has been accumulated to establish the ultimate value of the SOMPA as a bias-free assessment procedure.

Since this text is concerned with all levels of mental retardation, it should be noted that the bias issue has been applied primarily to the assessment of individuals with mild mental retardation. The bias issue might also be a factor in the assessment of youngsters with moderate mental retardation. The level of behavioral dysfunction in individuals with severe and profound mental retardation, however, normally precludes the possibility that their very low levels of function could be explained solely in terms of sociocultural disadvantage or unfair testing practices.

Introduction to Case Studies: Sample Assessments

It could be that assessment is as much an art as it is a science. As such, it can only truly be appreciated when its principles and techniques are put to the service of helping us to understand the conditions and experiences of individuals with disabilities. The purpose of this section is to illustrate assessment concepts and procedures through the presentation of sample assessments of eight cases with varying degrees of mental retardation. The same eight individuals will be followed throughout the course of this text. The assessments of the first two students, Tony and Sonia, will be presented in depth in order to provide examples of a comprehensive assessment report at different levels of mental retardation. The remaining assessments, which are more concise, are included to provide background information on the other six students who will be featured in case study examples in the chapters to follow.

At the time of these assessments, each of the eight cases was reviewed to specify the basis for their classification in light of the new, 1992 AAMR definition and classification system for mental retardation. Step 1 report forms for each case, except Tanisha, appear in Appendix A. Appendix B includes completed sample report forms for Tanisha for Steps 1, 2, and 3 from the 1992 AAMR Diagnosis, Classification, and Systems of Supports Workbook (1992).

CASE STUDY: Tony

At sixteen years of age (16–0), Tony lives at the Sullivan Avenue Group Home, which also houses three other residents. Like Tony, they have been classified as having mild mental retardation. Tony presently attends a self-contained classroom in a suburban high school where he is mainstreamed into one class (shop/woodworking). He is adept at many tasks involving basic carpentry, furniture repair, and grounds keeping. His father, a single parent for the past ten years, includes Tony in work for his lawn maintenance business during summer weekends.

Table 3-1 presents results of a battery of psychological and educational tests administered to Tony, consisting of the Wechsler Intelligence Scale for Children—Revised (WISC-R), the Peabody Individual Achievement Test—Revised (PIAT-R), the Spache Diag-

TABLE 3-1   Tony's Test Profile

Identifying Information

Chronological Age: 16–0

Program: Self-contained special education class in a comprehensive high school with mainstreaming for shop class.

Wechsler Intelligence Scale for Children—Revised (WISC-R)—Test Date: 11/2/92

Verbal IQ	64
Performance IQ	71
Full Scale IQ	65

Peabody Individual Achievement Test–Revised (PIAT-R)—Test Date: 11/9/92

Subtest	Grade Equivalent	Standard Score	Percentile Rank	Stanine
General Information	1.2	55	1	1
Reading Recognition	3.8	63	1	1
Reading Comprehension	2.5	55	1	1
Reading (Total)	3.4	55	1	1
Mathematics	2.6	55	1	1
Spelling	2.7	55	1	1
Total Test	2.6	55	1	1

Written Expression: Grade-Based Stanine: 1

Note: All standard scores except Reading Comprehension represent the lowest possible score derived from Tony's raw scores.

Spache Diagnostic Reading Scales—Test Date: 11/3/92

Instructional Level:	Grade 3.5
Independent Level:	Grade 3.5
Potential Level:	Grade 4.5

Vineland Adaptive Behavior Scales (Interview Edition)—*Test Date*: 11/10/92

Domain	Standard Score	Percentile Rank	Stanine	Age Equivalent
Communication	42	< 0.1	1	7–4
Daily Living Skills	52	0.1	1	7–9
Socialization	52	0.1	1	6–5
Composite	45	< 0.1	1	7–2

nostic Reading Scales, and the Vineland Adaptive Behavior Scales. On the latter survey, Tony and his group home manager both served as informants.

The WISC-R is a measure of general intelligence normed on children between ages six and sixteen. The difference between Tony's Verbal and Performance IQ scores is not significant, though nonverbal abilities enjoy a slight advantage. Not included in Table 3-1 is the list of scores for the twelve subtests that together comprise the WISC-R. However, the subtest score profile revealed three trends. One pattern pertained to Tony's problems with numerical computation and manipulation. Another trend was his relative proficiency in retaining, organizing and using visual-spatial information. A third trend revealed a deficit that concerns his judgment and problem solving in social situations.

Results of the PIAT-R reveal a very low level of academic achievement compared to his age peers, keeping in mind that the mean standard score on any test of the PIAT-R is 100. His highest score is in reading recognition where he achieved a standard score of 63 and a percentile rank of 1, meaning that 99 percent of the sample of students Tony's age taking the test obtained scores higher than his. All of Tony's percentile ranks fell within the first (and lowest) of nine stanines. Grade equivalents suggest that mathematics is particularly deficient, while reading recognition, his highest level of achievement, produced a grade equivalent approaching the fourth–grade level. Observations and results from the Spache Diagnostic Reading Scales also indicate that instructional and independent reading levels reached the Grade 3.5 level, and much work was required to read aloud even phonetically regular words which were unfamiliar to him. (The "instructional level" refers to reading proficiency which combines complete and accurate verbalization of printed text with adequate comprehension during oral reading, where classroom instruction is most appropriate. The "independent level" refers to grade-level comprehension of material read silently, which is suitable for reading on one's own.) Also on the Spache Diagnostic Reading Scales, Tony's comprehension of material read to him reached the Grade 4.5 level, his "potential level." Perhaps the time and effort required to decode unfamiliar words, or the failure to recognize some words altogether, detracts from his opportunity to understand what he is trying to read.

Four scores, based on interviews with Tony and his group home manager, are reported from Tony's Vineland Adaptive Behavior Scales. The most informative is probably the standard score, which, like the IQ, is best understood as a deviation from a sample mean of 100. Tony's highest standard scores are in the domains of daily living skills and communication, which are slightly more than three standard deviations below the mean. His communication score hovers almost four standard deviations below the mean.

What do these scores say about Tony? Two notes of caution are in order. First, scores should not be considered in isolation from each other, and second they should never be treated as abstractions distilled and separated from real-life observations of Tony's everyday behavior. The remaining discussion is a description of his skills and behavior, gleaned largely from test observations and Vineland interviews.

Several trends are important. First, he readily acquires daily living competencies through a consistent routine (in his home, in his father's business, in his leisure interests, etc.), provided that his routine is stable and predictable. Where judgment and problem solving are required for more ambiguous or unusual situations, he has more difficulty. Second, his retention, organization, and use of visual-spatial information is a key resource for him. Third, his difficulty with numerical reasoning imposes notable limitations on him. It should be noted that Tony's health, motor skills and social-emotional adjustment are not problematic, and will not be discussed below.

Perhaps Tony's most overlearned behaviors are those routinely performed in the daily living domain. This is particularly true in the personal subdomain where he has mastered all self-help skills with some qualifications pertaining to needed refinements in dressing. He often fails to exercise sound judgment in selecting clothing appropriate to season and weather. Sometimes, he also needs reminders to shave. He is almost as proficient in the domestic subdomain where he has mastered most domestic chores (e.g., vacuuming, bathroom cleanup), preparation of simple meals (e.g., soups, salads, sandwiches, pancakes and eggs, etc.), as well as laundry, though he is careless about folding and hanging clean clothes and neglects to throw used bathtowels in the hamper. Community living skills also are in his repertoire, including observation of pedestrian safety precautions, attention to survival signs, and routine use of bus service to reach various destinations in town.

Predictably, Tony has more difficulty in those daily living skills that require judgment and adjustments to new situations, as well as problem solving in practical situations. His problems are exacerbated where numerical skill is required. Just as Tony's performance in math was consistently depressed in the Arithmetic and Mathematics components of the WISC-R and the PIAT-R, respectively, it has consistently interfered with money, time-telling, and measurement applications in his daily routine. Though he can identify coins and state various coin equivalences, he has difficulty counting change to a dollar unless he uses a calculator. He is not adept at pricing items and anticipating the total cost of a purchase when shopping for several items at a nearby convenience store, and he requires supervision if he is expected to spend more than a few dollars. He has facility in handling the mechanics of filling out withdrawal and deposit slips and, although he understands basic banking concepts, he lacks an appreciation of interest and he is poor at planning a budget. He tells time at 15-minute intervals but not consistently at 5-minute intervals. Measurement skills are also weak, which sometimes interferes with following recipes with which he is unfamiliar when he assists in meal preparation. It also interferes with some of his woodworking projects at school, a source of considerable distress to him.

Visual-spatial skills, as measured by the WISC-R, represent an area of strength for Tony. This is sometimes evident in his woodwork and lawn maintenance work. On the other hand, results of intelligence tests and adaptive behavior surveys also point to Tony's somewhat immature social judgment, evidenced in his tendency to interrupt conversations, to place phone calls to family friends late at night in order to invite himself over for dinner, and his inclination to acquaint himself readily with strangers. He is somewhat unassertive and eager to please, so that he sometimes runs errands for others when it is personally inconvenient for him to do so. He accepts criticism well.

A recent fire safety training program at Tony's group home brought into sharp contrast his skills and deficits. In one exercise, he readily found and later recalled the location of two sockets containing overloaded circuits, another socket containing a cord with frayed insulation, and still another cord covered by a carpet. Given the existence of well over thirty sockets in his residence, this was a testament to his facility with recall of visual-spatial information. Yet, during the evacuation drill, it was also Tony who scrambled down the stair-

CASE STUDY: Tony (continued)

case as he pushed other residents aside, exclaiming: "Bail out, everybody, there's a fire in this place!"

CASE STUDY: Sonia

Sonia, a nonverbal girl aged seven years, seven months, was observed at the Olton Center, a school for children with profound mental retardation. The Vineland Adaptive Behavior Scales were administered, with Sonia's mother, an articulate and intelligent woman, serving as informant. An attempt was made to administer some of the subtests of the Stanford Binet Intelligence Scale and the Leiter International Performance Scale, but Sonia's use of test objects was limited to mouthing and throwing them. Her IQ was estimated to be less than 15.

On the Vineland Adaptive Behavior Scales, Sonia's results, based on an interview with her mother, placed her in the profound range of mental retardation. Four different scores were computed for Sonia on this instrument, and they are presented in Table 3-2. A standard score compares Sonia's results with a representative sample of children her age, with the sample's average (or mean) performance represented by a score of 100 and with departures from this mean marked in 15-point intervals called standard deviations. In all domains, Sonia's standard score was less than 20, or more than five standard deviations below the mean. The percentile rank indicates that, in all areas, Sonia's adaptive behavior scores are exceeded by more than 99.9 percent of the national sample of her chronological age peers. Percentiles are sometimes blocked into nine intervals called stanines, with the ninth stanine representing the sample's highest percentile ranks while the first stanine contains the lowest percentile ranks, such as Sonia's. It is not always easy to compare one child's percentile rank to that of another since the distances between such scores are different, just as the distances between runners in a marathon vary. (In most distributions, scores are concentrated near the middle and spread apart

TABLE 3-2   Sonia's Test Profile

Identifying Information:

Chronological Age: 7–7

Program: Olton Regional Center for Mental Retardation

Vineland Adaptive Behavior Scale Score (Interview Edition)—*Test Date*: 11/4/92

Domain	Standard Score	National Percentile Rank	Stanine	Age Equivalent
Communication	< 20	< .01	1	0–5
Daily Living Skills	< 20	< .01	1	0–10
Socialization	< 20	< .01	1	0–4
Composite	< 20	< .01	1	0–5

Note: Additional summary data such as confidence bands were left out for purposes of simplification and clarity.

with decreasing frequency at the extreme ends.) The advantage of stanines is that they help to equalize these intervals somewhat by grouping scores into more comparable categories.

Sonia's age equivalents reflect the average age level of the sample of children whose scores most closely approximated her own. Most of Sonia's scores are similar to children four or five months of age, though her skill competence in the Daily Living Activities Domain is at the ten-month level. Age equivalents have a good deal of intuitive appeal to many parents and professionals since they are easy to understand. However, they also have serious problems as accurate measures of behavior and should be regarded with extreme caution. It is misleading, for example, to characterize Sonia as an infant because she has scores on a particular survey similar to those of a sample of very young children. A discussion of problems inherent in age-equivalents can be found in Salvia and Ysseldyke (1991).

Three other caveats should be noted: First, information such as Sonia's adaptive behavior score-profile is seldom gathered for its own sake. To repeat what was said at the beginning of this chapter, the purpose of an assessment is to gather information useful for making decisions about a child's education. So in any assessment, descriptions of Sonia's behavior, skills, and abilities should also be prefaced by the reasons for her assessment, as well as background information and recommendations pertinent to those reasons.

Second, one might be disappointed by how little he or she is informed by Sonia's scores. Except for age equivalents, which are questionable measures of development in any case, all other scores are the same, so that nothing is disclosed about her relative strengths and weaknesses. Indeed, in the few norm-referenced instruments for individuals like Sonia, obtained scores do not, for the most part, tell even the casual observer much more than he or she readily can see; namely, that Sonia is a child with extremely atypical limitations. This is to disparage neither adaptive surveys per se nor the adaptive gains that people with disabilities like Sonia's have made. The point here is that such gains are often incremental and too subtle to be detected by broad lifespan surveys of adaptive behavior.

Finally, scores can never fully describe what the individual can and cannot do. An assessment should therefore also include descriptions of Sonia's behavior, derived from the examiner's direct observations as well as those of reliable informants like Sonia's mother. Indeed, interviews that are based upon adaptive behavior surveys are valuable not just because of the scores they generate but, perhaps more importantly, because of the wealth of descriptive data that is made available. Interviews based on adaptive surveys are often valuable because they help to collect and organize this information. Accordingly, the following paragraphs describe Sonia's full profile of skills and deficits. It should be noted that, in most assessments, such a comprehensive description would be narrowed to address issues raised in the reasons for the evaluation.

Sonia was observed to walk with a flat-footed gait, with precarious balance, and without consistently watching where she was going. She reached for objects frequently. Strength of grip and wrist-rotation skills were sufficient to turn a knob to open a door but she had difficulty turning on a faucet. Oral motor control was somewhat weak. She sometimes drooled and her tongue was slightly thrust beyond her lips which, in turn, appeared hypotonic. She was reported not to chew her food thoroughly. If it is not thoroughly cut for her, she may occasionally choke or cough. Spillage from her cup while drinking is quite common.

Eye-hand coordination was observed to be very poor. She did not look at her hands when soap was placed in them for hand washing, for example. However, she would gaze momentarily at nearby Leiter blocks and some buttons as she reached for them, showing a preference for neither hand. She seldom used a pincer grasp to pick up small objects and her manipulation of those objects was largely limited to throwing them or placing them in her mouth. Descending stairs, Sonia places both feet on each step, one foot following the other while holding the bannister firmly. She appears hesitant and apprehensive on the stairs.

Sonia wears diapers under her pants and is not toilet trained, though sometimes she eliminates while seated on the toilet. She required hand-over-hand manipulation to wash her hands after toileting during the observation session but she was also observed to make an attempt, not very successfully, at turning the faucet on her own when she approached the sink. She is reported to attempt removal of her socks while undressing, being most successful when her sock has been pulled below her heel by her mother. She sometimes anticipates being undressed and cooperates during the task, as when she raises her arms for removal of a pull-over shirt. She uses no utensils for feeding herself, briefly viewing a built-up spoon long enough to pick it up but looking away and dropping it almost immediately thereafter. She will reach for and grasp a cup with both hands, usually with physical guidance but she often releases the cup after drinking its contents. She has no other hygiene, eating, or dressing skills in her repertoire.

Regarding cognitive and communication skills, Sonia's attention span is very limited. She is unable to cooperate on any task for more than a minute. She looked toward the examiner when he called her name but she was easily distracted by extraneous noises and nearby objects available to her grasp. She tended not to look for objects that had fallen out of her view and she had difficulty remaining seated for more than a few minutes during the observation period. She sometimes responded appropriately to commands like "please sit," "come here," and "please stand," which were accompanied by gestural signs, but she may have been attending to other, situational cues (e.g., the appearance of her mother carrying her coat when told to "come here"). Sonia could not identify even familiar objects by pointing to them or picking them up when requested to do so. She vocalized some sounds but this seemed to serve more of a self-stimulatory than a communicative function. She had no conventional means of communicating her needs.

Sonia is an attractive, cheerful and affectionate girl who readily hugs anyone around her who attends to her. She readily smiles at others once eye contact is engaged. Her sociable nature works to her advantage since teachers and caregivers find it rewarding to interact with her and this increases her access to learning and recreational activities. Though she often ignores her age peers, she will play in their presence when given the opportunity. Her favorite reinforcers include adult affection, music, outdoor activities (excluding anything that involves climbing or height), large toys (e.g., beach balls) which she only briefly uses but often returns to if available, and almost any kind of food. In fact, pica sometimes is a problem, since she attempts at times to ingest, chew, or swallow inedible substances like toothpaste, cigarettes, and crayons.

CASE STUDY: Alicia

At three and a half years of age, Alicia's last assessment included administration of the Bayley Scales of Infant Development, normed on infants to two and a half years of age. Her standard score on the Mental Scale was 20 and her score on the Motor Scale was 15, with the mean on both scales being 100 and the standard deviation being 16. Alicia has been classified as having profound mental retardation.

Table 3-3 presents a profile of scores from Alicia's Vineland Adaptive Behavior Scales. Because she is younger than six years of age, results on the Motor Scale are reported as well as results from the Communication Skills, Daily Living Skills, and Socialization Skills domains. Standard scores must be interpreted with some caution, since even a single point earned on any given scale can result in a standard score of 40 or 50 for a child of Alicia's age. More revealing of the extent of her mental retardation is her percentile rank. In all domains, more than 99.9 percent of a sample of children her age obtained scores equal to or higher than hers. This demonstrates the relationship between percentile ranks and standard scores based on a mean of 100 and a standard deviation of 15. Fewer than 3 percent of a representative sample of people will have scores which fall below the 70th percentile (or two standard deviations below the mean), the cutoff score in many tests that define performance in the range of mental retardation. Fewer than 1 percent of the sample will have standard scores which, like Alicia's, fall below the 50th percentile. This is considerably more than three standard deviations below the mean.

Alicia's communication skills are limited to occasional brief glances, smiles, and vocalizations in apparent response to the presence of anyone interacting with her, especially when the person is talking to her. She typically smiles readily at the appearance of her mother. Differentiated vocalizations include mirthful laughter, often during play, and distressful moaning when uncomfortable (e.g., when soiled).

Socially and emotionally she is a placid child who passively accepts physical contact and handling by her caregivers. At the Early Childhood Center, she tends not to pay atten-

TABLE 3-3   Alicia's Test Profile

Identifying Information:

Chronological Age: 3–6

Program: Early Childhood Center for Children with Multiple Disabilities

***Bayley Scales of Infant Development*—*Test Date*: 11/5/92**

| Mental Scale | 20 |
| Motor Scale | 15 |

Vineland Adaptive Behavior Scales (Interview Edition)—***Test Date*: 11/6/92**

Domain	Standard Score	National Percentile Rank	Stanine	Age Equivalent
Communication	53	< 0.1	1	0–2
Daily Living Skills	54	< 0.1	1	0–8
Socialization	49	< 0.1	1	0–1
Motor Skills	44	< 0.1	1	0–1
Composite	46	< 0.1	1	0–3

CASE STUDY: Alicia (continued)

---

tion to children nearby. She will momentarily turn in the direction of a sound and visually follow a moving object. On such occasions, she may reach for objects with her right hand (there is some constriction of the left extremities). She may hold objects momentarily but stops gazing at them quickly and soon discards them. If they make sounds she may shake them briefly before dropping them. She usually handles objects only on her own initiative. She generally drops objects placed in her hand. Her attention span extends only a matter of seconds. She eats no solid food but she anticipates feeding by turning her head and opening her mouth as she views the spoon approaching and touching her lips. Lip closure is poor, so that she only partially removes the contents of a spoon. There is much spillage as she swallows from the contents of a cup which she sometimes holds with hand-over-hand guidance. She has no other self-care skills, though she may occasionally cry in distress when she has wet or soiled herself. She sometimes cooperates during dressing by raising her arms during removal of a pullover shirt. Reinforcing activities include bathing, water play, and feeling the vibration and air current from a hair dryer. She enjoys television, apparently more for its visual stimulation than for its sound, since she generally ignores the stereo.

Motor skills were mentioned in passing above but it should be added that Alicia will turn her head from side to side and sit up with support, holding her head upright for frequent but brief (5 to 10 second) intervals. She will reach for objects she sees on occasion, briefly handling them with her right hand using an overhand grasp only. In a reclining position she will often shift from her back to her side (predominantly her left side), which she does in order to watch television. This is one of the few but very obvious purposive behaviors which she demonstrates when the television is turned on in the morning.

CASE STUDY: Scott

Scott, classified as having severe mental retardation, was re-evaluated shortly after his eighteenth birthday. The Stanford-Binet Intelligence Scale, which consists of a series of short test batteries, was adminstered. Each battery is designed for administration at a particular age level. (The first battery of tests, for example, is usually administered to children between two and two and a half years of age.) Typically children begin by taking tests from a battery close to their chronological age level, or at a point where the examiner feels the child can achieve mostly successful results. Testing proceeds forward, in the direction of more advanced age levels, until the child reaches the point at which all tests in the battery are failed. This is the child's ceiling level. It is also often necessary to "work backward" from the starting point on this test to obtain a basal level, the age-level at which the entire battery of tests is passed. It is assumed that all tests beneath the basal level are within the child's capacity to pass, so they are not administered. Likewise, more advanced tests above the ceiling are not administered since the child is expected to fail them.

Relative strengths were evident on tests that measured perceptual skills and expression of previously learned material (e.g., vocabulary), while deficits were found in tests that called for judgment, comprehension and abstract reasoning, or concept formation.

TABLE 3-4   Scott's Test Profile

Identifying Information:

Chronological Age: 18–0

Program: Transition Center

Stanford-Binet Intelligence Scale (Fourth Edition)—*Test Date*: 11/25/92

IQ   33

Vineland Adaptive Behavior Scales (Interview Edition)—*Test Date*: 11/25/92

Domain	Standard Score	National Percentile Rank	Stanine	Age Equivalent
Communication	20	< 0.1	1	5–0
Daily Living Skills	20	< 0.1	1	5–5
Socialization	24	< 0.1	1	3–9
Composite	20	< 0.1	1	4–9

A profile of adaptive behaviors obtained in an interview with Scott's mother using the Vineland Adaptive Behavior Scales is presented in Table 3-4. Scott's communication skills are adequate in terms of following simple instructions, communicating his needs in simple but clearly understood sentences, and a command of a basic vocabulary. Beyond expressing himself at a very concrete level, however, he has difficulty conveying longer messages, such as giving directions or narrating a story about the day's events. Nor can he follow a conversation or a series of instructions for more than a few minutes. He can identify familiar survival words such as signs for the men's room, and writing is restricted to printing his name, address, and his telephone number (the latter of which is still not perfectly done).

His daily living skills are more advanced, with all self-care skills and many domestic skills being within his repertoire. There remain, however, significant deficits in some independent living areas such as shopping, meal preparation, and community travel. He has no opportunity to develop banking skills since he earns only a very small weekly allowance for some household responsibilities. Scott has just begun to learn to operate a washing machine at a nearby coin-operated laundromat, though he continues to require occasional supervision.

Scott tends not to socialize much and his parents and his teacher at the Transition Center both describe him as a "loner." He has an interest in caring for pets, including a dog and a parakeet. He is well-mannered but somewhat passive and gullible which sometimes makes him the object of practical jokes. Indeed, he unwittingly gets himself into mischief when other students set him up for pranks such as the delivery of towels to the girls' locker room.

CASE STUDY: Karen

At age fifteen, Karen, classified as having moderate mental retardation, attends a special class in a comprehensive high school. Results of Karen's examination on the Wechsler Intel-

CASE STUDY: Karen (continued)

ligence Scale for Children–Revised (WISC-R) are presented in Table 3-5. Note should be made of the consistency between her IQ scores. The five subtests that together comprise the Verbal battery of the WISC-R (not tabulated here) yielded consistently low scores for Karen. A representative sample of children obtains an average "scaled" score of 10 on each of these subtests, while Karen obtained a score of only two per scale. Her scores on the Performance subtests were also low, but they were slightly more variable, ranging from a high score of 4 to a low score of 1. She demonstrated relatively greater proficiency in perceptual-motor tasks such as assembly of designs and puzzles, which requires considerable analysis and integration.

An attempt was made to administer the Peabody Individual Achievement Test-Revised (PIAT-R) but there were too few correct responses in her protocol to generate scores. The Vineland Adaptive Behavior Scales were also administered and results are included in Table 3-5.

Karen's communication skills favor reception more than expression. Her receptive vocabulary is quite good. When given an array of pictures, she will often point to the one that best depicts an object, event, or description. She will attend to, remember, and follow two-step and sometimes three-step instructions as well. Yet, she is slow to verbalize, partly because she appears to have difficulty finding the words that best capture her intended meaning, partly because she has trouble assembling words beyond the most basic sentences, and largely because her articulation is slow and labored. She seems to have trouble activating and regulating the motor components of speech. In the process, she may sometimes lose track of what she is trying to say. In reading, word recognition is close to an early first grade

TABLE 3-5 Karen's Test Profile

Identifying Information:

Chronological Age: 15–1

Program: Special class in a comprehensive high school with mainstreaming for lunch, gym, and assembly.

Wechsler Intelligence Scale for Children–Revised (WISC-R)—Test Date: 11/16/92

Verbal IQ	51
Performance IQ	52
Full Scale IQ	47

Vineland Adaptive Behavior Scales (Interview Edition)—*Test Date*: 11/19/92

Domain	Standard Score	National Percentile Rank	Stanine	Age Equivalent
Communication	34	< 0.1	1	5–6
Daily Living Skills	38	< 0.1	1	6–6
Socialization	48	< 0.1	1	5–5
Composite	37	< 0.1	1	5–9

level and she can use letter-sound correspondence rules to pronounce only the most basic (CVC) words; a process too inefficient to support functional reading. She can, however, sight-read numerous signs in the community.

Karen is meticulous both in self-care and in housekeeping. Besides the vocational domain, her major deficits are in the area of money skills, time telling, and leisure activity. Although she enjoys domestic activities like cooking and rug hooking, and although she clearly enjoys the company of others, she appears to be at a loss during dances and other social functions. She often retreats to a corner of the room to watch others enjoy themselves.

CASE STUDY: Juan

Juan's parents moved from Puerto Rico to his present home four years before his birth. Juan is presently nine years old and classified as having mild mental retardation. English is his primary language, so his psychological and educational tests were administered in English. However, the impact of the student's cultural background should be considered when evaluating his or her academic and social competencies.

Table 3-6 presents results of Juan's intelligence and academic achievement tests. Results of his adaptive behavior survey are also presented. There is no significant discrepancy between his WISC-R Verbal IQ and Performance IQ, though the profile of the ten WISC-R subtest scores (not presented in the table) reveals a particular deficit in his general fund of information. This is evident in his low Vocabulary score and his difficulty in answering such questions as "How many months are in a year?"[1]

Juan is presently in the fourth grade, so his overall performance on the Peabody Individual Achievement Test—Revised (PIAT-R), a general screen of academic performance, is nearly four years behind grade level. His percentile ranks indicate that 99 percent of a representative sample of classmates obtained scores equal to or higher than his. Consistent with his WISC-R profile, his score on the General Information subtest is particularly low. This raises the question of the possible impact of cultural differences.

Results of the Vineland Adaptive Behavior Scales suggest that Juan's adaptive behaviors generally lag about three years behind his chronological age. This is a level matched or exceeded by more than 99 percent of a national sample of his age-peers. Although his listening skills are appropriate to his chronological age, reading and written communication are particularly limited; a finding consistent with his PIAT-R results. In the daily living skills domain, Juan's self-care and domestic skills are generally commensurate with age expectancies but his community skills are somewhat undeveloped, especially with respect to money skills, time telling, and telephone use. Sources for these deficits may be cognitive or they may be social in nature.

Although Juan is an amiable individual, his socialization skills are immature with needed refinements in coping skills. He becomes easily discouraged and sullen when he is confronted by school challenges which he perceives as threatening and humiliating. When frustrated and under stress, he may sometimes withdraw into a brooding silence. At other times, however, he may lose his temper.

---

[1] This hypothetical item is not actually included in the WISC-R.

CASE STUDY: Juan (continued)

TABLE 3-6   Juan's Test Profile

Identifying Information:

Chronological Age: 9–0

Program: Elementary school, mainstreamed part-time with two hours spent daily in resource room, Grade 4.

Wechsler Intelligence Scale for Children–III (WISC–III)—Test Date: 11/17/92

Verbal IQ   59
Performance IQ   58
Full Scale IQ   55

Peabody Individual Achievement Test–Revised (PIAT-R)—Test Date: 11/18/92

Subtest	Standard Score	National Percentile Rank	Grade Equivalent
General Information	55	< 1	1.2
Reading Recognition	55	< 1	2.0
Reading Comprehension	56	< 1	2.5
Reading (Total)	55	< 1	2.1
Mathematics	55	< 1	1.5
Spelling	55	< 1	1.8
Total Test	55	< 1	1.9

Vineland Adaptive Behavior Scales (Interview Edition)—*Test Date*: 11/20/92

Domain	Standard Score	National Percentile Rank	Stanine	Age Equivalent
Communication	54	< 0.2	1	6–7
Daily Living Skills	56	< 0.2	1	6–4
Socialization	56	< 0.1	1	4–10
Composite	51	< 0.1	1	5–11

CASE STUDY: Tanisha

Results of psychological and educational testing are presented in Table 3-7. Tanisha's IQ of 58 places her in the range of mild mental retardation. An analysis of test items passed on the Stanford-Binet Intelligence Scale reveals relative strength in vocabulary and memory, as well as comparative weaknesses in concept formation and visual discrimination.

In her inclusive second grade classroom placement, Tanisha's relative strength in school work appears to be on tasks that require long-term memory. This is suggested by rel-

TABLE 3-7   Tanisha's Test Profile

Identifying Information:

Chronological Age: 7–3

Program: Elementary school, inclusive classroom Grade 2.

Stanford-Binet Intelligence Scale (**Fourth Edition**)—*Test Date*: **11/23/92**

IQ   58

Peabody Individual Achievement Test–Revised (PIAT-R)—Test Date: 11/24/92

Subtest	Standard Score	National Percentile Rank	Grade Equivalent
General Information	87	19	1.1
Reading Recognition	82	12	1.3
Reading Comprehension	68	2	1.0
Reading (Total)	75	5	1.0
Mathematics	75	5	K.9
Spelling	64	1	K.8
Total Test	73	4	1.0

Vineland Adaptive Behavior Scales (**Classroom Edition**)—*Test Date*: 11/23/92

Domain	Standard Score	National Percentile Rank	Age Equivalent
Communication	70	2	3–10
Daily Living Skills	71	3	4–7
Socialization	81	10	3–9
Composite	68	2	4–1

atively high scores (compared to her own average performance) on the General Information and Reading Recognition subtests of the PIAT-R. Also consistent with intelligence test results, however, is her difficulty understanding what she reads. Overall, her standard scores on the PIAT-R are 27 points (almost two standard deviations) below a sample mean of 100. Compared to children at her grade level, 96 percent obtained scores equal to or higher than her own.

Results of the Vineland Adaptive Behavior Scales, based on a questionnaire completed by her teacher, also suggest that Tanisha's social competencies are approximately three years behind her chronological age (7–0). Verbal language reception and expression are well developed for her age but deficits are quite evident in the school-related skill areas of reading and writing. She cannot read simple stories, for instance, nor can she write basic four-word sentences. Personal self-care skills are generally in her repertoire although she may require some refinements in hair combing and neatness of appearance and possessions. She is somewhat careless and sloppy around the house, leaving her shoes,

CASE STUDY: Tanisha (continued)

school work, and jacket wherever she drops them when returning home. With frequent and persistent reminders, she will pick up after herself and tend to a few household chores like setting the dinner table, taking out the trash, and, sometimes, washing the dishes. She is a gregarious, cheerful, active child who seeks out the company of children and adults alike, sometimes demanding a good deal of attention from the latter. She occupies herself with many outdoor activities and she will watch anything on television on rainy days. She exercises poor judgment in managing her activities, often becoming unmindful of the time while playing with others. This often results in lateness for dinner and neglect of homework. Her mother fears that she also exercises equally poor judgment in the company of strangers with whom she may too openly and frequently engage in conversation.

CASE STUDY: Norman

Norman was tested on the Stanford-Binet Intelligence Scale. The Vineland Adaptive Behavior Scales were also administered. Results are presented in Table 3-8. On the Stanford-Binet, on which he obtained an IQ of 64, Norman demonstrated comparative strength in tasks involving perceptual discrimination and comprehension. On the other hand, he fared poorly on tasks requiring perceptual-motor coordination such as copying and folding. His chronological age is five years, five months and he has been classified as having mild mental retardation.

Socially, Norman is a polite, affable youngster who is quite aware of the activities of others at his mainstreamed preschool program and eager to join in them. He enjoys group

TABLE 3-8   Norman's Test Profile

Identifying Information:

Chronological Age: 5–5

Program: Fully Mainstreamed Preschool Program

Stanford-Binet Intelligence Scale (Fourth Edition)—*Test Date*: 11/12/92

IQ   64

Vineland Adaptive Behavior Scales (Interview Edition)—*Test Date*: 11/13/92

Domain	Standard Score	National Percentile Rank	Stanine	Age Equivalent
Communication	76	5	1	3–10
Daily Living Skills	67	1	1	3–5
Socialization	72	3	1	3–1
Motor Skills	39	< 0.1	1	1–8
Composite	58	0.3	1	3–8

games and activities, though he is somewhat shy and quiet around unfamiliar people. His participation in activities is sometimes limited by poor gross motor functioning.

Communication skills are probably the most advanced in his repertoire. Although he speaks slowly, and his speech is sometimes slurred, he expresses himself in phrases and short but syntactically adequate sentences. His receptive vocabulary is quite well developed to the extent that he can point to and, to a lesser extent, name most familiar household objects. He learned some time ago to identify colors and shapes but he has difficulty coordinating verbal information simultaneously. He becomes easily confused, for example, when asked to pick up the red square from an array of colored shapes. He enjoys browsing through his older sister's school books to look at the pictures, though he lacks supple wrist-turning facility and he is poor at grasping the pages with his fingers. He turns pages by using the palm of his left hand, a source of constant irritation to his sister who finds the pages often wrinkled and torn. He also tends to turn pages backward from the end of the book to the beginning since he prefers to handle each page with his left hand while situating the book left of midline. While browsing through books, he attempts to name pictures and illustrations. He knows the names and sounds of several letters. He also has learned to identify the numerals one and two and he can match them to their respective quantities. He is far less consistent with other numerals. He enjoys marking with crayons but he generally scribbles, handling his crayon with an overhand grasp.

Norman's expressive language is more deficient. It is generally limited to nouns, adjectives, and verbs combined into simple but syntactically adequate phrases and sentences. Often, he requires some time to name familiar objects. His articulation is poor.

Norman's motor development is delayed in some important respects. He walks with an awkward gait. Balance is often precarious and he tends to descend stairs both feet per step, the right foot following the left. Movement in the right extremities (particularly the right hand) can be somewhat constricted. His tendency not to spontaneously use his right arm restricts his activities at times. For example, when a puzzle is placed directly before him with pieces placed to the right, he turns his trunk and shifts his weight to the right in order to pick them up with his left hand. Puzzles have to be large and simple because of his difficulty handling small pieces and inserting them into a board.

Norman's daily living skills also tend to be delayed. Typically, he dresses in a slow, dawdling fashion. His mother feels that it is often easier simply to "get him started" by placing each of his arms through the sleeves of his pullover shirt while leaving him to the task of pulling the shirt down to his waist. She adopts a similar strategy for pulling on his pants. She does put on his shoes and socks for him. Norman will remove all of his clothes except, predictably enough, his right sock.

While eating, he uses an overhand grasp to manipulate his spoon and fork. He enjoys assisting his mother in preparation of meals. He follows her requests to retrieve items within reach in the refrigerator and counter drawers, then placing them on the table.

He avoids locating items in the cupboards which are a bit less accessible. He has many hygiene skills in his repertoire. He will wash his face with only a few reminders and, during bathing, he soaps and rinses most of his body parts. Once again, he requires only a few verbal reminders to do so. However, his parents continue to wash his back as well as his feet and ankles. He tends not to dry himself thoroughly.

Recommendations

Over the past decade, professionals in the field of special education have labored diligently to remove the "assessment stigma" from the referral, diagnosis, and placement process. That stigma has been expressed in two ways: (1) that assessment procedures, particularly intelligence testing, lead to the educationally unnecessary classification and labeling of individuals as having mental retardation; and (2) that sociocultural, racial, and ethnic bias have contributed heavily to that classification and labeling.

Practitioners have responded to these charges by indicating that most states require classification and even labeling before services can be provided and funding sources released. Having "fed the assessment dragon" to meet state identification requirements, it is contingent upon school psychologists and special educators alike to temper their interpretation of test scores by their knowledge of children's cultural and linguistic background, prior instructional experience, personality patterns, behavior problems, and school-related motivation (Messick, 1979). These tempered interpretations of formal test scores, combined with more culture fair tests and classroom-relevant forms of informal and curriculum-based assessment (Duffey, Salvia, Tucker, & Ysseldyke, 1981), should increase the validity of the special education assessment process.

Some specific recommendations that emerge from the assessment issues raised in this chapter include:

1. Assessment programs should be oriented toward how to include children in educational programs rather than on whether to exclude them from such programs.

2. Assessment data should be acquired from both formal norm-referenced instruments and informal or criterion-referenced procedures.

3. Assessment programs should begin to look at the capacity of students with mental retardation across a range of intellectual domains.

4. Assessment procedures should focus as much on how children process information as they now do on their ability to retrieve stored products.

5. Assessment procedures should include opportunities for children with mental retardation to exhibit their learning skills and potential for remediation on contemporary problems.

6. Group testing should be used infrequently as a screening device only under highly controlled conditions.

7. Assessment instruments should be selected that have adequate reliability, validity, and standardization.

8. Bias should be minimized and sensitivity to cultural and linguistic diversity should be maximized on assessment instruments both in terms of their content and administration.

9. Educators should become familiar with evolving theories on the construct of intelligence so as to appreciate the significance of intelligence test scores and their implications for curricular adaptations.

10. Conclusions drawn from test scores should be informed by information obtained from observation, interviews, and a close relationship with the children as well as their teachers and families.

References

American Association on Mental Retardation, Ad Hoc Committee on Terminology and Classification. (1992). *Mental retardation: Definition, classification, and systems of supports: Workbook.* Washington, DC: American Association on Mental Retardation.

Anastasi, A. (1976). *Psychological testing* (4th ed.). New York: Macmillan.

Baca, L. M. & Cervantes, H. T. (1984). *The bilingual special education interface.* St. Louis, MO: Times/Mirror Mosby.

Balthazar, E. E. (1976). *Balthazar Scales of Adaptive Behavior.* Palo Alto, CA: Consulting Psychologists Press.

Bayley, N. (1969). *Bayley scales of infant development.* New York: Psychological Corporation.

Binet, A. & Simon, T. (1908). Le développement de l'intelligence chez les enfants. *L'Année Psychologique, 14,* 1–94.

Binet, A. & Simon, T. (1905). Upon the necessity of establishing a scientific diagnosis of inferior states of intelligence. In M. Rosen, G. R. Clark, and M. S. Kivitz (Eds.) (1976), *The history of mental retardation: Collected papers,* (vol. 1). Baltimore: University Park Press.

Blackman, L. S. (1988). A review of Spitz, H. H., The raising of intelligence: A selected history of attempts to raise retarded intelligence. *Teachers College Record, 89*(3), 446–450.

Blackman, L. S. & Lin, A. (1984). Generalization training in the educable mentally retarded: Intelligence and its educability revisited. In P. H. Brooks, R. Sperber, & C. McCauley (Eds.), *Learning and cognition in the mentally retarded.* Hillsdale, NJ: Erlbaum.

Boehm, A. E. (1986). *Boehm test of basic concepts-Revised.* San Antonio: Psychological Corporation.

Budoff, M. (1968). A learning potential assessment procedure: Rationale and supporting data. In B. W. Richards (Ed.), *Proceedings of the 1st congress of the International Association for the Scientific Study of Mental Deficiency.* Reigate (Surrey): M. Jackson.

Burgemeister, B., Blum, L. G., & Lorge, I. (1972). *Columbia Mental Maturity Scale.* New York: Harcourt, Brace, Jovanovich.

Cain, L. F., Levine, S., & Elzey, F. F. (1977). *Manual for the Cain-Levine Social Competency Scale.* Palo Alto, CA: Consulting Psychologists Press.

Cattell, R. B. (1971). *Abilities: Their structure, growth, and action.* Boston: Houghton Mifflin.

Cervantes, R. A. (1974, April). *Problems and alternatives in testing Mexican American students.* Paper presented at the annual meeting of the American Educational Research Association, Chicago, Illinois. ERIC #ED 093 951.

Conoley, J. C. & Kramer, J. J. (Eds.) (1989). *The tenth mental measurements yearbook.* Lincoln: University of Nebraska Press.

CTB/McGraw-Hill. (1985, 1986, 1987). *California Achievement Test.* Monterey, CA: CTB/McGraw-Hill.

De Avila, E. A. & Havassy, B. (1974). Testing of minority children: A neopiagetian approach. *Today's Education, 63,* 71–75.

Detterman, D. K. & Sternberg, R. J. (Eds.) (1982). *How and how much can intelligence be increased.* Norwood, NJ: Ablex.

Dew, N. & Perlman, R. (1980). *Protection in evaluation procedures for linguistically different minority children.* Paper presented at the annual meeting of the Council for Exceptional Children, Philadelphia, Pennsylvania.

Duffey, J. B., Salvia, J., Tucker, J., & Ysseldyke, J. (1981). Nonbiased assessment: A need for operationalism. *Exceptional Children, 47,* 427–434.

Dunn, L. M. (1981). *Manual for the Peabody Picture Vocabulary Test-Revised.* Circle Pines, MN: American Guidance Service.

Dunn, L. M. & Markwardt, F. C. (1970). *Peabody Individual Achievement Test.* Circle Pines, MN: American Guidance Service.

Feuerstein, R. (1980). *Instrumental enrichment: An intervention program for cognitive modifiability.* Baltimore: University Park Press.

Feuerstein, R. (1979). *The dynamic assessment of retarded performers: The learning potential assessment device, theory, instruments, and techniques.* Baltimore: University Park Press.

Flavell, J. H. (1977). *Cognitive development.* Englewood Cliffs, NJ: Prentice Hall.

Gardner, E. F., Rudman, H. D., Karlsen, B., & Merwin, J. C. (1982). *Stanford Achievement Test* (7th ed.). San Antonio, TX: Psychological Corporation.

Gardner, H. (1983). *Frames of mind: The theory of multiple intelligences*. New York: Basic Books.

Gardner, H. & Hatch, T. (1989). Multiple intelligences go to school: Educational implications of the theory of multiple intelligences. *Educational Researcher, 18,* 4–10.

Guilford, J. P. (1967). *The nature of human intelligence.* New York: McGraw-Hill.

Guilford, J. P. (1959). Three faces of intellect. *American Psychologist, 14,* 469–479.

Halpern, A. S., Lehman, J. P., Irvin, L. K., & Heiry, T. J. (1982). *Contemporary assessment for mentally retarded adolescents and adults.* Baltimore: University Park Press.

Hieronymus, A. N., Hoover, H. D., & Lindquist, E. F. (1986). *Iowa Tests of Basic Skills.* Chicago, IL: The Riverside Publishing Company.

Honzik, M. P., Macfarlane, J., & Allen, L. (1948). The stability of mental test performance between 2 and 18 years. *Journal of Experimental Education, 4,* 309–324.

Jastak, J. F. & Wilkinson, G. (1984). *Wide Range Achievement Test-Revised.* Wilmington, DE: Jastak Assessment Systems.

Lambert, N., Nihira, K., & Leland, H. (1992). *AAMR Adaptive Behavior Scales-School* (2nd ed.). Austin, TX: ProEd.

Laosa, L. M. (1977). Historical antecedents and current issues in non-discriminatory assessment of children's abilities. *The School Psychology Digest, 6,* 48–56.

Markwardt, F. C. (1989). *The Peabody Individual Achievement Test-Revised.* Circle Pines, MN: American Guidance Service.

McCarthy, D. (1972). *Manual for the McCarthy Scales of Children's Abilities.* New York: Psychological Corporation.

McKinney, J. D. & Hacutt, A. M. (1988). The need for policy analysis in evaluating the regular education initiative. *Journal of Learning Disabilities, 21,* 12–18.

McLoughlin, J. A. & Lewis, R. B. (1986). *Assessing special students* (2nd ed.). Columbus, OH: Charles E. Merrill Publishing Co.

Mercer, J. R. (1979). *System of multicultural pluralistic assessment: Technical manual.* Cleveland: The Psychological Corporation.

Mercer, J. & Lewis, J. (1977). *Systems of multicultural pluralistic assessment: Parent interview manual.* New York: Psychological Corporation.

Messick, S. (1979). Potential uses of noncognitive measurement in education. *Journal of Educational Psychology, 71,* 281–292.

Meyers, J., Pfeffer, J., & Erlbaum, V. (1985). Process assessment: A model for broadening assessment. *Journal of Special Education, 19,* 73–89.

Mussen, P., Dean, S., & Rosenberg, M. (1952). Some further evidence on the validity of the WISC. *Journal of Consulting Psychology, 16,* 410–412.

Passow, A. H. (1984). *Reforming schools in the 1980s: A critical review of the national reports.* Teachers College, Columbia University: Clearinghouse on Urban Education, Institute for Urban and Minority Education.

Payne, J. S. & Patton, J. R. (1981). *Mental retardation.* Columbus, OH: Merrill.

Pearson, K. & Moul, M. (1925). The problem of alien immigration into Great Britain, illustrated by an examination of Russian and Polish Jewish children. *Annals of Eugenics, 1,* 5–127.

Piaget, J. (1972). Intellectual development from adolescence to adulthood. *Human Development, 15,* 1–12.

Piaget, J. & Inhelder, B. (1947). Diagnosis of mental operations and theory of intelligence. *American Journal of Mental Deficiency, 51,* 401–406.

Prescott, G. A., Balow, I. H., Hogan, T. P., & Farr, R. C. (1985, 1986, 1987). *Metropolitan Achievement Tests* (6th ed.). San Antonio, TX: Psychological Corporation.

Raven, J. C., Court, J. H., & Raven, J. (1977). *Colored Progressive Matrices.* London: Lewis.

Reis, E. M. (1986). Minority disproportionality in special placements as an assessment and programming issue. *Journal of Instructional Psychology, 13,* 135–140.

Salvia, J. & Ysseldyke, J. E. (1991). *Assessment* (5th ed.). Boston: Houghton Mifflin.

Siegler, R. S. & Richards, D. D. (1982). The development of intelligence. In R. J. Sternberg (Ed.), *Handbook of human intelligence.* Cambridge: Cambridge University Press.

Simeonsson, R. J. (1986). *Psychological and developmental assessment of special children.* Newton, MA: Allyn & Bacon.

Spache, G. D. (1972). *Diagnostic Reading Scales.* Monterey, CA: CTB/McGraw-Hill.

Sparrow, S. S., Balla, D. A., & Cicchetti, D. V. (1984). *Vineland Adaptive Behavior Scales.* Circle Pines, MN: American Guidance Service.

Spearman, C. (1927) *The abilities of man.* London: Macmillan.

Spitz, H. H. (1986). *The raising of intelligence.* Hillsdale, NJ: Erlbaum.

Sternberg, R. J. (1979). The nature of mental abilities. *American Psychologist, 34*, 214–230.

Sternberg, R. (1984). Macrocomponents and microcomponents of intelligence: some proposed loci of mental retardation. In P. H. Brooks, R. Sperber, & C. McCauley (Eds.), *Learning and cognition in the mentally retarded.* Hillsdale, NJ: Erlbaum.

Terman, L. M. & Merrill, M. A. (1937). *Measuring intelligence.* New York: Houghton Mifflin.

Terman, L. M. & Merrill, M. A. (1973a). *Stanford-Binet Intelligence Scale, 1972 norms edition, Form L–M.* Boston: Houghton Mifflin.

Terman, L. & Merrill, M. (1973b). *The Stanford-Binet Intelligence Scale.* Chicago: Riverside Publishing Company.

Thomson, G. H. (1939). *The factorial analysis of human ability.* London: University of London Press.

Thorndike, R. L., Hagen, E. P., & Sattler, J. M. (1986). *The Stanford-Binet Intelligence Scale: Fourth edition.* Chicago, IL: Riverside Publishing Company.

Thurstone, L. L. (1938). *Primary mental abilities.* Chicago: University of Chicago Press.

Thurstone, L., & Thurstone, T. (1965). *Primary Mental Abilities Test.* Chicago: Science Research Associates.

Wechsler, D. (1991). *Manual for the WISC III.* New York: The Psychological Corporation.

Wechsler, D. (1989). *Manual for the Wechsler Preschool and Primary Scale of Intelligence-Revised.* San Antonio, TX: The Psychological Corporation.

Wechsler, D. (1974). *Manual for the Wechsler Intelligence Scale for Children-Revised.* Cleveland: Psychological Corporation.

Wechsler, D. (1967). *Manual for the Wechsler Preschool and Primary Scale of Intelligence.* Cleveland: Psychological Corporation.

Wechsler, D. (1944). *The measurement of adult intelligence.* Baltimore: The Williams and Williams Co.

Weisz, J. R. & Kigler, E. (1979). Cognitive development in retarded and nonretarded persons: Piagetian tests of the similar sequence hypothesis. *Psychological Bulletin, 86*, 831–851.

Chapter 4

Assessment for Educational Programming

Before a teacher of students with mental retardation can properly begin to decide what to teach and how to teach it to insure maximum progress, he or she must be comfortable with at least some basic assessment issues, as well as how to link assessment with curriculum and instruction (Bigge, 1988). This chapter is intended to be a first exposure to assessment for teachers and future teachers. The first section of this chapter is a discussion of the impact of Public Law 94–142 and its regulations on the content and form of the assessment process. The second section describes an assessment model designed to assist the classroom teacher in determining what to teach and how to teach it. In the third section, characteristics of standardized assessment instruments are discussed. The fourth section discusses the use of informal tests as a means of exploring student achievement in relation to the demands of the environment and the task, instead of in relation to the normative group. In the fifth section, guidelines for constructing a criterion-referenced test are described and applied to the *Case Study of Tanisha*. In the final section, the utilization of data that has been collected as a means of monitoring and implementing an educational program is discussed, and recommendations are made.

Public Law 94–142 and Assessment

The content and form of the assessment process is governed by regulations that specify procedures that must be followed in order to comply with Public Law 94–142 and its amendments. Some of the basic rights and procedures guaranteed by the law and its regulations relevant to assessment include: (1) screening and identification; (2) due process and procedural safeguards; (3) quality of assessment procedures; and (4) individualized education programs. For each of these areas, references to both the law and its regulations are described in order to provide the classroom teacher with a more complete understanding of the rights of students with mental retardation and their parents as these students become involved in the educational assessment process. Although the term *handicap* was replaced by the term *disability* in the 1990 Amendments, the Individuals with Disabilities Education Act (IDEA, PL101–476), we have retained the original terminology throughout this text for direct references to PL94–142. Where relevant, the implications of the federal law and its regulations for the classroom teacher are stressed.

Screening and Identification

Public Law 94–142 requires the identification and screening of all handicapped children between the ages of three and twenty-one (provided state laws do not limit education for all children aged three to five). The specific language of the law requires that states assure that:

> All children residing in the State who are handicapped, regardless of the severity of their handicap, and who are in need of special education and related services are identified, located, and evaluated, and . . . a practical method is developed and implemented to determine which children are currently receiving needed special education and related services are identified, located, and evaluated, and that a practical method is developed and implemented to determine which children are currently receiving special education and related services (Sec. 612 (2) (c)).

This provision has resulted in the implementation of large-scale preschool screening and identification programs. The regulations pertaining to screening and identification of students with handicaps require that a file be kept with both the original screening plan and a detailed report on the student served in the screening plan [121a.128]. However, before students can be screened and identified as possible candidates for special education services, they must either be brought to the screening location or the program must have some systematic way of reaching out to those in need (Lillie, 1975).

The most common way in which programs have reached out to find possible candidates in need of special education and related services has been through child-find projects. Most child-find projects rely heavily upon public awareness campaigns as a means to finding children in need of services. However, the need for research to document the best avenues for early identification of children who need special education and related services is critical (Patton, Beirne-Smith, & Paine, 1990). Currently, the responsibility for "finding" most children with mild mental retardation rests with the classroom teacher. One of the ways in which classroom teachers identify students who demonstrate learning difficulties is through observation. Two types of observations that teachers can utilize are narrative and rating (Brandt, 1972). Narrative observations require teachers to write down exactly what they are observing. In a written narrative, the record of behavioral occurrences should be devoid of interpretation. Kepp has described the most common forms of narrative data as "(1) anecdotes, which describe certain episodes of behavior over long periods of time (e.g., tantrums since birth); (2) ecological descriptions, which report the size, number and arrangement of chairs, tables, books, and toys, etc.; and (3) running narratives, which describe behavior continuously over a short period or time" (Kepp, 1985, p. 109).

A rating scale (Kerlinger, 1973) refers to measuring instruments that require the rater or observer to assign the rated behavior to categories or to continua based on a numerical scale. Four types of rating scales that teachers of students with mental retardation could utilize are described in Table 4-1.

Observation coupled with knowledge about child development can provide teachers of students with mental retardation with hunches about how learning can best be facilitated (Farlow & Snell, 1989). An assessment model, described in the next section, will need to be utilized to determine if these hunches are on target. The importance of relating specific behaviors to the ongoing development of the child is based on the belief that the child with mental retardation, like all children, is more than the sum of his or her behaviors at any one time.

Due Process and Procedural Safeguards

Due process in the context of PL94–142 may be defined as "a procedure which seeks to insure the fairness of educational decisions" (Turnbull, Strickland, & Brantley, 1978, p. 5). In Section 615 of PL94–142, Congress specified procedures that schools must follow to insure due process in decision making:

> Any State educational agency, any local educational agency, and any intermediate educational unit . . . shall establish and maintain procedures in accordance with subsection

TABLE 4-1   Four Types of Rating Scales

Type	Description	Example
Checklist	There are two kinds of checklists: (1) static descriptions; and (2) action checklists. Static descriptions describe conditions, not behavior; action checklists provide records of actual behavior.	Static descriptions include age, sex, and degree of retardation. Action checklists could include how many times a student leaves his or her seat.
Category	Presents the observer or judge with several categories. The task is to pick the category that best characterizes the behavior being rated.	One of the characteristics rated is attentiveness. A category item might be: How attentive is she? (check one) Very attentive Attentive Not attentive Not at all attentive
Numerical	Numbers, such as 4, 3, 2, 1, can be affixed to the attentiveness item. It should be noted that Kerlinger (1973) suggests that verbal descriptions accompany the affixed numerals.	Select the number which best describes the individual. Frequency of attentiveness: 1. Always 2. Often 3. Occasionally 4. Rarely 5. Almost Never
Graphic	Lines or bars are combined with descriptive phrases. The task is to select a place on the continuum that best describes an individual's attentiveness.	See below for an example of how the attentiveness item would look on a graphic scale.

_____/_____/_____/_____

| Very attentive   Attentive | Not attentive | Not at all attentive |

(b) through subsection (e) of this section to assure that handicapped children and their parents or guardians are guaranteed procedural safeguards with respect to the provision of free appropriate public education by such agencies and units.

The regulations that were implemented to insure that children with handicaps and their parents or guardians received the due process rights to which they are entitled include a number of provisions.

For purposes of offering an overview, many of the most important regulations are listed below; however, the reader should refer to the official regulations for a complete description.

1. Parents must be informed in writing when a teacher or anyone else has referred their child for possible assessment [121A.504].

2. The written notification that the parents receive requesting permission to assess their child must include an explanation of the various procedural safeguards, a clear explanation of the reason for assessment, and a description of the procedures that are to be used in conducting the assessment [121a.505(a)].

3. In addition to the request for permission to begin the assessment process, all related communications with parents must be written in understandable language and in the native language of the parents [121a.504].

4. If the parents disagree with the evaluation that the school has conducted and the school system does not or cannot prove that its own evaluation was appropriate, they are entitled to an independent educational evaluation at public expense [121a.503].

5. Parental access to all school records pertinent to their child's identification and assessment is mandated [121a.502].

6. With regard to the issue of parental access to their child's records, the regulations specify that it is within the rights of the parent to ask the school system to answer questions they may have regarding the information that they find in their child's records [121a.562(b) (1)]. If, after the school has answered the parents' questions, the parents feel that the information does not accurately represent their child's needs, then it is within their due process rights to ask the school system to amend the records [121a.567].

7. Issues regarding access to a child's records, the securing of consent from parents for the use of certain records on their child for specific purposes, and the decision as to whether records should be destroyed when a system feels that it no longer needs such information are also regulated [121a.561–121a.571].

8. In those instances where the parents and the school system cannot agree on identification, evaluation, educational placement or the provision of a free appropriate public education, both the school and the parents have the right to request a due process hearing [121a.507]. For a detailed discussion of impartial hearings and litigation, see Podemski, Price, Smith & Marsh (1984).

Quality of Assessment Procedures

In order to evaluate what makes for a good assessment, the "fit" between the types of formulated questions being asked and the types of information that an assessment instrument or procedure can impart needs to be closely examined (Wilcox, 1986). If eligibility is the concern, for example, the questions and responses used to determine eligibility should not be used to help determine what to teach the students; new evaluation instruments should be used. The information gathered for the purpose of determining eligibility typically does not constitute a "good fit" for deciding what to teach.

Regardless of the questions that the assessment process is designed to answer, PL94–142 sets the standards for assessment. Some of the parameters of assessment that are required by additional regulations include:

1. The materials and procedures used in the course of the assessment process must not discriminate against a student on the basis of race or culture [121a.530(b)].
2. Tests and other evaluation materials must

    (a) Be provided and administered in the child's language or other mode of communication, unless it is clearly not feasible to do so;
    (b) Have been validated for the specific purpose for which they are used;
    (c) Be administered by trained personnel in conformance with instructions from the publisher;

3. Tests and other evaluation materials must be tailored to assess specific areas of educational need, and not merely designed to provide a single general intelligence quotient;
4. Tests must be selected for and administered to any child with impaired sensory, manual, or speaking skills so as to insure that the test results accurately reflect the child's aptitude, achievement level, or whatever other factor the test purports to measure, rather than reflecting the child's impaired sensory, manual, or speaking skills (except where those skills are the factors which the test purports to measure);
5. No single procedure may be used as the sole criterion for determining an appropriate educational program for the child;
6. The child must be assessed in all areas related to the suspected disability, including, where appropriate, health, vision, hearing, social and emotional status, general intelligence, academic performance, communicative status, and motor abilities [121a.532].

Individualized Education Programs

Once an assessment has been performed, the next step is to arrange for a meeting of professionals, the student's parents, and the student (when appropriate) to discuss the information that has been collected through the assessment process. This information is discussed with the purpose of deciding whether the student has a disability and is eligible for special education services, and to begin to formulate or design an Individualized Educational Program (IEP) (see Chapter 6). Public Law 94–142 mandates that parents and school personnel share in the design and formulation of a student's IEP. Some of the areas covered by the regulation [121a.345] that insures that this partnership be formed include the following:

1. Parents must be notified in advance of the meeting's purpose, time, and location, as well as the number and names of participants. The meeting should be scheduled at a mutually agreed upon time and place.
2. If the parents cannot attend, other means of communication (for example, conference telephone calls) should be used.
3. If the parents do not attend in spite of requests, records of all efforts to encourage their presence must be kept.
4. At the meeting, every effort must be made to insure that parents understand the proceedings. This may involve the use of interpreters.

In addition to these areas pertinent to the parent-school partnership, other substantive issues that have been regulated include but are not limited to:

1. The basic features that all IEPs must contain [121a.346]. These features are described in Chapter 6 of this book.
2. A listing of who should be present at an IEP conference [121a.344]. Such a list is provided in Chapter 6 of this book.
3. The time frame in which an IEP meeting must be held once a determination is made that the student is disabled and in need of special services [121a.343(c)]. This time frame is 30 calendar days.
4. The relationship between the completed IEP and the delivery of related services (e.g., an IEP must be developed before related services can be delivered), and the statement that an IEP must be implemented without any undue delay after the IEP meeting [121a.342].
5. The requirement that a meeting must be held at least annually, with the purpose of re-examining the appropriateness of the IEP and determining whether revision is necessary [121a.343(d)].
6. The student's needs as specified in the IEP must form the basis for the consideration of least restrictive environments that are discussed and investigated as possible educational environments for that student [121a.552]. A detailed discussion of the types of least restrictive environments available to meet the needs of students with disabilities is included in Chapter 8 of this book.

An Assessment Model

An assessment model that the classroom teacher of students with mental retardation can utilize in gathering more information about the strengths and weaknesses of his or her students is shown in Table 4-2.

The nine components that make up the assessment model are phrased as questions. This is in order to emphasize the importance of having a purposeful and systematic plan to guide the process of assessing the needs of learners with mental retardation. For each

TABLE 4-2 An Assessment Model

1. What are the learning characteristics of my students?
2. What is the scope and sequence of the skill areas that need to be taught?
3. What area or areas need to be assessed?
4. What kinds of formal (standardized tests) and informal procedures should be administered?
5. What kinds of errors did the student make?
6. What record keeping device or devices need to be prepared for noting student performance?
7. Should program changes be made?
8. What specific short- and long-term instructional objectives can be generated based on the data that has been collected?
9. How should the assessment information be updated?

question, a description of the procedures that the classroom teacher should follow in gathering the relevant information is outlined.

1. *What are the characteristics of my students?*

As the classroom teacher looks more closely at the characteristics of his or her students with mental retardation, these three areas should be of concern: (1) social characteristics; (2) learning characteristics; and (3) affective characteristics (MacMillan, 1977). In thinking about each of these areas, the classroom teacher will need to subdivide it into its subcomponent parts. To assist the classroom teacher with this task, some of the subcomponents within each area are specified under the heading *domain* or *domains* (see Table 4-3). In addition to these domains, scales are provided that can be used to obtain information related to each characteristic.

Beginning an assessment by closely examining the characteristics of the students enables the teacher to keep these factors in mind as he or she tries to obtain the best possible "fit" between the individual needs of a student with mental retardation and the types of tests that should be selected to establish the entry-level skills of that student. In this initial phase, the identification of learner characteristics is conducted by an interdisciplinary team

TABLE 4-3   Social, Learning, and Affective Characteristics of Students with Mental Retardation

Social Characteristics

Domain:	Adaptive Behavior
Defined:	Refers to the ability to cope with the demands of the environment; includes self-help, communication, and social skills (McLoughlin, 1977).
Scales:	AAMD Adaptive Behavior Scale Public School Version; Vineland Social Maturity Scale; Cain-Levine Social Competency Scale; and Balthazar Scales of Adaptive Behavior.

Learning Characteristics

Domains:	Cognitive Development; Motivational Variables; Attentional Variables; Memory; Paired-Associate Learning; Learning Set; Incidental Learning; Operant Learning; Observational Learning; Language Behaviors (Payne, Polloway, Smith & Payne, 1981)
Defined:	Factors that influence the learning potential of students with mental retardation.
Scales:	The Wechsler Scales; The Stanford-Binet; Peabody Picture Vocabulary Test-Revised; and Clinical Evaluation of Language Fundamentals-Revised.

Affective Characteristics

Domain:	Self-awareness and personality factors
Defined:	Refers to those skills that enable one to understand and cope with their own and others' social and emotional behavior.
Scales:	The Martinek-Zaichkorsky Self-Concept Scale for Children and The Piers-Harris Children's Self-Concept Scale.

as well as the teacher. Data provided by both the interdisciplinary team and the teacher should provide a fairly comprehensive overview of a student's learning and behavioral characteristics that might influence instruction.

2. *What is the scope and sequence of the skill areas that need to be taught?*

A teacher must be knowledgeable about the scope and sequence of skill areas that need to be taught to individuals with varying levels of mental retardation. This is in order to insure that functional skills are acquired that meet the demands of each student's current environment, as well as any future environment in which the student is expected to participate. Otherwise, the lesson topics and planned activities will not contribute to appropriate sequential learning for the student's short-term objectives and related annual goals. Scope and sequence skill lists that may be useful to the classroom teacher as he or she monitors progress across academic areas are presented by Mercer and Mercer (1993, pp. 657–675).

3. *What area or areas need to be assessed?*

As the classroom teacher decides on which area or areas to include in an assessment plan for a learner with mental retardation, the decision-making process should not be based on the identification of deficit areas but rather on an inventory of skills and abilities. One assessment alternative that may guide the teacher's selection of areas to assess and, at the same time, offer a format for the subsequent management of instruction is curriculum-based assessment (CBA). CBA uses curriculum as a diagnostic tool and is based on three themes: (1) that examining the curriculum to be used with students who have been classified at various levels of mental retardation offers a very meaningful avenue for assessment; (2) that the curriculum must place explicit demands on the learner (Gickling & Thompson, 1985); and (3) that in order to insure successful learning by students with mental retardation the curriculum must emphasize the needs, both current and future, of the group for which it is intended (Bailey & Simeonsson, 1988). Chapter 5 provides a detailed discussion of curriculum models in mental retardation and guidelines for establishing educational priorities for people with mental retardation.

4. *What kinds of formal (standardized tests) and informal procedures should be administered?*

To determine which formal and informal procedures should be utilized in collecting information about specific skills for the purpose of defining the focus of instruction, the teacher must determine what kinds of information he or she needs in order to learn more about a student's strengths and weaknesses. Table 4-4 presents some of the additional questions that can be used to guide the selection of both formal and informal procedures.

5. *What kind of errors did the student make?*

Whether a formal or an informal scale is used as part of the assessment plan for a student with mental retardation, an analysis to determine what kind of errors were made should be done. The error analysis requires that the teacher: (1) score all responses; (2) search for an error pattern; (3) categorize the error patterns; (4) summarize the types of errors that were made; and (5) hypothesize as to what may have led the student to arrive at such a response. Later in the chapter, Table 4-13 on page 111 provides a list of factors that are useful in conducting an error analysis on manuscript writing.

TABLE 4-4   Additional Questions to Guide the Selection of Both Formal and Informal Procedures

1. What kind of information is needed?

2. How close is the "fit" between the content of the test and the specific objectives that I need to examine?

3. Can the information I need be more effectively obtained with a commercially prepared instrument or with a professionally validated (explained in the third section of this chapter) data collection procedure?

4. How will this information add to the emerging picture of a student's strengths and weaknesses?

5. In the case of a formal test, has the test been critiqued favorably in the Tenth Mental Measurements Yearbook (MMY) (Conoley, 1989)?

6. *What record keeping device or devices need to be prepared for noting student performance?*

It is crucial that student performance data be graphed (Mirkin, Fuchs, & Deno, 1982) to insure easy access to information contributing to the emerging picture of a student's abilities. Alberto and Troutman (1990) have discussed several alternative procedures that can be used in graphing student performance data; however, there is little empirical evidence that supports one graphing procedure over another (Fuchs, 1982). Choosing a system of data collection (for some examples, see Table 4-5) is important and depends largely upon which area or dimension (White & Haring, 1980) is being measured. Of course, the teacher must have previously developed an understanding of the different dimensions on which behavior can be changed (see Table 4-6 on page 104). For a detailed discussion of data collection systems, the reader is directed to Alberto and Troutman (1990, pp. 95–145) and Rusch, Rose, and Greenwood (1988, pp. 167–215).

7. *Should program changes be made?*

Two approaches that the teacher of students with mental retardation can utilize to determine if program changes are needed include goal-oriented and program-oriented analysis (Evans, 1992; Fuchs, 1982; King & Evans, 1991). In the case of a goal-oriented approach to data interpretation, the performance of a student with mental retardation is compared to a prespecified goal to be reached by a certain date. In a program-oriented analysis, on the other hand, programs for students with mental retardation undergo frequent changes or modifications based on what the collected data say about the effectiveness of a given approach (Munger, Snell, & Lloyd, 1989). Fuchs, Wessen, Tindal, Mirkin, and Deno (1982) suggested that teachers prefer a combination of the two approaches to data interpretation. Regardless of the approach utilized for data interpretation, the teacher will need assistance when behavior changes are sporadic (Cooper, Heron, & Heward, 1987). An applied behavior analysis approach that can be used to interpret graphic data accurately and meaningfully is called visual analysis. Visual analysis involves exploring data to better enable the answering of these two questions: (1) Did a meaningful change in behavior take place? and (2) To what extent can that change in behavior be attributed to the method of instruction? For a systematic presentation of how to apply visual analysis, the reader is directed to Cooper et al. (1987, pp. 130–141).

TABLE 4-5   Three Categories for Classifying Data Collection Systems

1. *Observing Tangible Products*

   Data Collection System: Permanent Product Recording

   Definition of this system: Refers to those tangible items or environmental effects which are the result of a behavior's having occurred.

2. *Observing a Sample of Behavior*

   Date Collection System: Event Recording; Interval Recording; Time Sampling; Duration Recording; or Latency Recording

   Definitions of these systems:

Event Recording	Interval Recording	Time Sampling
Recording the exact number of times a behavior occurs.	Dividing a period of observation into a number of short intervals. The focus is on recording the number of intervals in which a given behavior occurs rather than the instances of the behavior.	Dividing a period of observation into equal intervals. Observation is made at the end of each interval.

Duration Recording	Latency Recording
Recording the amount of time between the initiation of a response and its conclusion.	Recording the amount of time between the presentation of a stimulus and the initiation of a response.

3. *Analyzing Written Records*

   Data Collection System: Anecdotal reports

   Definition of this system: Refers to continuous data recording that provides information about the behavior and the environment in which the behavior occurred.

8. *What specific short- and long-term instructional objectives can be generated based on the data that have been collected?*

Having collected a great deal of information through the first seven components of this assessment model, the teacher should now use the data to devise instructional objectives that build on the strengths displayed by a student with mental retardation and simultaneously remediate areas of weakness. The technique of writing both short- and long-term instructional objectives is covered in Chapter 6 of this book.

9. *How should the assessment information be updated?*

Once the teacher of students with mental retardation begins to plan instruction based on current assessment information, it is crucial that ongoing monitoring of progress made by the students be systematically recorded. One means of systematically monitoring student performance is to use a Daily Monitoring Sheet System (see Figure 4-1 on page 105) (Sugai, 1985). Four rules that the classroom teacher should keep in mind when using a Daily Monitoring Sheet System include (Sugai, 1985):

TABLE 4-6   Different Dimensions In Which Behavior Can Be Measured and Changed

1. Rate

Definition: Refers to the number of times a behavior occurs during a specified period of time.
Example: Yolanda completed 4 math problems per minute.

2. Duration

Definition: Refers to the length of time that a behavior occurs.
Example: John stayed out of his seat for 22 minutes.

3. Latency

Definition: Refers to how long it takes a student to begin performing a certain behavior.
Example: After the teacher said, "Louise turn to page 8 in your reading book," it took Louise 10 minutes to begin to locate page 8.

4. Topography

Definition: Refers to the physical form or description of motor behavior.
Example: Danny writes all his s's backwards on his language arts assignment.

5. Force

Definition: Refers to the strength with which a behavior is performed.
Example: Margie squeezes the pencil so tightly as she writes that the pencil often breaks.

6. Locus

Definition: Refers to the location where a behavior occurs.
Example: Charlie wet his pants in the lunchroom.

1. Based on a student's previous day's performance, the teacher should make a decision regarding the focus for the next day's daily objective and accompanying instructional activities.
2. If the student's performance does not meet the specified daily objective criteria for three consecutive days, one of the components of the daily objective (conditions, terminal behavior, or the criteria), or the entire daily objective, will need to be changed.
3. The student's performance data should be graphed immediately.
4. Data should be interpreted and a decision regarding the focus of the next day's objective should be made.

Characteristics of Standardized Assessment Instruments

The purpose for administering standardized assessment instruments is to obtain information about a student's abilities so that more informed decisions can be made (DeStefano & Metzer, 1991; Mehrens & Lehmann, 1987). As classroom teachers examine standardized assessment instruments, they should pay close attention to the type of information that the instrument will generate. In selecting the best "fit" between what the classroom teacher needs to know and what the test instrument can deliver, the teacher must be knowledgeable about assessment characteristics, some of which are presented in Table 4-7 and are then discussed.

FIGURE 4-1 Daily Monitoring Sheet System

Student's Name _____

Teacher's Name _____

Date	Obj. #	Behavior	Condition	Criteria	Data	Comments

Norm-Referenced vs. Criterion-Referenced

The purpose for conducting a given assessment determines whether the standardized assessment instrument that is selected should be norm-referenced (NRT) or criterion-referenced (CRT). Table 4-8 on page 106 presents an overview of the purpose and use that NRT and CRT measurement can fulfill.

TABLE 4-7 Characteristics of Standardized Assessment Instruments

1. Norm-Referenced vs. Criterion-Referenced

2. Formal vs. Informal

3. Group vs. Individual

4. Aptitude vs. Achievement

5. Student-Oriented vs. Environment-Oriented

TABLE 4-8 Purposes and Uses of Norm-Referenced Testing (NRT) and Criterion-Referenced Testing (CRT)

Norm-Referenced Testing	Criterion-Referenced Testing
Purpose: To compare an individual's performance to that of peers.	*Purpose:* To determine whether a student has mastered a particular skill or not.
Use: Helpful in screening for learning problems, in program evaluation, and in the placement of students with disabilities.	*Use:* Helpful in planning instruction because these tests enable the teacher to know not only the specific point at which to begin instruction, but also which instructional aspects follow directly in the curricular sequence (Salvia & Ysseldyke, 1991).

Cronbach offers some useful insight for the classroom teacher who is grappling with the appropriateness of NRT and CRT measurements:

> In course evaluation, we need not be much concerned about making measurement instruments fit the curriculum. However startling this declaration may seem, and however contrary to the principles of evaluation for other purposes, this must be our position if we want to know what changes a course produces in the pupil. An ideal evaluation would include measures of all types of proficiency that might reasonably be desired in the area of question, not just the selected outcomes to which this curriculum directs substantial attention. If you wish only to know how well a curriculum is achieving its objectives, you fit the test to the curriculum; but if you wish to know how well the curriculum is serving the national interest, you measure all outcomes that might be worth striving for (Cronbach, 1963, p. 680).

Formal vs. Informal

Assessment can be formal or informal. These are the two ways in which teachers of students with mental retardation can obtain information that may be helpful for instructional planning or evaluating student progress (Zigmond & Silverman, 1984). Simply stated, formal tests involve the use of commercially prepared published tests. Although the test items on formal tests are not designed to reflect the areas of emphasis of any single curriculum, the content of the test items does reflect knowledge or skills (e.g., computation) across a domain (e.g., addition). Formal tests may be either norm-referenced or criterion-referenced; however, most are norm-referenced. Formal tests are the assessment tools of choice for most classroom teachers, who welcome the ready-made supply of tightly organized test materials and prepared directions for the administration and scoring of the test (Thurlow & Ysseldyke, 1982). However, as illustrated in Table 4-9, there are several limitations in

TABLE 4-9   Limitations of Formal Assessment Instruments for Instructional Planning and Evaluation of Student Progress

1. They yield little information about the kinds of conditions under which the student can correctly respond to test items.

2. Scores obtained from formal assessments may not be reliable.

3. The standardization sample has often not included students with handicaps.

4. The content of test items on formal assessment instruments often does not reflect content areas that the classroom teacher has taught.

the use of formal assessment instruments for instructional planning and evaluation of student progress.

Informal assessment procedures include teacher-made tests, observation protocols and interviews. The items that comprise informal assessments are driven by the curriculum, with the purpose of determining whether a specific skill or item of information, rather than general knowledge or a general skill, has been acquired. Informal assessment procedures do not yield norm-referenced scores. The following section, Informal Assessment Procedures, describes procedures that teachers of students with mental retardation can use in planning instruction and in evaluating student progress.

Group vs. Individual

In deciding whether to administer a given test individually or to a group of students, the classroom teacher must keep in mind that although any group test may be administered individually, no test intended for individual administration may be administered to a group of students. In Table 4-10 the characteristics that comprise both individual and group-administered tests are listed. When choosing between an individual or a group test, class-

TABLE 4-10   Characteristics of Individually Administered Tests vs. Group Administered Tests

Individually Administered Tests	Group Administered Tests
1. Questions and demands are provided orally.	1. Directions are provided orally for younger children but for children beyond 4th grade, directions are usually written.
2. Tester is able to match tempo and pace to the testee's individual needs.	2. Tester attempts to match tempo and pace to the group's needs.
3. Monitor progress of only one test taker.	3. Monitor progress of several test takers simultaneously.
4. Readily lends itself to the collection of qualitative information (uses fingers for counting).	4. Difficult to obtain qualitative information.

room teachers of students with mental retardation should keep in mind that the administration of individual tests, while more time consuming, will better enable them to observe how a student approaches an individual task, which can be valuable in planning modifications in the presentation of new material to these students.

Aptitude vs. Achievement

In deciding whether to utilize an aptitude test or an achievement test, we should guard against what Anastasi (1982) has called the naive assumption that achievement tests measure the effects of learning, while aptitude tests measure "innate capacity," independent of learning. This assumption fails to recognize that as we measure an individual's current behavior, the score obtained inevitably reflects the influence of prior learning.

Use of the term *ability* has been suggested by some researchers as a useful way to replace the traditional categories of aptitude and achievement in psychometrics (Green, 1974; Lennon, 1980; Mehrens & Lehmann, 1988). Such a movement away from the traditional terms *aptitude* and *achievement* toward the use of the word *ability* has been reflected in test and title modifications. For example, the Lorge-Thorndike Intelligence Tests, which first appeared in 1954, were further developed and renamed as The Cognitive Abilities Tests (CogAT) in 1986 (Thorndike & Hagen, 1986).

Although both aptitude and achievement tests measure behavior, Mehrens and Lehmann (1988) emphasize that there are several dimensions in which aptitude and achievement tests differ. Table 4-11 presents some of those differences.

Student-Oriented vs. Environment-Oriented

As the classroom teacher decides which test should be used for which purpose, it is important that the overall focus of the assessment instrument not be overlooked. For example, student-oriented assessment instruments, which directly measure a student's level of skill, may not measure environment-oriented aspects of the learning process that might be at the root of the student's learning difficulties (e.g., appropriateness of tasks assigned; quality of instruction delivered).

EXAMPLE: When examining the *Case Study of Tanisha* introduced in Chapter 3, it becomes apparent that Tanisha's teacher could benefit from additional information

TABLE 4-11   Dimensions on Which Aptitude and Achievement Tests Differ

1. Typically the breadth of coverage is greater for aptitude tests than it is for achievement tests.

2. Achievement tests (e.g., test of knowledge in English) tend to be more related to particular school subjects.

3. Studies generally indicate a higher heritability index for aptitude tests than achievement tests.

4. The purpose of aptitude tests is to predict performance, whereas the purpose of an achievement test is to obtain a measure of a student's present level of skill or knowledge.

regarding Tanisha's handwriting competencies. This information can be obtained by administering the Zaner-Bloser Evaluation Scales (1984). These scales, which are of the student-oriented type, provide a global estimate of a student's overall handwriting competencies. To better enable Tanisha's teacher to systematically observe Tanisha's handwriting behavior across various school-related tasks that require handwriting competence, the use of handwriting checklists, an environment-oriented scale, would be beneficial. Howell and Kaplan (1980) and Ruedy (1983) provide a detailed listing of such observational checklists.

Informal Assessment Procedures

Because of the limitations of formal tests (see Table 4-9 on page 107), teachers of students with mental retardation will need to be knowledgeable about how informal assessment procedures can help them get a more complete picture of their students' needs. In gathering information about a student's performance through informal assessment procedures, the teacher of students with mental retardation is presented with opportunities that allow: (1) samples of student behavior to be evaluated in relation to specific instructional concerns; (2) modifications of administrative procedures, content, materials, and scoring criteria to meet the needs of a particular assessment situation (Bennett, 1982); (3) measurement of student performance within the context of the natural classroom setting; (4) the collection of data that formal tests cannot provide; and (5) manipulation of the conditions under which the student can perform.

Specific techniques or approaches that are included under the heading informal assessment procedures are presented in Table 4-12 (McLoughlin & Lewis, 1994) and are then described. The first five informal procedures are directly concerned with student performance, while the last three informal procedures are types of assessment devices that tap the opinions and perceptions of individuals that play or have played a significant role in the life of a student with mental retardation (e.g., parents, care givers, grandparents, current and former teachers). For each informal procedure, examples using the information presented in the *Case Study of Tanisha* (see Chapter 3) will be used to illustrate the point discussed.

TABLE 4-12   Informal Assessment Techniques

1. Observation

2. Work sample analysis

3. Criterion-referenced tests

4. Informal inventories

5. Task analysis

6. Checklists

7. Rating scales

8. Interviews and questionnaires

Observation

Observing students is something that teachers of students with mental retardation do all the time. When a planning stage and a record system for the collection of specific data within a designated time period are added to that observation, then observation becomes a very powerful tool that helps the teacher specify, record, and analyze the potential problem behavior. During the planning stage, the teacher will need to determine what behavior will be the focus of the observation. After the behavior has been described in behavioral terms (i.e., verifiable through direct observation), the teacher will need to decide whether direct observation will be done with a behavior checklist or whether the observation will be anecdotal. The behavior checklist describes specific skills (usually in hierarchical order) and the conditions under which each skill should be observed (Cooper, Heron, & Heward, 1987). Anecdotal observation requires that the classroom teacher produce a written narrative of a student's behaviors for a specified time period, as well as a description of the

FIGURE 4-2   Example of an Anecdotal Observation Recording Form

Student's Name: *Tanisha (T)*   Date: *Nov. 28*

Observer: *Mr. Gerzog*   Time of Observation: *10:05-10:14*

Time	Antecedents	Student's Response	Consequences
10:05	Books are being passed out for reading.	T is rummaging through her desk.	Mr. G. says, "Tanisha, please get ready for reading."
10:09	Task is to silently read one paragraph and answer two comprehension questions.	T begins talking to the girl in front of her.	The girl says, "Stop talking, I can't read while you talk."
10:11	Class is reading.	T has left her reading book and desk and has gone to the science area.	Mr. G is giving reading assistance to one of the students.
10:12	"	"	"
10:14	"	T lets the hamster out of his cage.	Mr. G announces that T will stay after school and she will make up her reading work at that time.

environmental conditions under which the behaviors were emitted (Cooper, 1981). An example of an anecdotal observation record form is illustrated in Figure 4-2. The data reflected in this anecdotal observation illustrates the need for Tanisha to stay in her seat during reading unless given permission to leave it.

Work Sample Analysis

For a work sample analysis, assignments that students complete are routinely collected for purposes of evaluation. The teacher must then note the number of errors made by each student as well as analyze the types of these errors. Table 4-13 presents some of the factors that a teacher should keep in mind when conducting an error analysis of the progress that Tanisha is making on the following short-term objective:

> When instructed to print her first name, Tanisha will print all of the letters legibly in the correct order on 9 out of 10 trials.

In addition to analyzing the types of errors that Tanisha made when asked to print her name, the teacher might also analyze the correctly formed letters. This kind of work sample analysis, equally concerned with analyzing errors as well as correct responses, is called a response analysis.

Criterion-Referenced Tests

When a student's performance is interpreted by comparing it to some specified behavioral domain or criterion of proficiency, the test is called criterion-referenced. The criterion-referenced test focuses on what an individual student can do, and on what might be needed to better enable the student to achieve the specified behavioral goal. Using Tanisha as an example, information obtained from criterion-referenced testing can be used to answer questions such as: How much improvement does Tanisha need in order to write ten words

TABLE 4-13   Factors to Guide an Error Analysis of Manuscript (Print) Handwriting

Slant	Manuscript letters are perpendicular to the baseline and have a straight up-and-down appearance.
Letter Size & Proportion	Examine the height relationship of one letter to the next letter.
Alignment	Letters should sit on the baseline. For example: the *d* and *g* letters are not sitting on the baseline
Spacing	Consistent spacing should be examined: • between letters within words • between words • between sentences
Line Quality	Consistent thickness and steadiness in the lines used to form each letter.

per minute? What letters of the alphabet (lower case) can Tanisha produce upon hearing the words, "Print the letter ____."?

Later in this chapter, a step-by-step procedure that teachers can follow in constructing a criterion-referenced test is described (Popham & Husek, 1971) and applied to Tanisha's case study.

Informal Inventories

Informal inventories are used to characterize the performance of a student with mental retardation in relation to the demands of curriculum. In this regard, informal inventories appear similar to criterion-referenced tests. However, when a teacher selects the use of an informal inventory instead of criterion-referenced tests, the intent is to examine broader issues within the curriculum.

In the case of Tanisha, informal inventories that could be administered in order to obtain more information about her present academic level of functioning include arithmetic, reading, and handwriting. For each of these broad curriculum areas, an informal inventory would provide answers to the general question, "How far has Tanisha progressed in the skill sequence for this area?"

Task Analysis and Error Analysis

The term *task analysis* has been used to describe a number of processes (see Chapter 7). For purposes of this section, task analysis will be defined as "the process of isolating, sequencing, and describing all the essential components of a task" (Howell, Kaplan, & O'Connell, 1979, p. 81).

If, for example, Tanisha's teacher has determined that Tanisha has difficulty printing her own name, the teacher could observe Tanisha's performance of a task which has been task analyzed into those component steps necessary for mastery. This would facilitate an error analysis through which the teacher could determine which steps of the task the student can and cannot perform. The factors to guide an error analysis of manuscript handwriting, shown in Table 4-13, can also be used as a guide to observing how Tanisha prints her own name.

Checklists

The content that is tapped in a checklist can include academic performance, classroom behavior, or developmental milestones. The purpose behind administering checklists, which can be completed by the student's parents, past teachers, or some other significant person, is to obtain additional information that would assist the teacher in trying to meet the student's educational needs.

In addition to obtaining information that is not readily available in the classroom, checklists that describe areas of difficulty for specific subjects can provide the teacher with a device for systematically recording current areas of difficulty. These areas of difficulty can be task analyzed and used as the basis for generating instructional objectives.

Rating Scales

The information collected on a rating scale can be said to take the notion of a checklist a step further. Individuals completing a rating scale do not merely report that they have observed a student with mental retardation engaged in a given activity but rate or evaluate the student's performance. For example, Tanisha's teacher could ask Tanisha's parents to report on how much television their daughter watches, by completing the following rating scale item:

Time spent watching television:
1. Most of the day
2. Some of the day
3. At least once a week
4. Less than once a week
5. Never

For a discussion of additional types of rating scales, see Table 4-1.

Interviews and Questionnaires

The purpose of conducting interviews and giving questionnaires is to obtain information from people close to students with mental retardation to better enable the classroom teacher to meet the needs of those students. An example of the application of the interview technique would be for Tanisha's teacher to observe her pressing the number on her keyboard that corresponds to the number of items that are on the computer screen. As Tanisha continues to work on this activity, her teacher would ask her questions during or immediately after the activity. The teacher's questions are geared toward exploring what strategies the student is utilizing as she performs the activity.

The use of a questionnaire offers the classroom teacher a comprehensive and quick way to obtain information about a topic beyond the immediate experience of the classroom. For example, a teacher might want information about a student's experience and attitudes toward "gross motor" activities, such as jumping rope, skipping, and hopping.

Guidelines for Constructing a Criterion-Referenced Test

The intent of this section is to provide teachers of students with mental retardation with specific guidelines that can be used in the construction of a criterion-referenced test. To clarify the purpose of each step, a description of what that step should entail is followed by a specific example describing how that step can be applied, once again using the *Case Study of Tanisha*. One specific annual goal and the short-term objective that goes with it will be used, namely:

Annual Goal	*Short-Term Objective*
Tanisha will decode new words.	When presented with a new one-syllable word consisting of familiar letter sounds, Tanisha will blend the sounds and say the word correctly on 4 out of 5 trials.

Step 1: Delimit the area to be tested

Description: Based on this annual goal, the area in need of improvement is decoding. In order to monitor performance in the area of decoding, a reading scope and sequence skills list (see Mercer & Mercer, 1993) in which skills pertinent to decoding will need to be consulted. Skills pertinent to decoding are often listed under the heading "word attack skills." Under this heading, a hierarchical presentation of subskills (e.g., relates spoken sounds to written symbols; recognizes all initial and final consonant sounds) that are needed for good word attack skills is listed.

Example: In order to monitor the progress that Tanisha is making as a decoder and at the same time be in keeping with the content specified within her short-term objective, the area to be tested has been limited to one syllable words that involve familiar letter sounds.

Step 2: State the objectives and define them in specific terms

Description: The stating of objectives proceeds in a global sense—in this example, knowledge of decoding strategies—and moves through a process in which learning outcomes are delineated. These learning outcomes should be clearly stated in behavioral, or performance, terms so that interpretation errors with respect to how well a student performs on a particular set of learning tasks can be avoided.

Example: In delineating more specific learning outcomes for the global objective of improving knowledge of decoding strategies, Tanisha's current short-term objective might be extended to include:

> When presented with a new one-syllable short vowel word, Tanisha will substitute different vowels to form new words (e.g., bad: substitute e = bed) and say the word correctly on 4 out of 5 trials.

Step 3: Make a content outline

Description: The information in a content outline for Tanisha would indicate the topics relevant to decoding that a teacher might decide to assess and teach at a later date.

Example: Drawing from the Word Analysis and Phonics Tests of the *Diagnostic Reading Scales* (Spache, 1981), examples for each of the topics in the content outline are illustrated in Table 4-14.

Step 4: Prepare a table of specifications

Description: A table of specifications for a criterion-referenced test includes both instructional objectives and the content areas that are to be covered. For each instructional objective and each content area, the teacher will need to decide the relative importance of the goal (e.g., amount of instructional time used), so that a decision can be made regarding the number of test items to be allotted to each objective and each area of content.

Example: A table of specifications for a test on word analysis is presented in Table 4-15. Nine items are to be constructed for the first content area (initial consonant). Of these, five are on pronouncing the letter sound and four are on pronouncing the word. The remainder of the table is read in the same way. A more detailed test plan can be obtained by including all the topics relevant to decoding that were generated in the previous step (see Table 4-14).

TABLE 4-14   Sample Content Outline for Constructing a Criterion-Referenced Test on Decoding

1. Initial Consonants
   Examples: **b**am; **v**an; **g**em

2. Final Consonants
   Examples: te**p**; te**z**; te**d**

3. Consonant Digraphs
   Examples: **ch**ay; sa**ck**; **th**in

4. Consonant Blends
   Examples: ba**lt**; **qu**el; **fl**en

5. Initial Consonant Substitution
   Examples: • Here is the word *ball*. If we drop the *b*, we have _____ (point to *all*).

     If we add a *c*, we have _____ (point to *call*).

   • Here is the word *man*. If we drop the *m*, we have _____ (point to *an*).

     If we add a *c*, we have _____ (point to *can*).

6. Initial Consonant Sounds
   Recognized Auditorily
   Examples: Examiner reads a word to the student and the student is required to tell the examiner what letter the word starts with.

7. Auditory Discrimination
   Examples: Examiner reads some pairs of words. In some of the pairs the words will be exactly the same. In other pairs, the words will be different. When the words sound the same, the student is required to say, "same." When the words sound different, the student is required to say, "different."

8. Short and Long Vowel Sounds
   Examples: Student reads pairs of words and tells the examiner which word has the short vowel sound.

9. Vowels with *r*
   Examples: Student reads phonograms that have the r-controlled vowel sound such as: bolor (boler); derm (term); witor (witer).
   (Acceptable pronunciations are indicated by the phonograms in parentheses.)

10. Vowel Diphthongs and Digraphs
    Examples: Student reads words and the examiner listens for accurate analysis and pronunciation of the vowel combinations in words such as: tray (play); coy (toy).
    (Only pronunciations indicated in parentheses are accepted.)

11. Common Syllables or Phonograms
    Examples: Student is directed to read phonograms such as: ail (pail); se (seat or set); ick (thick).
    (Acceptable pronunciations of the phonograms are shown in the parentheses following each test item.)

12. Blending
    Examples: Student is directed to pronounce each of the parts of a nonsense phonogram (se-ter); then to blend the parts into a blended phonogram. Additional examples include: con-ell; and sh-ay-ter.

TABLE 4-15   **Table of Specifications for a 57-Item Test on Decoding a New One-syllable Word Consisting of Familiar Letter Sounds**

Instructional Objectives	Pronounces the letter sound	Pronounces the word	Total Items
Content Area Initial Consonants	5	4	9
Initial Consonant Sounds Recognized Auditorily	5	6	11
Initial Consonant Substitution	6	5	11
Final Consonants	4	4	8
Consonant Diagraphs	4	6	10
Consonant Blends	3	5	8
Total Items	27	30	57

Step 5: Set standards of performance

Description: In order to set standards of performance, one should examine the research to determine what the mastery standard for a given task should be for a student with mental retardation. Bloom (1976) has extensively analyzed the components of mastery learning. His work emphasizes the importance of individualizing instruction through a rigorous program of educational assessment for all learners. This is relevant to learners both with and without mental retardation. Bloom calls upon the teacher to explore the interrelationship of these three components: (1) the student's current level of performance; (2) the student's affective entry characteristics (e.g., self-concept and motivational factors); and (3) the quality of instruction.

Example: In deciding what standard of performance to set for Tanisha, the interrelationship of each of the previously listed factors would need to be considered fully to ensure that learning success is being fostered.

Step 6: Select the item types to use

Description: In preparing items for a criterion-referenced test on decoding, the first step would be to look at Table 4-15 for an indication of the number of test items to construct for each content area, as well as what the student is expected to demonstrate (learning outcome). Next, a decision regarding the types of test items to be written needs to be made. Basically, test items can be classified into two major types: (1) the *supply* type (e.g., short answer, essay), which requires that students provide their own responses; and (2) the *selection* type (e.g., multiple choice, true/false, matching), which requires that students choose their responses from presented alternatives.

Example: In deciding what test type should be used to evaluate whether Tanisha has met the objective for a given skill area, the teacher needs to consider whether a particular test type will allow Tanisha to accurately demonstrate her knowledge of a particular subject matter.

Step 7: Write the test items

Description: As test items are written for each of the content areas, it is important that the teacher observe these guidelines: (1) the test item should relate directly to the specific learning outcome that is of interest; (2) the test item should be written so that the task to be performed is clear and definite; (3) information irrelevant to the main purpose of the test item should be minimized; (4) material that is included in one test item should not answer or give a partial answer to another test item; (5) the test item should be written in the positive form except in those instances in which the learning outcome calls for the identification of the exception; and (6) enough test items should be written to adequately sample the learning outcome that is of interest. For more information on writing test items the reader is directed to Gronlund (1973) and Hambelton, Swaminathan, Algina, and Coulson (1978).

Example: Using these guidelines to write test questions will help Tanisha's teacher to minimize the number of poorly constructed questions. Questions that measure whether Tanisha has achieved a specific learning outcome will be maximized.

Step 8: Assemble the items into a test

Description: As the test items are assembled into a test, it is important that the teacher keep in mind these organizational tips: (1) write the questions on index cards so that you can reuse the questions and change the order in which you ask them; (2) on the back of the card in the upper right hand corner indicate the content area that is being assessed so that you may file test items by content; (3) on the back of the card rewrite the test item along with its answer so that the correction of the test can be done quickly; (4) arrange the test items from easy to difficult within the entire test and within each section of the test; and (5) laminate or cover the cards with some kind of plastic covering so that additional time will not be used redoing previously constructed cards.

Step 9: Provide for test interpretation

Description: Interpreting performance on a criterion-referenced test (CRT) involves comparing the percentage of items answered correctly for each objective to the percentage previously specified for mastery that was indicated for each objective. From such a comparison, the teacher can determine which objectives have been satisfactorily mastered.

FIGURE 4-3   Sample Report Form for Criterion-Referenced Test

Content Area: *Initial Consonants*   Student: *Tanisha*

Objective	Number Correct	Percentage Correct	Mastered (X)
1. Pronounces letter sound (5)*	2	40	____
2. Pronounces the word (4)*	1	25	____

*Number of test items for each objective.

Example: A sample report form like the one in Figure 4-3 can be used to enable Tanisha's teacher to record information that specifies the percentage of items answered correctly as well as whether a particular objective has been mastered.

Recommendations

When undertaking the assessment of students with mental retardation, teachers may want to keep these specific recommendations in mind:

1. Assessment must not be undertaken without first identifying what kinds of questions should be asked, as well as what decisions will be based on the data that are collected.

2. In order for an assessment strategy to become manageable and meaningful for classroom teachers of students with mental retardation, school systems need to provide teachers with the time and opportunity for the continuous collection and analysis of data related to the goals of instruction.

3. When trying to determine a student's level of proficiency in a given skill area, it is crucial that these three steps be conducted: (1) carefully examine the types of errors that a student has made; (2) develop a hypothesis for the cause of each error; and (3) create a probe to gain more information about whether or not the hypothesis was on target.

4. When conducting an assessment for students with mental retardation, it is important that nonacademic skill areas be included.

5. It is important that achievement tests be kept in perspective when used with students with mental retardation. Achievement testing is a method to quickly determine general learner problems. It can also determine directions for more specific testing. However, achievement tests are not sensitive to measuring daily progress or program effectiveness for learners with mental retardation.

6. Before questions are formulated regarding areas that the assessment process should address, a listing of the kinds of information contained in a student's cumulative record should be examined.

7. When determining what a test measures, the teacher should look beyond the name of the test or subtests and carefully examine both the test items and the test manual.

8. When applying criterion-referenced measurement as a means of monitoring performance, the teacher should develop a checklist to evaluate the adequacy of the test to insure that test items relate to the specific learning behaviors that are of interest.

References

Alberto, P. A. & Troutman, A. C. (1990). *Applied behavior analysis for teachers* (3rd ed.). New York: Merrill/Macmillan.

Anastasi, A. (1982). *Psychological testing* (5th ed.). New York: Macmillan Publishing Company.

Balthazar, E. (1976). *Balthazar scales of adaptive behavior*. Palo Alto, CA: Consulting Psychologists Press.

Bailey, D., Jr. & Simeonsson, R. J. (1988). Investigation of use of goal attainment scaling to evaluate individual progress of clients with severe and profound mental retardation. *Mental Retardation, 26,* 289–295.

Bennett, R. E. (1982). Cautions for the use of informal measures in the educational assessment of exceptional children. *Journal of Learning Disability, 15,* 337–339.

Bigge, J. (1988). *Curriculum based instruction for special education students.* Palo Alto, CA: Mayfield Publishing Company.

Bloom, B. (1976). *Human characteristics and school learning.* New York: McGraw-Hill.

Brandt, R. M. (1972). *Studying behavior in natural settings.* New York: Holt, Rinehart & Winston.

Conoley, J. C. & Kramer, J. J. (Eds.) (1989), *The tenth mental measurements yearbook.* Lincoln: University of Nebraska Press.

Cooper, J. Q., Heron, T. E., & Heward, W. L. (1987). *Applied behavior analysis.* Columbus, OH: Merrill.

Cronbach, L. J. (1963). Course improvement through evaluation. *Teachers College Record, 64,* 672–683.

DeStefano, L. & Metzer, D. (1991). High stakes testing and students with handicaps: An analysis of issues and policies. In R. E. Stake (Ed.), *Advances in program evaluation: Vol. 1A. Using assessment policy to reform education* (pp. 281–302). Greenwich, CT: JAI Press.

Evans, K. M. (1992). *An outcome-based primer.* Minneapolis: University of Minnesota, Center for Applied Research in Educational Improvements.

Farlow, L. J. & Snell, M. E. (1989). Teacher use of student performance data to make instructional decisions: Practices in programs for students with moderate to profound disabilities. *Journal of The Association for Persons with Severe Handicaps, 14,* 13–22.

Fuchs, L. S. (1982). Data utilization. In P. K. Mirkin, L. S. Fuchs, & S. L. Deno (Eds.), *Considerations for designing a continuous evaluation system: An integrative review* (Monograph #20). Minneapolis, MN: University of Minnesota, Institute for Research in Learning Disabilities.

Fuchs, L., Wesson, C., Tindal, G., Mirkin, P., & Deno, S. (1982). *Instructional changes, student performance, and teacher preferences: The effects of specific measurement and evaluation procedures* (Research Report No. 64). Minneapolis: University of Minnesota, Institute for Research in Learning Disabilities.

Glickling, E. E. & Thompson, V. P. (1985). A personal view of curriculum-based assessment. *Exceptional Children, 52,* 205–218.

Green, D. R. (Ed.) (1974). The aptitude–achievement distinction. *Proceedings of the Second CTB/McGraw-Hill Conference on Issues in Educational Measurement.* New York: McGraw-Hill.

Gronlund, N. E. (1973). *Preparing criterion-referenced tests for classroom instruction.* New York: Macmillan.

Guerin, G. & Maier, A. (1983). *Informal assessment in education.* Palo Alto, CA: Mayfield Publishing Company.

Hambelton, R. K., Swaminathan, H., Algina, J., & Coulson, D. B. (1978). Criterion-referenced testing and measurement: A review of technical issues and developments. *Review of Educational Research, 48*(1), 1–47.

Howell, K. W. & Kaplan, J. S. (1980). *Diagnosing basic skills.* Columbus, OH: Merrill.

Howell, K. W., Kaplan, J. S., & O'Connell, C. V. (1979). *Evaluating exceptional children: A task analysis approach.* Columbus, OH: Merrill.

Kerlinger, F. N. (1973). *Foundations of behavioral research* (2nd ed.). New York: Holt, Rinehart & Winston.

King, J. A. & Evans, K. M. (1991). Can we achieve outcome-based education? *Educational Leadership, 49*(2), 73–75.

Lennon, R. T. (1980). The anatomy of a scholastic aptitude test. *Measurement in Education, 11,* 1–8.

Lizzie, D. (1975). *Identification and screening.* Paper presented at the Infant Education Conference, San Antonio, TX.

McLoughlin, J. A. & Lewis, R. B. (1994). *Assessing special students* (4th ed.). Columbus, OH: Merrill.

MacMillan, D. L. (1977). *Mental retardation in school and society.* Boston: Little, Brown and Company.

Martinek, T. & Zaichkorsky, L. (1977). *The Martinek-Zaichkorsky self-concept scale for children.* Jacksonville, IL: Psychologists and Educators, Inc.

Mehrens, W. A., & Lehmann, I. J. (1987). *Using standardized tests in education* (4th ed.). New York: Longman.

Mercer, C. D. & Mercer, A. R. (1993). *Teaching students with learning problems* (4th ed.). New York: Macmillan.

Mirkin, P. K., Fuchs, L. S., & Deno, S. L. (Eds.) (1982). *Considerations for designing a continuous evalua-*

tion system: An integrative review (Monograph #20). Minneapolis: University of Minnesota, Institute for Research on Learning Disabilities.

Munger, G., Snell, M. E., & Lloyd, B. H. (1989). *How often do you need to collect student data? A study of the effects of frequency of probe data collection and graph characteristics on teachers' visual inferences.* Unpublished manuscript, University of Virginia.

Piers, E. & Harris, D. (1969). *The Piers-Harris children's self-concept scale.* Nashville: Counselor Recordings and Tests.

Podemski, R. S., Price, B. J., Smith, T. E. C., & Marsh, G. E., II. (1984). *Comprehensive administration of special education.* Rockville, MD: An Aspen Publication.

Popham, W. J. & Husek, T. R. (1971). Implications of criterion-referenced measurement. In W. J. Popham (Ed.), *Criterion-referenced measurement.* Englewood Cliffs, NJ: Educational Technology Publications.

Payne, J. S., Polloway, E. A., Smith, J. E., & Payne, R. A. (1981). *Strategies for teaching the mentally retarded* (2nd ed.). Columbus, OH: Merrill.

Repp, A. C. (1983). *Teaching the mentally retarded.* Englewood Cliffs, NJ: Prentice-Hall.

Ruedy, L. R. (1983). Handwriting instruction: It can be part of the high school curriculum. *Academic Therapy, 18,* 421–456.

Rusch, F. R., Rose, T., & Greenwood, C. R. (1988). *Introduction to behavior analysis in special education.* Englewood Cliffs, NJ: Prentice-Hall.

Salvia, J. & Ysseldyke, J. E. (1991). *Assessment in special and remedial education* (5th ed.). Boston: Houghton Mifflin Company.

Semel, E. & Wiig, E. (1987). *Clinical evaluation of language fundamentals—revised.* San Antonio: The Psychological Corporation.

Spache, G. D. (1981). *Diagnostic reading scales.* Monterey, CA: CTB/McGraw-Hill.

Sugai, G. (1985). Case study: Designing instruction from IEPs. *Teaching Exceptional Children, 17,* 232–239.

Thorndike, R. & Hagen, E. (1986). *Cognitive abilities test.* Chicago, IL: The Riverside Publishing Company.

Thurlow, M. L. & Ysseldyke, J. E. (1982). Instructional planning: Information collected by school psychologists vs. information considered useful by teachers. *Journal of School Psychology, 20,* 3–10.

Turnbull, A. P., Strickland, B. B., & Brantley, J. C. (1982). *Developing and implementing individualized educational programs.* Columbus, OH: Merrill.

Wallace, G. & Larsen, S. C. (1978). *Educational assessment of learning problems: Testing for teaching.* Boston: Allyn & Bacon.

White, O. R. & Haring, N. G. (1980). *Exceptional teaching* (2nd ed.). Columbus, OH: Merrill.

Wilcox, B. (1986). Still struggling with assessment. *TASH Newsletter, 12*(6), 2–3.

Zaner-Bloser (1984). *Zaner-Bloser Evaluation Scales.* Columbus, OH: Zaner-Bloser.

Zigmond, N. & Silverman, R. (1984). Informal assessment for program planning and evaluation in special education. *Educational Psychologist, 19,* 163–171.

Foundations of Curriculum: Establishing Educational Priorities

Curriculum development is the process of establishing educational priorities. Curriculum decisions are, at their core, decisions about what to include and what not to include in educational programs. In describing the curriculum planning process as the specification of goals and objectives, Popham and Baker (1970) highlighted the priority-setting role of curriculum development. The extent of what can be covered in the curriculum of any educational program is necessarily limited by the number of instructional hours available. The extent of what can be covered in a curriculum for individuals with mental retardation is constrained even further by the limited learning potential of the students themselves. For example, in a purely quantitative sense a student with mental retardation could be expected to acquire only a fraction of the knowledge and skills acquired by a student without mental retardation during the course of a school year. Therefore, in order to maximize the impact of an instructional program for a student with mental retardation, it is essential that goals and priorities be selected with care and precision.

This chapter represents an effort to present models and strategies that will facilitate the selection and development of appropriate curriculum materials for students with mental retardation. Various definitions and curriculum models are examined in the first part of this chapter. In the next part, guidelines are presented for selecting and adapting existing curriculum resources for use with students with mental retardation. The third part shifts the focus to the application of curriculum design and evaluation principles in the development of new curricula for individuals with mental retardation. Recommendations for teachers are presented in the last part.

Curriculum Perspectives and Models

A wide variety of curriculum materials are now available for use with individuals with mental retardation. However, it is often difficult to find materials that are ideally suited to a particular instructional purpose. The following sections have been included to facilitate that process. First, curriculum development in mental retardation is viewed from the broader perspective of its roots in general education. In subsequent sections, the rationales underlying several of the major curriculum models in mental retardation are examined. Finally, strategies for the review and analysis of existing curriculum materials are presented.

Perspectives and Definitions

The term *curriculum* has been defined in a wide variety of ways. In fact, each treatment of curriculum in the literature seems to offer a unique definition of the term. The definitional debate has tended to focus upon two issues. First, educators disagree on whether definitions of curriculum should be limited to activities that take place in school, or broadened to include everything a child experiences between awakening and falling asleep (Doll, 1982). A second focus of the debate has centered upon whether the definition of curriculum should embrace both planned and unplanned activities. Planned activities are primarily those designed and directed by the teacher. Unplanned activities encompass all other experiences occurring within the school setting.

While the debate about these issues continues, for the purposes of this book we have defined curriculum as the content of instruction, which encompasses the following three dimensions:

(1) broad skill areas to be taught, (2) organization or sequencing of the skill areas, and (3) major tasks or steps contained within the skill areas (Van Etten, Arkel, & Van Etten, 1980, p. 208).

This definition does not confine curriculum to the school, but it does emphasize planned, as opposed to unplanned, activities. It is compatible with the fact that programming for people with mental retardation often extends beyond the boundaries of the school building into the home, community, or workplace. This working definition is consistent with the common conception of curriculum as the *what* of instruction. Instructional strategies, the *how* of instruction, are not, according to this conception, necessarily a part of the curriculum. In other words, a variety of alternative instructional strategies may be employed with a single curriculum. Instructional strategies, as defined in Chapter 7, may include teaching methods, behavior management techniques, and arrangements of the classroom/community environment.

Curriculum Models in Mental Retardation

Large-scale curriculum development efforts in the field of mental retardation were uncommon in the years prior to 1965 (Meyen & Horner, 1976). The need for comprehensive curriculum materials was acknowledged (e.g., Ingram, 1935; Inskeep, 1926; Martens, 1950). However, it was unusual for curriculum development efforts to proceed in a systematic manner, to include field-testing and evaluation, and to culminate in a commercial product. Most curriculum development occurred at a local level through the collective efforts of teachers responding to a local need for materials. Many of these products were either limited in scope or poor in quality.

Beginning around 1965, there was a significant increase in systematic curriculum development activity in mental retardation. Several large-scale curriculum projects, funded by the Bureau of Education of the Handicapped of the United States Office of Education, were initiated in the late 1960s. Some of them culminated in systematic, field-tested, commercial products that are still in use today, such as the *Social Learning Curriculum* developed by Goldstein and his associates at Yeshiva University, *Project MATH* developed by Cawley and his associates at the University of Connecticut, and the *I CAN* curriculum designed by Wessel and her colleagues at Michigan State University (Meyen & Horner, 1976).

In spite of this increase in curriculum development activity, the quality of curriculum guides in use throughout the United States still left much to be desired in 1971 when the National Association for Retarded Children (NARC) reported the findings of their nationwide survey (cited in Polloway, Payne, Patton, & Payne, 1985). In response to a request for curriculum guides from state education agencies and local school districts throughout the United States, NARC received 227 guides spanning all levels of mental retardation. Their key findings included the following:

1. Most of the guides had been developed for students with mild or moderate mental retardation in primary or secondary level self-contained classes.
2. The guides were extremely varied in format, organization, and construction.
3. The guides were notably similar in content.
4. The guides revealed a general absence of behavioral terms.
5. Most guides were not based upon any modern theory of learning.

In addition to issuing ten specific recommendations to guide future curriculum development efforts in mental retardation, NARC concluded that further curriculum development was needed to provide an individualized educational experience for all persons with mental retardation. They proposed that an adequate curriculum should be aimed at increasing the complexity of behavior, increasing personal control over the environment, and increasing culturally appropriate behaviors. Activities should be age-appropriate and relevant to the practical aspects of daily living and integration into the community. Vocational and leisure skills should be emphasized (Polloway et al., 1985).

Many of the NARC recommendations were incorporated into subsequent curriculum development efforts. Perhaps the most dramatic progress was seen in the development of curricula for children with severe and profound disabilities. A wide variety of curriculum materials are now available for use with individuals at all levels of mental retardation. Most of these curricula represent one or more of the curriculum models discussed below. The models, each of which reflects a different philosophical approach to curriculum development, have tended to focus upon either students with severe/profound mental retardation or students with mild/moderate mental retardation.

Models for Students with Severe and Profound Mental Retardation

Curriculum materials developed for use with individuals with severe and profound mental retardation can generally be characterized as either developmental or functional. The developmental model takes as its standard the elements, organization, and sequence of normal development. The functional model, on the other hand, takes as its standard the skills essential to independent adult functioning.

The Developmental Model

The first full-scale attempts at curriculum development for individuals with severe and profound mental retardation were based on a developmental model. It is not surprising that these initial efforts to develop educational programs for individuals with severe and profound mental retardation began with the careful assessment of skills relative to the well-known milestones of normal development. Program development, then, consisted primarily of an effort to fill in the undeveloped skills. A key assumption of this model is that many skills appearing early in the developmental hierarchy are prerequisites for skills appearing later in normal development. Programs following the developmental model have typically involved the painstaking training of discrete steps along a developmental continuum specified by one or another model of normal development. For example, Stephens (1977) carefully outlined the application of a Piagetian framework to curriculum development for individuals with mental retardation. At the present time, early intervention programs for infants and children with severe and profound mental retardation continue to rely heavily upon the developmental model (see Bricker and Iacino, 1977). Because it is based upon the universal sequence of normal development, the developmental model is classified as a universally-referenced curriculum model (see Chapter 7).

The adaptive/prosthetic approach (Van Etten et al., 1980), is sometimes applied as an adjunct to the developmental approach to accommodate the needs of people with multiple disabilities. That approach encourages the use of alternatives to the developmental skills unattainable by a particular person because of a motor or sensory disability. For example, a teacher using the adaptive/prosthetic approach might encourage a child to develop wheel-chair mobility skills as a substitute for walking. The application of the developmental cur-riculum model in conjunction with the adaptive/prosthetic approach for a child with profound mental retardation is illustrated in the *Case Study of Alicia*.

The most widespread application of the developmental model with children with men-tal retardation is in early childhood programs. At the preschool age level, the developmen-tal model is also appropriate for children with mild/moderate mental retardation, as illustrated in the *Case Study of Norman*.

CASE STUDY: Alicia (CA = 3–6, IQ = 20)

Case Summary

Alicia was diagnosed at birth, after a difficult delivery, as having cerebral palsy with pos-sible mental retardation. It soon became apparent that her development in all areas was seri-ously delayed. Now at the age of three and a half, Alicia has been classified as having profound mental retardation on the basis of obvious delays in adaptive behavior and an esti-mated IQ of 20 on the Bayley Scales of Infant Development. Alicia attends an Early Child-hood Center for children with multiple disabilities.

When Alicia's physical development is compared with the sequence of normal devel-opment, it is apparent that she has mastered most of the motor skills, within her physical limitations, that precede sitting upright. Alicia's low muscle tone and poor head control have generally precluded her sitting unsupported in an upright position.

Her parents and her teacher are concerned that Alicia's failure to sit upright will inter-fere with her continued physical/motor development as well as her development in other areas. For example, they fear that not being able to sit upright might interfere with the development of her ability to grasp and manipulate objects, the acquisition of self-feeding skills, and oppor-tunities to observe and imitate appropriate cognitive and social behaviors. Consequently, Ali-cia's parents and teacher have arranged for a specially-designed supporting chair in which Alicia can be comfortably positioned in an upright position. They want to insure that as much of her programming as possible takes place while Alicia is sitting upright.

Curriculum Model

Alicia's program emphasizes activities to foster development in the five areas designated by PL99–457: physical, self-help, language and speech, cognitive, and psychosocial. The

CASE STUDY: Alicia (continued)

above description of Alicia's case reflects close adherence to a developmental philosophy and curriculum model. One curriculum that has served as a guide in designing Alicia's program is *A Curriculum for Profoundly Handicapped Students: The Broward County Model Program* (Sternberg, Ritchey, Pegnatore, Wills, & Hill, 1986). Alicia's program is designed to follow the normal developmental sequence to the greatest extent possible. Whenever Alicia's physical limitations preclude the attainment of a developmental milestone, adaptive/prosthetic approaches (e.g., the supporting chair) are employed to help Alicia achieve a functional equivalent of that milestone.

CASE STUDY: Norman (CA = 5–5, IQ = 64)

Case Summary

At five and a half years of age, Norman is presently mainstreamed into a preschool program in his neighborhood. His IQ, measured on the Stanford-Binet Intelligence Scale, is 64, and he has been placed in the mild range of mental retardation. In many ways, Norman's adaptive behavior is consistent with his level of intellectual development, especially with regard to his communication and social skills. However, constricted movement of his right extremities has attenuated somewhat the development of motor skills and daily living skills. An interdisciplinary approach will probably be most advisable to facilitate collaboration between Norman's teacher and parents in the development of a program plan that integrates improved motor functioning with increased daily living competencies.

Curriculum Model

Norman's preschool instruction draws upon *The Developmental Resource* (Cohen & Gross, 1979), with developmentally sequenced, behaviorally defined target areas in cognitive, motor, and self-help competencies. In preschool programs, the distinction between developmental and functional curricula is not as useful as it is with older children, especially with respect to preschool children with mild disabilities who may not lag developmentally far behind their peers without disabilities. In Norman's case, instruction is designed to teach behaviors that are age-appropriate, adaptive, and relevant to the demands of his milieu (functional curriculum), but which at the same time are sequenced as a progression of skills which provide the prerequisite foundations for more advanced skills to be acquired later (developmental curriculum). His curriculum, therefore, reflects a combination of the functional and developmental models.

The Functional Model

The functional model of curriculum development may have emerged partly out of frustration at the slow progress often manifested by individuals with severe and profound mental retardation. It soon became apparent that if a strict developmental approach were followed, most adults with profound mental retardation would be limited to a repertoire of early developmental skills, many of which would have no practical application in their everyday lives. For example, the ability to stack cubes may have important developmental implications, but it cannot be expected to enhance the everyday functioning of an individual with profound mental retardation. In addition, because in the past such individuals had been excluded from the public schools, many of those entering programs for the first time were already adolescents or adults. Brown, Branston, Hamre-Nietupski, Pumpian, Certo, and Gruenewald (1979) pointed out the extreme inappropriateness of exposing adolescents and adults with mental retardation to curricula developed for infants and young children. They advocated the functional model as an alternative and proposed the following three components:

1. *Functional Skills*. Functional skills are defined as those most likely to be required in the everyday life of an adult with mental retardation. They may include any skills that can influence a person's ability to function independently and productively in the community.
2. *Natural Environments*. Natural environments refer to those least restrictive environments—domestic, vocational, or community—in which a person with mental retardation is being trained to function. They may serve as guides for selecting appropriate curriculum content as well as preferred settings for training.
3. *Chronological-age-appropriate Skills*. Chronological-age-appropriate skills are simply those skills that would be performed by normal adults in the community. Although many of the more complex skills are beyond the reach of individuals with severe and profound mental retardation, there are numerous everyday activities that are both simple and appropriate (e.g., eating, shopping, making phone calls).

The *Case Study of Sonia* and the *Case Study of Scott* both illustrate the application of the functional model. Both the major strength and the major weakness of the functional model is that it is highly individualized. At the opposite extreme from universally-referenced models like the developmental model, the functional approach has been classified as individually-referenced because it takes the individual as its point of reference (see Chapter 6). It is expected that the teacher will assess the adult living prospects of each student and design each student's curriculum accordingly. On the positive side, this approach lends itself directly to the development of the IEP. On the negative side, the demands upon the teacher's time may be prohibitive.

CASE STUDY: Sonia (CA = 7–7, IQ < 15)

Case Summary

Sonia is a seven year and seven month old girl with profound mental retardation. Her IQ is estimated to be below 15, based on largely unsuccessful attempts to administer the Stanford-Binet Intelligence Scale and the Leiter International Performance Scale. Her self-care skills are very limited, to the extent that she is not yet toilet trained and she does not dress herself or tend to her personal hygiene. She also requires physical prompting to feed herself. She has no speech and understands little of what is said to her. Gross motor develop-

---

CASE STUDY: Sonia (continued)

---

ment is adequate, but visual-motor coordination is poor and she demonstrates infrequent manipulation and use of objects when attempts are made to engage her in a task. Sonia attends a school for children with profound mental retardation.

Curriculum Model

Sonia's school has a strong functional orientation, emphasizing the acquisition of behaviors that enable the child to adapt to the requirements of her environment. It has a strong behavioral orientation with much emphasis on task analysis, differential reinforcement, and prompting sequences. Sonia's IEP contains goals and objectives for toilet training which are derived from Foxx and Azrin's *Toilet Training the Retarded* (1973). The school also draws upon the *Murdoch Center C & Y Program Library* (Wheeler, Miller, Duke, Salisbury, Merritt, & Horton, 1977). This source is particularly valuable to Sonia's school because of its emphasis on data-based approaches with recording systems to monitor behavioral progress.

CASE STUDY: Scott (CA = 18–0, IQ = 33)

Case Summary

Scott, who has been classified as having severe mental retardation, has a Stanford-Binet IQ of 33. He has no major sensory or motor problems and his adaptive behavior is generally consistent with his IQ. Scott, who is now eighteen years old, attends a secondary school program at a Transition Center that serves students with mental retardation between eighteen and twenty-one years of age.

Scott's Individualized Transition Plan (ITP) has been designed in light of his teacher's predictions about his most probable adult opportunities. Scott's teacher expects that Scott may be able to obtain a position in the cafeteria of the local hospital, and that he will continue to live at home with his parents. In order to qualify for a job at the hospital, Scott must be able to travel independently between his home and the hospital. At the present time, Scott has no independent travel skills. He travels to school and his job training site in a special transportation van.

Curriculum Model

The Transition Center program emphasis is upon providing students with the skills and supports they will need for a successful transition to an adult life in the community. The Center's program concentrates primarily upon the following areas: domestic, vocational, recreational/leisure, community functioning, and interaction with nondisabled persons. Falvey's (1989) *Community Based Curriculum* as well as *Impact: A Functional Curriculum Handbook for Students with Moderate to Severe Disabilities* (Neel & Billingsley, 1989) are used to guide programming. Scott's program illustrates the application of a functional curriculum that is individually designed to prepare him for his most probable adult needs. The activities in his program are functional, chronological-age-appropriate, and are taught in the natural environment to the greatest degree possible.

Wilcox and Bellamy (1982) have proposed a modification which they have called the community-referenced approach. Using this approach, they have proposed a structure for a high school curriculum based upon a survey of local opportunities for adults with mental retardation in a particular community. Wilcox and Bellamy's approach provides a basis for developing curriculum materials that address the common needs of a group of learners, offering a potentially time-saving adjunct or alternative to the functional approach (see Chapter 6).

Models for Students with Mild and Moderate Mental Retardation

Perhaps the central question in curriculum development for students with mild and moderate mental retardation is the extent to which their curriculum should, or should not, differ from that of the mainstream in regular education. Existing curricula for this population span the entire continuum from the totally different life-centered and process-training approaches to the regular academic curriculum itself. All three of the curriculum models for persons with mild and moderate mental retardation discussed in this chapter may be classified as universally-referenced. Neither individually- nor community-referenced models have been widely applied with individuals with mild and moderate mental retardation. However, there is nothing to preclude such applications as will be seen in the illustrative case studies.

The Life-Centered Model

The life-centered model contains many elements of the functional model, although the latter model was developed specifically for individuals with severe and profound disabilities. The life-centered model is an outgrowth of a longstanding emphasis on the importance of life skills in curriculum development for individuals with mental retardation. According to this model, the curriculum should emphasize the essential and practical skills needed for survival in the community. A comprehensive articulation of the life-skills emphasis is manifested in the career education movement. Although it began in regular education in the early 1970s, the career education concept was readily embraced by special educators, particularly in the area of mental retardation. In 1978, The Council for Exceptional Children issued a position paper on career education defining it in the following way:

> the totality of experiences through which one learns to live a meaningful life . . . providing the opportunity for children to learn, in the least restrictive environment possible, the academic, daily living, personal-social and occupational knowledges and skills necessary for attaining their highest level of economic, personal, and social fulfillment. The individual can obtain this fulfillment through work (both paid and unpaid) and in a variety of other societal roles and personal lifestyles (cited by Kokaska, 1983, p. 194).

Career education is different from vocational education, which focuses upon the training of specific technical skills for employment, and which usually does not begin until the secondary level. The concept of career education is much broader and encompasses all levels of schooling and all aspects of preparation for life. Brolin and Kokaska (1979) proposed that a career education curriculum for individuals with disabilities should include the following three areas:

1. Daily living skills
2. Personal-social skills
3. Occupational competencies

The *Social Learning Curriculum* (Goldstein, 1974) is a well-known, classic example of a life-skills curriculum. This curriculum was based on research indicating that social behavior was a central problem for individuals with mental retardation who were seeking and attempting to maintain employment. The curriculum was designed to focus on social development, while integrating instruction in language, math, and motor skills. The *Social Learning Curriculum* was developed and extensively field-tested with individuals with mild mental retardation. An application of the life-centered model with a community-referenced approach is illustrated in the *Case Study of Karen*. The *Case Study of Tony* provides another example of an application of the life-centered model.

CASE STUDY: Karen (CA = 15–1, IQ = 47)

Case Summary

Karen was diagnosed shortly after birth as having Down Syndrome. She has been classified in the moderately mentally retarded range on the basis of her adaptive behavior and a WISC–R IQ of 47. At the age of fifteen years and one month, Karen attends a special education class in a large comprehensive high school with mainstreaming for lunch, gym, and assembly. The emphasis in her program is upon preparation for adult life, and most learning activities fall into one of the following three curriculum areas: vocational, independent living, and leisure. Many of these skills are taught in a simulated apartment in the high school, as well as through frequent trips into the community. Sometimes, Karen is introduced to new skills through computer simulations of an activity. Karen is being prepared for a work-study placement in the kitchen of a local college.

Curriculum Model

The above description of Karen's program illustrates the implementation of a life-skills program. The program is guided by the career education philosophy of providing "the totality of experiences through which one learns to live a meaningful life" (cited by Kokaska, 1983, p. 194). In conjunction with this curriculum model, Karen's program has been planned within a community-referenced framework. Her long-term goals were selected on the basis of a catalogue of opportunities available in Karen's community. Many of her short-term objectives and program activities have been drawn from *The Syracuse Community-Referenced Curriculum Guide* (Ford, Schnorr, Meyer, Davern, Black, & Dempsey, 1989).

CASE STUDY: Tony (CA = 16–0, IQ = 65)

Case Summary

Tony is sixteen years old, has a WAIS–R Full Scale IQ of 65, and has been classified as having mild mental retardation. He resides in a group home and spends most of his school day in a special education class with other students with mild and moderate mental retardation. He possesses some very basic writing, arithmetic and reading competencies, as well as some skills in basic carpentry, furniture repair, and lawn maintenance. Although sociable, Tony needs to learn to be more assertive.

Although Tony's school placement consists primarily of a self-contained special education classroom (with one hour of mainstreaming in wood shop), the program emphasis is on the acquisition of functional skills necessary for integration into the community. Tony is receiving instruction in functional academics, and his transition team anticipates placing him in a work-training station in a nearby furniture repair shop.

Curriculum Model

Tony's curriculum is based on the life-centered model, which emphasizes the development of skills useful for survival in the community. His teacher draws heavily upon *Teaching Functional Academics* (Bender & Valletutti, 1982) as well as Westaway and Apollini's (1978) *Becoming Independent* curriculum, which consists of eight units. Before instruction began, the curriculum's checklists were completed to assess Tony's entering skills. Tony's IEP emphasizes goals and objectives that are derived primarily from three of the eight units, including job readiness, academic skills, and social skills. Tony's teacher works with the group home staff to implement his goals and objectives in the "community activities" unit. Consistent with a "community-referenced" approach to instruction (Wilcox & Bellamy, 1982), much of Tony's curriculum focuses on the acquisition of specific independent living skills that he is likely to need as an adult in his own residence, neighborhood, and prospective workplace.

The Process-Training Model

A recurrent theme in special education has been the remediation of deficits or the training of mental processes (see Chapter 11). A substantial body of research with individuals with mental retardation has accumulated on the training of cognitive strategies, much of which is directly relevant to the development of curriculum and teaching methods (see Borkowski and Konarski, 1981 or Kramer, Nagle, and Engle, 1980). In one sense, this research has produced instructional techniques that are almost content-free, and as such, more relevant to a consideration of instructional strategies than curriculum. On the other hand, in the sense that process training requires instructional time that might be devoted to other curriculum areas, it becomes a curriculum issue. Many of the training techniques were developed with laboratory tasks selected because they seemed to represent relatively pure measures of the process to be trained. Initially, it was hoped that if a process deficit could be remediated, then the newly acquired skill would be automatically employed in the wide variety of tasks to which it contributed. Because such generalization was not readily obtained, the emphasis in process training research shifted to a more global effort to identify the conditions favorable to generalization and, ultimately, to improving intelligence (Blackman & Lin, 1984). The relevance of this work to curriculum stems from its emphasis upon allocating a portion of the curriculum to activities directed toward the training of process rather than the teaching of concrete skills or academic content.

One example of a process-training curriculum is Meeker's (1969) translation of Guilford's (1956) structure of intellect theory into remedial instructional exercises. Another example of a process-training approach is Feuerstein's (1980) *Instrumental Enrichment Program* (see also Chapter 7). Originally developed in Israel for use with socially disadvantaged adolescents, the program has been applied widely with schoolchildren with mental retardation in the United States. Feuerstein's program includes more than 400 paper-and-pencil exercises aimed at improving problem-solving tactics and motivation. Attention is also given to "bridging" from the content-free process-training tasks to their life-relevant applications. Although program evaluation efforts have reported gains on nonverbal/performance measures of intelligence, the program has not been associated with consistent gains in school achievement (e.g., Brainin, 1984; Rand, Tannenbaum, & Feuerstein, 1979; Savell, Twohig, & Rachford, 1986). The *Case Study of Juan* provides an illustration of the process-training approach.

CASE STUDY: Juan (CA = 9–0, IQ = 55)

Case Summary

Juan is nine years old and has been classified as having mild mental retardation on the basis of his adaptive behavior and a WISC–III IQ of 55. Juan attends an inner-city elementary school where he is mainstreamed for part of the day. In addition, he spends two hours per day in a resource room receiving small-group and individualized instruction.

In the mainstream classroom, Juan's teacher reports that Juan is easily discouraged. For example, if he is presented with an unfamiliar math problem, Juan quickly gives up and says that he cannot do the problem. He does not spontaneously attempt to apply possible solution strategies.

Curriculum Model

Juan's program is devoting a significant portion of the curriculum to process training. During Juan's time in the resource room, he receives Feuerstein's *Instrumental Enrichment Program* (1980). The key to the success of this approach will be the integration of Juan's repertoire of cognitive strategies into his academic activities. Special "bridging" activities are being employed in the Instrumental Enrichment training sessions to facilitate the application of the acquired cognitive strategies to academic content. As another approach to process training, Juan is also receiving computer-based instruction in the use of LOGO, a computer graphics programming language developed to encourage thinking and problem solving in children (Papert, 1980).

The Academic Model

Most children with mild or moderate mental retardation will be exposed to the academic curriculum during at least some portion of their school careers. It makes good sense to foster the acquisition of basic academic skills, such as reading and arithmetic, for most of these children. Adhering to the regular education curriculum as closely as possible is, in fact, most compatible with the inclusion of children with mental retardation in regular education programs (e.g., Childs, 1979; Stainback & Stainback, 1992; Stainback, Stainback, & Forest, 1989). Although inclusion does not preclude the use of a specialized curriculum for an individual with mild mental retardation, it can increase the complexity of applying it. Many of the specialized curricula were developed with the self-contained special class in mind, and are not readily adapted for application by the regular classroom teacher or resource room teacher on an individualized basis. Ideally, however, some specialized materials can be utilized to increase the appropriateness of instruction even in a fully inclusive environment, as shown in the *Case Study of Tanisha.*

CASE STUDY: Tanisha (CA = 7–3, IQ = 58)

Case Summary

Tanisha has been classified as having mild mental retardation on the basis of her adaptive behavior and a Stanford-Binet IQ of 58. At age seven years and three months, Tanisha is enrolled in an inclusive elementary school program. The program emphasizes the basic academic skills of reading, writing, and arithmetic.

Although Tanisha can produce the sounds of most letters and letter combinations, she still cannot blend these sounds to decode new words. When a new word is taught to her and sufficient practice is provided, Tanisha usually retains and recognizes the word in later lessons. However, her parents and teacher feel that it is important for her to be able to figure out new words as she encounters them.

Curriculum Model

Tanisha's program is a fully mainstreamed regular academic program. Because she is classified as handicapped, she is required to have an IEP. Fortunately, her teacher is adept at individualizing her approaches to meet the needs of each student. For example, in order to provide a concrete and carefully sequenced math program for Tanisha, her teacher has been presenting her with exercises from the *I CAN Arithmetic Program* (Kramer & Krug, 1980). Another strategy used by Tanisha's teacher to provide individualized instruction is to involve Tanisha in activities on the microcomputer. So far, most of these activities have utilized either tutorial or drill and practice software.

Slightly more problematic is the fact that, as children with mental retardation grow older, the urgency of incorporating a life-skills emphasis into the curriculum tends to increase. This is often reflected in a shift from pure academics to functional academics. In functional academics, the emphasis is on academic skills with applications to everyday life (e.g., money skills) rather than on academic skills as precursors to more advanced study (e.g., pre-algebra).

Selecting Curriculum Materials

A visit to the exhibit hall at the annual convention of the American Association on Mental Retardation (AAMR), Council for Exceptional Children (CEC), The Association for Persons with Severe Handicaps (TASH), or other national or regional professional organization will quickly reveal that curriculum materials designed for individuals with mental retardation have proliferated in recent years. With this array of options, the education professional responsible for curriculum selection is faced with some difficult decisions. There are many factors to consider in determining the potential appropriateness of educational materials. Sometimes, a single set of materials may be found that entirely meets the curriculum needs of a particular program. More often, it will be necessary to combine or adapt materials from a variety of sources to meet the individual needs of a diverse group of students. In some cases, it may be necessary to design and develop new curriculum materials to supplement those that already exist. However, before taking on the often Herculean task of new curriculum development, the teacher should conduct a thorough review and analysis of existing curricula for possible adoption or adaptation to meet the needs of individual students (e.g., Salend, 1994).

Finding Existing Curriculum Materials

An exhaustive search of existing curriculum materials will not be readily accomplished. As mentioned earlier, in addition to published curriculum materials, many of the existing materials have been developed through the efforts of local educational programs and may not have been widely disseminated. The general suggestions listed below may aid in the initial stages of a search. However, they will not exhaust all possible sources of curriculum materials in any specific locality. The following sources may be helpful:

1. A university library is a good place to begin. Commercially published and many unpublished curriculum guides and materials are listed in comprehensive indices, such as the Fearon-Pitman Index or the Kraus-Thompson index. In addition, *Resources in Education* (RIE), published by the Educational Resources Information Center (ERIC), indexes and abstracts "report literature" (documents other than journals) from the ERIC Clearinghouses, one of which is devoted to literature on the Handicapped and Gifted. Most of this report literature is accessible through the ERIC Document Microfiche Collection. Journal articles are also indexed by ERIC in the *Current Index to Journals in Education* (CIJE). A local librarian may be consulted for other possible sources of curriculum materials.

2. Computerized retrieval systems can provide access to numerous databases, including ERIC and *Exceptional Child Education Abstracts*. Most university libraries have access to one of the major information retrieval systems, such as DIALOG Information Retrieval Service, Bibliographic Retrieval Service, or Systems Data Corporation (Schumacher & McMillan, 1993). Increasingly, libraries are allowing patrons to perform their own searches using interactive systems, such as CD-ROM. Again the librarian is probably the best source of up-to-date information on available options.

3. National and regional conferences of professional organizations concerned with mental retardation (e.g., AAMR, CEC, TASH) are excellent sources of the most recent commercially available materials. The exhibit halls of these conferences provide an opportunity for hands-on examination of most of these materials.

4. State, regional, and local instructional materials centers are excellent resources. Their availability and comprehensiveness, however, varies from one location to another.

Curriculum Review and Analysis

In 1979, Klein, Pasch, and Frew asserted that a commercial system can never meet a student's needs as well as an appropriate teacher-made system designed with that particular student in mind. Although this assertion may continue to apply for some students, the need for teacher-made materials is steadily declining. With the increasing variety of commercially available curriculum materials, it is more and more likely that existing materials will meet the educational needs of individual students, freeing valuable teacher time for teaching.

The process of selecting curriculum materials can be facilitated by applying decision-making criteria such as those illustrated in the sample curriculum review/analysis form in Table 5-1. The form, which can be modified to fit the specific characteristics of a situation, is included to provide a general guide for the analysis and selection of curriculum materials for students with mental retardation.

Multicultural Considerations

Dramatic increases are projected in the proportion of the school population that is nonwhite and for whom English is not the primary language. For example, it is anticipated

---

TABLE 5-1   Sample Curriculum Review/Analysis Form

---

1. Clearly identify the curriculum to be reviewed. Specify the name of the curriculum, the author(s), the year of publication, the place of publication, and the publisher.
2. Clearly specify the target population(s), in terms of functioning level and age, for whom this curriculum was developed. Is this information explicitly provided in the guide?
3. Identify the philosophical model represented by the curriculum (e.g., functional, developmental, process training, etc.).
4. Are the overall goals and instructional objectives clearly specified? Provide examples.
5. Briefly summarize the broad skill area(s) covered in the curriculum. Is the curriculum sufficiently comprehensive in terms of those areas?
6. Are the skill areas appropriately sequenced or organized? Provide examples.
7. Are appropriate materials, tasks, and activities provided? Provide examples.
8. Is the format clear and well-organized? Are instructions clear and detailed? Does the guide include a table of contents? Are appropriate assessment and evaluation forms included?
9. Has the curriculum been field tested? Are data available on the effectiveness of the curriculum/program? (Response to this item may require a search of the literature.)
10. Do you recommend the use of this curriculum with individuals with _____ mental retardation? Age? ____
    No ____   Yes ____   Yes, with modification ____
11. If your answer to #10 was *No*, specify the reason(s) for your recommendation.
12. If your answer to #10 was *Yes* or *Yes, with modification*, specify the following:
    a. the age and functioning levels of learners for whom it would be appropriate
    b. the conditions under which it should be used (e.g., group, individual, etc.)
    c. any necessary modifications

---

that by the year 2020, about 25 percent of the school population will be Hispanic, about 16.5 percent will be black, and an additional 4.2 percent will represent other nonwhite races. By that same year, about 7.5 percent of the school population will have a primary language other than English. That these children have not been well served by the schools is reflected in the fact that they are often labeled "educationally disadvantaged," or at risk for school failure (Pallas, Natriello, & McDill, 1989).

The quality of educational programming for students from ethnic and language minority groups is dependent, at least in part, upon societal values. The "melting pot" metaphor, which characterized the period of massive immigration to the United States early in the twentieth century, reflected the society's wholehearted endorsement of the goal of assimilation at the expense of cultural diversity. More recently, however, there has been a shift toward a philosophy of "cultural pluralism." The vision of society embraced by cultural pluralism is multiethnic and assumes equal rights, mutual respect, and the preservation of cultural traditions for diverse groups. According to Suzuki (1979), this shift was triggered by many forces including the black civil rights movement, the resistance of working-class ethnic groups to continued discrimination, and the feminist movement's attack on sexism. Within the framework of cultural pluralism a high value is placed upon multicultural education.

Suzuki suggested that the complete realization of the ideal of cultural pluralism will require a change in the social structure of society. Accordingly, he encouraged teachers to "help students conceptualize and aspire toward alternative social structures and to acquire the necessary knowledge and skills for creating this change" (Suzuki, 1979, p. 48). His six guidelines are intended to help teachers with the implementation of multicultural education:

1. Begin multicultural education by encouraging each student to explore his or her own ethnic background.
2. Encourage students to "decenter" or look for parallels between the experiences of their own ethnic group and those of others.
3. Incorporate a multicultural framework into the curriculum. Concentrate upon increasing understanding among ethnic groups in the community.
4. Vary teaching practices and classroom structure to empower students and create a more democratic classroom climate.
5. Encourage students to deal with their feelings and to develop sensitivity and empathy toward others.
6. Examine possible causes and remedies for oppression, racism, sexism, and poverty.

It is obvious that Suzuki's guidelines, which are equally applicable for students with and without mental retardation, envision multicultural education as much more than the celebration of ethnic foods, holidays, and music. He concludes that "multicultural education basically amounts to sound educational practice coupled with a vision of a better society" (Suzuki, 1979, p. 50). Clearly, multicultural education is essential for all students with mental retardation in order to prepare them for full participation in society. The need to establish multicultural education as an integral part of the curriculum for students with mental retardation derives an added urgency from the fact that disproportionately large numbers of students of minority ethnic status have been classified as having mental retardation (Reis, 1986; Reschly, 1988).

Computer-Based Curriculum Materials

With the increasing presence of microcomputers in the classroom, the role of computer-based materials in the curriculum has expanded steadily. The applications of microcomputers in special education generally fall into one of the following three categories: computer-assisted management, computer-managed instruction, and computer-assisted instruction (Behrmann, 1984). Computer-assisted management comprises the various applications that allow school administrators to track and manage student and staff schedules and records. Computer-managed instruction involves the use of microcomputers by teachers to aid in assessment, IEP development, and the recording of student progress. It is computer-assisted instruction (CAI), however, that is most directly relevant to a consideration of curriculum. CAI refers to the uses of microcomputers in the classroom for direct student instruction, both as an instructional medium and as a tool (Behrmann, 1984).

Types of Computer-Assisted Instruction

The types of computer-assisted instruction listed below are those most often advocated for students with disabilities. The first four types are examples of uses of the microcomputer as an instructional medium. The fifth approach illustrates the use of the microcomputer as a programming tool.

Drill and Practice.   Although drill and practice probably represents the most common instructional application of microcomputers, it is the most limited. It does not tap the potential of the computer as a medium of instruction and, in fact, offers little beyond the traditional workbook approach. Proponents do point out that even this application can facilitate the individualization of instruction, freeing teacher time for more essential teaching activities. Also, it is possible that computer-based activities may offer a motivational boost to some students who have experienced repeated failure with other forms of instruction.

Tutorial Instruction.   Tutorial instruction goes one step beyond drill and practice. Instruction in a particular skill may be provided entirely on the computer, offering opportunities for self-pacing, branching for remediation, optimal sequencing, and immediate and individualized reinforcement. This application uses some of the capabilities of the computer in that it is interactive, but does not go much beyond the opportunities for instruction presently found in most classrooms. Again, it may free teacher time or facilitate individualized, remedial instruction in the mainstream.

Games.   The use of computer-based games for instruction has been shown to have some unique advantages for students with disabilities. Chaffin, Maxwell, and Thompson (1982) identified several of the variables responsible for the general popularity of arcade games and proposed that they be exploited to enhance the learning situation for students with disabilities. On that premise, they developed an ARC–ED curriculum with the following characteristics: (1) fast-paced and requiring high response rates; (2) immediate feedback;

(3) unlimited ceiling; (4) errors viewed as opportunities for improvement; (5) repetition that is fun and motivating; (6) mastery based on both speed and accuracy; and (7) feedback as the basis for selecting instructional strategies. Clearly, games such as these do begin to take advantage of the power and flexibility of the computing medium.

Simulations.   Microcomputer simulations have been welcomed with enthusiasm by both regular and special educators. With simulations it is possible to teach a set of skills (e.g., banking, shopping, fire safety) in the context of a life-like situation—a clear advantage for learners with mental retardation. Interactive video disc technology offers expanded possibilities for enhancing the power of simulations. Simulated life-like situations can provide a context for the teaching of skills, such as decision making and problem solving, that are often limited in students with mental retardation.

Programming.   It has been proposed that teaching children to apply a specially designed computer programming language, such as LOGO, can facilitate their acquisition of problem-solving and thinking skills (Papert, 1980). In this type of learning environment, children can construct, correct, and execute a set of instructions, thus creating their own programs to accomplish tasks in graphics, language arts, or other areas. This application offers the advantage of allowing the child to actively direct the computer rather than passively responding to the directives of prepackaged software. It has been argued that the active, sequential, trial-and-error interaction with the computer that takes place in a LOGO environment may be particularly helpful to students with mild disabilities who tend to have difficulties with attention, organizational skills, and problem solving (Turkel & Podell, 1984). Although this approach seems to hold promise for at least some students with mental retardation, most supporting evidence to date has been anecdotal (Turkel & Podell, 1984).

Review and Analysis of Computer-Based Materials
A general note of caution seems in order. Although computer applications are sometimes promoted as a panacea for students with disabilities, this technology is still in its infancy. Powerful computer-based materials that could constitute a major portion of the curriculum have yet to be developed. Although we are still a long way from having a comprehensive array of computer-based materials to meet every need of students with mental retardation, the availability of potentially appropriate, or readily adaptable, hardware and software increases daily. Comprehensive overviews of promising applications of microcomputers in special education have been provided by both Behrmann (1984) and Hagen (1984). More recently, Gearheart, Mullen, and Gearheart (1993) have summarized the rapidly expanding array of applications of various types of technology in special education.

An even more important cautionary consideration is that the effectiveness of computer-based instruction has, for the most part, yet to be demonstrated (Walker & Hess, 1984). In exploring the usefulness of computer applications for individuals with mental retardation, it will be important to incorporate plans for the evaluation of these applications that consider: (1) their compatibility with the educational process; (2) their instructional adequacy;

TABLE 5-2   Sample Computer Software Review/Analysis Form

1. Clearly identify the software being reviewed. Specify the name of the program, the publisher, the address of the publisher, and the hardware and memory requirements of the software.
2. Clearly specify the overall goals and/or instructional objectives of the software. Is this information explicitly provided?
3. What type of educational software does this program represent? Check one of the following:

   ____ drill and practice

   ____ tutorial instruction

   ____ game

   ____ simulation

   ____ programming tool

   ____ other (describe)

4. Clearly specify the target population(s) for whom this software was developed. Is this information explicitly provided? Was it developed for individuals with disabilities? Type? Specify the targeted age and/or functioning level.
5. Estimate the approximate reading grade level required for use of this program.
6. Estimate the approximate arithmetic grade level required for use of this program.
7. Are the instructions clear and easy to follow? Provide examples.
8. Are the activities appropriately sequenced? Provide examples.
9. Is appropriate feedback and reinforcement provided? Give examples.
10. Does the program appear to be technically adequate (i.e., free of "bugs")?
11. Are data available on the effectiveness of this program? (Response to this question may require a search of the literature.)
12. Overall, would you recommend the use of this software with individuals with mental retardation? In light of the above criteria, specify the range of age and functioning levels for which it might be appropriate (if any).

and (3) their technical adequacy (Hannaford & Taber, 1982). A variety of tools for software evaluation can be found in the literature. For example, one system, developed in conjunction with the Huntington-Commack Software Evaluation Project, stands up well to Hannaford and Taber's (1982) criteria (Shanahan & Ryan, 1984). However, even this system is not geared specifically to the needs of people with mental retardation. The sample review form in Table 5-2, which incorporates many of the features of the Shanahan and Ryan system, was designed to be used as a guide in the selection of software for use with students with mental retardation.

Curriculum Design and Evaluation

In striving to meet the diverse educational needs of students with disabilities, most teachers will, sooner or later, be confronted with the need to design new curriculum materials. For some, this curriculum design activity will be limited to the impromptu construction of a circumscribed curriculum segment for an individual student. For example, it may be necessary for a teacher to develop materials for training an adolescent with blindness and mental retardation to work with and care for her guide dog. Other teachers may have the opportunity to participate in a large-scale curriculum development project geared to the needs of an entire program. For example, the staff of a residential program serving individuals with profound mental retardation may be called upon to develop a fire safety curriculum that is appropriate for their setting and participants. In a rapidly changing society, the need for curriculum development is continuous. A working knowledge of the principles of curriculum design and evaluation is essential for regular and special educators alike.

Principles of Curriculum Design

Establishing the guiding principles of effective curriculum development has long been a priority in education. An early formulation of the curriculum development process by Ralph W. Tyler in 1949, which embodied many elements of the progressive educational thinking of that period, continues to be influential today. Tyler raised four questions to be answered in this curriculum development process. His original questions have been translated into the following four-step curriculum development sequence: "(1) identifying objectives, (2) selecting the means for the attainment of these objectives, (3) organizing these means, and (4) evaluating the outcomes" (Tanner & Tanner, 1975, p. 57). Tyler's model has served as a curriculum planning guide for countless school districts across the United States and has even been considered by some to be "as American as baseball, hotdogs, and apple pie" (Ondrejack & Cochran as cited in Doll, 1982, p. 166). However, the model has been criticized by others. The two most common criticisms are that Tyler failed to provide a clear basis for the selection of objectives, and that he failed to appreciate the inevitable interdependence of the four elements in his linear model (Doll, 1982; Tanner & Tanner, 1975). A modification of Tyler's model, acknowledging the necessity of an underlying philosophy as a basis for objective selection and recognizing the interdependence of the four elements, has been presented by Tanner and Tanner (1975, p. 59). This model is reproduced in Figure 5-1.

Doll (1982), building upon existing curriculum development models, proposed eight steps to be included in the curriculum design process. The following steps have been adapted from those proposed by Doll (1982), and may be used as general guidelines for the development of curriculum materials for students with mental retardation.

1. *Determine the Need*. State the desired outcomes and seek the reactions of appropriate persons outside the planning group (e.g., student, parents, potential employer).

2. *Review Overall Program Goals*. Make sure that the new curriculum is compatible with the overall aims of the school or program. If those aims have never been specified, see that these aims are articulated at this stage in the planning process.

3. *State Specific Project Objectives*. Within the framework of the general aims of the program, clear, instructional objectives should be stated. These pupil objectives must be stated in precise, behavioral terms (see Chapter 6).

4. *Identify Evaluation Means*. In order to determine whether objectives have, in fact, been attained, criteria and means for their evaluation must be specified (e.g., observation schedules, rating scales, interviews).

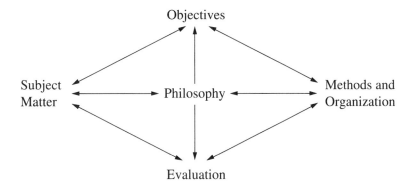

FIGURE 5-1   Modification of Tyler Model

Reprinted with the permission of Macmillan Publishing Company from *Curriculum Development: Theory into Practice* by Daniel Tanner and Laurel N. Tanner. Copyright 1975 by Macmillan Publishing Company.

5. *Choose a Curriculum Model.* Guided by the philosophical orientations of the planners, a curriculum model should be selected. For example, the individually-referenced functional model might be chosen for a twenty-year-old woman with profound mental retardation.

6. *Select Learning Content.* Base the selection of content upon the stated goals and objectives.

7. *Select and Organize the Learning Experiences.* Experiences with high educational values must be selected in light of all of the above considerations. Experiences can then be organized in ways compatible with the selected curriculum model.

8. *Evaluate the Effectiveness of the Project.* The worth of a curriculum design must be gauged through a comprehensive and ongoing evaluation of the project.

Most of the above guidelines can be applied directly to the development of curriculum segments for individual students with mental retardation. However, anyone undertaking a large-scale curriculum development project will need to acquire additional in-depth knowledge of the curriculum design process.

Methods of Curriculum/Program Evaluation

If curriculum is viewed as distinct from instructional strategies, as in our working definition, there is reason to question whether curriculum evaluation is possible at all. Popham and Baker have taken a clear stand on this issue:

Instructional questions usually are amenable to empirical solutions, curricular questions generally are not (Popham & Baker, 1970, p. 14).

The basis for this statement rests upon the key role of goals and objectives in the curriculum development process. Popham and Baker emphasize that the selection of goals and objectives is, by necessity, a value-based process, which cannot be objectively evaluated. However, once the goals and objectives have been selected, it is possible to empirically evaluate the effectiveness of various methods, materials, and/or activities employed to foster their attainment.

If, on the other hand, curriculum is viewed as part of a broader enterprise encompassing the entire educational program as it relates to a particular goal or objective, then evaluation is not only possible, but essential. In spite of the emphasis upon individualized educational programming within special education, many situations continue to exist where the evaluation of an entire program is required. For example, in a situation where a generic core of common employment-preparation goals and objectives have been selected for a group of high school students with mild mental retardation, several program options may be available within a school district. The relative effectiveness of these program options would, in this case, be a prime target for evaluation.

For example, Perotti (1984) compared the adult adjustment of individuals with mild mental retardation who had participated in one of three high school programs: (1) a work/study program in a comprehensive high school; (2) a resource room program in a comprehensive high school; or (3) a vocational/technical high school program. Individuals who had been out of school from two to six years were interviewed to assess their levels of independent living, occupational success, and social adjustment. The individuals who had participated in a work/study program were clearly superior in the occupational area, with the vocational/technical program graduates showing some advantage over the other groups in the social adjustment area. The least satisfactory levels of adult adjustment were observed among those who had participated in a resource room program. Although this study illustrates the continuing need for overall program evaluation in special education, its results must be interpreted with caution. Because it was not possible to assign students to programs randomly, it was not possible to employ a true experimental design in the Perotti study. Thus, it cannot be concluded with certainty that the type of high school program caused the differences in adult adjustment. It is safe to conclude only that a relationship existed between type of high school program and adult performance.

Evaluation Framework

Assuming that program objectives have been selected and appropriately stated, the evaluation of program effectiveness requires a clear evaluation framework. The evaluation framework consists of a plan, or organizational format, for gathering the information necessary to determine whether the objectives have been attained and, in a more general sense, whether the program has accomplished what it set out to accomplish. Numerous frameworks, or models, have been proposed (see Doll, 1982). For example, according to the evaluation framework proposed by Wolf (1984, 1987), a program evaluation effort should be organized around information on the following aspects of the program: (1) initial status of the learners (e.g., pretest performance); (2) learner status after a period of instruction (e.g., posttest performance); (3) implementation of the program; (4) costs; and (5) supplemental information.

Evaluation Design

In addition to a comprehensive evaluation framework, a rigorous evaluation design is required in order to determine whether the outcome is actually attributable to the effects of the educational program as opposed to other extraneous events. Two designs are described briefly below as illustrations of simple, yet rigorous, group experimental designs that can be employed for evaluation purposes (see Chapter 7 for a discussion of single-subject designs). These prototype designs may need to be extended or modified to accommodate the realities of a particular field situation.

The Pretest-Posttest Control Group Design.   This design allows a comparison of the mean performance of two groups which have received different treatments (e.g., phonics instruction programs). First, each student is randomly assigned to one of the two groups by picking names out of a hat or using a table of random numbers. This is the best way to insure that the two groups are roughly comparable before they receive the different treatments. Next, both groups receive a phonics pretest. After the pretest, one group receives the experimental intervention (e.g., computer-based phonics instruction) and the other group receives an alternative, or control, treatment (e.g., traditional phonics instruction). Upon completion of the program, both groups receive a phonics posttest. Application of statistical techniques permits the determination of whether group differences on the posttest are greater than one would expect by chance alone. If the computer-based instruction group obtains significantly higher posttest scores than the traditionally instructed group, then it may be concluded that computer-based instruction is superior to traditional instruction for teaching phonics.

One-way Analysis of Variance Design.   This design is simply an extension of the preceding one that can be used to compare the effectiveness of three or more programs (e.g., computer simulation vs. computer drill and practice vs. workbook drill and practice) to which students have been randomly assigned. First, all three groups received the same problem-solving pretest. Again, though the pretest is not an essential aspect of this experimental design, in an evaluation study all groups should be pretested. Then the three interventions are implemented and followed by a problem-solving posttest. Statistical analyses allow a determination of whether group mean differences in problem-solving performance exceed what would be expected by chance. More extensive discussions of these and other useful evaluation designs are provided by Wolf (1984) or, in the context of PL94–142, by Dunst (1979).

Recommendations

Some of the material covered in this chapter is highlighted in the following recommendations:

1. Select a definition of curriculum. In the proposed working definition, planned activities were emphasized, but the conception of curriculum was not limited to school-based content. It was suggested that curriculum be specified in terms of the following elements:

(a) broad skill areas; (b) sequencing, or organization, of skill areas; and (c) the steps, or tasks, within each skill area.

2. Select a curriculum model that is compatible with your educational philosophy. Most curriculum models for individuals with severe and profound mental retardation fall somewhere along a continuum from *developmental* to *functional*. Curriculum models for individuals with mild and moderate mental retardation range from "nothing different," as in the *regular academic* model, to "totally different," as exemplified in the *life-centered* and *process-training* models.

3. Before undertaking the development of new curriculum materials, conduct a thorough search of existing curriculum materials, including available computer-based materials, to identify any existing materials that may be well-suited to your purpose. A successful search can result in a considerable savings of time and resources.

4. Conduct a critical analysis of any potentially appropriate curriculum materials. On the basis of this analysis, materials may be either accepted, adapted, or rejected as inappropriate.

5. If curriculum development has been deemed essential, the principles of sound curriculum design should be taken into careful consideration. In addition, any large-scale curriculum to be employed with students with mental retardation must be designed so that circumscribed segments can be easily extracted to meet individual needs.

6. Regardless of whether curriculum/program development is to proceed on a large or small scale, it is essential to incorporate a well-controlled evaluation design to assess the effectiveness of the program. It is only through this final step that we can build the data base needed for the continued improvement of educational programs for individuals with mental retardation.

References

Behrmann, M. (1984). *Handbook of microcomputers in special education*. San Diego, CA: College-Hill Press.

Bender, M. & Valletutti, P. J. (1982). *Teaching functional academics: A curriculum guide for adolescents and adults with learning problems*. Baltimore: University Park Press.

Blackman, L. S. & Lin, A. (1984). Generalization training in the educable mentally retarded: Intelligence and its educability revisited. In P. H. Brooks, R. Sperber, & C. McCauley (Eds.), *Learning and cognition in the mentally retarded*. Hillsdale, NJ: Erlbaum.

Borkowski, J. G. & Konarski, E. A. (1981). Educational implications of efforts to train intelligence. *Journal of Special Education, 15*, 289–305.

Brainin, S. S. (1984). *Mediating learning: Pedagogic issues in the improvement of cognitive functioning*. Unpublished manuscript.

Bricker, D. D. & Iacino, R. (1977). Early intervention with severely/profoundly handicapped children. In E. Sontag (Ed.), *Educational programming for the severely and profoundly handicapped*. Reston, VA: The Council for Exceptional Children.

Brolin, D. E. & Kokaska, C. J. (1979). *Career education for handicapped children and youth*. Columbus, OH: Merrill.

Brown, L., Branston, M. B., Hamre-Nietupski, S., Pumpian, I., Certo, N., & Gruenewald, L. (1979). A strategy for developing chronological-age-appropriate and functional curricular content for severely handicapped adolescents and young adults. *Journal of Special Education, 13*, 81–90.

Chaffin, J. D., Maxwell, B., & Thompson, B. (1982). ARC-ED curriculum: The applications of video game formats to educational software. *Exceptional Children, 49*, 173–178.

Childs, R. E. (1979). A drastic change in curriculum for the educable mentally retarded child. *Mental Retardation, 17*, 299–301.

Cohen, M. A. & Gross, P. J. (1979). *The developmental resource, Vol. 8*. New York: Grune & Stratton.

Doll, R. C. (1982). *Curriculum improvement: Decision-making and process*. (5th ed.). Boston: Allyn & Bacon.

Dunst, C. J. (1979). Program evaluation and the Education for All Handicapped Children Act. *Exceptional Children, 46*, 24–31.

Falvey, M. A. (1989). *Community-based curriculum* (2nd ed.). Baltimore: Brookes.

Feuerstein, R. (1980). *Instrumental Enrichment: An intervention program for cognitive modifiability*. Baltimore: University Park Press.

Ford, A., Schnorr, R., Meyer, L., Davern, L., Black, J., & Dempsey, P. (1989). *The Syracuse Community-Referenced Curriculum Guide*. Baltimore: Brookes.

Foxx, R. M. & Azrin, N. H. (1973). *Toilet training the retarded*. Champaign, IL: Research Press.

Gearheart, B., Mullen, R. C., & Gearheart, C. J. (1993). *Exceptional individuals: An introduction*. Pacific Grove, CA: Brooks/Cole.

Goldstein, H. (1974). *The Social Learning Curriculum*. Columbus, OH: Merrill.

Guilford, J. P. (1956). The structure of intellect. *Psychological Bulletin, 53*, 267–293.

Hagen, D. (1984). *Microcomputer resource book for special education*. Reston, VA: Reston Publishing Company.

Hannaford, A. E. & Taber, F. M. (1982). Microcomputer software for the handicapped: Development and evaluation. *Exceptional Children, 49*, 137–142.

Ingram, C. (1935). *Education of the slow learning child*. New York: The Ronald Press.

Inskeep, A. D. (1926). *Teaching dull and retarded children*. New York: Macmillan.

Klein, N. K., Pasch, M., Frew, T. W. (1979). *Curriculum analysis and design for retarded learners*. Columbus, OH: Merrill.

Kokaska, C. J. (1983). Career education: A brief overview. *Teaching Exceptional Children, 15*, 194–195.

Kramer, T. & Krug, D. (1980). *I CAN arithmetic program*. Portland, OR: ASIEP Educational Co.

Kramer, J. J., Nagle, R. J., & Engle, R. W. (1980). Recent advances in mnemonic strategy training with mentally retarded persons: Implications for educational practice. *American Journal of Mental Deficiency, 85*, 306–314.

Martens, E. H. (1950). *Curriculum adjustments for the mentally retarded*. Washington, DC: U.S. Department of Health, Education, and Welfare.

Meeker, M. (1969). *The structure of intellect: Its interpretation and uses*. Columbus, OH: Merrill.

Meyen, E. L. & Horner, R. D. (1976). Curriculum development. In J. Wortis (Ed.), *Mental retardation and developmental disabilities, Vol. 8*, 258–296. New York: Bruner-Mazel.

Neel, R. S., & Billingsley, F. F. (1989). *Impact: A functional curriculum handbook for students with moderate to severe disabilities*. Baltimore: Brookes.

Pallas, A. M., Natriello, G., & McDill, E. L. (1989). The changing nature of the disadvantaged population, current dimensions and future trends. *Educational Researcher, 18*(5), 16–22.

Papert, S. (1980). *Mindstorms*. New York: Basic Books.

Perotti, F. (1984). *A comparison of the vocational adjustment of educable mentally retarded adults after completion of work-study, vocational/technical, and regular high school programs*. Unpublished doctoral dissertation, Teachers College, Columbia University.

Polloway, E. A., Payne, J. S., Patton, J. R., & Payne, R. A. (1985). *Strategies for teaching retarded and special needs learners* (3rd ed.). Columbus, OH: Merrill.

Popham, W. J. & Baker, E. L. (1970). *Establishing instructional goals*. Englewood Cliffs, NJ: Prentice-Hall.

Rand, Y., Tannenbaum, A. J., & Feuerstein, R. (1979). Effects of Instrumental Enrichment on the psychoeducational development of low-functioning adolescents. *Journal of Educational Psychology, 71*, 751–763.

Reis, E. M. (1986). Minority disproportionality in special placements as an assessment and programming issue. *Journal of Instructional Psychology, 13*, 135–140.

Reschly, D. J. (1988). Minority MMR overrepresentation and special education reform. *Exceptional Children, 54*, 316–323.

Salend, S. J. (1994). *Effective mainstreaming* (2nd ed.). New York: Macmillan.

Savell, J. M., Twohig, P. T., & Rachford, D. L. (1986). Empirical status of Feuerstein's "Instrumental

Enrichment" (FIE) technique as a method of teaching thinking skills. *Review of Educational Research, 56*(4), 381–409.

Schumacher, S. & McMillan, J. H. (1993). *Research in education* (3rd ed.). New York: Harper Collins.

Shanahan, D. & Ryan, A. W. (1984). A tool for evaluating educational software. *Teaching Exceptional Children, 16,* 242–247.

Stainback, S. & Stainback, W. (1992). *Curriculum considerations in inclusive classrooms.* Baltimore: Brookes.

Stainback, S., Stainback, W., & Forest, M. (1989). *Educating all students in the mainstream of regular education.* Baltimore: Brookes.

Stephens, B. (1977). A Piagetian approach to curriculum development. In E. Sontag (Ed.), *Educational programming for the severely and profoundly handicapped.* Reston, VA: Council for Exceptional Children.

Sternberg, L., Ritchey, H., Pegnatore, L., Wills, L., & Hill, C. (1986). *A curriculum for profoundly handicapped students: The Broward County model.* Rockville, MD: Aspen.

Suzuki, B. (1979). Multicultural education: What's it all about? *Integrated Education, Issue 97–98, 17,* (1–2), 43–50.

Tanner, D. & Tanner, L. N. (1975). *Curriculum development.* New York: Macmillan.

Turkel, S. B. & Podell, D. M. (1984). Computer-assisted learning for mildly handicapped students. *Teaching Exceptional Children, 16,* 258–262.

Tyler, R. W. (1949). *Basic principles of curriculum and instruction.* Chicago: The University of Chicago Press.

Van Etten, G., Arkell C., & Van Etten, C. (1980). *The severely and profoundly handicapped.* St. Louis: Mosby.

Walker, D. F. & Hess, R. D. (1984). *Instructional software.* Belmont, CA: Wadsworth.

Westaway, A. M. & Apolloni, T. (1978). *The developmental resource, Vol. 1.* New York: Grune & Stratton.

Wheeler, A. J. Miller, R. A., Duke, J., Salisbury, E. W., Merritt, V., & Horton, B. (1977). *Murdoch Center C & Y program library.* Butner, NC: Murdoch Center.

Wilcox, B. & Bellamy G. T. (1982). *Design of high school programs for severely handicapped students.* Baltimore: Brookes.

Wolf, R. M. (1987). A framework for evaluation. *International Journal of Education Research, 11*(1), 21–29.

Wolf, R. M. (1984). *Evaluation in education.* (2nd ed.) New York: Praeger.

The Individualized Education Program (The IEP)

Although it is essential to know the principles of curriculum development in order to design educational programs for students with disabilities, it is not sufficient. Designing programs for people with mental retardation and other disabilities in compliance with the requirements of PL94–142 and its subsequent amendments involves the consideration of a host of additional factors. First, PL94–142 insures the right of *all* children with handicaps to a free, appropriate education, precluding the exclusion of children who do not benefit readily from standard instruction. Thus, the curriculum must be adapted to meet the needs of each student. Secondly, PL94–142 mandates that the children with handicaps are to receive their education in the least restrictive environment (LRE). Consequently, children with mental retardation may receive some, or all, of their education in a regular classroom with learners without disabilities. In this situation, in which the regular class teacher is delivering the educational services in the context of a large number of students without disabilities, it is often difficult to implement a specialized curriculum. The third aspect of PL94–142, with all-encompassing implications for program development, is the individualized education program (IEP).

As stated in PL94–142, the IEP is defined as follows:

The term "individualized education program" means a written statement for each handicapped child developed in any meeting by a representative of the local educational agency or an intermediate educational unit who shall be qualified to provide, or supervise the provision of, specially designed instruction to meet the unique needs of handicapped children, the teacher, the parents or guardian of such child, and whenever appropriate, such child, which statement shall include:

(A) a statement of the present levels of educational performance of such child,

(B) a statement of annual goals, including short-term instructional objectives,

(C) a statement of the specific educational services to be provided to such child, and the extent to which such child will be able to participate in regular educational programs,

(D) the projected date for initiation and anticipated duration of such services, and

(E) appropriate objective criteria and evaluation procedures and schedules for determining, on at least an annual basis, whether instructional objectives are being achieved (PL94–142, 1975).

The most obvious implication of the IEP requirement is that it precludes approaching curriculum development solely in terms of the needs of a *group* of learners. The IEP requires the specification of a unique program geared to the specialized educational needs of each individual learner. As illustrated in the case study examples in Chapter 5, the IEPs of students in a particular educational setting may draw upon instructional sequences from published curricula to meet particular IEP goals (e.g., a toilet training curriculum segment). However, it may be necessary to supplement existing curriculum materials with teacher-designed curriculum segments tailored to the needs of individual learners (e.g., a program to train an adolescent to travel independently in her own community).

TABLE 6-1   Comparison of the Components of Individualized Educational Program (IEP) Development and Commonly Cited Elements of Sound Curriculum Design

Components of IEP Development	Elements of Sound Curriculum Design
Description of present levels of educational performance	Determination of need (Doll, 1982)
Statement of annual goals and short-term objectives	Identification of aims and objectives (Doll, 1982; Tanner & Tanner, 1975; Tyler, 1949)
Description of educational and related services to be provided and extent of participation with nonhandicapped children	Selection, organization, and sequencing of learning activities (Doll, 1982; Tanner & Tanner, 1975; Tyler, 1949)
Statement of projected dates for initiation and duration of services	———
Description of evaluation procedures	Evaluation of outcomes (Doll, 1982; Tanner & Tanner, 1975; Tyler, 1949)

In practice, the IEP functions as a curriculum design guide for children with disabilities. Although an IEP specifies an educational program for a single individual, the IEP is structured in such a way as to incorporate virtually all of the most commonly advocated principles of sound curriculum design, as illustrated in Table 6-1. As shown in the table, there is striking overlap between the mandated guidelines for IEP development and the recommended elements of sound curriculum design that were discussed in Chapter 5.

In the remaining sections of this chapter, the IEP process and each of the components of the IEP are examined in light of their role in the design of individualized instructional programs for people with mental retardation. In the final section, recommendations for practice are offered.

The IEP Process

Participatory decision making has been a long-standing ideal of government in the United States. This refers to the right of those affected by the decisions of a public agency to participate in those decisions (Turnbull & Turnbull, 1982). For many years, programming decisions for children with disabilities fell far short of this ideal, with most decisions being made unilaterally by school personnel and other professionals. Parents, as many of them have eloquently pointed out, were rarely consulted (Turnbull & Turnbull, 1985). Since the passage of PL94–142, parents have been recognized as legitimate partners in the decision-making process. The law also encourages participation by the person with disabilities.

The IEP meeting, mandated by PL94–142, is the mechanism through which parents and professionals share in program decisions. The purpose of that meeting is to generate the written individualized educational program. The participants in the meeting make use of the information and recommendations of the evaluation and placement team to construct a detailed program plan. In practice, the IEP meeting can be anything from a constructive planning session to an empty ritual. Considerable time, effort, and good will are needed on the part of parents and professionals to fulfill the true potential of the IEP process. For example, frequent contact between home and school for the purpose of building rapport and a shared perspective can go a long way toward eliminating potential barriers to effective communication at IEP meetings. Educators continue to seek ways to make the IEP process a meaningful one that goes beyond mere compliance with the law (e.g., Heward & Orlansky, 1992; Strickland & Turnbull, 1990).

The rules and regulations pursuant to PL94–142 designate that the following persons must be present at the IEP conference: (1) a representative of the local education agency, other than the child's teacher, who is capable of supervising or providing special education; (2) the child's present teacher or receiving teacher, or both; (3) other specialists (e.g., nurse, speech therapist, physical therapist), if appropriate; (4) one or both parents; and (5) the child, if appropriate. In addition, if the child has just been evaluated for the first time, a member of the evaluation team, or other person knowledgeable about the evaluation procedures used with the child, must attend the IEP conference. At the request of either the agency or the parents, other individuals may also attend.

A clear emphasis upon active parent participation is reflected in PL94–142. It is stipulated that the parents must be informed, in their native language, of the time, date, location, and purpose of the IEP conference, as well as the names of the other participants. The meeting must be held at a time and place convenient to the parents. After at least three serious and documented unsuccessful attempts to involve the parents, the school may proceed with the meeting. In this event, the school must provide the parents with a copy of the IEP and information about the placement decision. Parent involvement programs that are sensitive to the real needs of parents can effectively increase the likelihood that parents will play a meaningful role in the IEP process (Turnbull, 1983). Turnbull and Turnbull (1990) have provided a variety of strategies aimed at fostering the development of effective partnerships between professionals and families of individuals with disabilities.

Components of the IEP

In this section, the five major components of the IEP that are mandated by PL94–142 are examined in light of some of the central issues and educational considerations involved in their implementation.

Statement of Present Levels of Educational Performance

PL94–142 clearly specifies the conditions and procedures for the required individual assessment of the educational needs of any child suspected of having a handicapping condition. Assessment procedures must not discriminate on the basis of cultural, ethnic, or handicapping differences. No single test may be used as the basis for determining a child's educational program; rather, assessment information must come from a variety of sources. Due process, safeguarding the rights of the children and their parents, must be followed throughout the assessment process. Children who are identified and placed must be reevaluated at least every three years (Fiscus & Mandell, 1983). The implications and implementation of the requirements of PL94–142 regarding assessment have already been discussed in some detail in Chapter 4.

Statement of Annual Goals and Short-Term Instructional Objectives

The IEP, as mandated by PL94–142, must contain a statement of both annual goals and short-term instructional objectives. These goals and objectives must be agreed upon at the IEP conference by teachers, parents, and other relevant individuals.

Selecting Goals and Objectives

Establishing a clear basis for the selection of goals and objectives is, perhaps, the essence of successful IEP development. The selection of an educational philosophy, usually in conjunction with a curriculum model, is a necessary starting point. The assumptions inherent in the curriculum models discussed in Chapter 5 generally serve as the basis for the selection of educational goals and objectives for individuals with mental retardation. In addition, the process of selecting these goals and objectives differs somewhat depending upon whether the curriculum model is universally-referenced, individually-referenced, or community-referenced. The eight case study examples introduced in Chapter 3 have been further developed in the present chapter to illustrate the selection and statement of a few of the long-term goals and short-term objectives that might be included in each student's IEP.

The Universally-Referenced Model.   As noted in Chapter 5, universally-referenced curricula are based upon some universal norm of learning or development. The developmental, academic, and process-training curriculum models fall into this category. In most of these models, the content and sequence of instruction is predetermined. Goal selection and individualization consist of determining where in the sequence a particular student falls and how much can be accomplished in a given year. Assessment usually consists of comparing the student to some universal developmental or academic yardstick to identify gaps and weaknesses. It focuses upon discrete skills in specified domains (e.g., language). The environment in which the individual will be expected to function is generally ignored in the assessment process (Sailor & Guess, 1983). The logic of a universally-referenced approach is most compelling when children are very young, have only mild disabilities, or both. For young children, even those with mental retardation, attainment of the major developmental milestones (e.g., grasping, sitting, walking) is usually accepted as a desirable goal. This universally-referenced basis for goal selection is reflected in the illustrative goals and objectives for the *Case Study of Alicia*, which were based on a developmental curriculum model.

CASE STUDY: Alicia (CA = 3–6, IQ = 20)

	Annual Goals	*Sample Short-Term Objectives*
Physical	Alicia will manipulate small objects with her hands.	While sitting upright in a supporting chair, Alicia will grasp a rattle from a tray directly in front of her on 7 out of 10 trials.
Self-Help	Alicia will drink from a cup independently.	When a cup is placed in her hands while she is sitting upright in a supporting chair, Alicia will bring the cup to her mouth without spilling on 5 out of 5 trials.
Language	Alicia will respond to simple verbal messages.	Upon hearing her name while sitting upright with support, Alicia will turn her head in the direction of the speaker on 9 out of 10 trials.
Cognitive	Alicia will search for an object where it was last seen.	When a toy that she is holding while supported in an upright position is hidden behind a screen, Alicia will look at the screen on 4 out of 5 trials.
Psycho-Social	Alicia will imitate an adult model.	After observing an adult touch a musical toy, Alicia, while supported in an upright position, will touch the toy within 5 seconds on 4 out of 5 trials.

For individuals with mild mental retardation, acquisition of the majority of the regular academic skill sequences may be a reasonable expectation as reflected in the illustrative goals and objectives for the *Case Study of Juan* and the *Case Study of Tanisha*. However, for older persons with severe or profound disabilities who have not yet attained all of the early developmental skills, the value of some of these developmental milestones may be questionable when compared to other skills of direct functional significance to the individual.

CASE STUDY: Juan (CA = 9–0, IQ = 55)

	Annual Goals	*Sample Short-Term Objectives*
Academic	1. Juan will solve verbal addition problems.	Given a single-digit verbal addition problem, Juan will say the correct answer on 3 out of 5 trials.

	2. Juan will read at the first grade level	Given a first grade basal reader, Juan will read one paragraph aloud with no more than 5 errors.
Social	Juan will request help with academic tasks as needed.	Given an unfamiliar addition problem, Juan will request help after unsuccessfully attempting the problem on 9 out of 10 trials
Physical	Juan will learn to swim	When instructed to float, Juan will float on his back for 10 seconds.
Cognitive	1. Juan will apply flexible problem-solving strategies on a variety of cognitive tasks.	When given a worksheet on the organization of dots, Juan will successfully complete 90% of the items within 10 minutes.
	2. Juan will produce simple graphics on the computer monitor.	Given a LOGO program loaded on the microcomputer, Juan will instruct the computer to draw a triangle on 2 out of 3 trials.

CASE STUDY: Tanisha (CA = 7–3, IQ = 58)

	Annual Goals	***Sample Short-Term Objectives***
Academic	1. Tanisha will count out any number of items between 1 and 20.	Given 5 items on the computer screen, Tanisha will press the correct number on 4 out of 5 trials.
	2. Tanisha will decode new words.	When presented with a new, one-syllable, printed word consisting of familiar letter sounds, Tanisha will say the word correctly on 4 out of 5 trials.
	3. Tanisha will print her full name.	When instructed to print her first name, Tanisha will print all of the letters legibly in the correct order on 9 out of 10 trials.
Social	Tanisha will stay in her seat unless given permission to leave it.	During reading period, Tanisha will ask permission before leaving her seat without exception on 4 out of 5 days.
Physical	Tanisha will play kickball.	When instructed to kick, Tanisha will kick the ball on 7 out of 10 trials.

The Individually-Referenced Model.   The individually-referenced approach has been offered as an alternative to the universally-referenced model, especially for adolescents and adults with severe and profound mental retardation. This approach is exemplified in the functional curriculum model advocated by Brown, Branston, Hamre-Nietupski, Pumpian, Certo, and Gruenewald (1979) and described in Chapter 5. Brown, Falvey, Vincent, Kaye, Johnson, Ferrara-Parrish, and Gruenewald (1980) have proposed a strategy for IEP goal selection that is compatible with individually-referenced models such as the functional model. Their strategy consists of six phases:

1. *A strategy for organizing curricular content.* The underlying premise of this approach to IEP development is that curricular content should be oriented toward the direct teaching of skills needed "to function as independently and productively as possible in the least restrictive current environment and subsequent community environment" (Brown et al., 1980, p. 203). They propose that five functionally-relevant domains be used as a basis for program organization: (1) the domestic domain; (2) the vocational domain; (3) the recreational/leisure domain; (4) the general-community-functioning domain; and (5) the inter-action-with-nonhandicapped-persons domain.

2. *Ecological inventory strategies.* It is recommended that the teacher gather information about the current and anticipated subsequent natural environments of each student. A framework for gathering this information, as described by Brown et al., 1979, consists of the following five steps: (1) identify the relevant curriculum domains; (2) determine relevant current and future environments within each domain for each student; (3) divide the environments into subenvironments; (4) delineate the activities within each subenvironment; and (5) specify the skills needed for participation in the maximum number of activities.

3. *Student-repertoire inventory strategies.* This process is aimed at determining the skills currently present in the student's repertoire (Brown et al., 1980). A sample strategy consisting of four steps is presented. First, the teacher should conduct an inventory to determine the skill sequences used by people without disabilities to perform a particular activity (e.g., making a "collect" telephone call). Second, the teacher should conduct another inventory, in either a natural or simulated environment, to identify skills in a particular sequence that the student with disabilities can already perform. Third, by comparing steps one and two, the skills missing from a particular student's repertoire can be determined. The fourth step involves the adaptation of materials, skill sequences, and environments to increase the possibilities for participation.

4. *Parent/guardian inventory strategies.* This strategy is predicated on the assumption that all parents or guardians have important information to contribute, and requires the establishment of a close working relationship with them. Brown et al. (1980) have suggested that this phase include at least four steps: (1) inform the parents or guardians of the identified domains and ask them to suggest additional domains or priorities within domains; (2) present delineated environments and subenvironments to the parents or guardians and solicit their input regarding possible additional environments; (3) discuss results of the student-repertoire inventory with the parents or guardians and solicit information from them on functioning, and possible adaptations in additional environments; and (4) secure any other potentially useful information the parents or guardians can provide.

5. *Strategies for putting curricular content in order of priority.* During this phase, priorities are assigned to curricular content. Brown et al. (1980) suggest that at least the following sixteen dimensions be considered in determining IEP priorities and goals: (1) teacher preferences; (2) administrator preferences; (3) ancillary staff preferences; (4) parent or guardian preferences; (5) student preferences; (6) unique student characteristics; (7) commercial-publisher preferences (as reflected in available teaching materials); (8) presumed logistical and practical realities; (9) the number of environments in which a skill is required; (10) the number of occurrences or the frequency with which a skill is required; (11) social significance or potential effect on social acceptability; (12) probability of skill acquisition; (13) minimization of physical risk; (14) functional nature of a skill; (15) chronological-age-appropriate nature of a skill; and (16) relevant research. These dimensions should be carefully considered in terms of the needs of a particular student. It is expected that different dimensions will need to be emphasized for different students. Except for the guiding theme of selecting curriculum content "to teach chronological-age-appropriate functional skills for application in the least restrictive environment," Brown et al. did not specify guidelines for setting priorities among the sixteen dimensions for an individual student.

6. *The design and implementation of instructional programs.* After a teacher has implemented the first five phases, the following sequence of components has been suggested for organizing the instructional interactions necessary to teach a new skill sequence: (1) a description of the selected skill sequence; (2) a statement of why it is important to teach that skill sequence to a particular student; (3) a description of the instructional strategies; (4) a description of the performance criteria; (5) a description of the instructional materials; and (6) a description of how student progress will be measured.

The Brown et al. approach offers a detailed framework for the development of individually-referenced instructional programs. Its application is recommended especially, but not exclusively, with adolescents and adults with severe and profound mental retardation. Goal selection based on a functional, individually-referenced model is illustrated by the *Case Study of Scott.* As noted earlier, the weakest element in the framework presented by Brown et al. (1980) is its failure to elaborate upon a clear, systematic approach for setting priorities in the process of goal selection. Although consideration of the sixteen specified dimensions may, indeed, enrich the instructional program, the teacher or the IEP committee may easily become overwhelmed in an effort to assign relative weights to these dimensions in the selection of goals for a particular student. Sailor and Guess (1983), building upon the work of Brown and his colleagues, have proposed the use of a *priority matrix* which deals directly with this problem.

Constructing a priority matrix requires the identification of *critical functions.* These critical functions are behaviors that are central to increasing an individual's ability to function independently in multiple environments. For example, performing household chores might be considered a critical function, while sorting cubes would most likely not be so considered. In the priority matrix, reproduced in Table 6-2, eight critical functions common to all students with disabilities are listed at the left of the matrix. Four environmental domains are specified across the top of the matrix. In setting instructional priorities, Sailor

CASE STUDY: Scott (CA = 18–0, IQ = 33)

	Annual Goals	*Sample Short-Term Objectives*
Domestic	Scott will perform household chores.	When presented with a full bag of groceries, Scott will put each item in its correct kitchen location without error within 10 minutes.
Vocational	Scott will travel independently to and from his job location.	When told, "Go to the hospital," Scott will take the correct bus to the hospital without error on 5 out of 5 trials.
Recreational/ Leisure	Scott will play volleyball.	When a volleyball is served to Scott, he will return it over the net on 1 out of 5 serves.
Community Functioning	Scott will order food at restaurants.	Upon hearing the instruction, "Order your lunch, Scott," Scott will order a Big Mac, coke, and french fries at McDonald's without error on 5 out of 5 days.
Interaction with Non- handicapped Persons	Scott will interact appropriately with co-workers.	At his work-study site, Scott will ask work-related questions to coworkers in a way that is clearly understood on 5 out of 5 trials.

and Guess recommend first teaching those skills that represent critical functions in multiple environments and that increase the student's independence in those enviornments. Sailor and Guess also suggest that the use of a series of questions, originally presented by Brown, Branston-McClean, Baumgart, Vincent, Falvey, and Schroeder (1979), can aid in determining priorities. The answers to these questions can help determine which critical functions to match with environmental domains in setting educational goals:

1. What are the *present* environments available to the student for instruction; that is, which environmental domains on the matrix?
2. What are potential future environments for this student in the following year?
3. What are the requirements of these environments as a function of the student's *chronological age*?
4. What does this student need to assist *sensory* efficiency?
5. What does this student need to assist *motor movement* efficiency?
6. What does this student need to assist *communication* (Sailor & Guess, 1983, p. 110)?

A detailed illustration of the application of the priority matrix in the selection of instructional goals for a particular student is provided by Sailor and Guess (1983).

TABLE 6-2   Priority Matrix for Goal Selection

Critical Functions	Environmental Domains			
	School	Vocational	Domestic	Community
Eating				
Toileting				
Mobility				
Expressive Communication				
Receptive Communication				
Hygiene/ Appearance				
Recreation/Leisure				
Horizontal Social Interactions				

Adapted from Wayne Sailor and Doug Guess *Severely Handicapped Students: An Instructional Design.* Copyright 1983 by Houghton Mifflin Company. Used with permission.

The strategies proposed by Brown and his colleagues and Sailor and Guess, although developed particularly for young adults with severe disabilities, probably come very close to representing an ideal set of procedures for individualizing instruction for anyone with mental retardation. However, as even Brown et al. (1980) have acknowledged, "the IEP process suggested will probably require more time, effort, etc., than is typically expended by teachers and others" (Brown et al., 1980, pp. 214–215). Because the individually-referenced approach is so time-consuming, the fiscal constraints and staff-shortages of today's schools may preclude its full application in many educational settings. Wilcox and Bellamy (1982) developed the community-referenced model in response to some of these concerns.

The Community-Referenced Model.   The community-referenced model, although devised for high school students with severe disabilities, is potentially applicable to individuals at any age and with any level of mental retardation. Like the individually-referenced model, the community-referenced model is not based upon traditional developmental or academic sequences. Instead, the selection of instructional goals is based on the demands of adult functioning in the local community. This orientation was prompted by the observation that the adult behaviors required for independent functioning differ for individuals in different parts of the country. In a 1980 study by Fischer, Haney, and David (cited by Wilcox & Bellamy, 1982), subjects with varied backgrounds were asked to rank the priority of competencies needed for success in adult life. Priority rankings of competencies varied as a function of "rural/urban situation, geographic region, ethnic background, employment status, and income" (Wilcox & Bellamy, 1982, p. 31). An obvious implication of these findings is that in one community it may be relevant to prepare students for farm work, whereas in another, training in assembling electronics parts may be more relevant. The environmental inventory approach recommended by Wilcox and Bellamy may be viewed as an extension of the work of Brown and his colleagues. However, the Wilcox and Bellamy approach is responsive to the fact that the cost of an entirely individually-referenced strategy may be prohibitive. Wilcox and Bellamy argue that the community-referenced approach represents a balance between expensive individually-referenced curricula and a potentially inappropriate universally-referenced curriculum. Rather than being based on predetermined sequences as in the universally-based model, decisions about goals and priorities in the community-based model are guided by the values of parents, teachers, and students in a particular setting.

Wilcox and Bellamy recommended a three-step process for developing locally-referenced curricula: (1) catalog local opportunities; (2) select activity objectives for individual students; and (3) design instructional programs for target activities. The catalog of local opportunities is intended to consist of a list of activities that could enhance "productivity, participation, or independence" in the daily lives of individuals with mental retardation (Wilcox & Bellamy, 1982, p. 36). The organizational framework for this catalog, proposed by Wilcox and Bellamy, is reproduced in Table 6-3. Although admittedly arbitrary, an attempt has been made to organize activities that reflect meaningful aspects of adult life along two dimensions, domains of functioning and environments. The cells of the matrix are intended to be filled with activities appropriate to a particular community. Suggested strategies for gathering this information, including observation,

TABLE 6-3   Catalog of Local Opportunities Matrix for Community-Referenced Programs

	Domain		
Environment	**Vocational**	**Independent Living**	**Leisure**
Home			
School			
Community			

Adapted from Wilcox, B. and Bellamy, G. T., 1982, *Design of high school programs for severely handicapped students*. Baltimore: Brookes.

interviews, and logical analysis, are described by Wilcox and Bellamy (1982). The next step in the process is to make value-based decisions in selecting those activities to be targeted for a particular individual. Finally, using the catalog of opportunities and selected activities, the instructional program may be developed. The *Case Study of Karen* illustrates goal-selection, within the Community Environment only, based on a community-referenced approach. Tony's goals and objectives are also based on the community-referenced approach (see the *Case Study of Tony*). Each of the three domains is represented (e.g., vocational, leisure, and independent living), and learning activities were selected from the school and community environments. Notice that what is being taught to Tony is the management and mastery of *activities*, such as renting a video. Discrete skills such as counting change, printing one's name, and reading are taught as integral components of such activities.

Stating Goals and Objectives

The selection of appropriate goals and objectives is only a first step. It is essential that these goals and objectives be stated in a form that can meet the requirements of the IEP and enhance the instructional process. Each IEP is required to include a statement of both annual goals and short-term instructional objectives.

Annual Goals.   Annual goals are intended to describe what a particular child can be expected to accomplish in an educational program within one calendar year (Fiscus & Mandell, 1983). Sailor and Guess (1983) have recommended the specification of from four to six annual educational goals for students with severe disabilities. In many instances, how-

---

CASE STUDY: Karen (CA = 15–1, IQ = 47)

	Annual Goals	*Sample Short-Term Objectives*
Vocational	Karen will acquire skills appropriate for jobs in the food service industry.	When asked to fill the sink for dishwashing, Karen will fill the sink to the halfway point with warm water without error on 9 out of 10 trials.
Independent Living	1. Karen will place local telephone calls.	Given a written telephone number, Karen will push the correct buttons on the telephone without error on 4 out of 5 trials.
	2. Karen will safely cross a busy street at a traffic light.	Given a computer-simulation of a busy street corner with a traffic light, Karen will press the correct YES/NO response button on the computer on 10 out of 10 trials.
Leisure	Karen will buy movie tickets.	Upon arriving at the movie box office, Karen will successfully purchase a ticket for her preferred show without error on 5 out of 5 trials.

CASE STUDY: Tony (CA = 16–0, IQ = 65)

	Annual Goal	*Sample Short-Term Objectives*
Employment	Tony will construct four birdhouses per contract with the local hardware store.	After his teacher positions the wood at the proper angle, Tony will accurately cut out all pieces of the birdhouses 4 out of 5 times.
Leisure	Tony will rent a video from the local video store.	Upon receiving the video from the clerk, Tony will count out the correct amount of money to pay for his video 5 out of 5 times.
Community Living	Tony will read the news-paper for useful infor-mation.	Upon delivery of the newspaper, Tony will independently and without error locate the page of the weather forecast by the front-page index for 5 consecutive days.

ever, it may be appropriate to specify a larger number of goals. An educational goal has been conceptualized as "a specific functional skill or cluster of skills that the student should be able to attain in one year under existing instructional conditions and that will significantly enhance the student's progress toward reduced dependency upon adult caretakers" (Sailor & Guess, 1983, p. 102). This view emphasizes the description of a discrete skill or skill cluster as a framework for the specification of a "*sequence* of short-term instructional objectives that will culminate in some real act of greater independence" (Sailor & Guess, 1983, p. 103). This sequence should consist of the steps necessary for acquisition of a skill or skill cluster judged by the IEP committee to be important to the individual. Although there is some variability in the recommended form for stating annual goals, general guidelines have been provided by Fiscus and Mandell (1983) and are as follows:

A. *Annual goals should be based on assessment data.* The assessment process should be utilized to determine the specific needs of the individual.

B. *Annual goals should reflect past achievements and current performance.* Examination of an individual's past achievements should be used to gather information about the individual's rate of mastery of previous skills. This information is invaluable in estimating how much can reasonably be accomplished in one year.

C. *Annual goals should be considered high-priority items by members of the IEP team.* The varied perspectives of the members of the IEP committee are intended to insure that the annual goals will not be irrelevant to the needs of the individual.

D. *Annual goals should include the cognitive, psychomotor, and affective domains as well as deal with vocational and self-help skills when applicable.* The specific areas to be emphasized continue to be the focus of debate. However, the essence of this statement is that annual goals should span a number of areas.

Short-Term Objectives.   Short-term objectives, the "measurable intermediate steps between the present levels of performance and the annual goals" (United States Department of Education, 1980, as cited by Fiscus & Mandell, 1983, p. 188), have been identified as key components of the instructional process. Research has shown that the teacher's ability to clearly specify short-term objectives can be a major determinant of the success of instruction (Valletutti & Salpino, 1979). Although precisely stated short-term objectives may be viewed as the fulcrum of the IEP, concern about how to state objectives is not unique to special education. Guidelines for the statement of instructionally useful short-term objectives came, initially, from the field of educational measurement and evaluation (e.g., Payne, 1974). The value of these guidelines, however, was quickly appreciated in the field of special education. Since the passage of PL94–142, clearly stated short-term objectives have become a sine qua non of the individualized program for every child classified as handicapped. A good general introduction to the specification of instructional, or behavioral, short-term objectives is provided in a classic programmed text, first published by Mager in 1962, and revised in 1975. Most guidelines for writing instructional objectives in special education have been based upon Mager's criteria. According to Mager, "an objective describes an intended *result* of instruction, rather than the *process* of instruction itself" (Mager, 1975, p. 5). To be useful, an objective must clearly communicate the instructional intent of the writer, and have the following three characteristics:

A. *Performance* (*or Behavior*). An objective must specify, in behavioral terms, precisely what the learner is expected to *do*. The key to a precise specification of performance is selection of a verb that is open to few, as opposed to many, interpretations (e.g., to write, to point to, to kick). Mager indicated that either overt or covert behaviors are acceptable as long as the covert behavior (e.g., addition) is assessable in terms of an indicator behavior (e.g., a correct written solution to the problem). Although this view has been accepted by some educators, it is generally preferable for the sake of clarity to state the objective in terms of an observable behavior. Even the most complex cognitive skill can be assessed only in terms of observable behavior. Stating the objective in terms of observable behavior also avoids any ambiguity stemming from the fact that many cognitive skills (e.g., problem solving) can be measured in terms of more than one observable behavior (e.g., accuracy or response latency).

B. *Conditions*. An objective must clearly specify the conditions under which the behavior is to occur. Conditions may include *givens* (e.g., Given five written addition problems . . .) or *limitations* (e.g., With physical prompting . . .) under which the behavior is to occur (Fiscus & Mandell, 1983).

C. *Criteria*. An objective must specify the level of acceptable performance. This is the standard by which attainment of the objective is measured. Criteria may be expressed in terms of speed (e.g., within 5 minutes), accuracy (e.g., 9 out of 10 correct), or quality (e.g., drinking from a cup without spilling).

Examples of short-term objectives for a variety of functional skills are provided for the *Case Study of Sonia* and the *Case Study of Norman*.

CASE STUDY: Sonia (CA = 7–7, IQ < 15)

	Annual Goals	*Sample Short-Term Objectives*
Self-Help: Toileting	Sonia will eliminate only in the toilet.	Given only a verbal cue, Sonia will sit on the toilet 6 times per day for 10 consecutive school days.
Self-Help: Dressing	Sonia will remove her coat without assistance.	After her coat has been unzipped and pulled to the elbows of both arms, Sonia will pull her coat entirely off both arms when given a gestural cue for 5 consecutive sessions.
Self-Help: Eating	Sonia will drink independently from a glass.	Given a physical prompt (teacher's hand supporting her wrist), Sonia will place her glass on the table after drinking, without dropping the glass or spilling its contents, for 5 consecutive lunches.
Receptive Language	Sonia will identify articles commonly used during hygiene.	Given a choice of towel, comb, or soap, Sonia will pick up the comb, upon request, for 5 consecutive sessions.

CASE STUDY: Norman (CA = 5–5, IQ = 64)

	Annual Goals	*Sample Short-Term Objectives*
Social	Norman will demonstrate cooperative behavior with peers during group activities.	When asked to do so, Norman will pass food from the person seated on his right to the person seated on his left, for 10 consecutive snack breaks at school.
Self-Help	Norman will independently eat with spoon and fork.	When handed a spoon, Norman will hold it between his thumb and index finger to scoop food for 10 consecutive lunches.
Academic	Norman will read, count, and name the values of numbers 1 through 10.	When presented with 5 cards, each containing a printed number between 1 and 5, Norman will achieve 100 percent accuracy per session for 5 consecutive sessions in naming the number.

Statement of the Specific Educational Services and the Extent to which the Child Will Participate in Regular Educational Programs

PL94–142 specifies that each child classified as handicapped should be provided with "a free appropriate public education which emphasizes special education and related services designed to meet their unique needs." Special education refers to instruction specially designed to meet the unique needs of a child with one or more handicapping conditions and may include classroom instruction, specialized physical education, home instruction, and instruction in hospitals and institutions. The term, related services, is defined as follows:

> transportation, and such developmental, corrective, and other supportive services (including speech pathology and audiology, psychological services, physical and occupational therapy, recreation, and medical and counseling services, except that such medical services shall be for diagnostic and evaluation purposes only) as may be required to assist a handicapped child to benefit from special education, and includes the early identification and assessment of handicapping conditions in children (PL94–142, Sec. 19, 1975).

It is in this component of the IEP that the details of the instructional program are specified. Two important aspects of the instructional program, the specification of instructional strategies and placement in the least restrictive environment, are discussed in Chapters 7 and 8, respectively. The third key aspect, curriculum, has been discussed in Chapter 5.

Statement of Projected Dates for Initiation and Duration of Services

The standard IEP is written in terms of one calendar year. The inclusion of specific dates makes possible clear accountability for the attainment of goals and objectives.

Statement of Objective Criteria and Evaluation Design

PL94–142 clearly requires the objective evaluation of the effectiveness of each IEP. It stipulates that the IEP should include "appropriate objective criteria and evaluation procedures and schedules for determining, on at least an annual basis, whether instructional objectives are being achieved" (PL94–142, Sec. 4, 1975). As discussed earlier, "objective criteria" are an integral part of properly stated instructional objectives, which should constitute the core of any well-constructed IEP. However, the specification of appropriate "evaluation procedures and schedules" has been more problematic.

In practice, evaluation has often meant little more than gathering information on posttest performance which is then compared with initial performance to determine the degree of progress. However, as Dunst (1979) has pointed out, there are at least two important aspects of evaluation. First, as most educators would agree, it is essential to assess the degree to which goals and objectives have been attained. Second, although this aspect is often ignored, it is just as essential to determine the cause of the observed outcomes. While gathering performance data is an appropriate way to assess the attainment of goals and objectives, determining the cause of any change requires the careful application of an evaluation design calculated to rule out alternative explanations for the change.

Of the many well-controlled evaluation designs that are available for application to educational problems, single-subject designs lend themselves most readily to the evaluation of the effectiveness of the components of an IEP. At least three widely used single-subject designs are well-suited to this purpose: (1) the reversal (or withdrawal) design; (2) the multiple baseline design; and (3) the changing criterion design. Refer to Chapter 7 for descriptions and applications of each of these designs.

Recommendations

The focus of the present chapter has been upon the individualized education program. The IEP is a central requirement of PL94–142. In this chapter, discussion has been limited to the universal aspects of IEP development covered by the federal legislation. In actual practice, the steps of IEP development are further delineated by policies and procedures set forth in state plans and local regulations. Each school district has its own IEP forms and guidelines with which the new teacher will need to become familiar. However, these local variations will not generally alter the core features of the federally mandated IEP. Some general recommendations based on the material discussed in this chapter are as follows:

1. The key to the success of the IEP process is *meaningful* participation by all participants in the IEP Conference. This requires careful preliminary efforts to make sure that all participants are well-prepared to play an effective role in the decision-making process.

2. Although the selection of long-term, annual goals is necessarily a value-based process, the selection of goals may be aided by the explicit adoption of one of the following frameworks:

 (a) The *universally-referenced* framework is most readily applicable as a basis for early educational programming aimed at minimizing developmental delays in young children at all levels of mental retardation. In addition, a universally-referenced framework emphasizing academic content is appropriate for many school-age children with mild or moderate mental retardation.

 (b) The *individually-referenced* framework, although developed for adults with severe and profound mental retardation, may be used as a basis for designing individualized programs for individuals of any age and functioning level. However, the advantage of using this approach increases with age and severity of mental retardation.

 (c) The *community-referenced* framework, developed for high school-aged individuals with severe disabilities, can fruitfully be applied with individuals with mental retardation at any functioning level. Both the individual- and community-referenced frameworks are sensitive to the demands of the environment in which the individual is expected to function. The community-referenced approach offers the additional advantage of being less demanding of teacher time and resources.

3. In stating annual goals, keep in mind that they should: (a) be based on assessment data; (b) reflect past and current performance; (c) be considered high-priority items; and (d) span several curriculum areas.

4. Short-term instructional objectives should be stated so that they include the following clearly specified elements: (a) behavior; (b) conditions; and (c) criteria.

5. The effectiveness of each IEP must be evaluated from both of the following perspectives: (a) the degree to which goals and objectives have been attained; and (b) the cause of these changes. The single-subject designs, discussed in Chapter 7, are ideally suited to these purposes.

References

Brown, L., Branston, M. B., Hamre-Nietupski, S., Pumpian, I., Certo, N., & Gruenewald, L. (1979). A strategy for developing chronological-age-appropriate and functional curricular content for severely handicapped adolescents and young adults. *Journal of Special Education, 13,* 81–90.

Brown, L., Branston-McClean, M. B., Baumgart, D., Vincent, L., Falvey, M., & Schroeder, J. (1979). Utilizing characteristics of current and subsequent least restrictive environments in the development of curricular content for severely handicapped students. *AAESPH Review, 4,* 407–424.

Brown, L., Falvey, M., Vincent, L., Kaye, N., Johnson, F., Ferrara-Parrish, P., & Gruenewald, L. (1980). Strategies for generating comprehensive, longitudinal and chronological-age-appropriate individualized educational programs for adolescent and young-adult severely handicapped students. *Journal of Special Education, 14,* 199–215.

Doll, R. C. (1982). *Curriculum improvement: Decision-making and process* (5th ed.). Boston: Allyn & Bacon.

Dunst, C. J. (1979). Program evaluation and the Education for All Handicapped Children Act. *Exceptional Children, 46,* 24–31.

Fiscus, E. D. & Mandell, C. J. (1983). *Developing individualized education programs.* St. Paul: West Publishing Company.

Heward, W. L., & Orlansky, M. D. (1992). *Exceptional children* (4th ed.). New York: Macmillan.

Mager, R. F. (1975). *Preparing instructional objectives* (2nd ed.). Belmont, CA: Pitman Management and Training.

Payne, D. A. (1974). *Curriculum evaluation.* Lexington, MA: Heath.

Sailor, W. & Guess, D. (1983). *Severely handicapped students: An instructional design.* Boston: Houghton Mifflin.

Strickland, B. B. & Turnbull, A. P. (1990). *Developing and implementing individualized education programs* (3rd ed.). Columbus, OH: Merrill.

Tanner, D. & Tanner, L. N. (1975). *Curriculum development.* New York: Macmillan.

Turnbull, A. P. (1983). Parent professional interactions. In M. E. Snell (Ed.), *Systematic instruction of the moderately and severely handicapped* (2nd ed.). Columbus, OH: Merrill.

Turnbull, A. P. & Turnbull, H. R. (1990). *Families, professionals, and exceptionality: A special partnership* (2nd ed.). Columbus, OH: Merrill.

Turnbull, A. P. & Turnbull, H. R. (1985). *Parents speak out: Then and now* (2nd ed.). Columbus, OH: Merrill.

Turnbull, H. R. & Turnbull, A. P. (1982). *Free appropriate public education: Law and implementation.* Denver: Love.

Tyler, R. W. (1949). *Basic principles of curriculum and instruction.* Chicago: The University of Chicago Press.

Valletutti, P. J. & Salpino, A. O. (1979). *Individualizing educational objectives and programs.* Baltimore: University Park Press.

Wilcox, B. & Bellamy, G. T. (1982). *Design of high school programs for severely handicapped students.* Baltimore: Brookes.

Chapter 7

Foundations of Instruction

In 1966, when Maria was a year old, she was placed in an institution for persons with mental retardation and labeled "custodial." That label meant that she was considered unteachable and would be ineligible for any instructional programs. Her parents were told that she would require life-long residential care. In 1976, one year after the passage of the Education for All Handicapped Children Act (PL94–142), Maria was deinstitutionalized at the age of 11 and sent back to live at home with her family. For the next 10 years, she attended a public school program for students with severe mental retardation. In 1986, upon completion of her school program at the age of 21, Maria could feed, dress, and groom herself independently. She could read and write her name and several other "survival" words. She had also mastered some basic numerical skills, including using coins to make a telephone call and dialing her home phone number. With the assistance of the transition and supported employment services in her school and community, Maria obtained employment at a fast food restaurant. Now, at the age of 29, she has been successfully employed at the same job for eight years. Maria lives in a supported apartment with two friends and she is an enthusiastic participant in community activities.

What happened between 1966 and now to account for the massive discrepancy between Maria's prognosis and her accomplishments? Clearly, the passage of PL94–142 in 1975, entitling *all* children with handicaps to a free, appropriate education, was a major force in changing the lives of individuals like Maria. The law itself was a reflection of improved attitudes toward persons with disabilities and a societal acknowledgement of their right to education. However, it is the premise of this chapter that the dramatic expansion of legal rights and societal opportunities embodied in the law was largely enabled by the development, beginning in the 1960s, of a cadre of powerful instructional strategies. Though many of the instructional strategies described in this chapter were developed specifically for individuals with severe and profound mental retardation, the basic principles underlying those strategies are the cornerstones of effective instruction for all children.

In Chapter 5, instructional strategies were defined to include teaching methods, behavior management techniques, and the arrangement of classroom and community environments. The present chapter concentrates upon the application of teaching methods and behavior management techniques, while environmental arrangements are covered in Chapter 8. This chapter introduces some of the basic principles upon which a complex and powerful technology of instruction has been built (e.g., Englert, Tarrant, & Mariage, 1992; Greer, 1991). Prospective teachers should follow up this conceptual introduction with one or more courses and practicum experiences designed to develop hands-on proficiency in the delivery of effective instruction to students with mental retardation.

Teaching methods are covered in the first part of this chapter, with an emphasis on the basic behavior increase techniques that constitute the underpinnings of effective instruction. The second part of this chapter focuses on specific techniques for managing behavior, including behavior decrease operations. The third part provides a more global discussion of the application of some comprehensive instructional systems. The fourth part of this chapter discusses how to insure the effectiveness of instructional interventions. The final section presents recommendations.

Instructional Strategies

In the selection of instructional strategies, it is important to consider at least four distinct stages of learning: *acquisition*, *proficiency*, *maintenance*, and *generalization*. *Acquisition* refers to the initial learning of new skills not previously in the student's repertoire. *Proficiency*, also called mastery or fluency, is the stage following acquisition in which the speed of performance increases to the point where the behavior appears to be automatic. For example, a person who has just learned to type may be accurate, but slow and uncoordinated. However, after practicing this skill for a period of time, the person's performance is likely to become smoother and much more rapid. *Maintenance* refers to the continued application of a skill or strategy over time under identical task conditions, but with changed materials (Blackman & Lin, 1984). For example, maintenance would be demonstrated if a student, tested six months after acquisition, continued to use a particular strategy to solve a specific type of arithmetic word problem which contained number combinations different from those used during acquisition. *Generalization* is the performance of a learned skill or strategy, or some modification of it, in a new situation. The task structure, task demands, task context, or some combination of these variables may be significantly altered (Blackman & Lin, 1984). If the previously mentioned student applied a modified version of the acquired strategy to a new problem type, he or she would be demonstrating generalization. Because the appropriateness of particular instructional strategies depends on the stage of learning, the discussion of these techniques is divided into two sections. In the first section, strategies that are appropriate for use during the acquisition and proficiency stages are discussed. In the second section, strategies that facilitate maintenance and generalization are described.

Acquisition and Proficiency: Behavior Increase Techniques

Effective strategies for the acquisition and proficiency stages of learning typically include three general components: an analysis of the task to be performed, the manipulation of antecedent conditions, and the manipulation of the consequences of the behavior. In the following sections, specific strategies within these three general categories are discussed.

Task Analysis

One strategy that has found broad application in the instruction of individuals with mental retardation is task analysis. Task analysis consists of dividing a complex task into its component steps. The technique has its roots in industry, where it has been used to determine the best, or most efficient, way to perform an industrial task. In the education and training of people with mental retardation, this approach has been adapted to enable step-by-step instruction in the performance of a complex task. In the vocational area, the application of this approach has made it possible for workers with mental retardation to achieve proficiency with highly complex assembly tasks, such as the assembly of bicycle brakes (Gold, 1976) and electronics circuit boards (Boles, Bellamy, Horner, & Mank, 1984). The approach has also facilitated the instruction of the complex chains of behavior which constitute many of the activities of daily living (e.g., using the toilet, brushing teeth, dressing, using a washing machine).

Although writing a task analysis is usually a simple, straightforward procedure, the following guidelines may be helpful:

1. Before attempting to write a task analysis, either observe someone perform the task or perform the task yourself.
2. Write each step in terms of observable, student behavior.
3. Write each step as a simple, declarative sentence, with a single verb depicting a single action.
4. Write steps that are approximately equal in difficulty.
5. Write steps in the order in which the task will be performed.
6. Construct a data recording form for each task analysis.

A sample task analysis and recording form, based upon one of Scott's behavioral objectives, is presented in the *Case Study of Scott.*

In addition to following the above guidelines, it is important to consider the number and size of the steps to be included in a task analysis. Although industrial applications of task analysis generally assume that there is one optimal way to perform a task, this assumption has not prevailed in special education. In fact, the question of whether ease of acquisition is related to the number and size of steps has become a focus of debate. The positions taken in this debate, well summarized by Crist, Walls, and Haught (1984), have ranged from acceptance of a single best task analysis for each task to the recommendation that a unique task analysis be written to match the characteristics of each learner.

To help resolve the issue, Crist et al. (1984) conducted a research study on the effects of variations in the number of steps in a task analysis. In their study, three groups of adults, classified as having mild, moderate, or severe mental retardation, were taught to assemble three complex pieces of machinery: a lawn mower engine, an electric drill, and a carburetor. Each group was taught to perform each of these tasks using a task analysis with one of the following levels of specificity: 28 steps, 14 steps, or 7 steps. Results of the study showed that the total amount of time needed for training did not differ across the three levels of task analysis specificity. However, fewer errors were made during training using the long (28 steps) and medium (14 steps) task analyses than using the short (7 steps) task analysis. This difference was especially pronounced for individuals with severe mental retardation. Thus, there is at least some evidence to support the contention that as severity of mental retardation increases it may be beneficial to break down a task into many very small steps rather than fewer large steps. If a task is extremely complex, it may be necessary to break it down into several simpler tasks before subjecting it to task analysis. On the other hand, it goes without saying that if a task is very simple, the task may be taught without performing task analysis at all.

Although task analysis has most often been used to teach concrete tasks to people with severe or profound mental retardation, similar principles have been used to break down complex cognitive tasks and strategies into teachable steps. Most of this research has involved teaching people with mild mental retardation and learning disabilities to use deliberate strategies in order to enhance their performance of cognitive tasks involving memory, comprehension, and problem solving (Blackman & Lin, 1984; Masters & Mori, 1986).

CASE STUDY: Scott (CA = 18–0, IQ = 33)

Sample Task Analysis and Recording Form

Student *Scott*   Date *December 7–9, 1992*

Short-Term Objective *Upon hearing the instruction, "Order your lunch, Scott," Scott will*

order a Big Mac, a coke, and french fries at McDonald's, without error, on 5 out of 5

days.

Steps	Days				
	1	2	3	4	5
1. Take place at end of line.					
2. Step forward one step at a time as the line moves toward the counter.					
3. Move up to counter.					
4. Establish eye contact with counter person.					
5. Say: "I want to order a Big Mac, a small coke, and small fries to eat here."					
6. When the cost is stated by the counter person, take $5 bill from wallet.					
7. Give $5 to counter person.					
8. Take change.					
9. Put change in wallet.					
10. Take straw.					
11. Take napkin.					
12. When all three items are on tray, take tray.					
13. Walk to empty table.					
14. Sit at table.					
15. Eat lunch.					

RECORDING KEY: Correct   +

                    Incorrect   –

Antecedent Approaches

Most behavior increase and behavior decrease techniques involve manipulating the consequences of behavior. However, before the consequences can be manipulated, a behavior must occur. In order to elicit a behavior, it may be necessary to manipulate the antecedents, or the events that precede, that behavior. One way of doing this is through the use of prompts. Most prompts fall into one or more of the following three categories: *physical prompts*, *verbal instructions*, or *modeling*. *Physical prompts* consist of providing as much physical guidance and assistance as is needed to get the student to perform the task. For example, one way to teach a child to hit a ball with a baseball bat is to hold the bat with the child so that the child can get the feel of how to hit the ball with it. *Verbal instructions* consist of verbally telling the student what to do. These instructions may be as simple as telling the child to hit the ball, or they may consist of complex step-by-step descriptions of the behavior to be learned. It is important to keep in mind, however, that the lower the functioning level of the student, the simpler the verbal instructions must be. Thus, the receptive language ability of the student may place severe restrictions on the extent to which verbal instructions may be used to elicit new behaviors. Finally, *modeling*, or demonstration, is a useful technique for eliciting new behaviors in students at all functioning levels. As long as a student shows some imitative behavior, modeling may be an effective teaching tool. For example, many children learn to swing a baseball bat simply by imitating the actions of others.

The above three approaches may be used in combination as well as singly. Several prompt hierarchies have been developed which specify sequences of prompt levels useful for accomplishing certain instructional goals. The systems of *graduated guidance* and *least prompts* are two widely used types of prompt hierarchies (Snell, 1993). Of these two systems, the graduated guidance hierarchy is more useful for getting a totally new behavior to occur for the first time. Graduated guidance usually begins with full physical assistance. This assistance is then gradually faded, and only as much physical and/or verbal assistance is given as is necessary until the student is able to perform the task independently. In the *Case Study of Alicia*, an example is provided of how the graduated guidance method could be employed to teach Alicia to drink from a cup.

The least prompts method, on the other hand, begins with a minimal prompt and then provides increasing amounts of assistance as needed to get the student to perform the task. Usually, the level of assistance provided progresses from: (1) verbal instructions only; to (2) verbal instructions with modeling; to (3) verbal instructions with physical assistance. This method allows the student to perform as much of the task as possible without assistance and is most useful for eliciting a behavior already in the student's repertoire. The use of the least prompts method is illustrated in the *Case Study of Juan*.

Although prompts may be needed to elicit a new or infrequently occurring behavior, the goal of most instruction is to teach the student to perform the behavior independently under natural conditions. Ultimately, stimulus control of the behavior must be transferred from the prompting stimulus to a discriminative stimulus (S^D)—that is, a stimulus which signals the availability of reinforcement. S^Ds may be either artificially established conditions (e.g., a flashing light) or conditions which occur naturally in the environment (e.g., the presence of a cup of milk on the table). Ideally, prompts should be used only in the early stages of training. They should then be faded so that the student performs the behavior independently in the presence of an appropriate, naturally occurring S^D.

CASE STUDY: Alicia (CA = 3–6, IQ = 20)

Sample Application of Graduated Guidance Method of Prompting

Student *Alicia*   Date *November 23, 1992*

Short-Term Objective *When a cup is placed in her hands while she is sitting upright in a supporting chair, Alicia will bring the cup to her mouth without spilling on 5 out of 5 trials.*

Prompt Sequence

1. While saying, "Drink the milk," Alicia's teacher places her hand over Alicia's hand and helps her guide the cup to her mouth.
2. While saying, "Drink the milk," Alicia's teacher places her hand lightly on Alicia's wrist and guides the cup to her mouth.
3. While saying, "Drink the milk," Alicia's teacher places her hand lightly on Alicia's forearm and guides the cup toward her mouth.
4. While saying, "Drink the milk," Alicia's teacher places her hand lightly on Alicia's elbow and guides the cup toward her mouth.
5. While saying, "Drink the milk," Alicia's teacher places her hand lightly on Alicia's shoulder and gently guides her to bring the cup to her mouth.
6. Alicia's teacher instructs Alicia to "Drink the milk," with no physical prompts.

CRITERION: The teacher should begin with step one and proceed to each subsequent step only after the prior step has been performed correctly three times in a row.

CASE STUDY: Juan (CA = 9–0, IQ = 55)

Sample Application of Least Prompts Method of Prompting

Student *Juan*   Date *November 30, 1992*

Short-Term Objective *When instructed to float, Juan will float on his back for 10 seconds.*

Prompt Sequence

1. Juan's teacher verbally instructs Juan by saying, "Float on your back, Juan," with no other physical or verbal prompts.
2. If Juan does not respond, or if he performs the task incorrectly, Juan's teacher repeats, "Float on your back, Juan," followed by more specific verbal prompts, such as "Spread your arms" or "Hold your legs out straight."
3. If Juan still does not respond, or if he performs the task incorrectly, Juan's teacher demonstrates the task while Juan watches, then repeats the instruction to Juan.
4. If Juan still does not respond, or if he performs the task incorrectly, Juan's teacher provides as much physical assistance as Juan needs in order to perform the task.

PROCEDURE: On each trial, the teacher should proceed to the minimum prompt level needed to enable Juan to perform the task correctly.

Consequence Approaches

Once a behavior has been acquired by a student, the likelihood and frequency of its occurrence will be determined by its consequences. The consequences of a behavior are most precisely described in terms of the principles of reinforcement. *Positive reinforcement* is defined as an event the presentation of which is associated with an increase in the occurrence of a target behavior. For example, praising a child each time he or she uses a napkin during a meal may function as a positive reinforcer, but only if the praise is associated with an increase in napkin use. Positive reinforcement is an extremely powerful teaching tool with a wide range of applications. As in the above example, positive reinforcement may be used to increase the frequency of a behavior that is already present in a student's repertoire (e.g., use of a napkin). It may also be used to encourage successive approximations of a behavior during the early stages of its acquisition. This latter process, called "shaping," involves initially reinforcing a rough approximation of a target behavior (e.g., reaching). Gradually, closer and closer approximations of the desired behavior are required as a condition for reinforcement (e.g., reaching for an object) until the child succeeds at performing the target behavior correctly (e.g., grasping a toy). *Negative reinforcement* is defined as an event the removal, or avoidance, of which is associated with an increase in the occurrence of a target behavior. For example, a child may be negatively reinforced for cleaning his or her room by the cessation of a parent's nagging. Negative reinforcement is generally less effective than positive reinforcement, yet it is frequently employed by parents and teachers. Negative reinforcement is often confused with punishment, which is an event that is associated with a decrease in the occurrence of a behavior. However, because the focus of this section is upon behavior increase techniques, the discussion of punishment has been deferred until the next part of this chapter.

Selection of Reinforcers.   Care must be taken to select reinforcers that will be effective for each individual student. An item may be considered a positive reinforcer for a particular student only if it is associated with a behavior increase for that student. For example, raisins may function as a positive reinforcer for one child, but not for another. One or more of the following approaches may be used in the selection of reinforcers for individual students. First, the teacher may simply ask the student or his or her parents what the student likes. Second, the teacher may observe the student's preferences in the natural environment. Third, the teacher may set up some trial situations in which the student has a choice of reinforcers.

Reinforcers may be either primary or secondary. Primary reinforcers are those which spontaneously function as reinforcers (e.g., food). Secondary reinforcers are those which acquire their reinforcing qualities through repeated pairing with primary reinforcers (e.g., money). Although specific primary reinforcers may be very powerful, the student may eventually become satiated with them over the many trials that are typically required to change behavior. Generalized secondary reinforcers, such as tokens that may be traded for a variety of primary reinforcers, are more likely to find long-term applicability in a classroom situation.

Schedules of Reinforcement.   When initially teaching a new behavior, it is usually necessary to deliver reinforcement on a continuous schedule—that is, a schedule in which one reinforcer is given for each occurrence of the behavior. However, once the behavior has become established in the student's repertoire, it is usually possible to gradually reduce the delivery of reinforcement to an intermittent schedule so that the behavior can be maintained with less frequent reinforcement.

Intermittent reinforcement may be delivered on either a *ratio schedule* or an *interval schedule*. With a *ratio schedule*, the reinforcer is administered after a specified number of occurrences of the target behavior. With an *interval schedule*, the reinforcer is administered after a specified period of time. In addition, ratio and interval schedules may be either *fixed* or *variable*. Reinforcement is delivered on a regular basis with *fixed schedules* and on an irregular basis with *variable schedules*. For example, according to a fixed ratio schedule, a student might receive a piece of popcorn for every fifth correct response. According to a variable ratio schedule, the student would still receive popcorn for every firth correct response on the average, but on an irregular schedule. According to a fixed interval schedule, the student might receive a piece of popcorn every five minutes for working in his or her workbook. With a variable interval schedule, the student would receive one piece of popcorn on the average of every five minutes, but on an irregular schedule. The selection of a reinforcement schedule is dependent upon the characteristics of the child and the particular behavior being taught.

Chaining.   So far, we have discussed the use of reinforcement with single, isolated behaviors. However, many real-life activities require the performance of a series of related behaviors. *Chaining* is a technique for linking component behaviors together into a meaningful sequence of steps. Each step becomes the S^D, or discriminative stimulus, for the next step. Task analysis is used to break up the activity into a series of teachable steps. Steps may be taught one at a time, using repeated trials until each step is mastered before going on to the next step, or all steps may be taught simultaneously by reinforcing the correct performance of each step only within the context of the whole activity. Teaching one step at a time is most useful when the chain contains some particularly difficult steps, whereas teaching steps simultaneously more closely approximates the actual conditions of performance in the natural environment. Chains can be taught either in a forward order, following the natural sequence of the activity, or in a backward order, beginning with the last step. In backward chaining, the teacher may begin by performing the earlier steps in the sequence so that the student can perform the final, and often the most intrinsically reinforcing step (e.g., drinking the milk).

Maintenance and Generalization: Systematic Approaches

Whenever a student with mental retardation acquires and masters a new behavior, there is always a danger that the new behavior will be soon forgotten, or that it will not be generalized beyond the teaching situation to other appropriate situations. In fact, insuring that instruction will result in adequate maintenance and generalization has been one of the most elusive goals of researchers seeking to develop effective behavioral (e.g., Meichenbaum, 1980) and cognitive (e.g., Blackman & Lin, 1984) training techniques. The maintenance and generalization of new behaviors cannot be left to chance. Instructional planning must include specific strategies aimed at insuring long-term maintenance and appropriate generalization.

Maintenance

The likelihood that a behavior will be maintained over time can be increased by following certain procedures. First, maintenance is enhanced when training is extended over multiple sessions rather than being concentrated within a single long session (Blackman & Lin, 1984). Second, after a behavior has been acquired and it is being performed at an acceptable level of proficiency, maintenance can be fostered by gradually fading the high levels of reinforcement needed for training (Polloway & Patton, 1993; Snell, 1993). Consideration should be given to fading at least the following three dimensions of reinforcement: *immediacy*, *quantity*, and *frequency*. *Immediacy* can be faded by gradually increasing the delay between the behavior and the delivery of reinforcement. *Quantity* can be faded by progressively reducing the amount of reinforcement given for each performance of the behavior. *Frequency* can be faded by shifting from a continuous schedule of reinforcement to an intermittent one. The goal is to eventually shift control of the behavior to reinforcers occurring naturally in the environment.

In addition to the specific techniques discussed in the preceding paragraph, the cognitive behavior modification approach offers a useful method for fostering the maintenance of certain types of verbally mediated behaviors. The development of this approach represents a convergence of two formerly separate lines of research, behavior therapy and cognitive psychology. In the field of behavior therapy, frustration at the limited maintenance and generalization observed as an outcome of therapy led to efforts to supplement behavioral procedures with cognitive interventions (e.g., Kendall & Hollon, 1979; Meichenbaum, 1980). Meanwhile, trends in the field of cognitive psychology had rendered many mental retardation researchers in that field receptive to the emerging cognitive behavior modification techniques. Since cognitive research had shown that individuals with mild mental retardation could be trained quite easily to apply task-specific cognitive strategies, efforts to insure maintenance and achieve generalization of these strategies had become the focus of the research agenda (Blackman & Lin, 1984). Task-specific strategy training failed to produce automatic maintenance and generalization; therefore, attention began to shift to the possibility of directly training the more overriding, general, components of cognition known as metacognitive skills (e.g., Brown & DeLoache, 1978) or executive functions (e.g., Butterfield & Belmont, 1977). Metacognition has been defined as a person's understanding and control of his or her own cognitive system (Brown, 1987). Similarly, executive functions are those skills which allow the coordination, appropriate application, and flexible use of a variety of task-specific strategies (Belmont & Butterfield, 1977). Clearly, the goal of cognitive behavior modification, which was to teach the child to guide his or her own behavior so that he or she could function more effectively across situations (Meichenbaum, 1980, p. 272), corresponded very closely to the goals of the cognitive psychologists working in the field of mental retardation.

The cognitive behavior modification approach has been widely applied to ameliorate behavior problems, such as aggressiveness and hyperactivity (Meichenbaum, 1980). The approach has also been used in classroom settings with students with mental retardation to improve academic performance on a variety of tasks, including arithmetic problem solving and reading comprehension (Hughes, Korinek, & Gorman, 1991; Meichenbaum & Asarnow, 1979). With academic tasks, cognitive behavior modification typically consists of a sequence of self-instructional steps similar to those proposed by Meichenbaum and Goodman:

1. *Cognitive Modeling.* A model performs the task while talking out loud.
2. *Overt External Guidance.* The student performs the task with instructions from the model.

3. *Overt Self-Guidance.* The student repeats the instructions out loud while performing the task.
4. *Faded, Overt Self-Guidance.* The student whispers the instructions while performing the task.
5. *Covert Self-Instruction.* The student uses private, non-vocal speech to guide task performance (Meichenbaum & Goodman, 1971).

Although research has indicated that self-instruction is a highly effective method for enhancing maintenance, the outcomes of studies seeking generalization have been inconsistent and equivocal (e.g., Burger, Blackman, & Clark, 1981; Meichenbaum & Asarnow, 1979). A further caveat is that although self-instructional techniques have been used effectively with students with mental retardation, their use has been limited largely to those students who have fairly well-developed verbal skills. Recent research, however, has demonstrated that self-instructional routines can be taught to individuals with severe mental retardation and limited language skills (Hughes, 1992). An example of a self-instructional routine is provided in the *Case Study of Tanisha*.

CASE STUDY: Tanisha (CA = 7–3, IQ = 58)

Sample Self-Instruction Training Sequence

Student *Tanisha* _____   Date *December 3, 1992*

Short-Term Objective *During reading period, Tanisha will ask permission before leaving her seat without exception on 4 out of 5 days.*

Training Sequence

1. *Cognitive Modeling.* The trainer sits in a student seat in the classroom and raises her hand, saying aloud, "Each time I want to leave my seat, I must raise my hand and ask the teacher for permission." Then, the trainer says to the teacher, "May I go to the water fountain?"
2. *Overt External Guidance.* The trainer instructs and verbally prompts Tanisha to raise her hand and ask the teacher for permission to go to the water fountain.
3. *Overt Self-Guidance.* Tanisha raises her hand, saying to herself aloud, "Each time I want to leave my seat, I must raise my hand and ask my teacher for permission." Then Tanisha says to the teacher, "May I go to the water fountain?"
4. *Faded, Overt Self-Guidance.* Tanisha raises her hand, whispering to herself, "Each time I want to leave my seat, I must raise my hand and ask my teacher for permission." Then Tanisha says to the teacher, "May I go to the water fountain?"
5. *Covert Self-Instruction.* Tanisha raises her hand, and says to the teacher, "May I go to the water fountain?" This time, she uses private, nonvocal speech to remind herself that she must raise her hand and ask permission to leave her seat.

Generalization

Although some research studies have yielded evidence of generalization from one cognitive task to another for individuals with mild mental retardation, many other studies have failed to report this sought-after generalization (Blackman & Lin, 1984). This failure to find consistent evidence of generalization could, of course, be entirely attributable to the inadequacy of the training techniques employed. However, two alternative explanations have been suggested by Blackman and Lin (1984). First, it may be that the complexity of some of the cognitive tasks employed in this research made generalization exceedingly difficult given the presumed structural limitations of individuals with mental retardation. Second, the cognitive tasks selected to test generalization may have been inappropriate. For example, a task may have been too dissimilar from the original task to provide a reasonable test of generalization. Clearly, more research is needed to fully explicate the roles played by these factors in enabling generalized strategy use.

Meanwhile, generalization has also been a focal point of concern within behavioral psychology. While the cognitive literature on generalization in people with mental retardation has been concentrated largely upon individuals with mild disabilities, the behavioral literature on generalization has reflected a focus upon individuals with severe disabilities. In particular, these efforts have been motivated by a desire to insure that essential skills acquired in the classroom by individuals with severe disabilities would generalize to community settings (Horner, Dunlap, & Koegel, 1988). The following definition of generalization has provided a useful framework for work in this area:

> the occurrence of relevant behavior under different, nontraining conditions (i.e., across subjects, settings, people, behaviors, and/or time) without the scheduling of the same events in those conditions as had been scheduled in the training conditions (Stokes & Baer, 1977, p. 350).

The above definition implies that a savings in the amount of training required for the generalization task is an essential aspect of generalization. By specifying one of the following five types of generalization as the focus of instruction, targeted generalization programs can be designed. *Generalization across subjects* refers to the type of generalization that might occur if the presence of a peer who was trained to ask frequent questions led to an increase in question-asking behavior among other children in the class. *Generalization across settings* refers to the performance of a trained behavior in a non-training setting. For example, this type of generalization might occur if a child taught to initiate social interactions in the classroom spontaneously began to initiate social interactions on the playground. *Generalization across people* refers to the type of generalization that occurs when a child performs a trained behavior in the presence of an adult other than the teacher who performed the training. *Generalization across behaviors* refers to generalization from a trained behavior to other behaviors in that class. Generalization from a trained task to an altered form of that task, as reported in the cognitive studies, would fall into this category. Finally, *generalization across time* refers to the performance of a trained behavior at a time different from the training time. For example, reading skills acquired during one reading period might be spontaneously applied during the next reading period.

After identifying the type of generalization upon which to focus instruction, the next steps are writing appropriate behavioral objectives (see Billingsley, Burgess, Lynch, & Matlock, 1991) and selecting a programming strategy. The following eleven tactics for promoting generalization have been proposed (Stokes & Osnes, 1986):

1. Teach skills that are useful and adaptive.
2. Modify environmental contingencies that are maintaining undesirable behaviors.
3. Train the student to seek out opportunities for reinforcement from the natural environment.
4. Use a broad range of stimulus exemplars.
5. Use a broad range of response exemplars.
6. Train loosely, allowing training conditions to vary.
7. Make the consequences of the behavior progressively less discriminable.
8. Reinforce unprompted generalizations, if they occur.
9. Utilize stimuli that are common to both training and generalization settings.
10. Utilize social stimuli that are common to both training and generalization settings.
11. Use self-mediated stimuli (e.g., self-instruction).

One highly structured approach that incorporates many of the above tactics is *general case programming* (Becker, Engelmann, & Thomas, 1975; Chadsey-Rusch & Halle, 1992; Horner, Sprague, & Wilcox, 1982). General case programming was developed to increase the likelihood that skills acquired under one set of training conditions would be performed under conditions different from those present during training. The goal of training is that all members of a particular stimulus class will come to control the performance of a class of responses. To reach this goal, the student is reinforced for responding to relevant instances of the stimulus class, but not to irrelevant instances. The student is taught to ignore irrelevant stimulus variations and to avoid common error patterns. General case programming consists of the following six steps (Horner et al., 1982):

1. *Definition of the instructional universe.* Define the target behavior and the stimulus class.
2. *Definition of the range of stimulus and response variation.* Identify the chain of generic responses, the generic stimulus, stimulus and response variation, and potential errors.
3. *Selection of examples for teaching and probe testing.* Select the minimum number of positive exemplars that represent the full range of stimulus and response variation. Also select negative exemplars and significant exceptions.
4. *Sequencing of teaching examples.* Present multiple exemplars within each session, teaching exceptions last.
5. *Teaching of examples.* Use behavioral teaching techniques.
6. *Testing with untrained examples.* Conduct probes and modify teaching examples to correct any error patterns.

CASE STUDY: Karen (CA = 15–1, IQ = 47)

Sample General Case Analysis Form (Adapted from Horner, Sprague, & Wilcox, 1982)

Student *Karen*   Date *May 2, 1993*

Short-Term Objective *When asked to fill the sink for dishwashing, Karen will fill the*
sink to the halfway point with warm water, without error on 9 out of 10 trials.

Activity *Fill Sink for Dishwashing*

Instructional Universe *All large sinks at home and school*

Generic Responses	Generic Stimuli	Relevant Stimulus Variation	Relevant Response Variation	Exceptions
1. Turn on both hot & cold water faucet(s)	Water faucets	One hot & one cold lever; one center lever for both hot & cold; one center knob for both hot & cold	Turn on cold, then hot lever halfway; push center lever to middle; turn center knob clockwise to middle	Other type of faucet
2. Pause for 1 minute	Clock	Wall clock; digital wristwatch; stove timer	Watch second hand go all around; wait for number on watch to change; set timer	Clock without second hand
3. Check water temperature	Running water	——	Insert finger; insert thermometer	——
4. Adjust water temperature	Water faucets	(same as #1 above)	Move levers until finger is warm; move levers till thermometer hits red dot	No hot water
5. Close sink stopper	Sink stopper	Rubber plug; metal drain basket; metal plug with control lever	Place plug in drain hole; place drain basket in drain hole & turn; pull control lever	No stopper available
6. Turn off faucet(s)	Water reaching halfway mark in sink	(Same as #1 above)	Turn off hot, then cold faucets when water hits halfway mark; pull lever when water hits halfway mark; turn knob counter-clockwise	Fills sink too full before looking for halfway mark

Adapted from Horner, R. H., Sprague, J., and Wilcox, B., 1982, *Design of high school programs for severely hand-icapped students.* Baltimore: Brookes.

The planning phase (steps one and two) of a general case program is illustrated in the *Case Study of Karen*. The implementation phase of this program would require the application of steps three through six.

Behavior Management Strategies

As mentioned earlier in this chapter, our working definition of instructional strategies includes both teaching techniques and behavior management techniques. Although this distinction is somewhat arbitrary, it provides a useful framework for the present chapter. The focus of the first part of this chapter was upon teaching techniques aimed at augmenting the child's repertoire of knowledge and skills. The focus of the present part to techniques aimed primarily at the management of behavior rather than the teaching of knowledge and skills. Obviously, there is considerable overlap between the specific techniques used for teaching knowledge and skills and those used for managing behavior. The distinction is primarily one of emphasis as reflected in the key goals and objectives of a child's program. For instance, as indicated in Chapter 6, both instructional (e.g., Tanisha will decode new words) and behavior management (e.g., Tanisha will stay in her seat unless given permission to leave it) goals were included among Tanisha's annual goals. If Tanisha's IEP had consisted exclusively of instructional-type goals, the types of instructional strategies described in the first part of this chapter would probably have been sufficient for the design of an effective program for her. However, because Tanisha's IEP includes behavior management goals, the additional set of strategies and approaches described in the present part must be considered in designing her program.

Behavior decrease programs are most effective when conducted in the context of instructional programs aimed at increasing desirable behaviors and skills (e.g., Polloway & Patton, 1993). This part of the chapter begins with a section on establishing classroom rules and procedures that will maximize opportunities for positive behavior. Next, a method for performing a functional analysis of undesirable behavior is presented. Then, the principle of pairing behavior decrease objectives with behavior increase objectives is discussed. Finally, some specific behavior decrease techniques are described.

Classroom Rules

It is well-known that high levels of disruptive behavior are most likely to occur in unstructured, disorganized situations in which students have large amounts of unoccupied time. Therefore, an important first step in any effort to minimize disruptive behavior is to establish a highly structured instructional program in which instructional time is maximized. Clear classroom rules should be established and enforced. Setting clear boundaries of acceptable behavior can go a long way toward eliminating many negative classroom behaviors (Luftig, 1987; Polloway & Patton, 1993). Several rule-based systems of classroom management have been successfully applied with children with disabilities. For example, Kounin's (1970) group management system emphasizes techniques such as smooth transitions between activities, signals for maintaining group attention, concurrent praise, and the avoidance of satiation (Luftig, 1987; Polloway & Patton, 1993). Canter's (1976) assertive discipline approach also emphasizes the establishment and enforcement of a clear set of classroom expectations (Luftig, 1987).

Functional Analysis of Undesirable Behavior

The first step in designing a program to reduce or eliminate an undesirable behavior is to conduct a thorough functional analysis of that behavior. Such an analysis, sometimes referred to as an *ABC analysis* (Snell, 1993), examines the *antecedents*, the *behavior*, and the *consequences* in order to determine the environmental events that trigger and reinforce the behavior. The identification of the *antecedents* of a target behavior requires the careful and systematic observation of the environmental events (e.g., loud noises) or social events (e.g., teacher demands) that consistently precede occurrences of the behavior. Analysis of the *behavior* requires a careful, detailed description of the target behavior or class of behaviors in terms of its form, frequency, and duration (e.g., Charley hits smaller students repeatedly on the head). The functional analysis is completed by a thorough description of the naturally occurring *consequences* of the behavior (e.g., reprimand by the teacher). Thus, the functional analysis in our example suggests the possibility that the behavior is being maintained by the individualized attention of the teacher which invariably follows the hitting behavior.

The functional analysis can then provide the basis for several intervention alternatives. For example, it may be that the hitting behavior could be forestalled if individualized teacher attention were given to Charley immediately after each teacher request to make sure that he understood what was being asked of him. Another possible intervention would be to change Charley's seat in the classroom so that he is surrounded entirely by students who are bigger than he is. A third alternative would be to withhold teacher attention following hitting behavior. After identifying the most promising of the possible alternatives, a program can be designed and its effectiveness evaluated.

The Fair Pair Rule

Consistent with the idea that behavior management is best accomplished in the context of a total instructional program, the "fair pair" rule has been offered as a guiding principle (Snell, 1987). Essentially, this rule states that whenever an undesirable behavior is targeted for decrease, that behavior should be paired with a desirable behavior slated for increase. If the desirable behavior (e.g., handshaking) is incompatible with the undesirable behavior (e.g., hitting), then a DRI (differential reinforcement of incompatible behavior) procedure may be employed. If the desirable behavior (e.g., a verbal greeting) is compatible with the undesirable behavior, a DRO (differential reinforcement of other behavior) procedure may be used. These approaches may be accompanied as necessary by techniques specifically aimed at decreasing the frequency of the undesirable behavior. The *Case Study of Norman* provides an example of a classroom arrangement designed to foster applications of the "fair pair" rule.

CASE STUDY: Norman (CA = 5–5, IQ = 64)

Norman liked to rummage through whatever available shelves, containers, and storage spaces he could find when he was not engaged in structured activity. He enjoyed handling objects and toys and he had a particular fascination for leafing through books to look at their illustrations and photographs. Because of his fine motor deficits (see Chapter 3), page turning was difficult and he would sometimes leave behind torn, ragged, or wrinkled pages. Books and other objects were occasionally misplaced, lost, or broken. Although Norman was attentive and cooperative, he was more active than most of the other children in his program.

Norman's teacher prepared an area in the classroom consisting of materials that would maintain his interest when he was not engaged in a structured task. It included crafts materials, books, and magazines, as well as a favorite photo album with sturdy pages that were easy for Norman to turn. The area was located a distance from the shelves, boxes, and closets that he might otherwise explore. When he wandered to these areas, he was redirected to his own "resource area," which quickly engaged his attention.

The arrangements made for Norman in this instance are a demonstration of the principle of *differential reinforcement of incompatible behavior* (DRI). Leafing through a photo album in his own "resource area" and dismantling stored program materials elsewhere are mutually exclusive: Norman cannot do the latter activity while doing the former. In this manner, Norman's unintentionally destructive behavior was replaced by more appropriate behavior. Notice also that the appropriate behavior was enjoyable to him so that his teacher could rely on "natural" reinforcers to modify his behavior.

Behavior Decrease Techniques

Techniques that have been employed to decrease the occurrence of undesirable behaviors span at least three categories: drugs, punishment techniques, and nonpunitive techniques. The use of drugs to change and control behavior is beyond the purview of this text. Although teachers typically have little input into decisions about whether or not a child is placed on medication, it is essential for teachers to be informed of the name of the medication and any possible side effects. In addition, by doing their best to deliver highly effective instructional and behavior management programs, teachers are in a position to minimize the situations in which medication will be called for. Clearly, the full implementation of promising behavioral interventions should precede the introduction of pharmacological interventions, many of which are associated with potentially harmful side effects. The remainder of this section is devoted to an explication of punitive and nonpunitive techniques for reducing the occurrence of undesirable behaviors.

Punitive Techniques

In many societies, the time-honored way of eliminating undesirable behavior has been punishment—often corporal punishment. This is no longer considered acceptable educational practice. Although some forms of punishment are still employed, their use has become the focus of criticism and controversy. Serious questions have been raised regarding both the ethical acceptability and the effectiveness of punishment as a technique for reducing or eliminating undesirable behavior. The use of punishment with people with mental retardation is now viewed as a last resort, for use with only the most recalcitrant behaviors that pose a danger to the self or others. In those instances, extensive human rights safeguards must be applied to insure that the least intrusive technique possible is employed, and to guard against abuse. An additional problem with the use of punishment is that its effectiveness is often limited by the fact that it can have a variety of unintended effects upon behavior. Punishment often triggers immediate outbursts of intense emotional or aggressive behavior. It has also been linked to the long-term effects of negative modeling that can result in lifelong patterns of aggressive and abusive behavior (e.g., Foxx, 1982; Jenson, Sloane, & Young, 1988).

In the rare instances where the application of punishment may seem to be warranted, it can take one of two forms. The first type of punishment consists of the presentation of an aversive consequence contingent upon the occurrence of the undesirable behavior. Overcorrection is an example of this type of punishment. Positive practice overcorrection involves requiring the student to repeatedly perform a specified behavior (e.g., raising his or her hand) whenever the undesirable behavior occurs (e.g., talking out in class). Restitutional overcorrection involves requiring the student to repeatedly remedy the effects of the undesirable behavior on the environment (e.g, repeatedly wiping the table whenever the student spills his or her drink). Both of these procedures can be aversive to staff as well as students. The second type of punishment consists of the removal of positive reinforcement contingent upon the occurrence of the undesirable behavior. Time out from positive reinforcement is an example of this type of punishment. A typical application of time-out procedures might consist of the contingent removal of the student from the classroom, with its opportunities for positive reinforcement, for a period of time. It is critical that this technique not be used in ways that provide opportunities for students to harm themselves or to avoid unpleasant classroom demands (Kerr & Nelson, 1989).

Nonpunitive Techniques

For the previously mentioned reasons, the present focus in the field is upon the development and employment of nonpunitive approaches to the reduction of undesirable behavior. The most well-known of these approaches is extinction, which consists of simply withholding positive reinforcement or ignoring the occurrence of the undesirable behavior. Extinction, however, is often slow to take effect and is relatively weak, especially when the consequences maintaining the behavior are not within the control of the teacher (e.g., peer attention for acting out in class). Extinction is most effective when combined with positive reinforcement of other behaviors (e.g., Kerr & Nelson, 1989). Accordingly, the major thrust of nonpunitive behavior management is to design programs that emphasize using positive methods to increase the frequency of desirable behaviors, and to structure the environment so as to minimize opportunities for the occurrence of undesirable behaviors. Comprehensive discussions of nonpunitive/nonaversive intervention approaches are provided by Brigham, Bakken, Scruggs, & Mastropieri (1992), Horner, Dunlap, Koegel, Carr, Sailor, Anderson, Albin, and O'Neill (1990), and Meyer and Evans (1989). The *Case Study of Tony* provides an example of a nonpunitive approach to managing a behavior problem.

CASE STUDY: Tony (CA = 16–0, IQ = 65)

On Friday afternoons, Tony typically returned from school to his group home. He then often liked to accompany a staff member to the video store. Browsing through the "new releases" section to rent a movie for the evening was an errand that he enjoyed. Upon returning home, Tony usually ate dinner and then talked on the telephone for over an hour with a cousin, who had apparently tried unsuccessfully to limit the length of the phone conversations. The conversations were a source of conflict with Tony's housemates, who resented the way Tony monopolized the telephone. By mid-evening when Tony was ready to view the video, he typically became sullen and angry when reminded by a staff member that he had to do his laundry. His laundry could not be postponed until later in the weekend because Tony spent that time with his father.

At a residential interdisciplinary team meeting, the teacher from Tony's school program offered some programmatic recommendations, which Tony and the other team members agreed to implement. Tony's Friday routine was reorganized. He could go to the video store only after his laundry was finished and after he had called his cousin. All three activities had to be completed before dinner. The schedule had two advantages: First, lengthy phone calls and visits to the video store were *incompatible behaviors* and second, the schedule utilized the *Premack Principle*. According to that principle, a preferred, high-frequency activity depends on the prior completion of a less preferred, low-frequency activity (Bernstein, Ziarnik, Rudrud, & Czajkowski, 1981). Thus, both Tony's phone calls and his trips to the video store were made contingent upon his first having completed his laundry.

By adjusting his activity schedule, both a behavior deficit (doing laundry) and a behavior excess (telephone use) were successfully addressed. Activity schedules are useful in behavioral interventions because they contain not only the problem behaviors, but the reinforcers that can be employed to bring about and maintain the desired changes. Activity reinforcers, unlike tokens or other tangible reinforcers, are effective precisely because they fit naturally into the individual's ongoing routine.

Instructional Systems

The first two parts of this chapter were devoted to a discussion of an array of specific instructional strategies from which teachers may "pick and choose" to meet the needs of a particular situation. Most of the techniques described are based on behavioral research establishing their effectiveness for changing and controlling behavior. The application of these techniques typically requires repeated trials over time with individual students. Although the desirability of individualized instruction and small teacher-student ratios has generally been acknowledged in programming for individuals with severe and profound mental retardation, group instruction is the typical mode of instruction for individuals with mild and moderate mental retardation. In an effort to facilitate and systematize instruction in group settings, behavioral and other techniques have been combined and packaged into instructional programs or systems which have found widespread applicability in special education. Two examples, with particular applicability for students with mental retardation, direct instruction and instrumental enrichment, are discussed in the following sections.

Direct Instruction

Direct instruction has been defined in both a narrow and a broad sense. In its most restrictive meaning, direct instruction refers to the approach developed for Project Follow Through, which was designed to maintain gains made by low SES preschool children in Project Head Start into their early elementary school years. In that context, the Direct Instruction Follow Through model was developed by Becker, Engelmann, Carnine, and Rhine (1981) for the purpose of teaching reading, language, and mathematics. This model was marketed as DISTAR. The more generic definition of direct instruction (Rosenshine, 1979), not tied to any particular curriculum, focuses upon teacher behavior. As a primarily behavioral approach, it incorporates many of the techniques described in the first two parts of this chapter. In addition, direct instruction is associated with the following distinguishing features delineated by Gersten:

> (a) the explicit teaching of "general case" problem-solving strategies whenever possible; (b) an emphasis on small group instruction as opposed to students working alone; (c) a systematic technology of correction procedures; (d) principles for cumulative review of previously learned material; and (e) insistence on mastery of each step in the learning process (Gersten, 1985, p. 42).

Direct instruction has been widely applied with students with disabilities, including students with mental retardation. In the evaluation of Project Follow Through, which was conducted with economically disadvantaged kindergarten through third-grade students, the outcomes for direct instruction were highly favorable. By the end of third grade, the children who had received direct instruction were performing as well as average students and better than students who had received language experience, child development, open education, discovery learning, or Piagetian approaches (Stebbins, St. Pierre, Proper, Anderson, & Cerva, 1977). There is some evidence that children who had participated in the direct instruction component of Project Follow Through maintained their superiority to nonparticipating control students into their high school years (Meyer, 1984).

Several studies have provided evidence of the effectiveness of the direct instruction approach with children with mental retardation. Maggs and Morath (1976) conducted a two-year study comparing DISTAR with a more general language-based approach as a method of teaching concepts to children with moderate and severe mental retardation. They found that the DISTAR group gained in MA months on the Stanford-Binet intelligence test at a nearly average rate during the two-year period (i.e., 22.5 months), while the control group gained only 7.5 months. In another study, Gersten and Maggs (1982) followed the cognitive and academic performance of students with moderate mental retardation receiving DISTAR language programs over a five-year period. They reported that these children gained at a faster rate than their peers without disabilities. Usually, the opposite is found. Further support for the direct instruction approach was found when Gersten, Becker, Heiry, and White (1984) examined the performance of low-IQ (below 70) children from the original Project Follow Through sample. They found that the academic growth rate of the direct instruction group was no slower than that of the higher-IQ students in the sample.

Instrumental Enrichment

At the opposite end of the instructional continuum from direct instruction is the Instrumental Enrichment (IE) approach developed by Feuerstein (1980) and his colleagues, which was introduced in Chapter 5. While direct instruction focuses upon the teaching of basic skills, IE emphasizes the training of cognitive processes. Although IE was originally developed to remediate the learning deficiencies of culturally disadvantaged adolescents in Israel, it has been widely applied and fieldtested with children and adolescents with mental retardation. The program consists of 14 instruments consisting of approximately 400 paper and pencil exercises designed to remediate thinking skills impaired by inadequate mediated learning experiences. The program was developed on the premise that many disadvantaged children lack full access to adult interpretation and guidance of their learning activities. Unlike standard workbooks, these exercises can be presented to students only by teachers who have undergone extensive training in the instructional methods of IE. "Bridging," a key component of those instructional methods, consists of procedures for relating the principles acquired through the abstract cognitive exercises to academic content and real-life situations. A child's regular teacher is generally in the best position to accomplish meaningful bridging; therefore, there has been an effort to provide IE training and monitoring for regular teachers rather than sending specialized trainers into the classroom solely to conduct the IE program. Feuerstein (1980) has recommended that IE activities be included as a portion of the curriculum on a long-term basis (i.e., 2–3 years or 300–350 hours) before program effectiveness is assessed.

The IE approach has engendered considerable interest among educators and researchers in the field of mental retardation, perhaps because it is aimed at thinking processes, the area of greatest limitation for people with mental retardation. During the past ten years, a number of major evaluation projects have been undertaken in Israel, Venezuela, Canada, and the United States, most of them involving adolescents with mental retardation and other mild disabilities. After reviewing these studies in detail, Savell, Twohig, and Rachford (1986) offered four general conclusions:

1. Positive effects of IE have been observed in all four countries.
2. Positive effects have most commonly been reported on measures of nonverbal intelligence. Effects on school achievement and other measures have been either inconsistent or not clearly interpretable.
3. Positive effects have been most often reported with individuals who were between 12 and 18 years old at the time of their exposure to IE.
4. Studies reporting positive effects of IE tended to have the following three features in common:

    * a minimum of one week of training for instructors
    * a minimum of 80 hours of exposure to IE over 1–2 years
    * IE taught in conjunction with other school content

Insuring Effectiveness

The process of insuring that an instructional intervention is effectively accomplishing the desired change in performance is a two-part process. First, assessment procedures must be employed to monitor ongoing progress. In-depth treatment of assessment approaches and procedures is provided in Chapters 3 and 4. Second, as noted in Chapter 6, PL94–142 requires the evaluation of the effectiveness of each IEP. In addition to a careful monitoring of performance, such evaluation requires the use of a design that can establish a functional relationship between an instructional intervention and a change in student performance. In Chapter 6, it was suggested that single-subject designs lend themselves well to that purpose. It is rarely feasible to evaluate the effectiveness of an entire IEP. Instead, it is usually necessary to evaluate the effectiveness of instructional strategies, individually or in combination, in relation to particular behavioral objectives within the IEP. Single-subject designs can be used to determine whether a particular strategy is powerful enough to cause an improvement in performance and whether that strategy is more effective than other available strategies. It is only by demonstrating the effectiveness of the instructional strategies employed to attain individual objectives that the overall effectiveness of an individual student's instructional program can be accurately assessed.

Single-Subject Evaluation Designs

At least three widely used single-subject designs are well-suited to evaluating the effectiveness of instructional strategies. Each of these designs takes into consideration the need for rigorous experimental control, but can be used for evaluation purposes with a single individual. Although these designs have been described in detail elsewhere (e.g., Hersen & Barlow, 1976; Jenson et al., 1988; Rusch, Rose, & Greenwood, 1988), they will be described briefly here.

The Reversal or Withdrawal Design

This design, also known as an ABA design, consists of three phases: baseline 1, intervention, and baseline 2. This design is simple and straightforward as well as rigorous. It is especially useful in situations where an increase or decrease in the frequency of a particular behavior is the desired outcome. For example, it might be a good design to use if one wished to determine whether playing rock music could lead to an increase in the rate of pen assembly by an adolescent with severe mental retardation in an employment training setting. The first step would be to observe and record the student's rate per minute of assembling pens in the training setting for several days until a stable baseline rate, without music, could be established. Then, during an intervention period of several days, rate of pen assembly with music would be observed. Finally, during a second baseline period, rate of pen assembly without music would again be observed. If the rate of pen assembly is markedly higher with music (during the intervention period) than without music (during the two baseline periods), then it can be concluded that the treatment was effective.

The use of this design is sometimes precluded in situations in which a return to the baseline is either impossible (e.g., a new response has been learned and cannot be unlearned) or undesirable (e.g., return to baseline levels of a self-injurious behavior, such as head banging, would be undesirable). Although the three phases described above (ABA) satisfy the requirements of a well-controlled evaluation design, a fourth phase, return to intervention, is often added when the design is employed in treatment settings. This expanded version of the design (ABAB) allows any beneficial intervention conditions to be reinstated at the conclusion of the evaluation study.

Multiple Baseline Design

This design can be applied across subjects, behaviors, or settings. Following the establishment of a baseline for the target behavior or behaviors, an intervention is introduced for only one subject, behavior, or setting, and any changes in performance are observed. The intervention is then introduced for the other subject, behavior, or setting. For example, if the target behavior were the rate of verbal requests made by a child with moderate mental retardation, baseline performance might be recorded in two settings, the classroom and the home. Then, a reinforcer (e.g., a peanut) might be given each time the child made a verbal request, first in the classroom and, several sessions later, in the home. This would constitute the intervention. If the rate of verbal requests noticeably increases relative to the baseline immediately upon introduction of the intervention in each setting, evidence for the effectiveness of the intervention has been provided. This design is generally considered to be an excellent one for evaluation purposes.

Changing Criterion Design

This design is especially well-suited to situations in which a return to the baseline is not feasible. This design consists of repeated applications of a two-phase baseline/intervention sequence. Instead of returning to the initial baseline level, each new baseline is established at a progressively higher level of performance. Evidence of an effective intervention is provided by a marked improvement in performance, relative to the baseline performance, each time the intervention is introduced. For example, the target behavior might be the number of arithmetic problems solved by a child with mild mental retardation in a ten-minute period. Under baseline conditions, no reinforcement would be given. However, during intervention, token reinforcement might be given for each problem solved. Although the overall number of problems solved in a ten-minute period may continue to increase as a function of increased problem-solving proficiency, a sharp increase in rate each time the token conditions (intervention) are reinstated would be considered evidence of an effective intervention.

Combining Strategies: A Final Example

Typically, behavior change intervention strategy does not involve the use of a single approach. Many procedures may be used in combination. Techniques are integrated according to the child's needs and the teacher's ingenuity. A creative teacher with sharp observation skills and facility with behavioral principles will be particularly adept in the design of integrated instructional programs. The concluding *Case Study of Sonia* reveals how one teacher combined data collection and evaluation procedures with a behavioral intervention strategy to reduce Sonia's pica. The intervention strategy included stimulus control and differential reinforcement procedures.

CASE STUDY: Sonia (CA = 7–7, IQ < 15)

Pica refers to the ingestion of non-nutritive substances (Winton & Singh, 1983), though definitions vary somewhat, with some researchers including eating food off the floor and mouthing objects (Danford & Huber, 1982). Different causes have been suggested and certain nutritional deficiencies appear to be associated with particular types of pica (Snowdon, 1977). As with other maladaptive behaviors, its frequency may be influenced by the outcomes it produces.

For Sonia, pica was not a problem until recently. She occasionally chewed on napkins or swallowed the contents of an uncapped tube of toothpaste. But last spring at school she discovered nicotine, and her consumption of discarded cigarettes became a serious problem.

In the morning after getting off the school bus, it was Sonia's routine to mill around the sidewalk area with her peers, just outside the school's front door where the bus had dropped them off. Staff members were typically busy moving wheelchairs and assisting children into the building. During this time, Sonia began to pick up and mouth discarded cigarette butts. A similar pattern developed at noontime after recess and again in the afternoon as Sonia waited for the bus ride home. Soon it was not uncommon for Sonia to pick up cigarette butts off the curb and put them in her mouth before being stopped by staff (attempted cigarette swallowing) at a rate of one or two times per morning, noon, or afternoon period. Staff members were cautioned to toss cigarettes down nearby sewers or elsewhere, and maintenance staff tried to keep the area clean, but passersby often discarded cigarettes on the roadside anyway and Sonia continued to find some.

Sonia's teacher observed, counted, and modified Sonia's pica over a four-week period:

Baseline

During Week 1, Sonia's teacher counted attempted cigarette swallowing before implementing a program to reduce it. This baseline revealed that Sonia attempted cigarette swallowing six times altogether during the mornings that week, five times altogether during recess, and six times altogether in the afternoons, for a grand total of 17 attempted target behaviors. See Figure 7-1.

Intervention

The addictive properties of nicotine may have played a contributing role in the acquisition of this habit. Yet, the sharp increase in cigarette swallowing attempts during so brief a time period suggested that other factors may have been at work. Staff attention seemed to be the most likely candidate. Sonia's passive waiting behavior decreased as staff attended to other, more active children, while pica, apparently reinforced by staff attention, rapidly increased.

Sonia learned that, in the presence of certain cues (antecedents or discriminative stimuli), certain behaviors were predictably reinforced. In this instance, the availability of cigarette butts signaled that reaching for them would engage the immediate attention of staff. Other related cues included the curbside location, the presence of staff members, and the concurrent activities of other children. In contrast, there were very few stimuli to cue appropriate behaviors that would be reinforced.

Sonia's teacher devised an intervention strategy, originally introduced by Foxx and Shapiro (1978), that combined reinforcement procedures with manipulation of antecedent

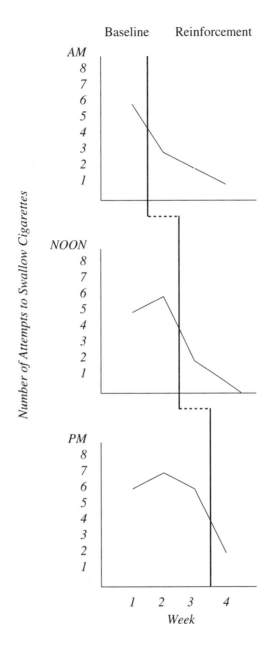

FIGURE 7-1   Reduction of Cigarette Pica in Sonia: A Multiple-baseline Design

cues. First, she identified appropriate behaviors to be reinforced as positive alternatives to pica. One such behavior was tossing bread crumbs to pigeons (Interestingly, Sonia showed little interest in eating the bread crumbs herself.). Second, at various times of the day when Sonia had been participating in her school routine and refraining from pica, Sonia's teacher conducted brief sessions during which a bracelet was placed on Sonia's wrist. She engaged Sonia in a few minutes of activity and then gave her a glass of juice (a favorite beverage). As Sonia drank her juice, her teacher pointed to her bracelet and remarked, "Nice working, Sonia," or "Good girl, Sonia; see, you are wearing your bracelet." The assumption was that the bracelet would become a cue for the reinforcement of targeted appropriate behaviors. A bracelet was used instead of the "timeout ribbon" employed by Foxx and Shapiro (1978), who recognized the advantages of using stimulus material that looked more normalized.

Week 2 saw the inauguration of the intervention program during the morning arrival period. Sonia's teacher greeted Sonia promptly, immediately placed the bracelet on her wrist, and arranged for her to feed the birds. The bracelet was a cue not only to Sonia but a reminder to other staff to praise Sonia for feeding the birds and behaving well during this time. As long as the bracelet remained on her wrist, the glass of juice was minutes away. On the other hand, when she attempted cigarette swallowing, her bracelet was removed and she was told, "No butts!" with no further comment or interaction in the remaining minutes before entering school. No juice was given when the bracelet was removed. The bracelet became a "discriminative stimulus," signaling the behaviors to be reinforced in its presence, and the behaviors to be extinguished upon its removal. Figure 7-1 shows that by the end of Week 2, Sonia's morning attempts at cigarette swallowing were reduced to three incidents altogether.

Evaluation

During Week 2, no attention was paid to modifying Sonia's noontime and afternoon behaviors. There was a good reason for this. Sonia's teacher anticipated the skepticism of some of her colleagues who doubted that Sonia would "make the connection" between bracelet, behavior, and reinforcement. Any reduction in her pica, they might argue, certainly must be coincidental. To evaluate the efficacy of her reinforcement strategy, Sonia's teacher used a *multiple baseline across settings evaluation design*. During Week 2, when the reinforcement procedure was introduced into the morning routine, baselines were continued and recorded during the noontime and afternoon periods. At the same time that pica during morning sessions was reduced from a baseline level of six cigarettes to an intervention level of three cigarettes, the noontime and afternoon baselines remained virtually unchanged from their original levels.

During Week 3, Sonia's teacher began to implement the reinforcement procedure at noontime, and pica at this time was reduced to two incidents. Also during Week 3, Sonia continued to make progress on her morning reinforcement program, with attempted cigarette swallowing reduced to a total of two behaviors. The only setting during Week 3 which did not include implementation of the reinforcement procedure was the afternoon session, during which pica maintained a level very close to its original baseline.

Sonia's teacher finally introduced the reinforcement procedure during the afternoon, having arranged for Sonia's mother to offer the reinforcing beverage to Sonia upon her return home if she was wearing her bracelet. This took place in Week 4, which concluded with the reduction of pica to near-zero levels.

Figure 7-1 graphically represents the stages of the multiple baseline across settings design described in this vignette. A behavior (pica) was observed and recorded on three separate occasions (morning, noontime, and afternoon). Inspection of the graphs convincingly suggests that the behavior was reduced only after the reinforcement procedure was applied. Otherwise, the behavior remained at its original baseline frequency. Multiple baseline evaluation designs can enable teachers to assess the effectiveness of their interventions with individual students.

Recommendations

In this section, some of the material covered in this chapter is highlighted in a series of brief recommendations:

1. In order to teach new material to high levels of proficiency, or mastery, select instructional strategies which involve analysis of the task, the manipulation of antecedent conditions, and the manipulation of consequences.

2. Cognitive behavior modification and self-instruction are recommended as techniques that foster the maintenance of learned skills and behaviors over time.

3. When instructing individuals with mental retardation, it is essential to provide direct training for generalization. General case programming is recommended as an effective way to accomplish this.

4. When it is necessary to reduce or eliminate an undesirable behavior, emphasize techniques aimed at increasing the child's repertoire of desirable behaviors, and minimize the use of techniques aimed specifically at decreasing the undesirable behavior.

5. Consider using available instructional programs (e.g., DISTAR, IE) to deliver goal-directed instruction to groups of learners.

References

Becker, W. C., Engelmann, S., Carnine, D. W., & Rhine, R. (1981). The Direct Instruction Model. In R. Rhine (Ed.), *Encouraging change in America's schools: A decade of experimentation*. New York: Academic Press.

Becker, W., Engelmann, S., & Thomas, D. (1975). *Teaching 2: Cognitive learning and instruction*. Chicago: Scientific Research Associates.

Belmont, J. M. & Butterfield, E. C. (1977). The instructional approach to developmental cognitive research. In R. Kail & J. Hagen (Eds.), *Perspec-*

tives on the development of memory and cognition. Hillsdale, NJ: Erlbaum.

Bernstein, G. S., Ziarnik, J. P., Rudrud, E. H., & Czajkowski, L. A. (1981). *Behavioral habilitation through proactive programming*. Baltimore: Brookes.

Billingsley, F. F., Burgess, D., Lynch, V. W., & Matlock, B. L. (1991). Toward generalized outcomes: Considerations and guidelines for writing instructional objectives. *Education and Training in Mental Retardation*, *26*(4), 351–360.

Blackman, L. S., & Lin, A. (1984). Generalization training in the educable mentally retarded: Intelligence and its educability revisited. In P. H. Brooks, R. Sperber, & C. McCauley (Eds.), *Learning and cognition in the mentally retarded,* 237–263. Hillsdale, NJ: Erlbaum.

Boles, S. M., Bellamy, G. T., Horner, R. H., & Mank, D. M. (1984). Specialized training program: The structured employment model. In S. C. Paine, G. T. Bellamy, & B. Wilcox (Eds.), *Human services that work: From innovation to standard practice,* 181–205. Baltimore: Brookes.

Brigham, F. J., Bakken, J. P., Scruggs, T. E., & Mastropieri, M. A. (1992). Cooperative behavior management: Strategies for promoting a positive classroom environment. *Education and Training in Mental Retardation, 27*(1), 3–12.

Brown, A. (1987). Metacognition, executive control, self-regulation and other more mysterious mechanisms. In F. E. Weinert & R. H. Kluwe (Eds.), *Metacognition, motivation, and understanding,* 65–116. Hillsdale, NJ: Erlbaum.

Brown, A. L. & DeLoache, J. S. (1978). Skills, plans, and self-regulation. In R. Siegler (Ed.), *Children's thinking: What develops?* Hillsdale, NJ: Erlbaum.

Burger, A. L., Blackman, L. S., & Clark, H. T. (1981). Generalization of verbal abstraction strategies in EMR children and adolescents. *American Journal of Mental Deficiency, 85,* 611–618.

Butterfield, E. C. & Belmont, J. M. (1977). Assessing and improving the executive cognitive function of mentally retarded people. In I. Bialer & M. Sternlicht (Eds.), *The psychology of mental retardation.* New York: Psychological Dimensions.

Canter, L. (1976). *Assertive discipline: A take-charge approach for today's educator.* Seal Beach, CA: Canter & Associates.

Chadsey-Rusch, J. & Halle, J. (1992). The application of general-case instruction to the requesting repertoires of learners with severe disabilities. *Journal of the Association for Persons with Severe Handicaps, 17*(3), 121–132.

Crist, K., Walls, R. T., & Haught, P. A. (1984). Degrees of specificity in task analysis. *American Journal of Mental Deficiency, 89*(1), 67–74.

Danford, D. E. & Huber, A. M. (1982). Pica among mentally retarded adults. *American Journal of Mental Deficiency, 87,* 141–146.

Englert, C. S., Tarrant, K. L., & Mariage, T. V. (1992). Defining and redefining instructional practice in special education: Perspectives on good teaching. *Teacher Education and Special Education, 15*(2), 62–86.

Feuerstein, R. (1980). *Instrumental Enrichment: An intervention program for cognitive modifiability.* Baltimore: University Park Press.

Foxx, R. M. (1982). *Decreasing behaviors of severely retarded and autistic persons.* Champaign, IL: Research Press.

Foxx, R. M. & Shapiro, S. T. (1978). The timeout ribbon: A nonexclusionary timeout procedure. *Journal of Applied Behavior Analysis, 11,* 125–136.

Gersten, R. (1985). Direct instruction with special education students: A review of evaluation research. *Journal of Special Education, 19*(1), 41–58.

Gersten, R. M., Becker, W. C., Heiry, T. J., & White, W. A. T. (1984). Entry IQ and yearly academic growth of children in direct instruction programs: A longitudinal study of low SES children. *Educational Evaluation and Policy Analysis, 6*(2), 109–121.

Gersten, R. & Maggs, A. (1982). Teaching the general case to moderately retarded children: Evaluation of a five-year project. *Analysis and Intervention in Developmental Disabilities, 2,* 329–343.

Gold, M. W. (1976). Task analysis of a complex assembly task by the retarded blind. *Exceptional Children, 43,* 78–84.

Greer, R. D. (1991). Teaching practices to save America's schools: The legacy of B. F. Skinner. *Journal of Behavioral Education, 1*(2), 159–164.

Hersen, M. & Barlow, D. H. (1976). *Single-case experimental designs: Strategies for studying behavior change.* New York: Pergamon.

Horner, R. H., Dunlap, G., & Koegel, R. L. (1988). *Generalization and maintenance: Life-style changes in applied settings.* Baltimore: Brookes.

Horner, R. H., Dunlap, G., Koegel, R. L., Carr, E. G., Sailor, W., Anderson, J., Albin, R. W., & O'Neill, R. E. (1990). Toward a technology of "nonaversive" behavioral support. *The Journal of the Association for Persons with Severe Handicaps, 15*(3), 125–132.

Horner, R. H., Sprague, J., & Wilcox, B. (1982). General case programming for community activities. In B. Wilcox & G. T. Bellamy (Eds.), *Design of high school programs for severely handicapped students.* Baltimore: Brookes.

Hughes, C. (1992). Teaching self-instruction utilizing multiple exemplars to produce generalized problem-solving among individuals with severe mental retardation. *American Journal on Mental Retardation, 97*(3), 302–314.

Hughes, C. A., Korinek, L., & Gorman, J. (1991). Self-management for students with mental retardation in public school settings: A research review. *Education and Training in Mental Retardation, 26*(3), 271–291.

Jenson, W. R., Sloane, H. N., & Young, K. R. (1988). *Applied behavior analysis in education: A structured teaching approach.* Englewood Cliffs: Prentice-Hall.

Kendall, P. C. & Hollon, S. D. (1979). *Cognitive-behavioral interventions.* New York: Academic Press.

Kerr, M. M. & Nelson, C. M. (1989). *Strategies for managing behavior problems in the classroom* (2nd ed.). Columbus, OH: Merrill.

Kounin, J. S. (1970). *Discipline and group management in classrooms.* New York: Holt, Rinehart, & Winston.

Luftig, R. L. (1987). *Teaching the mentally retarded student.* Boston: Allyn & Bacon.

Maggs, A. & Morath, B. A. (1976). Effects of direct verbal instruction on intellectual development of institutionalized moderately retarded children: A two-year study. *Journal of Special Education, 10*(4), 357–364.

Masters, L. F. & Mori, A. A. (1986). *Teaching secondary students with mild learning and behavior problems.* Rockville, MD: Aspen.

Meichenbaum, D. (1980). A cognitive-behavioral perspective on intelligence. *Intelligence, 4*(4), 271–283.

Meichenbaum, D. & Asarnow, J. (1979). Cognitive-behavioral modification and metacognitive development: Implications for the classroom. In P. C. Kendall & S. D. Hollon (Eds.), *Cognitive-behavioral interventions.* New York: Academic Press.

Meichenbaum, D. H. & Goodman, J. (1971). Training impulsive children to talk to themselves: A means of developing self-control. *Journal of Abnormal Psychology, 77*, 115–126.

Meyer, L. A. (1984). Long-term academic effects of the Direct Instruction Project Follow Through. *Elementary School Journal, 84*(4), 380–394.

Meyer, L. H. & Evans, I. M. (1989). *Nonaversive intervention for behavior problems.* Baltimore: Brookes.

Polloway, E. A. & Patton, J. R. (1993). *Strategies for teaching learners with special needs* (5th ed.). New York: Merrill/Macmillan.

Rosenshine, B. V. (1979). Content, time and direct instruction. In P. L. Peterson & H. J. Walberg (Eds.), *Research on teaching: Concepts, findings and implications.* Cambridge, MA: Harvard University Press.

Rusch, F. R., Rose, T., & Greenwood, C. R. (1988). *Introduction to behavior analysis in special education.* Englewood Cliffs, NJ: Prentice-Hall.

Savell, J. M., Twohig, P. T., & Rachford, D. L. (1986). Empirical status of Feuerstein's "Instrumental Enrichment" (FIE) technique as a method of teaching thinking skills. *Review of Educational Research, 56*(4), 381–409.

Snell, M. E. (1993). *Instruction of students with severe disabilities* (4th ed.). New York: Merrill/Macmillan.

Snell, M. E. (1987). *Systematic instruction of persons with severe handicaps* (3rd ed.). Columbus, OH: Merrill.

Snowdon, C. T. (1977). A nutritional basis for lead pica. *Physiology and Behavior, 18*, 885–893.

Stebbins, L., St. Pierre, R. G., Proper, E. C., Anderson, R. B., & Cerva, T. R. (1977). *Education as experimentation: A planned variation model (Vols. IV A–D).* Cambridge, MA: Abt Associates.

Stokes, T. F. & Baer, D. M. (1977). An implicit technology of generalization. *Journal of Applied Behavior Analysis, 10*, 349–367.

Stokes, T. F. & Osnes, P. G. (1986). Programming the generalization of children's social behavior. In P. S. Strain, M. Guralnick, & H. Walker (Eds.), *Children's social behavior: Development, assessment and modification,* 407–443. Orlando, FL: Academic Press.

Winton, A. S. W. & Singh, N. N. (1983). Suppression of pica using brief-duration physical restraint. *Journal of Mental Deficiency Research, 27,* 93–103.

Education in the Least Restrictive Environment: Placement Options

Placement decisions for students with mental retardation today involve a conscious effort by interdisciplinary teams to find environments which are both educationally suitable and the least segregated from peers without mental retardation. Or course, this has not always been the case. During the 1950s, school placements even for students with mild mental retardation were in classrooms so segregated that regular teachers in the same school often did not know where the classes for students with mental retardation were held. Even worse, some students with moderate mental retardation, as well as many students with severe and profound mental retardation, were denied the right to even a segregated education, and were often warehoused in state "homes." These homes were often run more like prisons than the charitable facilities they were originally intended to be. Finally, some courageous parents began to demand change and improved education for their children with mental retardation. Realizing that the same principles that were used to break down racial segregation in *Brown v. Board of Education* (1954) could be used to combat exclusion based on handicaps, parent and other groups began to press their case through Congress and the courts. Not until the 1970s, however, was significant progress made in bringing special education students into the mainstream (hence the term "mainstreaming") of regular school programs; and it took court action to do it.

Interested in the needs of their children, parents in Pennsylvania brought a class-action lawsuit, *Pennsylvania Association for Retarded Children* ("PARC") *v. Commonwealth of Pennsylvania* (1972), challenging the exclusion of children with mental retardation from free public school programs. The landmark decision of the United States District Court in Pennsylvania affirmed the right of children with mental retardation to appropriate education from preschool through all their developing years. In addition, the Court ruled that this right must be administered in the "least restrictive setting," one of the first uses of this now familiar phrase. While parents in Pennsylvania were going to court on behalf of their children with mental retardation, a class-action suit brought to insure the appropriate participation of all exceptional children in the public schools of the District of Columbia (*Mills v. Board of Education of the District of Columbia*, 1972) was also being won.

While the outcomes of these cases were heartening (see Table 8-1), activists knew that the approach was too piecemeal. Parents from many states began to lobby in Washington for the passage of a federal law that would guarantee all children with handicaps a free, appropriate public school education in the least restrictive environment. Lobbying efforts bore fruit in 1975 when Congress passed PL94–142, *The Education for All Handicapped Children Act.* In 1990, PL94–142 was amended for the third time (see Chapter 1). One of the changes was in the title, which was changed from "Education of the Handicapped Act" to the "Individuals with Disabilities Education Act (PL101–476).

Although much debate continues about what constitutes both an appropriate and least restrictive environment for students with disabilities, PL94–142 had the effect of requiring school systems to develop a continuum of services—that is, a range of placement options to meet the individual needs of students with disabilities. This continuum has been most frequently portrayed as a pyramid. The wide base, which signifies the least restrictive placements, symbolizes the belief that most individuals with disabilities should be served in regular classrooms. The number of individuals who require a more restrictive educational setting decreases as we move up the pyramid.

TABLE 8-1   Summary of Outcomes for Three Landmark Cases

Landmark Cases	Outcomes
Brown v. Board of Education (1954)	Mandated desegregation of the Topeka schools. Established the principle of equal opportunity for education.
Mills v. Board of Education (1972)	Ruled that no child be denied a free public education because of such handicaps: • mental • behavioral • emotional • physical
Pennsylvania Association for Retarded Children (PARC) v. Commonwealth of Pennsylvania (1971)	Stipulated that all children with mental retardation had a right to a "free program of education and training" regardless of the degree of deficit

The Regular Education Initiative, or REI, has been proposed as a way of providing the most appropriate education in the least restrictive environment (Will, 1986). This initiative calls for educators and researchers to look for ways to serve as many special education children as possible in the regular classroom; in essence, forming a partnership between special education and regular education. The objective of this partnership is for special educators to use their knowledge and expertise to support regular education for children with learning problems, rather than using it to set up separate programs for them.

Proponents calling for the restructuring of special and regular education for students with learning disabilities and other mild disabilities argue that the categorical system for classifying students and providing services for them has created a dual educational system that is dysfunctional, ineffective, and excessively costly (Lilly, 1986; Reynolds & Wang, 1983; Stainback & Stainback, 1984). Others are cautious about proposals such as REI,

FIGURE 8-1   Continuum of Educational Services for Students with Disabilities

Most Restrictive
Learning Environment

LEVEL 5: Special Residential Facility

LEVEL 4: Special Day School

LEVEL 3: Full-time Special Class

LEVEL 2: Regular Classroom with Resource Room

LEVEL 1: Regular Education Classroom

Least Restrictive
Learning Environment

fearing that these proposals are not the logical extension of mainstreaming, but rather a subtle way to de-emphasize special education. They believe that the REI is an attempt to cut back on funds needed to help special education students reach their full potential. These concerns are coupled with the lack of empirical evidence to support the basic assumption underlying the REI—that once adaptations are made in the regular class-room, learners with special needs will be able to learn as they would have been able to in a special education environment.

Credence may be added to this view when one considers that the 1980s have seen increasing and widespread criticism of regular education. Reports such as *A Nation At Risk* (National Commission on Excellence in Education, 1983), *Horace's Compromise* (Sizer, 1984), and *High School* (Boyer, 1983) have all concluded that schools are not functioning well, and that serious problems exist in the nature and quality of educational services that are being delivered. If the system cannot provide quality education to reg-ular students, it is argued, the system will be even further taxed when it is asked to take on the greater burden of educating students that have specific learning difficulties (Keogh, 1988).

However, in the 1990s, the discussion regarding REI has become more future-oriented (Fuchs & Fuchs, 1994; Thousand & Villa, 1991). This new orientation emphasizes the need to document, further refine, and disseminate organizational, technological, and instruc-tional approaches that allow local neighborhood schools to respond to the diverse educa-tional and psychological needs of all learners (Williams, Villa, Thousand, & Fox, 1990). This initiative has been called *inclusion*. The call for full inclusion, which has been cham-pioned by the Association for Persons with Severe Handicaps, perceives separate educa-tion (e.g., special education settings) as inherently unequal, and contends that educational agencies should not erect barriers between students based solely on their differences in abil-ity and achievement. However, the effects of mental retardation cannot be denied or mini-mized. Indeed, if individuals with mental retardation are to achieve their maximum potential for functioning in integrated community environments, then it seems likely that some of the educational services that they need would differ from those offered to students without mental retardation. In order to provide a full range of services for students with mental retardation, a continuum of placement options including fully inclusive settings, is essential (The Council for Exceptional Children, 1993).

The first three parts of this chapter describe the continuum of programs available for educating learners with mental retardation. This continuum of programs, and the models used to implement them, should most certainly not be viewed as static. Each such program must constantly be reviewed, and new models created to meet the needs that preexisting models do not address. If this is not done, the number of individuals with mental retardation who fail to receive effective educational programming will increase. The first section of this chapter describes programs for infants and preschool-aged children. The second section describes programs for elementary school-aged students, and the third section describes programs for adolescents and adults.

The fourth part of this chapter discusses the role of collaborative teams within the context of creating schools that are more responsive to the needs of all students. The final section offers recommendations for those involved in making and implementing place-ment decisions.

Programs for Infants and Preschool-Aged Children

Infants and some preschool-aged children cannot receive all needed services at school. Rather, services must be provided to them under a variety of service delivery models. Service delivery models are defined as "replicable patterns or designs of getting assistance to those who need it, such as families of young children with handicaps" (Bailey & Wolery, 1984, p. 14). The service delivery models used for infants and preschool children include home-based, center-based, a combination of home- and center-based, and hospital-based programs. This section describes each of these models, including implementation, advantages and disadvantages, and an illustrative example.

Home-Based Programs

As the term home-based indicates, this type of service is delivered in the child's home. Typically, the service provider visits approximately once a week. These home visits provide the perfect opportunity for the service provider and the parent (typically the mother) to establish and maintain rapport, as well as to discuss the effectiveness of previously planned and implemented activities. The service provider uses the techniques of *modeling, behavior rehearsal,* and *feedback* to help to train the parent (Neisworth & Bagnato, 1987). The first step in the training is for the service provider to verbally instruct the parent while simultaneously demonstrating how to do the activity with the child. This is called *modeling.* In the second step, the parent performs the activity with the child in order to practice and internalize the tasks demonstrated by the service provider. This is called *behavior rehearsal.* In the third step, the parent is asked to perform the same activity with the child; however, this time the service provider gives corrective feedback and encouragement as he or she observes the parent performing the activity. This is called the *feedback* stage. In addition to insuring that the parent knows how to carry out planned activities, it is the service provider's responsibility to teach the parent how to correct errors and record data on their child's progress. The breadth and depth of the direct services that home-based programs provide can be enriched, however, by the expertise of an interdisciplinary team as described later in this chapter.

Home-based programs have several advantages. First, they allow for individualized parent training. Second, they allow parents to become actively involved in meeting cooperatively planned goals for their child. Third, because the planned activities are conducted in the natural environment of the child and his or her parents, the opportunity to generalize learned skills to daily activities in the home is maximized. Finally, home-based programs provide a consistent weekly schedule. Many parents, because of work schedules or other external pressures, cannot travel to sites. With this model, issues regarding parent and child travel time are eliminated since the service provider does the traveling.

Of course, home-based programs have disadvantages as well. Among these are: (1) the placement of additional stress on the parent, who provides most of the actual instruction; (2) the restriction of opportunities for social interaction with other children; and (3) the use of valuable service provider time, which otherwise could be used for instruction, in traveling to and from the home-based site.

One well-known home-based program is the Portage Project in Wisconsin. This program emphasizes teaching parents to use behavior modification techniques with their children with disabilities (Shearer & Shearer, 1972). Approximately half of the children served in this program have mental retardation (Karnes & Zehrbach, 1977), but the project also serves children with behavior problems, physical disabilities, visual or hearing impairment, speech or language difficulties, or cultural disadvantage. The Portage Project staff developed an instructional guide, *The Portage Guide to Early Education* (Bluma, Shearer, Frohman, & Hillard, 1976), to assist in modifying existing goals and writing new ones based on data that had been collected and charted. This helps parents to understand the purpose of keeping records, as well as allowing for revision of goals based on actual performance.

Center-Based Programs

Center-based programs require that the child be brought to a center (e.g., a hospital, university, or preschool) to receive instruction and services. Typically, children with mental retardation who are enrolled in center-based programs attend the center for a few hours a day for 2 to 5 days a week. In this type of program, teachers, not parents, are the primary providers of instruction. Parents are encouraged, however, to participate as volunteers in the program. The advantages of having a child attend a center-based program include the following: (1) team members can work closely with and have easy access to children; (2) parents have the opportunity to share experiences and seek support, or to receive respite from their daily caregiving responsibilities; and (3) teachers can observe how an individual child interacts with other children in structured environments that include small- and large-group instruction.

However, a center-based program also has some disadvantages. One cause of much concern to staff and families is the potentially expensive and time consuming transportation to and from the center. Another disadvantage of center-based programs is that, unlike home-based programs, money must be allocated to the construction and maintenance of the facility itself. A third disadvantage is the apparent difficulty in involving the parents whose children attend center-based programs.

One example of a successful center-based program known for its active parental involvement component (Hayden & Dmitriev, 1975) is the Down Syndrome Program (now called Programs for Children with Down Syndrome and Other Developmental Delays), located at the University of Washington's Experimental Education Unit. Parents who enroll their child in the Down's Syndrome Program are required to participate in the classroom on a regular basis. Skills that parents are taught include how to manage and supervise play activities, how to prepare instructional materials, and how to observe and record behaviors. Communication between parents and the center is ongoing, and is augmented by the scheduling of at least one parent-teacher conference per academic quarter. The additional scheduling of an evening meeting held once each quarter provides an opportunity for parents to share concerns and data they have collected on their child's behavior, or to view and discuss videotapes of the preschool program.

Combination Home- and Center-Based Programs

Combination home- and center-based programs are typically one of two types: (1) programs that serve younger children at home while meeting the needs of older children at the center; and (2) programs that serve children in accordance with their individual needs (Bailey &

Wolery, 1984). Since one child may receive both home- and center-based services, while another child may receive only one of these, this model offers a wider range of flexibility in determining how best to meet the needs of the child and the family. Obviously, this model has some of the advantages and disadvantages of both the home- and center-based models.

A combination home- and center-based program, the Teaching Research Infant and Child Center in Eugene, Oregon, serves children from age one to eighteen with moderate to severe disabilities (Fredericks, Baldwin, Moore, Templemena, & Anderson, 1980). The curriculum uses task analysis and developmentally sequenced materials, and is based on the *Teaching Research Curriculum for Moderately to Severely Handicapped* (Fredericks, Rigges, Furey, Grove, Moore, Jordan, Hansen, Baldwin, & Wallow, 1976).

Residential Hospital-Based Programs

Residential hospital-based programs encourage the provision of services that meet the educational and developmental needs of the medically fragile child. It has been demon-

TABLE 8-2   Advantages and Disadvantages of Programs for Infants and Preschool-Aged Children with Mental Retardation

Program	Advantages	Disadvantages
Home-Based	Individualized parent training	Additional stress associated with parent being the "teacher"
	Natural environment	
	Parents actively involved	Restricted opportunities for interaction with nonhandicapped children
Center-Based	Team approach	Transportation to and from the center can be time consuming and costly
	Support groups for parents	
	Respite for parents	A proportion of money collected must be used to construct and maintain the center
	Opportunities for observing how a child interacts with other children in a structured environment are available	Reduced parental involvement
Combination Home- and Center-Based	Combined advantages of home- and center-based programs	Combined disadvantages of center-based programs
Residential Hospital-Based	Interdisciplinary team working together	Residential hospital environment
	Monitoring of needs around the clock	Stress on the family unit
	Immediate adjustment to treatment plan	Interacting with a large number of professionals

strated that an interdisciplinary team approach for infants and young children in a pediatric rehabilitation program in a hospital setting can promote significant developmental and behavioral progress (Bagnato & Neisworth, 1985). The interdisciplinary team generally includes a developmental school psychologist, a speech and language therapist, an occupational therapist, a physical therapist, a recreational therapist, a developmental pediatrician, a pediatric nurse, and an early childhood special educator.

The advantages of this program option include the following: (1) a team of experts available around the clock to cater to the needs of the child; (2) a systematic approach that maximizes communication among team members; (3) a flexible treatment plan that can be immediately adjusted to meet the current needs of the student; and (4) the opportunity for some families to receive needed respite from the responsibilities of care.

Some of the disadvantages of the hospital-based program include the following: (1) the hospital environment can be extremely stressful to parents who may feel overwhelmed by its impersonal, perhaps even frightening, nature; (2) the parents and their child must interact with large numbers of professionals; and (3) the separation of child from parents and siblings can, in some instances, place stress on the family unit.

Table 8-2 on page 203 presents a summary of some of the advantages and disadvantages of programs available for meeting the needs of infants and preschool-aged children with mental retardation.

Programs for the School Years

Under the mandate of PL94–142 and its amendments, the continuum of programs available for meeting the needs of students with mental retardation has broadened. Specifically, this federal law assures the availability of an appropriate public education for all children with handicaps at no cost to parents, and requires that special education services are to be delivered to children with handicaps in the "least restrictive" environment possible. Less restrictive models, commonly referred to as mainstreaming alternatives, involve placing students with mental retardation in contact with their peers without mental retardation for as much of the school day as is educationally sound for the learner with mental retardation. Some of the placement options available to elementary school-aged students with mental retardation are the regular education classroom, the regular education classroom with resource room, the full-time special class, the special day school, and the special residential facility. A description of each placement option coupled with a brief discussion of some of the issues and concerns surrounding it is provided.

Regular Education Classroom

The option of regular education classrooms as the least restrictive environment has more commonly been used with learners that have been classified as having mild mental retardation (Vitello & Soskin, 1985). This use of the regular education classroom embodies the spirit of the federal mandate, which calls for a more integrated or mainstreamed setting for these students. Nevertheless, the placement of learners with mild disabilities in the regular education classroom continues to be debated. At the forefront of the debate is the question of which environment—the special education classroom or the regular classroom—can, in fact, better facilitate growth by students who have been classified as having mild mental retardation. Project PRIME (Programmed Re-entry into Mainstreamed Education) (Semmel, Gottlieb, & Robinson, 1979), funded by the Office of Special Education and Rehabilitative Services, was a comprehensive study comparing the performance of students with mental retardation in regular classes with that of students with mental retardation in special classes. This investigation represented a return to the efficacy studies, done in the 1950s and 1960s, which tried unsuccessfully to demonstrate the superiority of special over regular class placement in terms of academic and social adjustment outcome variables (Blackman & Heintz, 1966; Kirk, 1964). The results of these early studies were taken to mean that, despite the apparent advantages of special classes with respect to limited enrollments, specially trained teachers, adapted curricula and methods, and higher per capita expenditures, children with mental retardation fared no better in them than they did in supposedly less responsive regular classes. These negative results contributed greatly to the "disestablishment" of the segregated special delivery system for children with mild levels of mental retardation (Dunn, 1968). If segregated education was not delivering the benefits promised, then there was no point to spending extra dollars without apparent results, especially because special education could potentially stigmatize children and their families, and erode their self-esteem.

Now that the "right values" could be found in regular rather than in special classes, it was important to determine whether positive achievement would follow. Project PRIME found that whether children were instructed in integrated or segregated settings made little difference. As might have been expected, irrespective of administrative ideology, good outcomes were related to effective teaching, administrative support, and easy access to high quality programmatic resources. After reviewing the impact of segregated settings on children with learning problems, Leinhardt and Pallay (1982) concluded similarly that it is the issue of effective practices, not placements, that should be the concern of educators. Calberg and Kavale (1980) performed a meta-analysis of 50 studies comparing the efficacy of special versus regular class placement. Their results must be considered equivocal in that special classes were found to be less effective than regular classes for children with below average IQs. On the other hand, special classes were found to be superior to regular classes for children with behavior disorders and learning disabilities.

The realization that students with disabilities are being taught the same academic content regardless of their placement (Smith & Dexter, 1980), coupled with the "back to basics" movement in regular education, has had some professionals calling for the development of curricula that will allow students to learn and practice skills applicable to community life. Interestingly, the Regular Education Initiative (REI) and the call for *full inclusion* bring the field of special education full circle, once again placing the spotlight on *where* a learner with disabilities should receive his or her education.

Resource Room Programs

There are at least four different types of resource room programs that serve the needs of learners with mental retardation: the categorical, the cross-categorical, the noncategorical, and the itinerant. Resource room programs did not become popular in the schools until serious questions regarding the educational and social ramifications of segregated special self-contained classes and schools were raised (Dunn, 1968; Christopolos & Renz, 1969; Lilly, 1970; Garrison & Hammill, 1971; Hammill & Wiederholt, 1972). The objective of resource room instruction is to remediate, on a regularly scheduled basis, deficits in language, reading, arithmetic, and social behaviors so that a child can perform more effectively in the regular classroom. Therefore, resource room teachers have two tasks: (1) assisting the student in performing effectively in the regular class; and (2) designing instruction that will help remediate the student's area or areas of deficit.

Categorical Resource Room Programs

Categorical resource room programs, like self-contained special education classes, separately serve students who are officially diagnosed as having mental retardation, a learning disability, or a behavior disorder. In some school districts, self-contained special education classes for children with mild mental retardation have been replaced with categorically-based resource rooms (Barksdale & Atkinson, 1971). Other districts have maintained their self-contained special education classes for each type of disability as back-up for their categorical resource room programs.

Cross-Categorical Resource Room Programs

Cross-categorical resource room programs serve students from two or more disability categories. In some districts, the special education resource room teacher's program is arranged so that although the program services two or more disability categories, not more than one disability category occupies the resource room at the same time. In other districts students are scheduled for the cross-categorical resource room program based on instructional needs rather than diagnostic label. In this instance, a special education resource room teacher might have a group of children with learning disabilities, mental retardation and behavior disorders scheduled to be in the resource room at the same time to develop skills appropriate to all of them (e.g., how to resolve conflicts).

Noncategorical Resource Room Programs

Noncategorical resource room programs serve students with and without disabilities. About 70 to 80 percent of the students in noncategorical resource programs do not have disabilities and have never received any type of special education service (Wiederholt, Hammill, & Brown, 1987). The advantage of having a noncategorical resource room program is that students do not have to be diagnosed as having a disability in order to receive appropriate services. Therefore, students get the assistance they need without the stigma that goes with being labeled as having mild mental retardation. For a detailed review of arguments that present both the positive and negative sides to the practice of labeling see MacMillan, Jones, and Aloia (1974) and Smith, Neisworth, and Hunt (1983). However, before the noncategorical resource room program can be used as a bridge between special and regular education, important questions need to be investigated. Using what criteria, if any, do teachers decide to schedule a student for noncategorical resource room assistance? Who should provide the instruction —a teacher who has been trained as a special educator? Or is an educator without special education training sufficient? Where will the funding come from to support such a program? Will there be too many teacher referrals made for students judged to be in need of noncategorical resource room assistance?

Itinerant Resource Room Programs

Itinerant resource room programs, in which the resource room teacher travels from school to school, can use a categorical, cross-categorical or noncategorical format. Although each of these formats have been discussed, there are additional issues involved in operating an itinerant resource room program. One major difficulty is that the itinerant teacher may have large numbers of students whom he or she sees only periodically. Time is also a factor—if a teacher must spend ten minutes of a period reorienting the student, teaching time is reduced.

Table 8-3 presents a summary of some of the resource room programs available for learners with special needs.

Special Class Programs

Special class programs provide self-contained (segregated) instructional environments. Although students with mental retardation who have been placed in self-contained special classes may have their instructional time divided between part-time self-contained class instruction in certain subjects and regular class instruction in others, most students with mental retardation tend to receive instruction segregated from the mainstream of education (e.g., self-contained special class) (Patton, Beirne-Smith, & Payne, 1990; U.S. Department of Education, 1990). Several concerns have been raised about the use of a segregated approach for the delivery of instruction for elementary school-aged students with mental retardation. They include the fact that students may not have adequate opportunities to observe and attain the higher levels of academic proficiency and social skills development that are needed to successfully adjust to an increasingly complex community (Brown, Long, Udvari-Solner, Davis, Van Deventer, Ahlgren, Johnson, Gruenewald, & Jorgensen, 1989; Dunn, 1968; Garrison & Hammill, 1971; Kaufman, Agard, & Semmel, 1985; Lilly, 1970). As discussed earlier in this chapter, Project PRIME investigated the complexities involved in providing services to children with mild mental retardation utilizing both segregated and integrated approaches. The three groups of students who were contrasted in Project

TABLE 8-3　Resource Room Programs Available for Meeting the Needs of Special Education Learners

Resource Room Program	Learner Served
Categorical	In a categorical resource room program, the needs of *only* one special education group are met. The students in the group would have a diagnosis of mentally retarded, learning disabled, or behavior disordered.
Cross-Categorical	A cross-categorical resource room program meets the needs of two or more special education groups.
Non-Categorical	The needs of students both with and without disabilities are met in a non-categorical resource room program.
Itinerant	In an itinerant resource room program, the teacher travels from school to school meeting the needs of learners that are experiencing difficulty in learning. The students might be grouped categorically, cross-categorically, or noncategorically.

PRIME included: (1) mainstreamed students; (2) nonmainstreamed or segregated learners with mild mental retardation; and (3) learners without disabilities. The important findings of this massive data collection effort, summarized in Table 8-4, suggest that adequate resources and better coordination between regular and special educators needs to precede consideration of placement.

Special Day School Programs

At one time, it was common practice for school districts to place the majority of their students with mental retardation in a special school. Therefore, a student's day began by being bussed out of his or her immediate neighborhood to a special school program that had been specifically designed to serve students with mental retardation. Although an advantage of the special school was total control over the child's curriculum and daily life, the absence of any contact with peers without mental retardation was unrealistic and limiting in that opportunities to observe and acquire socialization skills from contact with peers without mental retardation was impossible. Today, few school districts place students with mild or moderate mental retardation in special schools. However, many districts retain special school programs as an option for students with severe and profound mental retardation.

Special Residential Facilities

Congregate residential facilities that are completely segregated may appear not to meet the least restrictive environment criterion mandated by PL94–142 and its amendments. For some students with severe and profound mental retardation who require around the clock attention, however, this environment may in fact represent the least restrictive learning environment currently available in which they may function effectively. It is hoped that an increasingly flexible array of options (e.g., community residences) will broaden the choices of persons requiring continuous attention.

TABLE 8-4   The Major Conclusions of Project PRIME

1. Public schools and teachers significantly contribute to explaining the variations in nonhandicapped and EMR learner academic and social competence.

2. The regular and special education services being provided in alternative settings are delivered in distinctly different ways.

3. Variations in learner background and classroom environments were differently associated with academic and social competence.

4. Mainstreamed EMR learners' academic achievement was markedly associated with the extent to which regular and special education services were coordinated.

5. EMR learners, though homogenous in relation to Federal/state eligibility criteria, present very heterogeneous educational profiles for purposes of placement and programming.

Programs for Adolescents and Adults

Patton, Beirne-Smith, and Payne (1990) believe that there are three treatment orientations available for meeting the needs of adolescents and adults with mental retardation. They suggest that the three treatment orientations involve changing the environment, changing the individual, or changing both the environment and the individual. A brief description and rationale for each of these orientations follows, with an illustrative example for each.

Changing the Environment

Some programs have been put into place that have, in essence, created communities in which people with mental retardation can be protected and at the same time acquire the sense of belonging and self-esteem that comes with striving for self-sufficiency. An example of a program, more accurately called a movement, that changes the environment to meet the needs of individuals with mental retardation is Camphill Village. This movement is based on the teachings of Rudolf Steiner and was begun in Europe. It was promoted by his former student, Karl Konig. It was Konig that guided the application of Steiner's teachings into an approach for teaching individuals with mental retardation that became known as *curative education*. As stated by Patton, Payne, and Beirne-Smith (1986, p. 373), the basic beliefs of curative education include the following:

1. Every child has a right to be educated; there is no justification for speaking of ineducable children, with the exception of a very small minority (Konig, 1966).
2. Instead of embracing a high-pressured approach to treatment, curative education favors a humanistic approach which believes that the individual develops from stage to stage toward a sound maturity (Scientific Seer, 1969).
3. Students with mental retardation need a stable, supportive environment in which they know they are accepted as equals and are treated accordingly (Konig, 1966).

It was Carlo Pietzner who was responsible for bringing the concept of a village community (Camphill movement), incorporating staff and people with mental retardation into one family unit, to the United States in 1961. To be eligible for entrance into Camphill Village, all villagers, as they are called, must be able to care for their own physical needs and require no more than standard medical care. Although it is difficult to get a clear idea of what criteria are used, Camphill Village will not permit people with mental retardation to become villagers if they are able to meet the social standards of the "normal" community.

A typical day at Camphill Village includes villagers and co-workers (staff members) occupied in such work as: (1) wood-working and enameling; (2) weaving; (3) bookbinding; (4) baking; and (5) farming. Although this kind of productive and meaningful work is essential to Camphill, there is also a nondenominational spiritual emphasis that strengthens the bond between the villagers and their Camphill families.

Changing the Individual

Another way to meet the needs of adolescents and adults with mental retardation is to make changes in the individual, largely through providing academic instruction and employment preparation. For many students with mental retardation, instruction in functional academics continues to be an ongoing feature of the secondary program. In addition, most students will be exposed to one or more of the following employment preparation/vocational training models: (1) Special Education Employment Preparation; (2) Vocational Preparation; and (3) Vocational Rehabilitation.

Special Education Employment Preparation
Combination work/study programs, which grew out of model programs that were initiated in the 1950s and 1960s, were designed to have students spend part of the day or week acquiring work experience and job skills outside of the school environment. The impetus for the development of this program model, which combines the efforts of both special education and rehabilitation service personnel, was to respond to the criticism directed at secondary special education programs that focused on the development of "watered down" academics rather than on pragmatic skill areas that students need in order to function satisfactorily in the community. Many secondary school-aged students with mental retardation were given in-school work assignments (e.g., custodial assistant, library assistant, or office assistant) before they were considered for out-of-school work experiences (e.g., stocking shelves, messenger service, or bussing tables in a coffee shop).

More recently, the special education employment preparation model has been broadened to provide training opportunities in a range of job clusters that would present students and their families with a wider choice of employment opportunities upon completion of school (Bellamy, Rhodes, Mank, & Albin, 1988). However, despite the accomplishments of employment preparation programs for students with mental retardation, the effectiveness of many programs remains hampered by a selection of jobs that reflect what the coordinator was able to "get" rather than job sites that meet the individual's needs and abilities (Rusch, Mithaug, & Flexer, 1986). Far too often, students with disabilities encounter dead-end jobs that pay little and engender future dissatisfactions with the world of work (Gold, 1975). More research is needed to explore how special education personnel can work with vocational rehabilitation personnel to facilitate the transition from school to "best-fit" employment for students with mental retardation.

Vocational Preparation
The intent behind vocational preparation is to develop competencies for a particular trade (e.g., cosmetology, automotive mechanics, or carpentry) coupled with an emphasis on the kinds of worker attitudes and behaviors (e.g., being punctual or asking for assistance) that are important for entry into a specific industry in the community. As pointed out by Johnson (1980), the typical program structure usually consists of a laboratory class in which the students perform tasks similar to those required in the particular trade area that they are exploring, and a related class in which students learn safety procedures and pertinent concepts concerning the work they are learning to do. Mithaug, Horiuchi, and Fan-

ning (1985) have provided a data-based presentation of the value provided by vocational education programs.

Vocational Rehabilitation

Today, state vocational rehabilitation agencies play a major role in the vocational preparation of adolescents and adults with mental retardation (Bitter, 1979; Brolin, 1976). The passage of the Barden-LaFollette Act in 1943 (Public Law 113) entitled individuals with mental retardation to rehabilitation services. It was not until the passing of the Rehabilitation Act of 1973, however, that state vocational rehabilitation agencies began to deliver services to a sizeable number of individuals with mental retardation who were nearing completion of their educational training. Vocational rehabilitation agencies provide a variety of services, including vocational evaluation to determine the kind of work for which the individual might be best suited, psychological testing, vocational or on-the-job training, help in finding employment, and on-the-job follow-up services. The provision of on-the-job follow-up services is particularly important for persons with mental retardation who may need additional assistance in generalizing classroom or laboratory training to the real world of work.

Changing Both the Individual and the Environment

Traditionally, changing both the individual and the environment has been exemplified by sheltered workshops and, more recently, by the supported employment initiative. Sheltered workshops were designed to provide remunerative employment to those who could presumably not compete with workers without disabilities. In addition to the task of providing sheltered employment, workshop programs were also expected to function as a transitional service to move individuals into competitive placement. In trying to meet this two-pronged goal, sheltered workshops began to exclude individuals with severe and profound mental retardation. Thus, once again, parents of offspring with severe disabilities had to push for programs that would meet their youngsters' needs. From such efforts, work activity and day treatment centers for individuals with severe disabilities were established.

However, increasing evidence suggests that people with mental retardation can work competitively in nonsheltered employment settings when the appropriate support systems are available (Brickey, Browning, & Campbell, 1982; Kraus & MacEachron, 1982. The term *supported employment* has been used to describe this kind of work environment. The Developmental Disabilities Act defines supported employment as: paid employment which (1) is for persons with developmental disabilities for whom competitive employment at or above the minimum wage is unlikely and who, because of their disabilities, need ongoing support to perform in a work setting; (2) is conducted in a variety of settings, particularly work sites in which persons without disabilities are employed; and (3) is supported by any activity needed to sustain paid work by persons with disabilities, including supervision, training, and transportation (Federal Register, 1984). Additional information regarding employment options for individuals with mental retardation is provided in Chapter 14.

The Role of Collaboration and Consultation

Being able to create a school system responsive to the needs of all students (i.e., with and without disabilities), will require a new kind of interaction among regular educators, special educators, administrators, parents, and students that involves shared decision-making (Duke, Showers, & Imber, 1980; Nevin, Thousand, Paolucci-Whitcomb, & Villa, 1990). One way in which many schools have put shared decision-making into practice is to create "collaborative teams" (Stainback & Stainback, 1990; Thousand, 1990). A definition of a collaborative team, as well as a detailed discussion of the collaborative teaming process follow.

Definition of a Collaborative Team

Five components for defining a collaborative team have been proposed (Villa, Thousand, Stainback, & Stainback, 1992, p. 76). The team must:

1. Coordinate their work to achieve at least one *common, publicly agreed-upon goal* (Appley & Winder, 1977).
2. Hold a *belief system* that all members of the team have a unique and needed expertise (Vandercook & York, 1990).
3. Demonstrate *parity*, the equal valuation of each member's input (Falck, 1977), by alternately engaging in the dual roles of teacher and learner, expert and recipient, consultant and consultee (Villa, Thousand, Paolucci-Whitcomb, & Nevin, 1990).
4. Use a *distributed functions theory* of leadership in which the task and relationship functions of the traditional lone leader are distributed among all members of the group (Johnson & Johnson, 1987a, 1987b).
5. Employ a *collaborative teaming process* that involves face-to-face interaction; positive interdependence; the performance, monitoring and processing of interpersonal skills; and individual accountability (Johnson & Johnson, 1987a, 1987b).

Villa et al. (1992) have claimed that the collaborative teaming process encompasses the other four components when a collaborative team is operating successfully. Therefore, the discussion below is directed to the four elements that make up a collaborative teaming process. For each element a brief overview and discussion of how this element could foster a more inclusive school are provided.

The Collaborative Team Process

Frequent Face-to-Face Interaction
Frequent face-to-face meetings for collaborative teams provide the members with a forum to voice their concerns as well as listen to the concerns of others. Since these meetings occur frequently, members have an opportunity to get to know one another so that trust can be fostered. Other benefits of frequently planned meetings include the luxury of examining the complexities of an issue before deciding upon a possible problem-solving strategy.

Frequent face-to-face meetings also foster the integration of students with mental retardation because these forums enable regular and special education teachers to address the issue of what instructional needs and adaptations an individual student's learning style warrants. This kind of ongoing discussion of how best to meet the needs of a mainstreamed student with mental retardation could lead to a recommendation for team teaching between special education and regular classroom teachers. In a team teaching situation, teachers would share full responsibility for the same large group of students, and students with mental retardation would be permanent members of the class.

Positive Interdependence

Positive interdependence involves the belief among the members of the collaborative team that one cannot succeed unless they all succeed, and that each member's work benefits both that member and every other member of the team (Johnson & Johnson, 1987a, p. 399). A strategy for creating such a climate is to provide time for team members to explore the relevancy of group goals to each member's individual goals. Although this can be a time-consuming process, the experience fosters a sense of ownership of the team's purpose.

When this process of goal discovery is paired with a discussion of what each member of the team wants or needs from the group in order to work toward the common goal, then the best balance of special and regular education can be achieved. This balance can give enough support to enable a student with mental retardation to achieve his or her potential.

Interpersonal Skills for Collaboration

Some of the interpersonal skills that have been identified as important to the success of collaborative teams include: trust building, communication, leadership, creative problem solving, decision making, and conflict management (Johnson, Johnson, Holubec, & Roy, 1984). Since most of the members of a given team may not have had opportunities to develop these skills, it is important that the team create opportunities for members to: 1) see the need for the skill; 2) learn how and when the skill will be used; 3) practice the use of the skill; and 4) discuss and receive feedback on how well they are using the skill.

As team members create opportunities for developing interpersonal skills in the area of creative problem solving, the following ten guidelines should be considered (Meyen, 1990, p. 87):

1. Learn everything you can from the person you are invited to assist. For especial education teachers, this means learning about the operation of the general education classroom; for classroom teachers, this means learning how to construct individual interventions.

2. Assist, rather than lead, your colleague in clarifying the problem.

3. The teacher who initiates a request for assistance should take charge of the collaborative meeting; do not assume that you have to be the one in charge just because you have been asked to help.

4. Provide guidance, not ready-made answers.

5. Ask other staff members for assistance when you have a problem they can help you solve; do not always be in the position of giving but not receiving advice.

6. When planning informal meetings, the schedule of the classroom teacher should be accommodated as much as possible. Remember, classroom teachers have tight schedules, with responsibility for 25 to 30 students all day long!

7. Listen to your colleagues carefully.

8. Remember that you may routinely use terminology that a colleague trained in a different specialization may not understand; be sensitive to your own language during collaboration, and do not shut out others by using jargon.

9. Develop interventions jointly; if you impose a solution one-sidedly, your colleague may be either unwilling to implement it or unskilled at implementing it.

10. Trust your colleagues to be as committed as you are to the needs of the student you are discussing.

Individual Accountability

Individual accountability exists when the performance of each individual group member is assessed in order to:

1. Inform the group of which members need more assistance or encouragement in completing their work.
2. Increase members' perceptions that their contributions to the group effort are identifiable, and that they must fulfill their responsibilities in order for the group to be successful, as well as to be successful themselves (Johnson & Johnson, 1987a, p. 400).

One way in which group members can monitor individual accountability is to create and utilize prestructured worksheets that record decisions, identify individuals who will conduct the follow-up procedures, and establish a time frame in which follow-up measures need to be reported. This kind of structure has proven to be an effective tool for promoting individual accountability. For ideas about how to structure such a worksheet, team members should consult Thousand and Villa (Thousand & Villa, 1992, Figure 3).

Individual accountability is crucial to the fostering of more inclusive schools. Without input from all team members affected by a given issue, the implementation of a well-coordinated plan of action will be made more difficult.

Recommendations

The focus of this chapter has been to describe a number of placement options that are available for individuals with mental retardation. Placement decisions are influenced by the individual's learning characteristics (e.g., level of retardation, academic and social skills, management needs, and motivational factors). Other factors that influence placement decisions include parental awareness of available options and the breadth of school and community resources available to students with mental retardation. Some recommendations for those involved in making and implementing placement choices are as follows:

1. The continuum of placement models should be reviewed, and new models created to meet the needs that preexisting models do not address.

2. The quality of instruction for students with mental retardation should be emphasized regardless of their placement.

3. Whether the service delivery model used for infants and preschool children includes home-based, center-based, a combination of home- and center-based, or hospital-based programs, the many ways in which parents can be involved in their child's intervention should not be overlooked.

4. Before deciding what type of resource room program an individual student with mental retardation could benefit from, attention should focus on how the student's resource room instruction will be coordinated with the instruction that he or she receives outside the resource room.

5. As school systems implement *inclusion*, a new kind of interaction among teachers (regular educators and special educators), administrators, parents, and students that includes shared decision-making should be explored.

6. The use of collaborative teams should be explored as school systems become more responsive to the needs of all students, both with and without disabilities.

7. As collaborative teams are formed, frequent meetings should be scheduled so that members have an opportunity to get to know and trust one another.

References

Appley, D. G. & Winder, A. E. (1977). An evolving definition of collaboration and some implications for the world of work. *Journal of Applied Behavioral Science, 13*, 279–291.

Bagnato, S. J. & Neisworth, J. T. (1985). Efficacy of interdisciplinary assessment and treatment for infants and preschoolers with congenital and acquired brain injury. *Analysis and Intervention of Developmental Disabilities, 5*, 81–102.

Bailey, D. B. & Wolery, M. (1984). *Teaching infants and preschoolers with handicaps.* Columbus, OH: Merrill.

Barksdale, M. W. & Atkinson, A. P. (1971). A resource room approach to instruction for the educable retarded. *Focus on Exceptional Children, 3*, 12–15.

Bellamy, G. T., Rhodes, L. E., Mank, D. M., & Albin, J. J. (1988). *Supported employment: A community implementation guide.* Baltimore, MD: Brookes Publishing Company.

Bitter, J. A. (1979). *Introduction to rehabilitation.* St. Louis: C. V. Mosby.

Blackman, L. S. & Heintz, P. (1966). The mentally retarded. *Review of Educational Research, 36*, 5–36.

Blatt, B. (1987). *The conquest of mental retardation.* Austin, Texas: Pro-ed.

Bluma, S. M., Shearer, M. S., Frohman, A. H., & Hillard, J. M. (1976). *Portage guide to early education.* Portage, WI: Cooperative Educational Service Agency.

Board of Education of the Hendrick Central School District, Westchester Co. v. Rowley ex rel. Rowley. (1982). 458 U.S. 176.

Boyer, E. L. (1983). *High school: A report on secondary education in America.* New York: Harper & Row.

Brickey, M., Browning, L., & Campbell, K. (1982). Vocational histories of sheltered workshop employees placed in projects with industrial and competitive jobs. *Mental Retardation, 20*, 52–57.

Brolin, D. E. (1976). *Vocational preparation of retarded citizens.* Columbus, OH: Merrill.

Brown v. Board of Education. (1954). 347 U.S. Supreme Court 485.

Brown, L., Long, E., Udvari-Solner, A., Davis, L., VanDeventer, P., Ahlgren, C., Johnson, F., Gruenwald, L., & Jorgensen, J. (1989). The home school: Why students with severe disabilities must attend the schools of their brothers, sisters, friends, and neighbors. *The Journal of the Association for Persons with Severe Handicaps, 14*, 8–12.

Calberg, C. & Kavale, K. (1980). The efficacy of special versus regular class placement for exceptional children: A meta-analysis. *The Journal of Special Education, 14*(3), 295–304.

Christopolos, F. & Renz, P. A. (1969). A critical examination of special education programs. *Journal of Special Education, 3*, 371–379.

The Council for Exceptional Children. (1993, April). *Statement on inclusive schools and communities.* Reston, VA: Author.

Duke, D., Showers, B., & Imber, M. (1980). Teachers and shared decision-making: The costs and benefits of involvement. *Educational Administration Quarterly, 16*, 93–106.

Dunn, L. M. (1968). Special education for the mildly retarded—is much of it justifiable? *Exceptional Children, 35*, 5–22.

Falck, H. (1977). Interdisciplinary education and implications for social work practice. *Journal of Educational for Social Work, 13*(2), 30–47.

Fredericks, H. D. B., Baldwin, V., Moore, W., Templeman, T. P., & Anderson, R. (1980). The teaching research data-based classroom model. *JASH, 5*, 211–223.

Fredericks, H. D. B., Riggs, C., Furey, T., Grove, D., Moore, W., McDonnell, J., Jordan, E., Hansen, W., Baldwin, V., & Wadlow, M. (1976). *The teaching research curriculum for moderately and severely handicapped.* Springfield, Illinois: Charles C. Thomas.

Fuchs, D. & Fuchs, L. S. (1994). Inclusive schools movement and the radicalization of special education reform. *Exceptional Children, 60*(4), 294–309.

Garrison, M. & Hammill, D. (1971). Who are the retarded? *Exceptional Children, 38*, 13–20.

Gold, M. W. (1975). Vocational training. In J. Wortis (Ed.), *Mental retardation and developmental disabilities: An annual review, (Vol. 7)*, 254–264. New York: Brunner/Mazel.

Hammill, D. & Widerholt, J. L. (1972). *The resource room: Rationale and implementation.* New York: Grune & Stratton, Buttonwood Farms Division.

Hayden, A. H. & Dmitriev, V. (1975). The multidisciplinary preschool program for Down's Syndrome children at the University of Washington model preschool center. In B. Z. Friedlander, G. M. Sterritt, and G. E. Kirk (Eds.), *Exceptional infant; Vol. 3, Assessment and intervention*, 193–221. Jossey-Bass.

Johnson, C. M. (1980). *Preparing handicapped students for work: Alternative for secondary pro-*
gramming. Reston, VA: Council for Exceptional Children.

Johnson, D. & Johnson, R. (1984). Classrooms, learning structure, and attitudes toward handicapped students in mainstream settings: A theoretical model and research evidence. In R. Jones (Ed.), *Attitudes and attitude change in special education.* Reston, VA: Council for Exceptional Children.

Johnson, D. W. & Johnson, R. T. (1987a). *Joining together: Group theory and skills* (2nd ed.). Englewood Cliffs: NJ: Prentice-Hall.

Johnson, D. W. & Johnson, R. T. (1987b). *Learning together and alone: Cooperation, competition, and individualization* (2nd ed.). Englewood Cliffs, NJ: Prentice Hall.

Johnson, D. W., Johnson, R. T., Holubec, E., & Roy, P. (1984). *Circles of learning.* Arlington, VA: Association for Supervision and Curriculum Development.

Karnes, M. B. & Zehrbach, R. P. (1977). Alternative models for developing services to young handicapped children. In J. B. Kaufman, M., Agard, J. A., & Semmel, M. I. (1985). *Mainstreaming: learners and their environment.* Cambridge, MA: Brookline Books.

Keogh, B. K. (1988). Improving services for problem learners: Rethinking and restructuring. *Journal of Learning Disabilities, 21*, 19–22.

Kirk, S. A. (1964). Research in education. In H. A. Stevens & R. Heber (Eds.), *Mental retardation.* Chicago: University of Chicago Press.

Kraus, M. & MacEachron, A. (1982). Competitive employment training for mentally retarded adults: The supported work model. *American Journal of Mental Retardation, 86*, 650–653.

Leinhardt, G. & Pallay, A. (1982). Restrictive educational settings: Exile or haven? *Review of Educational Research, 52*(4), 557–578.

Lilly, S. M. (1986). The relationship between general and special education: A new face on an old issue. *Counterpoint, 10.*

Lilly, S. M. (1970). Special education: A teapot in a tempest. *Exceptional Children, 37*, 43–48.

MacMillan, D. L., Jones, R. L., & Aloia, G. F. (1974). The mentally retarded label: A theoretical analysis and review of research. *American Journal of Mental Deficiency, 86*, 650–653.

Mercer, J. R. (1974). *Labeling the mentally retarded.* Berkeley, CA: University of California Press.

Meyen, E. L. (2nd Ed.). (1990). *Exceptional children in today's schools*. Denver, Colorado: Love Publishing Company.

Mills v. Board of Education. 348 F. Supp. 866. (DDC), 1972.

Mithaug, D. E., Horiuchi, C. N., & Fanning, P. (1985). A report on the Colorado statewide followup study of special education graduates. *Exceptional Children*, *51*(5), 397–404.

National Commission on Excellence in Education. (1983). *A nation at risk: The imperative for educational reform*. Washington, DC: U.S. Department of Education.

Neisworth, J. T. & Bagnato, S. J. (1987). *The young exceptional child: Early development and education*. New York: Macmillan.

Nevin, A., Thousand, J., Paolucci-Whitcomb, P., Villa, R. (1990). Collaborative consultation: Empowering public school personnel to provide heterogeneous schooling for all. *Journal of Educational and Psychological Consultation*, *1*(1), 41–67.

Patton, J . R., Beirne-Smith, M., & Payne, J. S. (1990). *Mental retardation*. (3rd ed.). Columbus, OH: Merrill.

Patton, J. R., Payne, J. S., & Beirne-Smith, M. (1986). *Mental retardation* (3rd ed.). Columbus, OH: Merrill.

Pennsylvania Association for Retarded Children v. Commonwealth of Pennsylvania. 343 F. Supp. 279 (E.D., Pa.), 1972.

Reynolds, M. & Wang, M. C. (1983). Restructuring "special" school programs: A position paper. *Policy Studies Review*, *2*, 189–212.

Scientific Seer. Rudolf Steiner. (1969). MD, *The Medical News Magazine*, *13*, 245–250.

Semmel, M. I., Gottlieb, J., & Robinson, N. M. (1979). Mainstreaming: Perspectives on educating handicapped children in the public schools. In D. Berliner (Ed.), *Review of research in education* (*Vol. 7*). Washington, D.C.: American Educational Research Association.

Shearer, M. A. & Shearer, D. E. (1976). The Portage project: A model for early childhood education. *Exceptional Children*, *43*, 210–219.

Sizer, T. (1984). *Horace's compromise: The dilemma of the American high school*. Boston: Houghton Mifflin.

Smith, J. P. & Dexter, B. L. (1980). The basics movement: What does it mean for the education of men-

tally retarded students? *Education and Training of the Mentally Retarded*, *15*, 72–79.

Smith, R. M., Neisworth, J. T., & Hunt, F. M. (1983). *The exceptional child: A functional approach*. (2nd ed.). New York: McGraw-Hill.

Stainback, W. & Stainback, S. (1984). A rationale for the merger of special education: Implications for students. *Exceptional Children*, *53*, 327–329.

Stainback, W. & Stainback, S. (Eds.). (1990). *Support networks for inclusive schooling: Interdependent integrated education*. Baltimore: Brookes.

Thousand, J. S. (1990). Organizational perspectives on teacher education and renewal: A conversation with Tom Skrtic. *Teacher Education and Special Education*, *13*, 30–35.

Thousand, J. S. & Villa, R. A. (1991). A futuristic view of the REI: A response to Jenkins, Pious, and Jewell. *Exceptional Children*, *57*(6), 556–562.

Thousand, J. & Villa, R. (1992). Collaborative teams: A powerful tool in school restructuring. In Villa, R. A., Thousand, J. S., Stainback, W., Stainback, S. (1992), *Restructuring for caring, effective education: An administrative guide to creating heterogeneous schools*, 73–108. Baltimore: Brookes.

U.S. Department of Education. (1990). *Twelfth annual report to Congress on the implementation of the Education of the Handicapped Act*. Washington, DC: Author.

Vandercook, T. & York, J. (1990). A team approach to program development and support. In W. Stainback & S. Stainback (Eds.), *Support networks for inclusive schooling: Interdependent integrated education*, 201–218. Baltimore: Brookes.

Villa, R., Thousand, J., Paolucci-Whitcomb, P., & Nevin, A. (1990). In search of a new paradigm for collaborative consultation. *Journal of Educational and Psychological Consultation*, *1*(4), 279–292.

Villa, R. A., Thousand, S., Stainback, W., Stainback, S. (Eds). (1992). *Restructuring for caring and effective education: An administrative guide to creating heterogeneous schools*. Baltimore: Brookes.

Vitello, S. & Soskin, R. (1985). *Mental retardation: Its social and legal context*. Englewood Cliffs, NJ: Prentice-Hall.

Wiederholt, J. L., Hammill, D. D., Brown, V. (1978). *The resource teacher: A guide to effective practices*. Boston: Allyn & Bacon.

Will, M. C. (1986). Educating children with learning problems: A shared responsibility. *Exceptional Children, 52,* 411–415.

Williams, W., Villa, R., Thousand, J., & Fox, W. (1990). Is regular class placement really the issue? A response to Brown, Long, Udvari-Solner, Schwartz, VanDenventer, Ahlgren, *Journal of the Association for Persons with Severe Handicaps, 14,* 333–334.

Chapter 9

Early Intervention

This chapter summarizes and discusses the significance of intellectual delays and deficiencies in preschool children with mental retardation, as well as those placed at risk by poverty and disadvantage. The first section discusses the criteria for identifying those children who require early intervention. The second section reviews the research on the efficacy of early childhood intervention programs. The third section describes those cognitive strategies that are often the focus of training programs. The fourth section reviews some of the organized curricula that focus on cognitive development. The fifth section scans some examples of instructional activities often found in cognitively oriented curricula. The sixth section analyzes assessment techniques typically applied in this area. The final section makes some recommendations for early intervention efforts based on a review of the available literature.

Efforts to prevent or ameliorate cognitive deficits associated with mental retardation must focus on deterrents to satisfactory early childhood development and available interventions to counteract them. While the evidence is not unequivocal (Ferry, 1981), it has been suggested that the rapidity of central nervous system development in young children offers windows of opportunity for modifying cognitive functions in a way that might facilitate school learning and life adjustment later on (Hebb, 1949). Long before the advent of neurological theory, however, folk wisdom had already recognized the characteristic plasticity of the early developmental period. Illustrative of this recognition is Alexander Pope's often quoted line, "Just as the twig is bent, the tree's inclined."

Despite the widely accepted view that there is no such thing as "too soon" in dealing with the developmental and functional problems of children with disabilities, the first clear and comprehensive legislative mandate, PL94–142—The Education of All Handicapped Children Act—was not enacted until 1975. This act was designed to deal with the crisis in the schools caused by both an inability to manage the multifaceted problems of children with handicaps and, in some cases, an unwillingness to deal with those problems in the first place.

It was probably understandable that the first federal support thrust in the form of PL94–142 would be in the schools, where teachers and administrators, as well as parents, struggled to improve programs and services for children with handicaps. Still, it took eleven more years for the federal government to recognize formally that the roots of the schools' problems in providing for the large numbers of identified children with handicaps lay, to a great extent, in the inadequacy of preschool services for these children (Hebbeler, Smith, & Black, 1991).

This recognition came in the form of PL99–457—the Education of the Handicapped Act Amendments of 1986. Title I of this act responded to an urgent need "to enhance the development of handicapped infants and toddlers (birth–2 years) and to minimize their potential for developmental delay." Handicapped in this context refers to individuals who require remedial intervention because: (1) they have been diagnosed as experiencing developmental delays in cognition, physical status, language and speech, psycho-social skills, or self-help skills; or (2) they are deemed to be at risk of developmental delays if early intervention services are not provided. Title II of PL99–457 amended earlier provisions made for children with handicaps, ages three to five by: (1) establishing the conditions under which states may receive grants to support programs and services for preschool children; (2) specifying the amounts of funding available; and (3) indicating how grant funds may be distributed.

Identifying Children Who Require Early Intervention

According to Tjossem (1976), with the exception of those cases where disability is evident at birth, and later cognitive impairment is highly predictable (e.g., Down Syndrome), it is more desirable to speak of children at risk for developmental delay rather than making a possibly premature diagnosis of mental retardation. In identifying young children who may require systematic intervention programs, it is important to strike a balance between making parents and professionals aware of children exhibiting the kinds of delays in development that require preschool services while at the same time not oversensitizing parents to problems that may be transient and unrelated to future development. Striking that balance is obviously easier said than done. Good assessment devices, sound judgment, tact, respect for the views of parents, and professional humility are all important ingredients of a successful "child find" program.

Infants and young children who are especially vulnerable to delays in cognitive development fall into three types (Tjossem, 1976). The first, briefly noted earlier, are children with those conditions, often genetically determined, that are identified almost immediately after birth. Fragile X, for example, is one of those developmental pathologies that carry clearly established risks for cognitive deficits even though improved programs and training procedures have mitigated the severity of those deficits.

The second type includes those children who are at risk for cognitive deficits because of biological insults that occur before, during, or soon after birth. A variety of prebirth problems may cause low birth weight babies, as well as children born with Fetal Alcohol Syndrome, drug addiction, serious sensory impairments, and AIDS. With respect to the recent AIDS epidemic, it has been stated that "within 5 years, HIV infection is projected to become the largest infectious cause of mental retardation and brain damage in children" (Gray, 1989, p. 199). Medical mishaps that occur at the time of birth, including asphyxia and intracranial hemorrhage, might also result in cognitive impairment. After birth, serious infections of the central nervous system, such as encephalitis, may place children at risk for serious intellectual deficits. Finally, child abuse, head trauma resulting from accidents, poor nutrition, and excessive environmental lead levels have also been implicated as factors contributing to cognitive delays and deficits.

The third type is comprised of children who are at environmental risk because of socioeconomic factors. Whereas the specific dimensions of this problem have been difficult to pin down, poverty has been associated with an increased risk of mental retardation.

Types of Cognitive Inadequacy

If all children started school with their cognitive mechanisms intact for meeting the reading and arithmetic learning demands of the early grades, there would be little reason for this chapter. In fact, children who register for kindergarten at roughly the same chronological age often vary widely in their capacity to: (1) follow directions; (2) acquire, retain, and retrieve information; (3) comprehend fully both spoken language and stories read out loud; and (4) behave appropriately in the classroom.

The reasons for poor performance in school can often be traced to a cognitive infrastructure characterized by delay, deficit, and/or passivity. While, as a practical matter, it is often difficult to distinguish among these three types of cognitive malfunction, or to insist that they are mutually exclusive in any given child, it can be argued that they emanate from different etiological roots.

Cognitive delay, for example, may be something of a misnomer in some children. Although the child's intellectual readiness for the complexities of school learning may certainly seem delayed when viewed from the perspective of his or her more accelerated classmates, it may be right on time as far as the child's own biological clock is concerned. A preschool intervention for this child might focus more on realistically adapting educational objectives, choosing instructional strategies for achieving them, and determining the rates at which these objectives are expected to be accomplished rather than trying to force the child, at that particular stage and rate of development, into an educational trajectory that would overload his or her capacity and undermine his or her self-esteem.

A cognitive deficit suggests that a child was born on track for normal intellectual and academic functioning, but, as a result of a brain dysfunction caused by disease, accident, or malnutrition, has developed deficits in the operation of important cognitive processes that facilitate learning, memory, problem solving, and generalization. These underlying processes include cognitive strategies and metacognitive control functions, about which more will be said later. Here it should suffice to note that their absence or dysfunction predisposes children to academic failure and frustration. Appropriate preschool cognitive intervention might include training of these cognitive strategies when possible, or designing and applying compensatory instructional mechanisms that will allow children to reach pre-academic and academic goals despite deficits in cognitive strategies and metacognition.

Finally, cognitive passivity implies that a child's early environment neither encouraged cognitive development nor modeled the type of cognitive strategy activity that is required to support later classroom learning. Feuerstein (1980) has referred to this paucity of cognitive expectations in the child's early environment as a mediated learning deficiency. The cognitive passivity caused by this condition, while serious enough in its potential for causing cognitive deficits and academic failure later on, nevertheless appears to have the best prognosis for successful outcomes in early childhood cognitive intervention programs.

Drugs, Disease, and Trauma

Early childhood professionals, both in and out of preschool programs for children with mental retardation, are facing a growing epidemic of significant cognitive and attentional deficits that are traceable to "crack" addiction and Fetal Alcohol Syndrome. These children are born to mothers addicted to cocaine and alcohol, respectively, during their pregnancies. Many of these children are identified in the neonatal nurseries immediately after birth, showing evidence of drug- or alcohol-induced neurological dysfunction. These neurological problems continue to manifest themselves at the toddler and preschool stages in terms of distractibility, hyperactivity, and thinking disorders.

Children who have had AIDS transmitted to them by HIV infected mothers are also beginning to exert a major impact on preschool programs (Byers, 1989; Diamond, 1989). The children's distractibility, delays in cognitive development, and frequent illnesses, combined with the rigorous efforts to prevent spreading the disease as well as the specter of the children's early deaths, tax both the professional and emotional resources of preschool staffs. Close medical supervision, in-service training for teachers, and continuing professional and parent support groups are important components of these programs.

There is increasing evidence that child abuse is more prevalent in families in which there are children with disabilities (Zirpoli, 1986). Head trauma from violent shaking, striking, and dropping of children are increasing causes of brain damage with long-term developmental implications.

Research on the Goals and Efficacy of Early Childhood Intervention Programs

Goals of Early Intervention Programs

Early intervention programs for preschoolers with mental retardation, depending on the level of retardation for which the programs have been designed, have two main purposes. For some children with moderate mental retardation and all children with severe and profound levels of mental retardation, the emphasis is on reducing the delay in the acquisition of important developmental milestones. More seriously impaired children can also profit from early intervention programs with more functional objectives concerning the activities of daily living. For children with mild mental retardation or, more conservatively, at-risk children, the primary concern is with preparing them for successful academic performance (Haskins, 1989).

The major goals of early childhood programs for less impaired special needs children under five years of age are: (1) to minimize and, if possible, reverse the impact of delays or deficits in normal cognitive development on later school performance; and (2) to support family efforts to achieve desired intellectual, vocational, and social outcomes.

Efficacy of Early Intervention Programs

Perhaps the most reliable conclusion to be drawn from the many studies of the effectiveness of early childhood intervention programs is that, although it has been consistently demonstrated that IQ scores and measures of cognitive functioning can be significantly improved, the potential for parlaying these improved cognitive skills into better school performance and later life adjustment has yet to be firmly established. Clearly, there is still much to learn about the design and implementation of intervention programs.

The most recent illustration of the effectiveness of early intervention, particularly with at-risk, low birth weight babies, was reported by The Infant Health and Development Program (1990). This investigation followed the development of 985 infants who were born weighing less than 5.5 pounds each. One part of this sample was provided with intensive special education services, first at home, and later in special daycare centers. A comparison group was given regular pediatric care but no special education services. At age three, the group that had received special education services manifested significantly higher IQ scores and fewer behavior problems than the comparison group. The effects were more pronounced for a "heavier" subsample of babies, with birthweights between 4.4 and 5.5 pounds each, than they were for "lighter" babies who weighed less than 4.4 pounds each at birth.

The heavier group that received special services had mean IQ scores that were 13.2 points higher than the heavier comparison group. For the lighter babies, the special services group was 6.6 points higher in mean IQ scores than the comparison group that received no special education services. The enhanced effectiveness of this program with heavier babies might simply be a reflection of the principle that well-designed intervention programs will be relatively more successful with more neurologically intact children; if, in fact, weight correlates with degree of intactness. The children in the special services group were also 2.7 times less likely to have IQ scores in the range of mental retardation than the comparison group.

This study, like several others, has demonstrated that IQ and other cognitive capacity scores can be significantly improved for the short term. Most researchers, educators, and child advocates, however, would agree that the "proof of the pudding" is not just in improving IQ and other cognitive measures. Rather, the central issue is whether these newly acquired intellectual strategies that have germinated from an improved cognitive infrastructure will generalize to producing better school grades, the ability to be educated by ordinary means, and, ultimately, successful integration into community, vocational, and residential placements. Since The Infant Health and Development Program (1990) study has not yet had the opportunity to track these children through the school years, the question of whether the IQ differences between the special services and comparison groups will be maintained at age five, as well as the question of whether there will be a significant difference in school performance between the groups is as yet unanswered.

A previous and similar study by Garber (1988), already through its follow-up phases, may portend the findings of The Infant Health and Development Program when they become available. The main purpose of the Garber study, also known as the Milwaukee Project, was to determine whether mental retardation could be prevented or minimized in "at-risk" children. At-risk children were defined as children from disadvantaged backgrounds, whose mothers' IQs were below 75, and who evidenced no gross pathology. The early intervention program designed to prevent mental retardation was built around the principles of early environmental stimulation, changes in parental attitudes and practices, and the implementation of high-quality educational procedures.

The at-risk sample was divided into an Experimental Group (N=17) that received the early intervention program and a Control Group (N=18) that did not. In addition, a Low-Risk Contrast Group was added that was at no particular risk for mental retardation and that did not receive any intervention. At the infant level, the program provided to the Experimental Group was geared primarily toward the development of social, emotional, and perceptual skills. As the children increased in age, the program's objectives shifted gradually toward motor, cognitive, and language development.

Intellectual assessments were done regularly during the course of the study. By the age of 22 months, the Experimental Group was almost 27 points higher than the Control Group in their Gesell Developmental Quotient Scores. The Low-Risk Contrast Group fell between the other two groups. From twenty-four to seventy-two months, the Stanford-Binet (Form L–M) was administered. By the age of twenty-four months, there were highly significant differences in IQ scores among the groups. The Experimental Group had attained an impressive mean IQ score of 125; the Control Group's mean IQ score was 95, and the Low-Risk Contrast Group's mean IQ score was 112. Mean IQ score comparisons among the three groups, between forty-eight and seventy-two months, using the Wechsler Preschool and Primary Scale of Intelligence (WPPSI), revealed means of 110 for the Experimental Group, 85 for the Control Group, and 100 for the Low-Risk Contrast Group. From eighty-four to 120 months, this time using the Wechsler Intelligence Scale for Children (WISC) for estimating mean IQ scores, the means were 102 for the Experimental Group, 83 for the Control Group, and 101 for the Low-Risk Contrast Group. Although comparisons are risky because of the changes in the intelligence tests used, the program-enhanced IQ scores showed evidence of fading with increasing age.

Given that the Experimental Group children had been born to mothers with IQs less than 75, however, their significant improvement in IQ scores appears to speak to the power of environmental stimulation. This study is also in strong support of the work of many of the early environmentalists such as Skeels and Dye (1939), Skeels, Updegraff, Wellman, and Williams (1938), and Skodak (1938).

The potential significance of these findings has been questioned by Page's (1986) criticism of some of the methods used. Essentially, he argued that much of the educational program was geared toward developing competencies in children that were almost identical to those required to deal successfully with intelligence test items. If training-to-the-test actually occurred, one might expect improvements in IQ scores but would not necessarily expect to see those enhanced IQ scores reflected in either better classroom performance or improved postschool life adjustment skills.

The recently reported follow-up data in the Garber study may be instructive in this regard. Although the Experimental Group always remained ahead of the Control Group in grades one through four, both groups declined in percentile scores on the Metropolitan Achievement Test in both reading and math. Despite the uniform decline, reading scores held up relatively better than math scores for the Experimental Group. The Experimental Group never lost a 10 point IQ advantage over the Control Group but, by the age of fourteen, all three groups were similar with respect to school achievement. Despite having maintained normal IQs over the school years, the Experimental Group did not do as well in school as had been expected. They often performed below grade level and dropped out of high school at the same rate as those children who had not participated in this very early intervention program.

After a highly encouraging start, the results of the Milwaukee project demonstrate that more work is needed in early intervention programming. What is clear is that achieving an average IQ score against improbable odds did not guarantee the kind of school performance that an average IQ would normally predict. There are at least two possible explanations for this asynchrony between measured intelligence and academic achievement. The first is that Page (1986) may have been on target in his concern that teaching-to-the-test, if indeed that happened, would not develop the skills likely to generalize to more complex forms of classroom behavior. The second is that an average IQ, even if reflective of generalizable cognitive skills, still requires an environment that can maximize learning opportunities and support aspirations toward higher-level career goals.

If there is a message in all of this, it is that early identification of and intervention with children at risk or children with mental retardation, coupled with schools that are reformed and restructured to cater to the alternative learning styles of these children, are not enough. Unless the professional components of these remediation programs are fully complemented by social, economic, and health-maintenance structures that support families, assure social mobility, and promote access to the full range of appropriate careers, their benefits will continue to be limited.

Maintaining Early Gains

As evidenced by the two major studies just reviewed, the history of early intervention for children with mental retardation or those at risk for that condition has been characterized by early substantial advances in IQ scores and other cognitive measures followed by some evidence of a flattening improvement curve by the time the children reach school age. A meta-analysis, or integrative statistical summary, of a large number of individual studies involving primarily at-risk and disadvantaged children found that early intervention produced immediate benefits (Beauchamp, 1989; Castro & Mastropieri, 1986). By 60 months, however, these early benefits were less pronounced. According to Castro and Mastropieri (1986), the variables most impacted by a good early intervention program in declining order of effect are IQ, language, motor skills, social skills, and finally, academic achievement.

It is not entirely clear why it is difficult to both maintain enhancements in cognitive function and generalize those enhancements in order to improve academic achievement. In part, it may be that trajectories of intellectual growth are resistant to change and can be modified only with substantial and continuing efforts. The intervention rockets needed to boost a cognitive payload into a higher orbit must be both powerful and multi-stage. The need for remedial or developmental power at both the preschool and school levels suggests either the strong influence of genotypical factors in development or our inability to design powerful interventions with current concepts and curricula.

Since there is currently not much that we can do about genotypical factors, it behooves us as educators to continue to concentrate on designing powerful interventions. To compound the problem, as an educational establishment and as a society in general, we seem to be more attuned to "hit-and-run" programs designed to undo the sequelae of economic and social inequities, than we are to maintaining specialized "high gear" interventions throughout the educational career of the special-needs student. Part of the issue is cost, which is understandable within the context of other competing demands for resources. More debatable, however, is an emerging sense that many children, diagnosed as having mild mental retardation or as being at risk for that condition, have actually been misdiagnosed as requiring special educational intervention. To avoid inappropriate stigmatization, therefore, they would be best educated in the same programs that admit children who do not have mental retardation and who are not at risk.

Other studies have documented the decline phenomenon after early gains during and immediately after intervention. Gottfried's (1973) review of the effects of early intervention programs from 1966 to 1970 concluded that these effects were minimal. Specifically, Westinghouse's assessment of the highly visible Project Head Start found that the test results for Head Start graduates differed very little from their non-Head Start peers. Gray and Klaus' (1970) "Early Training Project" attempted to improve the educability of high-risk young children from disadvantaged homes. An important objective of this study was to counteract the progressive deterioration in elementary school performance that is typical of these children. An early superiority of the children in the intervention group over those in the control group on both intelligence and achievement measures was demonstrated; however, most differences disappeared by the age of seven.

In another review of the efficacy of early childhood programs, Haskins (1989) also observed the immediate, positive effects of early intervention on tests of intellectual performance and social competence. This effect declined, however, over the first few years of public schooling. Despite these declines in achievement during the first four grades, Haskins also noted some improvement in long-term adjustment measures of groups that had received early intervention. These included fewer teenage pregnancies, less delinquency, more graduates, and better employment records. What appears to be a U-shaped function of intervention effects—early improvement, fading in the early and middle elementary years, and an apparent resurgence of effect during the secondary period—was also noted by Lazar (1977), who found fewer intervention children enrolled in special classes. This "delayed fuse" effect, if real, seems to be associated primarily with cognitive intervention programs.

The Power Dimension of Early Intervention Programs

The finding that most early intervention programs produce immediate and short-term cognitive gains is encouraging and has been the prime impetus not only for continuing and expanding these programs but also for legislation (PL99–457) that makes early childhood identification and remediation programs for children with handicaps mandatory. The first-stage success of early intervention programs, however, does not mask the fact that significant problems remain in their design, implementation, and evaluation. The first and persistent indication that early intervention programming needed help (Guralnick & Bricker, 1987) was the observation that children retreated from early cognitive gains over time (Castro & Mastropieri, 1986). The response to this has been to try to upgrade the power of early intervention programs in the hope that effects could be extended over longer periods of time.

Although there has not been a complete consensus on what constitutes the power dimensions of early intervention programs, a number of factors have been identified as choice points from which more effective programming decisions may evolve. These include decisions about the relative value of: (1) home- versus center-based programs; (2) early versus late program onset; (3) intense versus less intense programming; (4) direct instruction of pre-academic content versus acontextual cognitive skill development; and (5) treatment versus service orientation in programming.

Home- Versus Center-Based Programming. The issue as to whether early intervention programs for children with mental retardation are best implemented in home- or center-based settings has been an active one (Bailey & Simeonsson, 1988). Logic suggests that home-based programs have some obvious advantages in rural areas where fragile children might have to be transported over long distances. Serious medical problems that require constant supervision or that might preclude children from leaving their homes, particularly in bad weather, would further recommend home-based programs. Financial considerations also seem to favor home-based programming.

Among other advantages cited for home-based instruction (Sheehan & Gradell, 1983) are that: (1) learning occurs in the child's and parents' natural environment; (2) little conflict develops between the program developers and the family's values and culture; and (3) there is some evidence that gains made in home instruction tend to be somewhat more tenacious than those made in center-based programs.

Center-based programs, on the other hand, appear to provide children with the following benefits: (1) more opportunities for the development of communication and socialization skills; (2) more convenient access to a multi-disciplinary professional team; (3) better and more varied educational materials; (4) trained teachers; (5) less tolerance for and more systematic response to inappropriate behavior; and (6) less reliance on parents who may have difficulty providing adequate instruction.

From a developmental perspective, professional opinion is heavily weighted toward the importance, both emotionally and educationally, of early high quality parent-child interactions (Castro & Mastropieri, 1986; Levinstein, 1970; Tjossem, 1976). Birth to two-year-old infant and toddler intervention programs rely heavily on parental involvement, while programs for three- to five-year-olds are primarily professionally driven and center-based (Bailey & Simeonsson, 1988). The resolution of the question of the relative superiority of home- versus center-based programs, therefore, seems to rest on developmental considerations about the differential roles of parent/child intimacy and peer socialization as important learning parameters at different maturational levels.

Early Versus Later Programming.   Both logic and cultural belief systems converge on the oft-quoted assumption that the earlier intervention programs are initiated, the more effective they are likely to be. Frantz's (1958) early work on the active approach of very young infants in their perception of visual patterns and Ferry's (1981) conjectures about the potential for greater neuronal modifiability in very young children offered at least theoretical support to that assumption.

The problem with assumptions is that they require confirming data before they can be elevated to the status of scientific principles. The few research studies that have analyzed the effects of early versus later onset programming have been largely unable to support the opinion that earlier is better than later. For example, studying the effects on emotional adjustment of enrollment in day care before versus after the age of three, Braun and Caldwell (1973) found no differences. Bronfenbrenner (1975) also reported that children entering intervention programs before the age of three did no better than later entrants. This lack of difference related to age of entrance into programs was also confirmed by Castro and Mastropieri (1986). In fact, in a few studies they found that later starters did better. One exception was reported in a review by Guralnick and Bricker (1987). They found that children who started intervention programs earlier were more likely to achieve higher levels of development.

Although the evidence is inferential at best, efforts made with children with Down Syndrome may suggest the value of very early intervention (Tingey, Mortensen, Matheson, & Doret, 1991). Many of these children are now admitted to infant stimulation programs soon after birth. In general, the effects of these programs appear to be salutary (Guralnick & Bricker, 1982). They seem to have halted the up-to-now anticipated decline in the cognitive functioning of Down Syndrome children with increasing age. It is even more encouraging that many children with Down Syndrome, traditionally classified as having moderate to severe mental retardation, are functioning at high enough levels to be admitted to programs for children with mild mental retardation.

In summary, when good sense and available theory come together in recommending earlier as opposed to later intervention it is difficult to interpret the meaning of ambiguous data. It is possible that we are choosing the wrong variables to measure the effects of early versus late intervention or, if the variables are appropriate, the available instrumentation may be insufficiently sensitive to detect important changes that have, in fact, occurred. When the data are ambiguous, prudence would suggest that the response to mental retardation should be the earliest and highest level of professional concern for the children and their families.

Intense Versus Less Intense Programming.   An important study that looked specifically at the issue of whether variation in program intensity would affect intellectual development emerged from Project CARE (Carolina Approach to Responsive Education) (Ramey, Bryant, Sparling, & Wasik, 1985). For this study, 64 infants were selected because they were considered to be at risk for mild mental retardation. This judgment was based on the families' disadvantaged socioeconomic and educational status. These children were randomly assigned to a high intensity intervention group that received educational day care plus family education, a low intensity group that received only family education, and a control group that received neither. After 36 months, the high intensity group obtained an average IQ score of 104.5, the low intensity group scored 88.4, and the control group scored 92.9. The significant difference between the high intensity and the other two groups was due primarily to a decline over three years in the scores of the low intensity and control groups while the high intensity group held its own. Thus, the high intensity program did not accelerate the trajectory of development for children in that group but rather allowed the group to maintain average IQ scores and a normal rate of intellectual development. On the other hand, the low intensity and control groups evidenced a decline in both the rate and level of their intellectual development.

The findings of the Ramey et al. study (1985) were supported by Castro and Mastropieri's (1986) metaanalysis of seventy-four studies that found that high intensity programming and length of exposure were associated with increased effectiveness in a number of different areas of development. What these findings seem to suggest is that early intervention programs for children with mental retardation at all levels, from mild to profound, should not be designed or expected to offer anti-mental retardation vaccinations. Rather, they should be viewed as first-stage preschool programs to be followed by highly specialized second-, third-, fourth-, and fifth-stage programs as the children move through the elementary, middle school, secondary, and work transitional aspects of their educational careers. Stemming the deteriorative effects of mental retardation, while expanding the educational and life options of individuals so diagnosed, must be a continuing effort shared by parents, professionals, and governmental advocates alike.

Direct Instruction Versus Cognitive Skill Development.   During the school years, curriculum builders for children with mental retardation have debated the relative effectiveness of directly teaching specific academic and life adjustment skills versus teaching those cognitive strategies that are ostensibly foundational to a broader range of learning and skill development (Blackman & Lin, 1984). Typically, cognitive strategy training is favored for younger children who may be more intellectually pliable and, therefore, more receptive to that training. They will also have a longer period of time to apply their newly acquired cognitive skills to the solution of a wider array of school and postschool problems.

Cognitive strategy training has more adherents for training children at higher levels of mental retardation, and direct behaviorally oriented instruction is the method of choice at the severe and profound levels of mental retardation. While direct instruction also has much to contribute to programs for children with mild mental retardation, cognitive strategy training is rarely appropriate for children with severe or profound levels of mental retardation. The prevailing wisdom, well supported by observation and experience, is that severe organic impairment, almost always associated with lower levels of mental retardation, limits the benefits that can be expected from cognitive training.

The push for direct instruction is based on the argument that the surest and shortest road to teaching reading or language skills is to teach reading or language skills. This position has some validity in that there is little dramatic evidence to date that cognitive strategies trained in one setting will generalize easily to others (Blackman & Lin, 1984; Mann, 1979). Still, if researchers were to succeed in remediating a limited number of key intellectual factors currently inoperative or deficient in individuals with mental retardation, it is possible that those improvements could infiltrate every aspect of academic functioning.

Belmont (1989) has observed that the development of effective thinking activities emanates from continuing and intimate interpersonal experiences between parents and children that gradually imprint the parents' conceptual strengths (or weaknesses) in the child. According to Feuerstein (1980), the process, referred to as mediated learning, works best when the parents are cognitively capable and approach the teaching task with motivation and intentionality.

Despite a common perception that cognitive development should be stressed early, the relationship of cognitive instruction to other competencies is controversial. The relative merits of cognitive readiness training as a prerequisite to the development of more effective functional behaviors, as compared to direct instruction to foster those behaviors (White, 1988), are still being contested. Bronfenbrenner's (1975) review of studies that were relevant to the effectiveness of early intervention found that highly structured, cognitively oriented programs produced the longest-lasting effects on children enrolled in those programs.

A few studies have compared the effectiveness of direct instruction and cognitive instruction for young children with disabilities. Cole, Mills, and Sale (1989) did a two-year follow-up of preschool graduates who had been enrolled either in a mediated learning (cognitive) or an academic (direct instruction) program. Little difference was found in that children from both programs showed evidence of maintaining or increasing both their academic and cognitive skills two years after the intervention. Similar findings were reported by Dale and Cole (1988), who compared preschoolers (CAs 3 to 5) who had been enrolled in direct instruction or mediated learning programs. Again, in the direct instruction program, the children were taught primarily academic skills, while in the mediated learning program, the children were taught the cognitive processes associated with the input, elaboration, and output of information in a classroom atmosphere that stressed reflectivity and encouraged cognitive self-esteem. The results indicated that neither program had a distinct advantage. The mediated learning group performed better on some measures of cognitive and early language development while the direct instruction group performed better on others. The most persuasive conclusion to be drawn from this study is that both programs improved performance to approximately the same extent.

While our ability to enhance performance is encouraging, researchers have been unable to generate convincing data that establishes the superiority of either direct or cognitive instruction for young children. This may be due, in part, to the commonly experienced research problem that it is easier to generate fine analytic differences between these instructional paradigms in theory but more difficult to see those distinctions in the context of classroom implementation. In the hands of "real-life" teachers and children, direct instruction can and frequently does include perceptible elements of cognitive instruction. The other side of this coin is that even though cognitive instruction is often designed to be acontextual in the sense that it can be free of any particular subject matter, it often bridges into illustrative academic material. In fact, so-called academic bridging activities are becoming more popular as educators who favor cognitive instruction confront obstacles to the generalization of trained cognitive skills (Brainin, 1982). It is reasonable to expect that the future will witness increased merging of cognitive and direct instructional techniques.

Treatment Versus Service Orientation.   The cornerstone of the approach to early intervention programs for children with more severe levels of mental retardation has been to identify significant deficits in early functioning and to design curricula and methods to treat those deficits in a way that allows the children to achieve developmental benchmarks sooner than they might otherwise. The approach was similar for children with mild mental retardation, or those considered at risk for that condition. For these children, the emphasis was on cognitive remediation leading to higher IQs and improved readiness for achieving at grade level in school.

After the Westinghouse evaluation of the Head Start program in 1969, four years after the initiation of Head Start, it became clear that this treatment perspective was not producing the intended results (Turner, Connell, & Mathis, 1980). For children with a limited exposure to Head Start, there was no difference in their school performance as compared to children in a control group. Children with more extended Head Start experience performed better than the control group in the first grade but then declined in the second and third grades to the point that those differences were no longer apparent.

Turner et al. (1980) suggested that the treatment model of early intervention was too narrow in its objectives, and too focused on short-term, measurable outcomes, to be responsive to the myriad of problems that were implicated in the poor school performance of these children. They proposed a service model to replace the treatment model. The service model shifts the emphasis from the child alone to the family as a unit. Instead of the highly specialized professional staff envisioned in the treatment model to teach pre-academic and cognitive skills to the child, the service model recommends experienced staff familiar with community issues and problems. The service model is also more committed to putting coordinated support services in place for the entire family, rather than identifying and remediating specific deficits in the children. In addition to early education, these support services include financial assistance, better housing, and improved health care (Bronfenbrenner, 1975).

The essential position taken in the service model approach to early intervention is that the school-related problems manifested by at-risk children and those with mild mental retardation are most appropriately addressed by attacking the economic, social, and health problems that may be the root causes of the cognitive deficits and school failures observed in many of these children. The service model is not only making headway in the at-risk and mild group, but is also having an impact on early intervention programs for children with severe to profound levels of mental retardation. It is not only the children who receive high-impact training. Parents and other family members receive training so that they too can play a role in the instruction of their children. Perhaps even more importantly, families are given support in the forms of immediate financial assistance, life-long guardianship planning, and counseling services. Evidence that the broader-gauged service model has achieved some preeminence in the field is the broadening from the PL94–142 requirement that each child have an Individualized Education Program (IEP), to the PL99–457 requirement that each child have an Individualized Family Service Plan (IFSP).

Cognitive Strategy Training

Preschool curricula for children with mental retardation have typically included as one of their major objectives the development of those cognitive skills or strategies that are likely to be supportive of the later acquisition of academic skills during the school years. In order to be effective in their support mission, those cognitive skills must be linked to a number of motivational, attitudinal, and learning style "peripherals" that act as the lubricants necessary to the smooth operation of the cognitive strategies. Cognitive strategies have received considerable attention, both in terms of research designed to identify how they work and programs developed for the purpose of teaching them to children. Sometimes the latter has proceeded in the absence of a good understanding of the former.

Illustrative Cognitive Strategies

Different cognitive strategies have been closely associated with different theoretical approaches. Since this stage of the discussion is better served by an explanatory overview rather than a sharp theoretical focus, a selection of those strategies noted frequently in both the research and practice literature follows.

Strategies	*Definition*	*Illustration*
Making Distinctions	Focuses on those aspects of objects or events that are most important in establishing differences among them.	"You can pour your milk into a cup or glass. Do you notice what is different about them? A cup has an ear that helps you hold on."
Induction	Looks for shared properties and functions in objects or events that are also different in many ways.	"Milk, cherry soda, and orange juice all have different colors. What's the same about them? You can drink all of them."

Strategies	*Definition*	*Illustration*
Concept Formation	Assigns a label to a class of items that share important common properties or functions.	"These animals can be big or small and have long or short hair. They all have four legs and a tail and they bark. We call all of them dogs."
Deduction	Uses a formed concept to decide whether any new item can be included as a member of that concept.	"We all know what animals and vegetables are. Now look at this (starfish). Is it an animal or vegetable? Why do you think so?"
Abstracting Relationships	Generating a list of associates to items for which a relationship is sought until common properties or functions appear on all lists.	"Tell me everything you know about a penny, a ball, a wheel. Now think about all the things that you have told me. Is there any word that is the same for penny, wheel, and ball? Right—they are all round."
Divergent Thinking	Extending the meaning of an object to include ever more remote examples of that concept.	"Tell me all the things that you can do with a brick."
Convergent Thinking	Focusing on a particular instance of a conceptual framework.	"On the 4th of July, we have parades, picnics, fireworks, and grown-ups making speeches. Which activity do you like the best? Why?"
Representing	Assigning a symbol or name to a familiar object so that it can be dealt with conceptually even in the absence of the object.	"Here is a kite. This is how you play with it and this is why it is able to fly." (Next day, kite not present.) "What did we learn about yesterday that flies? Do you remember why it can fly?"
Object Permanence	Knowing that the same object has the same meaning regardless of its orientation in space.	"Here is a cup. What do we do with it?" (Remove it. Later, show it again upside down.) "What is this? What do we do with it?"
Conservation	Knowing that the same volume or quantity remains constant even though it may be displayed differently.	Place 5 pennies in a line on a table spaced about one inch apart. "Count the pennies in this line." Spread the pennies until they are two inches apart. Now ask,

(continued)

Strategies	Definition	Illustration
		"Are there more pennies than there were before?" Count them to be sure.
Rehearsing	A strategy for remembering that requires repeated practicing of the material.	"We will memorize this sentence. I will say it first and then you repeat it after me. Now say it your-self and keep repeating it until you can remember it."
Grouping	A strategy for remembering in which stimuli are grouped based on their perceptual and/or re-dundancy characteristics.	"Let's remember your phone num-ber, 759–6622. First repeat the numbers before the dash until you remember them. Now repeat the numbers after the dash. Notice that there are only two numbers. Each is repeated twice."
Clustering	A strategy for remembering in which the items to be remembered are grouped according to their meaning.	"Let's remember the words shirt, pants, hammer, and pliers. First, remember the two clothing words. Now, remember the two tool words."
Retrieval	Retrieving material from memory by using verbal markers to access the locations in which that material is stored.	"We're studying animals today. Tell me all the animal names that you can remember."
Visual Imagery	Storing material to be remembered in visual forms to facilitate later retrieval.	"As I read this story about a dog's tricks, try to imagine a picture in your mind in which the dog is sitting up and begging for food."
Verbal Mediation	Different items to be stored and retrieved later are linked by meaningful sentences.	"The way to remember that a green light means walk is to say to yourself, 'Grass is green and it's fun to walk on it.'"
Analogical Reasoning	Establishing the relation-ship between two items as the basis for inferring a similar relationship between two others.	"If your brother is a boy, then your sister must be a (*girl*)."

Strategies	*Definition*	*Illustration*
Generalization	Recognizing that a strategy found effective in the solution of one problem is equally applicable to a new one even though that new one may differ from the original in task demand and materials.	"Yesterday, you remembered that green means walk by making up a little story about it. Now make up a story that will help you remember that + means add and – means take away."
Metacognition	A cognitive control mechanism that helps the child to understand the strengths and limitations of his or her cognitive system.	"I'm going to give you 10 numbers to remember. How many do you think you can remember?" The child says 8. The child tries and remembers 3. "You said you could recall 8 but only recalled 3. How many will you remember next time?"
Executive Function	A cognitive control mechanism which allows a child to scan his inventory of available cognitive strategies appropriate to a problem at hand, use one of them, and monitor outcome.	The child is given a piece of paper to make a boat. He is given a hammer, a paper clip, and scissors to help him. The competing strategies are to cut, pound, or clip together the edges of the paper. The cutting strategy is selected and is evaluated by the child and teacher as resolving the boat-making problem.

This list of strategies that often, either explicitly or implicitly, forms the basis for cognitive curricula for children with mental retardation is illustrative rather than exhaustive. A serious effort to list them all with accompanying recommendations for instructional activities would be a text in itself (Meeker, 1969).

Style Concomitants of Cognitive Strategy Training

It was noted earlier that strategies are acquired more efficiently and used more effectively in the presence of certain attitudinal or learning style catalysts. The more important of these catalysts include the capacity for self-regulation (Whitman, 1990; Zimmerman, 1990), appropriate attributions for success or failure in learning (Borkowski, Weyhing, & Turner, 1986), a reflective rather than an impulsive approach to solving problems (Lin, Blackman, Clark, & Gordon, 1983), and the capacity for intrinsic rather than extrinsic motivation (Haywood, 1989).

Self-Regulation

Self-regulation is demonstrated by children who assume that the solutions to problems, both academic and social, are achievable by recourse to their own repertoire of learned strategies, skills, and information. While outside resources may be requested to overcome specific obstacles, actions directed toward problem solving are self-initiated, self-monitored for appropriateness, and altered as required to achieve successful outcomes. The environment is not the primary source of problem solution or the reinforcement of behavior leading to problem solution. It is the context in which an autonomous, self-initiating, self-regulating, and self-reinforcing child deploys his or her inventory of cognitive strategies in an effort to achieve mastery over problems spawned in that environmental context.

Success and Failure Attributions

Attribution theory (Borkowski, Weyhing, & Turner, 1986) has suggested that children acquire information and solve problems best when "correct" intrapersonal assumptions are made about the reasons for success and failure in learning and problem solving. Good learners are characterized as children who attribute their successes to ability and their failures to task difficulty or lack of effort. Poor learners, on the other hand, attribute their successes to ease of task or luck and their failures to lack of ability. Although different attributional styles appear to be associated with successful and unsuccessful learners, it is difficult to establish a cause and effect relationship between them. The so-called correct attribution of having faith in one's own ability, however, does make sense as a better foundation for learning both in and out of the classroom.

There is clearly some overlap between ability-oriented attributions for success and the concept of self-esteem. The child who has learned self-esteem is typically confident in his or her ability to solve problems. When, on occasion, problem solutions prove elusive, he or she is able to tolerate the temporary frustrations associated with the effort. Self-esteem, or a sense of effort-based competence in learning situations, is an important characteristic of the successful learner. It develops in children whose learning environments have been tailored to their level of development and profile of intellectual strengths and weaknesses. Self-esteem also flourishes in an atmosphere of appreciation of the child's efforts, acceptance of the child's errors as opportunities for learning, and consistent praise for work correctly done.

Reflective Versus Impulsive

A dimension of cognitive style, more often talked about than studied in children with mental retardation, is that of reflection and impulsivity (Kagan, Rosman, Day, Albert, & Phillips, 1964). Reflection is described as the capacity to consider a variety of responses available for problem solution before selecting one, and then monitoring its outcome. Impulsivity, on the other hand, is defined as the tendency to select a response without scanning or weighing the potential benefits of alternatives. Children with mental retardation are more often described as impulsive than reflective. If cognitive training is to be successful, however, these children must begin to approach problems in a more reflective manner. Fortunately, there is some evidence that cognitive training programs do result in impulsive children becoming significantly more reflective in finding solutions to problems (Lin et al., 1983).

Intrinsic Motivation

Haywood (1986) has proposed that the ability to sustain intrinsic rather than extrinsic motivation is also an important component of successful learning and, ultimately, good school adjustment. Intrinsic motivation occurs when a child's rewards for good performance are self- rather than other-administered. While parents and teachers should always be responsive to children's honest efforts and successes, for the intrinsically motivated child that verbal praise or pat on the back triggers a confirmation of previously acquired internalized values about the importance of learning and the excitement of problem solving.

The Promise and Limits of Cognitive Strategy Training

The cognitive strategies and motivational catalysts described above are important ingredients of training programs for children with mental retardation at every stage of their development from preschool through secondary education. They represent important training objectives precisely because they are the intellectual skill areas in which children with mental retardation perform most poorly. If a low IQ score is an objective way of making a diagnosis of mental retardation from a psychometric perspective, then the relative inability to solve problems, see relationships, and generalize skills from one setting to another are the markers of mental retardation from an information processing perspective. Cognitive and motivational deficits, in their many forms, define mental retardation in the professional literature in the same way that IQs below 70 define it in the popular literature.

It should be noted that cognitively oriented training objectives are generally limited to children with mild mental retardation. These children typically have a non-organic etiology underlying their mental retardation and have adequate language skills. Moreover, from the point of view of observed thinking skills and academic expectations, they often appear to be just a step or two away from the performance of children without mental retardation. There is an implied promise that stimulating cognitive activities may push the performance of these children, both cognitively and academically, into the normal range of functioning.

Training objectives for children with more severe levels of mental retardation are not often couched in cognitive terms. The severity of involvement typically accompanied by evidence of wide-ranging brain damage makes it unlikely that self-regulated problem solving, with all of its cognitive strategy nuances, is a realistic expectation. Necessary behavioral enhancements for these children, typically in the areas of communication and daily living activities such as dressing, feeding, and using the toilet, require behavioral interventions. Specialists in behavior analysis, applying appropriate reinforcement contingencies, have designed sophisticated programs for implementing behavioral changes in areas that will facilitate the family adjustment, general social acceptability, and school readiness of these children. Chapters 7 and 10 are particularly instructive in this regard.

Returning to the impact of cognitive curricula on improving performance in preschool children with mild mental retardation or those considered at risk for that condition, it should be recognized that a cognitive training program requires that certain assumptions be made by the trainer. The most important of these is that cognitive functions are modifiable either in the sense that their development might be accelerated beyond the rate in evidence before cognitive intervention began or that specific deficits that had been identified are amenable to remediation. There are enough programs of this type in the field to indicate that such assumptions abound. At the current state of the professional literature, it is clear that cognitive training curricula do produce positive short-term changes in measures of cognitive function (Castro & Mastropieri, 1986). Follow-up studies tracking the stability of these changes over time are more sobering in their conclusion that the improvements in functioning found during and immediately after training are difficult to maintain.

The professional response to this enigma has fallen into two categories. One has suggested that, even though cognitive functions may be trainable, they are not likely to be reflected in improved performance on real-life tasks (Blackman & Lin, 1984). The second type of response takes heart from the temporary improvements that have occurred and continues to work toward that day when better theory and methods will both "lock in" cognitive enhancements and facilitate their generalization to the later acquisition of academic competencies (Feuerstein, 1980).

Curriculum

Up to this point in the chapter, we have listed and defined an inventory of useful cognitive strategies, their supporting attributional systems, and a rationale for making them a focus of training, at least for youngsters at mild and moderate levels of mental retardation. There have been a number of both comprehensive and more limited theory-based curriculum efforts that share the objective of enhancing cognitive development and improving behavior. They are described in this section.

Cognitive Curriculum for Young Children

One major curriculum effort is the Cognitive Curriculum for Young Children (CCYC) (Haywood, Brooks, & Burns, 1986). This curriculum relies heavily on theoretical support from Piaget's (1970) intellectual stage theory, Vygotsky's (1962) zone of proximal development, and Feuerstein's (1980) concept of mediated learning. The child's initial cognitive instruction emanates from his or her stage of intellectual development as defined by Piaget. There is some evidence that children with mental retardation can be trained to achieve higher levels of conceptual development (McCormick, Campbell, Pasnak, & Perry, 1990). Estimates of how far the child is likely to go are derived from his or her zone of proximal development. This is determined by comparing the child's actual level of performance to his or her performance under the teacher's direct supervision. Similar information is obtained from a procedure for determining the child's dynamic learning potential (Feuerstein, Rand, & Hoffman, 1979). This is essentially a test-teach-test procedure called the Learning Potential Assessment Device in which the child is tested, coached on errors made, and then retested to evaluate how much benefit has accrued from coaching.

The CCYC departs from a strictly developmental approach to cognitive intervention by building its instructional program, Mediated Learning, around the remediation of observed cognitive deficits (Feuerstein, 1980). A few of these deficits are blurred and sweeping perception, lack of spatial and temporal orientation, inability to consider multiple sources of information, an episodic grasp of reality, and lack of comparative, summative, and planning behavior. Training exercises germane to these and other deficits are fully explicated in Feuerstein's (1980) book.

Instrumental Enrichment

The mediated learning environment is structured around a pedagogical intimacy between child and tutor. The tutor orders, frames, schedules and, in general, interprets the child's environment in a way that facilitates the environment surrendering its important meanings to the child's intellectual purposes (Feuerstein, 1980). The child is supposed to develop a sense of intentionality and a feeling of competence. Learned problem-solving strategies are supposed to transcend the context in which they are learned so that they can be applied in other problem settings. The program is creative and has produced some reversal of cognitive deficits. As with most other intervention programs, however, improvements in cognitive functioning do not yet transfer reliably to the acquisition of academic skills (Blackman & Lin, 1984).

Montessori Method

The Montessori method has also been applied to the early education of both at-risk children and those with mild mental retardation. The method is based on the premise that the teacher is a resource to children engaged in the process of auto-education (Knudsen Lindauer, 1987). The curriculum objectives focus on perceptual and conceptual development, as well as on the acquisition of competencies in daily living activities such as floor sweeping, food preparation, and care of clothing. On a more affective level, the child is encouraged to develop a sense of self-mastery, mastery of the environment, and independence. Evaluations of Montessori programs have shown that they produce somewhat better results in performance than in verbal areas. In general, however, they appear to produce results similar to those obtained by other preschool education models.

The Ypsilanti Perry Preschool Project

The purpose of this project was to expose disadvantaged children with mild mental retardation, ages three and four, to the Cognitively Oriented Curriculum (Weikart, Bond, & McNeil, 1978). The curriculum and related instructional strategies were derived from Piaget's (1970) stage theory of intellectual development. Follow-up studies indicated an initial superiority on measures of aptitude of an experimental group over children in a control group. This effect diminished somewhat with increasing age. The project was declared a success, however, because differences in achievement between the experimental and control groups, in favor of the experimental group, persisted into eighth grade. As a result, the children who received the Cognitively Oriented Curriculum required fewer special services during their school careers. A later follow-up study (Schweinhart & Weikart, 1986), when the students were approximately nineteen years of age, showed that the experimental group was superior to the control group on a variety of life adjustment measures.

The Portage Project

The Portage Project (Shearer & Shearer, 1976) presented a home-based curriculum in language, self-help skills, cognition, motor skills, and socialization. The curriculum and accompanying instruction were mediated by the parent under the supervision of a home teacher who visited the home one day a week for 1.5 hours. The instructional procedure was based on a precision teaching model. Each week, three behaviors were targeted for instruction with the expectation that the child would reach criterion performance on those behaviors by the end of the week. Baseline data were recorded by the home teacher who also recorded post-intervention data for those behaviors at the end of the week. During the week, the parents implemented the teaching process using both reinforcement and extinction techniques. An evaluation study using some of the children as their own controls found average IQ increases of more than 18 points.

The Carolina Abecedarian Project

This project was designed to prevent developmental retardation in disadvantaged children from six months to 54 months. The Carolina Infant Curriculum is designed around the interaction of consumer opinions, Piaget's developmental theory, developmental facts, adaptive sets, and high-risk indicators (Ramey & Campbell, 1984; Ramey, Collier, Sparling, Loda, Campbell, Ingram, & Finkelstein, 1976). Consumer opinions refer to the goals that parents have for their children. Developmental facts are subsumed under four areas: language, motor, social/emotional, and cognitive/perceptive. Adaptive sets are thought of as "winning strategies" and refer to "that class of behaviors which predictably generate age-appropriate success." A few of these winning strategies are: uses adults as resources; uses receptive and expressive language extensively; exhibits high attention behavior; easily adapts to a changing environment; and uses cooperative behavior. The program also includes extensive parent training and the provision, as required, of social work services, nutritional supplements, medical care, and transportation. The program appears to have been effective because, after one year, using the Bayley Scales of Infant Development, the mean developmental index score of the intervention group was significantly higher than that of the control group. Again, long-range follow-up data are needed to confirm effect stability.

The Carolina Curriculum for Preschoolers with Special Needs (CCPSN)

The CCPSN (Johnson-Martin, Attermeier, & Hacker, 1990; Johnson-Martin, Jens, & Attermeier, 1991) evolved as an extension of the Carolina Curriculum for Handicapped Infants and Infants at Risk (CCHI). The CCPSN is designed for children from two to five years of age. The curriculum divides five major domains of development into detailed teaching sequences. These domains include cognition, communication, social adaptation, fine motor skills, and gross motor skills. Each of these domains carries detailed suggestions for classroom activities and materials. A special emphasis is placed on instruction likely to lead to generalization of skills acquired in the classroom to other environmental settings. The detailed nature of the curriculum makes it a very helpful classroom guide for teachers. No information with respect to evaluating the effectiveness of the curriculum is presented.

Instructional Activities

The preceding section has described a few of the better known preschool programs for children with mental retardation or those at risk for acquiring that condition. The activities, materials, and teacher strategies used in the pursuit of those objectives are legion, and are limited only by the experience, thoughtfulness, and creativity of classroom teachers. There are few learning activities generated by teachers that cannot be conceived of as contributing in some way to some aspect of cognitive development, whether it be inferring relationships, deploying attention effectively, implementing strategies for remembering, or facilitating the generalization of learned concepts and skills. The task has generally been to bring order to the early intervention enterprise by using some theoretical frame of reference, be it Piaget, Montessori, Feuerstein, or elements of information processing, to generate training activities likely to contribute to either helping a child reach the next stage of intellectual development or remediating cognitive deficits that have been identified.

Recognizing that the following represents only a fraction of potentially useful activities for both observing and training cognitive development, Williams and DeGaetano (1985) have suggested several such exercises that have been adapted for this presentation:

- identify and describe objects and events
- associate objects and events with one another ("things to wear when it's raining")
- group objects by shared properties ("all objects made of wood")
- describe the position of objects in space ("my boat went under the bridge")
- express sequential notions of time ("first you peel the apple, then you slice it")
- reproduce visual patterns ("doing a jigsaw puzzle")
- reproduce verbal patterns ("learn new songs or rhymes")
- reproduce motion patterns ("learn dances or games")
- predict the likely outcome of an activity ("what will happen if an egg rolls off the table?")
- pose alternative ways to solve a problem ("if the toy won't roll on the carpet, what else can you try?")

Bilingual Issues

Since there are both developmental parallels and important operational interdependencies between cognition and language, special problems are encountered in preschool programs for children with mental retardation when the dominant language of the school is different from that of the children and their families. Williams and DeGaetano, the developers of *Alerta: A multicultural and bilingual approach to teaching young children*, take the following position:

[if] the home language is respected and nurtured in an educational setting, there is a greater chance that the child will remain receptive to learning. The home language will be available for use as a foundation for continued concept development and will provide an avenue for learning a second language that may be needed for the child's access to the larger society (Williams & DeGaetano, 1985, p. 20).

Briefly, the child's development of necessary cognitive strategies cannot be held hostage to an instructional system that ignores or is insensitive to the language with which he or she is most comfortable. At the same time that the child's native language is given its respectful due in the training program, the second language representing the dominant culture must also be brought along. Ultimately, both languages should be equally capable of supporting the continued development of cognitive skills.

Cultural Diversity

How much influence do cultural factors have on the acquisition of cognitive skills in persons with mental retardation? Does cultural deprivation impose a barrier—perhaps a permanently insurmountable one—to the ability of the child with mental retardation to learn? Will it at least affect the efficacy with which she or he learns? Relating a child's cognitive functioning to his or her cultural or racial background or both has had an ugly history in America (Gould, 1981; Kevles, 1985). The practice of special education has no room for ethnocentrism—the often negative evaluation of another culture and its people according to one's own standards.

As long as a culture is intact, with its own organized family, political, social, economic, and belief systems, most social and behavioral scientists would not expect any culturally induced deficits in cognitive development prevalent in its people. To be sure, each culture will have its own language and its own way of attaching meaning to events in the world. Those differences must be taken into account and respected by special education teachers of children from ethnically diverse backgrounds. However, cognitive ability per se is not likely to vary from one stable culture to another.

But what about those communities in which the social and economic order is in flux? A culture transmits language, meaning, values, and concepts to children through the mediation of parents and other caregivers. When this arrangement breaks down for any reason, then cognitive development in the child with mental retardation can be even further jeopardized. The following *Case Study of Alicia* illustrates some of these issues.

CASE STUDY: Alicia

Culture and Cognitive Development

In Alicia's case, mental retardation and cerebral palsy were evident from early childhood. The extent of her developmental disabilities, however, was compounded by an impoverished and unstable milieu. Her mother assumed primary responsibility for Alicia's care. Her father was always a somewhat remote person in her life, and he recently left the household altogether. Alicia's mother works as a nurse's aide on the evening shift at Saint Francis Hospital. To earn some extra income she works whenever possible on a per diem basis at a nearby nursing home.

Alicia's day care center provides adequate supervision and activity for part of the day, but her care during evenings is usually entrusted to an adolescent baby sitter; a high school drop-out who also has a baby of her own and needs the extra money. She is reliable and tends to Alicia's basic needs, but tends not to interact with her verbally or playfully.

Alicia and her mother have very little time together. Typically, her mother arrives home from work when Alicia has already been asleep for several hours. She sees her briefly before Alicia leaves to attend her day care center. If work is available on weekends at the nursing home, their time together is further restricted. Alicia's mother has few social or family supports to help her. She has a couple of friends at work, but no contact with her family or her neighbors.

Cognitive skills develop best in a stable, socially stimulating environment. Despite her mother's best efforts, Alicia's home life is not very enriching. There is nobody at home to offer the kind of playful or conversational stimulation which, typically, sets the stage for much cognitive development. To name but a few deterrents to development, missing is a language model who can encourage turn taking, vocabulary acquisition, basic speech, and comprehension of language (e.g., following simple instruction). Missing are play activities that can incidentally teach concepts like object permanence (finding hidden objects); cause-effect relationships (anticipating the outcome of turning a light switch); and object functions (scooping with a toy spoon). Missing are opportunities to develop social skills bearing on cognitive development (eye contact and reciprocal play).

Most important, so many of Alicia's daily living activities are done for her that she does little for herself. For instance, Alicia may not wash her hands but she can place the soap in its tray, given a reminder. A child who discerns that her behavior produces no useful or effective outcomes can develop an orientation that Seligman (1975) called "learned helplessness," a pattern of thinking and behaving that discourages further attempts at learning. Thus, there are numerous factors in Alicia's home environment that tend to subvert her cognitive development.

It may be revealing to examine how Alicia's education program responded to this state of affairs. The staff at the center addressed precisely those areas of cognitive development that were unattended at home. But they were also mindful that the cognitive competencies that a child learns in the day care center do not automatically generalize to the home setting. In fact, the educational supervisor complained about this lack of transfer:

> *We've met with Alicia's mother on a number of occasions to review her daughter's needs, her progress, and her learning activities. Every time it's the same story. She agreed with all the programs and she expressed the best intentions of carrying them out at home. She agreed to chart Alicia's progress on a couple of programs. But our home observations were disappointing. She is polite and obliging at meetings, goes home, and promptly forgets about the programs and teaching activities.*

Alicia's mother has expressed a different point of view, laced with a small dose of resentment, at the patronizing attitude of the educational staff:

I'm out of this house ten hours a day. Maybe more. When I get home, Alicia's asleep in bed. So maybe we have an hour or two together, and maybe some more time on weekends. There's a house to clean, shopping to do, and bills to pay, so that's even less time to spend with Alicia. And, to be truthful, sometimes I'm just so tired that trying to get her to drink with nothing but a "physical prompt," or whatever you call it, is the furthest thing from my mind. And when they tell me to rush to the refrigerator door where her record sheets are supposed to be posted and write down her score every time she shakes her rattle . . . I mean, do you run your house like that? I'm not saying those things aren't important. I'm only saying that it is more than I can cope with.

Social deprivation plays a role in retarding the cognitive development of many children. This is particularly true of communities without resources to facilitate the cognitive development of their children. Early intervention programs can play a crucial role in preventing, curtailing, and perhaps correcting the destructive effects of social deprivation. The challenge to special education professionals is to provide the necessary services as an integral part of the community in which they teach and in a manner that is sensitive to the needs of both the students and their families.

Assessment

The problem of identifying children who might benefit from early intervention programs is both complex from a professional point of view and sensitive in terms of family acceptance. The formal assessment devices used most frequently with young children often suffer from problems of reliability and predictive validity. Their unreliability stems from the more limited range of behavior and language available to young children, particularly infants, and their difficulty in producing that behavior consistently when asked to do so. Inadequate predictive validity has been reported by Thorndike and Hagen (1977), who found little correlation between children's scores on infant intelligence scales and their scores on intelligence tests at age six. The weakness of infant and preschool intellectual measures in predicting performance during the middle elementary school years, for example, is attributable to: (1) the wider range of cognitive skills (e.g., problem solving, inference, abstractions, classificatory skills) available to older children that are not yet fully functional in the behavioral and conceptual repertoires of preschoolers; and (2) discrepancies in rate of maturation that allow "late bloomers" who might appear delayed in early testing to catch up with and even surpass "early bloomers."

The assessment of cognitive strengths and deficits in preschool children with mild mental retardation has been approached in a number of ways. Although oriented more towards product than process, standardized intelligence tests, yielding IQ scores, are probably the most frequently used instruments for evaluating general cognitive capacity. Then, there are a variety of measures of cognition that evaluate specific cognitive factors without intending to assess the more generic aspects of intelligence. Cognitive capacity has also been defined as a process rather than as a set of products. Measures of this type look at cognitive functioning in terms of the child's ability to benefit from coaching or the provision of cues leading to problem solution. Finally, cognition has been evaluated in a more informed and descriptive manner through observations of the child in both school and home settings, and by interviewing individuals who know the child best (e.g., parents, teachers, child care workers).

Intelligence Tests

The intelligence tests used frequently for preschool children are the Stanford-Binet Intelligence Scale: Fourth edition (Thorndike, Hagen, & Sattler, 1986) and the Wechsler Preschool and Primary Scale of Intelligence–Revised (WPPSI–R) (Wechsler, 1989). The Stanford-Binet can be given to children as young as two years of age, and provides both IQ and mental age scores. The WPSSI–R has been standardized for use with children from four to six and a half years; it offers verbal, performance, and full scale IQ scores.

Other instruments that have proven valuable as more generic measures of intellectual capacity are: the McCarthy Scales of Children's Abilities (McCarthy, 1972) (CA from 2.5 to 8.5 years), and the Coloured Progressive Matrices (Raven, Court, & Raven, 1977) (CA from 5–11 years).

For very young children, two of the most frequently used instruments are the Bayley Scales of Infant Development (Bayley, 1969) (CA from birth to 2.5 years) and the Denver Developmental Screening Test (Frankenburg, Dodds, Fandal, Kazuk, & Cohrs, 1975) (CA from birth to 6 years). The reader may wish to return to Chapter 3 to review concepts of general intelligence testing.

Specific Cognitive Tests

Other more specific measures of cognitive competence include the Test of Basic Concepts (Boehm, 1986) (CA from 5 to 6 years) and the Cognitive Abilities Scale (Bradley-Johnson, 1993) (CA from 2 to 3 years). For both the measurement of intelligence and more specific types of cognitive ability, there are many more instruments than have been noted here. For a more complete listing and treatment of these tests, see McLoughlin and Lewis (1990) and Salvia and Ysseldyke (1991).

Process Measures

There are approaches to assessing competence that view it less as a stored and decontextualized residue of life experience and more as cognition in action in a defined and carefully controlled context. For example, Vygotsky (1962) found it important to observe problem-solving skills ranging across a "zone of proximal development." The lower part of that zone defines what the child is able to do right now without assistance. The upper border of the zone represents what the child is capable of doing with some prompting and guidance. Similarly, Feuerstein et al.'s (1979) assessment of "dynamic learning potential" observes children's problem-solving performance before and after examiner coaching, in order to determine the child's ability to benefit from such help.

The premise underlying the assessment approaches of both Vygotsky and Feuerstein is that children's potential for profiting from cognitive intervention is not primarily a function of their achievement level after life experiences varying in opportunities for learning and enhancement of self-esteem. Rather, children's potential for instruction is more validly demonstrated in their current responsiveness to cognitive "stretching activities." Taking a contemporary function rather than a historical residue approach to assessment allows children to demonstrate their cognitive plasticity under maximally supportive conditions. Opportunities abound in this approach to assessment for building a sense of competence in children while elevating professional and parental expectations.

This section on process-oriented and more qualitative approaches to cognitive assessment would be incomplete without mentioning the large number of Piagetian assessment instruments which attempt to identify the level of a child's reasoning through more-or-less structured observations and interviews. Perhaps the best known of these is the Infant Psychological Development Scale constructed by Uzgiris and Hunt (1975). Although this device assesses progress only through the sensorimotor stage of intellectual development, others have been developed for succeeding stages. To the extent that Piaget's theory will continue to be used as a basis for preschool curriculum development in the future, assessment of where children's instruction should begin in that curriculum will be an essential part of that effort.

Recommendations

It would be satisfying to be able to report that the first and even the second generation of early childhood programs for young children with mild mental retardation has been an unqualified success. The reality, as extracted from many evaluation studies, is that early intervention programs seem to exert a positive impact on cognitive development during and immediately after training. The problem has been that the positive effects of early intervention have proven difficult to maintain.

There may be several reasons for this difficulty. First, professionals may not yet have developed sufficient expertise to design program objectives, curricula, and methods capable of: (1) locking in early cognitive gains; and (2) getting acquired cognitive skills to generalize to academic tasks. Teacher education programs should focus on needed competencies in this area. Part of the problem may be that so many early childhood programs were in formative stages over long periods of time. Since early childhood professionals often learned as they went along, programs were in a constant state of flux. An appropriate analogy might be to try to evaluate the performance of a car while continually changing its tires.

Second, it is conceivable that preschool programs, as suggested earlier, terminate too soon. Intensive special programs for children with mental retardation may be required all through the school and even postschool years to maintain and expand early gains. If it is as difficult as it appears to be to alter the trajectory of cognitive development in children with mental retardation, then a continuum of professional concern stretching from the preschool teacher at one end to the job coach at the other may be required.

Legislation mandating early childhood programs (PL99-457) has responded to the promise of early gains, which seems both appropriate and prudent. Intensive programming for special-needs children that includes support for stressed families is never out of place.

As more is learned from research and demonstration projects, we can expect to: (1) develop more sophisticated theories; (2) construct better curricula, instructional strategies, and behavior management techniques; (3) design better family support programs; (4) establish the most appropriate settings for preschool programs; (5) find ways to help children generalize the cognitive strategies that they have learned; and (6) develop more sensitive instrumentation that will detect intervention-related changes more efficiently.

In the context of these general observations about the effectiveness of early childhood intervention programs, the following recommendations seem to be in order:

1. Sound child-find programs should be based on the availability of good assessment instruments, close contact with parents, and effective communication among professional disciplines.

2. Alertness to medical conditions such as low birth weight and infectious diseases of the central nervous system, as well as factors such as child abuse and poor nutrition that may result in cognitive impairment should be maintained.

3. Early special education intervention, although often short-term in impact, is an important link in the chain of services that should be available to children with mental retardation.

4. Early special education intervention should be complemented by social and economic programs that support families and promote access to the full range of appropriate careers and life options.

5. Early childhood special educators need to acquire the competencies to design curricula, methods capable of locking in early cognitive gains, and techniques for getting cognitive strategies to generalize to both academic and extra-school tasks.

6. Intervention programs for young children with mental retardation should begin as early as possible and recruit the highest levels of professional competence.

7. Early intervention for children with mental retardation should be seen as a first-stage program that is followed by continuing high-impact programs as the children move through the elementary, middle, and secondary schools, as well as the work transitional aspects of their educational experience.

8. In early intervention, the service model that puts coordinated support services in place for the entire family should be an important partner of the child-oriented treatment model.

9. Young children with mild to moderate levels of mental retardation should learn self-regulation skills and develop attributions for their successful performances that emphasize the roles of ability and effort.

10. Bilingual programs and sensitivity to cultural diversity are important in helping children from ethnically diverse backgrounds to develop cognitive and academic skills.

References

Bailey, D. B., Jr. & Simeonsson, R. J. (1988). Home-based early intervention. In S. L. Odom & M. B. Karnes, *Early intervention for infants and children with handicaps: An empirical base,* 199–213. Baltimore: Brookes.

Bayley, N. (1969). *Bayley Scales of Infant Development.* New York: Psychological Corporation.

Beauchamp, K. D. (1989). Meta analysis of early childhood special education research. *Journal of Early Intervention, 13,* 374–380.

Belmont, J. M. (1989). Cognitive strategies and strategic learning: The socio-instructional approach. *American Psychologist, 44,* 142–148.

Blackman, L. S. & Lin, A. (1984). Generalization training in the educable mentally retarded: Intelligence and its educability revisited. In P. H. Brooks, R. Spencer, & C. McCauley (Eds.), *Learning and cognition in the mentally retarded.* Hillsdale, NJ: Erlbaum.

Boehm, A. E. (1986). *Boehm test of basic concepts–Revised.* San Antonio: Psychological Corporation.

Borkowski, J. G., Weyhing, R., & Turner, L. (1986). Attributional retraining and the teaching of strategies. *Exceptional Children, 53,* 130–137.

Bradley-Johnson, S. (1993). *Cognitive Abilities Scale.* Austin, TX: ProEd.

Brainin, S. (1982). *The effects of instrumental enrichment on the reasoning abilities, reading achievement, and task orientation of sixth grade underachievers.* Unpublished doctoral dissertation, Teachers College, Columbia University, New York.

Braun, S. J. & Caldwell, B. (1973). Emotional adjustment of children in day care who enrolled prior to or after the age of three. *Early Childhood Development and Care, 2,* 13–21.

Bronfenbrenner, V. (1975). Is early intervention effective? In B. Z. Friedlander & G. M. Sterritt (Eds.), *Exceptional infant: Assessment and intervention* (pp. 449–475). New York: Brunner/Mazel.

Byers, J. (1989). AIDS in children: Effect on neurological development and implications for the future. *The Journal of Special Education, 23,* 5–16.

Castro, G. & Mastropieri, M. A. (1986). The efficacy of early intervention programs: A meta-analysis. *Exceptional Children, 52,* 417–424.

Cole, K. N., Mills, P. E., & Sale, P. S. (1989). A comparison of the effects of academic and cognitive curricula for young handicapped children one and two years post-program. *Topics in Early Childhood Special Education, 9,* 110–127.

Dale, P. S. & Cole, K. N. (1988). Comparison of academic and cognitive programs for young handicapped children. *Exceptional Children, 54,* 439–447.

Diamond, G. W. (1989). Developmental problems in children with HIV infection. *Mental Retardation, 27,* 213–217.

Ferry, P. C. (1981). On growing new neurons: Are early intervention programs effective? *Pediatrics, 67*(1), 38–41.

Feuerstein, R. (1980). *Instrumental enrichment: An intervention program for cognitive modifiability.* Baltimore: University Park Press.

Feuerstein, R., Rand, Y., & Hoffman, M. (1979). *The diagnostic assessment of retarded performers: The learning potential assessment device, theory, instruments, and techniques.* Baltimore: University Park Press.

Frankenburg, W. K., Dodds, J. B., Fandal, A., Kazuk, E., & Cohrs, M. (1975). *Denver Developmental Screening Test.* Denver: LADOCA.

Frantz, R. L. (1958). Pattern vision in young adults. *Psychological Record, 8,* 43–47.

Garber, H. L. (1988). *The Milwaukee Project: Preventing mental retardation in children at risk.* Washington, DC: American Association on Mental Retardation.

Gould, S. J. (1981). *The mismeasure of man.* New York: W. W. Norton.

Gottfried, N. W. (1973). Effects of early intervention programs. In K. S. Miller & R. M. Oregon (Eds.), *Comparative studies of blacks and whites in the United States.* New York: Seminar Press.

Gray, C. D. (1989). Opening comments on the conference on developmental disabilities and HIV infection. *Mental Retardation, 27,* 199–200.

Gray, S. W. & Klaus, R. A. (1970). The early training project: A seventh year report. *Child Development, 4,* 909–924.

Guralnick, M. J. & Bricker, D. (1982). The effectiveness of early intervention for children with cognitive and general developmental delays. In M. J. Guralnick & F. C. Bennett (Eds.), *The effectiveness of early intervention for at-risk and handicapped children.* New York: Academic Press.

Haskins, R. (1989). Beyond metaphor: The efficacy of early childhood education. *American Psychologist, 44,* 274–282.

Haywood, H. C. (1988). Cognitive education for young handicapped children. In W.-T. Wu (Ed.), *Looking toward special education in the 21st century* (Proceedings of the 1988 International Symposium on Special Education), 99–118. Taipei Special Education Association of the Republic of China.

Haywood, H. C., Brooks, P., & Burns, S. (1986). Stimulating cognitive development at developmental level: A tested, non-remedial preschool curriculum for preschoolers and older retarded children. In M. Schwebel & C. Maher (Eds.), *Facilitating cog-*

nitive development: Principles, practices, and programs (pp. 127–147). New York: Haworth Press.

Hebbeler, K. M., Smith, B. J., & Black, T. L. (1991). Federal early childhood special education policy: A model for the improvement of services for children and disabilities. *Exceptional Children, 58,* 104–112.

Johnson-Martin, N. M., Attermeier, S. M., & Hacker, B. (1990). *The Carolina curriculum for preschoolers with special needs.* Baltimore: Brookes.

Johnson-Martin, N. M., Jens, K., & Attermeier, S. M. (1991). *Carolina curriculum for handicapped infants and infants at risk.* (2nd ed.). Baltimore: Brookes.

Kagan, J., Rosman, B. L., Day, D., Albert, J., & Phillips, W. (1964). Information processing in the child: Significance of analytic and reflective attitudes. *Psychological Monographs, 78*(1, Whole No. 578).

Kevles, D. J. (1985). *In the name of eugenics: Genetics in the uses of human heredity.* New York: Knopf.

Knudson Lindauer, S. L. (1987). Montessori education for young children. In J. L. Roopnarine & J. E. Johnson (Eds.), *Approaches to early childhood education.* Columbus, OH: Merrill.

Lazar, I. (1977). *The persistence of preschool effects.* Ithaca, NY: Community Service Laboratory, Cornell University.

Levenstein, P. (1970). Cognitive growth in preschoolers through verbal interaction with mothers. *American Journal of Orthopsychiatry, 40,* 426–432.

Lin, A., Blackman, L. S., Clark, H. T., & Gordon, R. (1983). Far generalization of visual analogies strategies by impulsive and reflective EMR students. *American Journal of Mental Deficiency, 88,* 297–306.

Mann, L. (1979). *On the trail of process.* New York: Grune & Stratton.

McCarthy, D. (1972). *Manual for the McCarthy Scales of Children's Abilities.* New York: Psychological Corporation.

McCormick, P. K., Campbell, J. W., Pasnack, R., & Perry, P. (1990). Instruction on Piagetian concepts for children with mental retardation. *Mental Retardation, 28,* 359–366.

McLoughlin, J. A. & Lewis, R. B. (1990). *Assessing special students* (3rd ed.). New York: Merrill/Macmillan.

Meeker, M. N. (1969). *The structure of intellect, its interpretation and uses.* Columbus, OH: Merrill.

Page, E. (1986). The disturbing case of the Milwaukee Project. In H. Spitz, *The raising of intelligence.* Hillsdale, NJ: Erlbaum.

Piaget, J. (1970). Piaget's theory. In P. H. Mussen (Ed.), *Carmichael's manual of child psychology, vol. 1* (pp. 703–732). New York: Wiley.

Ramey, C. T., Bryant, D. M., Sparling, J. J., & Wasik, B. H. (1985). Project CARE: A comparison of two early intervention strategies to prevent retarded development. *Topics in Early Childhood Special Education, 5*(2), 12–25.

Ramey, C. T., & Campbell, F. A. (1984). Preventive education for high risk children: Cognitive consequences of the Carolina Abecedarian Project. *American Journal of Mental Deficiency, 88,* 515–523.

Ramey, C. T., Collier, A. M., Sparling, J. J., Loda, F. A., Campbell, F. A., Ingram, D. L., & Finkelstein, N. W. (1976). The Carolina Abecedarian Project: A longitudinal and multidisciplinary approach to the prevention of developmental retardation. In R. D. Tjossem (Ed.), *Intervention strategies for high risk infants and young children.* Baltimore: University Park Press.

Raven, J. C., Court, H. H., & Raven, J. (1977). *Coloured Progressive Matrices.* London: Lewis.

Salvia, J., & Ysseldyke, J. E. (1991). *Assessment* (5th edition). Boston: Houghton Mifflin.

Schweinhart, L. J. & Weikart, D. P. (1986). What do we know so far? A review of the Head Start synthesis project. *Young Children, 41,* 49–55.

Seligman, M. E. P. (1975). *Helplessness: On depression, development, and death.* San Francisco: Freeman.

Shearer, D. E. & Shearer, M. S. (1976). The Portage Project: A model for early childhood intervention. In T. D. Tjossem (Ed.), *Intervention strategies for high risk infants and young children* (pp. 335–350). Baltimore: University Park Press.

Sheehan, R. & Gradell, L. (1983). Intervention models in early childhood special education. In S. G. Garwood (Ed.), *Educating young handicapped children.* Rockville, MD: Aspen Systems.

Skeels, H. M. & Dye, H. B. (1939). A study of the effects of differential stimulation on mentally retarded children. *Proceedings of the American Association on Mental Deficiency, 44,* 114–136.

Skeels, H. M., Updegraff, R., Wellman, B. L., & Williams, H. M. (1938). A study of environmental stimulation: An orphanage preschool project. *University of Iowa Study in Child Welfare, 15*(4).

Skodak, M. (1938). Children in foster homes. *University of Iowa Study on Child Welfare, 15*(4), 191.

The Infant Health and Development Program. (1990). Enhancing the outcomes of low-birthweight, premature infants: A multisite, randomized trial. *Journal of the American Medical Association, 263,* 3035–3042.

Thorndike, R. L. & Hagen, E. P. (1977). *Measurement and evaluation in psychology and education.* New York: Macmillan.

Thorndike, R. L., Hagen, E. P., & Sattler, J. M. (1986). *The Stanford-Binet Intelligence Scale: Fourth edition.* Chicago, IL: Riverside Publishing Company.

Tjossem, T. D. (1976). Early intervention: Issues and approaches. In T. D. Tjossem (Ed.), *Intervention strategies for high risk infants and young children.* Baltimore: University Park Press.

Tringey, C., Mortensen, L., Matheson, P., & Doret, W. (1991). Developmental attainment and young children with Down Syndrome. *International Journal of Disability, Development, and Education, 38,* 15–26.

Turner, R. R., Connell, D. B., & Mathis, A. (1980). The preschool child in the family: Changing models of developmental intervention. In R. R. Turner & H. W. Reese (Eds.), *Life-span developmental psychology: Intervention* (pp. 249–274). New York: Academic Press.

Uzgiris, I. C. & Hunt, J. McV. (1975). *Ordinal scales of intellectual development.* Urbana, IL: University of Illinois Press.

Vygotsky, L. S. (1962). *Thought and language* (E. Haufmann & G. Vakar, Trans.). Cambridge, MA: MIT Press. (Original work published 1934.)

Wechsler, D. (1967). *Manual for the Wechsler Preschool and Primary Scale of Intelligence—Revised.* San Antonio, TX: The Psychological Corporation.

Weikart, D. P., Bond, J. T., & McNeil, J. T. (1978). *The Ypsilanti Perry Preschool Project: Preschool years and longitudinal results through fourth grade.* Ypsilanti, MI: High/Scope Educational Research Foundation.

White, W. A. (1988). A meta-analysis of the effects of direct instruction in special education. *Education and Treatment of Children, 11,* 364–374.

Whitman, T. L. (1990). Self-regulation and mental retardation. *American Journal of Mental Retardation, 94,* 347–362.

Williams, L. R., & DeGaetano, Y. (1985). *Alerta: A multicultural, bilingual approach to teaching young children.* Menlo Park, CA: Addison-Wesley.

Zimmerman, B. J. (1990). Self-regulated learning and academic achievement: An overview. *Educational Psychologist, 25,* 3–17.

Zirpoli, T. J. (1986). Child abuse and children with handicaps. *Remedial and Special Education, 7,* 39–48.

Chapter 10

Basic Life Skills:

The Motor and Self-Help Domains

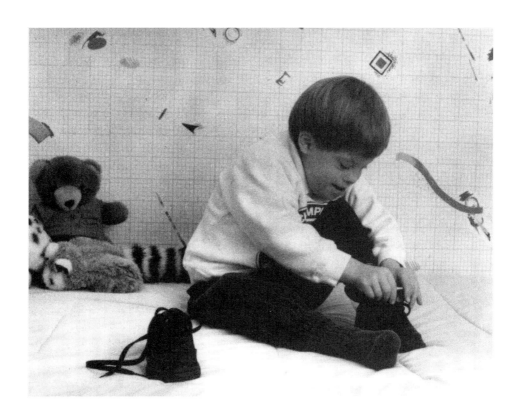

The passage of Public Law 99–457, the 1986 amendments to PL94–142, reflected a growing public awareness that the adverse effects of developmental delays can be minimized by early intervention, thus reducing future costs to society for educational and residential services. This law, which extends the entitlements of PL94–142 to preschool children with handicaps aged three to five, also provides early intervention services to handicapped and at-risk infants and toddlers from birth through age two. The "physical" and "self-help" domains, covered in this chapter, are two of the areas targeted by PL99–457 for early intervention services.

The first part of this chapter provides a brief overview of the areas of physical development and motor skills acquisition. This is intended to sensitize the teacher to some of the problems that may be manifested by young children with mental retardation. In the second part of the chapter, the focus shifts to self-help skills, their relationship to prerequisite motor skills, and approaches for fostering their acquisition. Specific recommendations are summarized in the final section.

Physical Development and the Acquisition of Motor Skills

In this section, an overview of typical and atypical physical development is followed by a discussion of approaches available to the teacher for assessing motor skills performance. Sections on motor skills curriculum components and instructional strategies are also included.

Physical Development and Mental Retardation

It is useful to view physical and motor development in the context of two developmental principles. The first of these asserts that motor development follows a fairly uniform sequence in children. For example, most children crawl before they walk. The second principle states, however, that the rate of motor development varies widely, even among children whose development falls within the normal range. The rate of motor development can be influenced by any of the following factors: size or type of physique, overall rate of maturation, childrearing practices, and socioeconomic level (e.g., Ersing, Loovis, & Ryan, 1982, p. 65; Peterson, 1987, p. 148).

The rate of motor development in children with mental retardation is often delayed beyond what would be considered a normal variation (e.g., Ersing et al., 1982; Rarick, Widdop, & Broadhead, 1970). However, the sequence of development is less likely to be disrupted by mental retardation (e.g., Kral, 1972), though constitutional or environmental factors can sometimes preclude the emergence of particular skills. With respect to the rate of motor development, even mild mental retardation is associated with developmental delays. However, with mild and moderate mental retardation, motor delays are often less pronounced than intellectual delays. On the other hand, severe and profound mental retardation is often associated with pronounced motor deficits stemming from extensive central nervous system involvement (Kral, 1972; Robinson & Robinson, 1976, pp. 351–352).

Research has indicated that the impact of motor delays and deficits can be reduced by appropriate early intervention (e.g., Horn, 1991). Such intervention can often prevent the occurrence of further physical damage, such as bone deformities and muscle contractures. Also, because the areas of development are highly interrelated, untreated delays in motor development can interfere with the emergence of skills in cognitive, social, and other areas. Specific motor skills may be prerequisites for the acquisition of self-help skills. For example, the child must acquire some form of ambulation or mobility before independent toileting behavior can occur (Smith, 1989, p. 303).

PL94–142 provides children with handicaps with access to "related services," which can include the services of physical and occupational therapists. These specialists typically play a major role in the design and implementation of interventions to enhance physical and motor development. However, it is essential that the teacher be sufficiently knowledgeable to identify potential problems and to refer the child to an appropriate specialist for assessment and services. The teacher must also be sufficiently skilled to carry out the recommendations of a physical or occupational therapist as part of the child's educational program.

Motor Development

Motor development has been defined as "the *process* of acquiring the necessary postural control and movement components to perform purposeful volitional movements" (Smith, 1989, p. 303). Progress in motor development has typically been measured by the attainment of developmental milestones, which have been extensively documented as to the usual sequence and age of emergence (e.g., Inge, 1987). The motor performance of children with mental retardation has often been compared with these milestones to determine the degree of motor delay. However, this approach is of only limited usefulness in providing a basis for effective interventions. In addition to monitoring the attainment of milestones, or marker events, it is essential to look closely at specific components and sequences of motor development to better understand the nature and impact of specific motor delays and disabilities.

There are two general types of movement. *Reflex* movement, normally dominant until about three months of age, consists of involuntary movement patterns that occur in response to specific types of environmental stimuli. *Voluntary* movement gradually replaces reflex movement, making possible intentional, purposeful activity (Kraemer, Cusick, Bigge, 1982). The production of movement involves the interaction of two major bodily systems. The *joints* support specific types of motion and various ranges of motion in different areas of the body. For example, the ball-and-socket joint at the shoulder allows rotation and a wide range of motion, while the hinge joints in the fingers allow only limited flexion and extension. The joints work in conjunction with the skeletal *muscles*, which provide the force behind each movement. The degree of tension in the muscles when they are at rest is known as *muscle tone*, which can vary from relaxed (as in sleep) to taut (as in fear). Movement proficiency is often viewed in terms of the following three components: stability, gross motor functions, and fine motor functions. *Stability* is postural control, achieved when the muscles contract simultaneously to form a base from which movement can occur. The *gross motor* component is concerned primarily with locomotion activities, such as creeping, standing, and walking. The *fine motor* component concerns manipulation skills, such as reaching and grasping (Inge, 1987; Smith, 1989).

Motor Delays and Disabilities

As noted earlier, motor delays and disabilities are a common accompaniment of mental retardation. These motor problems, attributable to a wide range of known and unknown causes, are manifested in a variety of forms and combinations. The focus of the present section is upon only a few of the most common types of motor delays and disabilities that are associated with mental retardation. The impact of motor problems upon children with mental retardation is considered in terms of the following four dimensions: (1) abnormal reflexes; (2) abnormal muscle tone; (3) restricted movement; and (4) weakness, or paralysis.

Abnormal Reflexes

If brain dysfunction inhibits normal neurological maturation, reflex patterns may fail to progress normally. Adaptive reflexes may either fail to appear at the appropriate time or they may fail to disappear when they should. Either type of disturbance can interfere with the normal course of motor development. The persistence of primitive reflexes is a common accompaniment of cerebral palsy (Peterson, 1987).

Abnormal Muscle Tone

Ideally, muscle tone should be taut enough to allow stability and loose enough to allow movement of the joints. Damage to the central nervous system can result in abnormal muscle tone. Muscle tone abnormalities are a common source of motor delays and disabilities in children with mental retardation. As pointed out by Smith (1989), they deserve special attention for at least three reasons. First, muscle tone abnormalities are encountered frequently in the classroom. Second, if ignored, muscle tone abnormalities can threaten the acquisition of skills in other domains. Finally, muscle tone abnormalities are amenable to early intervention. Extremely low muscle tone is called *hypotonia*. Extremely high muscle tone is referred to as *hypertonia* or *spasticity*. Fluctuating muscle tone is known as *athetosis*. One of the most common motor impairments found in children, *cerebral palsy*, involves severe impairments in muscle tone. Approximately 60 percent of children with cerebral palsy also have mental retardation (Robinson & Robinson, 1976). Although cerebral palsy can be associated with either extreme of muscle tone, or a combination of the two extremes, the most prevalent form is spastic cerebral palsy, involving abnormally high muscle tone (Peterson, 1987, p. 207). If the muscles of children with spasticity are not appropriately stimulated, they may atrophy or decrease in size, resulting in *contractures*, which can permanently restrict movement (Peterson, 1987, p. 215). *Down Syndrome* is also associated with muscle tone abnormalities, in this case, abnormally low muscle tone. Consequently, the muscles of children with Down Syndrome are often described as flaccid or floppy.

Restricted Movement

Limited range of motion, deformities, or the absence of limbs can severely restrict the degree to which a child can explore the environment. These limitations can involve either gross motor development, fine motor development, or both (Kraemer et al., 1982; Peterson, 1987). Because the ability to move and explore is essential to the development of cognitive, social, and self-care skills, limb deficiencies can be devastating to overall development unless appropriate interventions are initiated early.

Weakness and Paralysis
Movement may be prevented or greatly reduced by severe weakness or paralysis. These conditions are associated with spina bifida and other spinal cord injuries, which are sometimes accompanied by mental retardation. Additional complications may involve loss of sensation, or bowel and bladder incontinence (Kraemer et al., 1982).

Assessment of Motor Development

Interventions designed to enhance the motor development of a young child with mental retardation must be based upon the results of a thorough educational assessment of the child's current patterns of motor performance. It is essential that such an assessment be firmly based in the context of normal child development (Connor, Williamson, & Siepp, 1978). In most instances, a significant portion of the assessment should be carried out by an experienced physical therapist or other movement specialist, rather than by the teacher. The teacher, however, must make sure that the assessment is sufficiently educationally oriented to yield the types of information needed to guide educational programming decisions.

As discussed in Chapter 4, it is often necessary to include both formal and informal approaches in the educational assessment of a child with mental retardation. This is especially true in the assessment of young children with motor delays and disabilities. Formal, published tests can provide general information on the extent to which the child has attained developmental milestones, and on patterns of motor strengths and weaknesses. Informal assessment procedures, however, are necessary to describe the qualitative aspects of movement.

Formal Assessment Procedures
Although many formal instruments are available to measure motor development, perhaps no single test is ideally suited to assessing motor development in young children with mental retardation. Most norm-referenced tests were standardized on infants and children without disabilities, and although the child with mental retardation may fall within the chronological age range covered by the instrument, his or her developmental level may be considerably lower than that targeted by the test. Useful listings of some of these instruments and their characteristics have been provided by both Peterson (1987) and Smith (1989). Both of their listings provide examples of screening instruments, diagnostic instruments, and educational programming instruments.

Screening.   Screening is conducted, often by the teacher, to determine whether the child is exhibiting developmental delays severe enough to warrant referral for thorough diagnostic testing. The *Denver Developmental Screening Test* (Frankenburg, Dodds, Fandal, Kazuk, & Cohrs, 1975) is an example of a widely employed screening instrument, cited in both listings. It is designed to span the age range from zero to six and it includes assessments of both gross motor and fine motor skills.

Diagnostic Assessment.   Diagnostic assessment is conducted in order to obtain a detailed analysis of the type and extent of the problem. It is at this stage that the services of a specialist, such as a physical therapist, are most often employed. An example of a diagnostic instrument, cited in both listings, is the *Battelle Developmental Inventory* (Newborg, Stock, Wneck, Guidubaldi, & Suinicki, 1984). This test spans the zero to eight age range and includes an assessment of motor performance as part of a comprehensive developmental battery.

Educational Programming Assessment.   Educational programming assessment is conducted to pinpoint the child's learning needs, and to provide a detailed basis for designing and monitoring an appropriate intervention. For this purpose, both listings emphasize criterion-referenced instruments (see Chapter 4 for the definition of this term). At this stage, teachers may again play a central role in the assessment process. The *Brigance Diagnostic Inventory of Early Development* (Brigance, 1978) spans the age range from zero to six years, and includes gross and fine motor skill areas. Another widely used instrument in this category is the *Carolina Developmental Profile* (Lillie & Harbin, 1975). It spans the two to five year age range and also includes gross and fine motor skill areas.

Informal Assessment Procedures

As noted earlier, informal assessment procedures are a necessary supplement to formal assessment procedures. In the motor domain, they can provide qualitative descriptions of the child's status along the various dimensions of movement. This type of information is critical at the *diagnostic* assessment phase. For example, variations in muscle tone may be assessed by clinical observation and, sometimes, by rating scales. Reflexes may be assessed by observing the child's response to relevant environmental stimuli. In addition to noting the presence or absence of the reflex, qualitative information on the intensity or consistency of the reflex is usually gathered. Qualitative information is also essential in the assessment of gross and fine motor development (Smith, 1989). These informal assessment approaches are best carried out by an experienced physical therapist or other movement expert. Ideally, the teacher and the therapist will work closely, as members of a team, to share and utilize the information yielded by all phases of the assessment.

As pointed out in Chapter 4, informal assessment procedures are the primary source of information during the *educational programming*, or monitoring, phase of assessment. Monitoring the child's ongoing progress requires the regular collection of performance data relevant to each instructional objective. This is primarily the responsibility of the teacher and can include the use of checklists and rating scales as well as the graphic recording of direct behavioral measures (e.g., frequency of reaching) (Peterson, 1987).

Interventions to Enhance Motor Development

This section includes a discussion of curriculum as it relates to motor development and motor disabilities in young children with mental retardation. Management procedures and instructional strategies designed to foster the acquisition of motor skills are also discussed.

Curriculum in the Motor Domain

Of the curriculum models described in Chapter 5, the model which is most often applied with children with mental retardation at the preschool level is the Developmental Model. According to that model, the content of instruction should follow the organization and sequence of normal development. This model typically leads to the generation of curriculum sequences in fairly discrete skill clusters, generally including gross motor, fine motor, and self-help skills. Objectives within each of these clusters are typically sequential, generally assuming that earlier skills in the sequence are prerequisites for the acquisition of more advanced skills. While the Developmental Model can provide a valuable blueprint for curriculum development, rigid adherence to this model for children with mental retardation and motor impairments can lead to certain difficulties. Children with severe and profound disabilities may fail to adequately synthesize skills across skill clusters. In addition, motor impairments may preclude the acquisition of certain skills that are assumed to be prerequisites for more advanced skills. Furthermore, the emphasis in a developmental curriculum may be on "form" rather than "function" (Orelove & Sobsey, 1987). These and other limitations of the Developmental Model have led to the application of alternative curriculum models in the motor domain.

The alternative curriculum model presented in Chapter 5 for children at lower functioning levels is the Functional Model, first advocated by Brown and his colleagues (e.g., Brown, Branston, Hamre-Nietupski, Pumpian, Certo, & Gruenewald, 1979). The three features emphasized by the Functional Model are *functional skills*, or those skills most likely to be required in everyday life, *natural environments*, that is, those environments in which the child is being trained to function, and *chronological-age-appropriateness* of the skills to be acquired. The fact that these three features were often disregarded in the application of developmental curricula limited the usefulness of those curricula, especially for adolescents and adults with severe and profound mental retardation, and gave rise to a shift to more functionally oriented curricula for these groups. Though less often recommended for young children, a functional curriculum approach offers some advantages for this group also. For example, because skill clusters are subsumed within larger functional domains (e.g., community skills), the burden upon the child to synthesize isolated skills is reduced. In addition, this model emphasizes those skills that are most needed to improve the child's functioning in his or her environment, thus reducing the need to teach for generalization (Orelove & Sobsey, 1987). The main disadvantage of this model is that it is extremely time-consuming for staff who must design an individualized curriculum that is based on the present and future needs of each child. The increasing availability of curriculum materials, such as the *Activities Catalog*, that are well-suited for use with the functional approach promises to alleviate these demands somewhat (e.g., Wilcox & Bellamy, 1987).

Most often, for young children with mental retardation accompanied by motor delays and disabilities, it is advisable to combine the features of the Developmental and Functional Models. This can be facilitated by following Bigge's 1982 suggestion that a curriculum for children with physical and multiple disabilities should have at least three features. It should be *functional* in order to aid students in functioning as well as possible in their current and future environments. It should be *cumulative*, in the sense that it builds upon earlier learning and that it progressively increases in complexity. Finally, it should be *foundational*, to the extent that it includes any skills and adaptive behaviors that are true prerequisites for the acquisition of later skills.

Management and Instruction of Motor Behavior

Most intervention approaches designed to remediate motor delays and disabilities may be classified as either passive management (noninstructional) approaches or active instructional approaches (Campbell, 1987). Passive management approaches include therapeutic handling and positioning to improve muscle tone and posture. Active instructional approaches, in contrast, are aimed at developing specific movement responses and motor skills.

Passive Management Approaches.   According to Campbell (1987), physical management has three general goals. First, the student should be handled in ways that will promote normalized muscle tone and prevent the development of contractures and other secondary disorders. Second, the student should be handled and positioned in ways that achieve and maintain normal body alignment. Third, the student should be handled and positioned in ways that facilitate attainment of the goals of the active instructional program in as many situations as possible.

A number of approaches have been developed to enhance the motor (and sometimes cognitive) performance of children with motor disabilities, such as cerebral palsy, that involve abnormal muscle tone. These approaches include the Rood techniques, sensory integration therapy, vestibular stimulation, and the neurodevelopmental (NDT) approach. The Rood techniques, developed by Margaret Rood, have been used extensively by physical therapists. They involve using various types of sensory input to activate or inhibit specific muscle responses. Sensory integration therapy, developed by Jean Ayres, involves using various types of sensory stimulation to improve motor functioning and, ultimately, learning. Vestibular stimulation, which encompasses such activities as spinning in a swing or rolling on a ball, involves stimulating the vestibular system to improve motor functioning (e.g., Kuharski, Rues, Cook, & Guess, 1985; Ottenbacher & Petersen, 1985). The neurodevelopmental approach, developed by Berta and Karl Bobath as an alternative to purely orthopedic and surgical treatments of cerebral palsy, is perhaps the most widely used management approach for children with mental retardation and physical disabilities. This approach is designed to inhibit abnormal posture and movement patterns and to facilitate the development of normal ones (Bobath & Bobath, 1967). It involves frequent positioning and handling of the child throughout the school day.

Recent meta-analysis research on the use of developmental therapies with preschool children, reviewed by Harris (1988), has indicated generally positive effects of sensory integration, vestibular stimulation, and the neurodevelopmental approach (e.g., Ottenbacher, 1982; Ottenbacher, Biocca, DeCremer, Bevelinger, Jedlovec, & Johnson, 1986; Ottenbacher & Petersen, 1985). These findings should be interpreted with caution, however, because of the relatively few methodologically sound studies available. None of these approaches should be employed by a teacher without guidance and supervision by a physical therapist who has been trained in their use. Teachers should, however, be prepared to implement and monitor such programs when proper guidance is provided. These approaches can be a valuable adjunct to the active instructional program.

Active Instructional Approaches.   In the remediation of motor delays and disabilities, active instructional approaches are typically employed to accomplish two general goals (Campbell, 1987). The first goal, the establishment of coordinated movement patterns, falls largely in the domain of the occupational or physical therapist and may involve a variety of range of motion exercises performed in conjunction with positioning and handling procedures to normalize muscle tone. The second goal, the establishment of the functional use of movement, is primarily the responsibility of the classroom teacher. This goal involves learning to use coordinated movement skills to perform functional tasks in the self-care, cognitive, social and other domains, and should be taught in conjunction with instruction in each of those areas rather than as an isolated skill. Attainment of this second goal can be assisted by the use of two techniques. First, by controlling environmental influences by gradually introducing a stimulus (e.g., noise) known to increase muscle tone for a particular child, the child may be taught to maintain normal tone by gradual desensitization to the stimulus. Second, by utilizing adaptive equipment for positioning and other procedures for normalizing muscle tone, the student's efforts at coordinated movement may be facilitated (Campbell, 1987).

The basic principles of instruction and the instructional strategies described in Chapter 7 are the building blocks of effective instruction in the motor skills area, as in all other curriculum domains. The behavioral techniques described in Chapter 7 have been widely applied within the motor skills domain with children with mental retardation. For example, successful applications of a variety of behavioral techniques have been reported for teaching such skills as walking with crutches in a child with spina bifida (Horner, 1971), playground skills in a child with cerebral palsy (Hardiman, Goetz, Reuter, & LeBlanc, 1975), and walking for a group of children with profound mental retardation (O'Brien, Azrin, & Bugle, 1972). The specific techniques presented in Chapter 7 will not be repeated here. However, those techniques can be drawn upon as needed for instructional programming in the motor skills area. Six general principles, highlighted by Orelove and Sobsey (1987), are presented here as a general guide for instructional decisions in the motor area:

1. *Functional Tasks and Materials.* Give priority to skills selected through environmental inventories and judged to be critically important for the child's day-to-day functioning by the family and professional team members.
2. *Natural Settings and Cues.* Teach skills in the settings where they will be used, and select cues from the natural environment.
3. *Transdisciplinary Services and Integrated Therapy.* Particularly in the motor area, where programming typically involves therapists from other disciplines as well as educators, it is essential that therapeutic goals and activities be integrated into the instructional routine rather than delivered in isolated therapy sessions.
4. *Group Instruction.* Although group instruction is often preferable to individual instruction, some therapy interventions require individual sessions.
5. *Interaction with Individuals without Disabilities.* Opportunities for positive interactions with individuals without disabilities should be systematically arranged.
6. *Data-Based Instruction.* Instructional decisions should be based upon detailed student performance data.

In addition to the basic strategies for increasing and decreasing behavior that were described in Chapter 7, two general principles should be kept in mind when working with children with motor impairments or pronounced motor delays. First, finding ways for students to function independently should be an instructional priority that spans all curriculum areas. Second, in situations in which completely independent task performance is not possible, invoke the principle of partial participation.

Functional Independence. Helping each student achieve functional independence will challenge a teacher's ingenuity. However, numerous computer-based (e.g., Behrmann, 1984) and noncomputer-based (Bigge, 1991; York & Rainforth, 1987) adaptive devices and strategies are available for use as training aids. In using such training aids (e.g., pencil holders, adaptive switches) there are two important cautions. First, only aids that encourage coordinated movement should be employed; never aids that foster abnormal movement patterns. Second, aids should be employed with the intent that they will be removed or faded when the student can perform the task independently.

Partial Participation. The principle of partial participation, as advocated by Baumgart, Brown, Pumpian, Nisbet, Ford, Sweet, Messina, and Schroeder (1982) and revisited by Ferguson and Baumgart (1991), asserts that people with severe disabilities can perform a wide range of important skills, at least partially, with the assistance of individualized adaptations. This principle is based upon the premise that even partial participation in chronologically-age-appropriate community activities can offer important benefits to people with disabilities. For example, a person with severe disabilities might derive pleasure, increased self-esteem, and a more normalized image by going shopping at the mall even if he or she is unable to acquire some of the skills that are usually considered prerequisites for the independent performance of that activity. Among the individualized adaptations that might be necessary are adaptive devices (e.g., wheelchair), personal assistance (e.g., someone to accompany them to the mall), and adapted skill sequences (e.g., use of a department store charge card to bypass the need for money skills). Baumgart et al. (1982) proposed the following eight-phase strategy for applying the principle of partial participation in a particular situation.

1. Conduct an inventory to identify the sequence of skills used by a person without disabilities to perform the task.
2. Conduct a second inventory to determine which of the relevant skills the target student with disabilities can already perform in an acceptable manner.
3. Determine the skills that the target student can probably acquire.
4. Determine the skills that the target student probably cannot acquire.
5. Generate adaptation hypotheses consisting of adaptations that might allow performance of the missing skills, or their substitutes.
6. Conduct an adaptation inventory to test empirically the adequacy of the possible adaptations.
7. Decide upon the individualized adaptations.
8. List the selected adaptations.

In summary, it is important to emphasize that successful programming requires the integration of passive management techniques and active instructional techniques. The benefits of positioning and handling procedures are maximized only when they are used to enable and facilitate the acquisition of functional skills and independent behaviors (Campbell, 1987).

Working with Families

Because motor skills are a part of all of the activities of daily living, it is essential to find ways to extend gains achieved at school into the home environment. Family involvement in training activities should be encouraged because the acquisition of motor skills often requires extensive practice, and because children with mental retardation and physical disabilities may have difficulty synthesizing and generalizing isolated skills on their own (Rainforth & Salisbury, 1988). Rainforth and Salisbury point out that the following barriers often interfere with meaningful home–school collaboration: lack of information available to parents, a mismatch of program demands and family needs, and the exclusion of parents from program development and decision making. They propose the use of the "Family Daily Routine Model," developed in 1979 by Vincent, Salisbury, Laren, and Baumgart (cited by Rainforth & Salisbury, 1988) to extend the benefits of movement therapy and training into the home environment. This model involves the following steps:

1. Assess the daily routines and teaching resources of the home.
2. Select instructional targets, in consultation with the family, that can be taught at convenient times.
3. Implement the home program.
4. Work with the family to collect data.
5. Evaluate program effectiveness.

Many other guides are available to assist families in their efforts to remediate motor delays and disabilities (e.g., Connor, Williamson, & Siepp, 1978; Hanson & Harris, 1986).

The Acquisition of Self-Help Skills

In this section, essential self-help skills are identified and discussed in conjunction with their relationship to important, underlying motor behaviors. This section is followed by a consideration of issues relevant to the assessment of self-help skills in young children with mental retardation. A discussion of curriculum considerations is followed by an examination of instructional strategies that have been identified as effective for teaching skills in toileting, eating, dressing, and grooming.

Essential Self-Help Skills and Motor Prerequisites

Self-help skills are among the highest-priority skills to be acquired by most children with mental retardation. A repertoire of basic self-help skills is a key to independence and opportunities to enjoy full community participation through employment, living, and leisure options. Most individuals with mental retardation, regardless of its severity, are able to acquire the basic self-help skills of toileting, self-feeding, and dressing. Most can learn to perform these activities independently; others, especially those with motor impairments, can achieve at least "partial participation." These basic self-help skills can often be augmented with the related skills associated with personal hygiene, mealtime routines, and grooming.

Specific motor skills are often clear prerequisites to the acquisition of self-help skills. For instance, the development of grasping is generally a prerequisite for the acquisition of self-feeding skills. In addition, physiological readiness may be an important consideration in the acquisition of self-help skills, particularly toilet training, with most investigators suggesting that success will be maximized if training is delayed until predictable patterns of elimination and daily periods of dryness are observed (Snell, 1993). For most children with severe and profound mental retardation, this will mean waiting until at least the age of five. However, the training of self-help skills should not be delayed while waiting for the emergence of related skills that are not true prerequisites. Many of these skills, such as walking, can be taught concurrently with self-help skills. To illustrate this point, objectives geared toward the integrated teaching of motor and self-help skills are provided for the *Case Study of Norman*.

Assessment of Self-Help Skills

Goals and objectives in the self-help area are typically linked to a systematic assessment of the child's current level of functioning in each of the skill-cluster areas. Assessments of self-help skills can be performed by the teacher using both formal and informal approaches.

Formal Assessment Procedures

A wide variety of assessment devices may be used to provide information on self-help skill performance. Comprehensive adaptive behavior scales typically contain subscales on self-help skills. Widely used adaptive behavior scales, which may be particularly helpful at the *screening* phase of assessment, include the *AAMR Adaptive Behavior Scales–School* (Lambert, Nihira, & Leland, 1992) and the *Vineland Adaptive Behavior Scales* (Sparrow, Balla, & Cicchetti, 1984). The more detailed analysis of strengths and weaknesses that is needed during the *diagnostic* phase of assessment may be provided by scales and checklists such as the scale associated with the *Portage Guide to Early Education* (Shearer, Billingsley, Froham, Hilliard, Johnson, & Shearer, 1976), which uses a checklist to assess current functioning in children zero to six years old across several areas, including motor development and self-help. Assessment for *educational programming* is conducted to identify the child's specific learning needs as a basis for program design and monitoring. At this stage, the *Balthazar Scales* (Balthazar, 1976) may provide a helpful guide.

Informal Assessment Procedures

In the assessment of self-help skills, informal assessment plays a particularly key role. Children's gaps in self-help skills are often all too apparent, both at home and at school. Formal and informal observations may provide the best guide for the selection of programming goals and priorities. The most frequently used and most needed skills should be taught first.

CASE STUDY: Norman (CA = 5–5, IQ = 64)

Consultations between Norman's teacher and his occupational and physical therapists revealed that his limited motor skills are interfering with his performance of many daily living activities. Particular areas of need in the motor domain include difficulty with the active range of motion in the upper extremities, crossing midline from left to right, wrist rotation, and pincer manipulation. These motor delays appear to be limiting his performance of self-care activities, such as dressing, self-feeding at meals, and personal hygiene.

The following instructional objectives were developed by Norman's instructional team to expand upon some of his IEP goals (presented in Chapter 6), and to illustrate how integrated teaching can be incorporated into Norman's educational program.

Integrated Instruction of Norman's Motor and Self-Help Objectives

Motor	Self-Help		
	Dressing	*Meals*	*Hygiene*
Upper Range of Motion	Norman will fully extend each arm forward while inserting them into the sleeves of the pullover shirt his mother is holding, for 5 consecutive days.	For 5 consecutive days, Norman will reach for one food item in the kitchen cupboard during meal preparation upon request.	For 5 consecutive baths, Norman will dry all body parts except his back with a towel after bathing.
Crossing Midline	For 10 consecutive days, Norman will use both hands to remove his right sock, given a verbal reminder and hand-over-hand prompting.	For 10 consecutive meals, Norman will pass food from the person on his left to the person on his right when asked to do so.	For 10 consecutive baths, Norman will use a soaped wash cloth to wipe both feet, using his left hand to hold the wash cloth.
Wrist Rotation	For 5 consecutive mornings, Norman will turn the knob of his closet door when requested to do so, in order to locate his clothes.	For 10 meals in a week, Norman will, with hand-over-hand guidance, un-screw the lid of a jar, the contents of which are needed for the meal.	For 5 consecutive baths, Norman will turn off each water faucet upon request as soon as the tub is full.
Pincer Grasp	For 5 consecutive days, Norman will zip his coat once the zipper is engaged for him.	For 10 consecutive meals, Norman will hold his spoon between his thumb and finger once it is placed there by his teacher.	For 5 consecutive sessions, Norman will remove the cap from the toothpaste tube once it has been unscrewed.

As a basis for program design, observations should be guided by careful task analyses of each of the self-help skills to be taught. Published task analyses are available for most of the common self-help skills, such as toileting and toothbrushing. Existing task analyses can then be adapted to correspond to the functioning level of the individual and the specific features of the situation.

Interventions to Enhance the Acquisition of Self-Help Skills

This section begins with a brief discussion of issues relating to the selection of a self-help skills curriculum model for young children with mental retardation. This discussion is followed by descriptions of specific instructional strategies and procedures for training self-help skills within the areas of toileting, feeding, and dressing and grooming.

Curriculum in the Area of Self-Help Skills
As in the motor skills area, it is recommended that a curriculum model that combines the features of the Developmental and Functional Models be applied in teaching self-help skills to young children with mental retardation. This is another area in which the organization and sequence of normal development can provide a helpful guide for program design. Program priorities can, however, emphasize those skills most needed to allow the child to function independently in his or her environment as suggested by the Functional Model. Bigge's (1991) suggestion that a motor skills curriculum should be functional, cumulative, and foundational can be readily extended into the self-help curriculum area.

Instruction of Self-Help Skills

Toilet Training. For many centuries, individuals with severe and profound mental retardation received, at best, only custodial care. These individuals were often incontinent, lacking even the most rudimentary self-help skills. Families or institutional care providers faced the demanding task of continually changing, cleaning, feeding, dressing, and grooming the child, and ultimately the adult, with mental retardation. This situation has changed dramatically in the past thirty years. Now, people with even profound mental retardation can be taught basic self-help skills.

A major breakthrough came in 1963 with the publication of Ellis's theoretical and task analysis of toileting behavior, aimed at providing a basis for the development of training programs for the "severely defective." Ellis described his target group of institutionalized individuals with mental retardation in the following way:

> Typically they spend most of their waking hours milling about the dayroom or sitting on the floor. They have no toilet habits, are unable to dress or bathe themselves, and may show only minimal skill in feeding themselves. Language is usually absent or reduced to a few words. One of the most degrading features of the care of such patients is associated with the absence of toilet habits (Ellis, 1963, p. 98).

Ellis's article initiated a concerted effort to devise effective techniques to train independent toileting behavior in individuals with mental retardation. His stimulus-response (S-R) model and training sequence were readily adapted by researchers exploring the feasibility of applying operant conditioning principles to the toilet training of people with mental retardation (e.g., Giles & Wolf, 1966). Those early explorations paved the way for the development of the effective procedures that are currently available for teaching both daytime and nighttime toileting behaviors to individuals with mental retardation across functioning levels.

Daytime Toilet Training.   Building upon groundwork provided by numerous earlier studies, Azrin and Foxx (Azrin & Foxx, 1971; Foxx & Azrin, 1973a; 1973b) devised an effective and efficient, though fairly complex, method for teaching independent toileting skills. They provided clear research evidence that daytime toileting accidents could be reduced to near zero in about four days for adults with severe and profound mental retardation (Azrin & Foxx, 1971). A subsequent research study provided evidence that young children without mental retardation could acquire independent toileting behaviors through a similar training regime in an average of four hours. Children between twenty and twenty-five months of age required approximately five hours, while children between twenty-six and thirty-six months required a little over two hours of training.

Azrin and Foxx viewed toileting as a "complex operant and social learning process." They hypothesized that the failure of many people with mental retardation to acquire appropriate toileting skills was related to reduced learning ability and the conditions imposed by institutionalization. Their method involves the use of increased fluid intake to increase the number of training opportunities. Two signaling devices are also used. The first device, a "pants-alarm," consists of two moisture detecting snaps in the crotch of the underpants that activate an alarm and allow the immediate detection of accidents. The second device is a plastic bowl fitted with moisture-detecting studs. When placed in the toilet, this device signals the beginning of elimination so that consequences can be delivered immediately.

Each resident in the training program was given as large a quantity of water, tea, or coffee as he or she would consume every half-hour. In addition, each resident was required to sit on the toilet every half-hour. Dressing and undressing behaviors were shaped during each visit to the toilet. Residents were reinforced with edibles and social reinforcers for each elimination in the toilet, and for each five minutes that they remained dry away from the toilet. Accidents were followed immediately by verbal reprimands, cleanliness training that consisted of washing the soiled clothing and mopping the floor, and time-out from any positive reinforcement for one hour. To reduce opportunities for behaviors incompatible with toileting, residents were required to remain in the toilet area during the entire eight-hour session on each day of training. Training was followed by a posttraining program designed to insure maintenance of the newly acquired toileting behaviors in the context of the daily ward routine. This involved dry pants checks and cleanliness training procedures administered by ward attendants for at least a one-month period with no accidents.

Research involving the Azrin and Foxx approach has helped resolve the issue of whether toilet training sessions must be timed to coincide with the child's schedule of elimination. The method proposed by Ellis and several other experimental approaches were based on this premise. For example, Mahoney, Van Wagenen, and Meyerson (1971) reported high rates of success for children with and without mental retardation with a training package utilizing a urine-signaling device. In that study, children were taught to go to the bathroom each time they heard an auditory signal which was triggered by a urine-detecting device in their underpants. Smith (1979) conducted a study which compared an individualized "timing" method based on the Mahoney et al. (1971) procedures with a "regular potting" method based on the Foxx and Azrin (1973b) approach. They defined "regular potting" methods as those in which the child uses the toilet at "arbitrarily set intervals of time." In that study, an individualized and a group version of the "regular potting" approach were compared with the individualized "timed" approach. They found that both of the individualized methods were considerably more successful than the group approach. The two individualized methods had a similar high rate of success. They concluded that the "regular potting" method was clearly the method of choice because it eliminated the need for complex urine-sensing equipment and procedures.

In spite of its reported success, the intensity, complexity, and general aversiveness of the Azrin-Foxx technique precludes its application in some situations. For example, it was reported that parents attempting to apply the technique with very young children without disabilities between twenty and twenty-six months of age encountered screaming, crying, and tantrums (Matson, 1975). An even more serious danger arises from the fact that uncontrolled increases in fluid intake can cause overhydration and electrolyte imbalance leading to "nausea, emesis, muscular twitching, grand mal seizures, and coma" (Thompson & Hanson, 1983, p. 140). These investigators advise a careful medical examination before instituting increased fluid intake procedures with anyone. Individuals with any risk factors, such as seizures, hydrocephaly, or heart, liver, or kidney abnormalities should be excluded from such programs. In addition, guidelines for maximum amounts of fluid intake should be carefully followed (see Thompson & Hanson, 1983).

Subsequent research has focused upon determining the extent to which the effectiveness and efficiency of toilet training can be maintained when some of the more cumbersome or aversive features of the Azrin-Foxx and other successful approaches are removed (see reviews of research by Anderson, 1982 and McCartney & Holden, 1981). While the full Azrin-Foxx (1971) regime may be necessary to insure the rapid training of an adult with mental retardation who might otherwise lose an employment opportunity, it is rarely justified for a preschool child with or without mental retardation. One of the simplified, less stressful approaches should be tried first—even if a longer time period will be required to reach the criterion of independent toileting.

An example of a less stressful approach was described by Williams and Sloop (1978), who reported that self-initiated toileting behavior was achieved by six adults with profound mental retardation after nine days of training with a modified version of the Azrin-Foxx (1971) procedure. The procedure used by Williams and Sloop involved no urine-sensing devices, used regular staff members as trainers, and arranged training sessions around regularly scheduled ward activities.

Similarly, Richmond (1983) built upon Smith's (1979) earlier findings by investigating the effectiveness of a "regular potting" method aimed at simplifying the Azrin-Foxx (1973b) procedure. This simplified method was designed to be more readily incorporated into the routine of a preschool setting for children with severe and profound mental retardation. Richmond reported that this approach virtually eliminated daytime toileting accidents for the four children who participated in his study. The approach involved taking the children to the toilet at gradually increasing intervals, dry-pants checks, and providing prompting and praise for appropriate pretoileting behaviors. Toilet use was reinforced with a preferred liquid and praise. Accidents were followed with a brief reprimand and a simple correction procedure requiring the child to get a clean set of clothes, change, wash him- or herself, dress, and dispose of the dirty clothes. Because Richmond's approach seems well-suited to applications in preschool settings with young children with mental retardation, its main features are summarized in Table 10-1. It should be noted, however, that this program did not teach independent, self-initiated toileting behavior; it merely reduced accidents when children were taken to the toilet at regular intervals.

Although most of the research has concentrated upon training toileting behavior in a single setting, two recent studies have focused upon the generalization of toileting behaviors. In one of the studies, Heyward (1988) described the application of a procedure for gradually extending the range of discriminative stimuli controlling the toileting behavior of a six-year-old boy with multiple disabilities. Using a stepwise procedure, control was faded from the child's mother in the home setting to the classroom assistant in the school setting. After about a month of training, the target behaviors were established and it was reported

TABLE 10-1   Daytime Toilet Training Procedure

I. *BASELINE PHASE*
Take child to toilet every hour.
Praise child for using toilet.
Record the frequency of accidents.

II. *TRAINING PHASE*
First Week: Every 15 Minutes
Conduct dry-pants check.
    Praise child for clean/dry pants, or
    Consequate accidents with a brief reprimand and simple correction procedure.
    Record the frequency of accidents.
Ask child if he/she needs to use toilet.
Prompt child to respond and/or go to bathroom.
Praise child/give preferred liquid for toilet use.
Praise child for related toileting behaviors.

Second Week: Every 30 Minutes
(Same as above)

Third Week: Every Hour
(Same as above)

Fourth Week: Every Hour
(Same as above)

III. *POSTTRAINING PHASE*
Take child to toilet once every two hours.
Praise child for using toilet.
Record the frequency of accidents.

Reprinted from "Shaping bladder and bowel continence in developmentally retarded preschool children," by G. Richard, *Journal of Autism and Developmental Disorders, 1,* pp. 197–205, Copyright 1983, with permission from Plenum Publishing Corp.

that the child spontaneously began to use other toilets at the homes of relatives and at restaurants. A four-year follow-up failed to reveal any toileting problems.

In the other study, Dunlap, Koegel, and Koegel (1984) reported success for a set of procedures aimed at generalizing appropriate toileting behavior across all of a child's daily environments. Like Richmond, Dunlap et al. developed procedures that could be easily incorporated into the child's daily routine. Their approach included frequent opportunities for toileting, praise for successful toileting, dry-pants checks, and minimal prompting. Two of the four children wore pants-alarms to insure immediate detection of accidents. Accidents were treated with a mild reprimand and positive practice requiring the child to repeat the entire toileting sequence five times from the location of the accident. The key component of their approach was continuity of treatment across all of the child's daily environments. A treatment coordinator assigned to each child insured that regular communication took place with the trainer who had been designated in each setting. Communication took place via the telephone and written instructions carried by the child. As a result of training, accidents in all environments were greatly reduced. Maintenance of appropriate toileting behavior was reported by parents for periods ranging from two to five years. Parents also reported that, after training, their children spontaneously displayed self-initiated toileting. A final note of caution: although many simplified techniques have reported success, most have not had fully independent toileting as a goal.

Nighttime Toilet Training.   Daytime toilet training is not synonymous with nighttime training. In fact, it has been recommended that nighttime training not be instituted until daytime toileting is successful at least 75 percent of the time (e.g., Snell, 1993). It has been estimated that approximately 70 percent of people with severe retardation in institutions are bedwetters (Azrin, Sneed, & Foxx, 1973). Early treatments involved waking the bedwetter at intervals during the night and taking him or her to the bathroom in an effort to anticipate the accident. This approach was often aided by urine-sensing alarm devices placed on the bedsheet. Little information on the effectiveness of these procedures for individuals with mental retardation was available, leading Azrin et al. to develop and evaluate strategies specifically aimed at nighttime toilet training. Their intensive procedure, detailed in Table 10-2, was dramatically more successful than the traditional urine-alarm procedure. Bedwetting ceased for all twelve of their subjects; it stopped within one night for eight of them. Three required two nights of training, and one required three nights. The success of this procedure is tempered only by the fact that it requires intensive all-night intervention procedures that may exceed the stamina of many families.

Eating.   Proficiency with self-feeding and other mealtime skills can greatly increase the opportunities for social integration that exist for an individual with mental retardation. Prior to the 1960s, it was taken for granted that people with severe and profound mental retardation would always require assistance with even the most rudimentary self-care skills, including eating. The impact of that assumption was dramatically illustrated by the mealtime procedures that characterized most of the large, state institutions for people with mental retardation. Meals were typically delivered to a dining room full of residents, many of whom were tied to their chairs, waiting to be fed. As soon as the food arrived, usually pureed or mashed, the attendants hurriedly made their rounds trying to feed all of the residents in the time allotted. One haunting statistic from Geraldo Rivera's 1972 expose of con-

TABLE 10-2   Nighttime Toilet Training Procedure

I. *Intensive Training*
  A. *Before bedtime*
      1. Bedwetter drinks fluids
      2. Urine-alarm placed on the bed
      3. Potty-alert placed in toilet bowl

  B. *Hourly awakenings*
      1. Minimal prompt given for awakening the resident
      2. Resident instructed or guided to the toilet
      3. Resident seated on toilet bowl
          a. If urination does not occur within 5 minutes
              (i)   return resident to bed
              (ii) at bedside give resident fluids and praise as reinforcers
          b. If urination does occur within 5 min.
              (i)   give resident praise, snacks, and fluids as reinforcers
              (ii) return resident to bed
      4. Praise resident for having dry bed (require resident to touch the dry sheets)
      5. Resident returns to sleep

  C. *When accident occurs*—45 Minutes of Cleanliness Training and Positive Practice
      1. Disconnect the sound of the urine-alarm
      2. Awaken resident
      3. Reprimand resident for wetting and direct him to the toilet to finish urination
      4. Cleanliness Training
          a. Bedwetter changes wet linen
          b. Attendant reactivates urine-alarm
      5. Positive Practice in toileting
          a. Bedwetter lies down in bed for 3 minutes
          b. Bedwetter awakened with minimal prompt after 3 minutes
          c. Bedwetter directed to toilet
          d. Repeat steps a, b, c about 9 times
      6. Bedwetter returns to sleep when 45 minutes have elapsed since accident was detected

II. *Monitored posttraining phase*
  A. *Initiation of monitored posttraining*
      1. When resident has no more than 1 accident during a training night
      2. When the resident correctly toilets on at least 50% of all opportunities during a training night

  B. *Procedure*
      1. Urine-alarm on bed
      2. Whenever accident occurs, reprimand, Cleanliness Training and Positive Practice follow for 45 minutes
      3. No fluids, no hourly awakenings, no reinforcers

  C. *Termination of monitored posttraining*
      1. Terminated 7 nights after last accident

III. *Normal procedure*
  A. *Initiated after resident goes 7 nights without accident*
  B. *No urine-alarm, no reinforcers, no Positive Practice, etc.*
  C. *Bed inspected each morning*
      1. If bed wet, resident remakes and cleans bed (Cleanliness Training)
      2. If 2 accidents occur within a given week, the Monitored phase is reinstated

Reprinted from *Behavior Research and Therapy*, Vol. 11, Azrin, N.H., Sneed, T. J., and Foxx, R. N.; Dry bed: a rapid method of eliminating bedwetting (enuresis) of the retarded; pp. 427–434, Copyright 1973, with permission from Pergamon Press Ltd., Headington Hill Hall, Oxford OX3 OBW, UK.

ditions at the Willowbrook Developmental Center in New York City was that the average feeding time per resident was only three minutes. Clearly, these conditions raised serious quality of life as well as health issues. Fortunately, significant progress in our ability to teach self-feeding and other mealtime skills to individuals with all levels of mental retardation has been made in the past thirty years.

Inspired by Ellis's 1963 theoretical framework for toilet training, Bensberg, Colwell, and Cassel (1965) published a pilot study exploring the extent to which operant and classical conditioning methods could be used to teach self-help skills to children with severe mental retardation. The pioneer spirit of this endeavor is illustrated by the fact that one staff member was sent to a place called "Animal Behavior Enterprises, Inc." in order to learn how to apply operant conditioning techniques. That staff member then passed on what he had learned to the other members of the staff. After seven months of training, all six children had made noticeable gains in the areas of independent toileting, eating, and dressing. In the area of eating, the staff reported: "All eat with a spoon and five do so neatly" (p. 677). With this sketchy report of success as encouragement, numerous subsequent investigators have made considerable progress toward developing and refining a full complement of techniques for teaching independent eating skills.

Most of the research on this topic can be classified into three categories. Studies in the first category focused on identifying effective techniques for increasing children's repertoires of appropriate self-feeding skills. The focus of the second set of studies was upon eliminating inappropriate mealtime behaviors. The third set of studies concentrated on developing techniques for maximizing the maintenance and generalization of acquired eating skills.

The first of the three research thrusts was initiated by two studies aimed at developing step-by-step procedures for teaching self-feeding skills to children with profound mental retardation by Berkowitz, Sherry, and Davis (1971) and Song and Gandhi (1974). Although these studies employed weak research designs, they did demonstrate the feasibility of using shaping and fading techniques to teach children with profound mental retardation to feed themselves with a spoon within a period of about two months. Subsequently, using a group research design, Nelson, Cone, and Hanson (1975) compared the effectiveness of three methods for teaching utensil use to three groups of children with profound to mild mental retardation. The groups were taught by means of modeling, physical guidance, or physical guidance with immediate praise techniques. Nelson et al. reported that the two procedures based upon physical guidance were clearly superior to the modeling procedure, in which subjects watched while the experimenter demonstrated the procedures. It was suggested that the multisensory features of physical guidance may have facilitated skill acquisition.

These training approaches have all relied upon schedules that are dovetailed with regular mealtimes, typically resulting in a maximum of three training sessions per day and requiring several weeks of training for mastery of the target skills. Azrin and Armstrong (1973) introduced their "mini-meal" technique as a way of reducing the total time span needed for training while addressing the need of lower-functioning individuals for more intensive, concentrated training. Twenty-two individuals with profound mental retardation were randomly assigned to two groups, one of which received the mini-meal procedure and one of which received a control condition. Trainers for the control group were instructed to use whatever methods they thought were best during the regular 45-minute mealtime sessions.

The mini-meal procedure involved dividing each meal into three 15-minute sessions and using highly structured training procedures. The target skills for both the mini-meal group and the control group included napkin use, spoon, fork, and knife use, and drinking from a glass. Results indicated that all participants in the mini-meal group were trained within 12 days to a level of skill that was comparable to that of staff members. After 18 days of training, only four of the eleven control group residents had reached the training criteria. Clearly, the mini-meal approach is a powerful tool to use when other methods have failed or when time is of the essence. However, it does require a major disruption of normal mealtime procedures. The decision to use the mini-meal approach must be made in light of an individual's right to a normalized lifestyle, and his or her right to make personal choices.

Although most studies have assumed that food is the natural reinforcer to be used in self-feeding training, Richman, Sonderby, and Kahn (1980) questioned this assumption in research on teaching self-feeding to children with severe and profound mental retardation. Employing a multiple baseline design across subjects, they found that teaching prerequisite feeding skills in a simulated setting without actual food resulted in more rapid acquisition of fork use than an equivalent amount of training that occurred solely at mealtimes with food reinforcers. These and other studies on the training of self-feeding skills have been reviewed by Reid (1983). Although most of these studies were plagued by methodological weaknesses, they did suggest that eating skills could be taught across a variety of conditions.

The second focus of research on teaching eating skills to people with mental retardation is upon the reduction of inappropriate and disruptive mealtime behaviors. In several of the studies in the preceding section, procedures were included to deal with disruptive behaviors as they occurred so that they would not interfere with the training of target behaviors. Mealtime behaviors that are problematic in people with mental retardation include stealing and throwing food, eating with fingers, messy utensils, "pigging" or stuffing food into the mouth, and rapid eating.

A relatively early study by Barton, Guess, Garcia, and Baer (1970) employed time-out procedures to reduce the frequency of three mealtime behaviors that the researchers labeled "disgusting." These behaviors were: stealing food, eating with fingers, and "pigging." The consequence for stealing food was removal from the meal to another room for the duration of the meal. The consequence for "pigging" was tray removal for 15 seconds. It was found that the percentage of "disgusting" behaviors decreased dramatically during the five-month period of the study.

Another mealtime behavior problematic for many people with mental retardation is excessively rapid eating. According to a survey by McGimsey (cited by Favell, McGimsey, & Jones, 1980), approximately 28 percent of their institutionalized sample manifested this behavior. In that survey, fast eaters sometimes exceeded twenty bites per minute and finished their meals in one to three minutes. Favell et al. (1980) tested a treatment package to reduce rapid eating with three individuals with profound mental retardation. The training package consisted of reinforcing and shaping pauses of increasing length, and gradually fading manual prompts aimed at getting participants to pause after attempts at rapid eating. For all three participants, the treatment was successful at reducing the rate of eating to the target rate of 6 to 8 bites per minute.

The third focus of research on eating skills has been upon identifying techniques to insure the maintenance and generalization of acquired eating skills. After using a manual guidance procedure to train a six-year-old girl with profound mental retardation to eat with a spoon, O'Brien, Bugle, and Azrin (1972) employed an interruption-extinction procedure to foster maintenance. The procedure consisted of stopping the child's hand before it reached her mouth whenever she made an incorrect feeding response. A return to baseline immediately after training resulted in a total reversion to pretraining feeding behavior. However, a second return to baseline after an interruption-extinction phase revealed the maintenance of improved eating behavior.

Similarly, Albin (1977), reported success for a maintenance procedure used after training that utilized verbal and manual prompting to teach three children with profound mental retardation to eat with a spoon. The maintenance procedures involved gradually fading the presence of the training staff out of the dining area. Appropriate feeding behaviors were still being practiced eighteen months later.

Stimbert, Minor, and McCoy (1977) employed the mini-meal procedure with children (CA 3.5–13.5) with moderate to profound mental retardation. Maintenance procedures involved monitoring and praising self-feeding behavior on a reduced reinforcement schedule with overcorrection and tray time-out. Generalization to the home setting was fostered by gradually fading in parents as trainers. First, the parents observed training sessions through a one-way window; then they sat in the room; finally they took over training for some of the sessions. Follow-up observations indicated the continuation of correct feeding behavior in the home setting twelve months after training.

Sisson and Dixon (1986) reported training six children (CA 6.0–13.0) with mental retardation and severe behavior disorders in a range of mealtime behaviors, including chewing with mouth closed, utensil use, and napkin use. Training involved instructions, modeling, manual guidance, behavioral rehearsal, and feedback. Probes were administered throughout training to test for generalization to a hospital setting where the trainer was absent and where none of the training contingencies were in effect. Although modest generalization was obtained, generalization effects were less pronounced than training effects. This finding is perhaps a reflection of the absence of direct programming for maintenance and generalization.

Available evidence provides general support for the effectiveness of the techniques described in the preceding paragraphs. However, a serious drawback of most of the techniques is that they require extensive training time and a one-to-one staff to client ratio. Matson, Ollendick, and Adkins (1980) reported a study aimed at addressing some of these issues. In that study, they taught a range of mealtime behaviors (i.e., orderliness, eating, neatness, utensil use, and table manners) using a framework that they referred to as "independence training." Training strategies, summarized in Table 10-3, included social reinforcement, self-monitoring and evaluation, modeling, and practice supervised by other residents. All training was conducted in small groups comprised of four to six residents. Residents had profound to mild mental retardation and fellow residents served with staff members as co-trainers throughout the three-month training period. The training group outperformed a control group on the number of target behaviors correctly performed. Twenty-two of the forty trained participants, but none of the forty individuals in the control group, reached the highest level of the training sequence.

TABLE 10-3   Components of Dining Skills Training Program

1. Training in small groups (4–6 residents)

2. Assignment to one of five instructional dining levels

3. Explanation to each resident of system for advancing through the five dining levels

4. Verbal prompts in the event of an incorrect or omitted target behavior

5. Modeling of behavior by the trainer whenever verbal prompts are ineffective

6. Manual guidance by the trainer whenever modeling is ineffective

7. Prompting, modeling, and social reinforcement by other residents

8. Positive reinforcement (special privileges and certificates of recognition)

9. Self-monitoring and evaluation

Reprinted from *Behavior Research and Therapy*, Vol. 18, Matson, J. L., Ollendick, T. H. and Adkins, J.; A comprehensive dining program for mentally retarded adults; pp. 107–112, Copyright 1980, with permission from Pergamon Press Ltd., Headington Hill Hall, Oxford OX3 OBW, UK.

In some instances, children with motor impairments have difficulty with the motor responses involved in eating. Sobsey and Orelove (1984) evaluated a neurophysiological approach for facilitating responses such as lip closure, rotary chews per bite, spills per bite, and spills per drink. The facilitation procedures, which were developed in conjunction with a physical therapist, included rolling the student on a ball or mat, stroking the skin around the student's mouth, rubbing the student's palate and gums, brushing the skin on various parts of the student's face, applying ice near the student's mouth, vibrating various areas of the student's face, and tapping the student's tongue with a nylon spatula spoon. These procedures were administered for approximately 15 minutes prior to eating. Results indicated that the procedures were generally successful at facilitating the target behaviors, though there was considerable variability among subjects.

Dressing and Grooming.   The third basic area of self-help skills is dressing and grooming. Decisions regarding the restrictiveness of a person's living environment are often based on the degree to which a person with mental retardation can perform these skills independently. For example, the option of living in a supervised apartment, as opposed to a nursing home, is more likely to be open to people who can dress themselves, bathe themselves, brush their own teeth, and comb their own hair than to people who require assistance with these daily activities.

Most of the early studies in this area, published from the late 1960s to the early 1970s, contained serious flaws. Most obvious is the fact that these early studies predated the human rights standards and guidelines that are taken for granted today. For example, in a 1967 study by Minge and Ball that demonstrated the acquisition of dressing and other self-help skills by girls with profound mental retardation, breakfast and lunch were contingent upon performance in the training sessions. In another study (Martin, Kehoe, Bird, Jensen, & Darbyshire, 1971) that described the training of dressing skills in girls with severe mental retardation, the girls' fingers were slapped each time they engaged in disruptive behaviors such as grabbing reinforcers or hitting the experimenter. In addition, these early studies were generally lacking in experimental controls and internal validity, often making it impossible to unequivocally attribute any improvements to the intervention described. However, in spite of their flaws, these early studies did show that it was possible for people with severe and profound mental retardation to acquire and maintain a repertoire of independent dressing and undressing (Ball, Seric, & Payne, 1971), buttoning (Adelson-Bernstein & Sandow, 1978), and other grooming skills.

As in the other self-care areas, Azrin and his colleagues (Azrin, Schaeffer, & Wesolowski, 1976) analyzed the strengths and weaknesses of the procedures used in the early training studies, and devised an alternative training approach to teach dressing and undressing skills more effectively and in fewer total training hours. In that study, seven students with profound mental retardation learned to put on and take off five garments in an average of 12 hours of training time. Some of the innovations included in this approach were: concentrated training sessions, a forward training sequence, training with several articles of clothing simultaneously, using large sizes for training, and teaching the easier skill of undressing before dressing. Further support for the effectiveness of these procedures was reported by Diorio and Konarski (1984), who employed a multiple baseline design with three adults with profound mental retardation. Some initial indications of skill maintenance were observed, but most gains had disappeared after ten months.

Although most of these studies involved adults and older children with mental retardation, many of these approaches are also applicable with preschool children. Two relatively recent studies were conducted with preschool-aged children with mental retardation. In one of the studies (Young, West, Howard, & Whitney, 1986), a multiple baseline across behaviors design was used to test the effectiveness of a whole-task approach to teach dressing

TABLE 10-4   Components of Dressing Skills Training Program

I. *ACQUISITION*
Elicit full chain of responses on each trial, beginning with first step (whole-task training).
Give verbal instructions to put on or take off article of clothing.
Use physical, verbal, and/or gestural prompts as needed. (graduated guidance method).
Gradually withdraw prompts until performance is independent.
Intermittently praise completion of individual steps.
Reinforce completion of the whole chain of responses with praise, hugs, pats, and/or stickers.
Discourage inappropriate behaviors with a "no," interruption of the trial, and a 30-second time
    out.

II. *FLUENCY*
Begin fluency training as soon as the child responds consistently without prompts.
Identify steps in the chain where the child is experiencing the most difficulty.
Provide ten consecutive trials of practice on each step.

III. *GENERALIZATION*
Probe generalization to novel trainers and settings.

IV. *MAINTENANCE*
Conduct maintenance probes about one month after training in the generalization settings.

From *Education and Treatment of Children*, Vol. 9, Young, K. R., West, R. P., Howard, V. F., and Whitney, R.; Acquisition, fluency training, generalization, and maintenance of dressing skills of two developmentally disabled children; pp. 16–29, 1986.

skills to preschool children with moderate to profound disabilities (see Table 10-4). That study yielded evidence of one-month maintenance and limited generalization across people and settings, as well as evidence of acquisition and fluency. Kramer and Whitehurst (1981) manipulated several dimensions of button features to determine which of them influenced the difficulty of dressing for preschool children with mental retardation. They found that large buttons were easier than smaller buttons and the top button on a vest was easier than the lower buttons. The shape of the button did not affect performance.

Of course, grooming encompasses many skills in addition to dressing and undressing, including brushing teeth, showering, menstrual hygiene, hair care, etc. There is a clear need for additional research on these topics. Meanwhile, task analyses and training guidelines found in available curriculum guides may provide a helpful starting point, although most guides do not report data on effectiveness.

Recommendations

The material covered in this chapter suggests several recommendations that may be helpful. to teachers of children with mental retardation. An example of a context in which some of these recommendations might be applied is provided for the *Case Study of Norman*. The following recommendations are offered:

1. In both the motor and self-help domains, formal and informal assessment approaches should be used to determine the educational needs of the child. In the motor area, an occupational therapist or a physical therapist should typically play a central role in the assessment process.

2. For young children with mental retardation, a curriculum model should be selected for both the motor and self-help domains that combines the features of the Developmental and Functional Models.

3. In the motor domain, instructional strategies should include both passive management approaches and active instructional approaches. Passive management approaches, aimed at improving muscle tone and posture, should include one or more of the following approaches: sensory integration therapy, vestibular stimulation, and the neurodevelopmental approach. Active instructional approaches, aimed at training specific motor skills, should incorporate the behavior increase and decrease techniques described in Chapter 7. Training should be aimed at helping the child achieve functional independence or, if that is not possible, partial participation.

4. In planning self-help instructional programs, careful attention should be given to building in any necessary training for motor prerequisites.

5. For training daytime toileting skills, a method of demonstrated effectiveness should be selected and applied consistently. Richmond's (1983) approach is especially well-suited to training young children in a school setting. For nighttime toilet training, the method developed by Azrin et al. (1973) is recommended.

6. A number of different training techniques are available for training various eating skills. Again, an effective approach should be selected and applied consistently. The Matson

---

CASE STUDY: Norman (CA = 5–5, IQ = 64)

Norman's preschool program is based upon an *interdisciplinary team model*. According to this model, professionals complete their respective assessments independently; they then meet together with the child's parents to pool their findings. At the same time, they join forces to prepare or to review and update their plan for the child. Typically, the plan is then turned over to one person (usually the teacher) for implementation, with other team members available for consultation.

Norman's teacher works in close coordination with his physical therapist and his occupational therapist on the interdisciplinary team. Most importantly, Norman's mother is an active participant on the team. During the development of his Individualized Education Program (IEP), Norman's teacher identified needs in the areas of cognition and preacademic skills. His occupational therapist focused on needed improvements in his pincer grasp and crossing midline. His physical therapist also addressed crossing midline in addition to increasing his active range of motion. His mother was concerned with Norman's self-help skills (eating and dressing). Combining their ideas, objectives were developed that included: (1) reading numbers and counting objects aloud while pointing to stimulus items from the left to the right margins of the page; (2) arranging sequence cards in order from left to right (with the middle card at midline) while telling a story about them; (3) copying numbers from the left margin to the right margin of a paper; (4) scooping food servings from left to right; and (6) extension of arms while putting on a shirt or a coat. Norman's teacher is primarily responsible for data-based implementation of these activities, while his mother supervises mealtime and dressing activities at home.

---

et al. (1980) approach is recommended for training a variety of eating skills in a small group setting.

7. A variety of approaches are available for training dressing and grooming skills. In selecting an approach, consideration should be given to the whole-task training approach, which was reported to be effective for teaching dressing skills to preschool children with moderate to profound disabilities (Young et al., 1986).

References

Adelson-Bernstein, N. & Sandow, L. (1978). Teaching buttoning to severely/profoundly retarded multi-handicapped children. *Education and Training of the Mentally Retarded, 5*, 178–183.

Albin, J. B. (1977). Some variables influencing the maintenance of acquired self-feeding behaviors in profoundly retarded children. *Mental Retardation, 15*(5), 49–52.

Anderson, D. M. (1982). Ten years later: Training in the post-Azrin-and-Foxx era. *The Journal of the Association for the Severely Handicapped, 7*, 71–79.

Azrin, N. H., & Armstrong, P. M. (1973). The "mini-meal": A method for teaching eating skills to the profoundly retarded. *Mental Retardation, 11*(1), 9–13.

Azrin, N. H., & Foxx, R. M. (1971). A rapid method of toilet training the institutionalized retarded. *Journal of Applied Behavior Analysis, 4*, 89–99.

Azrin, N. H., Schaeffer, R. M., & Wesolowski, M. D. (1976). A rapid method of teaching profoundly retarded persons to dress by reinforcement-guidance method. *Mental Retardation, 14*(6), 29–33.

Azrin, N. H., Sneed, T. J., & Foxx, R. N. (1973). Dry bed: A rapid method of eliminating bedwetting (enuresis) of the retarded. *Behavior Research and Therapy, 11*, 427–434.

Ball, T. S., Seric, K., & Payne, L. E. (1971). Long-term retention of self-help skill training in the profoundly retarded. *American Journal of Mental Deficiency, 76*, 378–382.

Balthazar, E. E. (1976). *Balthazar scales of adaptive behavior.* Palo Alto, CA: Consulting Psychologist Press.

Barton, E. S., Guess, D., Garcia, E., & Baer, D. M. (1970). Improvement of retardates' mealtime behaviors by timeout procedures using multiple baseline techniques. *Journal of Applied Behavior Analysis, 3*, 77–84.

Baumgart, D., Brown, L., Pumpian, I., Nisbet, J., Ford, A., Sweet, M., Messina, R., & Schroeder, J. (1983). Principle of partial participation and individualized adaptations in educational programs for severely handicapped students. *The Journal of the Association for the Severely Handicapped, 7*, 17–27.

Behrmann, M. M. (Ed.). (1984). *Handbook of microcomputers in special education.* San Diego, CA: College-Hill Press.

Bensberg, G. J., Colwell, C. N., & Cassel, R. H. (1965). Teaching the profoundly retarded self-help activities by behavior shaping techniques. *American Journal of Mental Deficiency, 69*, 674–679.

Berkowitz, S., Sherry, P. J., & Davis, B. A. (1971). Teaching self-feeding skills to profound retardates using reinforcement and fading procedures. *Behavior Therapy, 2*, 62–67.

Bigge, J. L. (1991). *Teaching individuals with physical and multiple disabilities* (3rd ed.). New York: Merrill/Macmillan.

Bobath, K., & Bobath, B. (1967). The neuro-developmental treatment of cerebral palsy. *Physical Therapy, 47*(11), 1039–1041.

Brigance, A. H. (1978). *Brigance diagnostic inventory of early development.* North Billerica, MA: Curriculum Associates.

Brown, L., Branston, M. B., Hamre-Nietupski, S., Pumpian, I., Certo, N., & Gruenewald, L. (1979). A strategy for developing chronological-age-appropriate and functional curricular content for severely handicapped adolescents and young adults. *Journal of Special Education, 13*, 81–90.

Campbell, P. H. (1987). Physical management and handling procedures with students with movement dysfunction. In M. E. Snell (Ed.), *Systematic instruction of persons with severe handicaps* (3rd ed.) (pp. 174–187). Columbus, OH: Merrill.

Connor, F. P., Williamson, G. G., & Siepp, J. M. (1978). *Program guide for infants and toddlers with neuromotor and other developmental disabilities.* New York: Teachers College Press.

Diorio, M. A., & Konarski, E. A., Jr. (1984). Evaluation of a method for teaching dressing skills to profoundly mentally retarded persons. *American Journal of Mental Deficiency, 89*, 307–309.

Dunlap, G., Koegel, R. L., & Koegel, R. K. (1984). Continuity of treatment: Toilet training in multiple community settings. *Journal of the Association for Persons with Severe Handicaps, 9*, 134–141.

Ellis, N. R. (1963). Toilet training the severely defective patient: An S–R reinforcement analysis. *American Journal of Mental Deficiency, 68*(1), 98–103.

Ersing, W. F., Loovis, E. M., & Ryan, T. M. (1982). On the nature of motor development in special populations. *Exceptional Education Quarterly, 3*(1), 64–72.

Favell, J. E., McGimsey, J. F., & Jones, M. L. (1980). Rapid eating in the retarded: Reduction by nonaversive procedures. *Behavior Modification, 4*, 481–492.

Ferguson, D. L., & Baumgart, D. (1991). Partial participation revisited. *Journal of the Association for Persons with Severe Handicaps, 16*(4), 218–227.

Foxx, R. M., & Azrin, N. H. (1973a). Dry pants: A rapid method of toilet training children. *Behavior Research and Therapy, 11*, 435–422.

Foxx, R. M., & Azrin, N. H. (1973b). *Toilet training the retarded.* Champaign, IL: Research Press.

Frankenburg, W. K., Dodds, J. B., Fandal, A., Kazuk, E., & Cohrs, M. (1975). *Denver Developmental Screening Test.* Denver: LADOCA.

Giles, D. K., & Wolf, M. M. (1966). Toilet training institutionalized severe retardates: An application of operant behavior modification techniques. *American Journal of Mental Deficiency, 70*, 766–780.

Hanson, M. J., & Harris, R. R. (1986). *Teaching the young child with motor delays: A guide for parents and professionals.* Austin, TX: Pro-Ed.

Hardiman, S. A., Goetz, E. M., Reuter, K. E., & LeBlanc, J. M. (1975). Primes, contingent attention, and training effects on a child's motor behavior. *Journal of Applied Behavior Analysis, 8,* 399–409.

Harris, S. R. (1988). Early intervention: Does developmental therapy make a difference? *Topics in Early Childhood Special Education, 7*(4), 20–32.

Heyward, E. (1988). Generalisation of toilet training skills of a mentally handicapped boy. *Behavioural Psychotherapy, 16*(2), 102–107.

Horn, E. M. (1991). Basic motor skills instruction for children with neuromotor delays: A critical review. *Journal of Special Education, 25*(2), 168–197.

Horner, R. D. (1971). Establishing use of crutches by a mentally retarded spina bifida child. *Journal of Applied Behavior Analysis, 4,* 183–189.

Inge, K. J. (1987). Normal motor development. In F. P. Orelove & D. Sobsey (Eds.). *Educating children with multiple disabilities* (pp. 25–41). Baltimore: Brookes.

Kral, P. (1972). Motor characteristics and development of retarded children. *Education and Training of the Mentally Retarded, 7,* 14–21.

Kraemer, K. A., Cusick, B., & Bigge, J. L. (1982). Motor development, deviations, and physical rehabilitation. In J. L. Bigge (Ed.). *Teaching individuals with physical and multiple disabilities* (2nd ed.) (pp. 12–44). Columbus, OH: Merrill.

Kramer, L., & Whitehurst, C. (1981). Effects of button features on self-dressing in young retarded children. *Education and Training of the Mentally Retarded, 16*(4), 277–283.

Kuharski, T., Rues, J., Cook, D., & Guess, D. (1985). Effects of vestibular stimulation on sitting behaviors among preschoolers with severe handicaps. *Journal of the Association for Persons with Severe Handicaps, 10*(3), 137–145.

Lambert, N., Nihira, K., & Leland, H. (1992). *AAMR Adaptive Behavior Scales–School* (2nd ed.). Austin, TX: ProEd.

Lillie, D., & Harbin, G. (1975). *Carolina developmental profile.* Winston-Salem, NC: Kaplan.

Mahoney, K., Van Wagenen, R. K., & Meyerson, L. (1971). Toilet training of normal and retarded children. *Journal of Applied Behavior Analysis, 4,* 173–181.

Martin, G. L., Kehoe, B., Bird, E., Jensen, V., & Darbyshire, M. (1971). Operant conditioning in dressing behavior of severely retarded girls. *Mental Retardation, 9*(3), 27–30.

Matson, J. L. (1975). Some practical considerations for using the Foxx and Azrin rapid method of toilet training. *Psychological Reports, 37,* 350.

Matson, J. L., Ollendick, T. H., & Adkins, J. (1980). A comprehensive dining program for mentally retarded adults. *Behavior Research & Therapy, 18,* 107–112.

McCartney, J. R., & Holden, J. C. (1981). Toilet training for the mentally retarded. In J. Matson & J. McCartney (Eds.), *Handbook of behavior modification with the mentally retarded* (pp. 29–60). New York: Plenum Press.

Minge, M. R., & Ball, T. S. (1967). Teaching of self-help skills to retarded patients. *American Journal of Mental Deficiency, 71,* 864–868.

Nelson, G. L., Cone, J. D., & Hanson, C. R. (1975). Training correct utensil use in retarded children: Modeling vs. physical guidance. *American Journal of Mental Deficiency, 80,* 114–122.

Newborg, J., Stock, J., Wnek, L., Guidubaldi, J., & Suinicki, J. (1984). *Battelle developmental inventory.* Allen, TX: DLM Teaching Resources.

O'Brien, F., Azrin, N. H., & Bugle, C. (1972). Training profoundly retarded children to stop crawling. *Journal of Applied Behavior Analysis, 5,* 131–137.

O'Brien, F., Bugle, C., & Azrin, N. H. (1972). Training and maintaining a retarded child's proper eating. *Journal of Applied Behavior Analysis, 5,* 67–73.

Orelove, F. P., & Sobsey, D. (1987). *Educating children with multiple disabilities.* Baltimore: Brookes.

Ottenbacher, K. (1982). Sensory integration therapy: Affect or effect. *The American Journal of Occupational Therapy, 36,* 571–578.

Ottenbacher, K. Biocca, Z., DeCremer, G., Bevelinger, M., Jedlovec, K. B., & Johnson, M. B. (1986). Quantitative analysis of the effectiveness of pediatric therapy: Emphasis on the neurodevelopmental treatment approach. *Physical Therapy, 66,* 1095–1101.

Ottenbacher, K. & Petersen, P. (1985). A meta-analysis of applied vestibular stimulation research. *Physical and Occupational Therapy in Pediatrics, 5*(2/3), 119–134.

Peterson, N. L. (1987). *Early intervention for handicapped and at-risk children.* Denver: Love.

Rainforth, B. & Salisbury, C. (1988). Functional home programs: A model for therapists. *Topics in Early Childhood Special Education, 7*(4), 33–45.

Rarick, G. L., Widdop, J. H., & Broadhead, G. D. (1970). The physical fitness and motor performance of educable mentally retarded children. *Exceptional Children, 35,* 509–519.

Reid, D. H. (1983). Trends and issues in behavioral research on training feeding and dressing skills. In J. Matson & F. Andrasik (Eds.), *Treatment issues and innovations in mental retardation* (pp. 213–240). New York: Plenum Press.

Richman, J. S., Sonderby, T., & Kahn, J. V. (1980). Prerequisite vs. "in vivo" acquisition of self-feeding skill. *Behavior Research and Therapy, 18,* 327–332.

Richmond, G. (1983). Shaping bladder and bowel continence in developmentally retarded preschool children. *Journal of Autism and Developmental Disorders, 1,* 197–205.

Robinson, N. M. & Robinson, H. B. (1976). *The mentally retarded child* (2nd ed.). New York: McGraw-Hill.

Shearer, D. E., Billingsley, J., Froham, A., Hilliard, J., Johnson, F., & Shearer, M. (1976). *Portage guide to early education–Revised.* Portage, WI: Portage Project.

Sisson, L. A. & Dixon, M. J. (1986). A behavioral approach to the training and assessment of feeding skills in multihandicapped children. *Applied Research in Mental Retardation, 7*(2), 149–163.

Smith, P. S. (1979). A comparison of different methods of toilet training the mentally handicapped. *Behavior Research and Therapy, 17,* 33–44.

Smith, P. D. (1989). Assessing motor skills. In D. B. Bailey & M. Wolery (Eds.), *Assessing infants and preschoolers with handicaps* (pp. 301–338). Columbus, OH: Merrill.

Snell, M. E. (1980). Does toilet training belong in the public schools? A review of toilet training research. *Education Unlimited, 2*(3), 53–58.

Snell, M. E. (1993). *Instruction of students with severe disabilities* (4th ed.). Columbus, OH: Merrill.

Sobsey, R. J. & Orelove, F. (1984). Neurophysiological facilitation of eating skills in severely handicapped children. *The Journal of the Association for the Severely Handicapped, 9,* 98–110.

Song, A. Y. & Gandhi, R. (1974). An analysis of behavior during the acquisition and maintenance phases of self-spoon feeding skills of profound retardates. *Mental Retardation, 12*(11), 25–28.

Sparrow, S. S., Balla, D. A., & Cicchetti, D. V. (1984). *Vineland Adaptive Behavior Scales.* Circle Pines, MN: American Guidance Service.

Stimbert, V. E., Minor, J. W., & McCoy, J. F. (1977). Intensive feeding training with retarded children. *Behavior Modification, 1,* 517–530.

Thompson, T. & Hanson, R. (1983). Overhydration precautions when training urinary incontinence. *Mental Retardation, 21,* 139–143.

Wilcox, B. & Bellamy, G. T. (1987). *The activities catalog: An alternative curriculum for youth and adults with severe disabilities.* Baltimore: Brookes.

Williams, F. E. & Sloop, W. E. (1978). Success with a shortened Foxx-Azrin toilet training program. *Education and Training of the Mentally Retarded, 4,* 399–402.

York, J. & Rainforth, B. (1987). Developing instructional adaptations. In P. Orelove & D. Sobsey (Eds.), *Educating children with multiple disabilities.* Baltimore: Brookes.

Young, K. R., West, R. P., Howard, V. F., & Whitney, R. (1986). Acquisition, fluency training, generalization, and maintenance of dressing skills of two developmentally disabled children. *Education and Treatment of Children, 9,* 16–29.

Chapter 11

Cognitive Infrastructure of the Academic Program

The purpose of this chapter is to review the recent contributions of theory and research in cognition and information processing to the education of children with mental retardation. Since cognitive theory has had its greatest influence on the teaching of academic subjects, it follows that this chapter will highlight the educational efforts of children with mild mental retardation and, to a lesser extent, children with moderate mental retardation.

The first section examines the issue of academic versus life skills objectives for these students. Typically, that issue is expressed in terms of the appropriate curriculum balance between cognitive/academic and functional skill/community-referenced training. The second section reviews the role of cognitive training in support of the academic program. The third section discusses, in more general terms, the education of children with mental retardation from both cognitive/academic and life skills perspectives. The final section spells out some recommendations concerning the potential benefits of supporting both cognitive/academic and life skills objectives during the student's school career.

Curriculum Counterweights—Academics vs. Functional Skills

Whether children with mild mental retardation should be exposed to the regular academically oriented curriculum or be put on a separate educational track leading to social and vocational competence is an issue that concerns many educators. This issue is largely defined by our conception of what mild mental retardation means in terms of the limits that it imposes on intellectual capacity and potential for successful performance both in and out of school. What educators tend to expect from children with mild mental retardation is tied closely to our current definition of the condition, the faith we have in assessment procedures needed to make a diagnosis of mental retardation for any particular child, and our prognosis for that child's intellectual, academic, and vocational future.

When Doll (1941) included the criterion of "essential incurability" as part of his definition of mental retardation, educators took note by assuming that the condition was intractable and would manifest its symptoms at every stage of development from early childhood to later maturity. If mental retardation was assumed to be a permanent intellectual dysfunction, then academic and later vocational expectations would necessarily be limited. As a result, many of the early curricula for children with mild mental retardation stressed the development of functional skills. For example, Goldstein and Siegle (1958) produced a curriculum that focussed on introducing children to the following persistent life functions: citizenship, communicating, participating in home and family life, utilizing leisure time, management of materials and money, achieving occupational adequacy, maintaining physical and mental health, safety, social adjustment, and travel. Academic skills and other types of development were included in supporting roles to these critical life functions. These skills included arithmetic, fine arts, language arts, physical education, practical arts, science, and social relationships.

The well known Hungerford Core Curriculum (Dalton, 1975) was used extensively in the New York City Public Schools for decades to help children with mild mental retardation to progress with good adjustment through the concentric and expanding life circles of the home, the neighborhood, the larger community, and the city. The study of job areas, the development of prevocational and vocational skills, the ability to manage one's personal affairs, and the ability to contribute as a citizen were strongly emphasized. Again, academics played an "as needed" supporting role to the community-referenced skills that were foundational to this curriculum. Goldstein's (1969) Social Learning Curriculum worked backwards from desired adult behaviors as the basis for curriculum development. It reflected the perspective that special education served the purpose of training children with mental retardation to be well-adjusted adults with mental retardation. Thus, educational programs contributed to the self-fulfilling prophecy that mental retardation, even in its milder form, was essentially incurable and, while starting in childhood, would still exist at maturity (Doll, 1941).

The definitional and prognostic thrust that spawned functional curricula can be contrasted with the more recent definitions promulgated in the Manual on Classification and Terminology of the American Association on Mental Retardation (Grossman, 1983) and the new manual, Mental Retardation: Definition, Classification, and Systems of Support (AAMR, 1992). These definitions, while still retaining the essential criteria of significantly subaverage intellectual development, deficits in adaptive behavior, and onset during the developmental period, suggested that children diagnosed as having mental retardation today by the best professional personnel and instrumentation available, might be reevaluated as children without mental retardation tomorrow. This would be possible if an appropriate intervention, be it educational, psychological, medical, or some combination, could remediate the cognitive dysfunctions associated with mental retardation.

Since the definitional barrier to considering mild mental retardation as potentially remediable has been removed, a new curricular optimism is possible. Now, curriculum designers might more readily feel some obligation to introduce children to expanded opportunities for both cognitive and academic growth. Few would argue against the position that reinforcing the intellectual infrastructure of children with mental retardation could go a long way toward increasing academic competencies, expanding postschool life options, and eliminating stigma.

The Decline of the Influence of Testing

Prognostic and curricular optimism is also the legacy of debilitating attacks on the validity of intelligence tests as appropriate instruments for making the diagnosis of mental retardation. There is a growing reluctance to giving intelligence tests such a large weight in making decisions about placing children in the special services system of the public schools (MacMillan & Jones, 1972). Briefly stated, the disproportionately large numbers of minority children, primarily African-American and Latino, who were found in segregated special classes for children with mild mental retardation, particularly in large urban centers, suggested that the schools were not meeting their needs. This was manifested in "reflexive" referrals for psychological evaluations by teachers and administrators who misinterpreted the underachievement of these children and misunderstood their behaviors. It was compounded by the administration of tests considered unfair to children who were so different socioeconomically, culturally, and linguistically, from the white, middle-class children on whom many of the tests had been originally normed (Calnen & Blackman, 1992). Allegedly unfair referrals, testing practices, and placement decisions led to the charge that many children from racially and culturally diverse backgrounds had been misclassified as having mental retardation and, with the application of proper instructional support services, could succeed in regular classes.

Many educators, psychologists, and civil rights advocates, therefore, found common cause in the position that students classified as having mild mental retardation, arguably mistested and misclassified, had normal intellectual potential despite histories of poor achievement and often challenging classroom behaviors. This position was responsible, in part, for the least restrictive environment principle of PL94–142, the Education of All Handicapped Children Act and its subsequent amendments.

A significant fall-out of this policy has been that the number of children diagnosed as having mild mental retardation has dropped by more than 30 percent since 1975 (MacMillan, 1989). Some of these children have received, by administrative fiat, the more euphemistic labels of perceptually impaired or learning disabled. There is some evidence, however, that the majority of these youngsters have simply been declassified in the expectation that, by freeing them from the unjustly imposed bondage of the mental retardation label, they would be released to achieve the intellectual potential and school success that were always latent within them.

Curriculum Balance Between Academic and Functional Skills

When and how intensively cognitive and academic skills should be taught is a current focus of debate. How this issue is resolved will be directly reciprocal to when and how intensively the life skills needed for postschool vocational and social adjustment should be taught. Framing the issue in terms of academics and cognitive development as a serious pedagogical option would appear to limit the discussion of this curriculum analysis only to children with mild mental retardation. Later in this chapter, it will be noted that the cognitive and academic option for children with moderate mental retardation is also a matter of concern for some special educators.

If cognitive training or retraining is deemed to be an effective tool for facilitating academic skill development (Blackman, 1967; Feuerstein, 1980), it should start before or, at the very least, run concurrently with subject matter instruction at the earliest elementary level (Blackman, Burger, Tan, & Weiner, 1982). Many people accept as an article of faith that intact information processing skills will support and enhance the acquisition of academic skills. Although point-to-point correspondences between cognitive factors and requirements for learning particular academic skills have been difficult to identify, there are more than a few psychologists and educators who believe that students' self-awareness of cognitive strengths and weaknesses, as well as an accessible inventory of cognitive strategies, will provide the intellectual supports needed in the acquisition of reading and arithmetic skills.

These strategies will support, among others, the following cognitive skills: appropriate attentional deployment, memory, problem solving in a variety of formats, making comparisons, seeing relationships, deduction, inference, sequencing, and the ability to generalize useful strategies from one setting to another. Since the specific connections between cognitive strategies and academic tasks have been difficult to isolate empirically (Blackman, Bilsky, Burger, & Mar, 1976), some have questioned the "articles of faith" that opened this line of inquiry in the first place (Mann, 1979). Nevertheless, there is a clear

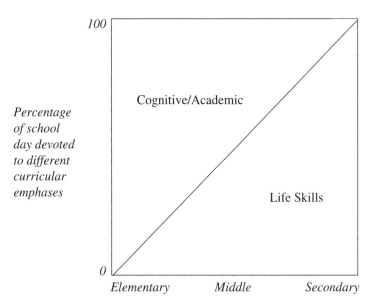

FIGURE 11-1   Balance between academic and life skills curricula across the school system.

need to include a cognitively oriented curriculum emphasis primarily for children with mild mental retardation in the elementary schools. By the time most students with mental retardation reach the middle and secondary schools, there is an increasing emphasis on social adjustment training, vocational evaluation, employment training, and placement services.

The aspiring special education teacher should be aware that curriculum planning is a "zero-sum" game. This means that the number of days in a public school career, even one extended to age twenty-one, is finite. The number of days devoted to strictly cognitive/academic instruction will necessarily subtract from the number of days available for social, vocational, recreational, sexuality, community living, and civic responsibility training. This polarity of curriculum objectives could be mitigated somewhat by teachers able to interweave academic and life skills objectives and programs.

Curriculum development for most students with mild mental retardation should emphasize cognitive/academic skill development in the early grades, and life skills in the later grades. Figure 11-1 provides a graphic representation of that curriculum balance.

The Role of Cognitive Training in Support of the Academic Program

Most experienced regular educators commonly observe that the acquisition of early reading and arithmetic skills is a difficult enterprise for some children. Perhaps as many as 15 percent of children in regular first grades quickly fall behind what the teacher considers to be an appropriate pace for instruction and learning. More ominously, this "lag rate" in developing academic skills often becomes even more pronounced as these children progress through the grades. If by the end of the second grade, the likelihood of these children "catching up" appears to be remote, concerned teachers, parents, and administrators begin asking the question, "What's wrong?"

Traditionally, the assumption has been that "what's wrong" can be found within the child. In support of that belief, the child was quickly referred for evaluation. Professionals from several helping disciplines probed the child's intellectual, emotional, neurological, and general health, as well as the child's ability to communicate, in an effort to locate the deterrent or deterrents to effective classroom learning.

Prior to the enactment of PL94–142, as soon as the "culprits" inhibiting learning had been isolated, alternative programming tracks were recommended. If the source of the deficit was judged to be intellectual, segregated classes for children with mental retardation was the placement of choice. Children with normal intelligence associated with diagnosable or presumed minimal brain dysfunction were assigned to classes for children with learning disabilities, perceptual impairments, or neurological impairments, depending upon the nomenclature preferred in a particular state and school district.

Since PL94–142 and its later amendments (PL98–199, PL99–457, & PL101–476), there has been a movement away from quick referrals for evaluation that lead almost inevitably to segregated class placements. Within the framework of the Regular Education Initiative (REI) (Will, 1986), the trend has been to delay referral for classification, labeling, and placement in favor of a process called prereferral consultation. This process reframes the question from what is wrong with the child to what is wrong with the educational connection between a child with problems and a classroom environment that seems, based on the child's continuing pattern of failure, to be unresponsive to that child's learning deficits and instructional needs.

The Cognitive Precursors of Successful Instruction

To take into account the recent reluctance to classify children, this section will enlarge the discussion to include children with special learning needs, whether they have been classified as having mental retardation or not. If special education, at least of children with mild and moderate levels of mental retardation, can be characterized in a simple and direct way, such a characterization should highlight the design of curriculum and instructional systems that take into account the cognitive capacities of the child and the cognitive demands placed on that child by the task to be learned (Blackman, 1967, 1977).

Before trying to explicate in detail what it means to design curriculum and instruction around the cognitive capacities of children and the cognitive demands placed on them by school tasks, it is first necessary to review a long-standing debate over an appropriate philosophy of curriculum in the special education of children with mental retardation. That debate concerns whether children with mental retardation should be educated through their intellectual strengths or weaknesses. Asking the question too simply, should children with mental retardation be educated by adapting the curriculum so as to cater to those cognitive capacities that are relatively unimpaired (teaching through strength), or should the curriculum be constructed to upgrade, to the extent possible, those cognitive capacities that are deficient in these children (teaching through weakness)? Illustrations of teaching through strength might include an emphasis on arts and crafts and lower level instruction in functional reading and arithmetic. That level would be approximately equivalent to educational expectations based on the children's mental ages, and would reflect fixed assumptions about the intractable nature of mental retardation (Spitz, 1986). Teaching through weakness might mean reserving part of each school day, at least in the early grades, for teaching children those cognitive skills and strategies that are considered to be the necessary prerequisites for developing academic skills at a level closer to chronological age expectations (Scheid, 1989). This approach speaks to the potential malleability of intellectual functions as a result of training, and the lack of fixed assumptions about the permanently limiting impact of mental retardation.

Teaching through strength has been the predominant mode for educating children with mental retardation since the inception of systematic special education programs. Empirical studies of the efficacy of these programs in terms of accelerating academic achievement and social skills have indicated that special classes for children with mental retardation, designed around a curriculum philosophy of exploiting strengths, were not fulfilling their promise (Blackman & Heintz, 1966; Dunn, 1968). Even if one argued that the strength curriculum could be characterized as a "delayed fuse" in that it focussed more on postschool adjustment than classroom competencies, Edgerton's (1967) work on this issue provided little comfort. He found that most of the adults with mental retardation who he interviewed were achieving very little life satisfaction and, indeed, devoted a great deal of time and psychic energy to trying to mask their retardation from friends and employers.

The curriculum philosophy that supports teaching children with mental retardation by attempting to overcome areas of intellectual weakness holds that most of the academic and some of the life skills difficulties of individuals with mental retardation are related to dysfunctions in metacognitive capacities and cognitive strategy competencies. These capacities and competencies are considered to be foundational to the development of appropriate school and extra-school behaviors.

Moving beyond the generic distinction between teaching through strength versus teaching through weakness, Heintz and Blackman (1977) did a more refined analysis of the three data sources that contribute to the development of special education curricula and methods. The first data source is subject matter itself. This data source is related to the hierarchy of knowledge inherent in subject matter, regardless of type. It also relates to sequencing instructional objectives in a way that reflects the interaction between developmental factors and the structural hierarchy of that knowledge (Bruner, 1960). Stated more directly, in order to design an instructional system that proceeds from easy to difficult skill development for any school subject, one should understand the pyramid of knowledge and skills inherent in that subject structure. One possible complication in this approach is that, after a careful epistemological analysis, what we believe to be an appropriate subject matter pyramid may become inappropriate when used with special needs learners with different types of cognitive dysfunction. For example, it might make good logical and pedagogical sense to give most children a sight vocabulary of 100 words before introducing phonics. For the child with a serious visual memory deficit or poor recall strategies, however, that particular sequence might be ill-advised.

The second data source contributing to the development of curriculum objectives for individuals with mental retardation is the expectations of society itself. This data source was studied carefully by Goldstein (1969) and his associates while they were constructing the

Social Learning Curriculum. At different levels of mental retardation, society expects varying levels of vocational competence, social interaction with family and peers, and assumption of citizenship responsibilities. In targeting desired behaviors of adults with mental
retardation as the basis for establishing children's curriculum objectives, we may be training children with mental retardation for what we predict they will become rather than for
what, under ideal instructional conditions, they might potentially achieve.

The third data source, and the one that has introduced cognitive theory into the pedagogical process, is the learner him- or herself. Understanding the pattern of cognitive abilities and disabilities in a particular learner with mental retardation as a basis for prescribing
instructional strategies that may be uniquely suited to that learner, represents the operational
thrust of those special educators who emphasize this data source. Bateman clarified the category of "learner as data source":

> [this approach] redirects our attention to question-asking as the foundation of teach-
> ing and curriculum planning, . . . to individual appraisal of patterns of cognitive abili-
> ties, . . . and to the need for direct teaching of the processes of thinking rather than the
> products of someone else's thinking (Bateman, 1967, p. 25).

Also emphasizing a "learner as data source" orientation to special education practices,
Blackman maintained that the effective modification of the classroom behavior of children
with mental retardation depends on the development of a "school-relevant taxonomy of their
psycho-educational characteristics." By psycho-educational characteristics he meant:

> An analysis of the retarded child's profile of abilities and deficits in a wide range of
> psychological processes such as perception, learning, retention, transfer, attention, dis-
> crimination, and language, among others (Blackman, 1967, p. 8).

The proposed taxonomic approach also maintains that knowledge of the disabilities of
a child with mental retardation has:

> little educational utility independent of its relevancy to school; that is, a comparable
> understanding of the psycho-educational prerequisites for acquiring specific school
> tasks (Blackman, 1967, p. 8).

The stress on understanding the nature of school tasks as the second anchor point in the
taxonomy reflects the relevance of the learner's psychological assets and disabilities to the
subject matter being acquired. Subject matter, therefore, must be understood not only in
terms of its own logical structure, but also in terms of the demands that it places on the cognitive abilities of the learner for whom it is targeted. The example cited earlier, in which a
particular child's cognitive deficit might necessitate omitting the acquisition of a sight
vocabulary before teaching phonics, is equally pertinent here. The final component of this
taxonomic system deals with the design of instructional systems predicated on the known
parameters of learner and task characteristics.

Basing instructional strategies for children with mental retardation on the learner's cognitive characteristics as well as on the cognitive demands placed on learners by specific

school tasks suggests a systematic approach. This approach includes three components. First, it is important to identify the cognitive prerequisites for the acquisition of particular school-related skills. Next, if these cognitive prerequisites are found to be deficient in learners with mental retardation, then evaluate their amenability to remediation. Finally, if these cognitive processes or strategies are remediable, then determine the extent to which the learning of the more complex skills related to school performance might be accelerated.

Cognitive Strategies: The Foot Soldiers of Cognitively Oriented Special Education

One of the contributions of cognitive psychology to the special education of school-age children with mental retardation has been to help teachers recognize that most children will use a variety of intellectual ploys, or "tricks," when confronted with learning tasks. The availability and quality of these ploys, frequently referred to as strategies, will vary depending upon the intellectual capacity of children. Some of these strategies will be sophisticated and right on target in terms of solving the problem at hand, while others will be primitive and ineffective. Some will be immediately available to respond to problem demands while others might be accessed only with great difficulty. In general, the relatively more able learner will have available an easy-to-access inventory of appropriate strategies ready to be selected and applied to the particular problem at hand.

These strategies can also vary in terms of the amount of intellectual energy required to assemble them as tools to facilitate the problem-solving process (Ellis, Woodley-Zarthos, Sularey, & Palmer, 1989). Blackman, Bilsky, Burger, and Mar, in a study of the interrelationships among a number of cognitive skills and reading performance in children with mental retardation, suggested that:

> cognition can be described in terms of a set of strategies for facilitating recall and the solution of problems that are either deliberately applied, spontaneously generated, or inherently available (Blackman et al., 1976, p. 125).

Deliberately Applied

Deliberately applied strategies are typically those that require the child to exercise a good deal of creativity or to reach deeply into his or her inventory of available but little-used strategies in order to help find a correct solution to a difficult problem. For example, a young child with mild mental retardation or an older child with moderate mental retardation may be asked to remember that a red traffic light stands for danger and means that you should not cross the street, whereas a green one means that it is now safe to cross. How should the child remember that red means danger and stop, and that green means safe and go?

One possible deliberately applied strategy would be for the child to generate a brief meaningful story that would connect the stimulus "red" with the concept of "danger" and the response of "stop." The child might say, "The color red makes a bull angry. That's dangerous. If I see an angry bull, I must stop." While this procedure may appear cumbersome, there is laboratory evidence that telling stories about unrelated words that need to be associated does facilitate their connection and recall (Burger & Blackman, 1976; Burger &

Blackman, 1978; Turnure & Walsh, 1971). This verbal mediation strategy was custom-designed to facilitate the arbitrary pairing of the previously unrelated words of red and stop. The reader might try a similar exercise in deliberate verbal mediation strategy design by connecting the word "green" with the meaning of "safe" and the response of "go."

Spontaneously Generated

Spontaneously generated strategies are easier to access than deliberately applied ones because their selection and use are often suggested by the problem materials themselves. Take, for example, a task that requires a child to memorize the following six words:

> milk
> car
> shirt
> train
> bread
> shoes

In scanning the list to find a way to facilitate the recall of these words, the child may discover that the six words actually fall into three conceptual categories. There are two food words (milk, bread), two clothing words (shirt, shoes), and two transportation words (car, train). In this case, the problem may trigger a clustering strategy in some children. Some laboratory research has shown that clustering conceptually related words may enhance the recall of those words (Bilsky, 1976; Bilsky & Evans, 1970).

Inherently Available

Inherently available strategies are those that operate as if they are "hard-wired" in the sense that they appear to be used without any conscious awareness by the child. This is best demonstrated by the child who can sort objects appropriately without being able to articulate the basis for that sort. For example, it is not unusual for a child with mental retardation, when given a number of toys (doll, truck), tools (hammer, screwdriver), and writing implements (pencil, crayon), to sort them into "piles that go together"—that is, to sort them correctly and efficiently according to the conceptual categories to which they belong. When asked how they knew to sort them in that way, the response, "I don't know" is not uncommon. It is, of course, not clear whether the child's inability to articulate the strategy used to sort correctly is a function of not being consciously aware of having used the sorting strategy, which would indicate that the strategy is inherently available, or a simple unwillingness to respond for fear that the response will be judged wrong.

Strategy Availability and Accessibility

If one accepts the premise that cognitive strategies are important catalysts that facilitate children's recall and problem solving, then it is important for teachers to monitor the use of these strategies regularly. Questions such as "How did you find the answer to that question?" or "Why did you give that answer?" or "How did you remember all that so well?" are, from an information processing point of view, more important to the teacher's understanding of the child's cognitive skills and capacity than simply asking, "What's the answer?" (Alper, 1985).

Detailed records of children's responses to the "how" and "why" questions will soon reveal the pattern of each child's cognitive activity with respect to different instructional tasks. From these data, the teacher should be able to infer: (1) which strategies are both available and accessible to a particular child; (2) which are available but not readily accessible; and (3) which are neither available nor accessible. An available strategy is one that is part of the child's cognitive inventory. Whether it is accessible will depend on whether the child can easily retrieve it from inventory and put it to work to solve a problem. For reasons not clearly understood, some available strategies are accessible, but others are not. Of course, a strategy that is not available is, by definition, not accessible. Making a distinction among the three possibilities listed above is easier said than done.

If a child informs you that she or he was able to remember a list of groceries to be purchased by repeating the list to her- or himself again and again, she or he shows evidence of both the availability and accessibility of an important rehearsal strategy. If a child fails to report the use of a rehearsal strategy, two possibilities exist: the strategy is available, but for some reason is inaccessible, or the strategy is unavailable and consequently also inaccessible. To make the determination, the teacher might suggest to a child that a rehearsal strategy could be helpful and might offer some instruction on how that strategy could be implemented. If the child responds by using the strategy with instructional assistance at first but later independently as well, that strategy can be characterized as available but needing some temporary instructional prodding to upgrade its accessibility. If instruction fails to promote the use of the rehearsal strategy, it is often judged to be both unavailable and inaccessible as a support to learning.

The child in whom a particular strategy can be made more accessible after training is said to have had a *production deficiency*. When training does not achieve appropriate strategy usage, the child's performance is described as a *mediation deficiency*.

The teacher who monitors his or her students' cognitive output carefully should be supporting and reinforcing strategy use that is self-generated and spontaneous. At the same time, deficiencies in strategy use should be pedagogically engaged and corrected on the premise that, unless the child demonstrates a continuing inability to learn, all failures to use strategies should be construed to be "trainable" production deficiencies that are worthy of the teacher's continuing remedial attention.

The *Case Study of Tanisha*, presented below, provides an illustration of a teacher training cognitive functions while providing instruction in the academic curriculum.

CASE STUDY: Tanisha

Using Cognitive Strategies

Instruction should focus on teaching the student with mental retardation the cognitive devices she will need to learn new material. First, the student needs to consider herself a learner, someone who can actively seek to replace uncertainty with information when she needs to do so. Second, she needs to know *what* she knows (metacognition) and, in people with mental retardation, this knowledge is by no means obvious. For example, think of the boy who is asked if he knows the days of the week. It is not uncommon for the student to

---

CASE STUDY: Tanisha (continued)

---

nod enthusiastically and then stand in disappointing silence when he is asked to recite them. Third, she must select a strategy which is appropriate for learning the new material. These competencies are typically lacking in children with mental retardation and instruction in these cognitive activities must be well-planned and proceed carefully.

Tanisha is learning the months of the year in their correct order. In addition, her teacher wants to proceed beyond this content and teach her how to learn such information. She begins first by planning her instructional objectives, and then she arranges her teaching interventions.

Tanisha is taught two goals in sequence. Within each goal-area, several objectives are taught, also in sequence. Sequencing has utility not only because Tanisha is required to learn the months one step at a time, but also because the order of objectives will provide support for later strategy use.

Goal 1. From her present level of naming three of four seasons out of order, Tanisha will correctly name all four seasons in order.

Objective 1.1. When asked to name the seasons, Tanisha will correctly name four seasons in order (beginning with winter) for two consecutive trials.

Objective 1.2. When asked to tell about a particular season, Tanisha will state two adjectives that correctly describe each season for two consecutive trials.

Goal 2. From her present level of naming four of twelve months of the year in incorrect order, Tanisha will correctly name twelve months of the year in order.

Objective 2.1. When asked to name the winter months, Tanisha will correctly name three winter months (December, January, February) in correct order for two consecutive trials.

Objective 2.2. When asked to name the spring months, Tanisha will correctly name three spring months (March, April, May) in correct order for two consecutive trials.

Objective 2.3. When asked to name the summer months, Tanisha will correctly name three summer months (June, July, August) in correct order for two consecutive trials.

Objective 2.4. When asked to name the fall months, Tanisha will correctly name three fall months (September, October, November) in correct order for two consecutive trials.

Objective 2.5. When asked to name all the months, Tanisha will correctly name all months of the year in order (beginning in January) for two consecutive trials.

From a cognitive perspective, there are two reasons why Tanisha's teacher began with learning the seasons. First, it will provide a meaningful framework for identification of the months, without which "month-listing" is a pointless recital of words. Material (especially a list of verbal material) is best learned when it has meaning and context. Second, learning and recall are made easier when information (months) is subsumed under a series of categories (seasons).

Assume that Tanisha has achieved mastery of the first goal and is about to proceed to the second. Keep in mind that her teacher will use some instructional intervention to teach her not only the months but a few associated cognitive skills as well.

Tanisha's teacher begins by giving her ample praise for having learned the seasons and reminding her that, if she had learned the seasons, then she can learn the months too. It is important to instill in Tanisha that she can actively affect and regulate the course of her own learning. Next, the teacher reminds Tanisha that there are twelve months and asks her how many she knows. Her teacher draws a blank for each month on the blackboard and writes the names of the months in their respective blanks as Tanisha names them. (She names four months.) Using the blackboard display as a cue, her teacher asks whether she knows *all* of the months, praising her when she replies that she does not. ("That's right, Tanisha, so we have to learn the rest of them.") She will correct Tanisha if she replies that she knows all of the months by filling in the remaining blanks and reminding her that there are eight months she still needs to learn. The purpose of this activity is to acquaint Tanisha with the extent and limitations of her knowledge, an awareness that can guide later learning. At this stage, metacognition is cued by the blackboard, but eventually Tanisha may simply reply, in response to the question, whether or not she is knowledgeable of new information. In some instances, she may even know without being asked that there are particular things she needs to learn.

Tanisha's teacher begins to teach the three months of winter, a season with which she is familiar (objective 2.1). She uses techniques from behavior analysis, such as praising Tanisha for reading the names of the three months from a card over a series of trials, and then praising her for reciting the months in order after fading the visual cue (removing the card). She corrects any errors by verbally modeling the correct response. She concludes the activity by telling Tanisha: "When you are just learning something, practice it over again," after which Tanisha rehearses the months a final time. Eventually, the teacher will fade cues for rehearsal by asking a leading question: "When you are just learning something, what do you do?" She praises Tanisha's correct response.

The next four objectives are taught in an identical manner, with cumulative review of material already learned. On the fifth objective, Tanisha learns to name all twelve months in sequence. In doing this, she can take advantage of two supporting circumstances: (1) she has already learned four triads of months; and (2) the months naturally "cluster" into seasonal categories. This can facilitate recall even if Tanisha "gets stuck" in the middle of the list. When this happens, her teacher may supply a "retrieval cue" (in this case, a category name) to guide her recall: "In what season does next month belong?" Gradually, Tanisha may begin to ask herself the same question and attempt to search for its answer. This review and recall of related bits of meaningful information is called "elaborated rehearsal." As the teaching activity concludes, the teacher may cue "rote rehearsal" of all twelve months by asking her: "When you have just learned something, what do you do?"

In summary, several features of this instruction should be noted. First, cognitive methods and behavioral approaches can join forces in an effective instructional coalition. Second, self-regulation begins with an orientation to oneself as an active and competent information-gatherer and problem-solver. Third, one must approach new learning situations with some awareness of the state and extent of her knowledge (metacognition).

The fourth and final point pertains to strategy use. Notice that acquisition and recall of material was facilitated by *clustering* related bits of information. In this instance, information clusters by category: some months "belong" in winter, some "belong" in fall, etc. Recall can be facilitated by the use of *retrieval cues* (e.g., "What season does the next month belong in?"). Acquisition of new material can be consolidated by elaborative or rote *rehearsal*. To the extent that Tanisha can select and use clustering, retrieval cues, and rehearsal as recall strategies with few or no reminders to do so, then instruction in naming the months of the year will have served a broader cognitive function.

Metacognition, Executive Function, and Self-Regulation: The Command Center of Cognitive Contributions to Classroom Learning

Much of the earlier discussion stems from the premise that the effective utilization of relevant cognitive strategies will go a long way toward helping students with mental retardation to solve school-imposed problems in the areas of academic skill development, social skill training, and vocational preparation. Among the more pervasive problems in the education of these children, however, is that compared to children without mental retardation, they tend to be relatively passive in the use of these strategies (Reichart, Cody & Borkowski, 1973). Unfortunately, children with mental retardation, when confronted with a problem, tend to do little "up front" intellectual planning. This leads to efforts at problem solving and eventual responses that are often disorganized and off-target. Adding to the teacher's consternation over children's answers to questions that often bear little resemblance to the expected answers, is that the children's self-monitoring and self-critical faculties seem nowhere in evidence.

One review of research (Blackman & Lin, 1984) suggested that the cognitive passivity of children with mental retardation can be ameliorated on a task-by-task basis. That is, a child who initially fails to apply a rehearsal or clustering strategy to a recall task can be trained to do so in relatively short order (Bilsky, 1976; Burger, Blackman, Holmes, & Zetlin, 1978; Burger, Blackman, & Tan, 1980). Another child who cannot infer the relationship among three words such as night, cave, and closet (answer: dark) can be quickly taught to use a strategy that requires generating associates to each word in the triad and then testing hypotheses until a word (in this case, dark) is found that is common to all three lists of associates (Burger, Blackman, Clark, & Reis, 1982).

It is widely recognized that children and adolescents with mild mental retardation can be taught to use a strategy or set of strategies appropriate to the solution of a particular problem. The teacher can also expect that the strategy, once learned, will be used again without further drill and practice over long periods of time when the child confronts the same problem (Blackman & Lin, 1984). Given that it is a positive development whenever a child with mental retardation moves from strategic passivity to activity in response to a particular task, that movement is nevertheless only a partial victory. It is partial in the sense that the strategy learned and maintained over time remains "welded" to the original task for which it was learned.

Generalization: Meaning and Mechanism

If cognitive strategy training in children with mental retardation is to become truly functional in terms of improving both classroom performance and life skills, children must be able to generalize cognitive strategies learned in one setting to other settings. Blackman and Lin characterized generalization as follows:

> Generalization . . . refers to the application of that learned strategy or some modification of that strategy (Campione & Brown, 1977) to a significantly altered task structure where both task demand and materials have been changed. The extent of generalization varies as a function of the degree of difference in task demands and stimulus materials. "Near" generalization reflects minimal changes whereas "far" generalization entails substantial change (Borkowski & Cavanaugh, 1979) (Blackman and Lin, 1984, p. 247–248).

An example of generalization would be a child who uses a rehearsal strategy initially learned to facilitate memorizing a series of brief facts important to a social studies lesson to memorize addition facts for numbers under 10. If the child recognizes that the same rehearsal strategy learned in the context of a social studies lesson is equally applicable in its original or, if necessary, some slightly modified form to this new context, then generalization has occurred. The intellectual efficiency inherent in a mature ability to generalize is reflected in the fact that there are probably a finite and manageable number of cognitive strategies that can lend support to the solution of an almost infinite range of academic, social, and vocational problems. The challenge is whether the child and later the adolescent and adult can achieve the fluent and versatile use of these strategies. These strategies will be available because they have received systematic instructional attention, and will be accessible because they have been organized in long-term memory storage in a meaningful and consequently easily retrievable way.

It is generally accepted that the ability to generalize is one of the essential components of intellectual normalcy (Blackman & Lin, 1984). For some time, investigators were relatively pessimistic about the possibility of training useful generalization skills in children with mental retardation (Blackman & Lin, 1984; Spitz, 1986). It was suggested that the ability to generalize and to make facile use of specific cognitive strategies in solving problems was probably a characteristic of an intact central nervous system. This intactness, in turn, was determined by genetic factors. In short, the capacity to generalize cognitive strategies from one learning situation to the next and to self-monitor the plausibility of responses was considered to be a "hardware" issue that was not likely to be improved by training.

An increasing number of investigators, however, have challenged the view that school-children with mental retardation cannot be taught to generalize (Belmont, Butterfield, & Borkowski, 1978; Brown, Campione, & Barclay, 1979; Burger, Blackman, & Clark, 1981; Burger, Blackman, Clark, & Reis, 1982; Kendall, Borkowski, & Cavanaugh, 1980; Lin, Blackman, Clark, & Gordon, 1983).

As training techniques have improved, evidence has been accumulating that students with mental retardation can be taught to generalize strategies learned in the solution of one laboratory task to another laboratory task that differs significantly from the original one (Day & Hall, 1988). This is a hopeful first step. It still falls short, however, of the long-pursued objective of training cognitive strategies in ways that will allow them to generalize broadly to the acquisition of school-related competencies in reading, arithmetic, science, and social studies. These strategies are also relevant to other important areas of the curriculum such as the arts, social development, and life skills education.

It has often been found that cognitive strategies trained in a laboratory setting will not generalize to the acquisition of academic skills. For example, Blackman, Burger, Tan, and Weiner (1982) attempted to accelerate the development of decoding skills in children with mild mental retardation by concurrently training cognitive strategies supportive of memory. Earlier research (Blackman & Burger, 1972; Blackman, Bilsky, Burger, & Mar, 1976) had concluded that strategies involved in memory tasks were more predictive of success in reading than the usual inventory of perceptual variables that dominated the "reading-prerequisites" literature. These memory strategies, trained successfully in learners with mental retardation, did not generalize spontaneously to the acquisition of reading skills.

What now seems clear is that it is not enough to train in isolation those strategies associated with academic tasks. Specific instruction must be provided that will help the student build bridges from his or her newly acquired cognitive strategies to those academic problems with which the strategies are associated (Feuerstein, Rand, Hoffman, & Miller, 1980). When careful instructional attention has been paid to bridging, better results have been achieved (Brainin, 1982).

The extent to which the acquisition of generalization skills in a child with mental retardation is an achievable education objective depends, to a large extent, on the child's ability to: (1) play a role in managing his or her own instructional environment; (2) be aware of the capacity of his or her own information processing system; and (3) know how to access, retrieve, apply, and self-monitor the effectiveness of an inventory of available cognitive strategies in the solution of problems. These three abilities are often referred to as self-regulation (Zimmerman, 1990), metacognition (Borkowski, Reid, & Kurtz, 1984; Flavell, 1979), and executive function (Belmont & Butterfield, 1977).

Self-Regulation

With respect to the issue of self-regulation, Whitman has suggested that "mental retardation might be better described as a self regulatory disorder" (Whitman, 1990, p. 348). A manifestation of this self-regulatory disorder in individuals with mental retardation is passivity in finding solutions to learning problems, either by withdrawing or relying too heavily on the assistance of the teacher. Discussing how this disorder developed would be a major work in itself. Suffice it to say that some important strategies were not learned. Examples of such strategies include: (1) repeating material to be remembered; (2) noticing that two or more objects may have something very important in common even though they do not look exactly alike; and (3) using language to organize a sequence of steps to follow in solving a problem.

Children who are fortunate enough to reach school age with a self-regulatory orientation toward learning have a greater chance of being successful (Hughes, Korinek, & Gorman, 1991). In the classroom, "self-regulated learning means that individuals manage their cognitive abilities and motivational effort so that learning is effective, economical and satisfying" (Paris & Oka, 1986, p. 103). A self-regulatory orientation to learning can be noted even in young children who believe at a developmentally appropriate level, that: (1) attending school is a positive, on-going commitment; (2) what is learned in school is important not only for the here and now but as stepping stones to a successful future; (3) they possess and have easy access to a variety of learning, recall, and thinking strategies useful in the acquisition of a wide range of competencies; (4) they are capable of evaluating realistically their own responses or proposals for problem solving which, if not completely correct on the first try, are sufficiently reasonable approximations that can be subsequently refined; (5) incentives for learning are value-driven and, therefore, internal or "built-in"; (6) self-generated reinforcements can be as potent as the externally provided type; and (7) success is a function of their ability (a stable and pervasive attribution) and failure is related to their lack of effort (a temporary and remediable attribution) (Borkowski, Weyhing, & Turner, 1986).

If self-regulation can be construed as the generic foundation for active and successful learning in the classroom, there are three cognitive subsets that nest within that construct. These include the high-level control functions of metacognition and executive function, and the operational cognitive strategies under their control.

Metacognition

Metacognition has been described as "knowledge concerning one's own cognitive processes and products or anything related to them" (Flavell, 1976, p. 232). For educational purposes, the child with an adequately functioning metacognitive system is aware of the capacity of his or her own cognitive system in relation to the complexity of problems with which he or she is confronted. This child, after being presented with a multiplication facts table or an issue in social studies, will ask him- or herself the question of whether the recall requirement of the arithmetic task or the inferential requirement of the social studies problem are likely to yield to his or her cognitive capacity. The child may conclude that only minimal effort will be required, and proceed to recall or problem solution with the cognitive tools immediately at hand. On the other hand, the child may understand that successful performance on these tasks will require stored strategies used so infrequently that the child may be initially unaware that they are actually available to him or her. Even more challenging, the child may realize that he or she simply does not possess those strategies necessary for problem solution. Under that unhappy circumstance, task failure is inevitable unless the child is able to learn and acquire those needed strategies.

When appropriate strategies are either difficult for the child to access, or were never learned and are therefore not in his or her inventory of available strategies, it is the task of the alert classroom teacher to recognize the signs of impending task failure and to act (Paris & Winograd, 1990; Scruggs & Brigham, 1990). This action typically has both substantive and process components (Lin, Blackman, Clark & Gordon, 1983). The substantive components are the actual strategies needed to perform the task successfully. For example, the child who is being asked to recall a list of six words might be instructed in how to apply a grouping strategy by first dividing the list into two groups of three. This would be followed by a rehearsal strategy in which the child would be encouraged to practice each shortened list three times; first in written form and then orally.

The process components generally fall into two categories: (1) to delay reflexive and nonthoughtful responding in favor of developing a preresponse cognitive plan for organizing and responding to the task; and (2) after the response has been made, to check its reasonableness against the student's own experience and the standards for problem solution set out by the teacher. If the response is appropriate in terms of that personal experience, and teacher standards, the student moves on. If the response proves to be inappropriate by those same criteria, the child must recycle through the problem, selecting or designing new cognitive plans for facilitating problem solution until the task has been successfully concluded.

Executive Function

The concept of metacognition concerns self-awareness of cognitive capacity (Brown & DeLoache, 1978; Brown & Campione, 1978) and the need for deliberate cognitive planning if that capacity appears to be unequal to the task posed by a particular problem. Executive function, on the other hand, controls the operations concerning "what to think." The executive function leads to selecting one or more specific strategies already available in the child's intellectual inventory (Belmont & Butterfield, 1977; Butterfield, 1979; Butterfield & Belmont, 1979). If specific strategies are not available, the child may require the custom design of new ones with the aid of the teacher.

Therefore, the sequence of hierarchical thinking activities to be included in a cognitive approach to special education is as follows: (1) self-regulation that requires a self-initiatory, active, resourceful, and confident approach to learning and problem solving; (2) metacognition that fosters a self-awareness of cognitive capacities and limitations as a precursor to planning the selection, design, and use of appropriate strategies; (3) executive function that controls the selection, use, and evaluation of the effectiveness of cognitive strategies available in the child's inventory, as well as modifying those strategies as the nuances of changes in problem structure require it; and (4) cognitive strategies that serve as the intellectual facilitators of problem solving that requires recall, seeing relationships, making discriminations, establishing sequences, and comprehending materials heard and read. These strategies must be effective not only for the problems to which they are initially assigned but also must be generalizable to other problems with surface dissimilarities but latent structure similarity.

Figure 11-2 attempts to organize some of these concepts. In the figure, self-regulation is characterized by the child's confident approach to learning within an attributional framework that suggests that success is due to ability and failure is due to not trying hard enough. In short, the reason for success is inherent and permanent. The reason for failure is temporary and correctable. Metacognition initiates a planning process based on the child's estimate of whether the cognitive tools required for solving problems are easily accessible or require considerable intellectual effort to bring them on line. Once those strategies with a high probability of contributing to successful problem solution have been identified, executive function selects the strategy most likely to succeed. In Figure 11.2, Strategy A is selected to acquire Task A_x. If, after applying strategy A to Task A_x, the monitoring mechanism of executive function determines that success has been achieved, that strategy is reinforced as the one to use again when that problem reappears. Generalization occurs when Strategy A, first successfully used with Task A_x, is applied with equal success to new tasks A_y and A_z. These tasks are new in the sense that they are made up of different materials and sometimes impose different demands. The way in which they are not different, allowing strategy generalization to work, is that the intellectual key that will open the door to Tasks A_y and A_z is the same or nearly the same as the key to Task A_x.

An example of strategy generalization would be a child who learned that a particular abstracting strategy was useful in determining what several words used in a classroom com-

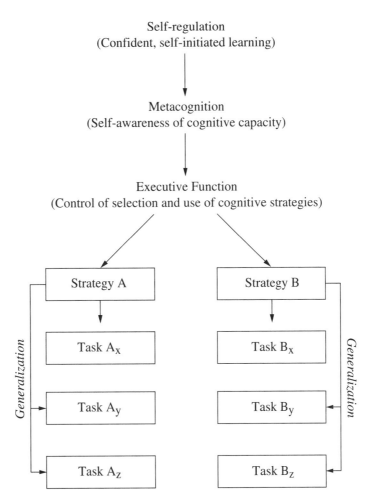

FIGURE 11-2   **The control and operational system for the application and generalization of cognitive strategies.**

prehension lesson had in common. If, on his or her own, he or she recognized that the same abstracting strategy could be applied to finding out, in a shop class, the functions that certain tools have in common, generalization would have occurred.

The Education of Children with Mental Retardation from a Cognitive Perspective

The previous section described how an intact cognitive system might function as a support to classroom learning. A major problem in the education of children with mild mental retardation, however, is that their cognitive systems typically do not function adequately. Under such circumstances, the educator must choose between two alternatives. The first, based on the premise that deficiencies in the cognitive system are remediable, is to design a curriculum and a set of instructional strategies that would upgrade the child's cognitive competencies in the context of developing academic skills. The second, derived from the belief that cognitive deficiencies are not remediable, would attempt to impart knowledge and skills without rehabilitating the cognitive system. In this case, instructional techniques would require engineering the classroom environment to be contingently responsive to the child's correct responses. The first part of this section will deal with the first alternative—a cognitive approach to the special education of children with mental retardation. We will return to the second alternative to present a brief overview of instructional techniques for children with moderate and severe mental retardation.

Cognitive Curriculum for Children with Mild Mental Retardation

Even among those who have championed cognitive approaches to special education (Kronick, 1988), there has been a lingering concern that training cognitive strategies as precursors to the successful acquisition of academic skills would not be effective. Much of this training, fractionated and isolated from knowledge acquisition, went on in laboratories far removed from classrooms. Generalizing strategies acquired in the laboratory to classroom learning proved difficult (Blackman & Lin, 1984). Later reflection would view with incredulity the optimism of many investigators who expected that the ability to generalize, a defining weakness of mental retardation, would somehow appear where it had never appeared before. Even when it became clear that strategy training would have to move to the classroom in order to weaken the generalization barrier, early studies did that training in parallel rather than integrated with subject matter acquisition and, again, did not succeed in producing positive results (Blackman, Burger, Tan, & Weiner, 1982).

The need for the full integration of cognitive system training into the curriculum for students with mental retardation was urgently supported by Harris and Pressley who stated that:

> Effective strategy instruction involves teaching students procedures that empower them to accomplish important academic tasks. Thus, educational researchers have identified strategies promoting reading comprehension, word decoding, composition, arithmetic computation, problem solving, and other skills (Harris & Pressley, 1991, p. 395).

To illustrate, Harris and Pressley reviewed studies by Pressley (1976) and Gambrell and Bales (1986) that investigated the role of mental imagery strategies in facilitating reading comprehension. Teachers instructed students to create images or "pictures in the head" to represent a section of text just read. It was found that students using that strategy had improved recall.

To guide the teacher committed to training the child's cognitive system, Harris and Pressley (1991) also outlined the following seven basic stages of self-instructional strategy development: Stage 1: development of preskills necessary to learn the strategy being taught; Stage 2: review the student's current status in terms of available strategies, both functional and dysfunctional, and commit the student to the acquisition of new strategies; Stage 3:

encourage the use of the executive strategy, which deals with what strategies should be used under what conditions; Stage 4: the strategy to be used is modeled by the teacher or other students in the class with subsequent discussions of how it might be modified for greater effectiveness; Stage 5: students memorize the strategy used; Stage 6: students use the strategy in the context of performing the task while also practicing the steps of self-regulation; Stage 7: students use the strategy independently and begin to consider ways in which the strategy can be generalized to other tasks.

The complete program for making strategy instruction an important part of both the academic and life skills curricula for children with mild mental retardation includes several components. The child should be committed to his or her role as a self-regulated learner who has confidence in his or her ability to learn, who has easy access to strategies that support learning and problem solving, and who relies as heavily on intrinsic or self-reinforcement as on extrinsic or environmentally controlled reinforcement. The child expresses learning-supportive attributions for experienced success and failure. From a metacognitive point of view, the child is aware of the capacity and limitations of his or her own cognitive system and responds with a plan to marshall the intellectual resources needed to meet particular task objectives (Palinscar, 1986). The child knows the library of cognitive strategies available to him or her through the control mechanism of executive function. He or she can select, apply, monitor, and evaluate the effectiveness of these strategies and ultimately find the right one for the target task. Impressing the child with the power of generalization, or the potential for multiple uses of the strategy in question, is a continuing part of the program.

Finally, the teacher makes sure that the melding of strategy usage with the knowledge and competency acquisition called for by the curriculum occurs in the "zone of proximal development" described by Vygotsky (1962). This is a learning zone just above the point at which the child can function independently and just below the maximum level that the child can achieve with full instructional support by the teacher. Instruction in this zone insures that the child is being "stretched" beyond his or her current level of independent skills. The new higher level of independent functioning will be reached as the teacher introduces appropriate strategies and gradually fades prompts and supports until the child achieves autonomy and mastery.

The Issue of a Cognitive Curriculum for Children with Moderate and Severe Mental Retardation

Most educational psychologists and special educators hold the view that enhancing the cognitive system in all of its components (self-regulation, metacognition, executive function, and generalizable cognitive strategies) is an effort more likely to be successful in children with mild mental retardation. The point, after all, in improving the quality of the cognitive system, is to provide the intellectual foundation that will give the child access to an ever-expanding range of life options. Even without cognitive training, most children with mild mental retardation will "pass" into postschool community and vocational life, albeit at a low level, because of their relatively intact social and language skills. Upgraded cognitive competencies would be a valuable third component that would allow these individuals to meet cognitive expectations at close to the same level at which they typically now conform to the community's social and language skills expectations.

Cognitively oriented psychologists and educators have expressed less optimism about achieving comparable results with youngsters with moderate and severe mental retardation. Most of these children have some form of brain dysfunction caused by heredity, trauma, or infection associated with their mental retardation. The issue then is whether the central nervous system "hardware" is sufficiently intact to accommodate the "software" associated with improving the various elements of the cognitive system.

Most of the effective pedagogy for children with mental retardation at this level has been behavioral in orientation. The curriculum is fashioned around the contingency teaching of those skills necessary for supervised vocational, social, and residential adjustment in the community. The development of so-called functional reading and arithmetic skills rarely goes beyond what is required for safety, preserving social amenities, assuring sufficient mobility skills, and functioning satisfactorily in closely supervised employment settings. As might be expected, the social and vocational objectives of the curriculum receive the greatest emphasis over the largest part of the youngsters' school careers.

While pedagogy derived from a traditional behavioral perspective has been widely identified with placing children under the control of a responsive environment, efforts have also been made to help people with mental retardation achieve self-control (O'Leary & Dubey, 1979, Rosenbaum & Drabman, 1979). Whitman has suggested that:

> By exercising self-control, persons with retardation can increase the probability that they will act effectively without external direction, maintain what they have learned, and generalize learned responses to situations where training contingencies have not been applied. Moreover, by self-regulating their behavior, they are more likely to be able to live in more normalized settings where close supervision is not possible (Whitman, 1990, p. 348).

According to Whitman (1990), language is the mechanism that brings cognitive and behavioral interpretations of self-control or self-regulation closer together. Covert or internal talk, from a behavioral point of view, is considered to be the counterpart of thought; a construct more compatible with a cognitive frame of reference. It is difficult to escape the conclusion, whether one forms that conclusion from a behavioral or cognitive perspective, that language, whether silent or spoken, is a vital support for directing all of those operations subsumed under self-regulation, metacognition, executive function, and the selection, monitoring, evaluation, and alteration of generalizable strategies (Harris, 1990).

The problem with using language to foster cognitive self-regulation and all of its component subprocesses is that more seriously involved individuals with mental retardation typically exhibit serious language deficits (Luria, 1961; Spradlin, 1963). This raises the question as to whether it makes sense to develop instructional programs that will use a weak language function to rehabilitate a weak cognitive system. Before this could be done, educators would have to develop curricula for mediating language skills before these skills could play their proper roles in the enhancement of the cognitive system. This might place students at more severe levels of mental retardation in a "double jeopardy" instructional situation where furthering cognitive development would rely heavily on training linguistic competencies. At the current state of the art and science of special education, most curriculum designers and teachers would prefer to remediate weakness from a stronger foundation.

At this time, the preferred approach to educating children with moderate and severe mental retardation is to apply the full range of behavior analytic techniques to the development of knowledge and competency structures that are likely to be useful to the youngsters in terms of succeeding in school and in making a satisfactory life adjustment as adults. This scenario recommends reverting to other regulation from self-regulation. It steps back from metacognition and executive function as self-initiated processes and makes them the subject of didactic instruction by alert teachers who will serve as remote control regulators of cognitive processes required to establish appropriate knowledge structures. If there is a concern that this approach abandons all efforts at cognitive enhancements for students with this level of mental retardation, some recent work eases that concern. Chi and Ceci (1987) and Peverly (1991) have suggested that the use of cognitive control processes and strategies in problem solution may be more a function of the complexity of a child's knowledge structure than it is a function of the size of his or her strategy inventory or sophistication in strategy selection and modification. In short, building comprehensive knowledge structures may be as sure a road to cognitive fluidity as the specific training of components of the cognitive system itself.

What seems clear as one scrutinizes the emerging psychological foundations of curriculum and methodology in the education of individuals with mental retardation is that behavioral and cognitive psychology are moving away from a commitment to theoretical orthodoxy, and toward a pragmatic integration that selects the most valuable contributions of both orientations in the service of educating children with mental retardation (Meichenbaum, 1977). In this integration, many contemporary behaviorists have accepted constructs such as "thought" and "thinking processes" back into their theoretical and instructional vocabulary. Cognitivists, in the same spirit, gratefully adopt behavioral techniques in the training of both the cognitive system and knowledge structures. If the history of science in general and psychology in particular can serve as a guide, the next decade will probably witness not only a continuation of the pragmatic integration that has already occurred but a real theoretical synthesis of the cognitive and behavioral positions.

A Specific Cognitive Curriculum for Children with Moderate Mental Retardation

A notable example of a cognitively oriented curriculum for children with moderate mental retardation has been described by the staff of the Rectory Paddock School (1983), under the leadership of its headmaster, Mark Roberts. Located in England, the school has prepared a publication entitled *In Search of a Curriculum*.

The curriculum is divided into core and applied segments. The core curriculum is dedicated primarily to developing cognitive skills that will support the applied curriculum. Figure 11-3 graphically represents the specifics of and the relationship between the two-part curriculum. It is suggested that teaching "key activities" represented in the cognitive core curriculum will:

> make a radical difference to our pupils' rate of development, resulting in altogether higher levels of performance across the curriculum and in their lives generally (Staff of the Rectory Paddock School, 1983, p. 9).

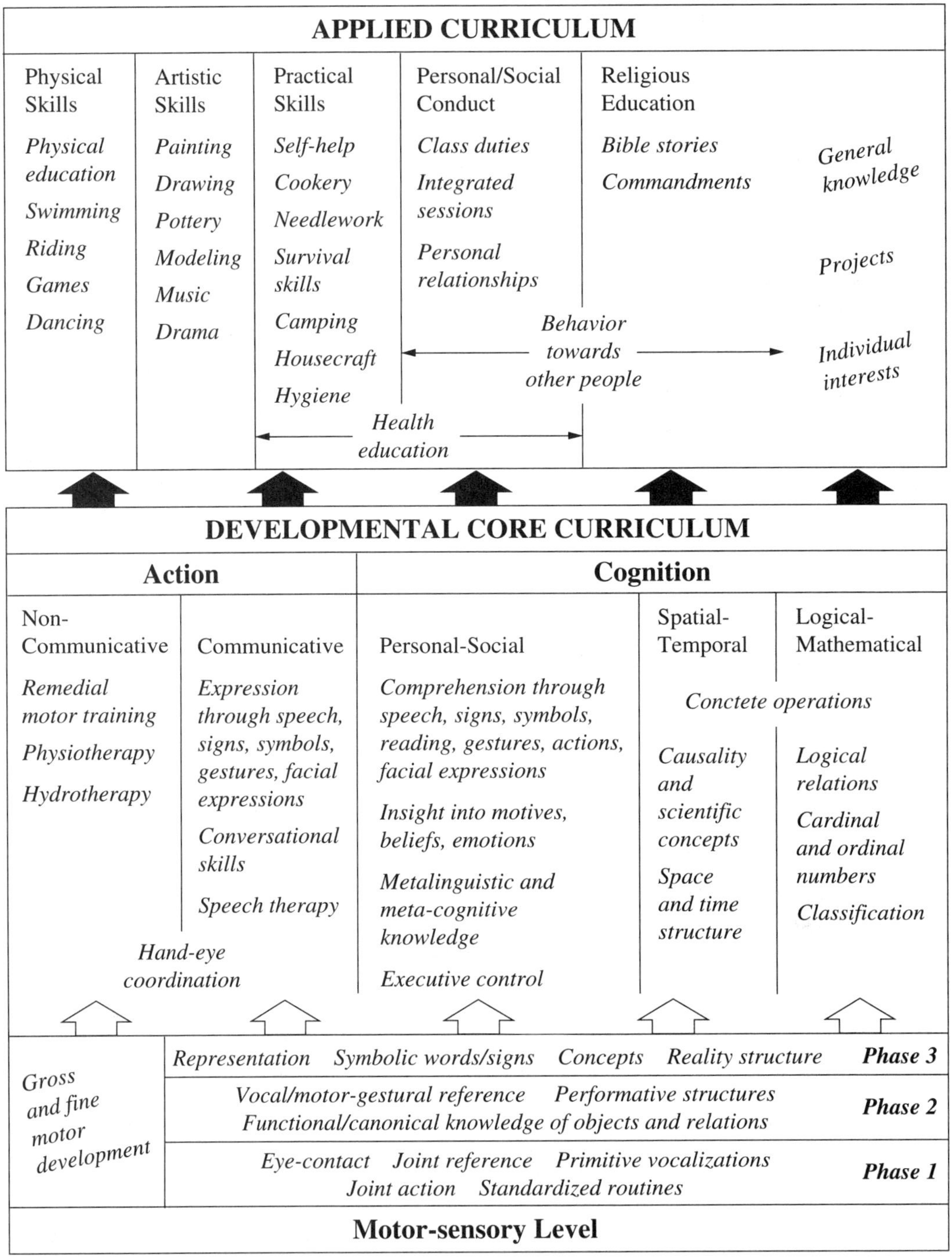

APPLIED CURRICULUM					
Physical Skills	Artistic Skills	Practical Skills	Personal/Social Conduct	Religious Education	
Physical education	*Painting*	*Self-help*	*Class duties*	*Bible stories*	*General knowledge*
Swimming	*Drawing*	*Cookery*	*Integrated sessions*	*Commandments*	
Riding	*Pottery*	*Needlework*	*Personal relationships*		*Projects*
Games	*Modeling*	*Survival skills*			
Dancing	*Music*	*Camping*	*Behavior towards other people*		*Individual interests*
	Drama	*Housecraft*			
		Hygiene			
		Health education			

DEVELOPMENTAL CORE CURRICULUM

Action		Cognition		
Non-Communicative	Communicative	Personal-Social	Spatial-Temporal	Logical-Mathematical
Remedial motor training	*Expression through speech, signs, symbols, gestures, facial expressions*	*Comprehension through speech, signs, symbols, reading, gestures, actions, facial expressions*	*Concrete operations*	
Physiotherapy			*Causality and scientific concepts*	*Logical relations*
Hydrotherapy		*Insight into motives, beliefs, emotions*		*Cardinal and ordinal numbers*
	Conversational skills	*Metalinguistic and meta-cognitive knowledge*	*Space and time structure*	*Classification*
	Speech therapy			
	Hand-eye coordination	*Executive control*		

Gross and fine motor development	*Representation Symbolic words/signs Concepts Reality structure*		***Phase 3***
	Vocal/motor-gestural reference Performative structures *Functional/canonical knowledge of objects and relations*		***Phase 2***
	Eye-contact Joint reference Primitive vocalizations *Joint action Standardized routines*		***Phase 1***

Motor-sensory Level

FIGURE 11-3   A Framework for Curriculum Development

Taken from *In search of a curriculum: Notes on the education of mentally handicapped children* (2nd edition). Sidcup, Kent, United Kingdom: Robin Wren Publications.

Part of the cognitive curriculum that deals with spatial-temporal and logical-mathematical operations derives from Piagetian theory (Piaget, 1970). The personal-social column, while emphasizing communication skills, awareness of self-motivation, and understanding of the motivation of others, also deals extensively with the training of what Roberts refers to as "learning to learn" processes. It is this section of the curriculum that has, as its primary objective, the training of executive function, metacognition, and cognitive strategies. Theoretically, these information processing components, functioning effectively, are necessary prerequisites to the successful acquisition and generalization of those competencies included within the applied curriculum.

Some early success reported in training youngsters with mild mental retardation to acquire and maintain important cognitive skills has had a ripple effect. It has encouraged both investigators and teachers (e.g., the staff of the Rectory Paddock School) to extend the cognitive training model to even more limited children. Future reports evaluating the success of those programs will attest to the wisdom of that extension.

A Suggested Service Delivery System

Although it is not always stated in these terms, a field-defining controversy in the education of schoolchildren with mild mental retardation is whether the educational symptomatology of mental retardation should be accepted as a predictable feature of their school and postschool adjustment or struggled against on the premise that it is, under the best educational circumstances, potentially remediable. Should the school careers of individuals with mental retardation be geared to helping them to maximize their performance within the context of their disability, or to liberating them from the stigmatization, school failure, and life constraints that it imposes?

Both the basic and applied research on which approach is likely to produce the best results is, at this time, incomplete and not yet sufficiently decisive to provide the kind of scientific support that significant changes in special education policy would require. However, the challenge of diminishing the incapacities and dysfunctions associated with mental retardation is so compelling that programs for remediating various deficits in the cognitive system have proliferated.

Many special educators have been unwilling to assign "cognitive blame" to youngsters with mild mental retardation, particularly those from racially and ethnically diverse groups. Instead, they have accepted for themselves the onus of "assessment blame." The net effect has been to replace the diagnosis of cognitive deficiency with concern for educational disadvantage. If children with apparent mental retardation do not "really" have a cognitive disability and are simply short on intellectually stimulating early experience and deprived of effective school programs, it may be argued that what they need is catch-up time in a more cognitively and academically enriched environment.

The general principle that classification, stigmatization, and special programming for children with mild mental retardation should occur only after a child has failed to make satisfactory progress in a regular curriculum suggests a particular service delivery concept. Whether or not a child has been identified as "at risk" at the preschool level, he or she is entitled to admission to a regular kindergarten with anticipatory support provided to children who exhibit problems likely to interfere with current or future learning. As the child progresses through the grades, the point at which it becomes clear that, whatever the etiological factors involved, he or she does not have the cognitive competencies required to perform successfully, the child is directed into a cognitive training program administered within the context of an academic curriculum. This should occur at about the end of the second grade when it is clear that the child is unable to meet the demands of learning to read, dealing with number abstractions, or both. The cognitive/academic program should take place in a regular class in which regular and consulting teachers have been trained in identifying and remediating deficits in the cognitive system. This remediation should also include helping the child to build bridges between newly acquired cognitive skills and the acquisition of academic knowledge.

The child in the cognitive training and academic phase of his or her program must be monitored carefully and frequently. If the gap between the child's achievement and the achievement of chronological age counterparts begins to narrow in the early part of the elementary school curriculum, and continues to do so as the child approaches the end of the elementary grades, the remedial program can be judged to be successful and the child retained in the regular curriculum of the middle and secondary school programs.

If the child does not flourish in the cognitive/academic program, he or she can be directed toward a middle and secondary school program that will stress life skills. The primary objectives of this stage of the curriculum will emphasize vocational evaluation, employment training, social skills training, and in general, developing those competencies required for: (1) living successfully in the community; (2) enjoying wholesome leisure time activities; (3) maintaining stable family relationships; (4) finding and keeping friends; (5) expressing sexuality appropriately; (6) managing financial affairs; (7) assuming citizenship responsibility; (8) using community transportation systems effectively; and (9) finding and keeping a job.

Consideration of a shift toward a life skills curriculum should take place by the time the child enters the middle school. By this time, educators have had an opportunity to observe the children through several years of the cognitive/academic curriculum. At this point, too, the regular curriculum often becomes departmentalized, resulting in a rapid acceleration in the skills needed to keep up with ever more challenging academic concepts and materials.

Moving toward a life skills curriculum will terminate cognitive training but will not bring an end to further development of academic skills. Academic skill development will continue as it is needed to support the objectives of the life skills curriculum. For example, vocational training and managing financial affairs will require credible arithmetic skills. Assuming citizenship responsibilities will require some reading skills as well as information typically included in the social studies curriculum.

This service delivery system suggests that a cognitive/academic curriculum for children with mild mental retardation is a reasonable first effort from which children may be gradually withdrawn if failure to flourish in that setting becomes apparent. Of course, it is hoped that children with mild mental retardation will be able to close the achievement gap while being exposed to the cognitive/academic curriculum. If that does not occur, however, emphasizing a life skills curriculum may better respond to the child's special developmental needs and postschool requirements.

With the exception of a few experimental programs, one of which, at the Rectory Paddock School, was mentioned in a previous section, almost all programs for children with moderate and severe mental retardation emphasize life skills accompanied by whatever level of academic achievement is needed to establish and reinforce those competencies. From the outset of their school careers, therefore, these children will be directed toward acquiring the social, vocational, recreational, and communication competencies necessary for life adjustment.

Recommendations

A number of recommendations relating to the cognitive infrastructure of the educational program flow from the material in this chapter.

1. In planning educational programs for children with mental retardation, effective teaching, administrative support, and high quality materials should be given greater weight than placement issues.

2. Cognitive training programs can facilitate children's performance in an academic curriculum.

3. Cognitive training should take place primarily in the elementary school.

4. The data sources that should be carefully monitored by curriculum developers in special education are the structure of subject matter, societal expectations, and a cognitive analysis of the learner him- or herself.

5. The design of a program to make changes in a child's cognitive infrastructure as a precursor to academic growth requires knowledge of: (a) the cognitive prerequisites for the acquisition of academic competencies; (b) whether the learner has these cognitive prerequisites in his or her repertoire; (c) methods for remediating these cognitive prerequisites if they are found to be deficient; and (d) knowledge of techniques for evaluating academic progress traceable to the remediation of these deficiencies.

6. Teachers will typically learn more about how their students process information by asking them how they arrived at solutions to problems than simply by asking for the right answer.

7. It is important for teachers to know which cognitive strategies are available and easily accessible to their students.

8. Although many cognitive strategies are learned fairly easily by students with mental retardation, teachers must continue to stress the generalization of these strategies to tasks and settings other than the one in which the strategy was originally learned.

9. Children should not be taught cognitive strategies in isolation. Bridging is an instructional technique that teaches these strategies in the context of learning academic and other skills.

10. Helping children to achieve self-regulation, metacognition, and competence in the use of executive function are important objectives of the teacher committed to improving their cognitive infrastructure.

11. Teachers can improve children's motivation and self-esteem by assuring them that the reasons for their success are intrinsic and permanent while the reasons for their failure are temporary and correctable.

12. Cognitive training programs are likely to be more effective in improving the performance of children with mild and moderate mental retardation than the performance of children with severe mental retardation.

13. Behavior analytic techniques continue to be the method of choice in educating children with moderate and severe mental retardation.

14. The education of children with mental retardation will be best served by both a pragmatic integration and, in the future, a theoretical synthesis of cognitive and behavioral approaches.

15. Upon entry to school, all children at risk for mild mental retardation should be admitted to a regular program.

16. At about the end of the second grade, children who are not making satisfactory progress should be directed into a cognitive training program administered within the context of an academic curriculum.

17. Children who do not benefit from the cognitive/academic curriculum may be directed, upon entry into the middle school, toward a life skills curriculum emphasis. This curriculum emphasis, supported by academic content as needed, can continue through the secondary school.

References

American Association on Mental Retardation Ad Hoc Committee on Terminology and Classification (1992). *Mental retardation: Definition, classification, and systems of support* (9th ed.). Washington, DC: American Association on Mental Retardation.

AAMR Newsletter Psychology Division. (1990). New AAMR definition on mental retardation proposed. *Vol. 1*(1).

Alper, S. (1985). The use of teacher questioning to increase independent problem solving in MR adolescents. *Education and Training in Mental Retardation, 20,* 83–88.

Bateman, B. (1967). Implications of a learning disability approach for teaching educable retardates. *Mental Retardation, 5,* 23–25.

Belmont, J. M. & Butterfield, E. C. (1977). The instructional approach to developmental cognitive research. In R. Kail & J. Hagen (Eds.), *Perspectives on the development of memory and cognition.* Hilldale, NJ: Erlbaum.

Belmont, J. M., Butterfield, E. C., & Borkowski, J. G. (1978). Training retarded people to generalize memorization methods across memory tasks. In M. M. Gruenberg, P. E. Morris, & R. N. Sykes (Eds.), *Practical aspects of memory.* London: Academic Press.

Bilsky, L. H. (1976). Transfer of categorical clustering set in mildly retarded adolescents. *American Journal of Mental Deficiency, 80,* 588–594.

Bilsky, L. H., & Evans, R. A. (1970). Use of associative clustering techniques in the study of reading disability: Effects of list organization. *American Journal of Mental Deficiency, 74,* 771–776.

Blackman, L. S. (1977). The contributions of research in cognition to the future of special education practices with the mentally retarded. In P. Mittler (Ed.), *Research to practice in mental retardation, vol. II.* Baltimore: University Park Press.

Blackman, L. S. (1967). The dimensions of a science of special education. *Mental Retardation, 5,* 7–11.

Blackman, L. S., Bilsky, L., Burger, A., & Mar, H. (1976). Cognitive processes and academic achievement in educable mentally retarded adolescents. *American Journal of Mental Deficiency, 81,* 125–134.

Blackman, L. S., & Burger, A. (1972). Psychological factors related to early reading behaviors of EMR and nonretarded children. *American Journal of Mental Deficiency, 77,* 212–229.

Blackman, L. S., Burger, A. L., Tan, N., & Weiner, S. (1982). Strategy training and the acquisition of decoding skills in EMR children. *Education and Training of the Mentally Retarded, 17*, 83–87.

Blackman, L. S. & Heintz, P. (1966). The mentally retarded. *Review of Educational Research, 36*, 5–36.

Blackman, L. S. & Lin, A. (1984). Generalization training in the educable mentally retarded: Intelligence and its educability revisited. In P. H. Brooks, R. Sperber, & C. McCauley (Eds.), *Learning and cognition in the mentally retarded.* Hillsdale, NJ: Erlbaum.

Borkowski, J. G. & Cavanaugh, J. C. (1979). Maintenance and generalization of skills and strategies by the retarded. In N. R. Ellis (Ed.), *Handbook of mental deficiency: Psychological theory and research* (2nd ed.), 569–618. Hillsdale, NJ: Erlbaum.

Borkowski, J. G., Reid, M. K., & Kurtz, B. E. (1984). Metacognition and retardation: Paradigmatic, theoretical, and applied perspectives. In P. H. Brooks, R. Sperber, & C. McCauley (Eds.), *Learning and cognition in the mentally retarded.* Hillsdale, NJ: Erlbaum.

Borkowski, J. G., Weyhing, R. S., & Turner, L. A. (1986). Attributional retraining and the teaching of strategies. *Exceptional Children, 53*, 130–137.

Brainin, S. (1982). *The effects of instrumental enrichment on the reasoning abilities, reading achievement and task orientation of sixth grade underachievers.* Unpublished doctoral dissertation, Teachers College, Columbia University, New York.

Brown, A. L., & Campione, J. C. (1978). Memory strategies in learning: Training children to study strategically. In H. Pick, H. Leibowitz, J. Singer, A. Sternschneider, & H. Stevenson (Eds.), *Application of basic research in psychology.* New York: Plenum Press.

Brown, A. L., Campione, J. C., & Barclay, C. R. (1979). Training self-checking routines for estimating test readiness: Generalization from list learning to prose recall. *Child Development, 50*, 501–512.

Brown, A. L. & DeLoache, J. S. (1978). Skills, plans, and self-regulation. In R. Siegler (Ed.), *Children's thinking: What develops?* Hillsdale, NJ: Erlbaum.

Bruner, J. S. (1960). *The process of education.* New York: Vintage.

Burger, A. L. & Blackman, L. S. (1976). Acquisition and retention of a mediational strategy for PA

learning in EMR children. *American Journal of Mental Deficiency, 80*, 529–534.

Burger, A. L. & Blackman, L. S. (1978). Imagery and verbal mediation in paired-associate learning of educable mentally retarded adolescents. *Journal of Mental Deficiency Research, 22*, 125–130.

Burger, A. L., Blackman, L. S., & Clark, H. T. (1981). Generalization of verbal abstraction strategies in EMR children and adolescents. *American Journal of Mental Deficiency, 85*, 611–618.

Burger, A. L., Blackman, L. S., Clark, H. T., & Reis, E. (1982). The effects of hypothesis testing and variable format training on the generalization of a verbal abstraction strategy in EMR learners. *American Journal of Mental Deficiency, 86*, 405–413.

Burger, A. L., Blackman, L. S., Holmes, M., & Zetlin, A. (1978). Use of active sorting and retrieval strategies as a facilitation of recall, clustering, and sorting by EMR and nonretarded children. *American Journal of Mental Deficiency, 83*, 253–261.

Burger, A. L., Blackman, L. S., & Tan, N. (1980). Maintenance and generalization of a sorting and retrieval strategy in EMR and nonretarded individuals. *American Journal of Mental Deficiency, 84*, 373–380.

Butterfield, E. C. (1979). *On testing process theories of intelligence.* Paper presented at NATO Conference on Intelligence and Learning, York, England.

Butterfield, E. C. & Belmont, J. M. (1979). *Instructional techniques that produced generalized improvement in cognition.* Paper presented at Gatlinburg Conference on Mental Retardation, Gulf Shores, Alabama.

Calnen, T. & Blackman, L. S. (1992). Capital punishment and offenders with mental retardation: Response to the Penry Brief. *American Journal on Mental Retardation, 96*, 557–564.

Campione, J. C. & Brown, A. L. (1977). Memory and metamemory development in educable retarded children. In R. V. Kail, Jr. & J. W. Hagen (Eds.), *Perspectives on the development of memory and cognition.* Hillsdale, NJ: Erlbaum.

Chi, M. T. H. & Ceci, S. J. (1987). Content knowledge: Its role, representation, and restructuring in memory development. In H. W. Reese (Ed.), *Advances in child development and behavior,* (vol. 20). Orlando, FL: Academic Press.

Dalton, M. (1975). *Core curriculum for use in classes for children with retarded mental development.*

Board of Education of the City of New York: Bureau for Children with Retarded Mental Development (reprinted).

Day, J. D. & Hall, L. K. (1988). Intelligence-related differences in learning and transfer and enhancement of transfer among MR persons. *American Journal of Mental Retardation, 93*, 125–137.

Doll, E. A. (1941). The essentials of an inclusive concept of mental deficiency. *American Journal of Mental Deficiency, 46*, 214–219.

Dunn, L. M. (1968). Special education for the mildly retarded—Is much of it justifiable? *Exceptional Children, 35*, 5–22.

Ellis, N. R., Woodley-Zarthos, P., Sulareg, C. L, & Palmer, R. L. (1989). Automatic-effortful processing and cognitive inertia in persons with mental retardation. *American Journal of Mental Retardation, 93*, 412–423.

Edgerton, R. B. (1967). *The cloak of competence.* Berkeley: University of California Press.

Feuerstein, R. (1980). *Instrumental enrichment: An intervention program for cognitive modifiability.* Baltimore: University Park Press.

Feuerstein, R., Rand, Y., Hoffman, M. B., & Miller, R. (1980). *Instrumental enrichment: Redevelopment of cognitive functions of retarded performers.* Baltimore: University Park Press.

Flavell, J. H. (1976). Metacognitive aspects of problem solving. In L. B. Resnick (Ed.), *The nature of intelligence.* Hillsdale, NJ: Erlbaum.

Flavell, J. H. (1979). Metacognition and cognitive monitoring: A new area of cognitive developmental inquiry. *American Psychologist, 34*, 906–911.

Gambrell, L. B. & Bales, R. J. (1986). Mental imagery and the comprehension-monitoring performance of fourth- and fifth-grade poor readers. *Reading Research Quarterly, 21*, 454–461.

Goldstein, H. (1969). Construction of a social learning curriculum. *Focus on Exceptional Children, 1*, 1–10.

Goldstein, H. & Seigle, D. M. (1958). *The Illinois plan for special education of exceptional children: A curriculum guide for teachers of the educable mentally handicapped.* A cooperative project of the Office of Public Instruction, State of Illinois and the Institute for Research on Exceptional Children at the University of Illinois. Chicago: Illinois Council for Mentally Retarded Children.

Grossman, H. J. (Ed.). (1983). *Classification in mental retardation.* Washington, DC: American Association on Mental Deficiency.

Harris, K. R. (1990). Developing self-regulated learners: The role of private speech and self-instructions. *Educational Psychologist, 25*, 35–50.

Harris, K. R. & Pressley, M. (1991). The nature of cognitive strategy instruction: Interactive strategy instruction. *Exceptional Children, 57*, 392–404.

Heintz, P. & Blackman, L. S. (1977). Psychoeducational considerations with the mentally retarded child. In I. Bialer & M. Sternlicht (Eds.), *The psychology of mental retardation: Issues and approaches.* New York: Psychological Dimensions, Inc.

Hughes, C. A., Korinek, L., & Gorman, J. (1991). Self-management for students with MR in public school settings: A research review. *Education and Training in Mental Retardation, 26*, 271–291.

Kendall, C., Borkowski, J. G., & Cavanaugh, J. C. (1980). Maintenance and generalization of an interrogative strategy by EMR children. *Intelligence, 4*, 255–270.

Kronick, D. (1988). *New approaches to learning disabilities: Cognitive, metacognitive, and holistic.* Philadelphia: Grune & Stratton.

Lin, A., Blackman, L. S., Clark, H. T., & Gordon, R. (1983). Far generalization of visual analogies strategies by impulsive and reflective EMR students. *American Journal of Mental Deficiency, 88*, 297–306.

Luria, A. R. (1961). *The role of speech in the regulation of normal and abnormal behavior.* New York: Liveright.

MacMillan, D. L. (1989). Equality, excellence, and the EMR populations: 1970–1989. *Psychology in Mental Retardation and Developmental Disabilities, 15*(1), 3–10.

MacMillan, D. L. & Jones, R. L. (1972). Lions in search of more Christians. *Journal of Special Education, 6*, 81–91.

Mann, L. (1979). *On the trail of process.* New York: Grune & Stratton.

Meichenbaum, D. (1977). *Cognitive-behavioral modification: An integrative approach.* New York: Plenum.

O'Leary, S. G. & Dubey, D. R. (1979). Application of self-control procedures by children: A review. *Journal of Applied Behavior Analysis, 12*, 449–465.

Palinscar, A. S. (1986). Metacognitive strategy instruction. *Exceptional Children, 53,* 118–124.

Paris, S. G. & Oka, E. R. (1986). Self-regulated learning among exceptional children. *Exceptional Children, 53,* 103–108.

Paris, S. G. & Winograd, P. (1990). Promoting metacognition and motivation of exceptional children. *Remedial and Special Education, 11,* 7–15.

Peverly, S. T. (1991). Problems with the knowledge-based explanation of memory and development. *Review of Educational Research, 61,* 71–93.

Piaget, J. (1970). Piaget's theory. In P. H. Mussen (Ed.), *Carmichael's manual of child psychology, vol. 1.* New York: Wiley.

Pressley, M. (1976). Mental imagery helps eight-year-olds remember what they read. *Journal of Educational Psychology, 65,* 355–359.

Reichart, G. J., Cody, W. J., & Borkowski, J. G. (1973). Training and transfer of clustering and cumulative rehearsal strategies in retarded individuals. *American Journal of Mental Deficiency, 78,* 292–299.

Rosenbaum, M. S. & Drabman, R. S. (1979). Self-control training in the classroom: A review and critique. *Journal of Applied Behavior Analysis, 12,* 467–485.

Scheid, K. (1989). *Cognitive and metacognitive learning strategies—Their role in the instruction of special education students.* The Instructional Methods Report Series, Information Center for Special Education Media and Materials. Columbus, OH: LINC Resources, Inc.

Scruggs, T. & Brigham, F. J. (1990). The challenges of metacognitive instruction. *Remedial and Special Education, 11,* 16–18.

Spitz, H. H. (1986). *The raising of intelligence: A selected history of attempts to raise intelligence.* Hillsdale, NJ: Erlbaum.

Spradlin, J. E. (1963). Language and communication of mental defectives. In N. R. Ellis (Ed.), *Handbook of mental deficiency.* New York: McGraw-Hill.

Staff of Rectory Paddock School. (1983). *In search of a curriculum: Notes on the education of mentally handicapped children* (2nd ed.). Sidcup, Kent, United Kingdom: Robin Wren Publications.

Turnure, J. E. & Walsh, M. K. (1971). Extended verbal mediation in the learning and reversal of paired associates by educable mentally retarded children. *American Journal of Mental Deficiency, 76,* 60–67.

Vygotsky, L. S. (1962). *Thought and language.* Cambridge, MA: MIT Press.

Whitman, T. L. (1990). Self-regulation and mental retardation. *American Journal on Mental Retardation, 94,* 347–362.

Will, M. (1986). *Educating children with learning problems—A shared responsibility* (pp. 1–23). Washington, DC: Office of Special Education and Rehabilitation Services, U.S. Department of Education.

Zimmerman, B. J. (1990). Self-regulated learning and academic achievement: An overview. *Educational Psychologist, 25,* 3–17.

C h a p t e r *12*

Reading

Preparing learners with mental retardation for meeting the many demands of reading is a multifaceted task. Some of the issues involved include: the recognition of words and symbols; the association of words and symbols with their sounds and meanings; the piecing together of meanings to form a complete idea or thought; and, ultimately, sharing with others the ideas that may have been fostered from the reading of printed materials (Kennedy, 1981). In addition to considering the tasks that are involved in the act of reading, teachers of students with mental retardation need to carefully weigh how their reading programs will address the individual needs and abilities of the students in their classroom.

After an initial emphasis on building the cognitive infrastructure, reading instruction for students with mental retardation will typically highlight the skills that foster independence in home, school, and other community environments. This emphasis on a functional model of a reading program for individuals with mental retardation ensures that the sequencing of skills needed for learning to read bridges the acquisition of skills to their applications in community environments (see Chapter 5 for a detailed discussion of the difference between a functional versus a developmental curriculum model).

A common goal inherent in teaching students with mild, moderate, severe, and profound mental retardation is to read for protection and for survival in the community. Exposure to this type of community-related vocabulary includes labels at the supermarket, signs on the street, associated symbols that denote poisonous substances, and other words that are selected with an individual student's needs in mind. Additional important goals for students with mild and moderate mental retardation include being able to read for information as well as for pleasure. Many books are available on teaching reading in general (Barr & Johnson, 1991; Gillet & Temple, 1994; Manzo & Manzo, 1993) and on teaching reading as well as other subjects to students with mental retardation (Polloway & Patton, 1993). The first part of this chapter discusses how characteristics of students with mental retardation might affect learning to read. The rest of the chapter uses the *Case Study of Tanisha* (see Chapter 3) as a vehicle for leading the reader systematically through the types of instructional decisions that need to be made for a fully mainstreamed seven-year-old girl with mild mental retardation who is learning to read. The second section of the chapter lists and describes components in the reading process. Pertinent assessment information is also highlighted. The third part describes word-recognition techniques. The fourth part presents a theoretical overview of reading comprehension, discussing both subsumption theories and schema theories. This section also presents research describing the effects of knowledge on comprehension for individuals with mental retardation. In the fifth part, three strategies for improving comprehension abilities are presented. The sixth part describes four developmental reading approaches. The final section presents recommendations for teachers.

Characteristics of Readers with Mental Retardation

To better facilitate reading instruction for students with mental retardation, both the cognitive and social characteristics of the individual learner need to be kept in mind. In looking at the cognitive characteristics of learners with mental retardation, Kirk, Gallagher, and Anastasiow (1993) noted that they have central processing limitations in

memory, classification, reasoning, and evaluation, as well as limits in executive functioning abilities.

In addition to the cognitive functioning of learners with mental retardation, the role that
personal and social characteristics play in the process of learning how to read cannot be
ignored. For example, the finding that inadequate social skills, not cognitive deficits, are
responsible for the degree to which learners with mental retardation are accepted in the
mainstream highlights the importance of considering an individual's personal and social
characteristics when planning a reading program. Other important personal and social factors that affect learning how to read include the student's attitudes toward reading and the
student' self-concept.

As . rly as 1964 Wattenberg found that measures of self-concept and of ego strength,
which were taken at the kindergarten level, were predictive of reading achievement two and
a half years later. This finding that there is a strong relationship between self-concept and
reading achievement has received widespread support (see Cecil, 1990; Gillet & Temple,
1994). In addition, Thompson and Hartley (1980) looked at the effects of a primary reading
difficulty on a student's social and emotional development. Although research has not
resolved whether a low self-concept leads to reading difficulty or vice versa, it is important to assess a student's self-concept. Formal norm-referenced measures for determining a
student's self-concept include: *Coopersmith Self-Esteem Inventories* (Coopersmith, 1982);
Multidimensional Self-Concept Scale (Bracken, 1992); *Self-Esteem Index* (Brown &
Alexander, 1991).

The Reading Process

At this point in the chapter, attention shifts from the capacity of learners with mental retardation (e.g., cognitive, personal, and social characteristics) to the demands that the reading
process places upon the learner. Eight components (Burns, Roe, & Ross, 1984) of the
reading process are highlighted to underscore the relation between demands of the task
and the capacity of the learner. Each of the following eight components will be related to
relevant information from the *Case Study of Tanisha*: (1) sensory; (2) perceptual; (3)
sequential; (4) experiential; (5) cognitive; (6) learning; (7) association; and (8) affective.

Sensory Component

The sensory component of the reading process encompasses the many ways in which our
senses assist us with the task of processing information. For example, in terms of Tanisha's
reading instruction, we know that she can produce the sounds of most letters and combinations but that she still has difficulty blending these sounds to decode words. To obtain a
clearer picture of the specific letter sounds and combinations that Tanisha can produce, a
closer look at the supplementary measures that make up the Ekwall Reading Inventory
(Ekwall, 1986) offers possible strategies for the evaluation of reading and readiness skills.
In addition, the use of the Analytical Reading Inventory (ARI) (4th edition) by Woods and
Moe (1989) provides an opportunity to explore both quantitative and qualitative analyses of
the types of decoding errors that Tanisha makes.

Perceptual Component

The term *perceptual* refers to the ability to perceive or to take in information. In examining the literature on perceptual abilities (Gough, Alford, & Holley-Wilcox, 1981; Patberg, Dewitz, & Samuels, 1981), the focus is usually on visual or auditory perception rather than perceptual abilities as a whole. A detailed list of some perceptual assessment measures can be found in McLoughlin and Lewis (1994). However, before the teacher actually subjects Tanisha to an assessment of her perceptual characteristics, he or she should weigh the Council for Learning Disabilities recommendation of a moratorium on perceptual assessment and training as a prerequisite for reading instruction. This recommendation, which was specifically directed toward students with learning disabilities, may be relevant for students with mental retardation as well.

Sequential Component

The basic ground rules for obtaining meaning from the printed page require an understanding that English print is read from left to right and from top to bottom. In addition, the understanding that language follows a sequential pattern of grammar and logic is another important aspect of this reading process component. Given that Tanisha is enrolled in a fully inclusive elementary school program, it is fair to assume that Tanisha has at least some such knowledge. To learn more about Tanisha's strengths and weaknesses regarding the sequential quality of the reading process, an assessment measure such as the Northwestern Syntax Screening Test (NSST) (Lee, 1971) might be considered. The NSST has two subtests that include both receptive and expressive dimensions of language. Receptively, the assessment measure is structured so that a page showing four drawings is presented to the student as the teacher reads a sentence. The student's task is to select the drawing that best depicts the meaning conveyed in the sentence. In terms of the expressive dimension, the assessment measure requires the student to look at two drawings while the teacher reads a sentence that describes each drawing. The sentence pairs that are used to describe the drawings differ in only one grammatical element (e.g., preposition, verb tense). The student's task is to recall the sentence that goes with the particular drawing that the teacher is focusing his or her attention on as the teacher asks, "Now, what's in this picture?"

Experiential Component

The experiential component of reading is based on the belief that both direct and indirect experiences are necessary for developing a student's vocabulary and comprehension. One way in which teachers can expand upon the experiences of their students is to plan field trips. The nature of the field trip should be selected in terms of its relation or fit with other ongoing classroom activities. For example, Tanisha's teacher might decide to plan a field trip that involves visiting a place or participating in an event that is not easily visualized through reading or discussion. Such a field trip could be planned at the beginning of a unit so that information could be gathered about specific problems or topics. Other field trips might be planned for the middle of a unit as a means of bringing new ideas or suggesting a new direction for study. A field trip could also be planned as a culminating activity. For planning a field trip, Hollingsworth and Hoover (1991) offer suggestions that include establishing problems to solve, evaluating the outing, and deriving generalizations from the data gathered.

Cognitive Component

A reader's cognitive competence plays a key role in his or her ability to comprehend what is read (Collins, 1991; Goodman, 1976). Some of the basic cognitive factors that Tanisha's teacher might investigate could include: (1) selective attention; (2) semantic processing speed; and (3) memory (e.g., the ability to identify words automatically). However, before an informal assessment is devised to learn more about Tanisha's cognitive abilities and how they affect the reading process, teachers should refer to Chapter 11 for a detailed discussion of cognitive processes and strategies that may have important implications for reading instruction.

Learning Component

The learning component of the reading process underscores the importance of being able to read in broadening a student's ability to learn. Tanisha's teacher can foster reading as a purposeful activity (Adams, 1990; Eldredge, 1990; Norton, 1991) by planning and implementing activities and projects that call for the use of a variety of reading materials that emphasize strategies for obtaining information (Blanchard & Rottenberg, 1990).

Association Component

The association component of the reading process refers to the link between ideas that are talked about and the awareness that these same ideas can also be found in written material. Tanisha's teacher could use word-association cues to assist her in retrieving words. For example, the activity of associating objects such as planes, kites, and helicopters with the action word *fly* enables the associated objects to be used as a cue should Tanisha have difficulty retrieving the word *fly*.

Affective Component

The affective component emphasizes the importance that a student's attitudes, self-esteem, and interests have for the reading process (Cecil, 1990). Both the classroom environment (Searfoss, 1993; Webb & Schwartz, 1988) and the home environment (Taylor & Strickland, 1986; Tierney, Readence, & Dishner, 1990) influence how a student feels toward reading. To learn more about how the classroom affects Tanisha's perception of herself as a reader, the assessment measures selected will need to investigate the role of the reading curriculum and the instructional methods and materials used for teaching that curriculum (Linn, 1983; Wood, 1992). If Tanisha's classroom environment is going to be thoroughly assessed, the interactions between students and teachers and students and students also need to be investigated. For a detailed listing of the types of questions that might make up such an investigation, see McLoughlin & Lewis (1994).

Word Recognition

As teachers design reading programs for students with mental retardation, the goal of increasing their ability to identify printed words is important. Students with mental retardation often resort to wild guessing and the substituting of inappropriate words as a way of getting around their inability to identify a word in print (Allington, 1980; Karsh, Repp, & Lenz, 1990).

Two interacting processes used to increase a student's ability to identify words in print include sight word recognition and phonetic analysis. For each of these processes, a brief description is provided with factors to keep in mind when meeting Tanisha's needs. A brief overview of contextual approaches to word recognition instruction follows these descriptions.

Sight Word Recognition

Sight word recognition involves being able to say a word immediately upon sight with little attention to letter-sound relationships. This process relies upon the ability to hold an image in working memory while physically moving past it to other words or images, to test whether the word should be called one thing or another (Manzo & Manzo, 1993).

Tanisha would benefit from being able to automatically identify whole words that are frequently used in basic reading material (e.g., *the, you, saw, in,* and *was*), to facilitate fluent reading. The three basic principles behind teaching sight words involve getting the student to see words and their distinguishing features, orally say those words, and find and silently practice those words until they are learned to 100 percent accuracy. For additional information on teaching sight words, see McNich (1981) and Manzo and Manzo (1993).

Phonetic Analysis

Phonetic analysis involves the application of knowledge about letter-to-sound (grapheme-phoneme) relationships until a hypothesis can be generated about the probable identity of the word (Harris & Sipay, 1985). That hypothesis is tested against the context in which the word is used. When the student is involved in phonic analysis, both various letter-sounds and the generalization rules or guidelines for using phonetic information are applied. Generally, when a phonics approach is being used, instruction is based either on a synthetic method (teaching individual letter sounds that are then blended into words) or the analytic method (teaching phonic principles from words the student already knows). However, as is true with any material that is being taught, instruction with phonetic analysis will be undermined if the teacher's knowledge of phonics and phonetic generalizations is poor (a concern worth noting based on the poor performance of fifteen licensed elementary teachers' knowledge of phonics (Reis, 1989) as measured on Lerner's (1985) fifty-item phonics quiz). Teachers in need of information about phonics and phonetic generalizations can consult: Cheek, Flippo, and Lindsey (1989); and Duffey and Roehler (1986).

Knowledge of the phonological structure of words has been shown to change as readers become more skilled. When less skilled readers were given a word pronunciation task to complete, it was found that the regularity of the vowel pattern structure of the words was not used effectively. Thus, it was postulated that a possible explanation for why students with mental retardation have difficulty learning to read is that they have problems using letter-sound patterns to identify words in print (Sing & Sing, 1988).

Because Tanisha's teacher recognizes the importance of determining how well Tanisha can translate printed symbols into spoken language or meaning, the administration of an informal assessment is essential. Such an informal assessment might include phonics and structural analysis, as well as syllabication. Directly upon administration of this informal assessment, the teacher would want to study the types of mistakes or errors (e.g., error analysis) that Tanisha made. From such an error analysis, factors such as whether Tanisha discounts vowel and even consonant information by guessing a common word that is somewhat similar would be apparent. If Tanisha does use this strategy, her teacher would recognize its futility because many common words contain irregular letter-sound patterns that do not form a satisfactory foundation for generalization (e.g., *was*, *there*, *have*, and *one*). Thus, the possible use of such a strategy would make it difficult for Tanisha to identify words correctly unless she had memorized every printed word.

Contextual Approaches

Contextual approaches emphasize reading for meaning. As a student tries to use contextual analysis, which involves the close examination of the context in which a word is used, his or her ability to figure out an unknown word is based on syntactic and semantic cues which evolve from the other words in the passage. Although the use of contextual analysis offers students an opportunity to experience reading as a meaningful language process, Tanisha may have difficulty in using context clues as a word-analysis procedure because of inadequate word-recognition skills. This might cause her to focus more on pronouncing words rather than on constructing meaning from printed words. As Tanisha's teacher plans instruction to effectively use contextual approaches for teaching the identification of unknown words, she might draw upon Dahl and Samuels' (1977) suggestion of a hypothesis-test strategy. Their hypothesis-test strategy includes the following steps: 1) use information from the passage; 2) make a prediction as to which word is more likely to occur; 3) test the hypothesis by comparing the printed and the predicted word; and 4) accept or reject the prediction.

Comprehension

Comprehension can truly be said to be the cornerstone of all learning. Exposure to information, regardless of the frequency of the exposure and the importance of information, is meaningless unless the receiver of the information can "get inside" it; that is, understand and comprehend its significance. In order to help teachers make decisions about how and where to modify instructional approaches and materials that foster comprehension, we include an overview of both subsumption theories and schema theories to provide a framework for planning instruction. This theoretical overview is followed by a discussion of the effects of knowledge on comprehension for individuals with mental retardation.

Subsumption Theories

Ausubel and others (Ausubel, 1960; Ausubel & Fitzgerald, 1961; Ausubel & Youssef, 1963), working within the theoretical framework of subsumption theory, have tested the hypothesis that learning and retention of unfamiliar but meaningful verbal material can be facilitated by the advance introduction of relevant subsuming concepts (organizers). According to Ausubel (1968) the function of the organizer was "to provide ideational scaffolding for the stable incorporation and retention of the more detailed and differentiated material that follows" (p. 148). This was accomplished by manipulating "the availability to the learner of relevant inclusive subsumers" (p. 136). Whether advance organizers for facilitating learning and retention of meaningful material are effective is inconclusive (Barnes & Clawson, 1975). Mayer's (1982) call for increased understanding of what constitutes a "good" advance organizer led us to consider the theoretical underpinnings of the advance organizer-subsumption theory.

Subsumption theory uses the hypothetical construct of *cognitive structure* as a mechanism for explaining how meaningful verbal learning and retention occur. Cognitive structure is viewed as an informational framework that makes possible the reception of new material and the emergence of meaning. Consequently, if meaningful learning of new material is to take place, there must be available in one's cognitive structure knowledge or ideas that act to subsume or include the new material (these ideas are called "subsumers").

A second characteristic of cognitive structure that is considered critical to meaningful learning within subsumption theory is the degree to which knowledge existing in cognitive structure can be discriminated from knowledge embedded in the new learning material. If the learner cannot distinguish degrees of importance from among these knowledge clusters, then he or she is likely to construct the wrong meaning.

Schema Theories

A set of theories, known as schema theories, emphasizes the important role of knowledge in the comprehension of a story. To understand the relationship between schema and comprehension, Rumelhart's (1977) definition of comprehension is useful. In Rumelhart's (1977) words, comprehension is the "process of selecting and verifying schemata to account for the situation (or text to be understood)" (p. 268). Compatible with Rumelhart's portrayal of the association between schema and comprehension is Winograd and Johnston's (1980) description of schema as providing a general outline for the comprehender to use as a guide in the processing of specific details from the text.

Effects of Knowledge on Comprehension for Individuals with Mental Retardation

Several studies (Blackhurst, 1966; Neisworth, 1967; Peleg & Moore, 1982; Reis, 1986) have investigated the facilitative effects of knowledge on the comprehension of individuals with mental retardation. Each of these studies investigated the facilitative effects of experimenter-provided information. In all three studies, experimenter-provided information was judged by the researcher to be knowledge necessary to process the story. A common issue in these studies, however, is the extent to which the format of experimenter-provided knowledge has influenced the results obtained. After each study is examined, the measures taken to control for this situation are discussed.

In Blackhurst's (1966) study, the effect of an oral advanced organizer (Ausubel, 1968) on the learning and retention of subsequently provided oral information was investigated. The subject matter concerned the process involved in passing legislation in the United States Congress. A modified posttest-only control group design was used. The advanced organizer group listened to a passage that briefly discussed the duties of a member of Congress. The control condition just informed the students that they were about to listen to a story detailing the processes involved in passing legislation in the United States. Students were randomly assigned to three groups (thirty students per group). One group received an advanced organizer, learning passage, and test. The second group received a control introduction, the same learning passage, and test, and the third group received unrelated material and the same test. All information was presented by way of a tape recording. Twelve days later, the test was readministered to obtain a measure of retention. Findings did not support the research hypothesis that individuals with mental retardation who listened to the advanced organizer would perform significantly better on criterion measures of learning and retention than individuals with mental retardation who listened to an introductory control passage and the same learning passage.

A number of explanations were proposed by Blackhurst for the failure to support the research hypotheses. One explanation he offered was that the material to be learned may have been too difficult for individuals with mental retardation, and thus, there was a gap between what the advanced organizer provided and what the comprehension task demanded (i.e., the understanding of subject matter describing the process involved in the passing of legislation in the United States). However, his explanation that learning characteristics of the individuals with mental retardation limited their ability to benefit from the advanced organizer may have been premature. At the very least, his findings are constrained methodologically because of the attrition of participants and the failure to employ a comparison group without mental retardation, in addition to the difficulty level of the material he used.

Neisworth (1967) explored the effects of a written organizer for individuals with mental retardation. Neisworth's advanced organizer dealt with the understanding, prevention, and treatment of accidental poisoning. He, like Blackhurst, failed to support the hypothesis that an advanced organizer would better facilitate learning and retention of the material to be comprehended. However, he placed an emphasis on the difficulties of constructing an advanced organizer, and suggested that further research be attempted to provide definitional clarity for what should make up an advanced organizer. In addition, he suggested that there is a need to operationalize these concerns so that direction can be provided as to the format and content that an organizer should entail.

Presentation of knowledge to individuals with mental retardation was tested by Peleg and Moore (1982). They investigated the effectiveness of the three types of introductions: (1) traditional introduction; (2) advanced organizer; and (3) no introduction. The traditional introduction, 130 words long, described the life of monkeys in the forest. The advanced organizer introduction, 150 words long, emphasized the similarities between human beings and monkeys. All students received a unit of instruction, one thousand words long, that discussed the use of monkeys in science as substitutes for human subjects. Introduction and unit were presented orally and in written form. Two levels of learning outcomes were tested:

high-level (inference) questions and low-level (memorization of a fact) questions. Results indicated that oral presentation is better for low-level questions, whereas a written presentation is slightly better for high-level questions. Peleg and Moore also found that the advanced organizer was detrimental to learning under an oral presentation, but may be helpful, or at least not disruptive, under a written presentation especially for high-level questions.

The two interpretations that the authors offer for these results are curious. The first interpretation suggests that the findings may derive from task differences, i.e., that written material must be read while orally presented material must be listened to. However, the authors are quick to add that "there is no available information to support or reject the idea directly; moreover, most evidence from studies with learners without mental retardation indicate no difference in comprehension when material is presented orally or in written form" (p. 625) (e.g., Elgart, 1978; Oaken, Weiner & Cromer, 1971; Weisberg, 1979). The second interpretation focuses on the fact that the students were classified as having mental retardation and that "a special difference may exist between the two modes of presentation for these students that may affect other learning variables" (p. 625). However, the relative ability of the students with mental retardation, as compared to students without mental retardation, could not be determined, since a comparison group without mental retardation was not included in their study.

In Reis' (1986) study, students classified as having mild mental retardation and an equal-mental age comparison group without mental retardation listened to tape recordings of two stories: 1) "The Raccoon and Mrs. McGinnis" (Clymer & Martin, 1976, level 7, 824 words); and (2) "The Donkey Egg" (Clymer & Martin, 1976, level 8, 783 words). There were four conditions: knowledge, purpose statements, knowledge plus purpose statements, and a control condition. For all experimental conditions, information was provided before one of the two stories but not during the other. The information given in the knowledge condition was in the form of a prose passage that (1) provided concepts, not merely by definition but by demonstrating relations and usage as specified in the to-be-comprehended story; and (2) entailed concrete and specific structure and content (Beck, Omanson, & McKeown, 1982). For example, the following passage was provided in the knowledge condition for the first segment of the raccoon story: "This part of the story talks about a raccoon. Let me explain what a raccoon looks like. A raccoon is an animal that has black markings around his eyes that make him look like he is wearing a mask."

The purpose statements condition was based on Beck et al.'s (1982) presilent reading unit preparation component and on schema theories in general. The purpose statements were phrased to highlight key upcoming events. Purpose statement information for the first segment of the raccoon story was delivered in the following format: "Listen to find out what Mrs. McGinnis wishes for and what she leaves for the raccoon every night." The knowledge plus purpose statements condition entailed the sum of the knowledge plus purpose statements condition administered together for each story. The control condition entailed the same tape recording of both stories; no supplemental information was provided, however.

Results indicated that the knowledge plus purpose statements condition enabled the students with mental retardation and the students without mental retardation to respond more accurately to comprehension questions than any of the other three conditions:

(1) knowledge; (2) purpose statements; and (3) control. This suggests that students bene-fitted from the combination of knowledge and purpose statements, but not from the knowl-edge or purpose statements conditions alone. In order to examine why students were able to correctly answer more comprehension questions when the knowledge plus purpose state-ments conditions were combined, consider first the specific role that each component of this condition plays in assisting the listener to process and comprehend orally presented sto-ries. In the knowledge component of the knowledge plus purpose statements condition, the student is provided with story concepts that are necessary for constructing meaning or comprehending the story. In the purpose statements condition, the student is provided with a purpose that should guide his or her processing and comprehension of the story. When both knowledge plus purpose statements components are combined, the student has a firmer foundation on which to build or construct his or her comprehension of a story, because potential roadblocks are addressed. Those may include a lack of a knowledge base for concepts that make up the story and difficulty in keeping attention focused or directed as the story is orally presented. When either the knowledge or purpose statements assistance is not provided, students both with and without mental retardation experience decreases in comprehension because they are not able to bridge the gap left when the knowledge or purpose statement components are presented separately (Pickert & Anderson, 1977; Schallert, 1976).

Strategies for Improving Comprehension

Studies involving individuals without mental retardation have yielded much empirical support (Kintsch, 1972; Johnson, Bransford, & Solomon, 1973; Pearson, Hansen, & Gor-don, 1979; Spillich, Vesonder, Chiesi, & Voss, 1979) for the importance of background knowledge in comprehension. It seems logical that knowledge should play an equally important role for students with mental retardation. However, results of studies on provid-ing the necessary knowledge through an advanced organizer technique for individuals with mental retardation have been equivocal. The global nature of the advanced organizer concept, as applied, makes it difficult to interpret the discrepant findings.

With this limitation in mind, teachers might consider the following three strategies to help their students bridge the gap between their own knowledge base for a particular topic with the necessary knowledge base that facilitates comprehension of that material. These strategies include: (1) The Pre Reading Plan (PREP); (2) a Paraphrasing Strategy; and (3) a Questioning-Answering Strategy. For each strategy there is a step-by-step presentation focusing on how this strategy could be implemented, as well as what kinds of information it could offer Tanisha's teacher.

The Pre Reading Plan (PREP)

The Pre Reading Plan (Langer, 1981) helps readers to activate knowledge they may already have about a topic that they are about to encounter in their reading and provides an oppor-tunity for assessing the adequacy of the reader's prior knowledge. In this three-phase process, the teacher first identifies key terms and then, (1) asks students for their associations to these terms; (2) builds a discussion around the question, "What made you think of that association?"; and (3) prompts further discussion by asking for any additional ideas. An example of a prereading plan is delineated below:

1. Teacher prereads the to-be-assigned reading material.
2. A word, phrase, or related photograph is selected as the stimulus that will be used for what Anderson & Ortony (1975) refer to as activating knowledge. For example, if a science selection was about the types of volcanoes, *volcanoes* might serve as a stimulus word.
3. After introducing the topic, volcanoes, these additional three steps are implemented:

   a. Involve the class in the process of freely associating or brainstorming what comes into their minds when they hear the word *volcanoes*. Write all responses on the board.
   b. Go back to each of the responses on the board and ask the respondee to elaborate on what he or she was thinking about when giving that particular response to the word *volcanoes*.
   c. Given that each student has had an opportunity to elaborate upon his or her initial response as well as to hear the explanations and elaborations of fellow students, ask if anyone has anything he or she would like to add or delete based on what the previous discussion might have triggered.

At this point in the prereading plan a series of ideas have been generated that relate in some way or another to volcanoes. However, Tanisha's teacher would need to know how to determine whether Tanisha has enough background knowledge or whether further concept building about volcanoes would need to be done prior to having Tanisha actually read the selection on volcanoes. To assist Tanisha's teacher in making such a determination, the following guidelines developed by Langer and Nicholich (1981) are suggested:

1. If the ideas generated included superordinate concepts, definitions, analogies, or appear to be a linking or an integration of one concept with another, then Tanisha is ready to read the selection on volcanoes.
2. However, if the list of generated ideas by Tanisha appears to be limited to examples, attributes, or defining characteristics, then Tanisha's teacher should devise instructional activities that foster Tanisha's ability to make the critical links between existing and new knowledge before Tanisha is ready to read the selection on volcanoes.
3. Of greater concern to Tanisha's teacher would be finding that Tanisha's free-association word list is limited to morphemes (prefixes, suffixes, root words), rhyming words, or unrelated experiences to the topic at hand. In this case, Tanisha's teacher would determine that Tanisha has demonstrated very little knowledge of the topic of volcanoes. Then the teacher would need to devise a series of firsthand experiences (e.g., constructing a volcano; studying the volcano exhibit at a museum). After these experiences the teacher would return to the first step of the Pre Reading Plan and have Tanisha free associate again in terms of what comes to her mind when she now hears the word *volcanoes*.

A Paraphrasing Approach

The Paraphrasing Approach was found to be effective for high school students with learning disabilities who had difficulty answering comprehension questions about material written at their grade level (Schumaker, Denton, & Deshler, 1984). This strategy provides a structured way of recalling the main ideas and specific facts of presented reading material. The simplicity of this strategy, as well as the basic nature of the skill being taught, makes it attractive for use as a springboard for instructing Tanisha to recall the main ideas and specific facts of materials that she reads. The steps to the paraphrasing strategy can be summarized using the acronym RAP. The first step, symbolized by the letter *R*, stands for READ the paragraph silently. The students are also instructed to think about what the words mean as they read the paragraph silently. The second step, symbolized by the letter *A*, stands for ASK YOURSELF, "WHAT WERE THE MAIN IDEAS AND DETAILS IN THE PARAGRAPH?" To better enable students to locate the main ideas and the details in the paragraph just read, the following two rules for finding the main idea are also taught (in advance of implementing the RAP strategy): (1) Look for the main idea in the first sentence of a paragraph; and (2) Look for repetitions of this same word or words throughout the paragraph. The third and final step to this strategy is symbolized by the letter *P*, which stands for PUT THE MAIN IDEAS AND DETAILS INTO YOUR OWN WORDS. Students are encouraged to provide at least two details related to the main idea.

The Questioning-Answering Strategy

The Questioning-Answering strategy (Raphael, 1984; Raphael, 1986) requires that the reader play an active role in the process of constructing meaning from what he or she reads. A possible advantage of this approach for students with mild mental retardation rests with the way in which the steps are designed to go from highly supportive to enabling the learner to carry out the strategy independently. Implementing this strategy requires that these steps be followed:

1. Teach the difference between a question that calls for specific information, referred to in this approach as *In the Book*, versus the application of information, referred to in this approach as *In my Head*. To accomplish an understanding of these two categories, provide several short passages, the questions, the answers, the label (*In the Book* versus *In my Head*), and the reason for why the label was appropriate.
2. Provide the same material as in the first step except elicit from the students the reason for the particular label that each question had been assigned.
3. Provide the same information in the first step except elicit from the students not only the reason for the particular label that each question should be assigned but the reason for the labels in general.
4. Provide only the text and the questions and have the students supply the answers, the labels and the reasons for the labels.

After students have learned the distinction between *In the Book* and *In My Head*, teach the next level of differentiation. This includes deciding whether in the case of *In the Book* the question requires the location of information that is in the text, or "Right There," or whether some "Thinking then Searching" through the text is needed before an answer for this question can be found. The *In my Head* category requires additional analysis to determine whether the question calls for the reader to use his or her background knowledge and relate it to the information used in the text (referred to as *Author and You* in this approach), or if the question calls for the reader to apply his or her own views or perspectives (referred to as *On Your Own* in this approach).

Developmental Reading Approaches

Because a number of reading approaches used to teach reading to students with mental retardation are basically developmental methods and materials that have been modified to meet specific individual needs, the following developmental approaches are described in this section: (1) basal approach; (2) linguistic approach; and (3) language experience approach. This section concludes with a discussion of the whole language approach.

Basal Approach

A basal approach, which characterizes the majority of reading programs found in schools in the United States, provides a comprehensive reading curriculum that spans the preprimer through the sixth or eighth grade level and includes all of the materials (e.g., readers, texts, workbooks, and reinforcement activities) needed for carrying out instruction (Spache & Spache, 1977). The basal approach is included here because of the frequency with which regular-education classroom teachers characterize their reading approach as "the basal approach." However, the basal perspective undermines the fostering of comprehension abilities because learning to read is characterized as a sequential addition of one bit of knowledge to another and an overemphasis on the importance of being able to decode words to sound. For further details about these problem areas or concerns, see Reutzel (1991) and Reutzel and Cooter (1988).

If Tanisha's mainstreamed reading class is using a basal approach for the fostering of vocabulary growth, Tanisha's teacher will need to recognize that a particular basal lesson often has multiple objectives. He or she will need to adapt the lessons for Tanisha by selecting only a few objectives for each lesson. Thus, Tanisha will be less likely to be overwhelmed and will have many more opportunities to apply the same lesson objective in a variety of situations. A second adaptation of a basal reading approach includes the creation and use of supplemental materials that have been selected or devised with Tanisha's individual reading needs in mind. Table 12-1 illustrates a more-detailed listing of the strengths, as well as the limitations, of the basal reading approach. In addition, Searfoss and Readence (1994) have presented ways to modify the basal reading approach so that the focus of instruction shifts from the basal reader to the needs of individual children.

Linguistic Approach

Instruction from a linguistic approach emphasizes a sound-letter relationship with the intended purpose of improving the student's ability to see patterns across groupings of

TABLE 12-1   Strengths and Limitations of the Basal Reading Approach

Strengths	Limitations
1. Vocabulary in each reader is controlled so that the student has many opportunities to say and understand the new word.	1. Due to the emphasis on controlled vocabulary, the stories are often dull.
2. Teacher manuals offer many suggestions and may even include sample lesson plans.	2. Since the manual offers so much prescriptive information, the importance of meeting the specific needs of the students in your class may be overlooked.
3. A basal reading series entails important components of a reading program, such as: vocabulary development, word identification, oral and silent reading, recreational reading, and comprehension.	3. Stories in basal readers typically reflect middle-class experiences rather than presenting a diverse sociocultural perspective. In addition, there is too little emphasis on teaching the learner systematically how to comprehend or construct new understanding through an interaction between the learner and the material that is read.

words. For example, the word *rat* is used as a means for identifying similar *at* words like *bat*, *cat*, and *sat*. This approach might offer some assistance for Tanisha, who is able to produce the sounds of most letter combinations but cannot blend these sounds to decode new words. However, as is often the case in selecting approach(es) to meet the individual needs of a particular student, questions arise about whether the basis or orientation of the approach is well matched with the strengths and weaknesses of the learning. Because the linguistic approach draws heavily upon auditory memory skills, Tanisha's teacher would need to determine whether Tanisha's auditory memory skills are intact enough to benefit from a reading approach that draws so heavily upon those skills. As Tanisha's auditory memory skills are being assessed, however, the teacher needs to keep in mind that although auditory memory is an important skill for reading, the improvement of memory skills will not necessarily lead to a corresponding increase in reading ability. It may be helpful to provide memory training in the context of reading activities.

Language Experience Approach

Instruction from a language experience approach draws upon the student's own interests, speech, and past experiences. This approach is designed to integrate listening, reading, and writing skills development with the already existing language of the student. Because this approach builds upon the interest of the student and the language that the student has already mastered, the language experience approach was meant not to rely heavily on published materials but to grow out of the oral expressions of students that were stimulated through group or individual experiences.

As Tanisha's teacher uses the language experience approach, the exact words that Tanisha utters will be what is written down. These words are written on large paper with letters large enough (both lower and upper case letters should be used) that everyone in the group can easily see them. Upon completion of the story, Tanisha's teacher will read the story aloud, pointing at each word as the story is read. The story should be read aloud a second time so that the connection between the familiar spoken word and its unfamiliar graphic representation can be made, as well as providing an opportunity for students to join in if they are able to recognize any of the words.

At this point, Tanisha's teacher might decide to build on Tanisha's strength of print-awareness skills by focusing on word-recognition activities. For example, the teacher might ask students to find the word that rhymes with the word *cake* or to find the word that tells the color of Mary's ball. From these types of questions could come the making of vocabulary cards for significant words in the previously dictated story. Based on Tanisha's individual needs these cards might contain pictures or other cues that would make it easier for Tanisha to recognize these words.

For more details about how a lesson would actually be implemented using a language experience approach, consult Barr and Johnson (1991).

Whole Language Approach

Whole language can best be discussed as a movement rather than an approach (Goodman, Goodman, & Hood, 1989; Gunning, 1992). Although the whole language movement shares principles of and draws upon the language experience approach, it is also strongly rooted in scientific understanding of how language works in human learning and thinking (Goodman, Smith, Meredith, & Goodman, 1987). This emphasis on how language is learned is the first planning step for the teacher. To assist teachers in their exploration of how language is learned, the following are brief descriptions of each of the seven conditions that Brown and Cambourne (1987) ascribe to oral language learning. The first condition is called *immersion* and involves having the student totally immersed in language, which includes reading and writing activities. The second condition involves the actual *demonstration* of literacy activities by the teacher. For example, teachers would provide opportunities for students to observe their teachers reading and writing. The premise behind this condition is that teachers would explain and show what they are doing so that students could see how and why people read and write. The third condition highlights the importance of having *high expectations* for the development of literacy skills. These high expectations need to be shared by parents and teachers.

The fourth condition centers on the importance of *empowering students* to structure some of the tasks that are planned for literacy development. The fifth condition emphasizes the benefit of *positive reinforcement* for a student's language development. The sixth condition focuses upon the fact that all language learning is *a complex task that requires time, effort, and points of regression as well as advancement.* The seventh condition stresses the need for *feedback* that is accepting, caring, patient, and specific.

As teachers ponder how these seven conditions of oral language learning can be transferred to the classroom to foster the development of reading and writing skills within a whole language approach, they should keep in mind that the whole language approach is not a prescribed program or method but rather an approach that is sensitive to the emerging knowledge base of how literacy is acquired. To learn more about how several teachers have planned reading instruction within a whole language approach, consult Altwerger, Edelsky, and Flores (1987) and Goodman, Goodman, and Hood (1989).

Recommendations

The following recommendations are suggested by the material discussed in this chapter:

1. Use the experiences of the students in your class to guide the selection of stories to be read.
2. Provide many opportunities throughout the school day for the application of newly taught words.
3. Expand the experiential background of your students by going on field trips, looking at films and pictures, reading stories, and engaging them in music and art activities.
4. Teach students to follow this sequence of steps when they come to a word that they cannot name:

   a. Read to the end of the sentence.
   b. If they are available, use picture clues.
   c. Sound out the word.
   d. Ask for help.

5. Provide opportunities for students to role-play material that they have been asked to read silently.
6. Supplement the basal reading approach with an emphasis on the whole language approach. To learn more about implementing the whole language approach in your school call 800–922–4474.
7. Teach questioning strategies to students with mental retardation because they may lack the ability to spontaneously self-question or monitor their own comprehension.
8. Use brainstorming as a technique to get students to think about and apply what they already know to material that is to be read.
9. After reading, use follow-up activities such as:

   a. Discussions that focus on both the content of what was read as well as the organization or writing style that the author used.
   b. Discussions that generate additional questions and ideas that go beyond what was read.
   c. Modeling how to retell what was read.

References

Adams, M. J. (1990). *Beginning to read: Thinking and learning about print.* Cambridge, MA: MIT Press.

Allington, R. L. (1980). Word frequency and contextual richness effects on word identification of educable mentally retarded children. *Education and*

Training of the Mentally Retarded, 15(2), 118–120.

Altwerger, B., Edelsky, C., & Flores, B. M. (1987). Whole language: What's new? *The Reading Teacher, 41,* 144–154.

Anderson, R. C. & Ortony, A. (1975). On putting apples into bottles: A problem of polysemy. *Cognitive Psychology, 7,* 167–181.

Ausubel, D. P. (1968). *Educational psychology: A cognitive view.* New York: Holt, Rinehart & Winston.

Ausubel, D. P. (1960). The use of advance organizers in the learning and retention of meaningful verbal material. *Journal of Educational Psychology, 51,* 267–272.

Ausubel, D. P. & Fitzgerald, D. (1961). The role of discriminability in meaningful verbal learning and retention. *Journal of Educational Psychology, 52,* 266–274.

Ausubel, D. P. & Youssef, M. (1963). Role of discriminability in meaningful parallel learning. *Journal of Educational Psychology, 54,* 331–336.

Barnes, B. R. & Clawson, E. U. (1975). Do advance organizers facilitate learning? Recommendations for further research based on an analysis of 32 students. *Review of Educational Research, 45,* 637–660.

Barr, R. & Johnson, B. (1991). *Teaching reading in the elementary schools.* New York: Longman.

Beck, I. L., Omanson, R. C., & McKeown, M. G. (1982). An instructional redesign of reading lessons: Effects on comprehension. *Reading Research Quarterly, 17*(4), 462–481.

Blackhurst, A. E. (1966). *Auditory learning of retarded adolescents in subsumption theory context.* Unpublished doctoral dissertation, University of Pittsburgh, Pittsburgh.

Blanchard, J. & Rottenberg, C. J. (1990). Hypertext and hypermedia: Discovering and creating meaningful learning environments. *The Reading Teacher, 43*(9), 656–661.

Bracken, B. A. (1992). *Multidimensional self-concept scale.* Austin, TX: PRO-ED.

Bransford, J. D. & Johnson, M. K. (1972). Contextual prerequisites for understanding: Some investigations of comprehension and recall. *Journal of Verbal Learning and Verbal Behavior, 11,* 717–726.

Brown, L. & Alexander, J. (1991). *Self-esteem index.* Austin, TX: PRO-ED.

Brown, H. & Cambourne, B. (1987). *Read and retell.* Portsmouth, NH: Heinemann.

Burns, P. C., Roe, B. D., & Ross, E. P. (1983). *Teaching reading in today's elementary schools.* Boston: Houghton Mifflin.

Cecil, N. L. (1990). Diffusing the trauma: An exit interview for remediated readers. *Journal for Affective Education, 10,* 27–32.

Cheek, E. H., Flippo, R. F., & Lindsey, J. D. (1989). *Reading for success in elementary schools.* Chicago: Holt, Rinehart & Winston.

Clymer, T. & Martin, P. M. (1976). *The dog next door and other stories.* Lexington, MA: Ginn.

Collins, C. (1991). Reading instruction that increases thinking abilities. *Journal of Reading, 34*(7), 510–516.

Coopersmith, S. (1982). *Coopersmith Self Esteem Inventories.* Palo Alto, CA: Center for Self Esteem Development.

Dahl, P. & Samuels, S. J. (1977). Teaching children to read using hypothesis-test strategies. *The Reading Teacher, 30,* 603–606.

Duffy, G. G. & Roehler, L. R. (1986). *Improving classroom reading instruction: A decision making approach.* New York: Random House.

Ekwall, E. E. (1986). *Ekwall reading inventory* (2d ed.). Boston: Allyn & Bacon.

Eldredge, J. L. (1990). Increasing the performance of poor readers in the third grade with a group assisted strategy. *Journal of Educational Research, 84*(2), 69–77.

Elgart, D. B. (1978). Oral reading, silent reading and listening comprehension: A comparative study. *Journal of Reading Behavior, 10,* 203–207.

Gillet, J. W. & Temple, C. (1994). *Understanding reading problems: Assessment and instruction* (4th ed.). New York: Harper Collins.

Goodman, K. S. (1976). Reading: A psycholinguistic guessing game. In H. Singer and R. Ruddell, (Eds.), *Theoretical models and processes of reading.* Newark, DE: International Reading Association.

Goodman, K. S., Goodman, Y. M., & Hood, W. J. (1989). *The whole language evaluation book.* Portsmouth, NH: Heinemann.

Goodman, K. S., Smith, E. B., Meredith, R., & Goodman, Y. M. (1987). *Language and thinking in school: A whole-language curriculum* (3rd ed.). New York: Richard C. Owen.

Gough, P. B., Alford, J. A., Jr., & Holley-Wilcox, P. (1981). Words and contexts. In O. J. L. Tzeng & H. Singer (Eds.), *Perception of print: Reading research in experimental psychology.* Hillsdale, NJ: Erlbaum.

Gunning, T. G. (1992). *Creating reading instruction for all children.* Boston: Allyn & Bacon.

Harris, A. & Sipay, E. R. (1985). *How to increase your reading ability* (8th ed.). New York: Longman.

Hollingsworth, P. M. & Hoover, K. H. (1991). *Elementary teaching methods.* Boston: Allyn & Bacon.

Johnson, M. K., Bransford, J. D., & Solomon, S. K. (1973). Memory for tacit implications of sentences. *Journal of Experimental Psychology, 98*(1), 203–205.

Karsh, K. G., Repp, A. C., & Lenz, M. W. (1990). A comparison of the task demonstration model and the standard prompting hierarchy in teaching word identification to persons with moderate retardation. *Research in Developmental Disabilities, 11*(4), 395–410.

Kennedy, E. C. (1981). *Methods in teaching developmental reading.* Illinois: F. E. Peacock Publishers, Inc.

Kintsch, W. (1972). Notes on the structure of semantic memory. In E. Tulving & W. Donaldson (Eds.), *Organization of memory.* New York: Academic Press.

Kirk, S. A., Gallagher, J. J., & Anastasiow, N. J. (1993). *Educating exceptional children* (7th ed.). Boston: Houghton Mifflin.

Langer, J. A. (1981). From theory to practice: A prereading plan. *Journal of Reading, 25*(2), 152–156.

Langer, J. A. & Nicolich, M. (1981). Prior knowledge and its effects on comprehension. *Journal of Reading Behavior, 13*, 375–378.

Lee, L. L. (1971). *Northwestern syntax screening text.* Evanston, IL: Northwestern University Press.

Lerner, J. W. (1985). *Learning disabilities: Theories, diagnosis, and teaching strategies* (4th ed.). Boston: Houghton Mifflin.

Linn, R. L. (1983). Testing and instruction: Links and distinctions. *Journal of Educational Measurement, 20*, 179–189.

Luftig, R. L. & Greeson, L. E. (1983). Effects of structural importance and idea saliency on discourse recall of mentally retarded and nonretarded pupils. *American Journal of Mental Deficiency, 87*(4), 414–421.

Luftig, R. L. & Johnson, R. E. (1982). Identification and recall of structurally important units in prose by mentally retarded learners. *American Journal of Mental Deficiency, 86*, 495–502.

Manzo, A. V. & Manzo, U. C. (1993). *Literacy disorders: Holistic diagnosis and remediation.* New York: Harcourt Brace Jovanovich.

Marsh, H. W. (1988). *Self-Description Questionnaire I and II.* San Antonio, TX: The Psychological Corporation.

Mayer, R. E. (1982). Assimilation theory versus schema theory: Building a better theory of meaningful learning. *Journal of Structural Learning, 7*, 75–80.

McLoughlin, J. A. & Lewis, R. B. (1994). *Assessing special students* (4th ed.). New York: Merrill/Macmillan.

McNinch, G. H. (1981). A method for teaching sight words to disabled readers. *The Reading Teacher, 35*, 269–272.

Neisworth, J. T. (1961). *Use of advance organizers with the educable mentally retarded.* Unpublished doctoral dissertation, University of Pittsburgh, Pittsburgh.

Norton, D. (1991). *Through the eyes of a child: An introduction to children's literature* (3rd ed.). New York: Merrill/Macmillan.

Oakan, R., Weiner, M., & Cromer, W. (1971). Identification, organization, and reading comprehension for good and poor readers. *Journal of Educational Psychology, 62*, 71–78.

Patberg, J., Dewitz, P., & Samuels, S. J. (1981). The effect of context on the size of the perceptual unit used in word recognition. *Journal of Reading Behavior, 13*, 33–48.

Pearson, P. D., Hansen, J., & Gordon, C. (1979). *The effect of background knowledge on young children's comprehension of explicit and implicit information* (Tech. Rep. No. 116). Champaign-Urbana: University of Illinois, Center for the Study of Reading.

Peleg, Z. R. & Moore, R. F. (1982). Effects of the advance organizer with oral and written presentation on recall and inference of EMR adolescents. *American Journal of Mental Deficiency, 86*(6), 621–626.

Pichert, J. W. & Anderson, R. C. (1977). Taking different perspectives on a story. *Journal of Educational Psychology, 69*, 309–315.

Polloway, E. A. & Patton, J. R. (1993). *Strategies for teaching learners with special needs.* New York: Merrill/Macmillan.

Raphael, T. E. (1986). Teaching question-answer relationships revisited. *The Reading Teacher, 39*(6), 516–523.

Raphael, T. E. (1984). Teaching learners about sources of information for answering comprehension questions. *Journal of Reading, 27,* 303–311.

Reis, E. M. (1989). Phonics and reading: Do we know what we're teaching? *Journal of Instructional Psychology, 16*(1), 51–54.

Reis, E. M. (1986). Advance organizers and listening comprehension in retarded and nonretarded individuals. *Education and Training of the Mentally Retarded, 21*(4), 245–251.

Reutzel, D. R. (1991). Understanding and using basal readers effectively. In B. L. Hayes (Ed.), *Effective strategies for teaching reading* (pp. 254–280). Boston: Allyn & Bacon.

Reutzel, D. R. & Cooter, R. B. Jr. (1988). Research implications for improving basal skill instruction. *Reading Horizons, 28,* 208–216.

Rumelhart, D. E. (1977). Understanding and summarizing brief stories. In D. LaBerge & J. Samuels (Eds.), *Basic processes in reading: Perception and comprehension.* Hillsdale, New Jersey: Erlbaum.

Schallert, D. L. (1976). Improving memory for prose: The relationship between depth of processing and context. *Journal of Verbal Learning and Verbal Behavior, 15,* 621–632.

Schumaker, J. B., Denton, P. H., Deschler, D. D. (1984). *The paraphrasing strategy* (*Learning Strategies Curriculum*). Lawrence: University of Kansas.

Searfoss, L. W. (1993). Assessing classroom environments. In S. Glazer & C. Brown (Eds.), *Portfolios and beyond: Collaborative assessment in reading and writing* (pp. 11–26). Norwood, MA: Christopher-Gordon.

Searfoss, L. W. & Readence, J. E. (1994). *Helping children learn to read* (3rd ed.). Boston: Allyn & Bacon.

Sing, N. N. & Singh, J. (1988). Increasing oral reading proficiency through over correction and phonic analysis. *American Journal of Mental Deficiency, 93*(3), 312–319.

Spache, G. D. & Spache, E. B. (1977). *Reading in the elementary school.* Boston: Allyn & Bacon.

Spilich, G. J., Vesonder, G. T., Chiesi, H. L., & Voss, J. F. (1979). Text processing of domain-related information for individuals with high and low domain knowledge. *Journal of Verbal Learning and Verbal Behavior, 18,* 275–290.

Taylor, D. & Strickland, D. S. (1986). *Family storybook reading.* Portsmouth, NH: Heinemann.

Thomson, M. E. & Hartley, G. M. (1980). Self-concept in dyslexic children. *Academic Therapy, 16,* 19–36.

Tierney, R. J., Readence, J. E., & Dishner, E. K. (1990). *Reading strategies and practices: A compendium* (3rd ed.). Boston: Allyn & Bacon.

Wattenberg, W. W. (1964). Relation of self-concepts to beginning achievement in reading. *Child Development, 35,* 461–467.

Webb, M. & Schwartz, W. (1988). Children teaching children: A good way to learn. *PTA Today,* 16–17.

Weisberg, R. (1979). A comparison of good and poor readers' ability to comprehend explicit and implicit information in short stories based on two modes of presentation. *Research in the Teaching of English, 18,* 337–351.

Winograd, P. & Johnson, P. (1980). *Comprehension monitoring and the error detection paradigm* (Tech. Rep. No. 153). Champaign-Urbana: University of Illinois, Center for the Study of Reading.

Wood, J. W. (1992). *Adapting instruction for mainstream and at-risk students* (3rd ed.). Columbus, OH: Macmillan.

Woods, M. L. & Moe, A. J. (1981). *Analytical reading inventory.* Columbus, OH: Merrill.

C h a p t e r *13*

Number Skills and Arithmetic

Most individuals with mental retardation can acquire a useful repertoire of counting and arithmetic skills to apply in their everyday lives. In fact, arithmetic has been identified as an area of relative strength for them. Research evidence indicates that the arithmetic computation performance of individuals with mental retardation is generally comparable to that of their nonretarded equal-MA counterparts (e.g., Noffsinger & Dobbs, 1970; Vitello, 1976). It is only in the solution of word problems that deep and pervasive deficits emerge. However, recent research suggests that these deficits are more likely attributable to the language comprehension demands of the problems than to their computational requirements (e.g., Cruickshank, 1948; Bilsky & Judd, 1986).

The first part of this chapter considers theoretical issues, assessment options, curriculum models, and instructional approaches. The second part focuses upon basic match skills—early number skills, counting, and arithmetic computation. The emphasis in the third part is upon the solution of verbal math problems, or word problems. Applied math skills, such as money use, are the focus of the fourth part. Recommendations are presented in the final section.

The Instruction of Math Skills

Over the past twenty years, information processing theory and research has illuminated many of the processes involved in mathematics learning and instruction. Although information processing approaches have been applied to all areas of cognition, their application to arithmetic computation and problem solving has been particularly fruitful in yielding theoretical frameworks and models that capture the scope and sequence of skill acquisition.

Information Processing Theory

Arithmetic Computation
The information processing literature contains a growing number of useful models explicating various processes involved in arithmetic computation (e.g., Ashcraft & Battaglia, 1978; Carpenter, 1985; Fuson, 1982; Groen & Parkman, 1972; Mayer, 1985; Pellegrino & Goldman, 1987). One such model suggests that the successful performance of arithmetic tasks requires the learner to draw upon two types of knowledge: declarative and procedural (e.g., Ashcraft, 1982; Pellegrino & Goldman, 1987). Declarative knowledge consists of math facts that appear to be stored in a memory network. Procedural knowledge consists of methods or routines for performing specific types of tasks. The degree to which a child relies upon each type of knowledge shifts as the child becomes more proficient. During the early acquisition of addition and subtraction skills, children rely almost exclusively on procedural knowledge. Initially the application of this procedural knowledge is slow and effortful. The nature of the procedural knowledge also shifts from simple strategies for counting physical objects to more sophisticated mental addition and subtraction routines. Eventually, older children and adults acquire a repertoire of math facts that they can retrieve rapidly and automatically in response to most basic addition and subtraction demands. At this point, they can rely primarily on declarative knowledge, leaving their attentional

resources available for more complex task demands, such as borrowing in multicolumn subtraction problems.

Arithmetic Word Problems

Information processing research and theory has also shed light on the processes involved in the solution of word problems. Studies have shown that the difficulty of arithmetic word problems varies largely as a function of their comprehension demands (e.g., Bilsky & Judd, 1986; Greeno & Riley, 1987; Threadgill-Sowder, 1985). Most current models of arithmetic word problem solving divide the process into at least two major stages: problem comprehension/representation and problem solution (e.g., Baroody, 1987; Briars & Larkin, 1984; Greeno & Riley, 1987; Kintsch & Greeno, 1985; Mayer, 1985). The problem comprehension stage involves translation of the problem text into a mental representation of the problem that sets it up for solution. Computational strategies are then applied to generate a solution to the problem.

Assessment of Math Skills

The degree to which appropriate goals and objectives will be formulated is a function of the extent to which an accurate and fine-grained assessment of the individual's present repertoire of math skills can be accomplished. A fine-grained assessment of math skills requires, perhaps more than in any other area, a combination of formal and informal assessment procedures. Most of these procedures can be administered by either a teacher or an educational evaluator, depending upon the staffing pattern of a given school system.

Formal Assessment Procedures

The initial *screening* of math performance is most often accomplished by administering a standardized test of academic achievement. Many of these tests are appropriate for use with school-age children with mental retardation (see Compton, 1990; Salvia & Ysseldyke, 1991). However, the reading requirements and group administration procedures of some of the tests may render them inappropriate for many children with mental retardation. The *Peabody Individual Achievement Test–Revised* (PIAT-R) is an individually administered achievement test that may be useful with a wide range of students with mental retardation. The PIAT-R, applicable for grades K–12, can be administered by the classroom teacher in thirty to forty minutes. No reading is required for the Mathematics Subtest; problems are read to the student. The test spans a wide range of difficulty, from matching numbers to trigonometry. Both problem solving and computational skills are assessed (Compton, 1990). Of the many instruments available for use at the *diagnostic* phase of assessment, the *Key Math–Revised* has proved extremely useful for students with mental retardation. It spans a grade range from preschool to grade nine and can be administered by the classroom teacher in about an hour. It provides detailed diagnostic information in each of three areas: Basic Concepts, Operations, and Applications (Compton, 1990). Although information from tests such as the Key Math–R can provide assessment information to guide and monitor *educational programming*, the information that is most directly relevant to educational programming decisions often comes from the informal procedures described in the following section.

Informal Assessment Procedures

The application of information processing theory to the acquisition of math skills has resulted in a heightened appreciation of the significance of children's problem solving and computational errors. In the math area, informal assessment cannot be achieved through direct observations of behavior as it is in the self-care area. Rather it typically involves the sophisticated analysis of children's error patterns as a basis for effective individualized instruction. These error patterns, often referred to as "buggy" procedures (Brown & Burton, 1978; Burton, 1982), are systematic, consistent, procedural errors which result in, and can be inferred from, identifiable types of incorrect responses. According to Burton (1982), "bugs" can "be the result of deleting part of the correct procedure, of adding incorrect subprocedures, or of replacing correct subprocedures by incorrect ones" (p. 158). Burton gives the following example:

$$\begin{array}{r} 500 \\ -65 \\ \hline 565 \end{array}$$

It can be inferred that the student who solved the above problem was following a procedure that led him or her to write the bottom digit as the solution whenever the top digit was zero.

To make use of the rich information provided by students' errors, the scoring of math problems must go beyond judgments of correct or incorrect. Teachers who are skilled at identifying and analyzing error patterns to detect "buggy" procedures have a powerful informal assessment tool that can go a long way toward enabling effective instruction and remediation. Ashlock (1990), in a useful programmed text, provides instruction and practice in identifying and analyzing common error patterns in arithmetic computations.

The Math Curriculum

Although the math skills area may at first appear to represent a straightforward application of the academic curriculum model, this model is rarely applied in its purest form with individuals with mental retardation. For students without disabilities, the application of a purely academic curriculum model usually means that students learn basic math skills primarily because they are prerequisites to the acquisition of higher-level math skills. For most students with mental retardation, however, the acquisition of higher-level math skills, like calculus and trigonometry, will not be a realistic goal. Instead, the value of basic math skills for these students will rest in their functional applications to everyday life. Thus, a strong functional or life skills orientation is almost always present in applications of an academic curriculum model with individuals with mental retardation. Although students with mild mental retardation are more likely to be exposed to an academic curriculum than are students at lower functioning levels, useful quantitative skills can be acquired by most persons with moderate and severe mental retardation. Following are two examples that illustrate possible differences in the scope and content of appropriate math curricula for students with moderate or severe mental retardation and for students with mild mental retardation.

McClennen and Harrington (1982) described a functional math curriculum that was based on experience with students with moderate and severe mental retardation and autism. Because of the limited language skills of the students, the curriculum was divided into two parts. The first part, the Perceptual Correspondence Curriculum, required no expressive language ability. It consisted of sixteen levels of tasks aimed at teaching the student to deal with objects, including placing them into sets, constructing identical sets, excluding extra items, completing partial sets, and constructing remembered sets, and the concepts of "one/many" and "more." The second part, the Numerical Correspondence Curriculum, required at least sign, picture board, or electronic communication ability. This part was composed of thirty-one skill levels, involving seriation, functional addition, subtraction, multiplication, and division, and understanding the concept of "less." Interactions with the students during the development of the curriculum led to very careful control of the language used. The components of this curriculum are summarized in Table 13-1.

Cawley and his colleagues have engaged in extensive curriculum development efforts (Cawley, Miller, & Carr, 1989) for students with mild disabilities, including both mental retardation and learning disabilities. Their efforts have culminated in a model, called the Interactive Unit, which is designed to guide instruction in math. The model provides for sixteen combinations of teacher/learner interactions, composed of four possible modes of teacher input (i.e., manipulate, display, say, write) and four possible modes of student output behavior (i.e., manipulate, identify, say, write). These interactive combinations can be applied with a wide range of activities and content. According to their model, the curriculum should include the following areas: counting, computation, and problem solving. The basic elements of this model are summarized in Table 13-2.

TABLE 13-1   Ten Recommended Components of a Math Curriculum for Students with Moderate and Severe Mental Retardation

Recommended Curriculum Components

1. Based on accurate assessment of present math skills

2. Based on accurate assessment of present conceptual level

3. Based on assessment designed to identify specific next steps in a developmental instructional sequence

4. Adjusts for possible language deficiency relative to conceptual level

5. Provides assessment-based teaching instructions

6. Stresses functional applications of math skills

7. Builds in training for generalization of skills to a variety of persons, settings, and language cues

8. Includes instruction in problem-solving strategies

9. Includes specific criteria for mastery with respect to functional use, generalization, and problem solving applications

10. Uses age-appropriate methods and materials

From McClennen & Harrington, 1982

TABLE 13-2   The Interactive Unit Model for Arithmetic Instruction

Student Output Modes	Teacher Input Modes			
	MANIPULATE	DISPLAY	SAY	WRITE
MANIPULATE				
IDENTIFY				
SAY				
WRITE				

From Cawley, J., Miller, J. and Carr, S., 1989, Arithmetic, in G. A. Robinson, J. R. Patton, E. A. Polloway and L. R. Sargeant (Eds.) *Best practices in mild mental disabilities*, pp. 67–85, Reston, VA: The Division on Mental Retardation of the Council for Exceptional Children.

Instructional Strategies

As in the other chapters of this book, the principles of effective teaching and general instructional strategies presented in Chapter 7 form the basis of successful teaching of math skills. An added challenge in the math area, as with other cognitive skills, is that many of the processes and routines involved in math computation and problem solving are not directly observable. Fortunately, as mentioned earlier, there is a body of research and theory that provides a detailed analysis of many of those processes and routines. That literature has provided a basis for systematic instruction in the application of effective computational and problem solving strategies. In the subsequent sections of this chapter, specific techniques for teaching these strategies will be discussed separately for basic math skills, word problem solving, and applied math skills. Prior to those discussions, three general approaches that have been used with considerable success across a variety of math tasks will be described. These approaches are peer tutoring, computer-assisted instruction (CAI), and self-instruction. Each of these approaches is relevant to a different stage of learning (see Chapter 7 for definitions of each of the stages). Peer tutoring is generally geared toward the acquisition of new skills. CAI is aimed at increasing mastery/fluency. Self-instruction is most effective at promoting maintenance and generalization.

Peer Tutoring

Research has generally supported the widely held belief that peer tutoring can be an extremely valuable tool in math instruction (an article by Britz, Dixon, and McLaughlin [1989] contains a useful review of this research). The term *peer tutoring* has been used loosely to describe a variety of situations where one student teaches another student. However, as Britz et al. have pointed out, there are at least two versions of this approach: (1) when an older student teaches a younger student (cross-age tutoring); and (2) when a student teaches a same-age peer (peer tutoring). The majority of studies in their review involved cross-age tutoring. Findings were generally positive for both types of tutoring, regardless of whether tutoring was used to replace or supplement regular math instruction.

Gains in math achievement were consistently observed for tutees, with affective and cognitive benefits sometimes reported for tutors as well. The research suggested that the degree to which the tutoring situation is structured and the extent of training for the tutors may be important factors in determining the effectiveness of peer and cross-age tutoring.

Positive outcomes were also reported in two studies in which students with mental retardation were tutored by children without mental retardation. Lancioni (1982) reported beneficial effects of tutoring on performance with addition, subtraction, multiplication, and division word problems when children with mild mental retardation were tutored by third and fourth graders without mental retardation. In a study by Vacc and Cannon (1991), children with moderate mental retardation were tutored by sixth grade students without mental retardation. Improvements were observed on the beginning math skills treated in the study, which included counting, using number words, and identifying the month and day of the week. In the *Case Study of Scott*, an illustration is provided of how a simplified version of the Vacc and Cannon approach could be applied to teach Scott, who has severe mental retardation, some quantitative skills to apply in his everyday life.

CASE STUDY: Scott (CA = 18–0, IQ = 33)

Scott's functional math instruction was supplemented with a cross-age tutoring program for a period of six weeks. Scott's tutor was Jamal, a fourteen-year-old student volunteer without disabilities from the local junior high school. In a training program based on Vacc and Cannon's (1991) procedures, Jamal was trained in various instructional activities, such as how to present the instructional tasks to Scott, how to prepare instructional materials, when and how to give positive, social reinforcement, how to handle any behavior problems, and how to record performance data.

On the basis of Scott's previously acquired quantitative skills, some beginning mathematical skills were targeted for instruction and taught by following a clear learning sequence. For example, Jamal taught Scott to identify number words before matching them to their respective numerals (a previously learned skill). Jamal implemented the instructional activities in their predetermined sequence. Over the entire tutoring period, he consistently recorded the number of correct and incorrect responses made by Scott, including the specific items he missed during each tutoring session. At the end of the tutoring program, improvements in Scott's basic mathematical skills as well as his interpersonal competence were documented. Both Scott and Jamal reported that they had enjoyed working with each other.

Computer Assisted Instruction

It has long been known by good teachers that extensive drill and practice facilitates the rapid recall of basic math facts (e.g., 2 + 2 = 4). This common teacher observation is readily explained in terms of information processing theory which posits that, as the retrieval of basic math facts becomes rapid and automatic, attentional/information processing resources are freed to attend to the more complex aspects of problem solving, such as comprehension of the verbal statements and questions in word problems. If the math facts do not become automatic, then the cumbersome burden of computing the number combination each time it is encountered can reduce the amount of a person's finite information processing capacity available for solving word problems and performing daily living tasks involving numerical computation. Computer-assisted instruction (CAI) offers a practical way to provide the large amounts of individualized drill and practice that may be required to achieve automaticity of math facts for children with mental retardation (Podell, Tournaki-Rein, & Lin, 1992). If well designed, it can be highly motivating and fun. However, research has indicated that the effectiveness of CAI depends upon the attainment of certain prerequisites prior to the introduction of the computerized drill and practice activities. Hasselbring, Goin, and Bransford (1988) found that in order for CAI drill and practice to be effective, children must already be able to retrieve the relevant math facts from memory. Even extensive practice was ineffective if the children were still using counting strategies to compute the answers to the problems. Similarly, McCollister, Burts, Wright, and Hildreth (1986) reported that CAI was more effective than teacher-assisted instruction for teaching numeral recognition to children with good beginning knowledge, but that the opposite was true for children with poor beginning knowledge. The *Case Study of Tony* is included to show how CAI might be employed within a math instructional program.

CASE STUDY: Tony (CA = 16–0, IQ = 65)

Tony received computer-assisted instruction (CAI) training aimed at developing automaticity on certain previously acquired math facts. A CAI program with a drill-and-practice type instructional format was selected to provide repeated practice on skills for which Tony had already acquired a preliminary understanding. For example, the software package, *Arcademic Skill Builders in Math* (Chaffin & Maxwell, 1982) was used to strengthen Tony's ability to retrieve basic arithmetic facts. The program uses a game format with fast action and colorful graphics to provide practice with arithmetic facts. The teacher and/or student can change the parameters of the game to increase or decrease the task demands in terms of speed, problem difficulty, and game duration.

Tony's teacher taught him how to operate the computer and how to use the program. Now, Tony enjoys working independently on his counting skills with this interactive CAI program.

Self-Instruction

Leon and Pepe (1983) reported the successful application of self-instructional training in teaching arithmetic computation to students who were classified as having learning disabilities and mild mental retardation. The nine- to twelve-year-old students received daily fifteen-minute training sessions for seven weeks. The training was based upon Meichenbaum and Goodman's (1969, 1971) model and incorporated the following steps:

1. Modeling of overt self-instruction by the teacher
2. Overt self-instruction by the student with teacher guidance

3. Overt self-instruction by the student with monitoring by the teacher
4. Whispered self-instruction by the student with monitoring by the teacher
5. Covert self-instruction by the student

Both posttest and generalization performance were superior for the self-instruction group compared with a comparison group who received systematic instruction.

Murphy, Bates, and Anderson (1984) used the following self-instruction training sequence to improve the ability of preschool children with disabilities to count out ten objects:

1. Observation by the student with the researcher talking out loud while performing the task
2. Performance of the task by the student with the researcher overtly stating the instructions
3. Performance of the task by the student while he or she overtly self-instructs with minimal prompting
4. Fading of the student's self-instruction from quieter speech to private speech

Using a multiple baseline design, eight of the nine subjects improved. Generalization to functional objects and maintenance after six months were also reported.

Successful applications of self-instruction to teach addition and/or subtraction strategies to children with mental retardation were reported by Albion and Salzberg (1982) and Johnston, Whitman, and Johnson (1980). The *Case Study of Juan* is included to provide an example of a self-instruction sequence.

CASE STUDY: Juan (CA = 9–0, IQ = 55)

A self-instructional training program that incorporates the various steps suggested by Meichenbaum and Goodman (1969, 1971) was introduced to strengthen Juan's weight-discrimination skills, such as "heavy" and "light." Juan's program included the following steps:

Step 1. On presenting two objects, Juan's teacher says, "Point to the heavy one." The teacher points to the heavy object and says, "This is the heavy one," while Juan silently observes the teacher perform the task. The same sequence is repeated with the light object.

Step 2. On presenting the two objects, Juan's teacher says, "Point to the heavy one." The teacher points to the heavy object and says, "This is the heavy one." Juan imitates the teacher, pointing to the heavy object and saying, "This is the heavy one." The same sequence is repeated with the light object.

Step 3. On being presented with the two objects, Juan says aloud, "Point to the heavy one." Juan points to the heavy object and says, "This is the heavy one." The teacher observes silently and prompts only if Juan makes a mistake. The same sequence is repeated with the light object.

CASE STUDY: Juan (continued)

Step 4. On being presented with the two objects, Juan whispers, "Point to the heavy one." Juan points to the heavy object and whispers to himself, "This is the heavy one." The teacher silently observes and prompts only if Juan makes a mistake. The same sequence is repeated with the light object.

Step 5. On being presented with the two objects, Juan says to himself silently, "Point to the heavy one." Juan points to the heavy object and says to himself silently, "This is the heavy one." The teacher silently observes and prompts only if Juan makes a mistake. The same sequence is repeated with the light object.

Basic Math Skills

Acquisition of a variety of informal number skills precedes the acquisition of formal computational skills. The next section, which examines the development of some of these basic skills, is followed by a section on the acquisition of computational skills and strategies.

Early Number Skills

Prior to the recent spate of theory and research on basic math skills, initial instruction in counting and arithmetic was often based on absorption theory. According to Baroody (1987), this view assumed that the child entered school without any useful knowledge of mathematics and that an array of facts and skills would have to be taught and memorized. Baroody (1987) went on to point out that cognitive theory, on the other hand, posits that new information must be related to and integrated with preexisting knowledge structures (p. 9). Much of the recent research on the acquisition of math skills has been conducted from the perspective of cognitive/information processing theory and generally has been supportive of that orientation. In fact, there is considerable evidence that, before they ever enter school, children without disabilities possess a variety of mathematical skills and understandings. For example, Baroody and Ginsburg (1982) described four informal number skills that have been observed in preschool children.

Counting Words. By the time most children enter kindergarten, they are able to count to at least ten, with many children counting to fifteen or twenty. The numbers from one to twelve are acquired primarily by rote memorization, while acquisition of the numbers beyond ten involves the application of simple rules.

Enumeration. By kindergarten age, most children can count up to five objects and about half can count up to twenty objects. Enumeration involves labeling each object with one counting word.

The Cardinality Rule. Children who have acquired the cardinality rule understand that the final counting word indicates the number of items in a set. Baroody and Ginsburg

(1982) reported that of children entering kindergarten, 86 percent always applied the cardinality rule and 14 percent applied it correctly half the time with sets of one to five items.

Quantitative Comparison.   With sets of up to five, most children can determine the larger of two numbers by the time they enter kindergarten. Application of this rule involves knowing that the next number in a counting sequence is *more* than the one that precedes it.

Both Baroody and Ginsburg (1982) and McEvoy (1989) emphasized that mastery of these four skills is essential to the acquisition of the formal arithmetic skills taught in school. They advocate screening and remediation of any weaknesses before proceeding with formal instruction.

Unfortunately, it cannot be assumed that children with mental retardation will possess these basic number skills before they enter school or, in fact, that they will acquire them incidentally at any age (e.g., Baroody, 1986; Baroody & Snyder, 1983). Baroody (1986) surveyed groups of elementary-age and intermediate-age children with moderate and mild mental retardation on ten basic number skills which were commonly possessed by kindergarten children. He reported that the majority of children with moderate mental retardation had mastered only four of the ten skills, but that most of the children with mild mental retardation had mastered nine of the ten skills. Although Baroody did find that many of the children had acquired basic counting skills, it should be noted that he reported considerable variability within the groups. Also, the fact that the children in his study had already been in school for several years underscores the point that the acquisition of basic number skills prior to school entry cannot be taken for granted in children with mental retardation. Baroody advised that upon entry to school specific deficiencies should be carefully assessed. The possibility of successful remediation is supported by numerous studies which have demonstrated that basic number skills can be taught effectively to children with mild and moderate mental retardation (e.g., Brown, Bellamy, & Gadberry, 1971; Grimm, Bijou, & Parsons, 1973).

Computational Skills and Strategies

Developmental Trends in Strategy Acquisition

Cognitive theory on the development of arithmetic computational skills has been influenced by two well-known theories on how adults solve addition and subtraction problems. According to Groen and Parkman's (1972) "min" model, adults solve addition problems by counting up from the larger of the two addends. Ashcraft's (1982) "fact retrieval" model, on the other hand, specified that adults retrieve problem solutions from a mental network of math facts. Although Groen and Parkman's counting model fits the performance of first graders better than Ashcraft's model, Ashcraft's retrieval model was more able to account for the performance of fourth graders through adults (Ashcraft, 1982; Hamann & Ashcraft, 1985). Hamann and Ashcraft's findings with first through tenth graders suggested that by fourth grade, the memory network contains most of the basic whole-number facts stored as declarative knowledge and available for retrieval. Also by fourth grade, there was evidence that procedural knowledge, such as estimation and carrying routines, was beginning to establish itself in memory. Retrieval of procedural knowledge was more rapid in seventh and tenth graders, presumably a reflection of increasing automaticity. This research suggests a general developmental shift from reliance on counting strategies to reliance on retrieval strategies. However, it did not provide information on individual differences in performance within age groups.

Siegler and Shrager (1984) proposed that even children as young as four and five years old employ a variety of strategies in their efforts to solve addition and subtraction problems and that they choose strategies to match the difficulty level of the problem. They identified four strategies:

1. *Counting Fingers Strategy.* This strategy involved raising fingers to correspond to each addend and then counting them.
2. *Fingers Strategy.* This strategy involved raising fingers to correspond to each addend, but not counting them.
3. *Counting Strategy.* This strategy involved moving the lips or counting aloud.
4. *Retrieval Strategy.* This strategy involved recalling problem solutions from memory.

According to Siegler and Shrager's strategy choice model, the child first attempts to retrieve the correct answer to the problem. If those attempts are unsuccessful, the child will employ a counting strategy. Research support for this model was reported by Geary and Burlingham-Dubree (1989) who investigated its predictions with preschool and kindergarten children. Both studies reported that the "fingers" strategy was rarely used, but that many children used the "retrieval strategy" on easy problems and one of the counting strategies, either "fingers counting" or "counting," on difficult problems.

Other research has focused upon the variations among counting strategies. The earliest strategy to emerge developmentally has been referred to as the "concrete counting all" strategy. It involves using fingers or objects to count the items in one addend and then the other. Even this simple strategy was not employed spontaneously by the kindergarten children in Baroody's (1987) study. However, most could apply it after one or more demonstrations. With repeated practice, children went on to apply concrete counting strategies involving shortcuts, like beginning to count with the number in the larger addend. Eventually, some children made the transition to retrieval-based mental arithmetic strategies.

The strategies used in subtraction problems are similar to those used in addition problems. Children usually begin with a "counting down" strategy that is somewhat difficult to apply. Eventually, they tend to shift to an easier-to-apply "counting up" strategy (Baroody, 1984). Young children have been aided in making the transition from basic to more sophisticated strategies by learning to use one-handed finger patterns for both addition (Fuson & Secada, 1986) and subtraction (Fuson & Willis, 1988).

There is evidence that, as early as third grade, multiplication performance is based primarily upon the retrieval of information from long-term memory. Attempts to explain multiplication processes solely in terms of counting strategies have not generally been supported by research findings (e.g., Koshmider & Ashcraft, 1991). It is not surprising, therefore, that intervention strategies that have been associated with improvements in multiplication performance have emphasized drill and practice (e.g., Beattie & Algozzine, 1982; Ogletree & Ujlaki, 1976).

Strategy Deficits

According to Kirby and Becker (1988), research has suggested three possible sources of learning problems in arithmetic. The first possibility is the slow or inefficient encoding of the numbers in the problem. Another potential source of difficulty is the failure to select a correct strategy or problem-solving operation (e.g., addition or subtraction). The third possibility is the inefficient execution of the operation. Kirby and Becker (1988) conducted a study to determine the relative importance of these three sources of difficulty in the addition and subtraction performance of three groups of fifth-grade children, a group with arithmetic problems and two control groups (an average-achieving group and a group with reading problems). Kirby and Becker's study was based on a model of single-digit addition and subtraction (e.g., $2 + 3 = 5$) performance with the following components (p. 9):

- Encode first number
- Select operation
- Encode second number
- Execute operation (add or subtract)
- Encode given answer
- Compare calculated answer with given answer and respond

The results of Kirby and Becker's study indicated no significant differences among the three groups on either the encoding of numbers or the selection of the correct strategy or operation. However, the operational efficiency of the children with arithmetic problems was inferior to that of the other two groups. In other words, they were slow and inefficient at executing the selected operation. It was suggested that they had not sufficiently automatized the basic operations. The authors emphasized that this inefficiency with basic operations could greatly interfere with the execution of more complex problem-solving tasks. They recommended systematic practice, made as enjoyable as possible, with appropriate algorithms.

Fleischner, Garnett, and Shepherd (1982) compared children with and without learning disabilities between eight and twelve years old on their proficiency with addition, subtraction, and multiplication facts. They reported that the children with disabilities were less proficient than the children without disabilities, especially with respect to computation speed. Fleischner et al. suggested that the computational performance of the students with learning disabilities was less accurate and less automatized than that of the students without learning disabilities.

The above findings are consistent with Pellegrino and Goldman's (1987) observation that children with math disabilities are more likely than children without math disabilities to depend on counting strategies, as opposed to retrieval strategies, to solve basic arithmetic problems. In other words, it appears that in children with math difficulties, the shift from reliance on procedural to declarative knowledge is either delayed or impaired.

Although none of the above studies involved children with mental retardation, the findings of these studies suggest that inefficiency or lack of automaticity should be considered as possible sources of computational difficulty for these children as well. If basic math facts cannot be retrieved automatically, the need to allocate processing capacity to their calculation can interfere with the performance of complex math tasks. Hasselbring, Goin, and Bransford (1987) propose that increased emphasis be placed on teaching children with learning difficulties to "move from effortful computations to automatic retrieval of basic facts" (p. 31). They suggest the following four steps:

1. Assess the current extent of automaticity.
2. Build upon present knowledge.
3. Focus upon a limited set of facts until the student can retrieve them from memory.
4. Use "challenge times" by gradually reducing the retrieval time allowed.

After these four steps have been completed, math facts that have been mastered and can be retrieved within the "challenge time" can be added to the child's daily drill-and-practice materials. As noted earlier, the effectiveness of computer-assisted instruction and other drill-and-practice activities is determined by whether the math facts being practiced can be retrieved from memory. Practice is not beneficial if counting procedures must be applied to generate the answer. Baroody's (1988) research suggests that *practice* is not a sufficient explanatory mechanism for developmental changes in mental arithmetic proficiency. Rather, his findings point to sudden qualitative changes in learning as children acquire an understanding of relationships that allows them to solve a whole class of problems.

Estimation Skills

Sowder (1989) reports that although the teaching of computational estimation is often emphasized, estimation is a complex skill that may be beyond the reach of most children until they reach the age of eleven or twelve. True estimation has at least two components: mental arithmetic computation and approximation. Many individuals with mental retardation may not be able to acquire a complete and flexible repertoire of estimation skills. However, as Sowder suggests for children younger than age eleven, it may still be appropriate to teach them tasks involving one of the two components, which are useful skills in and of themselves and which can then provide a basis for the acquisition of full estimation skills wherever possible.

Solving Word Problems

The solution of arithmetic word problems is a major stumbling block for individuals with mental retardation. Studies have shown that even adolescents with mild mental retardation, who have been equated with children without mental retardation on mental age and computational performance, are significantly inferior in their ability to solve word problems. Although this deficiency was first noted by Cruickshank in 1948, systematic follow-up investigations were not reported until much later (Bilsky & Judd, 1986; Friedman, 1991; Judd & Bilsky, 1989; Narayanan, 1983). In all of these studies, sizable performance discrepancies on addition and subtraction word problems were found between adolescents with mild mental retardation and children without mental retardation of comparable MA and computational ability. Bilsky and Judd (1986) reported average performance of approximately 66 percent correct for the children without mental retardation in their study and 43 percent correct for the adolescents with mental retardation. Judd and Bilsky (1989), with a set of problems that was less difficult overall, reported an average of 87 percent correct for children without mental retardation as opposed to 70 percent correct for adolescents with mental retardation. Narayanan (1983) reported accuracy rates of approximately 62 percent and 38 percent correct for students with and without mental retardation, respectively. Friedman (1991) reported 87 percent correct for the children without mental retardation participating in her study and 59 percent correct for the adolescents with mild mental retardation. These performance differences are summarized in Table 13-3.

In order to identify possible sources of the verbal problem-solving difficulty experienced by individuals with mental retardation, it is useful to view the problem-solving process in the context of a theoretical model. Although several detailed models of the process have been proposed (e.g., Baroody, 1987; Briars & Larkin, 1984; Greeno & Riley, 1987; Kintsch & Greeno, 1985; Mayer, 1985), most of them seem to point to some version of these two major components: problem comprehension/representation and problem solution. Problem comprehension/representation involves understanding what is being asked for by the text of the problem and translating the text into a mental representation of the problem that sets it up for solution. Problem solution involves applying counting or retrieval strategies to solve the problem.

In light of this general theoretical framework, research studies pointing to possible sources of the word problem-solving deficit in persons with mental retardation are examined in the next section. That section is followed by a brief discussion of several additional factors that affect problem solving difficulty for students with and without mental retardation.

Possible Sources of the Word Problem-Solving Deficit

Available research has implicated the problem comprehension/representation component as the primary source of the marked word problem-solving deficit manifested by persons with mental retardation (e.g., Bilsky & Judd, 1986; Judd & Bilsky, 1989). This conclusion is based on the findings of studies that examined the effects of variations of the problem-solving task on solution accuracy. The task variations that differentially affected the performance of students with and without mental retardation were those most directly reflecting problem comprehension and the ease with which the problem could be set up

TABLE 13-3 **Percent of Correct Responses on Addition and Subtraction Word Problems by Adolescents with Mild Mental Retardation and Children without Mental Retardation with Comparable MA and Computational Skill**

	Percent Correct	
Study	**Adolescents with Mental Retardation**	**Children without Mental Retardation**
Bilsky and Judd, 1986	43	66
Friedman, 1991	59	87
Judd and Bilsky, 1989	70	87
Narayanan, 1983	38	62

for solution. In fact, recent evidence suggests that a training program that combines an emphasis on problem comprehension with general case instruction can be highly effective at teaching persons with mental retardation to expand their word problem-solving skills (Frisch, 1989).

To date, the task variations yielding possible sources of the word problem-solving deficit have involved characteristics of the problem text, in particular problem type and problem context, which are discussed in the following paragraphs.

Problem Type

Numerous classification schemes have been devised to characterize the range of possible textual presentations of addition and subtraction word problems. An example of the problem classification scheme proposed by Riley, Greeno, and Heller (1983) is presented in Table 13-4. Bilsky and Judd (1986) reported differences in difficulty between "change" and "combine" problems (see Table 13-4 for sample problems). for adolescents with mental retardation, but not for equal-MA children without mental retardation. Although the problems in their study were designated "dynamic" and "static" in accordance with Nesher and Katriel's (1978) terminology, for the sake of consistency, the Riley et al. terminology is used in the present discussion. Combine problems, which involve combining (or subtracting) quantities from different sets, were more difficult for the adolescents with mental retardation than were change problems, which involve an action causing a change in quantity. It was suggested that they may have had difficulty understanding and constructing semantic representations of the combine problems. According to Briars and Larkin's model of arithmetic problem solving, change problems can be represented and solved simply by following the action in the problem. However, combine problems require rerepresentation to set them up for solution. This suggests that problem representation may be a stumbling block in the word problem solving of individuals with mental retardation, especially with problems that cannot readily be represented for solution in a straightforward way.

Problem Context

In addition to their quantitative differences, word problems differ in their story contexts. In the Judd and Bilsky (1989) study, problem solving accuracy was affected by problem context for students with mental retardation, but not for students without mental retardation. The students with mental retardation had particular difficulty with abstract, or intangible, contexts like "miles run" and "hours worked." Problems with concrete contexts, like "pens given" and "candy sold" were significantly easier to solve. This finding suggested that individuals with mental retardation may not be adept at applying a strategy labeled the "generalization operator" posited by van Dijk and Kintsch (1983). According to their theory, proficient problem solvers strip problems of any narrative details that are irrelevant to setting up the quantitative relationships in the problem for solution. If the generalization operator is being applied consistently, problem context should not affect problem difficulty. The Judd-Bilsky findings suggested that the students with mental retardation may have been distracted by the narrative context of the problem. Explicit instruction on how and when to apply the generalization operator may facilitate problem comprehension for individuals with mental retardation. However, this suggestion must be viewed as highly speculative. The fact that the Judd-Bilsky finding was not replicated in a more recent study in which Friedman (1991)

TABLE 13-4 Four Classes of Word Problems*

Types of Word Problems

Action	Static

Action

CHANGE

Result Unknown

1. Joe had 3 marbles. Then Tom gave him 5 more marbles. How many marbles does Joe have now?

2. Joe had 8 marbles. Then he gave 5 marbles to Tom. How many marbles does Joe have now?

Change Unknown

3. Joe had 3 marbles. Then Tom gave him some more marbles. Now Joe has 8 marbles. How many marbles did Tom give him?

4. Joe had 8 marbles. Then he gave some marbles to Tom. Now Joe has 3 marbles. How many marbles did he give to Tom?

Start Unknown

5. Joe had some marbles. Then Tom gave him 5 more marbles. Now Joe has 8 marbles. How many marbles did Joe have in the beginning?

6. Joe had some marbles. Then he gave 5 marbles to Tom. Now Joe has 3 marbles. How many marbles did Joe have in the beginning?

EQUALIZE

1. Joe has 3 marbles. Tom has 8 marbles. What could Joe do to have as many marbles as Tom? (How many marbles does Joe need to have as many as Tom?)

2. Joe has 8 marbles. Tom has 3 marbles. What could Joe do to have as many marbles as Tom?

Static

COMBINE

Value Unknown

1. Joe has 3 marbles. Tom has 5 marbles. How many marbles do they have altogether?

Subset Unknown

2. Joe and Tom have 8 marbles altogether. Joe has 3 marbles. How many marbles does Tom have?

COMPARE

Difference Unknown

1. Joe has 8 marbles. Tom has 5 marbles. How many marbles does Joe have more than Tom?

2. Joe has 8 marbles. Tom has 5 marbles. How many marbles does Tom have less than Joe?

Compared Quality Unknown

3. Joe has 3 marbles. Tom has 5 marbles more than Joe. How many marbles does Tom have?

4. Joe has 8 marbles. Tom has 5 marbles less than Joe. How many marbles does Tom have?

Referent Unknown

5. Joe has 8 marbles. He has 5 more marbles than Tom. How many marbles does Tom have?

6. Joe has 5 marbles. He has 3 marbles less than Tom. How many marbles does Tom have?

*From Riley, M. S., Greeno, J. G., & Heller, J. I. (1983). Development of children's problem-solving ability in arithmetic. In H. P. Ginsburg (Ed.), *The development of mathematical thinking ability*. (p. 160). New York: Academic Press.

compared tangible, intangible, and stripped problems, leaves open some important questions. Further research will be needed to identify the variables which may interact with context to determine the extent to which the generalization operator will be needed and applied in the solution of word problems. Nevertheless, the above findings taken together do permit the tentative conclusion that the locus of the general word problem solving deficit in individuals with mental retardation is more likely to be found in the comprehension/representation phase of problem solving than in the problem solution phase. It is essential, therefore, that problem-solving instruction for individuals with mental retardation give careful attention to strategies for maximizing comprehension of the problem text.

Factors Affecting Word Problem Difficulty

The factors discussed in the following paragraphs have been found to affect problem difficulty similarly for individuals with and without mental retardation.

Mode of Presentation

The reading difficulties commonly experienced by individuals with mental retardation can introduce another dimension of difficulty to word problem tasks. By conducting problem-solving instruction with orally presented problems, this source of difficulty can be bypassed so that instruction can be targeted upon essential problem-solving skills. Oral presentation has the added advantage of more closely resembling the real-life problem-solving situations most likely to be encountered by individuals with mental retardation, most of whom have limited reading competence (Bilsky, 1985). For these reasons, the Bilsky and Judd (1986) and the Judd and Bilsky (1989) studies were conducted with orally presented problems.

Memory Aids

With oral presentation of word problems, it is necessary to consider the role of memory in the problem-solving process. During problem solution, key information must be extracted from the problem and held in working memory until a semantic representation of the problem is constructed and the necessary computations have been carried out. The memory demands of problem solving are exacerbated with oral presentation because it is not possible to scan back over the problem for forgotten information. In view of the frequently cited memory deficits manifested by individuals with mental retardation (e.g., Detterman, 1979), Bilsky and Judd (1986) and Judd and Bilsky (1989) examined the effects of memory aids on problem-solving performance. Bilsky and Judd found that presenting each problem twice led to significantly more correct responses on addition and subtraction problems than presenting each problem once for both adolescents with mild mental retardation and fourth-grade children without mental retardation. Clear-cut benefits were not obtained for aids aimed at facilitating the recall of the specific quantities mentioned in the problems. Bilsky and Judd reported that neither group made consistent use of numeral cards that were available to them during problem solution. Similarly, Judd and Bilsky reported that neither numerals nor dots presented on a computer screen facilitated the performance of students with and without mental retardation.

Operation

Most of the word problem-solving research with individuals with mental retardation has been conducted with single-digit addition and subtraction problems. Studies have consistently shown that subtraction is more difficult than addition, with the magnitude of this difference being greater for adolescents with mental retardation than for their equal-MA counterparts without mental retardation (Bilsky & Judd, 1986; Judd & Bilsky, 1989). These differences occurred in spite of the fact that participants had been screened for their ability to perform the computations required by the problems. Goodstein, Cawley, Gordon, and Helfgott (1971) offered a possible explanation of the subtraction difficulty of individuals with mental retardation in terms of a rote computational strategy consisting of a tendency to simply *add* all numbers in a word problem regardless of the text.

Cue Words

In problem-solving instruction, students are often encouraged to look for cue words, like "altogether" and "left," to help them solve the problem (e.g., McGlothlin, 1987). Goodstein (1973) has suggested that individuals with mental retardation may be overly dependent upon such cue words. Poor problem-solving performance can result if students rely so much upon these cue words that they are discouraged from trying to comprehend the overall meaning of the full problem text. Cue words taken out of context can be misleading. Judd and Bilsky (1989) and Narayanan (1983) reported that participants both with and without mental retardation were aided by appropriate cue words when they were available. However, when cue words were inappropriate (i.e., inconsistent with the rest of the text), the performance of individuals with and without mental retardation was impaired (Goodstein, 1973; Narayanan, 1983). Though cue words can facilitate performance in some situations, their use as instruction aids is not recommended. They can become a crutch that prevents the acquisition of strategies for problem representation that accurately and flexibly reflect the full meaning of the problem text.

Extraneous Information

On the basis of early studies involving only individuals with mental retardation, some investigators suggested that the inclusion of extraneous, or irrelevant, information in word problems creates particular difficulties for persons with mental retardation (e.g., Cruickshank, 1948; Goodstein, Cawley, Gordon, & Helfgott, 1971). However, more recently it was found that the presence of extraneous numbers similarly disrupts the performance of students without mental retardation (Bilsky & Judd, 1986). In fact, in the Bilsky and Judd study, the children without mental retardation made a greater proportion (53 percent) of their errors on problems with extraneous information than equal-MA adolescents with mental retardation (44 percent). Although these difficulties can be avoided by selecting problems without extraneous information, the important instructional implication of these findings is that both groups of students experience confusion with problem comprehension in the presence of misleading information much as they do in the presence of misleading cue words.

Applied Math Skills

The ultimate value of acquired math skills is determined by the extent to which they can be applied by an individual with mental retardation to enhance community participation. Many activities of daily living require some numerical skills. For example, independent use of the telephone requires the matching of digits from a phone number with the digits on the phone. The centrality of this requirement was emphasized in a study in which a thirty-six-year-old man with moderate mental retardation was taught independent use of the telephone (Lalli, Mace, Browder, & Brown, 1989). Similarly, cooking requires extensive use of numerical skills for measuring ingredients and setting and adjusting the oven temperature. Telling time and time management also rely upon an understanding of quantitative relationships (see Ford, Schnorr, Meyer, Davern, Black, & Dempsey, 1989, for a detailed curriculum sequence targeting these skills). The list of everyday activities requiring quantitative processing is, perhaps, infinite. However, the demand for some level of numerical competence is clearly most obvious with respect to the use of money. It is not surprising that the majority of research on the application of math skills has centered upon this activity.

Money Skills

Most available research focuses upon the use of coins or very small amounts of paper money. The sophisticated management of large amounts of money may be beyond the reach of many individuals with mental retardation. In fact, research suggests that even people with mental retardation who are living on their own in the community are likely to require assistance during times of financial crisis (e.g., Halpern, Close, & Nelson, 1986). This evidence notwithstanding, there is considerable potential for individuals with mental retardation to expand their repertoires of money management skills.

Several research studies have explored the coin use abilities of people with mental retardation. In an early study asking individuals with mental retardation to indicate their preference for various amounts of money, Blount (1967) noted considerable confusion, especially for the larger denominations used (i.e., a half dollar and one- and two-dollar bills). Even for the smaller denominations (i.e., pennies, dimes, nickels, and quarters), participants were often misled by the size or number of coins on display. A series of studies reported during the 1970s explored the feasibility of instructing people with mental retardation in the component skills of coin use. The equivalence of various combinations of coins was successfully taught to individuals with mental retardation both by using a teaching machine (Wundelich, 1972) and by modeling and reinforcement procedures (Trace, Cuvo, & Criswell, 1977). In a later study, Borakove and Cuvo (1976) compared two methods for teaching coin equivalence. They found that performance was superior when participants were allowed to move each coin during training as opposed to using a finger-counting method alone. Bellamy and Buttars (1975) reported a study in which adolescents with moderate mental retardation were taught a variety of counting skills and then successfully taught to apply them in counting coin combinations up to one dollar. In a study on coin names, Miller, Cuvo, and Borakove (1977) found that directly teaching the production of coin names facilitated comprehension, but teaching comprehension did not facilitate production.

Frank and McFarland (1980) developed and field-tested the effectiveness of a curriculum to teach coin skills to individuals with mental retardation. They reported that students exposed to their curriculum outperformed a control group and that one-to-one instruction was superior to group instruction. A revision of their coin skills curriculum (Frank & McFarland, 1988) provides detailed instructional sequences for coin naming, coin equivalence, coin summation, and coin selection for purchasing. The *Syracuse Community-Referenced Curriculum Guide* (Ford et al., 1989) provides three general money handling sequences. The *predetermined amount* sequence teaches the individual to make purchases by selecting an appropriate money envelope to make a specific purchase. The *money card* strategy teaches the individual to determine the affordability of an item by comparing available money to a money card. The most flexible strategy makes use of a *numberline* and *calculator*. Several research studies support the contention that the functional quantitative skills of individuals with mental retardation can be significantly expanded through training in calculator use (e.g., Horton, 1985; Koller & Mulhern, 1977; Mastropieri, Bakken, & Scruggs, 1991; Matson & Long, 1986).

Recommendations

The following recommendations are suggested by the material reviewed in this chapter:

1. For the screening and diagnostic assessment of arithmetic skills, standardized achievement and diagnostic tests are recommended. However, as a basis for individualized educational programming and remediation, teachers are advised to become proficient in the informal identification and interpretation of common error patterns.
2. The best framework for the arithmetic instruction of students with mental retardation will combine the features of academic and functional curriculum models.
3. Peer tutoring is an extremely useful technique for fostering the acquisition of math skills in students with mental retardation.
4. Once children have acquired the prerequisite ability to retrieve math computational facts from memory, computer-assisted instruction (CAI) is an effective way to improve fluency and automaticity.
5. Self-instructional routines are a highly effective way to promote the maintenance and generalization of acquired math skills.
6. Prior to formal instruction in computational skills, basic number skills should be assessed and any deficiencies remediated.
7. Computational instruction should guide students from primary reliance on counting strategies to the flexible and automatic application of fact retrieval strategies. Once retrieval strategies are in place, drill and practice should be provided, possibly through CAI, in order to minimize possible deficits in automaticity or efficiency that could interfere with the solution of more complex problems and applications.
8. Word problem-solving instruction for individuals with mental retardation should emphasize strategies to enhance comprehension of the problem and setting it up for solution.
9. Word problem-solving instruction for individuals both with and without mental retardation should incorporate the following features:

   • Practice with orally presented problems, with each problem presented at least twice
   • Additional instruction aimed at teaching strategies for knowing when to subtract, rather than add
   • Instructions encouraging comprehension of the full problem text and discouraging reliance on cue words

- Instruction on how to identify and ignore irrelevant information imbedded in word problems

10. The application of numerical and computational skills in community living activities (e.g., telling time, cooking, money use) should be emphasized in the curriculum for individuals with mental retardation.

References

Albion, F. M. & Salzberg, C. L. (1982). The effect of self-instructions on the rate of correct addition problems with mentally retarded children. *Education and Treatment of Children, 5*, 121–131.

Ashcraft, M. H. (1982). The development of mental arithmetic: A chronometric approach. *Developmental Review, 2*, 213–236.

Ashcraft, M. H. & Battaglia, J. (1978). Cognitive arithmetic: Evidence for retrieval and decision processes in mental addition. *Journal of Experimental Psychology: Human Learning and Memory, 4*, 527–538.

Ashlock, R. B. (1990). *Error patterns in computation: A semi-programmed approach* (5th ed.). Columbus, OH: Merrill.

Baroody, A. J. (1988). Mental addition development of children classified as mentally handicapped. *Educational Studies in Mathematics, 19*(3), 369–388.

Baroody, A. J. (1987). *Children's mathematical thinking*. New York: Teachers College Press.

Baroody, A. J. (1986). Counting ability of moderately and mildly handicapped children. *Education and Training of the Mentally Retarded, 21*(4), 289–300.

Baroody, A. J. (1984). The case of Felicia: A young child's strategies for reducing memory demands during mental addition. *Cognition and Instruction, 1*(1), 109–116.

Baroody, A. J. & Ginsburg, H. P. (1982). Preschoolers' informal mathematical skills. *American Journal of Diseases of Children, 136*, 195–197.

Baroody, A. J. & Snyder, P. M. (1983). A cognitive analysis of basic arithmetic abilities of TMR children. *Education and Training of the Mentally Retarded, 18*(40), 253–259.

Beattie, J. & Algozzine, B. (1982). Improving basic academic skills of educable mentally retarded adolescents. *Education and Training of the Mentally Retarded, 17*(3), 255–258.

Bilsky, L. H. (1985). Comprehension and mental retardation. In N. R. Ellis and N. Bray (Eds.), *International review of research in mental retardation, Vol. 13* (pp. 215–246). Orlando, FL: Academic Press.

Bilsky, L. H. & Judd, T. P. (1986). Sources of difficulty in the solution of verbal arithmetic problems by retarded and nonretarded individuals. *American Journal of Mental Deficiency, 90*, 395–402.

Blount, W. P. (1967). Naive male retardates and U.S. moneys: An exploratory study. *American Journal of Mental Deficiency, 72*, 487–491.

Borakove, L. S. & Cuvo, A. J. (1976). Facilitative effects of coin displacement on teaching coin summation to mentally retarded adolescents. *American Journal of Mental Deficiency, 81*, 350–356.

Briars, D. J. & Larkin, J. H. (1984). An integrated model of skills in solving elementary word problems. *Cognition and Instruction, 1*, 245–296.

Britz, M., Dixon, J., & McLaughlin, T. (1989). The effects of peer tutoring on mathematics performance: A recent review. *B.C. Journal of Special Education, 13*(1), 17–34.

Brown, L., Bellamy, T., & Gadberry, E. (1971). A procedure for the development and measurement of rudimentary quantitative concepts in low functioning trainable students. *Training School Bulletin, 68*, 178–185.

Brown, J. S. & Burton, R. R. (1978). Diagnostic models for procedural bugs in basic mathematical skills. *Cognitive Science, 2*, 155–192.

Burton, R. R. (1982). Diagnosing bugs in a simple procedural skill. In D. H. Sleeman & J. S. Brown (Eds.), *Intelligent tutoring systems* (pp. 157–183). London: Academic Press.

Carpenter, T. (1985). Learning to add and subtract: An exercise in problem solving. In E. A. Silver (Ed.), *Teaching mathematical problem solving: Multiple research perspectives*. Hillsdale, NJ: Erlbaum.

Cawley, J., Miller, J., & Carr, S. (1989). Arithmetic. In G. A. Robinson, J. R. Patton, E. A. Polloway, & L. R. Sargent (Eds.), *Best practices in mild mental disabilities* (pp. 67–85). Reston, VA: The Division on Mental Retardation of the Council for Exceptional Children.

Chaffin, J. & Maxwell, B. (1982). *Arcademic Skill Builders in Math*. Allen, TX: Developmental Learning Materials.

Compton, C. (1990). *A guide to 85 tests for special education*. Belmont, CA: Fearon Education.

Cruickshank, W. M. (1948). Arithmetic ability of mentally retarded children. II: Understanding arithmetic processes. *Journal of Educational Research, 42*, 279–288.

Detterman, D. K. (1979). Memory in the mentally retarded. In N. R. Ellis (Ed.), *Handbook of mental deficiency, psychological theory and research* (2nd (ed.), (pp. 727–760). Hillsdale, NJ: Erlbaum.

Fleischner, J. E., Garnett, K., & Shepherd, M. J. (1982). Proficiency in arithmetic basic facts computation of learning disabled students. *Focus on Learning Problems in Mathematics, 4*, 47–56.

Ford, A., Schnorr, R., Meyer, L., Davern, L., Black, J., & Dempsey, P. (1989). *The Syracuse community-referenced curriculum guide*. Baltimore: Brookes.

Frank, A. R. & McFarland, T. D. (1988). *Coin skills curriculum*. Bellevue, WA: Edmark.

Frank, A. R. & McFarland, T. D. (1980). Teaching coin skills to EMR children: A curriculum study. *Education and Training of the Mentally Retarded, 15*, 270–278.

Friedman, L. W. (1991). *The effect of problem content, semantic category, and difficulty in the solution of arithmetic word problems by learners with and without mental retardation*. Unpublished doctoral dissertation, Teachers College, Columbia University.

Frisch, S. A. (1989). *Generalization to arithmetic word problem types as a function of single exemplar and general case exemplar instruction with mentally retarded learners*. Unpublished doctoral dissertation, Teachers College, Columbia University.

Fuson, K. C. (1982). An analysis of the counting-on solution procedure in addition. In T. P. Carpenter, J. M. Moser, & T. A. Romberg (Eds.), *Addition and subtraction: A cognitive perspective* (pp. 67–82). Hillsdale, NJ: Erlbaum.

Fuson, K. C., & Secada, W. G. (1986). Teaching children to add by counting-on with one-handed finger patterns. *Cognition and Instruction, 3*(3), 229–260.

Fuson, K. C., & Willis, G. B. (1988). Subtracting by counting up: More evidence. *Journal for Research in Mathematics Education, 19*(5), 402–420.

Geary, D. C. & Burlingham-Dubree, M. (1989). External validation of the strategy choice model for addition. *Journal of Experimental Child Psychology, 47*, 175–192.

Goodstein, H. A., Cawley, J. F., Gordon, S., & Helfgott, J. (1971). Verbal problem solving among educable mentally retarded children. *American Journal of Mental Deficiency, 76*, 238–241.

Goodstein, H. A. (1973). The performance of educable mentally retarded children on subtraction word problems. *Education and Training of the Mentally Retarded, 8*, 197–202.

Greeno, J. G. & Riley, M. S. (1987). Processes and development of understanding. In F. E. Weinert & R. H. Kluwe (Eds.), *Metacognition, motivation, and understanding* (pp. 289–313). Hillsdale, NJ: Erlbaum.

Grimm, J. A., Bijou, S. W., & Parsons, J. A. (1973). A problem-solving model for teaching remedial arithmetic to handicapped young children. *Journal of Abnormal Child Psychology, 1*, 26–39.

Groen, G. J. & Parkman, J. M. (1972). A chronometric analysis of simple addition. *Psychological Review, 79*, 329–343.

Halpern, A. S., Close, D. W., & Nelson, D. J. (1986). *On my own*. Baltimore: Brookes.

Hamann, M. S. & Ashcraft, M. H. (1985). Simple and complex mental addition across development. *Journal of Experimental Child Psychology, 40*, 49–72.

Hasselbring, T. S. Goin, L. I., & Bransford, J. D. (1987). Developing automaticity. *Teaching Exceptional Children, 19*(3), 30–33.

Horton, S. (1985). Computational rates of educable mentally retarded adolescents with and without calculators in comparison to normals. *Education and Training of the Mentally retarded, 20*(1), 14–24.

Johnston, M. B., Whitman, T. L., & Johnson, M. (1980). Teaching addition and subtraction to mentally retarded children: A self-instruction program. *Applied Research in Mental Retardation, 1*, 141–160.

Judd, T. P. & Bilsky, L. H. (1989). Comprehension and memory in the solution of verbal arithmetic problems by mentally retarded and nonretarded individuals. *Journal of Educational Psychology*, *81*(40), 541–546.

Kintsch, W. & Greeno, J. G. (1985). Understanding and solving word arithmetic problems. *Psychological Review*, *92*, 109–129.

Kirby, J. R. & Becker, L. D. (1988). Cognitive components of learning problems in arithmetic. *Remedial and Special Education*, *9*(5), 7–15, 27.

Koller, E. Z. & Mulhern, T. J. (1977). Use of a pocket calculator to train arithmetic skills with trainable adolescents. *Education and Training of the Mentally Retarded*, *12*, 332–335.

Koshmider, J. W. & Ashcraft, M. H. (1991). The development of children's mental multiplication skills. *Journal of Experimental Child Psychology*, *51*, 53–89.

Lalli, F., Mace, F., Browder, D., & Brown, K. (1989). Comparison of treatments to teach number matching skills to adults with moderate mental retardation. *Mental Retardation*, *27*(2), 75–84.

Lancioni, G. E. (1982). Employment of normal third and fourth graders for training retarded children to solve problems dealing with quantity. *Education and Training of the Mentally Retarded*, *17*(2), 93–102.

Leon, J. & Pepe, H. (1983). Self-instruction training: Cognitive behavior modification for remediating arithmetic deficits. *Exceptional Children*, *50*(1), 54–60.

Mastropieri, M. A., Bakken, J. P., & Scruggs, T. E. (1991). Mathematics instruction for individuals with mental retardation: A perspective and research synthesis. *Education and Training in Mental Retardation*, *26*(2), 115–129.

Matson, J. L. & Long, S. (1986). Teaching computation/shopping skills to mentally retarded adults. *American Journal of Mental Deficiency*, *91*, 98–101.

Mayer, R. E. (1985). Mathematical ability. In R. J. Sternberg (Ed.), *Human abilities: An information processing approach* (pp. 127–150). New York: Freeman.

McClennen, S. & Harrington, L. (1982). A developmentally based functional mathematics program for retarded and autistic persons. *Journal of Special Education Technology*, *5*(3), 23–30.

McCollister, T. S., Burts, D. C., Wright, V. L., & Hildreth, G. J. (1986). Effects of computer-assisted instruction and teacher-assisted instruction on arithmetic task achievement scores of kindergarten children. *Journal of Educational Research*, *80*(2), 121–126.

McEvoy, J. (1989). From counting to arithmetic: The development of early number skills. *British Journal of Special Education*, *16*(3), 107–111.

McGlothlin, M. (1987). *Understanding math story problems: Book I.* Austin, TX: Pro Ed.

Meichenbaum, D. H. & Goodman, J. (1971). Training impulsive children to talk to themselves: A means of developing self-control. *Journal of Abnormal Psychology*, *77*, 115–126.

Meichenbaum, D. H. & Goodman, J. (1969). The developmental control of operant motor responding by verbal operants. *Journal of Experimental Child Psychology*, *7*, 553–565.

Miller, M. A., Cuvo, A. J., & Borakove, L. S. (1977). Teaching naming of coin values: Comprehension before production vs. production alone. *Journal of Applied Behavior Analysis*, *10*(4), 735–736.

Murphy, J., Bates, P., & Anderson, J. (1984). The effect of self-instruction training of counting skills by preschool handicapped students. *Education and Treatment of Children*, *7*(3), 247–257.

Narayanan, K. (1983). *Sources and order of difficulty in word problem solving in EMR and nonretarded individuals.* Unpublished Doctoral Dissertation, Teachers College, Columbia University.

Nesher, P. & Katriel, T. (1978). *Two cognitive modes in arithmetic word problem solving.* Paper presented at the second annual meeting of the International Group for the Psychology of Mathematics Instruction, Osnabruck, West Germany.

Noffsinger, T. & Dobbs, V. (1970). Teaching arithmetic to educable mentally retarded children (review). *Journal of Education Research*, *64*, 177–184.

Ogletree, E. J. & Ujlaki, V. (1976). A motoric approach to teaching multiplication to the mentally retarded child. *Education and Training of the Mentally Retarded*, *11*, 129–134.

Pellegrino, J. W. & Goldman, S. R. (1987). Information processing and elementary mathematics. *Journal of Learning Disabilities*, *20*(1), 23–32.

Podell, D. M., Tournaki-Rein, N., & Lin, A. (1992). Automatization of mathematics skills via computer-assisted instruction among students with mild mental handicaps. *Education and Training in Mental Retardation*, *27*(3), 200–206.

Riley, M. S., Greeno, J. G., & Heller, J. I. (1983). Development of children's problem-solving ability in arithmetic. In H. P. Ginsburg (Ed.), *The development of mathematical thinking* (pp. 153–196). New York: Academic Press.

Salvia, J. & Ysseldyke, J. E. (1991). *Assessment* (5th ed.). Boston: Houghton Mifflin.

Threadgill-Sowder, J. (1985). Individual differences and mathematical problem solving. In E. A. Silver (Ed.), *Teaching and learning mathematical problem solving: Multiple research perspectives* (pp. 331–343). Hillsdale, NJ: Erlbaum.

Siegler, R. S. & Shrager, J. (1984). Strategy choices in addition and subtraction: How do children know what to do? In C. Sophian (Ed.), *Origins of cognitive skills* (pp. 229–293). Hillsdale, NJ: Erlbaum.

Sowder, J. & Sowder, L. (1989). Research into practice: Developing understanding of computational estimation. *Arithmetic Teacher*, *36*(5), 25–27.

Trace, M., Cuvo, A. J., & Criswell, J. (1977). Teaching coin equivalence to the mentally retarded. *Journal of Applied Behavior Analysis*, *10*(1), 85–92.

Vacc, N. N. & Cannon, S. J. (1991). Cross-age tutoring in mathematics: Sixth graders helping students who are moderately handicapped. *Education and Training in Mental Retardation*, *26*(1), 89–97.

van Dijk, T. A. & Kintsch, W. (1983). *Strategies of discourse comprehension*. New York: Academic Press.

Vitello, S. J. (1976). Quantitative abilities of mentally retarded children. *Education and Training of the Mentally Retarded*, *11*, 125–129.

Wunderlich, R. A. (1972). Programmed instruction: Teaching coinage to retarded children. *Mental Retardation*, *10*, 21–23.

Chapter 14

Transition to Employment and Life in the Community

The ultimate goal of education is to enable each person—with or without disabilities—to live a full, satisfying life in the community. Attainment of this goal requires not only the acquisition of a complex array of skills across a number of domains, but also the accomplishment of a successful transition from school to adult employment and community living. Both of these tasks may pose special challenges for people with mental retardation. While much of this text has been concerned with educational programming to promote the acquisition of skills, the focus of the present chapter is upon transition.

McDonnell, Wilcox, Boles, and Bellamy have described transition as a bridge, which "is only as strong as the foundation on either side (the quality of school preparation on one side and the quality of adult service opportunities on the other) and the construction of the span itself (the planning process)" (McDonnell et al., 1983, p. 2). In this chapter, attention is given to both sides of the bridge—preparation as well as adult service opportunities—in terms of employment in the first section and in terms of community living in the second section. Within each of the two parts, adult service models and opportunities are presented first to provide a context for the subsequent discussion of preparation and training. The transition planning process itself is discussed in the third section. In the final section, recommendations based on the material in the chapter are presented.

Employment

Most adults with mental retardation are employable. However, most adults with mental retardation are unemployed—as many as 90 percent, according to some estimates. Concern over this situation was voiced as early as the 1950s and 1960s in the context of studies on the efficacy of special classes for individuals with mental retardation. It was a source of great disappointment that the employment rates of special class program graduates were just as dismal as those for individuals who had never had access to special education services. After an initial wave of criticism in which special education bore the entire blame for this failure (e.g., Dunn, 1968), models that more accurately reflected the multiplicity of factors influencing employability have emerged. Out of these models, a variety of intervention approaches have been developed and field tested in an effort to improve the employment picture for people with mental retardation.

Employment Placement Models

In this section, consideration is given to three employment placement models which have had a major impact on services for adults with mental retardation. For many years, the *Flow-Through Model* dominated employment services for these individuals. Over the past twenty years, it has been seriously challenged, first by the *Competitive Employment Model*, and, most recently, by the *Supported Employment Model*. These three models, which continue to vie for dominance, are illustrated in Table 14-1 and described and discussed in the following sections.

Flow-Through Model
According to the Flow-Through Model, most individuals with mental retardation should expect to begin their employment careers in a *sheltered employment* setting. Sheltered

TABLE 14-1   Employment Models for Adults with Mental Retardation

"FLOW-THROUGH" MODEL	EMPLOYMENT OPTIONS MODEL
Competitive Employment	Competitive Employment
↑	

Sheltered Workshop	Supported Employment
	  1. Supported Work
	  2. Enclaves
	  3. Mobile Crews
	  4. Benchwork Shops

↑	
Work Activity Center	
↑	
Day Activity Center	

employment typically consists of working for less than the minimum wage with coworkers with disabilities at a job with a therapeutic orientation and limited opportunities for advancement (Rusch, 1983). Nationally, the three most common sheltered employment settings are:

- *Sheltered Workshops*. Sheltered workshops are typically large employment centers that provide employment and therapeutic intervention for one hundred or more adults with mild or moderate mental retardation. Work is typically provided through work contracts in a variety of areas (e.g., benchwork assembly jobs, packing and shipping, messenger work). Pay is less than, but at least 50 percent of, the current federally established minimum wage.
- *Work Activity Centers*. Work activity centers provide prevocational and life skills training for individuals with moderate or severe mental retardation. Pay is less than 50 percent of the minimum wage.
- *Day Treatment Centers*. Day treatment, or day activity, centers serve the lowest-functioning adults with mental retardation—those who are ineligible for sheltered workshops or work activity centers. The program emphasis is typically nonvocational, with a focus on daily living skills. Again, any pay is less than 50 percent of the minimum wage.

The original conception of the Flow-Through Model was that individuals with mental retardation would begin their careers with temporary placement in a day treatment center. As their skills improved, they could move on through placements in a work activity center and a sheltered workshop until they were ready to graduate to competitive employment, or a regular job in the community. Although the Flow-Through Model was devised to fill an almost total gap in employment opportunities for people with mental retardation, it did not live up to its promise as a pathway to competitive employment. In fact, Bellamy, Rhodes, Mank, and Albin (1988) pointed out that a person who began his or her employment career at the age of twenty-one and spent the average amount of time in each of the three settings—thirty-seven years in a day activity center, ten years in a work activity center, and nine years in a sheltered workshop—would be seventy-seven years old by the time he or she was likely to obtain a regular job in the community. Although sheltered employment for people with mental retardation still exists in some communities, increasingly it has come under attack. Critics have asserted that sheltered employment cannot be justified as a route to competitive employment. Furthermore, it restricts the worker to substandard wages, extremely limited opportunities for advancement, and almost total segregation from workers without disabilities. For these reasons, the sheltered employment model is being replaced gradually by competitive and supported employment models (e.g., Bellamy et al., 1988; Kiernan & Stark, 1986; Rusch, 1983; Wehman, Moon, Everson, Wood, & Barcus, 1988).

Competitive Employment Model

During the past twenty years, it has been amply demonstrated that individuals with mental retardation can be successfully placed and maintained in competitive employment settings. Competitive employment has been defined as working for at least a minimum wage with coworkers without disabilities at a job that provides room for advancement in a setting that produces valued goods and services (Rusch, 1983).

Rusch's 1983 competitive employment training model is an example of an early model which has been widely applied with considerable success. Although Rusch, Chadsey-Rusch, and Lagomarcino (1987) have subsequently adapted Rush's 1983 model so that it can serve as a guide for supported employment applications tailored to the needs of people with severe disabilities, the original model still provides a useful program planning framework for people whose disabilities are mild enough to permit success in competitive employment.

Rusch's 1983 competitive employment model has the following four components: SURVEY, TRAIN, PLACE, and MAINTAIN. According to that model, the first step in setting up a competitive employment training program is to SURVEY the local community for possible jobs and needed skills. The next step is to TRAIN the worker in the needed competencies. Because individuals with mental retardation typically have limited ability to generalize, it is recommended that most training be conducted in training stations in actual business establishments in the community. The next step is to PLACE individuals in regular jobs in the community—either part-time or full-time. It is best to negotiate a specific number of job slots with each employer. Then, in the event that a specific worker fails in a given job, another program trainee can replace him or her. The fourth step in Rusch's 1983 model, MAINTAIN, is crucial to its successful implementation. Program follow-up services typically continue for a period of from three months to three years. These services may included direct on-the-job observations, consultation with employers and coworkers, advocacy, and additional training.

Competitive employment programs may involve close collaboration between businesses and agencies serving people with mental retardation. For example, Brickey and

Campbell (1981) described a project that was jointly sponsored by the McDonald's restaurant chain and a local association for citizens with mental retardation. McDonald's viewed this project as a possible solution to their extremely high rate of employee turnover (175 percent at the time of the study). The purpose of the project was to determine whether people with mental retardation could be trained so that they would have a better longevity record than other McDonald's employees. Seventeen individuals with mild and moderate mental retardation from sheltered workshops, ranging in age from twenty-one to fifty-two, were trained and placed in a variety of nonmanagerial positions. They were not placed in counter positions because of the money handling, writing, and social skills required. Jobs performed by the program participants included cleaning tables and grounds, heating pies and fish filets, making french fries, working with back room supplies, dressing buns, and night maintenance. Some task modifications were necessary, such as special counting systems to keep count of stock. Employees averaged twenty hours of work per week. At the end of two years, the turnover rate was 41 percent. All of those who left did so during the first year, three of them to take full-time jobs. The program was considered highly successful and has been replicated across the country.

Efforts to place and maintain individuals with mental retardation in competitive employment positions have been generally successful. For example, a 1985 nationwide survey indicated that of those individuals with developmental disabilities who entered competitive employment during the survey period, approximately 76 percent were still employed after 60 days (Kiernan & Ciborowski, 1985). Similarly, Beebe and Karan (1986) reported that out of one hundred and two people with developmental disabilities who were placed in competitive employment settings by the Vocational Educational Alternatives Program in 1983, 85 percent were working after 60 days and 73 percent were still working after one year.

These programs demonstrated beyond a doubt that people with mental retardation could be trained to work in competitive employment settings. However, these programs also revealed several problems that interfered with successful long-term employment. These problems fell into two categories: worker behaviors and service system disincentives. For example, of eighty-two adults with mental retardation placed into competitive food service jobs through the University of Washington Employment Training Program, 65 percent worked for at least one year. Of those individuals, only 7 percent did not need any intervention after the first 6 months. Intervention was necessary in many cases because vocational skills deteriorated after placement. Problems included insufficient speed, inadequate quality, the need for too much supervision, and poor compliance with instructions. Another major reason for intervention was inadequate social and life skills. These deficits included poor social interactions with employers and coworkers, inappropriate behaviors and emotional outbursts, poor grooming, money management, transportation use, and health care (Ford, Dineen, & Hall, 1984). The effects of these problems were exacerbated by the fact that most benefits and services to individuals with disabilities terminated shortly after placement in a competitive job.

The loss of benefits and services has operated as a major disincentive to competitive employment for adults with mental retardation and their families. Federal assistance programs include income support programs, health care programs, and employment programs. People with disabilities are eligible for most of these programs only if they are judged unable to engage in "substantial gainful activity" because of their disability. Substantial gainful activity is subject to a federally-defined upper limit on monthly income beyond which individuals lose eligibility for many benefits (Conley, Noble, & Elder, 1986). Furthermore, it is likely that once a person has been placed in a competitive job, even if he or she loses that job and cannot find another, he or she will have become ineligible for his or her former benefits. More recently, however, programs have been established by the federal and state governments, in conjunction with service agencies and employers, to reduce these disincentives. In this context, an alternative employment model, called "supported employment," was developed. The exact configuration of incentives and disincentives to the employment of persons with mental retardation continues to be in a state of flux and may vary considerably from state to state.

Supported Employment Model

In 1985, in an effort to address the problem of employment disincentives, ten states received five-year federal grants for Supported Employment Demonstration Projects. The intent was to encourage change in the ways that employment-related services were delivered to persons with developmental disabilities likely to need support for an extended period of time (Elder, 1986). The federal initiative was based, at least in part, on the early success of several university-based supported employment projects. For example, Wehman and Kregel (1985) reported the successful application of a supported work model over a six-year period. Of one hundred seventy individuals placed, 45 percent of them, most with moderate mental retardation, were still working after six years. The mean length of time employed was twenty months. They noted that the average length of employment for workers without mental retardation in similar jobs was only five months. Their program model was based on the four components of (1) job placement; (2) job site training and advocacy; (3) ongoing monitoring; and (4) follow-up and retention services that sometimes continued for several years.

Mank, Rhodes, and Bellamy (1986) proposed a continuum of supported employment alternatives, including the following four variations:

1. *Supported Work.* Workers are placed in regular competitive employment community jobs with long-term support.
2. *Enclave.* Groups of workers with disabilities are trained and supervised among workers without disabilities in an industry or business setting. This version of supported employment can accommodate relatively low-functioning individuals who require continuous supervision.
3. *Mobile Crew.* A van-based crew of people with disabilities is trained to perform service jobs in the community.
4. *Benchwork.* Small, single-purpose business operations are designed to replace day treatment centers and to provide long-term employment opportunities for low-functioning individuals.

All four variations are aimed at providing long-term employment for individuals with developmental disabilities. According to this model, payment is based upon individual productivity.

Preparation for Employment

Preparation for employment should begin in elementary school and continue throughout the school years. In fact, for many people with mental retardation, the need for some form of continuing employment training and support will probably persist well into adulthood. The assessment, curriculum, and instructional approaches described in the following sections are for the most part applicable in either a school or adult service setting, depending upon the age of the person being served.

Vocational Assessment

Two assessment models are discussed, each of which may be useful at different stages of the employment preparation process. The *Comprehensive Vocational Assessment Model* is most likely to be of value early in the preparation process to aid in the selection of a career focus. The *Targeted Employment Assessment Model* was designed to aid in matching a worker to a particular job and can be used at any time during the employment preparation process to assess the need for specific training, or job supports.

Comprehensive Vocational Assessment Model.   The Comprehensive Vocational Assessment Model is exemplified by a model developed by Brolin (1976) within the career education framework. According to Brolin's model, the main purpose of vocational assessment is to sort individuals into one of the following career tracks:

- immediate community job placement
- vocational training prior to community job placement
- placement in sheltered employment
- no employment placement (e.g., day activity center)

Although it is obvious that the original purpose of Brolin's 1976 model is somewhat out of step with the philosophies of the competitive and supported employment placement models, many of the assessment approaches encompassed by his model can be fruitfully employed to help formulate competitive and supported employment goals. As illustrated in Figure 14-1, Brolin's Comprehensive Vocational Assessment Model covers the following four domains:

1. *Clinical Assessment.* Within this first domain, it is recommended that each evaluation include relevant medical and social history information about the individual. In addition, educational diagnostic and achievement information should be gathered and compiled along with the outcomes of psychological assessments of intelligence and personality.

2. *Work Evaluation.* Within the second domain, the following four types of assessment are recommended:

- a. Intake and counseling interviews should be used to establish rapport with the individual and his or her family and to begin to informally assess abilities and interests.
- b. A situational assessment should be undertaken to observe performance in an actual or simulated work setting.

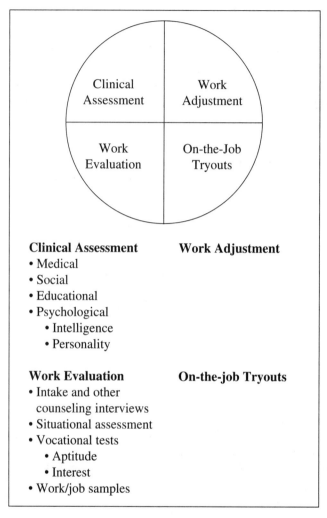

FIGURE 14-1 Brolin's Comprehensive Vocational Assessment Model

    c. Standardized vocational testing is recommended to provide formal assessment data on abilities and interests.

    d. Work/job samples, consisting of a battery of simulated job tasks, are also recommended. The *VIEWS* (Vocational Assessment for the Mentally Retarded) work sample battery was developed especially for use with individuals with mild, moderate, and severe mental retardation.

3. *Work Adjustment.* The third domain in Brolin's model differs from other conceptions of assessment. It was introduced in Brolin's model to acknowledge the possible need for a period of preparation before meaningful vocational assessment could be accomplished. Brolin (1976) proposed that the assessment process include a period of work adjustment that might involve such activities as counseling, instruction, or situational work experience aimed at improving work behaviors.

4. *On-the-Job Tryouts.* The fourth domain in the Comprehensive Vocational Assessment Model is the final phase of the assessment process. It is typically used to test the appropriateness of a recommended placement under actual employment conditions.

Targeted Employment Assessment Model.   The Targeted Employment Assessment Model, developed by Wehman (1981) in conjunction with the competitive employment model, is also compatible with the supported employment model. The Targeted Employment Assessment Model is summarized in Table 14-2. The Targeted Employment Assessment Model is organized around the following four elements:

1. *Vocational Skills.* Wehman (1981) proposed the assessment of six vocational skills that had been identified as essential to success in competitive employment. *Work proficiency,* or competence in performing a skill, is usually measured by the number of steps performed correctly. *Work rate* is the speed with which the task is completed. *Work quality* may be measured by number of errors or by a supervisor's rating. *Work perseveration level* is a measure of nonfunctional, perseverative behavior which can interfere with effective job performance. *Work repertoire* consists of the range of job skills that a person can perform before training. It is usually assessed through on-the-job observations. *Work endurance* addresses the extent to which a person possesses the physical stamina needed for specific job.

2. *Independent Living Skills.* Five independent living skill areas, identified as being important in maintaining employment, are recommended for assessment. *Transportation,*

TABLE 14-2   Wehman's Targeted Assessment Model

A. *Assessment of Client's Vocational Capabilities* (in terms of a specific job or job cluster)

1. Work Proficiency
2. Work Rate
3. Work Quality
4. Work Perseveration Level
5. Work Repertoire
6. Work Endurance

B. *Assessment of Client's Independent Living Capabilities*

1. Transportation
2. Communication
3. Self-Care and Appearance
4. Socialization
5. Functional Reading & Computation

C. *Assessment of Parent Attitudes and Behavior*

D. *Assessment of Job Requirements in the Work Environment*

From: Wehman, P. (1981). *Competitive employment.* Baltimore: Brookes.

as it relates to ability to get to and from the job, is essential. *Communication* can be assessed through worker interviews and observations, as well as parent interviews. Emphasis should be placed on the worker's ability to express needs and understand employer instructions. *Self-Care/Appearance* may be assessed by using a behavior checklist. *Socialization* is usually assessed through direct observations targeting both prosocial and antisocial behaviors. *Reading and Computational Skills* are best assessed in the context of actual job requirements.

   3. *Parent Attitudes and Behavior.* A structured interview with parents should be set up to assess parent attitudes, feelings, and behaviors that might be relevant to the worker's ability to maintain employment. Parent cooperation is an essential, although often overlooked factor, in the success of employment placements for individuals with mental retardation.

   4. *Job Requirements.* A work environment inventory should be conducted to identify the specific demands and requirements of a given job.

Curriculum

A strong curriculum designed to enhance employability is an essential component of adult employment preparation programs as well as school programs for individuals with mental retardation. The career education movement has yielded a framework which can provide a useful starting point for the development of a curriculum which incorporates key vocational survival skills.

Career Education.   Although the construct of career education originated in regular education (Marland, 1971), it quickly gained widespread support from special educators (see Chapter 5). Career education encompasses, but is not limited to, preparation for paid employment. According to Hoyt (1975), career education is the totality of experiences through which one learns about work as one aspect of building social skills appropriate to achieving adult status. One particularly expansive view of career education is that it constitutes all of education for children with mental retardation. It systematically coordinates all school, family, and community components to facilitate the realization of each individual's potential for economic, social, and personal fulfillment (Brolin, 1976). These conceptions are consistent with the definition adopted by the Council for Exceptional Children in 1978 which asserted that career education is "the totality of experiences through which one learns to live a meaningful life" (cited by Kokoska, 1983, p. 194). In spite of a strong emphasis on preparation for paid employment, the career education movement allows, indeed often encourages, alternative pathways to fulfillment in life. Work is only one of many competencies that can contribute to later life adjustment. The reverence for vocational preparation is tempered by the position that avocational pursuits, appropriate and productive family roles, and civic contributions are also important components of personal and social adjustment.

   Goldhammer (1972) suggested that full preparation for life would encompass five careers. These included: (1) a producer of goods and services; (2) a contributing and supportive member of the family; (3) a participant to the extent possible in the social and political life of the community; (4) a participant in avocational pursuits; and (5) a concern with aesthetic, moral, and religious issues. While some individuals with mental retardation might not be able to, or might not choose to, participate in all of the preceding five careers, these categories do suggest the potential breadth of career education goals.

   Similarly, Parnell (1973) recommended that each individual with mental retardation be taught how to function as a producer, a consumer, a learner, and a citizen. According to Parnell, the curriculum should stress daily living skills, occupational preparation, personal-social skills, and the development of academic skills not for their own sake but in close support of the other, more socially and vocationally oriented career education objectives.

Vocational Survival Skills.   It is essential that the curriculum for secondary level and transitional students include an emphasis on vocational survival skills, defined by Rudrud, Ziarnik, Bernstein, and Ferrara (1984) as skills that are directly work-relevant and essential to successful work performance. Vocational survival skills may be either *generic skills* or *specialized skills*. Generic skills, which are essential for most jobs, should be a central part of the school curriculum. Lists of generic skills have been compiled through research on the factors associated with job success or failure and through observational data on the general requirements of jobs in the community. The lists usually include skills relating to attendance, work habits, grooming, and social skills. Specialized skills, on the other hand, which are specific to a particular job (e.g., dishwashing), are best taught at the job site in on-the-job training.

Instructional Strategies

The instructional strategies presented in Chapter 7 are directly applicable to teaching both generic and specialized vocational skills. In addition, available books and manuals provide explicit guidelines for training employment-relevant behaviors (e.g., Rusch, 1986, Rusch & Mithaug, 1980). In a manual designed for use in secondary level school programs, Fredericks, Covey, Hendrickson, Deane, Gallagher, Schwindt, and Perkins (1987) have detailed procedures for providing community-based vocational training to students with moderate and severe disabilities. Fredericks et al. recommend that all training be conducted in the context of nonpaid community jobs. Their training strategy is directed toward accomplishing successful transitions from school to more than one concurrent part-time job in the community. They offered eleven reasons to justify concurrent part-time employment as an alternative to full-time employment as a transition goal, most of which can be summarized under availability, flexibility, diversity, and security. The manual provides materials and specific instructional strategies for training specialized job skills and associated work skills (e.g., hygiene, travel). Key instructional strategies include task analysis, prompting, and reinforcement.

Manuals designed for use in posttransition competitive and supported employment training programs are readily adaptable for use with secondary and transition age students with disabilities. For example, training materials and behavioral techniques similar to those described in Chapter 7 and the Fredericks et al. manual are presented in the supported employment training guides offered by Moon, Inge, Wehman, Brooke, and Barcus (1990) and Powell, Pancsofar, Steere, Butterworth, Itzkowitz, and Rainforth (1991).

Life in the Community

Employment success is only one facet of community adjustment. Living a full, satisfying life in the community also involves finding a suitable residential living arrangement, or a home, and acquiring the skills necessary for personal maintenance and safety as well as social and leisure participation.

Community Living Arrangements

The deinstitutionalization movement of the 1970s triggered a rapid expansion of the types of community living arrangements available for individuals with mental retardation. Although the need for these community-based residential alternatives has always exceeded their availability, the existing options do offer varying degrees of support for people with mental retardation. At the present time, in addition to the natural family, the most common supervised community living arrangements are family care homes, group homes, and intermediate care facilities. In addition, increasing numbers of people with mental retardation are living in semi-independent and independent living arrangements. Table 14-3 provides a list of these alternatives.

Although most research has focused on comparisons of institutional and community placements and/or general factors influencing the success of deinstitutionalization, a 1984 study by Willer and Intagliata reported some interesting comparisons among community living alternatives. Their sample consisted of individuals with mental retardation who had been released from New York State institutions. Only individuals who had lived in an institution for a minimum of one year and who were at least thirteen years old at the time of release were included in the study. Two or more years after release, questionnaires were mailed to the primary care provider and to the natural family. In cases where questionnaires were completed and returned, the deinstitutionalized individual with mental retardation was also interviewed. Their data revealed some of the advantages and disadvantages of three community-based settings: the natural family, family care homes, and group homes.

The Natural Family

Willer and Intagliata (1984) pointed out the irony in the fact that the natural family has often been viewed as an alternative to institutionalization rather than as the normal placement for individuals with mental retardation. They noted that, even at the peak of institutionalization in the United States, no more than 10 percent of people with mental retardation lived in institutions, with most of the rest remaining at home with their families. Willer and Intagliata went on to observe that the principle of normalization has often been interpreted to preclude the possibility of people with mental retardation continuing to live at home with their families once they reach adulthood. Nevertheless, in their study, 12 percent of the

TABLE 14-3   Alternative Living Arrangements for Adults with Mental Retardation

Independent Living

Semi-Independent Living

Natural Family

Family Care

Group Home

Intermediate Care Facility

Institution

deinstitutionalized individuals returned to live with their natural families. Individuals who returned to live at home tended to be younger, with more severe disabilities than those placed in other community settings.

In all cases the family member with mental retardation stated that home was where they wanted to be. They felt that they had an important role to fulfill and found satisfaction in being helpful to others. However, only about half of the mothers said that they were satisfied with their decision to have their son or daughter with mental retardation return home. This may have been due in part to the financial disincentives involved in returning an individual with mental retardation to their natural family. For example, natural families were eligible for smaller federal assistance benefits than other care providers. Willer and Intagliata also reported that the individuals who returned to their own homes were more likely to have behavior problems and less likely to use community services, attend day programs, and use recreational facilities than those in other settings. These findings suggested a pressing need for increased support to families.

Family Care Homes

Family care homes are family homes that are licensed to take in a few individuals with mental retardation. Of those people in the Willer and Intagliata study who were in family care, 60 percent had mild or moderate mental retardation and 40 percent had severe or profound mental retardation. All of the individuals interviewed said that they preferred life in their family care home to life in the institution. They felt like part of a family and valued the close relationships that they had formed. They were proud of their chores and responsibilities; 87 percent of them had assigned household chores. Individuals in family care exhibited few behavior problems and 90 percent of them attended day programs outside the home. Although they regularly used community resources (e.g., stores, restaurants, and movies), they typically were accompanied by a supervising adult. Care providers complained about the unavailability of special transportation services and difficulty in finding free time. Family care homes were generally well-accepted by neighbors. The greatest problem with these homes was that their quality was quite variable, indicating a need for improved systems for monitoring and providing training for care providers.

Group Homes

Group homes are houses or apartments in the community that typically house from three to fifteen people with mental retardation. In the Willer and Intagliata study, 71 percent of the individuals in the group home sample were classified as having borderline, mild, or moderate mental retardation. Just about all individuals preferred the group home to the institution. However, most expressed a desire to live with their own families and many expressed a desire to live independently. They also complained of overcrowding and not being liked by neighbors. Individuals in group homes were more likely to use community resources than those in other settings. Seventy-nine percent went out for daytime programs, but only 21 percent had housekeeping responsibilities in the home. Group home residents were much more likely to show gains in community living skills than individuals in any other setting. However, they were also more likely than those in other settings to develop behavior problems and, because of those problems, to return to institutions.

Intermediate Care Facilities

Intermediate care facilities (ICFs) are essentially licensed nursing homes for the care of individuals with mental retardation. They may house anywhere from ten to several hundred people, with larger facilities typically divided into smaller units. Because most ICFs are designed to meet the medical/safety regulations required for eligibility for Medicaid support, they tend to be the least normalized of the community living alternatives. Most states have redesigned their institutions so that they now qualify as ICFs. Shifts in state and federal funding policies will be required to reduce the number of people placed in these often unnecessarily restrictive settings.

Semi-Independent Living Programs

Halpern, Close, and Nelson (1986) reported a study of the lives of individuals being served by semi-independent living programs in various locations. The participants in their study were between eighteen and fifty-nine years of age, with a mean age of twenty-eight years. They ranged in ability from severe mental retardation to borderline intelligence, with a mean IQ of 66. These individuals were living in a variety of dwellings, but most lived in apartments in complexes housing mostly people without disabilities. In general, the individuals in the study functioned well in the community. They had few behavior problems, followed appropriate health practices, and kept their homes relatively clean. However, many of them did need help in planning well-balanced meals and suffered from teasing and harassment. Only 29 percent held regular employment in the community; 37 percent worked in sheltered workshops; 5 percent held temporary jobs (e.g., babysitting or yard work). The remaining 29 percent were unemployed. The major source of income was government assistance. The individuals received considerable help from the project staff, approximately fifteen hours per week of training and supervision and one crisis intervention per month to resolve money and health problems. During the course of the research, only 5 percent of the individuals moved to a more restrictive living situation because of health or behavior problems. Participants in the project reported that the most difficult aspects of living independently were money management, social skills, home maintenance, and food purchasing and preparation. When asked what advice they would offer another person with mental retardation about living on their own, project participants mentioned money management, home maintenance, and high self-esteem as important survival skills. In the words of one individual, "Be yourself, accept that you are retarded, and go for it!"

Independent Living

Many individuals who at one time in their lives have been labeled mentally retarded are living independently in the community. In fact, most individuals with mild mental retardation lose their label upon leaving school and simply disappear into society. Members of this group, because they are not easily identified, have been studied relatively infrequently. One study reported that of forty-two adults with mental retardation living in the Los Angeles area, twenty-four were married and eighteen were unmarried. Approximately 56 percent were employed. These individuals expressed varying degrees of satisfaction with their lives (Kaufman, 1984). In another study (Schalock, Harper, & Carver, 1981), graduates of an independent living training program in Nebraska were followed for five years. Whether individuals were initially placed in a staffed apartment (semi-independent) or independent housing did not affect the success of their community adjustment. Of the sixty-nine individuals originally placed, 80 percent had either remained in their original placement or moved into independent housing from a staffed apartment. The remaining 20 percent returned to a more restrictive living facility, including family care, natural home, or group home. The most common reasons for return included bizarre behavior, nutritional problems, illegal activities (e.g., bad checks or stealing), and inadequate home maintenance.

Preparation for Life in the Community

Preparation for life in the community should be a central part of the curriculum for all people with mental retardation throughout the school years. For many individuals with mental retardation, it is likely that community living skills acquired during their school years will need to be augmented by training and support activities during their adult years. Most of the assessment, curriculum, and instructional approaches discussed in the following sections are applicable in both school and adult service settings.

Assessment

Assessment as a guide to placement and preparation for community living should generally include at least two components. The first component is comprised of global measures of *adaptive behavior*. The second component consists of a *targeted assessment* which focuses upon the specific skills required for living in a particular community environment.

Adaptive Behavior.   As discussed in Chapter 3, several comprehensive instruments are available for measuring adaptive behavior in people with mental retardation. Of these scales, most of which are applicable to both children and adults, two are the most widely used. The *AAMR Adaptive Behavior Scales–School* (Lambert, Nihira, & Leland, 1992) was designed to provide information about "personal independence and social skills and to reveal areas of functioning where special program planning" is needed (Lambert, Windmiller, Tharinger, & Cole, 1981, p. 3). It consists of two parts, adaptive behavior and maladaptive behavior, each containing multiple domains. Similarly, the *Vineland Adaptive Behavior Scales* (Sparrow, Balla, & Cicchetti, 1984), designed to assess personal and social functioning, taps the domains of communication, daily living skills, socialization, motor skills, and maladaptive behavior.

Targeted Assessment.   The picture of overall functioning provided by the global measures of adaptive behavior described above is not sufficient to guide placement and programming decisions. As with employment, a more targeted approach is an essential supplement. Two of the four elements of Wehman's (1981) *Targeted Employment Assessment Model* can yield information with direct relevance to assessment for community living. As noted earlier in this chapter, the independent living skills element in this model covers the following five independent living skill areas: transportation, communication, self-care/appearance, socialization, and reading and computational skills. Although the emphasis in Wehman's model is upon how these skill areas relate to employment, it is also possible to assess competencies in each of these areas as they relate to functioning in the community. The second element in

Wehman's model with direct relevance to community living is the assessment of parent attitudes and behavior through structured interviews. Parent cooperation and support can be key factors in community adjustment, just as they are for employment.

Additional information to guide the design of individual instructional programs for community living can be provided by *ecological inventories* and *student repertoire inventories* (Falvey, 1989). Ecological inventories involve ascertaining the sequences of skills necessary for participation in specific community environments (Brown, Branston, Hamre-Nietupski, Pumpian, Certo, & Gruenewald, 1979). To conduct an inventory, target environments and subenvironments should be identified and the skills required for a person without disabilities to perform that activity should be delineated. This process should be followed by a student repertoire inventory in which a student's existing skills are compared with the skills required for participation in the activity (Falvey, Brown, Lyon, Baumgart, & Schroeder, 1980). This information can be used as a basis for one of the following options: teaching the skill, adapting the skill to allow partial participation, or teaching a related skill.

Curriculum and Instructional Strategies

Developing instructional programs to prepare individuals with mental retardation for life in the community requires the careful selection of curriculum materials and instructional strategies that are suited to the characteristics of the individual and his or her community. The following sections are included to highlight life skills and social and leisure participation as key areas to consider in planning individualized programs.

Life Skills.   In a 1988 American Association on Mental Retardation Monograph, Dever presented a taxonomy of "skills required for daily life in the community" (Dever, 1988, p. 7). The taxonomy is not a curriculum, but rather a compilation of goals for instruction in community living. It was intended to aid the process of curriculum development in specific settings by providing general goals on the premise that the actual steps needed to attain the general goals would vary from setting to setting. The taxonomy was developed and field tested within the context of an instructional paradigm which included the following steps: (1) establish the aim of instruction; (2) set the goals; (3) develop curricula leading to the goals; (4) develop individual programs; (5) teach; and (6) evaluate instruction (Dever, 1988, p. 15).

Dever's taxonomy includes the following five domains, which encompass the skills needed to live an unsupervised life in the community:

- *Personal Maintenance and Development*. This domain contains all of the standard self-help skills as well as skills for maintaining good relationships with family and friends. It also contains skills for coping with daily "glitches," or manifestations of "Murphy's Law" which states that, "If anything can go wrong, it will" (p. 23).
- *Homemaking and Community Life*. This domain includes skills relating to obtaining housing, managing money, and insuring adequate nutrition. It also encompasses the skills for maintaining good relationships in the community and dealing with the glitches of community life.
- *Vocational*. This domain is comprised of the skills needed to obtain and sustain employment, maintain good relationships at work, and deal with glitches in the workplace.

- *Leisure.* The focus of this domain is upon learning, selecting, and performing leisure activities. It also includes skills for maintaining good relationships during leisure activities and handling any glitches in these settings.
- *Travel.* This domain includes the skills needed for traveling within the community, maintaining good interpersonal relationships while traveling, and handling any glitches.

In addition to Dever's taxonomy, a wide variety of materials are available to aid in planning instructional programs aimed at preparing individuals with mental retardation for life in the community. Some examples are Falvey's *Community-Based Curriculum* (1989), *The Syracuse Community-Referenced Curriculum Guide* (Ford, Schnorr, Meyer, Davern, Black, and Dempsey, 1989), and *The Activities Catalog* (Wilcox & Bellamy, 1987).

Social and Leisure Participation.   Although social and leisure participation were among the areas included in Dever's taxonomy, their particular importance for people with mental retardation justifies singling them out for special attention in this text. One reason for this emphasis is apparent in a series of studies by Edgerton and his colleagues.

In *The Cloak of Competence* (Edgerton, 1967), a study of the lives of forty-eight adults with mild mental retardation who had been discharged from a state institution, Edgerton described their struggles to hide their mental retardation and build their own lives in the community. Twelve years later, Edgerton and Bercovici (1976) again interviewed and observed thirty members of the original group. At the time of follow-up, the rate of full-time employment had dropped from 44 percent to 31 percent and, of the eight who were employed, six were still receiving the same wages that they had received twelve years earlier. The rest of the individuals were either being supported by spouses or were receiving welfare. In spite of this bleak employment picture, most of the individuals said that they were either happier than twelve years ago or about the same. Their primary interests were recreation, hobbies, good times, friends, and family. A major insight of this study was that the criteria for quality of life differed for the project staff and for the individuals in the study. While the project staff tended to measure success according to degree of competence and independence, the people with mental retardation were more likely to judge their lives in terms of personal satisfaction.

Further follow-ups of members of the original sample have confirmed that successful coping with community life was much more dependent upon personal, social, and communicative abilities than upon the more standard measures of financial or career success (Edgerton, Bollinger, & Herr, 1984; Edgerton & Gaston, 1991). This research suggests that if we restrict our efforts to providing people with mental retardation with required skills for employment and independent living, we may be short-changing them in those very areas that are most important to them.

Social and leisure activities are critically important in the lives of people with mental retardation. There is ample evidence that social behavior can be the determining factor in whether a person with mental retardation is able to obtain and maintain employment (Brolin, 1976). Similarly, studies of the community adjustment of people with mental retardation by Edgerton and others point to social behaviors as crucial determinants of the ability to live independently. Even more important, social interactions may provide a crucial source of personal satisfaction for people with mental retardation. Data supporting this position are provided by research on friendship (e.g., Berkson & Romer, 1980; Landesman-Dwyer, Berkson, & Romer, 1979), which has found evidence of deep and lasting friendships among people with mental retardation at all ability levels. In addition to social interaction, many other leisure activities can play important roles in the lives of individuals with mental retardation.

The word leisure is derived from the Latin *licere*, meaning to be free. This definition suggests not only that leisure time is free time, but also that leisure activities must be freely chosen if they are to satisfy an individual's personal and social needs. For adults with mental retardation, free choice is often restricted. Restrictions may stem from a restrictive living arrangement, limited access to community recreation opportunities, and skills limitations. Although individuals without disabilities tend to acquire leisure interests and skills through incidental learning during the course of their daily lives, formal programming may be needed to provide people with mental retardation with an adequate repertoire of leisure skills.

Although leisure activities are sometimes taken for granted by individuals without disabilities, they may play a very important role in our lives. The same possibility—often unrealized—exists for people with mental retardation. For example, in the McDonald's employment training project described earlier in this chapter, one trainee nearly lost his job because he was unable to plan leisure activities for his after-work hours. He deliberately completed his work assignments two hours late because he did not want to go home to his empty apartment (Ford et al., 1984). Another individual with mental retardation in the Halpern et al. (1986) semi-independent living study, reported that he hated Mondays because he had nothing to do after work, which ended at 3 P.M. He usually coped with this problem by watching a little television, going out for a cup of coffee, and going to bed early. A wider repertoire of leisure activities could have solved the problems of both of these individuals.

Other justifications for training leisure skills have included positive effects in other curriculum areas, a reduction in negative and inappropriate behaviors, and better community adjustment (Dattilo & St. Peter, 1991; Voeltz, Wuerch, & Wilcox, 1982; Wehman, 1979; Wuerch & Voeltz, 1982). These positive effects, coupled with the finding that direct training in a particular leisure activity, such as rug hooking, can increase preference for that activity in a free-choice situation (Johnson & Bailey, 1977), emphasize the importance of providing opportunities for adults with mental retardation to acquire a repertoire of leisure activities.

This goal was emphasized in a program described by Salzberg and Langford (1981). In that program, individual adults with mental retardation were carefully matched with an adult without disabilities on the basis of leisure interests. The adults without disabilities were provided with orientation and training and encouraged to invite their companions with mental retardation to accompany them as they pursued some of their usual leisure activities. The program was enjoyed by the adults without disabilities as well as by the adults with mental retardation who expanded their leisure repertoires to include such activities as going on shopping trips, going to movies, going to nightclubs, eating in restaurants, hiking, and swimming. This program provided opportunities for adults with mental retardation to learn how leisure activities are performed by adults without mental retardation while participating in integrated community activities.

Transition from School to Adulthood

The concept of transition as a bridge from the school years to the adult years has provided the framework for this chapter. Up to this point, this chapter has discussed only the two sides of the bridge—school preparation programs on the one side and adult employment and community living options on the other. Although well-designed preparation programs and appropriate adult opportunities are essential, they are not sufficient to insure that people with mental retardation will live full, satisfying lives in the community. In addition, individuals with mental retardation must successfully negotiate the transition from school to adulthood. During the past ten years, there has been a growing appreciation of the extent to which that process can be facilitated by careful planning. Models and strategies for effective transition planning are the focus of this section.

Models of the Transition Process

The development of approaches to transition planning for people with mental retardation has been guided by two general models. The first model was proposed by Will (1984), who was then the Assistant Secretary of the United States Office of Special Education and Rehabilitative Services (OSERS). The model, referred to as the OSERS Model, is illustrated in Figure 14-2. The OSERS Model portrays the transition process as the successful negotiation of one of three bridges from school to employment. The transition team must select the most appropriate bridge for each student. Students with well-developed repertoires of vocational competencies may be able to find competitive employment opportunities with the assistance of only the generic services that are available to people without disabilities (e.g., state employment services), thus choosing the bridge of "no special services." Students with mild or moderate disabilities may require

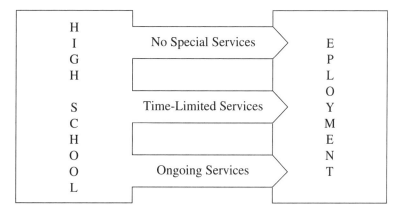

FIGURE 14-2   OSERS Transition Model

From: Will, M. C. (1984). *OSERS programming for the transition of youth with disabilities: Bridges from school to working life.* Washington, DC: Office of Special Education and Rehabilitative Services, U.S. Department of Education.

"time-limited services" designed specifically for people with disabilities in order to obtain and succeed in a competitive job. Finally, those with the most severe disabilities may require "ongoing services" throughout their careers, usually in the form of specialized supported employment services.

In 1985, Halpern proposed an alternative to the OSERS Model in which "community adjustment" replaced "employment" as the destination of the three bridges. In the Halpern Model, which is generally compatible with the goals of the present chapter, community adjustment is defined as including the residential environment and social and interpersonal networks as well as employment. The bridges in the Halpern Model, illustrated in Figure 14-3, are essentially the same as those in the OSERS Model.

Transition Planning

The establishment of effective transition services requires collaborative planning among schools, agencies, and employers in the community. Wehman et al. (1988) have suggested

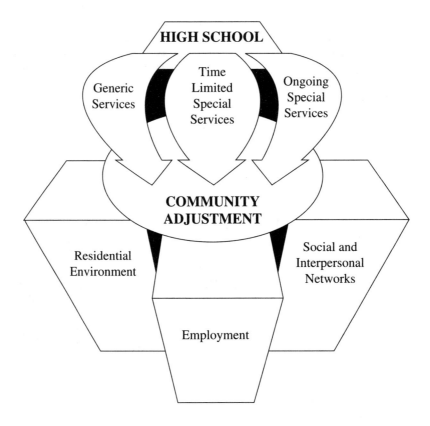

FIGURE 14-3 Halpern's Transition Model

From Transition: A look at the foundations, by Halpern, A. S., *Exceptional Children*, *51*(6), 1985, p. 481. Copyright 1985 by The Council for Exceptional Children. Reprinted with permission.

that this be accomplished through the formation of *local core transition teams*. Once school and community transition services are in place, planning for individual students is accomplished through the development of *Individualized Transition Plans* (ITP).

Local Core Transition Teams

Local core transition teams are interagency teams formed to establish and coordinate transition services in a community. According to Wehman et al. (1988), the team's goals should include at least the following activities:

- Survey existing services
- Provide guidelines for transition planning
- Work out local interagency agreements

Local core teams generally include representatives from the schools, the local vocational rehabilitation agency, the local mental retardation or developmental disabilities council, and a parent, advocate, and student. Members of the core team are responsible for developing all necessary agreements as well as the "action plans" needed to implement them. Team members are expected to represent their agency in team discussions and also to serve as the agent of change within their agency.

Individualized Transition Plans

The Individualized Transition Plan is a guide to transition planning for individual students with disabilities (e.g., Wehman, 1992). It is mandated by the IDEA (PL101–476) that a transition statement be included in the IEP by age sixteen. For most students, the ITP will differ from the IEP in that it specifies desired outcomes and required support services in terms of goals for employment, community living, and leisure. The IEP, on the other hand, concentrates upon skill acquisition. A sample ITP is provided for the *Case Study of Scott*. According to Wehman et al. (1988), the ITP should have the following characteristics:

- annual goals
- short-term objectives
- required services
- comprehensive scope
- individualized focus
- longitudinal development
- informed participation of parents

A four-part framework for the creation of ITPs has been proposed by Stowitschek and Kelso (1989). The framework includes the following components:

- *Relevance and Quality.* If ITPs are to have quality and to constitute "true bridges," then the content specified must foster entry into the workplace and integration into the community.

CASE STUDY: Scott (CA = 18–0, IQ = 33)
Individualized Transition Plan for Scott

I. EMPLOYMENT GOAL: To obtain a supported employment placement in a hospital cafeteria.

A. Educational Objectives:

1a. When placed as a dishwasher in a cafeteria of a local hospital, Scott will clean dishes with 80 percent accuracy, within 2 months of job placement.

1b. When placed as a tray-stacker in a cafeteria of a local hospital, Scott will stack dishes with 80 percent accuracy, within 2 months of job placement.

1c. When placed as a counter-server in a cafeteria of a local hospital, Scott will serve dishes at the counter with 80 percent accuracy, within 2 months of job placement.

Activities	*Persons Involved*
• Job site analysis to determine job skills needed for the three alternative positions targeted in the hospital cafeteria	Vocational Education Teacher, Special Education Teacher
• Assess Scott's job skills	Vocational Education Teacher, Special Education Teacher
• Target instructional goals and develop task analyses of skills to be trained	Vocational Education Teacher, Special Education Teacher
• Provide skill training on all three targeted positions in the hospital cafeteria	Vocational Education Teacher, Special Education Teacher, Job Coach
• Select job position for final placement	Vocational Education Teacher, Special Education Teacher, Job Coach, Scott

2. When instructed to use public transportation to travel from home to the job site (or return home from the job site), Scott will use the local bus system with 100 percent accuracy over 4 consecutive sessions.

Activities	*Persons Involved*
• Plan a transportation training schedule	Vocational Education Teacher, Special Education Teacher, Parent
• Locate training sites	Vocational Education Teacher, Special Education Teacher, Parent
• Assess Scott's travel skills and target training goals	Vocational Education Teacher, Special Education Teacher, Parent
• Implement training of travel skills and evaluate performance	Vocational Education Teacher, Special Education Teacher

B. Administrative Objectives:

1. Accomplish formal transition planning and referral to appropriate adult service agencies.

Activities	*Persons Involved*
• Obtain comprehensive assessment information	School Psychologist, Special Education Teacher, Vocational Education Teacher
• Obtain school administrative support and contact adult service providers such as OVR and OMRDD	Case Manager, Rehabilitation Counselor, Placement Specialist, School Staff
• Identify the extent of local support	Case Manager
• Set up an individualized transition planning (ITP) team	School Staff, Parent
• Formulate a plan for transition implementation; discuss and delineate responsibilities among ITP team members; write the ITP	ITP Team, Parent, Scott

2. Develop a transportation training program.

Activities	*Persons Involved*
• Meet with school district's transportation department; procure needed bus passes	School Administrator, Case Manager
• Set up a schedule for use of local bus transit and provide travel training	Special Education Teacher, Case Manager, Parent, Scott

3. Secure the necessary documents for enabling employment.

Activities	*Persons Involved*
• Apply for Social Security Income (SSI) benefits	Social Security Staff, Case Manager, Parent, Scott
• Discuss how employment will impact on Scott's SSI benefits	Social Security Staff, Case Manager, Parent, Scott
• Apply for DVR certificate	Case Manager, DVR Representative, Scott
• Apply for a work permit	Case Manager, School Administrator, Scott
• Obtain insurance for training period	Case Manager, Parent, Scott
• Assist Scott to have a medical examination; obtain job uniform and other prerequisites to employment	Case Manager, Parent, Scott

4. Build contract with a non-profit agency receiving federal, state, and/or local funds to provide ongoing support at employment site after placement.

Activities	*Persons Involved*
• Research local rehabilitation agencies	Case Manager, School Administrator
• Contact the agency and discuss Scott's placement needs	Case Manager, ITP Team, Parent, Advocates, Placement Specialist, Agency Representative

CASE STUDY: Scott (continued)

• Hold intake meeting	Case Manager, ITP Team, Parent, Advocates, Placement Specialist, Agency Representative

5. Locate appropriate employment training stations (dishwasher/tray-stacker/counter-server) and a supported employment job placement site for Scott in a local hospital cafeteria.

Activities	*Persons Involved*
• Screen the community and research local hospitals	Vocational Education Teacher, Special Education Teacher, Placement Specialist, Parent
• Initiate contacts with specific employers and discuss the possibilities of Scott's placement, fill out job applications	Vocational Education Teacher, Placement Specialist, Case Manager, Scott
• Assess alternative job positions in the local cafeteria and select one for final placement	Vocational Education Teacher, Special Education Teacher, Placement Specialist, Parent, Employer, Scott
• Complete a Job Placement Plan describing work schedule, wages, job duties, etc.	Placement Specialist, Case Manager, Employer, Scott

6. Review personnel-policies with employers at each of the sites.

Activities	*Persons Involved*
• Decide on overtime rates and/or compensatory pay for providing transition training	School Administrator, School District Superintendent
• Allow for flexible working schedules for school staff providing training or supervision at employment site	School Administrator, ITP Team, Employer

7. Provide for adequate monitoring and follow-along services after placement at each of the sites.

Activities	*Persons Involved*
• Prepare a progressive report on Scott's work performance	Vocational Education Teacher, Job Coach
• Determine problem areas by reviewing performance evaluation data	Vocational Education Teacher, Job Coach
• Develop and implement modification plans	Vocational Education Teacher, Job Coach
• Make accommodations at work site	Vocational Education Teacher, Job Coach
• Provide vocational counseling if needed	Vocational Counselor, Vocational Education Teacher, Case Manager, Parent

8. Coordinate follow-along and transfer of responsibilities from school staff to adult service agency when Scott is placed in his supported employment position.

Activities	*Persons Involved*
• Design a formal follow-up plan	ITP Team, Adult Service Agency Representative, Employer, Case Manager
• Identify persons responsible for continuing transition coordination	ITP Team, Adult Service Agency Representative, Employer, Case Manager

II. COMMUNITY LIVING GOAL: *To function semi-independently in the community, while continuing to live at home with his family.*

A. Educational Objectives:

1a. When asked to prepare a particular dish, Scott will make a list of the required ingredients with 95 percent accuracy on 4 out of 5 trials.

1b. When given the recipe and the ingredients required for the meal, Scott will correctly mix the ingredients on 4 out of 5 trials.

Activities	*Persons Involved*
• Assess present skill level	Special Education Teacher, Vocational Education Teacher
• Design instructional plan and develop task analyses of skills to be trained	Special Education Teacher, Vocational Education Teacher
• Implement training and evaluate performance; continue supervision	Special Education Teacher, Vocational Education Teacher

2. When given some money and asked to purchase a particular item from the grocery store, Scott will correctly select and pay for that item for 5 consecutive trials.

Activities	*Persons Involved*
Same as above	Same as above

3. When taken to a laundromat and given the requisites (money, washing soap, clothes), Scott will operate the washing machine with 100 percent accuracy for 4 consecutive trials.

Activities	*Persons Involved*
Same as above	Same as above

4. On reaching a bank when the amount of money to be withdrawn is specified, Scott will use his bank card to operate the ATM machine to withdraw the specified amount of money with 100 percent accuracy for 8 consecutive trials.

CASE STUDY: Scott   (continued)

Activities	*Persons Involved*
Same as above	Same as above

5. When instructed to use public transportation to travel from home to the bank/grocery store (or return home from the bank/grocery store), Scott will use the local bus system with 100 percent accuracy over 4 consecutive sessions.

Activities	*Persons Involved*
• Plan a transportation training schedule	Vocational Education Teacher, Special Education Teacher, Parent, Scott
• Locate training sites	Vocational Education Teacher, Special Education Teacher, Parent
• Assess Scott's travel skills and target training goals	Vocational Education Teacher, Special Education Teacher, Parent
• Implement training of travel skills and evaluate performance	Vocational Education Teacher, Special Education Teacher

B. *Administrative Objectives:*

1. Provide the necessary facilities/materials needed for training on the targeted community living skills.

Activities	*Persons Involved*
• Locate training sites in the community (groceries, laundry, bank)	Case Manager, Vocational Education Teacher, Special Education Teacher, Parent
• Seek support and supervision of staff at these community sites	Case Manager, Parent, Advocates
• Open a bank account	Case Manager, Parent, Scott
• Procure bus passes needed for travel training	School Administrator, Case Manager, Scott
• Set up a schedule for use of local bus transit and provide travel training	Special Education Teacher, Vocational Education Teacher, Case Manager, Parent, Scott

III. LEISURE GOAL: To establish a leisure program for Scott that increases his contact with nondisabled peers.

A. *Educational Objectives:*

1. When the game has been set up at the bowling alley, Scott will bowl, following the rules of the game with 75 percent accuracy for 4 consecutive trials.

Activities	Persons Involved
• Assess present leisure skills	Special Education Teacher, Vocational Education Teacher
• Assess and identify social skills needed for group participation	Special Education Teacher, Vocational Education Teacher, Parent
• Design instructional plan and develop task analyses of skills to be trained	Special Education Teacher, Vocational Education Teacher
• Develop Scott's ability to make choices for leisure activity	Special Education Teacher, Vocational Education Teacher, Parent, Scott
• Implement training and evaluate performance; continue supervision	Special Education Teacher, Vocational Education Teacher

2. When asked to participate in a badminton game, Scott will play badminton, following the rules of the game with 75 percent accuracy for 4 consecutive trials.

Activities	Persons Involved
Same as above	Same as above

3. On being given his harmonica and music book, Scott will play the harmonica, following the notes of a tune from his music book with 50 percent accuracy for 4 consecutive trials.

Activities	Persons Involved
Same as above	Same as above

4. On being presented with different leisure activities and asked to make a single choice, Scott will express a preference for one of the activities for 4 consecutive sessions.

Activities	Persons Involved
Same as above	Same as above

5. When instructed to use public transportation to travel from home to the leisure program sites (or return home from the program), Scott will use the local bus system with 100 percent accuracy over 4 consecutive sessions.

Activities	Persons Involved
• Plan a transportation training schedule	Vocational Education Teacher, Special Education Teacher, Parent, Scott
• Locate training sites	Vocational Education Teacher, Special Education Teacher, Parent
• Assess Scott's travel skills and target training goals	Vocational Education Teacher, Special Education Teacher, Parent
• Implement training of travel skills and evaluate performance	Vocational Education Teacher, Special Education Teacher

CASE STUDY: Scott   (continued)

B. Administrative Objectives:

1. Provide the necessary facilities/materials needed for training on the targeted leisure skills.

Activities	*Persons Involved*
• Locate training sites in the community (bowling areas, badminton clubs, etc.)	Case Manager, Vocational Education Teacher, Special Education Teacher, Parent
• Seek support and supervision of community members	Case Manager, Parent, Advocates
• Arrange trips in the community	Case Manager, Vocational Education Teacher, Special Education Teacher, Parent
• Arrange for funds for group leisure activities (trips, parties, etc.)	Case Manager, Parent, Advocates
• Procure bus passes needed for travel training	School Administrator, Case Manager, Scott
• Set up a schedule for use of local bus transit and provide travel training	Special Education Teacher, Vocational Education Teacher, Case Manager, Parent, Scott

Form adapted from: Wehman, P., Moon, M. S., Everson, J. M., Wood, W., & Barcus, J. M. (1988). *Transition from school to work*. Baltimore: Brookes.

- *Accountability.* An ITP must be more than words on paper. It is essential that the school actively monitor the ongoing implementation of the ITP while fostering the necessary links. Wehman, Kregel, Barcus, & Schalock (1986) have suggested that collaborative links across agencies and services can be enhanced through the pairing of an educational objective with an administrative objective for each transition goal.
- *Feasibility.* The effectiveness of ITPs is often jeopardized by the fact that no single service agency spans both youth and adulthood for a significant period of time. However, Stowitschek and Kelso (1989) have pointed out that parents and family members have a "vested interest" in as well as knowledge about their family member, which could be utilized by encouraging family members to mediate the transition process. Sharing the belief that the transition process should be planned with parents, not for them, Dattilo and St. Peter (1991) have included the family/friend support group as a component of their model of leisure education in transition services for young adults with mental retardation.
- *Preparedness.* Orientation and education programs for parents and teachers must be designed to insure the success of the ITP process.

Members of each student's ITP Team should include at least special and vocational educators, representatives of vocational rehabilitation agencies, representatives of mental retardation or other case management agencies, the parent, the student, and if possible, the potential employer.

Much of the preceding discussion is summarized in the following list of ten strategies for transition planning compiled by Rusch and DeStefano (1989):

1. Begin transition planning early (in middle school if possible).
2. Establish an ITP Team for each student.
3. Develop an ITP for each student.
4. Emphasize integration in school programs and in employment placements.
5. Teach community living skills.
6. Teach community living and employment skills in community-based settings.
7. Enlist parents, community members, and employers in finding jobs.
8. Place students in jobs that provide opportunities for advancement.
9. Develop an in-service program for training transition personnel.
10. Evaluate outcomes as a basis for program improvement.

Recommendations

Drawing upon the material in this chapter, the following recommendations are offered to teachers and parents:

1. Foster a career education curriculum orientation that begins in the elementary and continues through secondary school years. Special emphasis should be placed on life skills, vocational survival skills, and social and leisure skills.
2. Make an ongoing effort to gather both comprehensive/global and targeted assessment information for employment and community living.
3. Begin transition program planning for each student by age fourteen, by contacting or, if necessary forming, a Local Core Transition Team. This team will be responsible for establishing and coordinating appropriate transition services in your community.
4. Select a transition model (e.g., the Halpern Model) to use as a guide in transition planning for your students.
5. For each student, convene a transition team as early as possible in the secondary school years, and develop an Individualized Transition Plan (ITP) to guide program planning for that student.
6. Select transition goals for employment, living, and leisure that foster full participation in the community with as much independence as possible.

References

Beebe, P. D. & Karan, O. C. (1986). A methodology for a community-based vocational program for adults. In R. H. Horner, L. H. Meyer, & H. D. B. Fredericks (Eds.), *Education of learners with severe handicaps: Exemplary service strategies* (pp. 3–28). Baltimore: Brookes.

Bellamy, G. T., Rhodes, L. E., Mank, D. M. & Albin, J. M. (1988). *Supported employment: A community implementation guide.* Baltimore: Brookes.

Berkson, G. & Romer. D. (1980). Social ecology of supervised communal facilities for mentally disabled adults: I. Introduction. *American Journal of Mental Deficiency, 85,* 219–228.

Brickey, M. & Campbell, K. (1981). Fast food employment for moderately and mildly mentally retarded adults: The McDonald's Project. *Mental Retardation, 19*(3), 113–116.

Brolin, D. E. (1976). *Vocational preparation of retarded citizens,* Columbus, OH: Merrill.

Brown, L., Branston, M. B., Hamre-Nietupski, S. Pumpian, I., Certo, N., & Gruenewald, L. (1979). A strategy for developing chronological-age-appropriate and functional curricular content for severely handicapped adolescents and young adults. *Journal of Special Education, 13,* 81–90.

Conley, R. W., Noble, J. H., & Elder, J. K. (1986). Problems with the service system. In W. E. Kiernan & J. A. Stark (Eds.), *Pathways to employment for adults with developmental disabilities.* Baltimore: Brookes.

Dattilo, J. & St. Peter, S. (1991). A model for including leisure education in transition services for young adults with mental retardation. *Education and Training in Mental Retardation, 26*(4), 420–432.

Dever, R. B. (1988). Community living skills: A taxonomy. *AAMR Monographs, 10.*

Dunn, L. M. (1968). Special education for the mildly retarded: Is much of it justifiable? *Exceptional Children, 35,* 5–22.

Edgerton, R. M. (1967). *The cloak of competence: Stigma in the lives of people with mental retardation.* Berkeley: University of California Press.

Edgerton, R. M. & Bercovici, S. M. (1976). The cloak of competence: Years later. *American Journal of Mental Deficiency, 80,* 485–497.

Edgerton, R. M., Bollinger, M., & Herr, B. (1984). The cloak of competence: After two decades. *American Journal of Mental Deficiency, 88*(4), 345–351.

Edgerton, R. B. & Gaston, M. A. (1991). *"I've seen it all!"* Baltimore: Brookes.

Elder, J. K. (1986). *Supported employment demonstration projects* (Unpublished memorandum). Washington, DC: Department of Health and Human Services.

Falvey, M. A. (1989). *Community-based curriculum: Instructional strategies for students with severe handicaps.* (2nd ed.). Baltimore: Brookes.

Falvey, M., Brown, L., Lyon, S., Baumgart, D., & Schroeder, J. (1980). Strategies for using cues and correction procedures. In W. Sailor, B. Wilcox, &

L. Brown (Eds.), *Methods of instruction for severely handicapped students* (pp. 109–133). Baltimore: Brookes.

Ford, L., Dineen, J., & Hall, J. (1984). Is there life after placement? *Education and Training of the Mentally Retarded, 19*(4), 291–296.

Ford, A., Schnorr, R., Meyer, L., Davern, L., Black, J., & Dempsey, P. (1989). *The Syracuse community-referenced curriculum guide for students with moderate and severe disabilities.* Baltimore: Brookes.

Fredericks, B., Covey, C., Hendrickson, K., Deane, K., Gallagher, J., Schwindt, A., & Perkins, C. (1987). *Vocational training for students with severe handicaps.* Monmouth, OR: Teaching Research Publications.

Goldhammer, K. (1972). A careers curriculum. In L. Goldhammer & R. E. Taylor (Eds.), *Career education: Perspective and promise.* Portland, OR: Northwest Regional Educational Laboratory.

Halpern, A. S. (1985). Transition: A look at the foundations. *Exceptional Children, 51*(6), 479–486.

Halpern, A. S., Close, D. W., & Nelson, D. J. (1986). *On my own.* Baltimore: Brookes.

Hoyt, K. (1975). *An introduction to career education: A policy paper of the U.S. Office of Education.* Washington, DC: U.S. Government Printing Office.

Johnson, M. S. & Bailey, J. S. (1977). The modification of leisure behavior in a half-way house for retarded women. *Journal of Applied Behavior Analysis, 10*(2), 273–282.

Kaufman, S. (1984). Friendship, coping systems and community adjustment of mildly retarded adults. In R. B. Edgerton (Ed.), *Lives in process: Mildly retarded adults in a large city* (pp. 73–92). Washington, DC: American Association on Mental Deficiency.

Kiernan, W. E. & Ciborowski, J. (1985). *Employment survey for adults with developmental disabilities.* Washington, DC: National Association of Rehabilitation Facilities.

Kiernan, W. E. & Stark, J. A. (Eds.) (1986). *Pathways to employment for adults with developmental disabilities.* Baltimore: Brookes

Kokaska, C. J. (1983). Career education: A brief overview. *Teaching Exceptional Children, 15,* 194–195.

Lambert, N., Nihira, K., & Leland, H. (1992). *AAMR Adaptive Behavior Scales–School* (2nd ed.). Austin, TX: Pro Ed.

Lambert, N., Windmiller, M., Tharinger, D., & Cole, L. (1981). *Administration and instructional planning manual, AAMD Adaptive Behavior Scales—School Edition*. Monterey, CA: CTB/McGraw-Hill.

Landesman-Dwyer, S., Berkson, G., & Romer, D. (1979). Affiliation and friendship of mentally retarded residents in group homes. *American Journal of Mental Deficiency, 83*(6), 571–580.

Mank, D. M., Rhodes, L. E., & Bellamy, G. T. (1986). Four supported employment alternatives. In W. E. Kiernan & J. A. Stark (Eds.), *Pathways to employment for adults with developmental disabilities*. Baltimore: Brookes.

Marland, S. P. (1971). *Career education now*. Presentation at the Convention of the National Association of Secondary School Principals, Houston, TX.

McDonnell, J. J., Wilcox, B., Boles, S. M., & Bellamy, G. T. (1983). *Issues in the transition from school to adult services: A survey of parents of secondary students with severe handicaps*. Technical Report, University of Oregon, Eugene, OR.

Moon, M. S., Inge, K. J., Wehman, P., Brooke, V., & Barcus, J. M. (1990). *Helping persons with severe mental retardation get and keep employment*. Baltimore: Brookes.

Parnell, D. (1973). Career education and the school curriculum. In L. McClure and C. Buan (Eds.), *Essays on career education*. Portland, OR: Northwest Regional Education Laboratory.

Powell, T. H., Pancsofar, E. L., Steere, D. E., Butterworth, J., Itzkowitz, J. S., Rainforth, B. (1991). *Supported employment*. New York: Longman.

Rudrud, E. H., Ziarnik, J. P., Bernstein, G. S., Ferrara, J. M. (1984). *Proactive vocational habilitation*. Baltimore: Brookes.

Rusch, F. R. (1986). *Competitive employment issues and strategies*. Baltimore: Brookes.

Rusch, F. R. (1983). Competitive vocational training. In M. E. Snell (Ed.), *Systematic instruction of the moderately and severely handicapped* (2nd ed.) (pp. 503–523). Columbus, OH: Merrill.

Rusch, F. R., Chadsey-Rusch, J., & Lagomarcino, T. (1987). Preparing students for employment. In M. E. Snell (Ed.), *Systematic instruction of persons with severe handicaps* (3rd ed.) (pp. 471–490). Columbus, OH: Merrill.

Rusch, F. R. & Mithaug, D. E. (1980). *Vocational training for mentally retarded adults*. Champaign, IL: Research Press.

Rusch, F. R. & DeStefano, L. (1989). Transition from school to work: Strategies for young adults with disabilities. *Interchange, 9*(3), 1–2.

Salzberg, C. L. & Langford, C. A. (1981). Community integration of mentally retarded adults through leisure activity. *Mental Retardation, 19*(3), 127–133.

Sparrow, S., Balla, D., & Cicchetti, D. (1984). *Interview edition, expanded form manual, Vineland Adaptive Behavior Scales*. Circle Pines, MN: American Guidance Service.

Schalock, R. L., Harper, R. S., & Carver, G. (1981). Independent living placement: Five years later. *American Journal of Mental Deficiency, 86*(2), 170–177.

Stowitschek, J. J. & Kelso, C. A. (1989). Are we making the same mistakes with ITPs as were made with IEPs? *Career Development for Exceptional Individuals, 12*(2), 139–152.

Voeltz, L. M., Wuerch, B. B., & Wilcox, B. (1982). Leisure and recreation: Preparation for independence, integration, and self-fulfillment. In B. Wilcox and G. T. Bellamy (Eds.), *Design of high school programs for severely handicapped students*. Baltimore: Brookes.

Wehman, P. (1992). *Life beyond the classroom: Transition strategies for young people with disabilities*. Baltimore: Brookes.

Wehman, P. (1981). *Competitive employment*. Baltimore: Brookes.

Wehman, P. (1979). *Recreation programming for developmentally disabled persons*. Baltimore: University Park Press.

Wehman, P. & Kregel, J. (1985). A supported work approach to competitive employment of individuals with moderate and severe handicaps. *Journal of the Association for Persons with Severe Handicaps, 10*(1), 3–11.

Wehman, P. H., Kregel, J., Barcus, J. M., & Schalock, R. L. (1986). Vocational transition for students with developmental disabilities. In W. E. Kiernan & J. A. Stark (Eds.), *Pathways to employment for adults with developmental disabilities* (pp. 24–38). Baltimore: Brookes.

Wehman, P., Moon, M. S., Everson, J. M., Wood, W., & Barcus, J. M. (1988). *Transition from school to work*. Baltimore: Brookes.

Wilcox, B. & Bellamy, G. T. (1987). *The activities catalog: An alternative curriculum for youth and adults with severe disabilities*. Baltimore: Brookes.

Will, M. C. (1984). *OSERS programming for the transition of youth with disabilities: Bridges from school to working life.* Washington, DC: Office of Special Education and Rehabilitative Services, U.S. Department of Education.

Willer, B. & Intagliata, J. (1984). *Promises and realities for mentally retarded citizens,* Baltimore: University Park Press.

Wuerch, B. B. & Voeltz, L. M. (1982). *Longitudinal leisure skills for severely handicapped learners: The Ho'onanea curriculum component.* Baltimore: Brookes.

Appendix A

1992 AAMR Classification System-Step One Examples: All Cases

STEP 1. DIAGNOSIS OF MENTAL RETARDATION

Name _Tony_   Date _11/30/92_ DOB _11/16/76_

Team Members _Ms. Bates, Teacher_   _Ms. Foote, Group Home Manager_

Dr. Lisles, Psychologist   _Tony's Father_

---

1. IQ _65_ Test Administered _WISC-R_ Date _11/2/92_

2. Related limitations in two or more adaptive skill areas
   ☑ Yes ☐ No

Adaptive Evaluations _Vineland_ Date _11/9/92_ ; _PIAT-R_ Date _11/9/92_

SIGNIFICANT LIMITATION

	YES	NO		YES	NO
Communication	☑	☐	Self-direction	☑	☐
Self-care	☐	☑	Health & safety	☐	☑
Home living	☐	☑	Functional academics	☑	☐
Social skills	☑	☐	Leisure	☑	☐
Community use	☐	☑	Work	☐	☑

3. Age of onset _Childhood_

4. Diagnosis _Mental Retardation_

Diagnosis of mental retardation if:
- The person's intellectual functioning level is approximately 70 to 75 or below,
- There are related limitations in two or more applicable adaptive skill areas, and
- The age of onset is 18 or below.

Guidelines: Intellectual Assessment
1. The determination of subaverage intellectual functioning requires the use of global measures that include different types of items and different factors of intelligence. The instruments more commonly used include The Stanford Binet Intelligence Scale, one of the Wechsler scales (WISC-III, WAIS-R), or the Kaufman Assessment Battery for Children.
2. If a valid IQ is not possible, significantly subaverage intellectual capabilities means a level of performance that is less than that observed in the vast majority (approximately 97 percent) of persons of comparable background.
3. In order to be valid, the assessment of cognitive performance must be free from errors caused by motor, sensory, emotional, or cultural factors.

Guidelines: Adaptive Behavior
1. Adaptive skill assessment instruments should be used that are normed within the community environments on individuals who are the same age grouping as the individual being evaluated.
2. Validity can be increased through techniques such as reviewing case histories, interviewing key people in the individual's life, observing the individual in his/her environment, interviewing the individual directly, or interacting with him/her in their daily routine.

STEP 1. DIAGNOSIS OF MENTAL RETARDATION

Name *Sonia*   Date *11/30/92* DOB *4/17/85*

Team Members *Mr. Gonzales, Teacher*   *Sonia's Mother*

  Dr. Strong, Psychologist _____

---

1. IQ *<15* Test Administered *Stanford-Binet &* Date *11/4/92*
  Leiter attempted

2. Related limitations in two or more adaptive skill areas
   ☑ Yes ☐ No

Adaptive Evaluations *Vineland* Date *11/4/92* ; _____ Date _____

SIGNIFICANT LIMITATION

	YES	NO		YES	NO
Communication	☑	☐	Self-direction	☑	☐
Self-care	☑	☐	Health & safety	☑	☐
Home living	☑	☐	Functional academics	☑	☐
Social skills	☐	☑	Leisure	☑	☐
Community use	☑	☐	Work	☐	☐ *NA*

3. Age of onset *Birth*

4. Diagnosis *Mental Retardation*

Diagnosis of mental retardation if:

- The person's intellectual functioning level is approximately 70 to 75 or below,
- There are related limitations in two or more applicable adaptive skill areas, and
- The age of onset is 18 or below.

Guidelines: Intellectual Assessment

1. The determination of subaverage intellectual functioning requires the use of global measures that include different types of items and different factors of intelligence. The instruments more commonly used include The Stanford Binet Intelligence Scale, one of the Wechsler scales (WISC-III, WAIS-R), or the Kaufman Assessment Battery for Children.
2. If a valid IQ is not possible, significantly subaverage intellectual capabilities means a level of performance that is less than that observed in the vast majority (approximately 97 percent) of persons of comparable background.
3. In order to be valid, the assessment of cognitive performance must be free from errors caused by motor, sensory, emotional, or cultural factors.

Guidelines: Adaptive Behavior

1. Adaptive skill assessment instruments should be used that are normed within the community environments on individuals who are the same age grouping as the individual being evaluated.
2. Validity can be increased through techniques such as reviewing case histories, interviewing key people in the individual's life, observing the individual in his/her environment, interviewing the individual directly, or interacting with him/her in their daily routine.

STEP 1. DIAGNOSIS OF MENTAL RETARDATION

Name _Alicia_   Date _11/30/92_   DOB _5/1/89_

Team Members _Ms. Sullivan, Teacher_   _Alicia's Mother_

Dr. Wu, Psychologist

---

1. IQ _20_   Test Administered _Bayley Scales_   Date _11/5/92_

2. Related limitations in two or more adaptive skill areas
   ☑ Yes ☐ No

Adaptive Evaluations _Vineland_   Date _11/6/92_ ; _____ Date _____

SIGNIFICANT LIMITATION

	YES	NO		YES	NO
Communication	☑	☐	Self-direction	☑	☐
Self-care	☑	☐	Health & safety	☑	☐
Home living	☑	☐	Functional academics	☐	☐ _NA_
Social skills	☑	☐	Leisure	☑	☐
Community use	☑	☐	Work	☐	☐ _NA_

3. Age of onset _Birth_

4. Diagnosis _Mental Retardation_

Diagnosis of mental retardation if:
- The person's intellectual functioning level is approximately 70 to 75 or below,
- There are related limitations in two or more applicable adaptive skill areas, and
- The age of onset is 18 or below.

Guidelines: Intellectual Assessment
1. The determination of subaverage intellectual functioning requires the use of global measures that include different types of items and different factors of intelligence. The instruments more commonly used include The Stanford Binet Intellegence Scale, one of the Wechsler scales (WISC-III, WAIS-R), or the Kaufman Assessment Battery for Children.
2. If a valid IQ is not possible, significantly subaverage intellectual capabilities means a level of performance that is less than that observed in the vast majority (approximately 97 percent) of persons of comparable background.
3. In order to be valid, the assessment of cognitive performance must be free from errors caused by motor, sensory, emotional, or cultural factors.

Guidelines: Adaptive Behavior
1. Adaptive skill assessment instruments should be used that are normed within the community environments on individuals who are the same age grouping as the individual being evaluated.
2. Validity can be increased through techniques such as reviewing case histories, interviewing key people in the individual's life, observing the individual in his/her environment, interviewing the individual directly, or interacting with him/her in their daily routine.

STEP 1. DIAGNOSIS OF MENTAL RETARDATION

Name _Scott_   Date _11/30/92_   DOB _11/20/74_

Team Members _Ms. Miller, Teacher_   _Dr. Salter, Psychologist_

              Mr. Rigali, Job Coach   _Scott's Parents_

---

1. IQ _33_   Test Administered _Stanford-Binet_   Date _11/25/92_

2. Related limitations in two or more adaptive skill areas
      ☑ Yes   ☐ No

Adaptive Evaluations _Vineland_   Date _11/25/92_ ; _____ Date _____

SIGNIFICANT LIMITATION

	YES	NO		YES	NO
Communication	☑	☐	Self-direction	☑	☐
Self-care	☐	☑	Health & safety	☑	☐
Home living	☑	☐	Functional academics	☑	☐
Social skills	☑	☐	Leisure	☑	☐
Community use	☑	☐	Work	☑	☐

3. Age of onset _Shortly after birth_

4. Diagnosis _Mental Retardation_

Diagnosis of mental retardation if:

- The person's intellectual functioning level is approximately 70 to 75 or below,
- There are related limitations in two or more applicable adaptive skill areas, and
- The age of onset is 18 or below.

Guidelines: Intellectual Assessment
1. The determination of subaverage intellectual functioning requires the use of global measures that include different types of items and different factors of intelligence. The instruments more commonly used include The Stanford Binet Intelligence Scale, one of the Wechsler scales (WISC-III, WAIS-R), or the Kaufman Assessment Battery for Children.
2. If a valid IQ is not possible, significantly subaverage intellectual capabilities means a level of performance that is less than that observed in the vast majority (approximately 97 percent) of persons of comparable background.
3. In order to be valid, the assessment of cognitive performance must be free from errors caused by motor, sensory, emotional, or cultural factors.

Guidelines: Adaptive Behavior
1. Adaptive skill assessment instruments should be used that are normed within the community environments on individuals who are the same age grouping as the individual being evaluated.
2. Validity can be increased through techniques such as reviewing case histories, interviewing key people in the individual's life, observing the individual in his/her environment, interviewing the individual directly, or interacting with him/her in their daily routine.

STEP 1. DIAGNOSIS OF MENTAL RETARDATION

Name _Karen_   Date _11/30/92_ DOB _10/18/77_

Team Members _Ms. Rosenburg, Teacher_   _Karen's Mother_

           Dr. Johnson, Psychologist

---

1. IQ _47_   Test Administered _WISC-R_   Date _11/16/92_

2. Related limitations in two or more adaptive skill areas
     ☑ Yes ☐ No

Adaptive Evaluations _Vineland_ Date _11/19/92_ ; _____ Date _____

SIGNIFICANT LIMITATION

	YES	NO		YES	NO
Communication	☑	☐	Self-direction	☑	☐
Self-care	☐	☑	Health & safety	☑	☐
Home living	☐	☑	Functional academics	☑	☐
Social skills	☑	☐	Leisure	☑	☐
Community use	☑	☐	Work	☑	☐

3. Age of onset _Shortly after birth_

4. Diagnosis _Mental Retardation_

Diagnosis of mental retardation if:

- The person's intellectual functioning level is approximately 70 to 75 or below,
- There are related limitations in two or more applicable adaptive skill areas, and
- The age of onset is 18 or below.

Guidelines: Intellectual Assessment

1. The determination of subaverage intellectual functioning requires the use of global measures that include different types of items and different factors of intelligence. The instruments more commonly used include The Stanford Binet Intellegence Scale, one of the Wechsler scales (WISC-III, WAIS-R), or the Kaufman Assessment Battery for Children.
2. If a valid IQ is not possible, significantly subaverage intellectual capabilities means a level of performance that is less than that observed in the vast majority (approximately 97 percent) of persons of comparable background.
3. In order to be valid, the assessment of cognitive performance must be free from errors caused by motor, sensory, emotional, or cultural factors.

Guidelines: Adaptive Behavior

1. Adaptive skill assessment instruments should be used that are normed within the community environments on individuals who are the same age grouping as the individual being evaluated.
2. Validity can be increased through techniques such as reviewing case histories, interviewing key people in the individual's life, observing the individual in his/her environment, interviewing the individual directly, or interacting with him/her in their daily routine.

STEP 1. DIAGNOSIS OF MENTAL RETARDATION

Name _Juan_ Date _11/30/92_ DOB _11/26/83_

Team Members _Mr. Stevenson, Teacher_ _Dr. Gelb, Psychologist_

Ms. Rosa, Resource Teacher _Juan's Parents_

---

1. IQ _55_ Test Administered _WISC-III_ Date _11/17/92_

2. Related limitations in two or more adaptive skill areas
☑ Yes ☐ No

Adaptive Evaluations _Vineland_ Date _11/20/92_ ; _PIAT-R_ Date _11/18/92_

SIGNIFICANT LIMITATION

	YES	NO		YES	NO
Communication	☑	☐	Self-direction	☑	☐
Self-care	☐	☑	Health & safety	☑	☐
Home living	☐	☑	Functional academics	☑	☐
Social skills	☑	☐	Leisure	☐	☑
Community use	☑	☐	Work	☐	☐ _NA_

3. Age of onset _Early childhood_

4. Diagnosis _Mental Retardation_

Diagnosis of mental retardation if:
- The person's intellectual functioning level is approximately 70 to 75 or below,
- There are related limitations in two or more applicable adaptive skill areas, and
- The age of onset is 18 or below.

Guidelines: Intellectual Assessment
1. The determination of subaverage intellectual functioning requires the use of global measures that include different types of items and different factors of intelligence. The instruments more commonly used include The Stanford Binet Intelligence Scale, one of the Wechsler scales (WISC-III, WAIS-R), or the Kaufman Assessment Battery for Children.
2. If a valid IQ is not possible, significantly subaverage intellectual capabilities means a level of performance that is less than that observed in the vast majority (approximately 97 percent) of persons of comparable background.
3. In order to be valid, the assessment of cognitive performance must be free from errors caused by motor, sensory, emotional, or cultural factors.

Guidelines: Adaptive Behavior
1. Adaptive skill assessment instruments should be used that are normed within the community environments on individuals who are the same age grouping as the individual being evaluated.
2. Validity can be increased through techniques such as reviewing case histories, interviewing key people in the individual's life, observing the individual in his/her environment, interviewing the individual directly, or interacting with him/her in their daily routine.

STEP 1. DIAGNOSIS OF MENTAL RETARDATION

Name _Tanisha_ Date _11/30/92_ DOB _8/17/85_

Team Members _Mr. Drake, Teacher_ _Dr. Smiley, Psychologist_

Ms. Ortiz, Special Education _Tanisha's Mother_
Teacher Consultant

---

1. IQ _58_ Test Administered _Stanford-Binet_ Date _11/23/92_

2. Related limitations in two or more adaptive skill areas
   ☑ Yes ❑ No

Adaptive Evaluations _Vineland_ Date _11/23/92_ ; _PIAT-R_ Date _11/24/92_

SIGNIFICANT LIMITATION

	YES	NO		YES	NO
Communication	❑	☑	Self-direction	☑	❑
Self-care	❑	☑	Health & safety	☑	❑
Home living	☑	❑	Functional academics	☑	❑
Social skills	❑	☑	Leisure	❑	☑
Community use	☑	❑	Work	❑	❑ NA

3. Age of onset _Childhood_

4. Diagnosis _Mental Retardation_

Diagnosis of mental retardation if:

• The person's intellectual functioning level is approximately 70 to 75 or below,
• There are related limitations in two or more applicable adaptive skill areas, and
• The age of onset is 18 or below.

Guidelines: Intellectual Assessment
1. The determination of subaverage intellectual functioning requires the use of global measures that include different types of items and different factors of intelligence. The instruments more commonly used include The Stanford Binet Intelligence Scale, one of the Wechsler scales (WISC-III, WAIS-R), or the Kaufman Assessment Battery for Children.
2. If a valid IQ is not possible, significantly subaverage intellectual capabilities means a level of performance that is less than that observed in the vast majority (approximately 97 percent) of persons of comparable background.
3. In order to be valid, the assessment of cognitive performance must be free from errors caused by motor, sensory, emotional, or cultural factors.

Guidelines: Adaptive Behavior
1. Adaptive skill assessment instruments should be used that are normed within the community environments on individuals who are the same age grouping as the individual being evaluated.
2. Validity can be increased through techniques such as reviewing case histories, interviewing key people in the individual's life, observing the individual in his/her environment, interviewing the individual directly, or interacting with him/her in their daily routine.

STEP 1. DIAGNOSIS OF MENTAL RETARDATION

Name _Norman_   Date _11/30/92_   DOB _6/27/87_

Team Members _Ms. Brodsky, Teacher_   _Norman's Mother_

           Mr. Smith, Teacher Assistant   _Ms. Kelly, Physical Therapist_

---

1. IQ _64_   Test Administered _Stanford-Binet_   Date _11/12/92_

2. Related limitations in two or more adaptive skill areas
     ☑ Yes ☐ No

Adaptive Evaluations _Vineland_   Date _11/13/92_ ; _____ Date _____

SIGNIFICANT LIMITATION

	YES	NO		YES	NO
Communication	☑	☐	Self-direction	☑	☐
Self-care	☑	☐	Health & safety	☑	☐
Home living	☑	☐	Functional academics	☐	☐ _NA_
Social skills	☐	☑	Leisure	☐	☑
Community use	☑	☐	Work	☐	☐ _NA_

3. Age of onset _Early childhood_

4. Diagnosis _Mental Retardation_

Diagnosis of mental retardation if:
- The person's intellectual functioning level is approximately 70 to 75 or below,
- There are related limitations in two or more applicable adaptive skill areas, and
- The age of onset is 18 or below.

Guidelines: Intellectual Assessment
1. The determination of subaverage intellectual functioning requires the use of global measures that include different types of items and different factors of intelligence. The instruments more commonly used include The Stanford Binet Intelligence Scale, one of the Wechsler scales (WISC-III, WAIS-R), or the Kaufman Assessment Battery for Children.
2. If a valid IQ is not possible, significantly subaverage intellectual capabilities means a level of performance that is less than that observed in the vast majority (approximately 97 percent) of persons of comparable background.
3. In order to be valid, the assessment of cognitive performance must be free from errors caused by motor, sensory, emotional, or cultural factors.

Guidelines: Adaptive Behavior
1. Adaptive skill assessment instruments should be used that are normed within the community environments on individuals who are the same age grouping as the individual being evaluated.
2. Validity can be increased through techniques such as reviewing case histories, interviewing key people in the individual's life, observing the individual in his/her environment, interviewing the individual directly, or interacting with him/her in their daily routine.

© AAMR 1992

Appendix B

Complete 1992 AAMR Classifiction System Example: Tanisha

STEP 1. DIAGNOSIS OF MENTAL RETARDATION

Name _Tanisha_   Date _11/30/92_ DOB _8/17/85_

Team Members _Mr. Drake, Teacher_   _Dr. Smiley, Psychologist_

Ms. Ortiz, Special Education   _Tanisha's Mother_
Teacher Consultant

---

1. IQ _58_   Test Administered _Stanford-Binet_   Date _11/23/92_

2. Related limitations in two or more adaptive skill areas
   ☑ Yes ☐ No

Adaptive Evaluations _Vineland_   Date _11/23/92_ ; _PIAT-R_   Date _11/24/92_

SIGNIFICANT LIMITATION

	YES	NO		YES	NO
Communication	☐	☑	Self-direction	☑	☐
Self-care	☐	☑	Health & safety	☑	☐
Home living	☑	☐	Functional academics	☑	☐
Social skills	☐	☑	Leisure	☐	☑
Community use	☑	☐	Work	☐	☐ NA

3. Age of onset _Childhood_

4. Diagnosis _Mental Retardation_

Diagnosis of mental retardation if:
- The person's intellectual functioning level is approximately 70 to 75 or below,
- There are related limitations in two or more applicable adaptive skill areas, and
- The age of onset is 18 or below.

Guidelines: Intellectual Assessment
1. The determination of subaverage intellectual functioning requires the use of global measures that include different types of items and different factors of intelligence. The instruments more commonly used include The Stanford Binet Intelligence Scale, one of the Wechsler scales (WISC-III, WAIS-R), or the Kaufman Assessment Battery for Children.
2. If a valid IQ is not possible, significantly subaverage intellectual capabilities means a level of performance that is less than that observed in the vast majority (approximately 97 percent) of persons of comparable background.
3. In order to be valid, the assessment of cognitive performance must be free from errors caused by motor, sensory, emotional, or cultural factors.

Guidelines: Adaptive Behavior
1. Adaptive skill assessment instruments should be used that are normed within the community environments on individuals who are the same age grouping as the individual being evaluated.
2. Validity can be increased through techniques such as reviewing case histories, interviewing key people in the individual's life, observing the individual in his/her environment, interviewing the individual directly, or interacting with him/her in their daily routine.

STEP 2. CLASSIFICATION & DESCRIPTION

Name *Tanisha*   Date *11/30/92*

Dimension I: Intellectual Functioning & Adaptive Skills

Describe the individual's strengths and weaknesses in intellectual functioning and adaptive behavior based on testing or observation. Indicate source.

• Communication

Strengths	*Well developed, receptive, and expressive language skills*	*Vineland/Observation* Source
Weaknesses	*Limited reading and writing skills*	*Vineland/Observation* Source

• Self-Care

Strengths	*Can manage most self-care skills*	*Vineland/Observation* Source
Weaknesses	*Needs refinements in neatness of appearance*	*Vineland/Observation* Source

• Home Living

Strengths	*Performs some household chores*	*Vineland/Observation* Source
Weaknesses	*Needs prompting to pick up after herself*	*Vineland/Observation* Source

• Social Skills

Strengths		
	Gregarious, cheerful, and seeks out the company of children and adults	*Vineland/Observation* Source
Weaknesses		
	Too open with strangers	*Vineland/Observation* Source

• Community Use

Strengths		
	Uses community playgrounds and recreational resources	*Observation* Source
Weaknesses		
	Needs supervision in crossing streets	*Observation* Source

• Self-Direction

Strengths		
	Initiates own activities	*Observation* Source
Weaknesses		
	Poor planning of time needed for activities	*Observation* Source

• Health & Safety

Strengths		
	Is in good health	*Observation* Source
Weaknesses		
	Insufficiently cautious about strangers	*Observation* Source

• Functional Academics

Strengths		
	Relatively good performance on general information and reading recognition subtests	*PIAT* Source
Weaknesses		
	Less adequate performance in reading comprehension and mathematics	*PIAT* Source

• Leisure

Strengths		
	Enjoys outdoor activities and television	*Observation* Source

Weaknesses		
	Needs help in balancing time devoted to leisure and household chores	*Observation* Source

• Work   *Not Applicable*

Strengths	
	Source

Weaknesses	
	Source

Dimension II: Psychological/Emotional Considerations

Describe the individual's strengths and weaknesses using behavior observations, clinical assessments, or formal diagnosis (e.g., DSM-III-R). Indicate source.

Strengths		
	Emotionally stable and very sociable	*Psychological Examination* Source

Weaknesses		
	Overly demanding of adults	*Psychological Examination* Source

Dimension III: Physical/Health/Etiology Considerations

List health related diagnosis, primary etiology, and contributing factors based on behavioral observation, clinical assessment, or formal diagnosis (e.g., ICD 9).

Health related diagnosis   *Good Health* _____

_____

_____

Primary etiology   *Unknown* _____

Contributing factors _____

_____

_____

Dimension IV: Environmental Considerations

Describe the extent to which the individual's living, work and educational environments **facilitate** or **restrict** opportunities for community integration, social supports (family and friends), and material well-being (income, housing, possessions).

• Living Situations

Strengths		
	Very supportive home (mother)	*Observation*
		Source
Weaknesses		
	No apparent support system other than mother	*Observation*
		Source

• Work *Not Applicable*

Strengths	
	Source
Weaknesses	
	Source

• Educational

Strengths	
	Inclusive classroom in a neighborhood school
	Source
Weaknesses	
	Insufficient special education instructional support
	Source

Option Environment

Describe the optimal environment that would facilitate the individual's **independence/ interdependence, productivity,** and **community integration.**

1. Inclusive classroom in a regular elementary school

2. Adequate regular education teacher in consultation with special education resource teacher.

3. Community-based learning opportunities.

4. Education program focusing on communication, functional academics, social interaction, community use skills, and early vocational skills.

5. Behavior support services.

STEP 3. PROFILE & INTENSITIES OF NEEDED SUPPORTS

Name _Tanisha_   Date _11/30/92_

List the support function, the specific activity, and the level of intensities needed in each of the areas and/or dimensions. (See Activities listed on the back of this page.)

Levels of intensity are: I – Intermittent; L – Limited; E – Extensive; P – Pervasive

Dimension I: Intellectual Functioning & Adaptive Skills

Dimension/Area	Support Function	Activity	Level of Intensity I L E P
Communication	Befriending	Find adolescents and adults to read to her.	I
Self-Care	Health Assistance	Assist in refining independent grooming and hygiene skills.	L
Social Skills	Behavior Support	Provide modeling and social skills programming on how to react appropriately to strangers.	I
Home Living	Behavior Support	Provide incentives for putting away clothing and toys.	L
Community Use	Community Access and Use	Provide training in travel safety such as street crossing skills.	E
Self-Direction	Behavior Support	Teach time-management strategies.	L
Health & Safety	Health Assistance	Role-play appropriate reactions to strangers.	L

© AAMR 1992

407

Dimension I: Intellectual Functioning & Adaptive Skills *(continued)*

Dimension/Area	Support Function	Activity	Level I L E P
Functional Academics	*Student Assistance*	*Provide activity-based instruction in math, reading, and writing.*	*E*
Leisure	*Community Access and Use*	*Build on and expand existing repertoire of leisure activities.*	*I*
Work *NA*			*NA*

Dimension II: Psychological/Emotional Considerations

Dimension/Area	Support Function	Activity	Level I L E P
	Behavioral Support	*Role play appropriate interactions with adults.*	*I*

Dimension III: Physical/Health Considerations

Dimension/Area	Support Function	Activity	Level I L E P
	Health Assistance	*Procure annual physical examination.*	*I*

Dimension IV: Environment Considerations

Dimension/Area	Support Function	Activity	Level I L E P
	Community Access and Use	*Provide more community-based learning opportunities.*	*I*

1. Befriending

Advocating	Evaluating
Associating	Giving feedback
Befriending	Instructing
Car pooling	Socializing
Communicating	Supervising
Collecting data	Training

2. Financial Planning

Advocating for benefits
Assisting with money
    management
Budgeting
Income assistance
Planning considerations
Projection & legal assistance
Working with SSI-Medicaid

3. Employee Assistance

Counseling
Crisis intervention/assistance
Job performance enhancement
Job/task accommodation
Procuring/using assistive
    technology devices
Supervisory training
Redesigning job/work duties

4. Behavioral Support

Building environment with
    effective consequences
Emphasis on antecedent
    manipulation
Functional analysis
Manipulation of ecological &
    setting events
Minimizing use of punishments
Multicomponent instruction
Teaching adaptive behavior

5. In-House Living Assistance

Architectural modifications
Attendant care
Behavioral support
Communication devices
Dressing and clothing care
Eating and food management
Home health aids
Homemaker services
Housekeeping
Med alert devices
Personal maintenance/care
Respite care
Transfer and mobility

6. Community Access and Use

Car pooling/rides program
Community awareness
    opportunities
Community use opportunities
Interacting with generic
    agencies
Recreation/leisure
    involvement
Transportation training
Vehicle modification

7. Health Assistance

Assistance
Counseling appointments
Counseling interventions
Emergency procedures
Hazard awareness
Med alert devices
Medical appointments
Medical interventions
Medication taking
Mobility
Physical therapy
Safety training
Supervision

Subject Index

411